CONDITION: F/54+ (228731)

Edition: 1st   Prtg: DJ/NO

Red-(orange) DJ, black ltrs.

COMMENTS: 1/8" DJ tr'le, ~~DJ~~ very sly
Sealed (NOT ltrs) on spine, 115¢

IF05
1990

KEYWORDS: DRS, Social Structure, Sex
Role, Psychoanalysis, Feminism, UP,
Sociology, ~~~~, Neurosis,
Psychoanalytic

20.3

40 0 14

THE NEUROTIC FOUNDATIONS OF SOCIAL ORDER

PSYCHOANALYTIC CROSSCURRENTS
General Editor: Leo Goldberger

THE NEUROTIC FOUNDATIONS OF SOCIAL ORDER

Psychoanalytic Roots of Patriarchy

J. C. Smith

NEW YORK UNIVERSITY PRESS
New York and London

Library of Congress Cataloging-in-Publication Data

Smith, J. C. (Joseph Carman), 1930–
The neurotic foundations of social order / J. C. Smith.
p.   cm. — (Psychoanalytic crosscurrents)
Includes bibliographical references and index.
ISBN 0-8147-7903-4 (acid-free paper)
1. Social structure.   2. Sex role.   3. Psychoanalysis.
4. Psychoanalysis and feminism.   5. Sociological jurisprudence.
I. Title.   II. Series.
HM131.S567   1990
305.3—dc20   90-6146
CIP

New York University Press books are printed on acid-free paper,
and their binding materials are chosen for strength and durability.

For Lois

CONTENTS

FOREWORD

The *Psychoanalytic Crosscurrents* series presents selected books and monographs that reveal the growing intellectual ferment within and across the boundaries of psychoanalysis.

Freud's theories and grand-scale speculative leaps have been found wanting, if not disturbing, from the very beginning and have led to a succession of derisive attacks, shifts in emphasis, revisions, modifications, and extensions. Despite the chronic and, at times, fierce debate that has characterized psychoanalysis, not only as a movement but also as a science, Freud's genius and transformational impact on the twentieth century have never been seriously questioned. Recent psychoanalytic thought has been subjected to dramatic reassessments under the sway of contemporary currents in the history of ideas, philosophy of science, epistemology, structuralism, critical theory, semantics, and semiology as well as in sociobiology, ethology, and neurocognitive science. Not only is Freud's place in intellectual history being meticulously scrutinized, his texts, too, are being carefully read, explicated, and debated within a variety of conceptual frameworks and sociopolitical contexts.

The legacy of Freud is perhaps most notably evident within the narrow confines of psychoanalysis itself, the "impossible profession" that has served as the central platform for the promulgation of official orthodoxy. But Freud's contributions—his original radical thrust—reach far beyond the parochial concerns of the clinician psychoanalyst as clinician. His writings touch on a wealth of issues, crossing traditional boundaries—be they situated in the biological, social, or humanistic spheres—that have profoundly altered our conception of the individual and society.

A rich and flowering literature, falling under the rubric of "applied psychoanalysis," came into being, reached its zenith many decades ago, and then almost vanished. Early contributors to this literature, in addition to Freud himself, came from a wide range of backgrounds both within and outside the medical/psychiatric field, many later became psychoanalysts themselves. These early efforts were characteristically reductionistic in their attempt to extrapolate from psychoanalytic theory (often the purely clinical theory) to explanations of phenomena lying at some distance from the clinical. Over the years, academic psychologists, educators, anthropologists, sociologists, political scientists, philosophers, jurists, literary critics, art historians, artists, and writers, among others (with or without formal psychoanalytic training) have joined in the proliferation of this literature.

The intent of the *Psychoanalytic Crosscurrents* series is to apply psychoanalytic ideas to topics that may lie beyond the narrowly clinical, but its essential conception and scope are quite different. The present series eschews the reductionistic tendency to be found in much traditional "applied psychoanalysis." It acknowledges not only the complexity of psychological phenomena but also the way in which they are embedded in social and scientific contexts that are constantly changing. It calls for a dialectical relationship to earlier theoretical views and conceptions rather than a mechanical repetition of Freud's dated thoughts. The series affirms the fact that contributions to and about psychoanalysis have come from many directions. It is designed as a forum for the multidisciplinary studies that intersect with psychoanalytic thought but without the requirement that psychoanalysis necessarily be the starting point or, indeed, the center focus. The criteria for inclusion in the series are that the work be significantly informed by psychoanalytic thought or that it be aimed at furthering our understanding of psychoanalysis in its broadest meaning as theory, practice, and sociocultural phenomenon; that it be of current topical interest and that it provide the critical reader with contemporary insights; and, above all, that it be high-quality scholarship, free of obsolete dogma, banalization, and empty jargon. The author's professional identity and particular theoretical orientation matters only to the extent that such facts may serve to frame the work for the reader, alerting him or her to inevitable biases of the author.

The *Psychoanalytic Crosscurrents* series presents an array of works from the multidisciplinary domain in an attempt to capture the ferment of scholarly activities at the core as well as at the boundaries of psychoanalysis. The books and monographs are from a variety of sources: authors will be psychoanalysts—traditional, neo- and post-Freudian, existential, object relational, Kohutian, Lacanian, etc.—social scientists with quantitative or qualitative orientations to psychoanalytic data, and scholars from the vast diversity of approaches and interests that make up the humanities. The series entertains works on critical comparisons of psychoanalytic theories and concepts as well as philosophical examinations of fundamental assumptions and epistemic claims that furnish the base for psychoanalytic hypotheses. It includes studies of psychoanalysis as literature (discourse and narrative theory) as well as the application of psychoanalytic concepts to literary criticism. It will serve as an outlet for psychoanalytic studies of creativity and the arts. Works in the cognitive and the neurosciences will be included to the extent that they address some fundamental psychoanalytic tenet, such as the role of dreaming and other forms of unconscious mental processes.

It should be obvious that an exhaustive enumeration of the types of works that might fit into the *Psychoanalytic Crosscurrents* series is pointless. The studies comprise a lively and growing literature as a unique domain; books of this sort are frequently difficult to classify or catalog. Suffice it to say that the overriding aim of the editor of this series is to serve as a conduit for the identification of the outstanding yield of that emergent literature and to foster its further unhampered growth.

Leo Goldberger
Professor of Psychology
New York University

PREFACE

I view this book as one side of a dialogue. In writing it I have conceived of myself as having the opportunity to respond (at length) to those great thinkers of the past, such as Hegel, Nietzsche, and Freud, who have so much influenced my own intellectual life, and to a range of contemporary writers who have responded in their own way to those who have introduced new paradigms of thought. In like manner, it is my response and dialogue with radical feminism and postmodernism, "two of the most important political-cultural currents of the last decade."[1] These are, to me, the most intellectually exciting and rewarding movements in contemporary political and social thought. This book is also a part of a dialogue which I have had over the years with many students from whom I have learned much and to whom, I hope, I have imparted knowledge. This dialogue was particularly rewarding and intense with those students who assisted me in researching the book and with editing the manuscript.

The book, at the same time, represents my own struggle to understand the origins, history, and structure of the law, a quest which spans my thirty-year career as an academic. This quest led me to philosophy, psychoanalytic theory, and artificial intelligence, all of which I now view as a part of cognitive science. I have thus written for myself rather than with a particular audience in mind. It is my own summary of what, toward the end of an academic career, I now believe to be true about social order. I hope the reader will view this volume as conversation as well as dissertation.

The style in which the book is written, however, is not particularly conversational. It tends to be dogmatic and assertive. I have not found it possible to maintain both the appearance of detachment characteristic of academic works (where one argues both sides of an issue and includes one's own questions and doubts) and the strength of feeling which has motivated the book and energized the years of research preceding its writing. Since choice was necessary, I opted for passion over academic style. I have tried, however, not to allow feeling to interfere with scholarship. I have striven instead for a deeper form of objectiveness than I find in most academic works where prejudices are cloaked with an aura of objectivity.

In the spirit of postmodernism I wish to engage the modernists on their own ground. I seek to reveal the subjectivity of their objectivity by objectifying my own subjectivity. I hope to achieve this by demonstrating through this book that the distinction between the observer and the observed, which appears to me to be a basic presupposition of modern scholarship, is fallacious. It is as untrue for the social sciences as it is for physics. Just as in quantum mechanics we alter the state of a particle by forcing it into a definite position in order to measure its location, or we spread it over an infinite wave space or field in order to measure its frequency, so in our observation of the world around us do we conceptualize sensed experience in terms of our mental structures, and structure our views of ourselves as observers in terms of what we believe reality to be. The very act of observation entails a separation and denial of relatedness in the distinction between observer and observed, and the self and the other. I wish to use "the reality-constructing practices of psychoanalysis"[2] to challenge the appearance of reality underlying the theories which legitimate social order. By challenging the legitimacy of our institutions of social order, we make room for new dialogues within which voices now unheard can speak, interests now unrecognized can claim standing, and peoples now devalued and disempowered can fully participate.

The book takes the form of the overarching theory of history which postmodernists so often criticize. It does so, however, in order to turn the tool of metahistory against the metahistories of social order. It is framed and titled foundationally because social order is legitimated in foundational terms. I wish to respond to the claimed legitimacy of social order within its own framework of reference. I wish to turn foundationalism on foundationalism. I wish to attack the "grand narratives of legitimation"[3] with an overarching narrative of delegitimation.

This book grew out of three articles published in the *International Journal of Law and Psychiatry*. The first, "The Evolution of Western Legal

Consciousness" was co-authored with David N. Weisstub. I am grateful to him for an ongoing interchange of ideas and for awakening my interest in myth. This interest led to my writing "The Sword and Shield of Perseus: Some Mythological Dimensions of the Law," and "Gods and Goddesses of the Quadrant: Some Further Thoughts on the Mythological Dimensions of the Law." If one reads, or has read these three pieces, one will note a drift from a Jungian to a Freudian perspective. While many find Jung after having become familiar with Freud, my intellectual journey has gone in the opposite direction. As I gradually realized the limitations of Jungian psychology for social theory, I, at the same time, discovered the power of Freudian psychoanalytic theory for explaining why social order has taken the particular forms which it has. I have found, however, that Jung's concept of the archetypally structured collective unconscious manifesting itself in the conscious through complexes, to be essential for psychoanalytic social theory. This book, therefore, attempts to integrate Jung's theory of the collective unconscious, archetypes, and his related theory of complexes, into a Freudian analytical structure by showing how Freud's ego ideal takes as its objects manifestations of Jungian archetypes. On any other matter where Jung differs from Freud, I prefer Freud.

The book not only attempts to integrate the more valid parts of Jungian depth psychology into a Freudian analytical framework, it also seeks to integrate Freud and Hegel. The synthesis of Freud and Hegel is attempted by replacing in Hegel's theory of history, his theory of mind, with that of Freud's.

Lastly, and most importantly, the book attempts a reconstruction of psychoanalytic theory in terms of radical feminist critique. In this it follows in the tradition pioneered by such feminist theorists as Juliet Mitchell, Dorothy Dinnerstein, Nancy Chodorow, Jessica Benjamin, Jane Gallop, Janet Sayers, Luce Irigaray, and others. The feminist perspective which this volume takes has been particularly influenced by Catharine A. MacKinnon, Mary Daly, Andrea Dworkin, Marilyn French, Adrienne Rich, as well as many others. Feminism, however, has not yet developed an adequate theory of the etiology of patriarchy. I hope that this book will make a contribution toward a better understanding of the underlying causes which have produced male domination.

I owe a substantial debt of gratitude to the people who helped me as research assistants and as editors of the manuscript. At the point where I felt overwhelmed by the magnitude of the project and frightened by my own audacity in its undertaking, Karin Peedo, who had already spent two summers working as a research assistant, postponed graduate studies for a year to see the project through. I doubt that the book would have been finished without this help. James Andersen, who also worked with me as a research assistant brought many insights to the project, and our many ongoing discussions, then and since, allowed me to see a number of things in a different light. The editing skills of Paddy Arthur have immensely improved the final product. Finally, Barbara Rae-Yuen put the entire manuscript into the form desired by the publishers. I am also grateful for the help of Norm Riise of the University Book Store in Seattle, who for a good many years has kept me informed of the latest literature in my fields of interest. It is a delight to know a bookseller who is conversant with the contents which lie between the covers of what is sold.

I acknowledge with gratitude the generous financial support afforded me in this project by the Social Sciences and Humanities Research Council of Canada. Without their research grants, which extended over several years, this book would not have been possible. I am, as well, grateful to The Izaak Walton Killam Memorial Funds For Advanced Studies for a Senior Killam Fellowship and a Killam Research Prize, which also gave important financial support to this project.

Above all, this book owes its existence to Lois Maxwell Smith. Her encouragement, inspiration, and support are only the beginning of the list of ways in which she made it possible.

1.

LAW, SOCIETY, AND PSYCHOANALYSIS

HEGEL REVISITED

In the late twenties, Alexandre Kojève, a young Soviet Marxist scholar disillusioned with the path Communism had taken, decided that Marxism itself, as a theory, was basically flawed. To discover where Marx had gone wrong, he turned to a re-examination of Hegel, and eventually came to be recognized as one of the world's foremost Hegelian scholars. Kojève succeeded in reintroducing Hegel into the mainstream of contemporary political thought and theory, free from what had become its traditional association with Marxism.[1] Hegel was an idealist and Marx was a materialist. Marx adopted Hegel's dialectical system of historical change in terms of a thesis, its denial in the form of an antithesis, and the denial of the antithesis by the synthesis, which formulates a third position reconciling the valid parts of the thesis and the antithesis.[2] However, Marx rejected Hegel's idealism and postulated a materialist position, thus laying the foundation of Marxist political theory in dialectical materialism.[3]

In the early fifties, Milovan Djilas, a former Marxist revolutionary, political theorist, partisan general, and high-ranking leader in the Yugoslavian Communist party, also came to the conclusion that something was very wrong in Communist societies. He turned the Marxian method of class analysis onto Communist society in a book entitled *The New Class,* which resulted in his expulsion from the party and eventual imprisonment.[4] In a later book he directly targeted Marx's materialism as a major

1

deficiency in Marxist theory.[5] Again, like Kojève, Djilas rejected a Marxian modification of Hegel. Idealism, as a theory of history, focuses on mind and ideas as the generating force of historical change, as contrasted with materialism which emphasizes material conditions as the primary determining factor of history. A return to Hegel, free from Marxian materialism, entails a shift back to idealism in the sense that a theory of mind becomes fundamental to political theory. Like most philosophical debates, such as that between free will and determinism which postulates the necessity of a choice between two contrary positions, the truth lies, not at either pole, but in some form of reconciliation. Nevertheless, as in most theoretical positions, one or the other of the two poles must be chosen as primary if the theory is to have a coherent internal structure. A coherent theory of history must select a materialist, or an idealist or mentalist position as dominant and fundamental.[6]

One of the most challenging theories of the twentieth century, and the one I believe history will eventually reveal as the most significant, is radical feminism. The contemporary feminist movement, particularly radical feminism, owes much to Marxist theory.[7] Most feminist theories of history furnish explanations of the evolution of male domination over the female in terms of material conditions, and explain little by way of the dialectical process.[8] Such theories are neither adequate nor persuasive in that material conditions cannot account for either the universality or the pathology of patriarchy. The reason may well be that in moving beyond dialectical materialism, the wrong thing was jettisoned. Feminism should have emphasized the dialectics and rejected the materialism, rather than retaining the materialism and implicitly rejecting the dialectics. Dialectical materialism is not a sufficiently comprehensive or powerful conceptual tool to account for social order, whether one takes a feminist or some other view of it. While it is undeniable that material conditions have a profound effect on history, they are not sufficient nor determinative by themselves.

Marxist theory, on the other hand, has profoundly influenced critical thought through its exploration of the dialetical relationship between experience and ideas. Marxist methodology, whereby beliefs are tested experientially in terms of subordinate class relations, has led feminists to deconstruct male conceptions of reality and patriarchal ideology through women's experience of being situated in a subordinate position in a set of social relations based on sexual hierarchy. The exploration of the relationship between experience and ideas, while an essential part of Marxist

dialectical materialism, is not exclusively a Marxist, nor a materialist methodology. It is equally consistent with, and essential for, the contemporary
forms that idealism takes in cognitive theory. The dialectical relationship
between ideas and experience is what all epistemology is about. Although
implicit in Hegelian thought, it furnishes the common ground between
contemporary idealism and materialism. The relationship can be used by
each position to subsume that of the other. Material conditions can be
reduced to beliefs about experience, and knowledge can be explained in
terms of causal relationships between experience and beliefs.

A return to Hegel entails a return to a dialectical theory of the evolution of mind. We have learned much about the mind since the time of
Hegel, even if there is much that we still do not know. Assuming that we
accept a dialectical Hegelian mentalist position, in contrast to a dialectical
Marxian materialist position, we still need an up-to-date theory of the
mind. This book presents a dialectical theory of the evolution of social
order, based on contemporary psychoanalytic theory.[9] The psychoanalytic
view of mind assumes a dynamic unconscious. We must accept neurosis
rather than rationality as the driving force of history.

If we look at history in terms of the evolution of a universal or
collective mind we can recognize several different dialectics. One dialectic
comes out of our conception of ourselves in relationship to nature. Most
primal societies and early cultures viewed themselves as a part of nature.
They drew no fundamental distinction between the inanimate and the
various forms of life, whether plant, animal, or human. As human consciousness evolved, this unified world view was denied by the projection
of the uniqueness of man. This anthropocentric view is the antithesis of
the thesis of primal unity. Our own animality and dependence upon
nature have recently been forced upon us as the effects of the human
species on the environment start to be felt in terms of dying bodies of
water, oxygen depletion of the atmosphere, deterioration of the ozone
layer, and destructive climactic changes. In terms of the evolution of the
collective mind, we may now be in the process of formulating a synthesis
whereby humans recognize both their interconnectedness and identity
with nature, and their uniqueness as a sentient species.

Another dialectic of human consciousness is that relating to communitarianism and individualism. At one time, nearly all complex societies
were monarchies. People's identities were determined by their biological
status as male or female, first-born or later-born, highborn or lowborn.
Society was a family ruled over by the royal father. Monarchy was the

thesis which was denied by classical liberalism which postulated the equality and autonomy of the individual. At the conceptual level, classical
liberalism, as antithesis, has been denied by contemporary political theory,
whether conservative, socialist, or Marxist-Leninist, all of which decry the
alienation and isolation of selfish individualism, and proclaim the importance of community. Thus, the communitarian emphasis of the thesis has
been combined with the egalitarian emphasis of the antithesis, into a
synthesis centering on the corporate nation-state. This process has taken
place within the period of the antithesis of the first-mentioned dialectic,
the age of anthropocentricity.

In the process of individuation of the individual psyche, we can also
see a dialectic at work. In the thesis state of the psyche, the infant draws
no distinction between the self and (m)other.[10] The ego develops as a
negation of connectedness. A synthesis of separateness and connectedness
is achieved when the self is conceived of in terms of both individual
uniqueness and common identity as a member of various communities.

The psychoanalytic social theory developed in this book details a dialectical process in the evolution of the mind with the transition from the
pre-Oedipal to the Oedipal, to the post-Oedipal. It will also introduce the
notion of a trans-Oedipal stage which would mark the end of history in a
Hegelian sense. The theory thus interrelates Hegel and Freud by substituting a Freudian view of mind in place of the traditional Hegelian
phenomenology of spirit. The book seeks to develop a contemporary
dialectical mentalist and historical perspective of social order. As the
Freudian perspective is developed, Hegel is revisited.

TOWARD A PSYCHOANALYTIC EXPLANATION
OF SOCIAL ORDER

The central thesis of this book is that social order is primarily the product
of neurosis. Neurosis is not the only foundation, as social order serves a
variety of functions, some neurotic and others not. We could therefore
talk about the economic foundations of social order in terms of the role
social order plays in ensuring and protecting markets and organizing
humans for production. There is no doubt that social order plays some
part in reducing random violence. It does a fairly good job of protecting
the property of those who have from those who have not. Or we could
discuss the biological foundations of social order in terms of instincts,

hard-wired in the brain, to use a computer analogy. The book assumes that there are non-neurotic foundations for social order, but that these are merely secondary. Neurosis is the primary structuring principle.

This thesis may intuitively strike the reader as being wrong. However, consider one of the almost universal features of social order. Social order, from one end of the world to the other, is male-dominated. Even in Western democracies which have made a substantial commitment to equality, social order is highly patriarchal. Only 4.5 percent of the members of the United States Congress are female. There has never been a female American president or even a female presidential candidate nominated by a major party. When in the late twentieth century the Democratic party nominated a woman as vice-presidential candidate, it became a matter of special concern and comment. While Great Britain has a female Prime Minister, only 3.6 percent of the House of Commons are female, and in France, women make up only 4.4. percent of the National Legislature.[11] This is an extremely significant characteristic of social control. Who controls is as important a property of social order as is the content of the control because it will be a major factor in determining content.

Many take the patriarchal hierarchical structuring of social order as both natural and normal. Figures such as those above have only recently begun to distress us. Many still feel that there are good reasons for things being the way they are. We cannot account for the patriarchal characteristics of social order in terms of economic theory, nor can we explain it in utilitarian terms such as a natural division of labor between the sexes. We can, however, explain a great deal about the genderized nature of social order in terms of neurotic needs.

It is also true, of course, that black and native Americans have been excluded from political power. However, their exclusion stems from the same psychosocial roots. Sexism and racism are only two of the more glaring examples of hierarchy which cannot be accounted for by any "rational" explanation. Throughout the book an argument will be made that neurosis explains all of the major characteristics of social order better than any other explanation. The conclusion which follows from this is that social order is determined more from the unconscious mind than it is from the conscious.

As social order is primarily the product of neurosis and serves other human needs only secondarily, these other needs are not well served. Social order is as necessary and responsible for war and aggression as it furnishes a protection against it. It perpetuates violence as much as it establishes peace. It has legitimized domination more than it has guaranteed freedom. This is because non-neurotic needs come into play only after the neurotic needs are met, within the framework of neurosis and pathology. If, under certain conditions, social order is effective in serving non-neurotic needs, as is sometimes the case, it is because they converge with neurotic needs. However, if our neurotic and our non-neurotic needs require divergent social ordering, it will, in general, be the neurotic needs which prevail. Compare, for example, the budgets of nations for military-related expenditures with that for social programs. If the human needs which we think justify social order really did furnish its foundations, our social institutions would be of a very different nature and structure.

The forces behind the structure of social order are nonrational neurotic drives. However, social order would not be effective if it was justified in terms of neurotic needs. Therefore, we rationalize social order by focusing on the non-neurotic needs which social order serves badly, rather than on the neurotic needs which it serves well. Political and social theory preserves the illusion rather than exposes it. Consequently, we are constantly faced with the gap between political and social theory and the reality of social order. We are constantly trying to understand irrational human behavior and explain it in rational terms.

We need a special kind of conceptual tool to make what is fundamentally irrational appear rational; to make what is contingent appear necessary; to make what is self-serving appear natural; and to make that which is arbitrary appear right, just, and legitimate. That tool is to be found in the analysis of myth.

By analyzing the neurotic foundations of social order we can close the gap between theory and reality. When we understand that our neurotic needs are more powerful than our rational needs, it becomes clear that social order serves its foundational nonrational needs very effectively. The foundation science of social order therefore should be psychoanalytic theory rather than economics, sociology, law, politics, or philosophy. Human neurotic drives are expressed through will and not reason. Behind the triumph of the will lies the pathology of the will. The underlying thesis of this book is that the foundations of social order lie in the id, repression, and illusion as a denial of reality. One of the primary functions of myth is to replace reality with illusion. Social order, therefore, reflects an essential mythic structure.

THE LEGAL DIMENSIONS OF SOCIAL ORDER

Law is the central ideology of social order. Law determines what conduct will be regulated by the collective and what conduct will be left up to the discretion of the individual. It draws the line between who regulates and who is regulated. Law is central to social order because it is the conceptual framework through which society is ordered. If we are to understand the neurotic foundations of social order, we must understand the neurotic foundations of law, because they are the same. An analysis of the pathology which underlies and produces law and its related institutions furnishes the key to uncovering the neurotic foundations of social order. In our journey through the psychoanalytic looking glass we must move from Oedipus Rex to Oedipus Lex.

Law in Western industrial societies is in the midst of a crisis. Perhaps now more than at any other time in history there are large numbers of highly trained and specialized workers in the profession who perform their tasks without any acknowledgment of a common set of values and with no particular theoretical view of the nature and purpose of law. There is considerable disagreement about whether law is a repressive force in culture or whether it is a meaningful vehicle for establishing the emotional and physical well-being of citizens. The ambiguity of law's status is most heightened in the context of the state, and therefore much recent significant writing about law has concentrated on law's relationship to state authority, and on the mutual implications of law and political ideologies such as democracy and socialism.

Some critics have outlined the extent to which law is the mere servant of existing power and, in so doing, have relegated law to forms of rationalization and rhetoric.[12] More sympathetic observers have insisted that law represents an autonomous, intellectual, and ethical presence in Western society and is the best counterforce available to the questionable applications of political authority.[13] The fact that people have approached law so differently gives rise to the question of what it is that both attaches some individuals to legality and creates a reaction of frustration and rebuke in others.

Undoubtedly, law is the official and central historical organization of social order. The majority of persons in Western democracies have learned to live with the law, however ambivalently, and instinctively resist attacks on the legal system. Stability and prediction of behavior are assumed to be necessary conditions for fulfilled lives. It is safe to generalize that there is a considerable psychological investment in legitimating and protecting legal structures. An interesting tension in this regard arises when we are pushed to choose between the stability of autocracy and the laissez-faire quality of liberalism. The shadow of the Holocaust, the testimony of the survivors of the Gulag, the resurgence of religious fundamentalism, along-side the upsetting contemporary reverberations of terrorism, criminality, and political demagoguery, testify to the recurring tendency of human beings to escape from law into nonrational or unconscious oblivion.

Investigations of the foundations of our major theoretical legal structures reveal both contradictions and polarities. The classical dichotomies —between positivism and natural law, justice and mercy, formal justice and social justice, liberty and social equality, democracy and fundamental rights, legislative sovereignty and judicial review, judge-made law and legislation, the individual and the community—permeate our legal and political institutions and are reflected in the very structure of the conflicts which we attempt to resolve. It will be one of the themes of this book that these contradictions and polarities, when understood from a psycho-logical viewpoint, reflect deep-seated unconscious tensions and anxieties and fundamental archetypal patterns of the human psyche.

If this is the case, then it is meaningful to speak about the psychological dimensions of the law and to relate legal psychology to legal philosophy. It is in this link between philosophy and psychology that the justification of law is realized. What constitutes an argument for legitimacy, or logical justification of the consistent application of legal rules, remains clearly within the jurisdiction of philosophy. The need and quality of rationalization, however, may be understood through a parallel psychological inquiry. A psychoanalytic jurisprudence would entail the application of psychoanalytic social theory to law.

PSYCHOANALYTIC SOCIAL THEORY

While the psychoanalyst moves from the individual psyche to social structures, the psychoanalytic social theorist starts from the perspective of social practices and institutions in order to uncover the interrelationship between society, the family, and the individual psyche. There are very few people in the psychoanalytic community who have the training and experience to act as both analyst working with individual analysands, and social theorist studying societal behavior and institutions. Psychoanalytic theory, while developed from the analysis of individuals, has always been rooted in social theory.[14] Psychoanalytic theory continues to be a partnership between these two sources, with analysts using the work of psychoanalytic social theorists[15] and psychoanalytic social theorists using the work of the psychoanalysts.[16]

Because the practitioners of psychoanalysis and psychoanalytic social theory have different emphases, these two streams will always be semi-independent of each other, but both will feed into a common psychoanalytic perspective. This separation is worth maintaining. The practice of psychoanalysis is broken up into many different schools, such as Freudian, neo-Freudian, and schools of thought centering on the work of particular individuals such as Melanie Klein or Erik Erikson. There is also the more profound split between the Freudians and Jungians who speak of depth psychology rather than psychoanalysis. The fact that these two terms are often used interchangeably, the degree to which Jungian theory presupposes much of the work of Freud, the impact of Jung's ideas on Freud during the period of their close collaboration, and the degree to which Freudian and Jungian terms can be translated into very similar concepts, suggests that while there are fundamental differences, they are less important than the similarities. Psychoanalytic social theory should be sufficiently independent from psychoanalytic practice and the sectarian disputes which it has engendered, that it need not fragment itself over these different points of view. It should be free to draw from any or all where research and clinical studies are relevant to social theory. Psychoanalytic social theory is a nascent discipline which is not, as yet, sufficiently mature to split into schools. Psychoanalytic social theory must not rely on a potpourri of individual analytic insights, but on a fully developed psychoanalytic theory. The psychoanalytic social theorists, however, should feel free to construct their own psychoanalytic theory in the light of the societal and institutional materials with which they are working.

One of the objectives of this book is to forge a psychoanalytic social theory from the perspectives of legal and political institutions. Hopefully, it will have implications for the practitioners of psychoanalysis. They should freely draw upon psychoanalytic social theory and upon anthropology, history, or law, where such theories and disciplines carry implications for theories about the nature and structure of the individual psyche. In particular this book, while Freudian in its principal orientation, will rely upon writings, studies, and theories which come from the Jungian tradition, which has its own divisions.[17] It will suggest how important insights drawn from the abundant Jungian research and literature can be woven into and thus enrich a Freudian framework.

It is hoped that this study will help to achieve a better understanding of how social institutions and systems of thought affect the development of the individual psyche, and how the development and structure of the individual psyche is reflected in social institutions and ideologies. In this way a framework of analysis can be developed which will achieve a closer integration of what we have learned from clinical research with what we can learn from studying history and social institutions.

This study may also enrich psychoanalytic theory in a different way by integrating radical feminist theory with psychoanalytic theory. Both are powerful tools of deconstruction. One of the weakest points of psychoanalytic theory is its views on the nature of femininity and the female psyche. Radical feminism can be used to deconstruct and reconstruct psychoanalytic theory to rid it of its patriarchal bias.[18] At the same time, feminist theory can also be enriched. The weakest point of feminist theory is the lack of a theoretical explanation of the causes and dynamics of patriarchy. It is not difficult to understand why. Radical feminism, by its own definition comes out of the experience of women. Patriarchy is primarily a product of the male psyche. Yet traditional psychoanalytic theory has not fully faced the nature of male sexuality or the structure of the male psyche. This book strives to shed light on the nature of the male psyche and male sexuality by focusing on male social behavior. In so doing, psychoanalytic theory and radical feminist theory can be integrated in such a way that each is strengthened by the other.

AN OVERVIEW

It may be useful to the reader to provide an overview of the structure and theory of the book so that the reader can have some idea of how each succeeding chapter fits into the whole. The problem with such a strategy, however, is that overviews may be unclear or unpersuasive because more development of particular parts is required. If this is the case, the reader should not be disquieted, but encouraged to consider and delay judgment for fuller development and clarification in later chapters. If deemed desirable, the balance of this chapter, which may appear overly technical at this point, may be left to be read or reread at a later point such as after chapter 7.

The theory which will be developed in the following chapters can be summarized as follows. Repression is the foundation concept of the entire theoretical structure of psychoanalysis.[19] All of the other fundamental ideas and constructs of the Freudian mental universe such as neurosis, narcissism, the unconscious, the ego, the superego, the ego ideal, and the id, fit within its conceptual framework. Repression arises out of the conflict between the primary drives and the defenses which we build against them.[20]

The fetus exists in a prenatal state of narcissistic, undifferentiated, autonomous elation in which it is the universe. Consequently, there is no division between self and other, nor container and contained. It is omnipotent and immortal because it neither recognizes limitations nor measures time. The memory of this state continues to exist in the unconscious throughout a person's life, and will form a narcissistic nucleus so long as the person lives. After birth the child continues to dwell in a similar protonarcissistic realm where the sense of omnipotence is supported and encouraged through the care of loving parents.

Gradually, however, the child develops a sense of the self as separate from the (m)other. In so doing, the child shifts from a mental state of omnipotence to one of abject dependency, resulting in the creation of the narcissistic wound. The mother becomes an ideal object with which the child seeks to merge. At the same time the child is pushed by the drive to individuate. Throughout life, the individual seeks to regain the prenatal state of omnipotence and harmony or "oceanic feeling" by merging or inflating the self in order to heal the narcissistic wound. Civilization itself can be viewed as "a kaleidoscope of different attempts by man to restore *narcissistic omnipotence.*"[21]

Thus, there are two fundamental drives which determine the development of the individual psyche from birth to death. Both drives have their origin in the reality of human biology and the development of consciousness. The first is the drive to individuate. This has its origin in our necessary conscious awareness of the separateness of ourselves from the outer universe, the (m)other. This separateness is biologically determined in that each individual brain is encased in a separate body. Separate brains allow and require separate psyches.

The second drive is the drive to merge, which has its origin in the biologically determined fact that the fetus spends a lengthy period inside the womb during which mental life begins before birth. The individual seeks to heal the narcissistic wound by either merging the self in an external ego ideal which is other than the self, thus shading the distinction between the self and other, or by inflating the ego and extending it to incorporate the external other by patterning itself after an all-powerful ego ideal, and attempting to become like it.

"The ego ideal is a substitute for primary narcissistic perfection, but a substitute from which the ego is separated by a gulf, a split that man is constantly seeking to abolish."[22] The ego ideal takes several different objects in the life of the psyche. The first object is the mother; the second is the father, and for that period both the object of ego ideal and the superego are situated in the same archetypal figure of the father. The third object of the ego ideal is disembodied mind, and the fourth is that of the collective brotherhood. Another object of the ego ideal is the beloved. These various objects of the ego ideal can co-exist, to varying degrees, but not without some contradiction. In the movement from one object of the ego ideal to another, an object is never fully replaced, but can be repressed or limited in function, or function in conjunction with another object.

The Freudian concept of the ego ideal and the Jungian concept of the archetype furnish an important point of potential linkage between the two traditions. The ego ideal is an agency which is internalized in the psyche in that it serves a function through which the ego seeks narcissistic transcendency. Archetypes make up the structure of the collective unconscious. They furnish the ideals which the ego strives to merge with or emulate. It does not matter at this point whether we conceive of the ego ideal as a singular agency with several potential archetypal focal points as objects, or whether we look upon individual archetypes as individual ego ideals.

Individuation takes place when the drive to separate from an old object of the ego ideal and the drive to merge with a new one both pull in the same direction, away from the old object. The drive to separate alone is seldom powerful enough to move the psyche along the path of individuation without the pull toward a new merger. The drive to separate from the mother is reinforced by the drive to identify with the father. The drive to separate from the father, and thus to allow the ego to achieve the state of autonomous agency by rejecting the authoritative structure of the superego, can only move a male psyche to further individuation when it is reinforced by the drive to merge in the collective brotherhood. The merging of the ego in the object of the ego ideal as the beloved is the only drive which is powerful enough to separate a man from the collective brotherhood. It is for this reason that dictatorships fear and despise romantic love.[23]

The objects of the ego ideal for both male and female are not gender neutral. An object of the ego ideal will be either feminine or masculine. Since the psyche of both male and female is always, in its earlier stage, in a state of protofemininity, the object of the ego ideal will start as feminine because in the beginning the "other" is always the mother. The object of the ego ideal always remains a substitute for the state of primary narcissism, when there was no distinction between ego and ideal. The first object of the ego ideal is the mother and therefore feminine. This dictates that other objects of the ego ideal which draw the child to separate must be male or masculine. It also means that these other objects can never heal the narcissistic wound. It is a case of eating (merging) but always feeling hungry (isolated and alienated).

By substituting the father for the mother as object of the ego ideal, the father serves as an external focal point to separate the psyche of the child from the mother. Young females wish to replace the mother by merging with the father, and males wish to become like the father by identifying with him. They see the father as an all powerful figure who dominates and controls the mother. Becoming like the father, or adopting the father as object of the ego ideal in place of the mother, entails objectifying the other and dominating and controlling it as if it were an extension of the self, thereby receiving a narcissistic confirmation of the importance of the self as well as an illusion of omnipotence. When the ego seeks confirmation and narcissistic omnipotence through inflation, the male perceives women as objects to be dominated and controlled. The male now owns and controls the (m)other by possessing his own woman, and attempts to manipulate and control his environment. The ego of the male can also inflate itself by denying and transcending dependency on women for emotional and sexual satisfaction. Furthermore, it can deny the limitations of the body by conceiving of the self as a mental entity encased in a physical shell. The body will be viewed as "a worthless garment to be cast off in order to go beyond the bounds imposed by embodiment" to merge with the Divine as a spiritual essence.[24] The archetype of disembodied mind can take different forms. It can be differentiated as the *logos* of the Greeks, or it can be undifferentiated as the nirvana of Buddhism.

The attempts to heal the narcissistic wound can take one or more of four different methods: 1) through merging the ego into the other in the form of an external feminine object of the ego ideal; 2) through identifying the ego with, and patterning it after, an omnipotentlike masculine object of the ego ideal; 3) through inflating the ego to incorporate the other into an omnipotent disembodied self, or by merging the self in such a body; and 4) through merging the ego into the other in the form of an external masculine collective object of the ego ideal. The archetype of the mother or the female beloved, acts as a feminine object of the ego ideal. The archetype of the father or male beloved, acts as a masculine object of the ego ideal. The archetype of disembodied mind furnishes a different kind of masculine object of the ego ideal, as does the archetype of the collective brotherhood. It should not surprise us that a patriarchal world furnishes more masculine than feminine objects of the ego ideal or ego ideal archetypes.

The entire transition from narcissistic elation and completeness through the narcissistic loss and wound, and the seeking of a solution driven by the narcissistic memory of a state of well-being toward a merger with the ego ideal, all take place within a highly sexualized and genderized framework. Within this framework, female, body, and nature coalesce in meaning and conceptual structure in opposition to male, mind, and culture. The four methods of healing the narcissistic wound, therefore, are closely interrelated with sexuality and gender. In the second and third methods of attempting to heal the narcissistic wound, the male attempts to inflate the ego by incorporating the (m)other by dominating and controlling women, or attempts to transcend the (m)other by denying or transcending sexuality and the body. In the fourth method women are excluded by seeking union within the brotherhoods of the male. The sexualization and eroticization with which these four methods become infused is reflected in several well-known mental processes, neuroses, or perversions.[25] For example:

1. Merging of the self with the other—masochism
2. Incorporating the other into the self—sadism
3. Denying and transcending the other—sublimation
4. Losing the ego in the unity of male brotherhoods—some forms of homosexuality, destructive behavior toward women such as rape and murder.

The entire Oedipal passage starting in a pre-Oedipal state, through the Oedipal, to the post-Oedipal, is a journey from the state of primary narcissism, followed by a separation from the mother which shatters the infantile illusion of omnipotence. The separation creates the gap between the ego and the ego ideal, which is followed by a lifelong struggle to reunite ego and ego ideal to recover the lost omnipotent contentment felt in the womb. In the pre-Oedipal stage the child suffers a separation crisis in the emergence of the nascent self. The emergent self must establish its identity in terms of its generational and sexual identity and relationship with its parents. In this genderization crisis the male child must move from a psychological state of protofemininity to a state of masculinity. In the Oedipal stage the child is faced with acknowledging the difference between the sexes, and, therefore, sexuality enters into his relationship with his mother. However, the desire for union with the mother is not necessarily for the satisfaction of sexual tension but is to regain the primary narcissistic state of blissful harmony.

In the post-Oedipal stage of development the individual psyche is faced with the full realization of its limitations and its dependencies. For the male this entails the realization of the dependency of the ego on the body, on nature, and on females for emotional and sexual satisfaction, and the realization of the mortality of the ego which must terminate with death. The male faces the animality crisis when reality forces upon the conscious mind the fact that the individual is biologically locked into the procreative cycle of sexual arousal, sexual frenzy, birth, and death.

The ego of the adult male is drawn toward losing itself in a return to the mother through a merger of the ego with an object of the ego ideal in the form of a female archetype. This entails a loss of the self or the ego which is perceived as a form of castration which creates tension by conflicting with the drive toward individuation. The drive to lose the self and merge the ego within the ego ideal as other-mother-feminine creates a tension between the drive to individuate and the drive to regain the lost state of narcissistic elation and omnipotence. The tensions which the child suffers in the pre-Oedipal stage between separation and engulfment anxiety, and in the Oedipal and post-Oedipal stages become transformed into tensions between the desire to lose the self by merger and surrender of the ego to a particular female or females, and to preserve and inflate the ego through individuation or separation.

As the unconscious memory of this state of narcissistic pleasure arose from a union with a female—the mother, the urge to project the ego ideal onto a female, females, or the feminine is never lost. This drive to lose or surrender the ego to the other-mother-feminine object of the ego

ideal is repressed and countered by a drive to heal the narcissistic wound
through inflation of the ego by incorporation of females as objects into
the ego through dominating and controlling them, or by inflating the ego
through denying and transcending females, sexual desire, and the body.
Separation anxiety leads the male to project a counter masculine object of
the ego ideal in the form of the brotherhoods of the collective.

The concept of the complex furnishes a further link between Freudian
and Jungian theory. In Jungian depth psychology, complexes center on
archetypes. The heir to the Oedipus complex in the adult post-Oedipal
male is a set of four complexes within the context of which the individual
seeks the healing of the narcissistic wound. These four complexes have
their roots in the function of archetypes as objects of the ego ideal which
the ego strives to merge with or become. The heir to the tensions between
separation and engulfment anxiety of the pre-Oedipal period are the
tensions between these four complexes. In particular, the tensions are
manifested in the opposition of the drive to merge the ego with an other-
mother-feminine ideal (the Dionysian complex), with the drive to incorporate women into the ego as objects for the use and satisfaction of the
ego as omnipotent father (the Persean complex), the drive to deny and
transcend sexuality, the dependence on women, and the body, (the Apollonian complex), and/or the drive to merge the ego in a brotherhood of
the collective male (the Heraclean complex). These four complexes correspond to and incorporate four forms of objects of the ego ideal. The
Dionysian complex entails the archetypal mother as object of the ego
ideal, the Persean complex entails the archetypal father as object of the
ego ideal, the Apollonian complex entails disembodied mind as object of
the ego ideal, and the Heraclean complex entails the collective brotherhood as object of the ego ideal.

In the pre-Oedipal stage, the male child is in a Dionysian state, worshipping and wishing to merge with the mother. The Oedipal passage
begins the transition to Persean, Apollonian and Heraclean states of the
psyche through various forms of identification with the male. The child
becomes Persean when he exchanges the desire to merge with his mother
for a desire to possess his own woman as his father does. When the child
rejects female playmates for exclusively male companions we see the beginnings of the Heraclean complex. Yet in adulthood the child never
entirely loses the Dionysian complex, but only represses it because the
memory of the primary narcissistic state is one of a merger with a femi-

nine object of the ego ideal. The power of the Dionysian complex is reflected in the virulence of the other three complexes used to repress it.

Humans share a common genetic endowment and thus have a similar bimorphic sexuality. The differences between male and female regarding the nature of sexuality, the roles in procreation, the differences in kinds and quantity of hormones, result in different kinds of behavior as between the male and the female of the species. Humans concentrate in groups sharing common languages and symbolic systems within which different meanings are given to the differences of biological sex, procreation, and related human behavior. The ability of humans to communicate and store and transmit information between individuals and between generations leads to the development of what can be usefully conceived of as a collective psyche or a psyche or psyches of the collectives. The collective psyche formulates views of itself and the individuals which make it up, in terms of mythic systems. Myths are thus the manifestations of the collective psyche.

The four complexes by which the male psyche seeks the healing of the narcissistic wound are expressed or manifested in the collective psyche in the form of mythic structures which are externalized as social institutions. Thus myths, social practices, and institutions can be characterized as Dionysian, Persean, Apollonian, or Heraclean, or as varying combinations of these. These mythic structures are internalized by the individuals who make up the collective. When internalized, these myths and institutions furnish the energy for the psyche to separate from the mother, and to repress the Dionysian drive for a return or a remerger with the feminine. This is accomplished by a denigration of the feminine/mother/female/body/earth/other through negative archetypal images, and a positive reinforcement and inflation of the masculine/father/mind/culture/male ego. This creates both conscious and unconscious misogyny which furnishes the energy for the Oedipal passage and the process of individuation. The fear of castration (remaining or becoming feminine) interacts with the drive toward castration (surrendering the burden of ego-masculinity and merging with the feminine). Human culture is patriarchal because it has evolved to serve these functions.

Freud was the first to recognize that the path of individuation of the collective psyche follows that of the individual psyche. The individual Oedipal passage becomes externalized as an Oedipal passage of the collective psyche. History, therefore, can be usefully viewed in three stages, the pre-Oedipal, the Oedipal, and the post-Oedipal. In the pre-Oedipal stage of history the archetypal object of the ego ideal of the collective psyche is the figure of the mother, externalized as the Goddess or earth mother or mother earth. This is the age of matriarchal, fertility cult paganism. In the Oedipal stage of history the archetypal object of the ego ideal is the figure of the father, the paterfamilias, the royal father or monarch, and the heavenly father or father god. In the post-Oedipal stage of history the object of the ego ideal is disembodied mind as the rational, autonomous agent. It is the age of the nation-state founded on the equality of the citizens united in the brotherhood of the collective. The age of patriarchy is a negation of the age of matriarchal consciousness. The age of patriarchy covers both the Oedipal and the post-Oedipal stages of history. Patriarchy has its own dialectic. The age of monarchal father rule (thesis) is denied and negated by the age of liberal individualism within which man is conceived of as equally free from the authority of the father (the antithesis), which is in turn denied by the age of corporate state structures or male brotherhoods which restores the community which was negated by liberal individualism (the synthesis). The age of patriarchy produced the Persean, Apollonian, and Heraclean mythic systems and institutions which nurture the Persean, Apollonian, and Heraclean complexes of the individual male psyches. The process of individuation of the collective psyche whereby mankind separates from earth and nature and which produces the mind-body polar split, is thus interrelated and sexualized through a common set of misogynous mythic structures. It parallels the process of individuation whereby the individual psyche separates and individuates from the mother. The Dionysian complex which attracts the male ego toward a surrender and merger with the feminine (which would heal the masculine-feminine, mind-body, and culture-nature dualism) is in a dialectical tension with a coalescence of the Persean, Apollonian, and Heraclean complexes and institutions which drive one toward separation and individuation, and an exclusively male unification.

It would appear from this that patriarchy is an inevitable consequence of individuation. This would account for its universality. Such a view, however, is based on a simplistic concept of individuation as consisting only of separation. Individuation is the process by which the psyche or mind evolves. The psyche is more than the ego. The identity of the self is made up of identifications as much as it is made up of differentiations. Consciousness requires language and language requires common communities. Individual psyches are made up of both an individual and a collective consciousness and unconsciousness, or "I" consciousness and "We" consciousness.[26] The fully individuated psyche must integrate both ego and other. This is only possible in the context of a mythic system which heals the gender gap, and transcends mind-body and culture-nature dualism. This requires that patriarchy be negated through a new synthesis which returns our mythic structures to a positive perspective of the female, the feminine, the body, and nature.

The negation of patriarchy would require the object of the ego ideal to shift from the masculine back to the feminine. The Dionysian complex would need to be reinforced at the expense of the Persean, Apollonian, and Heraclean. The masculine archetype would then change from that of the father to that of the consort. Because it is biologically determined that humans are born of women, it is inevitable that the object of the ego ideal will commence as feminine, and it must remain so. Alienated individuality is not a stable state since the psyche will always be driven to merge the ego with the other in the course of its search for the healing of the narcissistic wound. However, such healing must be sought through men merging with women rather than merging in the brotherhood of the male. When the object of the ego ideal remains feminine for the male, misogyny will disappear from the psyche, and when it disappears from the collective psyche, then patriarchy will be transcended.

From the perspective of the history of the evolution of human consciousness, it may have been the case that the unconscious memory of the primary narcissistic union with the mother was so powerful that the process of individuation required a counter pole in the form of the father for both the male and the female. Similarly, given the uniqueness of the mental life of a brain having a fully developed cortex, the projection of a father figure may have enabled the collective psyche to separate from the animal world and nature. The collective psyche of humans in the post-Oedipal state of history, however, is sufficiently individuated that alienation is driving the individuals who make up the collective to seek forms of community. This individuated state has been externalized to such an extent in our political mythic systems and institutions that the father figure is no longer necessary as a counter polar attraction. The transference of the object of the ego ideal from the brotherhood of man to the feminine and solidarity with women and children, can eventually transform the mythic structures of the collective mind by rejecting and eliminating all misogynous content without in any way threatening the individuation of the individual or the collective psyche.

Both individuality and community are necessary conditions for full individuation of the psyche. Freedom is a necessary condition for individuality. The only way that freedom can be reconciled with community is if the forms of community and individual participation with them are con-sensual. Freedom is not possible for women without liberation from male authority and control. Human culture and institutions are patriarchal because the primary psychological forces which have been influential in producing the structures which permit or facilitate the domination by some males over others, were the complexes which led to the domination of the female by the male. The elimination of the myths and structures which permit and legitimize the dominion of males over females will, at the same time, abolish dominion of males over other males. The liberation of women is therefore a necessary condition for human liberation and further individuation of the collective psyche.

The nature and role of law has changed throughout history according to the role which it has played and continues to play in the process of individuation of the collective psyche. Law first arose as the externalization or reification of the will of the father. It therefore became a powerful mythic system and institution in the process of denying matriarchal consciousness, repressing women, and legitimizing male domination. Law and male authority were an essential part of the first stages of patriarchy. In the shift of the collective psyche from the father archetype to that of the projection and externalization of the ego as the autonomous and equal citizen, law guaranteed the necessary conditions for male independence. In the externalization and projection of the object of the ego ideal as the brotherhood of man, law has furnished the framework of the corporate structure of the state.

In the process of individuation of the female individual and collective psyche, women have sought refuge in the law and patriarchal legal and political structures. Yet law never meets the expectations of women, because it is a manifestation of the male collective psyche and a projection of the three complexes which repress and deny the Dionysian by the masculinization of the object of the ego ideal. Women will always be marginalized within such structures. The dilemma of feminism is that without patriarchal tools women have few mythic structures and institutions as instruments of liberation. The use of patriarchal structures for this purpose strengthens and adds legitimacy to them, thus guaranteeing their survival. Therefore, judicial and political action can be no substitute for consciousness-raising and awareness, nor for the deconstruction of patriarchal institutions.

Psychoanalytic theory itself is a patriarchal theory and the psychoanalytic communities are and always have been patriarchally dominated. Neither Freud or Jung's views and attitudes toward women nor the way in which they treated some of the women with whom they interacted are particularly commendable. However, this is only one of many criticisms which have been leveled at both Freud and Jung. In chapter 2, the fundamental criticisms of Freud, including those of Jung, will be briefly examined and evaluated.

According to Freud, the postulation of a "collective mind" is a necessary assumption for the existence of any social psychology.[27] Since there is no societal equivalent of the individual brain, the collective mind or psyche can best be viewed in terms of the stored information which constitutes cultures, subcultures and shared views of the world. Myth, as a product of the collective psyche, parallels dreams and fantasies as products of the individual psyche. Myth-creating is an extremely complex cultural phenomenon. Culture itself is a mythic system made of many interrelated subsystems. In creating a holistic world view, mythologizing gives meaning to the human condition. Myth as a product of the processes of projection and introjection, will contain psychological truths. Myth, however, is also a product of wish fulfillment and repression, and consequently contains a good deal of illusion. Culture, since it is in part a vast mythic system, will always contain a mixture of truth and illusion. Myth as methodology, linked with psychoanalytic social theory, enables us to recognize some of those aspects of culture which contain illusion in the Freudian sense. Therefore, in chapters 3 and 4, a theory of myth will be developed which should furnish the link between the collective and the individual psyche.

Psychoanalytic theory is subject to much debate. Freud's view of women, the feminine, and the development of the psyche in the female, have in particular come under a good deal of criticism. However, psychoanalytic theory ought to be viewed in terms of contemporary research and development. Chapters 5 and 6 will set out the revisions which must be made to Freud's theories in order to have an adequate psychoanalytic foundation for a psychoanalytic social theory, and the revisions which must be made to the theory of the Oedipus complex in order to incorporate contemporary psychoanalytic research and development. In chapter 5 a theory of the Oedipal passage will be postulated which, while remaining Freudian, will better conform to the revisions required in Freud's own views in order to develop an adequate foundation for a psychoanalytic theory of social order. Chapter 6 will examine the structure of the psyche and will discuss how Jung's interrelated concepts of archetypes and complexes can be used to enrich the Freudian concept of the ego ideal. The chapter will also argue for the position that the superego and the ego ideal are best conceived as separate and distinct agencies. The potential for confusion arises from the fact that the same archetype, that of the father, can serve as the focal point for both.

Psychoanalytic social theory requires a theory of the collective psyche. While Freud postulated the existence of the collective mind, he did not develop the concept in his writings.[28] The collective psyche should reflect the structure of the individual psyche. We should find analogues to parts of the individual psyche such as the ego, the ego ideal, and the collective unconscious.[29] Chapter 7 attempts to develop a theory of the collective psyche in terms of collected, stored, and shared information. The parallel between the view of mind entailed in psychoanalytic theory and that entailed in artificial intelligence, noted by others, is used to clarify the nature of archetypes and their function as objects of the ego ideal.

Chapter 8 develops the link between the theory of myth and psychoanalytic theory, thus showing the psychoanalytic dimension of myth. In this chapter an attempt will be made to show how myths with a particular kind of content furnish a psychological energy for the process of individuation in both the individual and collective psyche, and to show how social order fits into these mythic structures and how it reflects the presence of that particular kind of content.

In chapter 9 it will be argued that the male in the post-Oedipal stage oscillates between four different kinds of complexes which operate as defense mechanisms to deny dependency. Chapter 10 demonstrates the validity of the analysis of chapter 9 in terms of its power to explain male pathology and sexual fantasy. Chapter 11 further develops an analysis of patriarchal culture and institutions in terms of these four complexes, functioning either singly or in combinations.

Chapter 12 sketches a perspective of history which focuses on the development of mind in contrast to events, and which can support a psychoanalytic social theory which views history in terms of the development of the collective psyche. In this chapter a Hegelian theory of history will be combined with the Freudian view that the evolution of the collective psyche follows the pattern of the individual psyche. The resulting theory of history is described in terms of pre-Oedipal, Oedipal, and post-Oedipal stages which evolve in terms of a pattern of dialectical change. Chapter 13 examines the evidence and argues for the existence of an age of matriarchal fertility cult worship which parallels the pre-Oedipal stage of the individual psyche when the mother was the object of the ego ideal, and the process of separation was just beginning. The unity of humans with the earth and nature in the pre-Oedipal stage of history parallels the unity of child and mother before the separation entailed in the Oedipal passage. Chapter 14 describes the transition between the age of matriarchal consciousness and the age of patriarchy, marked by the shift from the worship of the Great Earth Goddess to the Heavenly Father or father gods, as a shift from the pre-Oedipal to the Oedipal stage of history. The shift is dialectical because the embracing of the father entails the negation of the mother. Chapters 15 and 16 detail the shift from the Oedipal to the post-Oedipal stage of history. It will be argued in these chapters that the killing of the father by the brotherhood did not occur at the beginning of history, as Freud postulated in *Totem and Taboo,*[30] but took place within history by the death of monarchy and of the paterfamilias with the rise of the republics made up of the male brotherhoods of equal citizens. The role that law plays in each of these stages will be briefly set out. Chapter 15 will discuss the role that disembodied mind as the archetypal object of the ego ideal plays in the process of individuation in both the individual and the collective psyche. Chapter 16 will analyze the role of the brotherhood of the collective as an archetypal object of the ego ideal in the post-Oedipal stage of history.

Chapter 17 will discuss the fundamental dilemma underlying nearly all legal and political theory—how to reconcile the autonomy of the individual with the necessary demands for community life, and will suggest a way in which it can be transcended by psychoanalytic jurisprudence. It will be argued in this chapter that the theoretical disputes of legal and political theory arise out of and are given their particular form and structure by underlying psychological considerations. The latter part of the chapter will examine two schools of jurisprudential thought, legal liberalism and radical feminist jurisprudence, from the perspective of a psychoanalytic jurisprudential approach. Legal liberalism has been selected because it is probably the theory which conforms most closely with Freud's own theory of law.[31] By using Freud's methodology to deconstruct legal liberalism, we can at the same time show where some of

Freud's theoretical conclusions are inconsistent with his own methodology. The concluding part of the chapter will outline the contributions to legal theory and to social theory in general which will come out of the development of a psychoanalytic social theory. It will reiterate a theme developed throughout the book, that psychoanalytic social theory needs radical feminist social theory. A particular similarity in approach and methodology brings these two streams of thought together, and makes them not only compatible with but necessary to each other.

In chapter 18, the final chapter, an attempt is made to relate all the various themes dealt with in the book in a discussion of social order in the contemporary world in terms of a struggle between Eros (life) and Thanatos (death). Theory should permit some degree of prediction by enabling us to project onto the future the patterns of change we recognize in the past. The psychoanalytic social theory developed throughout the book is used to suggest how the neurosis which has shaped the social order of today, may continue to shape it in the future. The question with which the reader is left, along with the author's own opinion, is whether or not, and to what degree, we can transcend neurosis.

Psychoanalytic social theory, lacking the clinical research and individual studies which are the raw materials from which psychoanalytic theory has been constructed, is somewhat speculative. In order to explain such contemporary events as the Holocaust, the insanity of nuclear armaments, the prevalence of the use of torture, the takeovers of government by military elites, and the staggering number of one hundred million deaths due directly or indirectly to governmental actions in the twentieth century,[32] traditional theories of social evolution and change in terms of class struggle, economic forces, ideological conflict, or other kinds of material conditions, are inadequate. Similarly, the traditional theories of and approaches to legal and political theory fail to provide a comprehensive framework within which social order can be related to the overall milieu of human existence. This book seeks to lay a foundation for the development of a psychoanalytic theory of social order by examining the mythic dimensions of law and politics, or to put it in another way, by viewing law as a mythic system. It is to be hoped that an understanding of the neurotic needs which law and politics have evolved to satisfy will lead to a better comprehension of why our legal and political institutions have taken the form and shape which they have. This, in turn, should enable us to provide a unifying foundation in psychology for the social sciences.

2.

STRUGGLING WITH FREUD'S LEGACY

PSYCHOANALYTIC SOCIAL THEORY

Freud first recognized the interrelationship of culture and neurosis in the context of religion. "[O]ne might venture," he wrote, "to regard obsessional neurosis as a pathological counterpart of the formation of a religion, and to describe that neurosis as an individual religiosity and religion as a universal obsessional neurosis."[1] Through the development of his analysis of religion as neurosis, Freud evolved the theoretical perspective that not only should we understand human history as neurosis, but the neuroses of individuals should also be understood in the context of history as a whole.[2] Psychoanalytic social theory takes the view that the evolution of human culture, with its corresponding institutions and ideologies, is the product of human neuroses which arise from awareness of certain biological imperatives, and that the neuroses of individuals are a product of institutions and ideologies. Freud concluded that there is a fundamental interrelationship between society and the individual psyche,[3] writing, "[C]ivilization is based on the repressions effected by former generations . . . each fresh generation is required to maintain this civilization by effecting the same repressions."[4]

He states elsewhere:[5]

A similar application of its point of view, its hypotheses and its findings has enabled psycho-analysis to throw light on the origins of our great cultural

25

institutions—on religion, morality, justice and philosophy. By examining
the primitive psychological situations which were able to provide the motive for creations of this kind, it has been in a position to reject certain
attempts at an explanation that were based on too superficial a psychology
and to replace them by a more penetrating insight.

Psycho-analysis has established an intimate connection between these
psychical achievements of individuals on the one hand and societies on the
other by postulating one and the same dynamic source for both of them.
. . . Our knowledge of the neurotic illnesses of individuals has been of much
assistance to our understanding of the great social institutions. For the
neuroses themselves have turned out to be attempts to find *individual*
solutions for the problems of compensating for unsatisfied wishes, while
the institutions seek to provide *social* solutions for these same problems.

An individual's private drives, emotions, repression mechanisms, wishes,
and illusions are too weak by themselves to serve their psychological
functions.[6] They work far more effectively when they can be reinforced
by group behavior.[7] Such reinforcement is possible where the patterns
tend toward the universal. Freud frequently referred to the processes of
the individual psyche when explaining the psychology of group processes,
and to the phenomena of group action in explaining the function of the
individual psyche. Toward the end of his life he wrote,

I perceived ever more clearly that the events of human history, the interac-
tions between human nature, cultural development and the precipitates of
primaeval experiences (the most prominent example of which is religion)
are no more than a reflection of the dynamic conflicts between the ego, the
id and the super-ego, which psycho-analysis studies in the individual—are
the very same processes repeated upon a wider stage.[8]

Thus, psychoanalytic social theory seeks the common patterns to be found
in the structure of society, the family, and the psyche.[9] Eli Sagan concludes his study of the transition between kinship and kingship in what
he calls "complex" societies, with the following paragraph:[10]

What seems plausible is that the great contradiction, the severe tension, in
primitive society was not economic, political, or social, but psychological.
The energy that drives the whole history of the world is the force of the
psyche struggling to fulfill its developmental destiny. That struggle is essentially an internal one against the energy of repression. The two great
elements of developmental drive and repression, at eternal war with each
other, dominate political life now as much as in the days when the first
lonely chief emerged out of the kinship-system world. Our understanding

of our present situation could be greatly enhanced if we would consider two questions about our society: What human drives and needs does it satisfy? And what needs and drives does it repress? We live at the intersection of those two questions.

Behind society, the family and the individual psyche, stands human biology as a given and the major determinant. This is what Freud was referring to when he stated, "Anatomy is destiny."[11] Psychoanalytic social theory presupposes what Freud called "metapsychology."[12] Metapsychology is based on the premise that there is an interrelationship between the pattern of the evolution of the individual psyche and that of the evolution of the collective psyche. Freud believed that all individuals contain within themselves, in some form or another, the psychological history of the human race, paralleling the way in which the development of the fetus appears to mirror the biological evolution of the human body.[13] In turn, the common pattern of development within each individual psyche furnishes the pattern for the evolution of human societies. Thus, there is a mutual interrelationship between the patterns of the evolution of the individual psyche and the psychological development of societies as a whole.[14] If this is so, we should be able to analyze any society as being in a pre-Oedipal, Oedipal, or post-Oedipal stage, or in transition between one to another.

The basic themes of psychoanalytic social theory were developed by Freud and have since been expanded upon in studies such as Herbert Marcuse's *Eros and Civilization*,[15] Norman O. Brown's *Life against Death*,[16] and *Love's Body*,[17] and Ernest Becker's *The Denial of Death*.[18] These are important and pioneering works and the author acknowledges a substantial debt to them. However, all such analyses remain trapped within the phallocentric boundaries of traditional psychoanalytic theory. This literature extensively discusses eros, sexuality, and death in the context of repression, illusion and neurosis, without seriously relating these themes to female bodies and male desire.

Phallocentricity itself is an illusion, born of repression, and a product of neurosis. By examining the characteristic psychoanalytic themes of eros, sexuality, death, illusion, repression, and neurosis in the concrete context of male desire and female bodies, phallocentricity becomes an object of study rather than a tool or category of analysis. Thus, this book seeks to transcend the phallocentric orientation of traditional psychoanalytic theory by turning Freud's methods onto some of Freud's doctrines.

In this way it seeks to be more Freudian than Freud, thus avoiding the dangers of revisionism without remaining trapped in the limits of a world view dictated by Freud's time and place in history.

The present work seeks to take psychoanalytic social theory beyond Marcuse, Brown, and Becker. At the same time it attempts to reclaim Freud's tragic vision of the future from the distortions of psychoanalytic utopianism such as that of Reuben Fine in *The Psychoanalytic Vision.*[19] It lies outside of their framework of analysis and is based on different presuppositions. To respond to their work or comment on the differences between them would be an unnecessary digression. The presuppositions upon which this study is based will be clearly set out, thus permitting the reader to contrast them with those of phallocentric psychoanalytic social theory.

THE VERIFICATION
OF PSYCHOANALYTIC THEORY

Psychoanalysis, according to two of its most eminent contemporary practitioners, is *"the* science fundamental to all human sciences."[20] This proposition would be a self-evident truth to a Freudian and a patent absurdity to a skeptic. Critics have proclaimed "the fall of the Freudian Empire," purported to have written its obituary, and described Freud's legacy as "a historical curiosity," which is "at best a premature crystallization of spurious orthodoxies; at worst, a pseudo-scientific doctrine that has done untold harm to psychology and psychiatry alike."[21]

The critics and criticisms of Freud's theories are numerous and varied. However, they generally fall into three categories. One set of critics argues that Freud's work is not scientific. A second kind of criticism has been summarized by the statement: "What is new in these theories is not true, and what is true is not new."[22] A third methodology of attack is to explain Freud's theories in terms of particular and idiosyncratic aspects of his personal life, such as his use of cocaine,[23] his Jewish cultural heritage,[24] or his own neurosis.[25]

Freud considered psychoanalytic methodology to be scientific.[26] Ernst Federn has pointed out, however, that Freud never called psychoanalysis a science, but used the German word *wissenschaft* which means the process of gaining knowledge.[27] Although it has been translated into English as "science," it doesn't have the same meaning as the English word which means a body of knowledge *(wissenschaftlichkeit* in German).[28] Karl R. Popper has argued that psychoanalysis is not a science since its propositions can neither be proven or disproved.[29] Adolf Grunbaum, on the other hand, is critical of Popper's position, arguing that Freudian hypotheses are in fact empirically testable, and in terms of such tests many of Freud's theories and doctrines can be shown to be false.[30] Both critics and defenders of Freud reject Popper's contention but hold instead that empirical evidence can refute or support the theories of Freud. There is, however, much disagreement about what would constitute proof or refutation.

There is a body of critical literature which asserts, to varying degrees, that psychoanalysis is unscientific because it has been proven in whole or in part to be false.[31] The best discussion of the issue of the status of psychoanalysis as a science is that of Kenneth Mark Colby and Robert J. Stoller.[32] They conclude that psychoanalysis is not a science because there is no objective or reliable data to be studied, since the reports of the analysts are subjective, hearsay, and interpretive. The study of the subjective is the very essence of psychoanalysis.[33] They view the term *psychoanalysis* as "a label for a number of ideas about mind that have a history extending indefinitely into the past and a future extending indefinitely forward. . . ."[34] Stoller asserts that "psychoanalysis need not claim to be a science to legitimate both its process of discovery and the discoveries that resulted."[35] He comments however, that "no other field not a science has so wanted to be one, has so watched the behavior of the unquestioned sciences, has so struggled to make itself a science."[36] After all, how can psychoanalysis be a science when there is as yet no such thing as a science of the mind? Colby and Stoller foresee psychoanalytic theory in the future eventually being absorbed by and as a part of the new discipline called *cognitive science*.[37]

There can be little question that Freud was wrong about some things. This should surprise no one, least of all his supporters, since his work was pioneering and revolutionary. Freud himself often changed his mind and later rejected a previous position. Figures like Freud, Marx, and Darwin are controversial because they all are responsible for bringing about paradigmatic shifts in human thought.[38] It is because of the profound impact of their work that there is almost a public disposition to expect perfection in their theories. Many tend to dismiss outright the significance of their writings when later events and scholarship have proved them wrong in some particular. Thus, some people talk as if Darwin, Marx, or Freud have been refuted, failing to realize that the paradigmatic shifts of thought which stem from their work have become so much a part of our world view that we lose sight of their original source.

This body of literature which is critical of all or part of Freud's theories, must be evaluated and weighed against the vast body of clinical material and research produced by the psychoanalytic community, and the vast influence that Freud has had on human thought. People from a wide variety of disciplines think that the many fundamental insights which Freud has brought to the study of the mind far outweigh his errors, most of which have already been recognized and corrected within the psycho-analytic community.

As psychoanalytic theory focuses on the mind or psyche, it raises problems which are not found in the standard sciences. These problems arise from the mind-body dualism which remains as yet unresolved in that there exists neither a valid comprehensive theory which can fully explain material and empirical phenomena in terms of mind, nor mind in terms of functions of the brain; neither is there yet a theory which can resolve the dualism by transcending both mind and body in terms of a synthesis. By linking biology to mental processes psychoanalytic theory makes an important contribution to the eventual resolution of the mind-body di-alectic.[39] Consciousness is both the source of the process of examination as well as a part of what is being observed. As consciousness is both observer and observed we are faced with a particular kind of epistemolog-ical difficulty. Psychoanalytic theory has had to resort to metaphor and analogy drawn from the physical world to describe the mental. Conse-quently it has had to borrow concepts from the physical sciences, such as drive and energy, and to draw maps and divide what is in fact not a physical territory. Many of the criticisms of psychoanalytic theory for not being sufficiently scientific miss the point of the epistemological difficul-ties. The psychological behaviorists, while purporting to maintain meth-odological and epistemological purity, cannot account for even simple mental processes such as memory which we now attribute even to com-puters.[40] The issue should not be whether psychoanalytic theory is "sci-entific" as there is no single view as to what constitutes a science or a scientific methodology. Structure and methodology differ from subject to subject even within the paradigmatic scientific world. Rather, the ques-tion should be whether mental phenomena or mind are worth studying, and if so, whether we are using the best conceptual tools. From this perspective, there can be little question about the value of continuing to struggle with Freud's legacy. Nevertheless, the critics do serve a purpose in making us aware of the problems of reifying psychoanalytic concepts and misusing analogy.[41]

Some consider the fact that the early claims of psychoanalysis to effect cures later proved to be far too optimistic as grounds for rejecting psychoanalytic theory. However, most people today who seek analysis do so for insight and understanding of themselves. If a mental condition improves, that is seen as a bonus. Freud himself finally came to recognize that his greatest contribution to human thought involved the implications of his theory of the mind for social theory, and not as a cure for certain forms of mental illness or individual therapy. Freud's place in the history of human thought is permanent and secure, and it is extremely unlikely that new developments in psychology or new revelations about Freud's personal life will change this.

There are, of course, critics who discount even this aspect of Freud's work. For example, Freud's use of psychoanalysis on historical figures has been subject to criticism.[42] In the area of anthropology, reactions have been mixed. Marvin Harris, for example, rejects all mentalist views of societal development and offers a nondialectical materialist theory of culture.[43] Malinowski claimed that the Oedipus complex is culturally specific since he found no evidence of it among the Trobriand Islanders.[44] Other anthropologists have found Freud's work to be an invaluable tool.[45] Geza Roheim finds substantial evidence of the Oedipus complex among matrilineal peoples such as the Trobriand Islanders, and shows how the uncle (the brother of the mother) plays the role of the father.[46] Recent anthropological studies have laid a great deal of stress on the importance of understanding a people's view of their sexuality and their gender structures if one is to have an in-depth comprehension of their culture as a whole.[47] Their work casts doubts on the validity of much of the views of earlier anthropologists about the sexuality of the people whom they studied. In most of these recent studies the influence of Freud's thought is prominent.

Opposition to psychoanalytic social theory has come from within the psychoanalytic community as well as from without, as a result of the medicalization of psychoanalysis in America. Freud believed strongly in the importance of having lay analysts as well as those with a medical background. "The use of analysis for the treatment of the neuroses," he wrote, "is only one of its applications; the future will perhaps show that it is not the most important one. In any case it would be wrong to sacrifice all the other applications to this single one, just because it touches on the circle of medical interests."[48] Freud lost this struggle in the United States, and the near monopoly over psychoanalysis by the American medical profession almost brought about the demise of psychoanalytic social theory in this country.

In Europe, on the other hand, psychoanalytic social theory was an influential movement, particularly among the second generation of European psychoanalysts with an interest in reconciling Freud and Marx. This ended with the rise of fascism and their forced exile from Europe. Many of these European psychoanalysts such as Otto Fenichel, Annie Reich, Edith Jacobson, Erik Erikson, Erich Fromm, and Bruno Bettelheim sought refuge in the United States. The interest in psychoanalytic social theory which they brought with them did not flourish in a psychoanalytic environment dominated by psychiatrists.[49] However, due in part to the influence of Jacques Lacan, psychoanalytic social theory has been enjoying a strong revival since 1968 in France.[50]

There is little question that analysis itself is very much on the decline. For most people lengthy sessions are a luxury. The best psychoanalytic techniques have been picked up and integrated into a wide variety of forms of pragmatic and eclectic psychotherapy. Nevertheless, in recent years there has been a revival of interest in North America in psychoanalytic social theory as is evidenced by the number of books and articles being published in the English language. Whether or not one wants to call psychoanalytic theory scientific, the reality is that it is very much alive and healthy, and its influence is spreading. When one understands the role of psychoanalytic social theory in deconstructing cherished views, it becomes clear why it meets such rabid and widespread resistance.

The criticisms of Freud claiming that what is original is not true and what is true is not original, are at worst false, and at best, trivial. Of course Freud did not discover the unconscious.[51] Neither did Marx invent socialism, nor Darwin originate the idea of evolution. One could make the same criticisms of either—that what was original was not true and what was true was not original—and it would be fallacious in much the same way as when applied to Freud. Freud developed a concept of the unconscious within a broad theory of the psyche. "He was the first systematically to connect the general idea with a wide range of particular distortions of behavior in a way that is manifestly valid to unprejudiced minds. Freud changed, perhaps irrevocably, man's image of himself."[52]

FREUD AND THE SEDUCTION THEORY

The criticisms of Freud which explain his theories in terms of his own neuroses or aspects or events of his personal life are not relevant to the issue of the truth or falsity of his work. The validity of psychoanalytic theory is independent of the historical events which led to its production. However, there is one explanation in terms of the idiosyncratic factors of Freud's life which is related to the validity of psychoanalytic theory, and that is the explanation of Jeffrey Masson.[53]

Most of Freud's early patients were women who suffered from hysteria. Almost without exception each revealed during analysis that she had been sexually molested as a child by an adult or older male, generally a member of the family and in most cases her father. Freud believed their accounts to be true and attributed the primary cause of their illness to the fact of these molestations. He set this out in a paper, "The Aetiology of Hysteria," where he writes,

> I therefore put forward the thesis that at the bottom of every case of hysteria there are *one or more occurrences of premature sexual experience,* occurrences which belong to the earliest years of childhood but which can be reproduced through the work of psycho-analysis in spite of the intervening decades. I believe that this is an important finding, the discovery of a *caput Nili* [source of the Nile] in neuropathology.[54]

Freud delivered this paper on the evening of 21 April 1896, to colleagues at the Society for Psychiatry and Neurology in Vienna. Freud describes their reaction in a letter written five days later to his friend, the Berlin surgeon, Wilhelm Fliess. "A lecture on the etiology of hysteria at the psychiatric society was given an icy reception by the asses, and a strange evaluation by Krafft-Ebing: 'It sounds like a scientific fairy tale.' And this, after one has demonstrated to them the solution of a more-than-thousand-year-old problem."[55] Most of the documentation we have on the development of what has become known as the seduction theory, Freud's growing doubts and his subsequent rejection of it, is to be found in the letters which Freud wrote during this period to Fliess.[56] In his 1933 lecture on femininity, Freud related that,

In the period in which the main interest was directed to discovering infantile sexual traumas, almost all my women patients told me that they had
been seduced by their father. I was driven to recognize in the end that these
reports were untrue and so came to understand that hysterical symptoms
are derived from phantasies and not from real occurrences. It was only later
that I was able to recognize in this fantasy of being seduced by the father
the expression of the typical Oedipus complex in women.[57]

What was it that drove Freud to believe in the end that these reports
were untrue or, in other words, fantasies? In the letter of 21 September
1897, in which Freud announced to Fliess that he was rejecting the
seduction theory, Freud gave as reasons, "[t]he continual disappointment
of my efforts to bring a single analysis to a real conclusion," and "the
surprise that in all cases, the *father* . . . had to be accused of being perverse
. . . whereas surely such widespread perversions against children are not
very probable."[58] At the same time Freud had reached the "insight that
there are no indications of reality in the unconscious, so that one cannot
distinguish between truth and fiction that has been cathected with affect."[59]

It does not follow from the fact that Freud was unsuccessful in curing
hysteria that the reports of his patients of sexual molestation in their
childhood were false.[60] Permanent cures appear to have eluded Freud
throughout all stages of the development of psychoanalysis. As far as the
prevalence of such perverse acts, what is now known about incest through
the reports of police officers and social workers, the results of interview
surveys, and the writings of people such as Judith L. Herman and Florence Rush,[61] strengthens rather than weakens the credibility of Freud's
patients. Finally, even if we accept that sexual fantasies can produce in the
unconscious the same kind of effect as an actual traumatic experience, this
would furnish no grounds for believing that memories of sexual abuse in
childhood were fantasies.

Marie Balmary has turned Freud's psychoanalytic method upon Freud
himself to argue that his rejection of the reality of childhood sexual abuse
and the creation of the Oedipus complex was an act of repression. It
stemmed from his deep sense of guilt which arose at the time of his
father's death and his inability to accept a hidden sin or "fault" in his own
father.[62] Jeffrey Masson, the former Projects Director of the Sigmund
Freud Archives, explains Freud's rejection of the reality of incest and child
abuse as a failure of courage in the face of strong professional opposition,

and an attempt to deny responsibility for what he permitted his close personal friend, Wilhelm Fliess, to do to one of Freud's patients.[63] Freud turned over his first patient, a young woman, Emma Eckstein, to his surgeon friend Fliess in order that Fliess could remove a bone from her nose to cure her of what was probably the habit of masturbation. Fliess had concocted a bizarre theory that there was a relationship between the mucous membrane of the nostrils and that of the female genital organs, such that treatment of the former could cure the problems related to the latter. To make matters worse, Fliess left a half meter of gauze in the nasal cavity, causing infection and a hemorrhage which nearly cost Eckstein her life. A very troubled Freud, in letters omitted from the first published volume of correspondence from Freud to Fliess, postulated that Eckstein bled out of longing to bring Freud to her side, thus denying not only Fliess's guilt but his own as well.[64] According to Masson, the idea of wish fulfillment, which underlies the Oedipus complex, was born at this time.[65] Another unpublished letter to Fliess, revealed by Masson, indicates Freud had subsequent doubts about his renouncement of the seduction theory.[66] Masson further reveals Freud's massive and partially successful efforts to suppress Sandor Ferenczi's last paper, in which he asserted that after years of practice as a psychoanalyst he had reached the conclusion that the memories of his patients of childhood sexual molestation were in fact true, and not Oedipal fantasies.[67]

According to Masson, Freud constructed the Oedipus complex using the idea of fantasy wish fulfillment and building on his analysis of his own psyche. Put very simply, the first object of a child's love is its mother. For the boy this remains so with the development of an unconscious hostility toward his father. A young girl, however, at a certain stage in her sexual development replaces her mother with her father as the object of her love. In the transference of her love to her father, the female child may fantasize that she is being seduced by her father. Later guilt may result in the fantasy taking the form of an act against the girl's will.

Balmary's and Masson's explanations of the unconscious motivation for Freud's change from belief to disbelief of many of his patients' accounts are not mutually exclusive.[68] In the letter to Fliess written 7 July 1897, Freud writes of a malaise which prevents him from completing the formulation of the seduction theory. "I still do not know what has been happening in me. Something from the deepest depths of my own neurosis set itself against any advance in the understanding of the neuroses, and you have somehow been involved in it. For my writing paralysis seems to me designed to inhibit our communication."[69] Nor does either explanation preclude the possibility of other motivational factors. Whatever the reasons for Freud's reversal, the fact remains that Freud's repression mirrors society's repression. Society in general has closed its eyes to the sexual abuse of children, and Freud has only made it easier for us to deny what we do not wish to accept.

Whether or not what has become known as the seduction theory is valid as a psychoanalytic theory of the origins of neurosis, as is argued by Masson and intimated by Balmary, is not relevant to my argument. I wish only to suggest that it is highly likely that many of the descriptions given by patients in analysis of sexual abuse as children are true and not fantasies, and a recognition of this fact should have led Freud to study the nature of male rather than female sexuality, and, further, that if psychoanalysis had taken this direction, we would have today a more solid foundation upon which to build an adequate psychoanalytic social theory.

Peter Gay, in his biography *Freud: A Life for Our Time,* points out that the abandonment of the seduction theory did not lead Freud to disbelieve all of his patients' accounts of childhood sexual abuse. Gay states, "Ceasing to believe everything his patients told him did not require him to fall into the sentimental trap of holding sober black-coated bourgeois incapable of revolting sexual aggression. What Freud repudiated was the seduction theory as a general explanation of how all neuroses originate."[70]

Zvi Lothane argues that both Masson and his critics were wrong in part.[71] Masson was wrong because Freud never abandoned the seduction theory, but always believed that some of the sexual child abuse related by some of his patients had actually taken place. Yet at the same time, a theory of fantasy was important to psychoanalytic theory. On the other hand, according to Lothane, Anna Freud and Eissler were wrong in assuming that the seduction theory would confuse or destroy psychoanalysis. Lothane persuasively demonstrates that the seduction theory is not inconsistent with the Oedipus complex and the fundamental structure of psychoanalysis.

It is probable that Gay and Lothane are correct in asserting that Freud did not discount all of his patients' accounts as fantasies. However, his general skepticism has facilitated the suppression of the reality of child abuse, and has helped shape the attitudes of the legal profession and psychiatrists toward women's testimony about sexual abuse and assault. The leading text in the English-speaking world on the law of evidence states:

> Modern psychiatrists have amply studied the behavior of errant young girls and women coming before the courts in all sorts of cases. Their psychic complexes are multifarious. . . . One form taken by these complexes is that of contriving false charges of sexual offenses by men. . . . *No judge should ever let a sex offense charge go to the jury unless the female complainant's social history and mental makeup have been examined and testified to by a qualified physician.*[72]

One medical practitioner even goes so far as to warn the legal profession that "the girl herself may tear her genitals to fabricate her story."[73]

If Freud did take seriously the testimony of at least some of his patients, he should have been led to confront the underlying but central question: how are we to understand the nature of the psyche of males who would sexually molest little children, including their own? Male sexuality should then have become the focal point of psychoanalytic theory. Instead, the Oedipus complex shifted the focus onto the female, turning the analysand from victim to psyche-defective. Freud wrote several essays on human, infantile, and female sexuality,[74] but none on male sexuality as such. He produced no male counterpart to his lectures on "Female Sexuality" and "Femininity." Freud constructed his theory of female sexuality around the Oedipus complex and penis envy. The entire development of the psyche of the female child is colored, according to Freud, by the feeling of incompleteness and inferiority because of the lack of a penis.[75] Freud thus accepts the male psyche as the norm and explains the female psyche in terms of a pathological reaction to masculinity. Thus, traditional psychoanalytic theory has avoided, denied and repressed the nature of male sexuality.

Much of the feminist literature critical of Freudian theory focuses its attack on Freud's view of female sexuality. The criticism is well taken but not fatal to psychoanalytic theory.[76] A reconstruction of Freud's theory in terms of a more accurate view of the nature of both female and male psychosexuality can, I believe, furnish an adequate foundation for social theory. Given the numerous significant examples of irrational human behavior in the twentieth century, it is imperative that the kind of work pioneered by Freud be kept vital.

FREUDIAN AND JUNGIAN
PSYCHOANALYTIC THEORY

A good depth psychologist, familiar with the works of Freud and Jung, will point out to the social scientist that Freud has given us an ego psychology focused on the individual psyche. An adequate foundation for a depth psychology requires consideration of Jungian analytical concepts such as archetypes and the collective unconscious. Jung was deeply influenced by the theoretical interpretation of history of the Swiss legal historian, J. J. Bachofen. Through his study of prehistory through myth, Bachofen revealed or uncovered the prehistorical period of matriarchal consciousness and Goddess worship which, though ferociously attacked by anthropologists of the day, has since been supported by archaeological evidence. This discovery permitted Jung to do for Paganism what Freud did for the Judaeo-Christian tradition. Jung set the archetypal mother alongside Freud's archetypal father. Norman O. Brown clearly recognizes the importance of what Jung saw in Bachofen's work, stating:

> The proper starting point for a Freudian anthropology is the pre-Oedipal mother. What is given by nature, in the family, is the dependence of the child on the mother. Male domination must be grasped as a secondary formation, the product of the child's revolt against the primal mother, bequeathed to adulthood and culture by the castration complex. Freudian anthropology must therefore turn from Freud's preoccupation with patriarchal monotheism; it must take out of the hands of Jungian *Schwärmerei* the exploitation of Bachofen's great discovery of the religion of the Great Mother, a substratum underlying the religion of the Father—the anthropological analogue to Freud's discovery of the Oedipal mother underlying the Oedipal father, and comparable, like Freud's, to the discovery of Minoan-Mycenaean civilization underlying Greek civilization.[77]

Another Freudian, Janine Chasseguet-Smirgel, writes "Bachofen's work . . . touches upon a profound psychological truth, because we can thus observe projected onto the history of civilizations the individual adventure of development in men and women."[78]

The differences between Freudian and Jungian theory, while substantial, are not as great as would appear from a mere superficial examination.[79] Many of the concepts are similar but a different terminology is used. There is no reason why some of the more important insights and clinical research of each tradition should not be used by the other. The almost religious fervor and narrow-mindedness of some of the practitioners of both schools is not appropriate in the context of research and scholarship. Books such as *The Origins and History of Consciousness,* by the Jungian scholar Erich Neumann, for example, are valuable sources for anyone interested in psychoanalytic social theory. Given the neglect of the Freudian tradition regarding the mother archetype, work already done by Jungian theorists in this field should be an essential starting point for psychoanalytic social theory within the Freudian tradition. Jungian scholarship in the field of myth is equally important. A useful starting point for linking the vast bodies of Freudian and Jungian psychoanalytic social theory is the work of Otto Rank on myth, particularly the myth of the hero.[80]

Nevertheless, because I think that Freud was correct about the importance of infantile sexuality, and that Jung was wrong in de-emphasizing the importance of human sexuality in the evolution of both the individual and the collective psyche, and because I think that Jung was wrong in rejecting the Oedipus complex as a useful analytic framework of analysis, Jungian scholarship will be used in this book to supplement a Freudian frame of reference rather than vice versa.

REVISING FREUD

Whatever position one takes toward the work of Freud, it is undeniable that his impact on twentieth century thought has been far-reaching and profound. We continue to struggle with the legacy of his writing. "The specter of psychoanalysis continues to haunt society."[81] The reason it does, and the reason why at least some consider it to be a foundation science, is that in Freud's lifetime psychoanalytic theory was transformed from a method of treatment of certain neurotic disorders into a "general theory of civilization."[82]

Freud's greatest weaknesses lie where he himself failed to apply his own methodology. Freud was very much a deconstructionist in the tradition of Nietzsche. Deconstruction is both a philosophical position and an intellectual strategy. As a philosophical position it entails setting up an opposition to the accepted or more popular philosophical theory or perspective.[83] As an intellectual strategy it entails taking a new and external perspective to describe what has been hidden, repressed, ignored, or excluded from the position which is being opposed.

Almost from the very beginning of the psychoanalytic movement, it became clear to the more creative and insightful among Freud's disciples that the pre-Oedipal period of the development of the psyche and the importance of the role of the mother in the development of the child were vastly underestimated by Freud. Jung pioneered the study of the role of the archetypal image of the mother in the development of the psyche.[84] Georg Groddeck wrote extensively about the role of the mother in the development of the child.[85] Otto Rank made the relationship between the child and the mother central to his psychoanalytic perspective.[86] Sandor Ferenczi placed much greater stress on the role of the mother than Freud.[87] Ruth Brunswick first coined the term *pre-Oedipal* and developed an analysis of the phases of child development.[88] In particular she examined the relationship between female children and their mothers in the pre-Oedipal stage of the child's development. Others such as Melanie Klein,[89] Harry Sullivan,[90] D. W. Winnicott,[91] Erik Erikson[92] and Margaret Mahler and her associates[93] have developed an extensive body of theory, research and literature on the role and place of the mother in the development of the psyche.

While Jung and Rank broke with Freud, the others all remained within the Freudian tradition to varying degrees. Although Freud reached an understanding of the importance of the pre-Oedipal stage in the development of the female psyche, he was less convinced of the relevance of the role of the mother in the development of the psyche of the male. Contemporary psychoanalytic theory fully recognizes the role of the mother and the importance of the pre-Oedipal stage for both males as well as females. It is now generally recognized that in terms of the development of the individual psyche the pre-Oedipal stage is at least as important as the Oedipal stage, if not more so. The Oedipal passage described in chapter 5 will take into account current research, and will be viewed as the stage in the ongoing process of individuation of the psyche during which the child completes the psychological break from the mother through establishing an identity in terms of the positions of, and the appropriate relationship to, the two parents. The interpretations and revisions of Freud to be found in the psychoanalytic writings of Margaret Mahler and her associates,[94] Robert Stoller,[95] Janine Chasseguet-Smirgel,[96] and Irene Fast,[97] furnish us with the basis of an Oedipal theoretical framework which can function as the foundation of a psychoanalytic social theory. I have chosen to focus on the interpretation of Freud developed in the work of these psychoanalytic theorists because their theoretical perspectives, interpretations, and modifications of Freud's theories are based on years of clinical psychoanalytic research and treatment (Mahler and her associates with psychotic infants, Stoller with genetically normal males suffering from gender ambiguities, and Chasseguet-Smirgel with sexual perverts).[98] Their work sheds much light upon pre-Oedipal development and the role that the mother plays in the process of the development of the psyche in the child, areas which Freud himself recognized were deficient in his writings and would need revision after further research. Not only does their work remain true to the spirit and methodology of Freud, but their conclusions are mutually consistent and supportive. Stoller and Chasseguet-Smirgel have written extensively about the implications of their work for psychoanalytic social theory, and the work of Mahler and her associates has been found to be highly relevant by other social theorists,[99] in particular by some radical feminists.[100] Thus, it could be said that struggling with Freud's legacy consists of remaining true to his methodology but revising his theories where current research suggests Freud was in error.

FREUD AND LACAN

Jacques Lacan (1901–1981) has had a profound influence on psychoanalytic theory in France, and upon some feminist psychoanalytic theorists.[101] His life as an analyst, theorist, and teacher has been surrounded by controversy.[102] Given the contention surrounding his work and the complexity of his use of language, it would be dangerous and presumptuous to summarize or restate his views.[103] Nevertheless, he is far too important a figure to ignore and many of his ideas are pivotal to some of the central themes of this book, particularly the issues which relate to patriarchy. Chasseguet-Smirgel, upon whose views this book heavily relies, rejects Lacan's view that infants are born into language which structures their unconscious, and finds his perspective far too phallocentric to be helpful in understanding female sexuality. She states: [104]

> I do not work with "language" as being there before the individual, as something that captures him like a net. But I must say that in general, as far as I understand Lacan, my views are very far from his. I must also add that I am very surprised that in some foreign countries Lacan is considered an

important reference for the feminists. I do not know of any psychoanalytic theory that is so strongly phallocentric. In fact, Lacan disliked women very much. When some of the women in his movement became feminist, he fired them.

In contrast, feminist psychoanalytic theorists such as Jane Gallop[105] and Juliet Mitchell[106] find Lacan's work central to feminist concerns. The psychoanalytic perspective taken in this book is not particularly Lacanian. On the other hand, the reading of Lacan has influenced important aspects of themes developed within it. In particular Lacan's view of the unconscious as structured is adopted,[107] and is found to be consistent with Jung's view of the unconscious as having an archetypally structured part which he called the collective unconscious.[108]

I have found Lacan's views about the nature of desire,[109] and his theory as to the nature of sexual differences to be particularly worthwhile. I also find that many of his views can be reconciled with those of Chasseguet-Smirgel, and their different perspectives can frequently be accommodated within the theoretical framework being developed here. One of the more significant differences between these authors relates to the nature of female sexuality. Lacan views female sexuality as phallus-centered,[110] while Chasseguet-Smirgel views female sexuality as womb and vagina centered.[111] In this regard Lacan's theory of female sexuality is more consistent with that of Freud than that of Chasseguet-Smirgel. Nevertheless, I prefer the view of Chasseguet-Smirgel, given that the nature and structure of feminine/female archetypal images seem to be womb- rather than phallus-oriented. It will later be argued that there are at least two different interrelated gender/sex archetypal structures of sexual difference in terms of which the self is formulated and structured. The first archetypal structure (Jehovah/Adam-Eve) is phallus-oriented with completeness and wholeness determined in terms of the absence or presence of the phallus in the archetypal image. The other (Goddess-consort) is womb-oriented and reproductive centered. Both contradictory sets of archetypal structures are rooted in the collective psyche and play primary or subsidiary roles in the formation of the self and sexual difference. Each determines the nature of desire in a somewhat different way. This analysis would permit some reconciliation between the Lacanian position and that of Chasseguet-Smirgel.

This book will be sympathetic to Lacan's attempts to undermine recent Freudian reconstruction by returning to a serious analysis of Freud's text.

At the same time, the book will incorporate recent developments in Freudian psychoanalytic theory where clinical research indicates that Freud was likely wrong. The delicate balance sought is to be true to the methodology and spirit of Freud, while being open to the ongoing development of psychoanalytic theory in a manner which is consistent with Freud's legacy to human thought.

PSYCHOANALYTIC THEORY AND PATRIARCHY

The most serious criticisms of Freud focus on his views on female sexuality and the patriarchal orientation of his theory.[112] Implicit in psychoanalytic theory, even in its most contemporary form which would in every way deny the inferiority of women, is an assumption of the necessity and inevitability of patriarchy, and consequently male domination. This necessity rests upon certain presuppositions which include the following:

1. In the human species there is a natural instinctive drive toward the individuation of the self. It is an inevitable consequence of having a cortex and the mental process of consciousness which the cortex makes possible.
2. The family is a natural social structure given the evolutionary developed capacities and biological structure of the male and female in the human species.
3. Masculinization is a necessary condition for the individuation of the males of the human species, otherwise they will not be able to separate from the mother and will remain in some form of femininity or protofemininity.
4. The role of archetypal figure of the father is a necessary focal point for the process of individuation in both the male and the female.
5. Misogyny will be an inevitable by-product of the process of individuation.

While nothing in contemporary psychoanalytic theory directly dictates that males must dominate, all the factors which have led to patriarchy are seen as necessary for the process of individuation.

Stoller even goes so far as to argue for the necessity of perversion. He finds males much more inclined toward perversion than females. In "The

Necessity of Perversion," the final chapter of his book, *Perversion: The Erotic Form of Hatred,* he argues: [113]

> Until the family no longer functions as the primal unit in the maintenance of society, perversion will serve four necessities: preservation of the individual's pleasure, preservation of the family, preservation of society, and preservation of the species. In claiming this, I am moving beyond Freud's fundamental discovery that the perverse person is a *casualty* of that necessity of society, the family, to the position that perversion is a *necessity* created by society and the family so as not themselves to become worse casualties. . . .
>
> As we know from studying oedipal conflict, intimacy causes erotic strains so severe that the family's stability is chronically endangered. Thus a second necessity: perversion must act as a repository of conservatism to stabilize otherwise explosive forces. It allows cruelty and hatred in the family to be contained before they become too destructive, and the resulting efficiency permits parents to secure themselves and their family by means of the presence of their perverse child.

Stoller goes on to argue, "[P]erversion has served—as a counter-revolutionary force—to allow the family to persist," and that "by preserving the family, perversion saves society." [114] He concludes that [115]

> In other words, like all other conditions produced by neurotic mechanisms so stabilized and efficient that we call them character structure, perversion serves as the only workable complex of compromises; it draws off enough rage and despair that society and the individual are not completely unstrung by the otherwise destructive tendencies arising from infantile frustration and trauma in the family.
>
> As long as there are infants, society will invent ways to raise them, and, in raising them, will shape their sexual desire. Not knowing what will come if the family disappears, we cannot know how human sexuality will, in adapting, be modified. My guess is that if all goes well for our race, perversion will die down and variance increase. Perhaps someday perversion will not be necessary.

However, there is something perverse about this very argument. Given that perversion is found mainly among males, and that it is generally females who are its victims, it follows that to argue for the necessity of perversion is to argue for the necessity of females as victims. While it is never directly articulated, it seems that at its very core the entire structure of psychoanalytic theory assumes that the welfare of women must be sacrificed for the sake of the family and society—indeed, for the welfare of the human race.

It also strikes me that not only is this argument perverse, but that it is in some way circular. The family and society are patriarchal by their very nature. The argument therefore becomes "patriarchy is necessary for the preservation of patriarchy." It is true that perversion is necessary for the continuation of male domination, patriarchy, and masculinity. The critical issue is whether there is anything in psychoanalytic theory which demonstrates that masculinity and gender bifurcation are still necessary for the process of individuation.

This raises several questions. First, is there any connection between the repression of the sense of self in females and the process of individuation in males? Second, if such a connection does exist, is it a necessary connection? Is female suppression the price of male individuation? If so, what is the relationship between male domination and male individuation?

These issues have been directly addressed in the writings of psychoanalytic theorist, Jessica Benjamin, in her book, *The Bonds of Love: Psychoanalysis, Feminism, and the Problem of Domination.*[116] In it she sets out in sharp focus the relationship between domination and individuation which is both express and implicit in Freud's theory of the Oedipus complex. "The three pillars of oedipal theory," according to Benjamin are "the primacy of the wish for oneness, the mother's embodiment of this regressive force, and the necessity of paternal intervention."[117] The Oedipus complex assigns gender to the polarity of the drive for individuation and the natural longing to return to the blissful symbiotic state which underlies the reluctance to differentiate. According to Benjamin, this polarity is closely interrelated to a second set of polarities, the split between autonomy and dependency and between nurturance and freedom, which also become bifurcated along gender lines. These two sets of polarities "all combine to create the paradox that the only liberation is paternal domination."[118]

Benjamin highlights the pivotal issue underlying the ambivalent but necessary relationship between feminism and psychoanalytic theory. Only feminist theory focuses on the problem which psychoanalytic theory "scarcely acknowledges" but which is central to both contemporary psychoanalytic theory and particularly psychoanalytic social theory. Psychoanalytic social theory can no longer be carried on independently of feminist theory. Benjamin's statement of the problem reveals why.[119]

The construction of difference . . . harbors the crucial assumptions of domination. Analyzing the oedipal model in Freud's original formulations and

in the work of later psychoanalysts, we find this common thread: the idea
of the father as the protector, or even savior, from a mother who would
pull us back to what Freud called the "limitless narcissism" of infancy. This
privileging of the father's role . . . can be found in almost every version of
the oedipal model. . . . Paradoxically, the image of the liberating father
undermines the acceptance of difference that the Oedipus complex is meant
to embody. For the idea of the father as the protection against "limitless
narcissism" at once authorizes the idealization and the mother's denigration.
. . . At the heart of psychoanalytic theory lies an unacknowledged paradox:
the creation of difference *distorts,* rather than fosters, the recognition of the
other. Difference turns out to be governed by the code of domination.

Benjamin suggests a way out of the paradox. "One step in the dissolution of this dualism," she writes "is to reinterpret the Oedipus complex in
such a way that it is no longer the summation of development."[120] Her
suggestion is that we need to develop a view of the process of individuation that takes us beyond successful separation, but includes a reintegration of self and other, and a recognition that our interrelatedness between
self and other is as much a part of reality as is our separateness. Such a
view "opens a place in the reality principle for bodily continuity with an
other; it includes the intersubjective experience of recognition and all the
emotional elements that go into appreciating, caring for, touching, and
responding to an other, many of which are developed in infancy.[121] Thus,
"a new perspective on the Oedipus complex might see it as only a step in
mental life, one that leaves room for earlier and later levels of integration."[122]

Chasseguet-Smirgel is also aware of the paradox of the Oedipus complex, but is unable to suggest a resolution because she identifies the
superego, which is the heir of the Oedipus complex, with the masculine/
father, and the ego ideal, which is the heir of primary narcissism, with the
feminine/mother. Benjamin is rightly critical of the genderization of these
two agencies of the psyche.[123] This book will attempt to reconcile her
view with that of Chasseguet-Smirgel by developing a theory of the ego
ideal in the context of Jung's concepts of archetypes. It will later be argued
that the objects which the ego ideal takes are archetypal. Thus, the ego
ideal, which has in and of itself no gender, can take either a masculine or
a feminine archetype as its object. It can have more than one object at the
same time, and the archetypal objects of the ego ideal can change in the
process of individuation. In the passage from the pre-Oedipal to the
Oedipal state, the object of the ego ideal of the child changes from that of

the archetypal mother to the archetypal father. Such an explanation allows us to retain Chasseguet-Smirgel's important analysis of the function of the ego ideal in contrast with the superego, while at the same time permitting us to develop a theory of individuation which culminates in the kind of reintegration argued for by Benjamin.

In the context of psychoanalytic social theory this allows us to develop a theory of the origins, development, and decline of patriarchy in terms of archetypal shifts in the objects of the ego ideal of the collective psyche. The moment that the family is seen as an institution where certain members have a legitimate right to dominate other members, then we are in the context of law. Law is not merely the externalization of the superego in the collective psyche, it is also the externalization of the archetypal father as object of the ego ideal. Law cannot be separated from patriarchy, and the moment that human families became patriarchal, law was born.[124] Because the extrojection of the male has been, and still remains, such a powerful projection, it becomes a part of our description of the world. It permeates nearly every aspect of human culture. It is the product of neuroses stemming from the biological imperatives which have, as Freud has shown, shaped the psyche of the male. Freud himself did not go far enough in uncovering the nature and shapes which male neuroses have taken. It was left to the theorists and writers of the feminist movement to take up the task. In so doing, they have brought about the beginnings of a paradigmatic shift even more radical than that introduced by Marx. Traditional liberal political theory limits the perimeters of political analysis to the functions of official governmental and legal institutions, excluding what transpires in the workplace. Marx expanded the arena of political analysis to include the economic sphere, thus including in the public arena what previously was considered to be an area of private social interaction. Marx has made economic politics a part of our conceptual framework. Whatever orientation on the spectrum of left to right of political theorists, their political analysis must now inevitably include, come to terms with, or interface with economics.

While Marx moved the line between the public and the private to include the economic arena, the feminists have eliminated the distinction between the public world of politics and the private world of the home which underlies both liberal and Marxist political analysis.[125] They have shown that not only is the structure of the family political, but it is the political structure of this private world which underlies the political structure of the public arena. Radical feminism challenges all traditional epistemological assumptions and requires us to re-evaluate what we consider to be the most self-evident ontological assumptions.[126]

Psychoanalytic social theory takes this deconstructionist methodology one step further, and for the purpose of political analysis, eliminates the distinction between the private world of the self and the public world of the other. An adequate psychoanalytic social theory must not only be able to explain political and economic forces in terms of a depth psychology, but must be able to explain why human culture is patriarchal. Therefore, psychoanalytic theory is the ultimate tool of deconstructionism which challenges all exclusionary lines and divisions between public and private, mind and body, self and community, masculine and feminine, normal and abnormal.[127]

Psychoanalytic social theory and radical feminist political and legal theory, while using different methodologies, have striking parallels. The corner stone of radical feminist political and legal theory is in the writings of Catharine A. MacKinnon.[128] That methodology "is neither materialist nor idealist"[129] but is based on consciousness-raising: "the collective critical reconstitution of the meaning of women's social experience, as women live through it."[130] Psychoanalytic social theory, on the other hand, uses the techniques of psychoanalysis to analyze collective behavior, social institutions, shared ideologies, and mythic systems. Radical feminism and psychoanalysis converge as their different methodologies end up focusing on the same thing: sex. As stated by MacKinnon, "Male dominance is sexual"[131] and men "sexualize hierarchy."[132] Nancy J. Chodorow clearly outlines the various congruencies that feminism and psychoanalysis share.[133] Gender and sexuality are central to both theories in that both are fundamentally concerned with femininity, masculinity, heterosexuality, and gender and sexual inequality. This common focus makes both theories essentially political. Both theories share a similar set of epistemological premises in that both recognize that what is believed to be reality is a construct, and in particular, both recognize "that sexual and gender development as we know them are not inevitable.[134] Feminist theory reveals how women have been objectified. As graphically stated by MacKinnon, "Man fucks woman; subject verb object."[135] Psychoanalytic theory furnishes a theory of object relations, which explains the psychological processes involved in the objectification of persons. Radical feminism recognizes that the power of patriarchy derives from and rests on the power to construct the world or define reality. According to MacKinnon, "Power to create the world from one's point of view, particularly from the point of view of one's pleasure, is power in its male form."[136] Psychoanalytic theory explores the mental processes underlying the formulation of the beliefs and constructs that constitute what is taken as being real.[137] The processes, fundamental to psychoanalytic theory, by which constructs of the self and the other are formed underlie all beliefs about reality. Radical feminism reveals that male power "is a myth that makes itself true."[138] Psychoanalytic theory reveals how and why myth and reality converge.

Contemporary psychoanalytic social theory must be able to subsume economic and sexual politics. Therefore, it would require an interpretation and revision of Freud which, while maintaining the integrity of Freud's methodology and the basic structure of his theory, would fully integrate the deconstructionist and epistemological paradigmatic shift which radical feminism has made possible.

The extrojections of the male have had such a profound effect on the shaping of our institutions that one can read the structure of the male psyche from them, and the nature of the institutions from the structure of the male psyche. Therefore, patriarchy is both an item of the psyche as a belief system, and a set of institutions. To fully understand patriarchy, we must see what is contained within the psyche which has been extrojected and what its relationships are to the biological imperatives which have determined the structure of the male psyche.

Patriarchy is not directly determined by biological imperatives. However, these imperatives have produced the psychic conflicts which give rise to the repression and wish fulfillment which have structured the male psyche. These include the belief in the inferiority of women and the legitimate right of the male to dominate them. These belief systems are intimately related to the psychic processes of separation from the mother, the process of genderization, and the passage through the Oedipus complex. These processes are instrumental in the development of the ego, the ego ideal, and the superego. Thus, patriarchy is a set of mythic systems which transforms a contingent history arising out of male wish fulfillment and repression, into an inevitable and consequently justified and legitimate natural state.

3.

THE MYTHOLOGICAL DIMENSIONS OF CULTURE

THE NATURE OF MYTHIC THOUGHT

Viktor E. Frankl argues that the "will to meaning" is "man's primary concern."[1] The search for meaning requires that we give order and significance to what we experience, and that we define the self in terms of its relationship to the external world. Order, significance, and definition require such properties as relatedness, differentiation, unification, and consistency. As people seek a unified or consistent view of the world, their view of society reflects their view of nature. To this extent, their view of the social order and the natural order form part of a unified view of the cosmos, or a world view. Any world view is a mythic structure, even that of a highly technical and scientifically oriented culture.[2]

Our fascination with society's relationship to nature is long standing, stemming from our psychological need to view the chaotic cosmos in which we find ourselves as an ordered whole. It reflects a desire to construct a society in a manner allowing the natural order to be represented in the social order. According to Roland Barthes, myth transforms history into nature.[3] He states, "[M]yth has the task of giving an historical intention a natural justification, and making contingency appear eternal. . . . What the world supplies to myth is an historical reality, defined . . . by the way in which men have produced or used it; and what myth gives in return is a *natural* image of this reality."[4]

The dominant mythic structure or world view shared by the members

50

of a culture gives them the belief that their social order is legitimate, that is to say, natural. Social orders presume or rest on mythic structures from which the belief in the legitimacy of that order is derived. Therefore, the relationship between social order and myth is fundamental to the understanding of culture and human behavior. The mythic structure furnishes the link between the natural and the normative, between what is and what ought to be—between the way things are and what we want. Given Barthes's definition of myth, natural law as philosophy, for example, must inevitably have a mythic dimension. Thus, it is difficult to mark where philosophy ends and mythic thought begins.[5]

The mythic structures of culture evolve unconsciously over a period of time. To the extent that the mythic structure is woven into the cultural fabric, it becomes a part of the cultural heritage of each person born into that culture.[6] The mythic structure is an important force in the formulation of the psychic identity and consciousness of the members who share the culture. The mythic structure is both the reflection of the psychic content of the peoples sharing a culture, and a formulating force in the shaping of that psychic content. Thus, a two-way relationship exists between people and their culture: the culture and its mythology are products of the psychic life of a people, and the people's psychic life is in large part the product of the culture.

Like branches of a tree, the disciplines of human knowledge differentiate from the common trunk of myth. Whether physics, mathematics, literature, philosophy, religion, history, medicine, or law, all are the children of this common mother. Yet no department of mythic studies is to be found in the university, and the study of myth is not recognized as an independent branch of learning. Many disciplines such as literature, anthropology, religious studies, classics, and history readily admit their debt to myth as a source of their subject matter, but often fail to recognize the essential mythic structure of the discipline itself.

There are other areas of human knowledge such as sociology and political theory where the function of myth is acknowledged historically, yet while such "scientists" observe mythic thinking in their subjects, they remain unaware of the mythic dimensions of their own thought and the degree to which myth colors their purportedly objective observations and conclusions.[7] Law is just such a discipline.[8] Legal scholars and lawyers are ready to admit the mythic origins of law, but few recognize the mythic dimensions of contemporary legal thought.

While it may appear that some disciplines such as mathematics or physics have entirely transcended their mythic origins, at their periphery thought begins to take on a mythic dimension when questions are posed which are as yet unanswerable.[9] Gilbert Ryle defines myth as a categorical error, as "the presentation of facts belonging to one category in the idioms appropriate to another."[10] When we are faced with the unknown we begin by seeing if it is like something in the realm of the known, and hence resort to metaphors, analogies, and models. It is at this point that the danger of categorical mistake can enter, and thought can take on a mythical dimension.[11]

The concept of myth has several levels of meaning.[12] Most commonly myth is used as an ancient story, the "truth" or "falsehood" of which is not relevant. Indeed, at this level when people say, "It is a myth," they mean it is merely a myth. By doing this, they have in fact demythified the belief and it no longer has the potency of a myth. However, at a deeper level of meaning we recognize that while the story is in mythic form, it contains important psychological truths about humans and their nature. Myths are generally not found in isolation, but exist rather as parts of mythic systems. The Old and New Testaments, for example, make up a unified mythic system.[13] The myths of classical Greece or sets of myths of ancient India, such as those of the Upanishads, form systems, or are at least systematically related. When myths form a system, they usually furnish answers for the basic questions of human existence such as, "What are we?" "Where do we come from?" and "Where are we going?" or "What is our destiny?" When writers such as Milton or Dante seek to give expression to such questions, the mythic dimensions of their work become apparent. Although less obviously, the writings of natural and social scientists, such as Darwin, Marx, Freud, and Jung, take on a mythic dimension when struggling with these same questions.

Taking these various levels of meaning into account we can conclude that mythic thought does not necessarily take the form of a narrative. Barthes's explanation of the role of myth, the transformation of history into nature, stresses the ontological aspect of mythic thought, while Ryle's definition of myth as, "the presentation of facts belonging to one category in the idioms appropriate to another," stresses its epistemological function. As well as the ontological and epistemological functions of myth, there is a psychological function or aspect by which the external world is seen in terms of internal psychological experience. The decisive characteristic of mythic thought, according to Tucker, is "that something by nature interior is apprehended as exterior."[14] The external world is organized and formulated from the projections of internal psychological experience.

MYTH AND PSYCHOANALYTIC THEORY

Barthes', Ryle's, and Tucker's definitions of myth are not mutually exclusive. As we organize disparate areas of human thought and experience into a unified world view, we require conceptual superstructures to interrelate these seemingly independent areas which have been organized around and according to the categories of the traditional disciplines, sciences, and arts. As we move outside the boundaries of these familiar classifications we enter into less-known conceptual territory. Even though our old categories, methodologies, and epistemologies are inadequate, they are all we have to work with, and consequently we seek analogies and similarities with the known. Thus, familiar patterns are projected onto the unknown. In this process of projection, it is inevitable that the external world is viewed, in part at least, as a reflection of the inner mental world. It is this projection which changes history into nature, and because of the kind of material which is projected from the psyche, a categorical mistake is made.

The fact that mythic thought is so revealing of the nature and structure of the human psyche explains the frequent reference to and use of myth by Freud, Jung, and Rank.[15] The revelatory force of myth for psychoanalysis lies not so much in its epistemological function as in its ontological role of making the contingencies of the historical "what was" and "what is" conform to what we wish that it had been and wish that it were. These wishes are then projected onto the external world. The categorical mistake or error is what allows illusion to appear as reality. According to Freud:[16]

> [A] large part of the mythological view of the world, which extends a long way into the most modern religions, *is nothing but psychology projected into the external world*. . . . One could venture to explain in this way the myths of paradise and the fall of man, of God, of good and evil, of immortality, and so on, and to transform *metaphysics* into *metapsychology*.

Ernest Becker writes that the great lesson of Freudian psychology is that "repression is normal self-protection and creative-self restriction . . . the essence of normality is the *refusal of reality*."[17] Mythologizing is an essential step in the repression of reality. History is turned into nature by the repression of reality and the projection of a wished-for world in the form of mythic structures which create the illusion that these wishes are truly fulfilled in the very nature of things. Thus, the mythic world view allows us to repress what we would otherwise know or should know to be the case.

Extrojection, that is, the projection of some aspect of the content of our own psyche onto the world, entails an ontological claim. It is a mistake to think that the natural order actually has these extrojective properties. Our world view or our view of nature will therefore almost always be a mixture of what actually is, to the degree that we can approach reality, and what we wish reality to be. It is in this illusionary element that the categorical mistake which Ryle finds characteristic of mythic thought is to be found. Transcategorical moves are a necessary and acceptable part of our epistemological and scientific advancement. However, a very special transcategorical move is involved when thought takes on a mythic dimension. Mythic thought starts with deeply embedded mental phenomena and a basic motivation to extroject them onto the ontological realm. What is repressed is an aspect of reality which it is the function of the extrojection to deny. What is also repressed is the fact of the repression. This ontological aspect of mythic thought is central to the role of myth in repression, manifested in the use of nature to justify history.

The psychoanalytic perspective views myth in the context of repression and wish fulfillment. This lies at the heart of the use of myth[18] in psychoanalytic theory as a tool to uncover the content of the unconscious. The human species, unlike others which have only brief recurring periods of sexual frenzy, is sexually active at all times from infancy on. Karl Abraham states, "We have established, that all mankind from the beginning, has given great weight to the sexual differences. Human sexuality displays a need of expansion far beyond the object of sexual satisfaction. Man permeates and impresses everything in his environment with his sexuality and language is the witness of his, at all times, creative sexual phantasy."[19] Thus, much of repression and wish fulfillment have their basis in human sexuality, and therefore myth generally has a repressed sexual dimension which is expressed symbolically.[20]

MYTH AND CULTURE

Not only does myth join different universes of discourse, and function as the vehicle for the convergence of the internal psyche with the external world, it also serves as the mediator between the past and the present. While we cast off outmoded ideologies as mere myth, we fail to see the mythic dimensions of our contemporary ideologies. Social order is as mythic today as it ever was. Yesterday's ideologies are seen as today's myths just as the mythic function of today's legal and political ideologies will be recognized by future generations, who will in turn consider their own mythic structures to be pure philosophy, science, or truth.[21] This is not to suggest that there is no difference between myth and science, or myth and philosophy. Rather, it is to suggest that we apply these disciplines to other areas of life or knowledge in an attempt to legitimize, that is, view a particular state of affairs as natural. By drawing inferences across the boundaries of discrete areas of knowledge, the opportunity for extrojection increases and thought takes on a mythic dimension.

No discipline has done more to reinstate the place of myth in the temples of learning than psychoanalysis. Not only did Freud meld myth to science, but science took on a mythic dimension when Freud-as-scientist created psychoanalysis, which itself has mythic aspects involving the projection of a patriarchal view of female sexuality onto women. Since for humankind the mythic dimensions of thought have their roots in the unconscious, the tools of psychoanalysis become indispensable for uncovering the mythic dimensions of any area of knowledge. Myth is the objectification of our deepest social experience, consciousness, and unconsciousness. Social order is the expression of our most fundamental values, needs, and psychological drives. Therefore, social order, if indeed it is not in itself a mythic system of thought, must have at least a pervasive mythic dimension. Thus, psychoanalytic theory may well hold the key to the revelation of the mythic dimensions of social order.

Myth creating is an extremely complex cultural phenomenon. Culture itself is a mythic system made up of many interrelated subsystems. Mythologizing as a means of creating a holistic world view is a method of obtaining truth and understanding about ourselves and our universe. Myth as a product of the processes of projection and introjection also contain psychological truths. Myths are the dreams of the collective psyche.[22] Mythologizing is as necessary for the mental health of the collective psyche as dreaming is for that of the individual. New myths save us from the destructive power of our older myths. When an old mythic system begins to be taken to its logical conclusion, the illusory content becomes pernicious. The deleterious potency of the older mythic system, which at its maturity pervades the social structure, calls forth the nightmares in the collective psyche from which the new myths arise. The new myths contain the seeds of the new paradigms of knowledge which contain the germs of destruction for the old. At the very height of the pervasiveness of Catholic Christianity, for example, the seeds of the Renaissance and the so-called Age of Enlightenment began to sprout. Often even older myths reappear in new forms and with new potency.

The human condition drives us to dream and to fantasize. Fantasies are as important for analysis as dreams are. Stoller writes: [23]

> I want to underline what analysts since Freud and Melanie Klein have endlessly shown: that our mental life is experienced in the form of fantasies. These fantasies are present as scripts—stories—whose content and function can be determined. And I want to emphasize that what we call thinking or experiencing or knowing, whether it be conscious, preconscious, or unconscious, is a tightly compacted but nonetheless separable—analyzable—weave of fantasies. What we consciously think or feel is actually the algebraic summing of many simultaneous fantasies.
>
> This position puts me on the side of those theorists who feel that psychoanalysis deals with meaning, not energy, and who insist that psychic energy and its resultant, psychic structure, are only metaphors, that meaning alone is the constant essence of mental function.

As we all, to varying degrees, share the human condition, our fantasies will have common archetypal content. Those archetypal images will shape our myths, and our myths will structure our social life. The hero myths of any society, for example, reflect the patterns of our individual daydreams and fantasies. Comics, television, movies, pornography have plots and images which feed shared patterns of fantasy. The human condition produces repression, repression produces neurosis and wish fulfillment, neurosis and wish fulfillment produce illusions which are expressed in a network of fantasies, the collective pattern of illusion produces myth, and the myth produces social cohesion and direction.

Like the paradigmatic shifts in science, our recognition of incongruity between our mythic systems and what reality forces onto our consciousness, will lead to shifts in these systems. It is not so much the power of reason which leads to cultural advancement as it is the power of the mythic systems in which reason was a factor in the paradigmatic shift. The predominant shifts in mythic systems in the past, such as from polytheism to monotheism, from *mythos* to *logos* in the rise of Western mathematics and science, and from naive realism to the Eastern systems of religious and philosophical thought such as in Buddhism and Taoism, all took place when a divergence developed between the old mythic paradigms and what people perceived to be dictated by reality.[24] The eventual spread and triumph of the new sets of myths came from their capacity to feed neurosis with new illusions, while at the same time carrying the elements of a newly perceived reality. The importance of myth lies in its dynamic potential for change. Stasis is to be feared over all else since when our myths rigidify, social change ceases, and the freezing of the collective psyche hinders the passage and development of the individual psyche. Illusion starts to feed upon itself and begins to erode that which reality dictates.

Myth might well be compared to a manure bed. It contains both decaying matter and the fuel for growth. The more ferment, the greater the potential for fertilizing new plant life. Freud defined illusion as a belief motivated by a wish fulfillment which sets no store by verification from reality.[25] Myth, containing as it does a mixture of truth (that which can receive some degree of verification from reality) and illusion, must be kept dynamic or it becomes destructive. Culture, since it is in part a vast mythic system, will always contain a mixture of truth and illusion. Myth as methodology, linked with psychoanalytic social theory, enables us to recognize some of those aspects of culture which contain illusion in the Freudian sense, and thus resist change in the collective psyche and become a threat to the health of the body politic.

MYTH AND IDEOLOGY

Our legal and political institutions, along with our legal and political ideologies, have a mythic dimension. In fact, the mythic dimension of social order is profound. Consequently, these institutions and ideologies have an illusionary content. Law and political order entail authority, authority entails legitimacy, legitimacy entails a mythic content, and a mythic content entails illusion.

The link between social order and illusion can best be illustrated by examining the relationship between social order and ideology. The link between ideology and illusion has been carefully traced by the French psychoanalysts and social theorists Janine Chasseguet-Smirgel and Béla Grunberger.[26] They arrive at the following definition of ideology: "[I]t is a system of thought which claims to be total, it is a historical and political interpretation whose (unconscious) aim is the actualization of an illusion, of illusion *par excellence,* that the ego and its ideal can be reunited by a short-cut, via the pleasure principle. The pleasure principle entails the immediate and complete discharge of the drives without any of the deferments and detours that characterize the path of its opposite, the reality principle."[27] They point out that Engels's definition of ideology ("Ideology is a process accomplished by the so-called thinker consciously, indeed, but with a false consciousness. The real motives impelling him remain unknown to him, otherwise it would not be an ideological process at all. Hence he imagines false or apparent motives"[28]) accords with their own. As ideology functions to legitimize legal and political orders, it is essential to authority. The belief that political authority can be justified in pure philosophical terms without any mythic dimension is in itself an illusion. Philosophy without myth would contain no illusions. Such a pure philosophy, if it is at all possible to achieve, could not serve the function of legitimizing social order.

Mythic thought becomes more scientific and philosophical as illusions are uncovered and our views shift to a greater conformity with reality. When we can recognize no illusion, we believe we are in the realm of science and philosophy. Such a belief does not mean that illusion is not present, but merely that it is not recognized. For example, Freud pointed out that Marxism, while it stripped away a great deal of illusion, still contained a substantial illusionary content, writing, "[A]lthough practical Marxism has mercilessly cleared away all idealistic systems and illusions, it has itself developed illusions which are no less questionable and unprovable than the earlier ones."[29] The Marxist belief in a natural human benevolence, which may be recovered through the abolition of institutions and practices such as private property or class structures, reflects a repression of the role which unconscious psychological forces play in creating human misery. Marxism thus promises an "easy" solution to the problem of human suffering and offers a utopian reconciliation, a return to the garden of lost unity. Wish fulfillment and projection replace reality. Yet Marxists believe that they have freed themselves from illusion and that their approach to political life is scientific.[30]

Psychoanalytic theory, as contrasted with Marxist theory, according to Chasseguet-Smirgel and Grunberger, "considers that primary drives— aggressivity and the hunger for love—determine the economic conditions themselves . . . [and] tends to see social institutions as the exosmosis of the unconscious, a projection of the drives and the defences against the drives."[31] Political ideologies, they point out, are projective systems which ascribe the source of human suffering and malignity to external factors such as capitalism or communism, rather than to the effect of the drives which constitute a part of the human condition. "Ideologies and their interpretations of social and political facts are thus, to varying extents, paranoid formations."[32] They add: [33]

> To summarize our argument, then: because political ideologies analyse sociopolitical facts in terms of a projective, and sometimes persecutory, system of interpretation, they tend to disconnect these facts from their unconscious roots. This disconnection opposes the reconnection that psychoanalysis tends to make. The latter connects disparate human activities and systems, understanding these as projections of the drives and their defences. . . . [H]uman beings can only act, and create, on the basis of their internal, psychosexual, model. We project this model out on to the world when creating political systems, institutions and economic structures, thus making them in our own image. In other words, this kind of projection is a translation of psychic space into social space. . . .
>
> At the heart of all ideologies lies the romantic and fashionable idea of "changing the world." Psychoanalytic understanding tends to act against this idea. By returning the creation (economic systems, social institutions, sociopolitical facts) to the creator (the human psyche) it burdens man with an unbearable responsibility and guilt. We not only have to bear the burden of acknowledging, and taking responsibility for, the drives we have tried to expel but we also have to tolerate having our narcissism undermined, since psychoanalysis dispels Illusion.

The inevitable regression of Marxist-Leninist societies to a class structure, so ably documented and explained by Milovan Djilas in *The New Class*,[34] confirms that primary drives determine economic conditions rather than the converse.

In the progression from mythic to scientific or philosophical thought, as in the field of science itself, changes generally take place in paradigmatic shifts rather than incrementally.[35] The creation of a new paradigm often entails revealing illusory content in the old, but the new paradigm will have its own share of illusionary content. In the pure sciences, such as

physics, people generally become aware of the nature and structure of a
paradigm and recognize its limits before change takes place. In politics
and law the paradigms are archetypal, having their roots deep in the
unconscious, and cannot be proved empirically false. Consequently they
will have a stronger grip on us. The only way to seek out the illusory
content of contemporary legal, political, or moral paradigms is through
the tools of psychoanalysis, and so, "psychoanalysis is not only an indispensable research tool, it comes to occupy the privileged place of being
the science fundamental to all the human sciences." [36]

Historically, psychoanalytic theory itself has had its share of wish
fulfillment and illusion. However, psychoanalysis is important not for its
particular content at a particular period of time, but as a tool for the
understanding of mental processes. There is no reason why the tools of
psychoanalytic theory cannot be turned onto psychoanalysis itself, in the
same way that Djilas turned the tools of Marxist analysis on Communist
states. [37] The mere use of psychoanalytic theory does not guarantee the
abolishment of all illusion. Chasseguet-Smirgel and Grunberger, in *Freud
or Reich? Psychoanalysis and Illusion,* have demonstrated that the contemporary "Freudo-Marxist" synthesis can be ridden with illusion. [38] The
minute that psychoanalytic theory is used in the service of ideology one
starts to enter the mythic dimension where illusion resides. The safest
course is to use psychoanalytic theory primarily as a tool of deconstruction.

Of course, one must realize that conventional methods of proof are not
adequate when dealing with the content of the unconscious. The dominant epistemology discriminates against dormant or delitescent factors or
interests. A case for the validity of the kinds of propositions which will be
set forth in this book will have to rest on an epistemology that can do
justice to knowledge which is latent and submerged, and which require
techniques other than those associated with positive methods of evaluation. The epistemological foundations of political and legal theories must
be critically examined in terms of psychoanalytic theory in order to uncover their mythic dimensions. At the same time, we must be consciously
aware of the epistemological implications of psychoanalysis itself.

The mythic dimensions of human thought can be seen as the product
of certain mental processes, in particular, projection or reification, and
introjection or internalization. Projection consists of the process by which
inner mental experience is unconsciously projected onto the outer world,
thus transforming inner subjective experience into an external objective

reality. By the process of introjection, patterns, structures, or properties generally considered to be an aspect of the external world, are unconsciously incorporated into the psyche and made an aspect of the person. This process reverberates back and forth to such a degree that it becomes impossible to differentiate the external world from mental processes, individuality from community, or even to conceive of the self independently from society, and vice versa. How, for example, can we conceive of the self without self-awareness or consciousness, self-awareness or consciousness without language, language without communities, communities without individuals, and language without individual speakers?

MYTH AND PSYCHOANALYTIC SOCIAL THEORY

To understand the interaction between projection and introjection in the formation of people's views of themselves and of what they perceive the external world to be, the tools of psychoanalytic methodology are essential. To understand the interaction between the structures of society, the family, and the individual psyche, the common archetypes which permeate mythic structures must be carefully analyzed. The function of psychoanalytic social theory is to uncover the relationships which exist between a) the human condition, including biologically determined factors such as the infant's long period of dependency on its parents, the sexual drive, the different procreative roles of the male and female, and the differences in male and female sexuality; b) the psychological tensions which are a product of the drives originating in the human condition and our repression mechanisms which arise from our conscious awareness of our own mortality; and c) our institutions of social order, such as law and government, conceptual structures and ideologies which implicitly and explicitly incorporate our repressions, denials of the human condition, and illusions. Thus, psychoanalytic social theory seeks to uncover the link between the unconscious and how society is structured.

One of the major themes of this book will be that the individual goes through three crises in the passage from the pre-Oedipal to the Oedipal, to the post-Oedipal: the separation crisis, the genderization crisis, and the animality crisis. In the first stage of the development of the self, the child separates from a symbiotic psychological union with its mother. In the second stage, the child achieves its sense of gender identity in relationship to the opposite sex, and in the context of the generation gap between itself and its parents. In the post-Oedipal stage the individual must come to terms with his or her sexuality and death. In each stage a person is affected by both separation anxiety and engulfment anxiety. The development within each stage is affected by that which takes place in the prior stage.

It will be argued that there is a remarkable similarity to this pattern in the evolution of our institutions of social order. They also can be viewed as pre-Oedipal, Oedipal, and post-Oedipal in the cultural evolution of the collective psyche. One of the central arguments of the book will be that not only societies as a whole, but their myths and mythic systems, rituals and sacraments, legal and political institutions and legal, political, religious, and moral ideologies can be classified and analyzed as pre-Oedipal, Oedipal, and post-Oedipal. Myths which portray the bifurcation of masculinity and femininity from a primordial unity, and myths which tell of a time long past when women were strong and dominated men who eventually prevailed over them, are pre-Oedipal in that they portray the separation of the male psyche from the original state of protofemininity when the infant does not differentiate itself from the mother. Those cultures where there is evidence of an age of matriarchal consciousness show characteristics which are pre-Oedipal. With the decline of matriarchal consciousness and the rise of patriarchy and kingship, the societies pass into an Oedipal stage, with a corresponding radical shift in the mythic systems whereby a son or consort of the fertility mother goddess becomes a superior father god. Myths which justify the inferior social position imposed by men on women, rituals of male children coming of age, patriarchal social orders such as the family or monarchy, and status systems of morality such as Confucianism are Oedipal in that they reflect the role of the father in the process of individuation, whereby the child emotionally and psychologically separates from the mother and the male child becomes genderized as masculine. Political, legal, and moral theories of equality, democratic or totalitarian states which postulate the equality of the citizen, and the body of Western law including classical Roman, the civil, and the common law, are post-Oedipal in that they reflect the psychological processes whereby the superego evolves and the self achieves full individuation. Indeed, some of these institutions and ideologies represent the superego of the collective psyche, which are in turn internalized by children as they go through the Oedipal passage and replace their father with their own superego.

In particular, the modern, Western, democratic state can be usefully viewed as post-Oedipal. While the ideology of equality arises out of a legal context, and law has been one of the most effective tools for removing or diminishing the impact of gender differentiation and generational differences, Western legal and political institutions, are still permeated by gender bifurcation and political father figures. The shift in Western law from status and authority to equality and contract reflects a major paradigmatic shift within Western legal consciousness. This, in turn, marks a cultural passage from an Oedipal to a post-Oedipal stage in societal psychological development. It marks the transition from monarchy and the reification of fathers in the cultural psyche as the Royal Father, to the rule of law and the reification of the ego. Just as the ego of the child is dependent upon the father in the Oedipal passage, and develops in the post-Oedipal stage into a fully individuated self which is now like the father and can be a father in his own right, so in the passage from the Oedipal to the post-Oedipal stage of societal development the organization of the social structure shifts from a hierarchical social order of domination and dependency to one of autonomous agents forming social relations through consensual contract.

The comparison of the evolution of the individual psyche with the evolution of society as a whole enables one to reach a deeper understanding of law, because the common patterns which can be recognized in the psychological development of different individuals will inevitably be reflected in social interaction. There appear to be many interesting parallels between neurotic patterns of behavior and perversions of individuals and many of our legal and social practices. Separation and engulfment anxiety take on a social dimension as individuals function in the context of communities. The attitudes which people take toward authority will be shaped in part by the nature of the family structure within which their psychological development takes place. Their neurosis regarding their sexuality and fear of death will affect their social interaction. These tensions are reflected in the context of conflicting legal and political ideologies and the institutions which they engender.

The most widespread pattern of human social interaction is the domination of the female by the male. This universal pattern is paralleled in our mythic systems by a content reflecting misogyny and gynophobia, which furnish a purported rationale and a ritual setting legitimizing male sexual perversion and aberrant patterns of sexual behavior. Pedophilia in ancient Greece, ritualized rape in some tribal societies, Chinese footbinding, Indian suttee, witch-burning, wife-beating, female genital mutilation such as clitoridectomies are but a few examples. There is an inter-relationship between sex and power. The foundation and legitimacy of social hierarchy rest on mythic structures and belief systems which make the biological distinctions between male and female central. The female is always relegated to an inferior position which is then used to justify male domination. The projection of inferiority onto the female represents wish fulfillment on the part of the male which manifests itself in illusion. One form this illusion takes is a categorical error whereby actual, but often imagined, biological properties are given social meaning within a mythic framework.

In the post-Oedipal stage the individuated self represses its consciousness of its fleeting transitory nature by denying death, and creating illusions of immortality.[39] The biologically determined processes of birth, procreation, and death are viewed as an enslavement which is denied and repressed through the illusion of autonomous agency. The mythic structures which carry the illusion often take the form of hero myths or ideologies of the heroic.

It will be argued that the four different kinds of complexes between which the male in the post-Oedipal stage oscillates are reflected in mythic systems which function to deny and repress our biologically determined animality. These mythic systems are expressed in ideologies and institutions which furnish the illusions required to feed one or a combination of the complexes, and thus in one way or another deny reality through false paradigms. One of the more central and critical paradigms is that of the male view of the female. This is a central part of male mythic thought, and it constitutes a construct filled with illusion and projection which has successfully resisted the impingement of reality. The denial of full autonomous agency for women, which the male imputes to himself, will be found at its core. This denial is a necessary condition for maintaining the view that male domination is legitimate. These post-Oedipal mythic systems continue to legitimize the social order through false paradigms of the natural order.

The crisis of social order, not only in Western industrialized societies but in the Third World, arises in part from our ambivalence toward institutions of law and politics. On the one hand, we attempt to use them to cure every social ill and problem, yet when they inevitably fail to produce the wished-for solution, our cynicism about law and politics increases. Still we press blindly on, seeking new lawmakers and new sets of laws. We seek legal-political solutions to problems which arise from the human condition and lie quite beyond the effects of legislative change. When we better understand the role which law has played and continues to play in the process of the individuation of the self, and when we become clearer about the drives and anxieties which have helped shape us as law-creating, -abiding, and -breaking creatures, we can gain a better understanding of both the limits and the possibilities of law. By linking social order and myth with the study of the unconscious, our utopian hopes will inevitably suffer but we will gain a more realistic appreciation of the nature of the problems which arise from our past and present forms of social order, and its capacity for meeting our non-neurotic needs.

While biology has been our destiny, our future is not completely predetermined. We may be able to make further paradigmatic shifts which will diminish illusion and move us toward reality. These shifts could have the effect of further modifying the process of the Oedipal passage, gender-ization, and individuation in the individual psyche, which in turn could affect the structure of the family, and our legal and political institutions. The critical issue is whether both males and females will be able to shed the illusion-filled mythic systems which deny full agency to women and make the social changes which this entails. If this happens, it will be one of the most important paradigmatic shifts in history, which should reflect further changes in the process of development of the collective psyche.

MYTH AND MEANING

The most fundamental difference between Freud and Jung, as well as between Freud and Rank or psychotherapists such as Viktor Frankl is whether "man's search for meaning is the primary motivation in his life and not a 'secondary rationalization' of instinctual drives" or whether "meanings and values are 'nothing but defense mechanisms, reaction formations and sublimations.' "[40] It is impossible to seek meaning in life or for life without entering the realm of myth and mythic thought. One cannot achieve meaning without unifying different areas of knowledge, using metaphor and analogy, and cross-categorization, all of which are fundamental to mythic thought. The very seeking of a meaning for the external cosmos and of the whole of which humans are only a part, entails projection of something internal onto the external, which again, is the essence of myth. Thus, Freud's atheism is counterposed against Jung's, Rank's, Frankl's, Becker's, and others' searches for purpose, God, the divine, or an objective or external meaning for life. They all lost their courage in the light of or darkness of Freud's tragic vision. The choice appears to be between myth and nihilism.

Consciousness is not possible without language and symbols; language and symbols are not possible without meaning. To be human, therefore, entails seeking meaning. Seeking meaning entails myth. There is, therefore, a mythic dimension to human thought which is an essential part of consciousness. Myth has a positive function which reaches from the creative leaps of imagination which lie behind the greatest scientific discoveries and breakthroughs[41] to the positive movements of history such as the suffragette movement, Gandhi's influence in gaining independence for India, and Martin Luther King Jr.'s charismatic leadership of the civil rights movement. The issue, therefore, has to be not whether we can avoid mythic thought, but whether mythic thought can be used as a tool for uncovering and discovering reality rather than repressing it.

However, the moment we conclude that life has a meaning to be sought out, we shift to the proposition that life has a purpose to be understood. Teleology is a human attribute, which when projected on the cosmos gives it a mythic dimension which distorts reality. Given the dangers of the use of mythic thought, we should keep close to the Freudian framework. Nevertheless, there is a very important element which Jung brings to the forefront. Humans are a part of nature, and only a part. We know from experience that wholes are often greater than their parts. The parts of reality which have been repressed through patriarchal culture are our links with the earth and nature, and the similarities and identifications we share with other animal species and forms of life. To try to understand our relationship to nature we must use a holistic form of thought rather than modes of thought suitable for differentiation only. These holistic approaches will inevitably be mythic. Myth does, therefore, have some role to play in the uncovering and discovery of reality. The Jungians can teach us much about the use of myth in this positive role. Jung recognized that the unconscious can play a positive role in the process of individuation, while Freud saw the unconscious more as a receptacle for repressed psychic conflicts which are too dangerous or painful for the ego to handle. For Freud, mental health is furthered by bringing the repressed material back into the conscious to be dealt with by the ego. Jung, on the other hand, tended to see the process of mental health furthered by an integration of conscious and unconscious. In this integration myth and symbols play a positive role.

Myth can only fully serve this positive function of integrating the unconscious with the conscious and giving meaning to reality when we recognize that it is myth, and that it is not to be taken literally. We must recognize that we do not find the meaning of life, but rather give a meaning to life. Meaning comes from within. It is not to be discovered externally. Myth best serves this end when it functions in conjunction with symbols. Myth provides a foundation for meaning which allows us to transcend repression, illusion, and other forms of denial of reality, when it serves as a tool for helping us to cope with and accept reality. It can only do so, however, when we are consciously aware of the mythic dimension and just how we are using it. Myth can help us approach reality and transcend illusion only so long as we recognize it as myth.

Myth can serve a useful function in helping us approach reality at the point where reason fails us. The neurosis and pathology which result from repression are often too powerful to be exorcised by mere rational processes of thought. Not all defense mechanisms are negative. Some, such as sublimation, can serve positive functions. Sadism is nearly always a destructive pathology because it generally entails harm to others. Masochism, on the other hand, while generally destructive of the self, can serve a positive function when it leads to self-sacrifice for the benefit of others.[42] It may take a neurosis to transcend a neurosis, or a pathology to transcend a pathology. If replacing one neurosis or pathology with another moves one closer to reality, then there should be an overall improvement in one's mental condition. Often the mental condition of an analysand is improved when a negative, harmful, or disruptive defense mechanism is replaced by a less harmful or more positive mechanism. Defense mechanisms can function and help the ego to protect itself from threatening material repressed in the unconscious, even when we are consciously aware that we are resorting to defense mechanisms.[43] Freud must have been well aware of his own form of denying death by achieving immortality through leaving the heritage of his thought. He certainly was well aware of his fear of his intellectual sons/disciples killing him as the father in terms of undermining or denying his soul/spirit in the form of his life's work. Heroism, for example, can sometimes be harmful, but other times is a positive defense mechanism. Freud played the role of the hero, and recognized that he did so, in his struggle against physical death in the form of his cancer, and intellectual death at the hands of his critics, some of whom were his former disciples.

In a later chapter the concept of collective defense mechanisms will be introduced. Collective defense mechanisms serve to protect the ego against shared or common psychic trauma. It is shared because the factors which give rise to it are a part of the biological genetic heritage of the human race living in a somewhat similar environment. Collective defense mechanisms have a mythic dimension which enforces their function within the individual psyche. Where a collective defense mechanism in mythic form can consciously be used to replace a more harmful collective defense mechanism, then the process of individuation in the individual can be carried a step forward, and myth can be used to serve a positive function.

Culture and myth simply cannot be separated. If all of the mythic dimension of culture were stripped away, there wouldn't be enough left for it to be recognizable as culture. So long as humans are born of mothers and remain subject to death they will be neurotic.[44] So long as they repress reality they will dream. So long as they live in communities and communicate, their shared neurosis will be manifested in the form of myth. Nevertheless, myth is a two-edged sword and while the work of Jung can help one to use myth as a positive tool of individuation, one must have one's feet resting on a firm foundation of Freudian principles and methodology. The Freudian methodology is essential for uncovering the illusions which myth inevitably entails.

A removal of the illusory content within the mythic structures which order society requires a literal gutting of the body politic, its institutions, and its ideologies. The result is a stripping away of our defense mechanisms and a restoration into consciousness of that which has been repressed, leaving us naked and frightened in the cold wind of the knowledge that we are merely fragile creatures caught in and buffeted by forces which we can never fully understand or control. Darwin revealed to us the animality of our bodies. This we can painfully and reluctantly accept. We can even honor him for helping to free us from our collective father complex. We can psychologically accept the death of God as we collectively move through the Oedipal passage toward self-directed autonomy, so long as we can maintain a heroic and illusionary view of the self. Freud revealed the animality of our soul to us. We have not forgiven him for this. His honor and praise is made possible by ignoring, trivializing, discounting, misinterpreting, and in other ways avoiding his central theme. Even he was only able to accept it with great difficulty.

4.

THE MYTHIC FOUNDATIONS
OF SOCIAL ORDER

MYTH AS METHODOLOGY

If myth turns history into nature, in the Barthesian sense, then political philosophy serves a mythic function when it maintains that a particular conception of a political order is either natural or reflects the nature of things as they truly are.[1] Every political philosophy contains express or implicit presuppositions about the nature of the person and about the nature of the world within which people find themselves, and draws conclusions from those assumptions about the way social orders ought to be. To this extent, they all serve a mythic function. The mythic dimension of political philosophy reflects Ryle's view of myth as "the presentation of facts belonging to one category" (nature) "in the idioms appropriate to another"[2] (social order). Hume, in pointing out that much moral and philosophical discourse makes a subtle shift from "is" to "ought" propositions, that is from descriptive to prescriptive discourse, clarifies how philosophy is made to serve a mythic role in naturalizing history.[3]

We can use mythic analysis as a method for deconstructing history, culture, and the belief systems and institutions which give history and culture their particular forms. The purpose of such deconstruction is to strip away illusion and come closer to reality.[4] Theories about myth, and the forms of analysis which can be developed from such theories, can furnish us with powerful tools to deepen our understanding of the human condition.

On the basis of the theory of myth developed in the last chapter, a series of questions can be formulated which serve as a structure for using myth as a form of analysis. These questions may be put as follows:

1. What is the nature and structure of the aspect of culture or history which we wish to examine or deconstruct, to demythologize?
2. What is the reality being repressed?
3. What is the illusion being projected?
4. What wish fulfillment is being served by the illusion?
5. What are the two sets of categories which are used to relate the natural order to the social order?
6. How are the categories used to turn historical contingency into natural inevitability?

1. The Nature and Structure of Culture and History

The essential feature of human culture and history is that it is patriarchal. An examination of the patterns of domination in the human species shows that the most widespread form is that which is exercised by the male over the female. Less than fifty percent dominates over fifty percent upon the basis of their biologically determined sex. From this duality gender roles are constructed for each sex, bifurcating almost every aspect of human activity, and going far beyond that which is prescribed by the bodily functions of procreation. Yet the literature of domination in the human race either ignores entirely, or at best treats as peripheral, this almost-universal pattern of the exercise of power. Nearly all studies of domination deal with patterns of power relationships between males. Most of these studies are relatively modern and a product of Western scholarship, and consequently reflect, expressly or implicitly, the presupposition that a state of autonomy is the ideal. Consequently, domination is viewed as an aberration or a necessary evil. With the exception of the rhetoric (as contrasted with the practice) of liberal and Marxist political theory, domination of the female by the male is perceived as the norm, or as a part of the natural order of things. Until very recently, serious examination of *male* domination has been considered to be an aspect of feminism or women's studies and consequently relegated to the status of ideology. However, we will never have an adequate understanding of domination in the human species until the most prevalent form and pattern of domination is made central to research, theory, and analysis. An adequate political, legal, and social theory must place the issue of male domination into a theoretical framework which will include all or most other forms of domination.

The essential nature and structure of history and culture reflect a fundamental ordering of values: the mind is more important than the body; culture is more important than the natural world; what males can do is more important than what they cannot do, that is, procreate the species by giving birth to new life; male interests are more important than female interests; and men are more important than women. It is the proper function of women to serve the needs and interests of men. This set of values and their ordering constitutes the underlying structure of patriarchy regardless of what particular cultural form it takes.

2. The Reality Being Repressed

The reality which patriarchy represses is that humans are a species of animals which, like any other with which it shares the earth, is chained to the biological cycle of birth, procreation, and death. The most important aspect of life is the continuation of the species. Two lines by the poet, T. S. Eliot, sum up the reality of nature and the nature of reality:

That's all the facts when you come to brass tacks:
Birth, and copulation, and death.[5]

The reality which is being repressed is our animality, the dependency of the mind upon the body, which in the end will inevitably fail the mind, and our dependence upon nature. The female, in this regard, has a tremendous psychological advantage over the male. She has the power to bring forth new life by giving birth. The female is a direct participant within the forces of life, the male only an observer. Females procreate while males preside. The comparison with the queen bee and the drone lies forever at the edges of male consciousness. While it is true that the male of the human species can play a significant role in protecting the female and obtaining food and shelter while the female is carrying a child or the child is young and highly dependent upon the mother, that role is nevertheless secondary when compared to that of the mother.

The primacy of the female in mammals has now been clearly established at the biological level.[6] Femaleness is the basic structure out of which maleness is secondarily derived. "The evidence has piled up that in mammals anatomical and physiological maleness does not even occur, regardless of chromosomal sex (XX in females, XY in males), unless the fetus secretes male hormones (apparently initiated by the Y chromosome). Even, and especially, the brain requires such masculinization in mammals or else femininity will result."[7]

Another aspect which is repressed in the relationship between the male and the female of the human species is the psychological dependency of the male on the female for emotional and sexual satisfaction. This dependency starts with the dependency of the child on the mother. In the female infant the dependency is transcended by the female child becoming a mother. However, in the male the dependency is never transcended but met by possessing another female who replaces the mother as a source of satisfaction.

3. The Illusion Being Projected

The illusion of male primacy and superiority is projected in various behaviors in patriarchal cultures. Production is elevated over reproduction. Scholarship, politics, war, hunting, sports, art, and other things which men do to occupy their time are given a social meaning entailing a higher value than those things which have traditionally been relegated to the sphere of women, in particular procreation and the nurturing of infants. Females have been viewed as incomplete males in that femaleness is defined in terms of the absence of male qualities.[8] The myth of the heroic, self-sufficient, independent male is perpetuated throughout patriarchal culture, while the female is viewed as dependent and clinging.

4. The Wish Fulfillments Being Served by the Illusion

The projected wish fulfillments are the negation of the repressed reality.[9] They include the illusion of immortality, the illusion of rationality (that all of our actions are the result of valid processes of reasoning), the illusion of the superiority of the male over the female (phallocentricity), the illusion that what constitutes the proper gender role for males is more important than what constitutes the proper gender role for females (gendercentricity), the illusion that the psyche or the soul is somehow independent of the body which is a mere shell within which the soul resides, the illusion that nature exists to be conquered, used, mastered, and shaped for the purposes of man (homocentricity).

Another set of illusions which incorporate most of the basic wish structures outlined in the previous paragraph is the set which makes up the heroic image. The fantasies of heroism are projected onto external reality in a wide variety of complex ways. The image of the hero helps us to repress our own actual weaknesses which are dictated by the reality principle—our dependency, our mortality, our sexuality, our fears, and our own irrelevance. A further set of illusions surround our sexuality. These illusions are fed through pornography and pornographic images which deny the personhood of women and project onto them the illusion that they achieve their fulfillment by serving the needs and interests of men.

While it is true that some of these illusions are held and projected by women, since women must also come to terms with their own animality, the kind, amount, and degree of wish projection would appear to be different between the two sexes. The reason that the projection of the male psyche dominates and monopolizes the human world view is that the pathology and neurosis of the male are more powerful. This will be developed more fully in later chapters. An indicator that this is the case can be found in the well-acknowledged fact that sexual perversion is much more extensive among males than it is among females.[10]

5. Categories Which Are Used to Relate the Natural Order to the Social Order

The mythic dimensions of human thought, which include mental processes such as projection (the process by which inner mental experience is unconsciously projected onto the outer world), introjection (the process by which perceived patterns and structures of the external world are unconsciously incorporated into the psyche in formulating one's view of the self and the inner world of consciousness), and conceptual unification (the process by which conceptual structures and patterns of one dimension of thought are applied to another, or two different dimensions are unified in terms of the structure and pattern of a third), involve both the differentiation of phenomena and concepts and their holistic unification. The most important step in the process of differentiation is that of bifurcation. This process starts with a bifurcation which establishes a polarity. Shades of differences and subdivisions are then carried out within the polar distinction. True-false, black-white, good-bad, up-down, near-far, are but a few examples. We give social meaning to perceived differences by choosing some as a basis for bifurcation and by finding commonalties among other perceived differences. What we choose to bifurcate and what we choose to relate are not biologically determined but reflect an evolutionary cultural development. It is extremely difficult to separate the complex interrelationship between nature and nurture.

Looking to the most rudimentary human cultures, it is readily observed that a human's physical being as a part of nature afforded biological differences and similarities which served as models for responding to the external world. One of the most fundamental distinctions in mythic thought and culture is the sex/gender bifurcation. Our own species is bifurcated into male and female on the basis of anatomical differences which are given a certain primacy over all other possible bases of differentiation. Thus, a dualistic structure is projected onto humankind and many other species of animal life. This dualism is introjected back into the psyche in the form of the dichotomy between the masculine and the feminine. The correlation of these two binary forms of differentiation gives us the basic quadrant:

male	feminine
masculine	female

This basic masculine/feminine dichotomy is used to give other bifurcations a hierarchical order. For example:

masculine	moon	masculine	night
sun	feminine	day	feminine

masculine	body	masculine	nature
mind	feminine	culture	feminine

masculine	yin	masculine	evil
yang	feminine	good	feminine
masculine	weakness	masculine	irrationality
strength	feminine	reason	feminine
masculine	submissive	masculine	obedience
dominant	feminine	authority	feminine

These bifurcations attest to the importance of human sexuality in mythic thought.

Gender, as the social meaning assigned to the sexual bifurcation between male and female, permeates almost every aspect of human culture from language to social roles. It need not necessarily have been so.[11] Our common humanity could have been made the fundamental criteria for social identity. However, this has not been the case. It is nearly impossible for humans to interrelate without sexual categorization. It is the first thing which we seek to know about a newborn human, and any person whose identity is ambiguous in these terms is in for a very difficult social passage. The very processes by which we know ourselves and the world are imbued with gender. Even epistemology does not escape the bifurcation of gender. Processes of differentiation such as logic and analysis have been assigned to the masculine gender, while processes related to identification, such as empathy, emotion, love, and the holistic approach to life, have been assigned to the feminine. We see aspects of this epistemological bifurcation in a wide variety of common attitudes and beliefs. Men are thought to be more rational and scientific than women, women are said to be more emotional and empathetic than men. These beliefs have determined traditional roles.

The entire mythic structure or structures of patriarchy are based on gender bifurcation. Gender bifurcation underlies and is the fundamental presupposition of patriarchy. Gender, as social meaning projected onto biological differences, serves the function of naturalizing social differences. These social differences are projected wish fulfillments and are, to a substantial degree, illusionary. Therefore, gender itself is essentially a mythic structure underlying all patriarchal mythic systems.

6. How the Categories Are Used to Turn Historical Contingency into Natural Inevitability

The underlying assumption of patriarchy is that the right of the male to dominate the female is natural, because females are by their nature believed to be inferior to males. This assumption is not based on fact, as the only qualities in regard to which the male may claim superiority are size, body weight, and possibly aggressiveness. Since it is almost universally rejected that might necessarily makes right, no legitimization of male dominance could be derived from the physical difference alone. Rather, the assumption of male superiority is an integral part of mythic structures which are a product of the psyches of males, and from which input of a feminine nature has been systematically excluded.

Patriarchal rule is the most pervasive and unconsciously enforced form of authority to be found. The parent-child relationship is probably the only authority which is universally accepted as legitimate. It is no wonder that civilizations have used the parent as the prototype for gods and kings and the family as the model of the tribe and state. In the nineteenth and twentieth centuries kingdoms have been replaced by republics and hereditary leaders overthrown, the power of the father has been weakened, and lip service has begun to be paid to the liberation of women. Nevertheless, the parental-domination archetypes, in particular patriarchy, persist in the human unconscious and from there continue to infuse our political and legal consciousness.

The contemporary, Western, democratic world remains essentially and fundamentally patriarchal, in spite of the fact that it is now possible for a few women to achieve positions of influence and power which are normally the prerogative of males. Only some privileged women who enjoy the role of the token female in the corridors of power, or a relatively small group of especially talented women who have been able to beat the male at his own game and think that if they can do it, any women can do it, or a few men who are dominated by women in their own personal lives, would deny the universality of male domination in even the most enlightened contemporary society. The measure of the degree of patriarchy which permeates contemporary society must be that of the lives of average women. Anyone who listens to their experience cannot fail to recognize that the so-called equality of the sexes promised by Western democracies has not changed the reality of male domination. It has only removed some of the more obvious forms of exploitation and abuse. The most efficient way to maintain power is to give a little where it shows a lot, and in fact patriarchy has been extremely efficient in maintaining the male monopoly of power.

The domination of the female by the male is not based on naked power. If it was, it would not be nearly so pervasive, complete, or effective. Generally, the authority of the male is accepted voluntarily by the female because both believe that rule by the male is legitimate. Authority is the normative justification for domination. It creates the right to rule in some and the duty to obey in others. It entails the right to use force to extract obedience, and thus, legitimizes the use of power. Male domination is believed to be legitimate because it is believed that the sexual difference reflects a natural hierarchy of superiority and inferiority. The myth of female inferiority is the foundation of male domination, and is the basic presupposition of all patriarchal systems. Since all prevailing mythic systems are patriarchal, this presupposition can be said to be universal.

THE NECESSITY FOR 'NATURALIZING' SOCIAL ORDER

The need for turning the contingencies of history into the determinations of nature is obvious. A political system can be seen as a social order made up of dominant and servient power relationships. For such a system to be effective, and economical, compliance with the exercise of power must be substantially voluntary. For compliance to be voluntary, the hierarchical ordering of the power relationships and the exercise of power must be considered legitimate by the subjects of that power. As Rousseau stated, "The strongest is never strong enough to be always the master, unless he transforms strength into right, and obedience into duty."[12] A social order is considered by its subjects to be legitimate when it is believed to reflect, comply with, or be in accordance with the natural order. This is how power relationships are legitimized. To this extent, all theories of political or legal obligation, or theories of the moral foundations of government, are directly or indirectly "natural" in the sense that they assume a particular view of nature. Even the supreme positivist, Jeremy Bentham, began his classic work, *An Introduction to the Principles of Morals and Legislation* with the words, "Nature has placed mankind under the governance of two sovereign masters, *pain* and *pleasure*."[13]

If there is a radical paradigmatic shift in our view of nature, it will inevitably lead to a radical shift in the nature of our legal and political institutions. When a particular view of nature is rejected as wrong or obsolete, any political or legal ordering which is dependent upon it for its legitimacy will also be rejected. It is not an accident of history that when the scientific world view was developed in Greece, a radical change took place contemporaneously in her political institutions and theory. Thus, Western science and mathematics and Western political institutions originated at the same time because the new view of nature could no longer legitimize the old form of political order.[14]

For a political system to remain stable, the power relationships of dominance and subservience must be clear, identifiable, and changeable only according to rule. Then certainty and stability of expectations may be maintained. The legal order furnishes the rules by which dominant persons are identified, and the rules which prescribe how those persons create law. Even those power relationships in a society which do not have a legal basis are subsidiary to the framework of legal power structures; they rest on the foundation of that framework and function within it.

The mythic structure upon which the law rests must justify the rules or selection processes which identify the law-makers, by selecting those who *by their very nature* are the "right" or "best" persons. If the right people make the law in the proper manner, then the law will be considered good or just. Thus, authority combines the functions of furnishing both legitimacy, and certainty and stability of expectations. It is the concept of authority which furnishes the link between law and myth. The mythic structure from which legal authority is derived must justify the existence of a social hierarchy in terms of power relationships. It must justify the right of certain persons to command, and of others to obey, and it must do so in terms that make it clear that this is the natural order of things.

An awareness of the difference between naked uses of power and authorized uses is essential if we are to understand the nature of authority. H. L. A. Hart brought this distinction sharply into focus in his well-known gunman analogy.[15] If a gunman points a gun at your head and demands your money you are obliged to hand it over, but it would be untrue to say that you have an obligation to do so or ought to in a normative sense (as contracted within a prudential use of the word). On the other hand, you have an obligation to pay your taxes, and you ought to do so.[16] The difference is that the gunman has no authority to take your money, but the government has the authority to take money from you as taxes.

In the political context, authority may be defined as the right to rule and consequently must entail the duty on the part of those subject to the authority to obey. Obedience is the correlative of authority. Nature or conformity with nature is the source of the right, which is why rights are, more often than not, referred to as "natural rights."[17]

THE TRANSCATEGORICAL RELATIONSHIP BETWEEN BIOLOGICAL DIFFERENCES AND SOCIAL RELATIONS

Every recorded society has dealt with material limitations by establishing hierarchies and by distributing material goods accordingly. Although it is clearly in the interests of the ruling class to maintain these hierarchies, the hierarchies and hence the distribution have been accepted by most of society. We have a psychological need to naturalize or mythologize the material distribution systems in order to view them as legitimate. Before one can perceive hierarchies, one must be able to perceive differences. Hierarchies are differences weighted with social meaning. In order for hierarchies to be effective, humans must be trained to recognize differences and to react psychologically to them. There is nothing natural about which perceived differences are given social significance, or what meaning may be attributed to those differences. These are learned social responses, just as connecting up one's identity with these differences is a learned social response.

Next to the sexual, the most fundamental human dichotomy is that between the parent and child. This generational difference is projected onto the external world, generally in conjunction with gender. God is not just male, but he is a father. This dominant father concept is reflected in the most universal pattern of domination-subservient relationships throughout history, the patriarchal family. It has been and remains the central institution in human social hierarchy. Through it the dominance of the male over the female and of the father over his posterity has been maintained.

Historically, social order has been based on the following biological orderings:

1. Sex-gender: male over female;
2. Generational differences: parent over progeny;
3. Order of birth: first born over second born;
4. Proximity: close relationship over distant relationship, kin over nonkin, highborn over lowborn.

Monarchy, aristocracy, and caste have been maintained on the basis of ranking between families and bloodlines according to descent from special "first families." Imperialism and racism have been maintained on the basis of racial distinctions and cultural differences which are seldom differentiated from race. The distinction between the propertied and the propertyless follows these other hierarchical patterns. There is a mutual relationship between property and social status in that social status gives an individual or a family a great advantage in the competition to accumulate property, and the possession of sufficient property over an extended length of time will generally lead to an enhanced social status.

Biology has traditionally furnished the link between the normative social order and the natural order. As Sir Henry Maine stated, "The history of political ideas begins, in fact, with the assumption that kinship in blood is the sole possible ground of community in political functions."[18] Humankind has always distinguished between the "we" of common blood, and the others—the strangers, the aliens, the gentiles. The closer the consanguine ties, the stronger is the social bond. "Kindred and kindness go together—two words whose common derivation expresses in the happiest way one of the main principles of social life."[19] The bond of blood is an ethical tie reflecting the basis for an entire morality. Therefore, the naturalistic "is" of blood relationship is transformed into the "ought" of social obligation.

The anthropologist, G. B. A. Coker, finds that "[A]ll along the West Coast of Africa, there is a universally accepted conception of the family set-up, involving identical or at least similar characteristics."[20] Anthropologists are in general agreement that the family lies at the heart of the social structure of all tribal societies.[21] In these cultures, the tribe is normally divided into major and minor lineages; the minor lineages are made up of extended families, and these in turn are broken down into nuclear units consisting of parents and children. Every society, whether tribal, city or nation-state, at some stage of its development has been socially organized on the basis of common lines of genealogical descent. It is significant that it appears that almost no society, no matter how much it might be committed to an ideology of equality, has been able to transcend entirely the morality of kinship. What Coker said of "primitive" law, that "almost every known legal concept began and ended with the family," is equally true of ancient and traditional social orders.[22] The clan, the tribe, the nation, and the race, are all seen as families of members of common blood.

Two incidents which occurred in the Cook Island Land Claims Court, and were related to the author by the judge of that Court, furnish excellent examples of how individuals in the now independent state of the Cook Islands still view themselves as a part of a family which reaches into the ancient past and will continue on into the indefinite future. Claims as to title to land in the traditional law of the Cook Islanders, like that of most Polynesians, rested on ancestral right which had its origins in either conquest or discovery and occupation. In one of the land disputes, one litigant turned to the other and shouted, "Were you in the canoe?" thus placing his claim on the basis of descent from ancestors who discovered and occupied land of which the disputed parcel was a part. In the other, the litigant cried out, "The bones of your father still stick in my teeth," thus making a claim based on ancestral conquest.

As extended families develop through natural increase into clans, there can be no living common ancestor such as a great-grandfather from whom all clan members are descended. Inevitably, the common ancestor will be dead. A living surrogate father must be found in the form of a clan head. This position may be hereditary, in that it falls on the oldest son of the oldest son, a direct descendant of the common ancestor, or it may be based on ability, so that some powerful and able warrior or wise man will be chosen or rise through circumstances into a position of leadership. Clans are made up of people of common lineages. As they split into subclans or minor lineages, they will tend to amalgamate into tribes, eventually to be led by hereditary chieftains. In the long run, the position of head or chief tends to become hereditary, probably because the struggle for leadership, with its inevitable civil strife, turns out to be too costly. It is far better to know who the king is than have the best man as king. A "right" to rule by descent is clear and precise as to identity and the time at which the right vests. On the other hand, a right vested on some ability such as merit, wisdom, or prowess in warfare is much more indeterminate as to who has the qualities and when they are sufficiently developed as to found a right to leadership.

Where a number of tribes of common racial origin, physical features, and language are contiguously located geographically, one powerful chief may gain sovereignty over the other tribes and unite them all into a single political unit. Eli Sagan describes societies at this stage of their evolution, as "complex societies."[23] Complex societies stand at the transition from tribes to kingdoms, and their leadership marks the transition from chief to monarch. Sagan gives as recent examples African kingdoms such as Buganda and the Polynesian kingdoms of Hawaii and Tahiti.

The transition from tribal society to kingship corresponds to a shift from kinship to class. According to Sagan, this transition, whenever and wherever it takes place, is marked by extensive anxiety and collective neurosis which are manifested in the form of institutionalized human sacrifice and infanticide. He notes that these practices are not extensively found in either kinship or kingship societies, but are only prevalent in the transition stage between the two, and compares this anxiety with that which children suffer when passing through the separation-individuation process described by Mahler.

Class distinctions within kingship societies replace lineage divisions within kinship societies. The ruling class is made up of the closest relatives of the royal family. The highborn and lowborn are measured in terms of the distance of relationship between the members of the class and the lineage of the royal family. One essential difference between kinship and kingship societies, noted by Sagan, is that kinship societies never attempt to incorporate into their political system the tribes which they conquer in war. A political bond is simply not feasible without a blood relationship. This is not so in a kingship society. The shift from lineages to classes furnishes a hierarchical political structure which does not require a common bloodline as a necessary condition for a political relationship. Conquered people form the lowest class in the class structure, often with the lowest status, that of slave.

Dominance is related to superiority, and subservience to inferiority. Therefore, the foundations of authority can be said to lie in the perceptions of superiority. Perceived differences between people are ordered according to superiority and inferiority, which in turn justify the dominant-subservient hierarchical ordering of people.

The human biological order allows us to differentiate between people in terms of properties which are genetically determined and are fixed from birth. The male is made dominant over the female, the parent over the child, and the first-born over the later-born. The criterion for making some families dominant over others and some races servient to other races has been the blood line of descent. This gives a stable "natural" social order with clear, straightforward and unchanging criteria for dominance and servience. The patriarchal family, in fact, is the archetypal paradigm for nearly all social hierarchies. While it is our biological nature which allows us to establish the criteria of differentiation, it is the mythic structures which furnish the ordering based on that criteria, thereby justifying or legitimizing the hierarchical social relations thus produced. Since patriarchy is universal, we are safe in assuming that at a fundamental level, there are some basic similarities in the mythic structures of totally different cultures and people.

Sir Henry Maine has used the term "law of status" to describe legal orders which achieve their legitimacy by prescribing a social order based on biological properties.[24] He wrote, "Ancient law . . . knows next to nothing of Individuals. It is concerned not with Individuals, but with Families, not with single human beings, but groups."[25] Maine's view was that the family included not only the living, but the dead and the yet to be born. Each individual was a continuation of his forefathers, just as his life in turn would be prolonged through his descendants. Michael Barkun has called such legal orders "genealogical-legal systems" because "[p]utative genealogical distance determines the meaning and consequences of action."[26] In such societies, "the need for genealogical expertise parallels the need for what in Western societies we would call traditional legal expertise."[27]

Authority is the normative justification for domination. It creates the right to rule in some and the duty to obey in others. It generally entails the right to use force to extract obedience, and thus legitimizes the use of power. Being subject to the authority of another is inconsistent with the autonomy of an individual. If, therefore, the source of authority is to be found in a biologically determined status, then the autonomy of the individual cannot be assumed to be the normative or natural condition of humankind. If, on the other hand, the autonomy of the individual is made the basic presupposition of legal and political theory, authority must be assumed to rest on a consensual foundation. The assumption that all persons are born free creates the necessity of the social contract to legitimize domination. Robert Paul Wolff argues persuasively that all justifications for authority fail and that authority and the autonomy of the individual simply cannot be reconciled.[28] No form of authority based on biological status can be reconciled with the autonomy of the individual.

Sir Henry Maine also states, "[T]he movement of the progressive societies has hitherto been a movement *from Status to Contract*."[29] If one takes this statement at face value it would suggest that the transition from kingship to democracy is as natural and as inevitable a transition as from kinship to kingship. This is not the case. Kinships have developed into kingships throughout the world and at various periods of time. However, the shift from kingship to democracy only took place spontaneously in classical Athens, and wherever it has taken place elsewhere, it has been as a direct result of the impact of Greek culture. The shift from kingship to democracy is of a radically different nature than the shift from kinship to kingship. The latter does not entail a radical shift in mythic structure. In both systems of social order, hierarchy is based on similar biological criteria. Kingship is a natural expansion of kinship. The role of the father develops, gradually replacing many of the functions which were previously served by the kinship communities. While the shift from kinship to kingship marks an advancement in the process of individuation, in that the sense of individual self or ego is more marked under kingship than it is within kinship, the concept of the person is not radically different. Genealogy is still the measure.

The shift from kingship to democracy was both radical and revolutionary. Genealogy became irrelevant. Biological sameness, rather than biological difference, was accentuated in the mythic system. The revolution in the view of the person was the result of a revolution in the view of nature—the shift from *mythos* to *logos*. The old world of gods and goddesses was replaced with a new mythic system based on a universe of natural and universal laws. If man-made laws are to follow the pattern of the laws of nature, then they must also be universal in the sense of applying to any person similarly situated. Therefore, if people were equal before the law, there was no meaning for a natural social hierarchy.

Political authority, in the sense of some people having a "right" to rule over others who have a "duty" to obey, is based on biological differences which are given social meaning through mythic systems. Political autonomy is based on the assumption of equality. When a group of people are considered to be autonomous or free, the assumption is that no social meaning is given to biological differences. Where political authority is exercised within a group of persons who are considered to be equal, that authority is not exercised as that of "right" but by consent. If the mythic system which supports the social order gives no meaning to biological differences between people, then the myth will prevail that the authority is exercised with the consent of the governed.

This helps us to understand one of the reasons why women have been excluded from the ambit of democratic political theory. Democratic political theory generally assumes that "all men are born free." Democratic societies have always been and still are highly patriarchal. The inconsistency would be obvious and the contradiction blatant if, on the one hand, women were proclaimed to be born free by the ideologies supporting the political system, and, on the other hand, it was also maintained that they are by their very nature subject to the authority of the male.

In contemporary Western democratic societies we have the myth that sexual differences between male and female have no social meaning, in the sense that they are irrelevant for purposes of social order. Yet, at the same time, we have the reality of male domination. This means that another conflicting mythic system underlies the myth of political equality As even the most democratic of Western nations are still highly patriarchal, we can assume that the mythic system which gives social meaning to the biological differentiation of sex is much more powerful than the mythic system which denies that the differentiation of sex has social significance. The mythic systems which legitimate democracies, whether libertarian or totalitarian, are based on two presuppositions. They are the equality of men, and the inequality of women with men. They are a form of patriarchy based on the brotherhood of man. Thus, the mythic systems of the brotherhood contain a fundamental contradiction. The equality of men entails the irrelevancy of biological criteria for social order, while the superiority of men over women entails that a fundamental biological distinction is critical for social order.

Nowhere can we find a better example of both the negative and positive force of myth than in the mythic systems which legitimize social order. Social order, it will be argued throughout this book, has a fundamental mythic dimension which underlies and determines legal and political philosophy and the economic, historical, social, and anthropological dimensions of society. Law, like religion, is one of the major mythic systems which make up human culture. It often serves a positive role in containing harmful conduct, facilitating social planning, regularizing and formalizing institutional practices such as property and market transactions, and generally organizing human behavior. However, it also serves a number of negative roles in repressing women and legitimizing the exploitation by humans of each other. We can only begin to gain a full comprehension of the function of social order when we recognize its mythic dimensions, its role as a set of collective defense mechanisms, and the human pathology which underlies and energizes its legal and political institutions.

5.

THE COURSE
OF INDIVIDUATION

Psychoanalytic social theory links collective behavior with psychological processes which take place within individuals. Psychoanalytic theorists are agreed that mythic thought furnishes the key to an understanding of the psychological processes which underlie collective behavior. "[M]yths," Freud once stated, "are distorted vestiges of the wishful phantasies of whole nations, the *secular dreams* of youthful humanity."[1] Rank viewed myths as the collective dreams of a whole people.[2] Abraham wrote that myth is "a retained fragment from the infantile psychic life of the race, and the dream is the myth of the individual."[3] Neumann regarded myth as "a projection of the transpersonal collective unconscious."[4] If this is so, then it is clear that myth furnishes an essential key to revealing the neurotic foundations of social order.

To understand the nature and structure of collective neurosis, we must first clarify the process of development of the individual psyche and its structure. This chapter will trace the individual psyche's pattern of development, while chapter 6 will examine its structure. Chapter 7 will develop a theory of the collective psyche, and chapter 8 will develop one of the essential roles myth plays in the evolution of the individual psyche. Myth furnishes one of the important links between individual and collective neurosis. By moving back and forth between individual and collective psychological processes, we can begin to understand the interrelationship between individual ego psychology and the psychology of collective behavior. Therefore, we must examine the process of individuation which

87

each individual psyche goes through, which furnishes the pattern for the process of individuation for the collective psyche. Jung defines individuation as follows: [5] "In general, it is the process by which individual beings are formed and differentiated; in particular, it is the development of the psychological *individual* as being distinct from the general, collective psychology. Individuation, therefore, is a process of differentiation having for its goal the development of the individual personality."

Mahler, Pine, and Bergman define individuation in a somewhat similar manner, stating, "[I]ndividuation consists of those achievements marking the child's assumption of his own individual characteristics." [6] Jung sees the process of individuation as including self-realization. As Jung's theory of the nature of the self has no counterpart in Freudian theory, the use of the term *individuation* in this book, while it conforms with Jung's definition above, will not necessarily conform to the broad Jungian view of that process.

THE PRE-OEDIPAL STAGE

The Theory of the State of Primary Narcissism

The centrality of the Oedipus complex to psychoanalytic theory suggests a threefold division which has become standard: pre-Oedipal, Oedipal, and post-Oedipal. In the prenatal state the fetus is in a condition of well-being and elation. It has no needs, tensions, or desires, due to the fact that wants are satisfied automatically. It is immortal since it has no sense of time or death. It is invulnerable because it knows no threat nor danger. It is autonomous as it lacks any feeling of dependency nor does it differentiate between the self and an external other. It is omnipotent since it has no sense of limitation or deprivation. [7] This is a state of "a cacophony of awareness of being and a total unawareness of objects." [8]

The probable state of mind of infants in the early stages of post-natal life, has been best described by Irene Fast in her analysis of the process of differentiation. [9] Infants, she states, do not differentiate between their experiencing, and that which is being experienced. Their experience itself is the only reality which they know. Consequently, "they are subject to two illusions, that of omnipotence (the notion that one's own experiencing (cognition) carries with it the relevant reality) and that of primary creativity (the notion that events exist only as they are being experienced)."[10] Fast writes:

> In such experience the self is central in two ways. In the earliest period of life only "experiencing" is known to the infant. All existence, therefore, is perceived as a function of this "experiencing." The infant is in this way absolutely central, though without a *sense* of its centrality. Within events the infant is central as well. It is its own experience (grasping, etc.) that determines which aspects of the human or nonhuman environment are included in a given event. In identity terms this implies that a narcissistic identity experience is one in which the infant has no sense that anything can occur independent of his own experiencing and in which only those aspects of the environment relevant to his actualization of an event will have reality for him. . . . In narcissistic "experiencing" infants cannot think beyond the present event: cognition is limited to the current actuality. Therefore, on the one hand, whatever is thought is accompanied by the relevant reality, and on the other, objects cannot be known to continue in existence when they are not being perceived. The illusion of the omnipotence of thought has its roots in the first of these, the illusion of primary creativity in the second. . . . In this formulation illusions of omnipotence and primary creativity do not accompany narcissism. They are its components: the infant's narcissistic experience is experience in which cognition is accompanied by the actuality to which it refers and actualities are perceived to exist only when they are being experienced.[11]

After birth the child continues to live in a similar "proto-narcissistic" state similar to that of its prenatal life, so long as all needs are quickly met and satisfied.[12] Loving parents tend to make this stage last as long as possible. Fast describes how the infant incrementally, through the recognition of patterns of similarity in discrete units of experience, begins to distinguish between phenomena which are unresponsive to the infant's control from those which appear to be responsive to her or his will. In this way the child begins to build up a sense of the independent existence of objects. A very young infant will cease to respond to an attractive object once it is out of its sight, but at a later stage of development will start to look for it.[13] The child thus, with the breakdown of primary narcissism, passes from a mental state of primary creativity and omnipotence to "an identity organization of self as center of thought and will in relation to a world independent of self."[14]

As the child gradually realizes its separateness from the mother and begins to develop an awareness of self in relation to an external 'other' in the form of the mother, the child becomes aware of its own weakness, limitations, and vulnerability. The infant passes very quickly from a stage where it has a sense of complete autonomy and omnipotence, to a stage of abject dependency. Freud deals extensively with the symbiotic union with the mother, and the traumatic separation. He saw its effects reaching into the post-Oedipal stage of life. Freudians refer to the effects of the separation as "the narcissistic wound."[15] According to Freud people often seek to regain the blissful state which lingers in their psyche as an unconscious memory. He suggests that the "oceanic feeling," which is sought through religion, meditation or drugs, may be an attempt to regain this blissful state.[16]

Béla Grunberger writes:

> The fetus . . . lives in a state of narcissistic regression, of spontaneous satisfaction, a state that is preambivalent by definition because it is unconflicted. After birth, the infant maintains, with the help of external factors and hallucinatory satisfaction, a somewhat similar position. This position is breached (abruptly or not) when his narcissism meets with failure, a trauma that is hard to bear. Only repression enables the child to overcome, though not completely, this narcissistic wound. What does one do to ease his passage through these rough waters? Formerly he was one with his source of satisfaction, and, in effect, gave pleasure to himself (the term bliss would be more appropriate); after birth, those around him help him to reconstruct that narcissistic oneness by loving him, that is, his narcissistic reflection of himself is replaced by *narcissistic satisfaction that now comes from outside*. It is a matter of "narcissistic gratification." At the same time, the child embarks on a process that will enable him to adapt still further to his new condition . . . and to reorganize his instinctual economy on a new basis, that of object mastery.[17]

Mahler and her associates, along with a number of other Freudian psychoanalysts, have done extensive research on the development of the psyche of the child in early infancy. After working for a number of years treating and studying many cases of schizophrenia, Mahler and her research group developed a theory of "the psychological birth of the individual" which is described as a "slowly unfolding intrapsychic process"[18] as contrasted with the sudden, dramatic, and observable biological birth of the infant. They refer to the psychological birth of the individual as the separation-individuation process. Separation and individuation are conceived as two complementary developments which are preceded by the period when the infant is in a symbiotic relationship with its mother.[19]

According to this theory the first few weeks of the infant's life are spent in a state of normal autism during which the infant is unable to differentiate between itself and its mother. As it gradually enters the symbiotic stage, the infant begins to function, "as though he and his mother were an omnipotent system—a dual unity within one common boundary."[20] The term symbiosis is used to describe "that state of undifferentiation, of fusion with mother, in which the 'I' is not yet differentiated from the 'not-I' and in which inside and outside are only gradually coming to be sensed as different."[21]

Separation and individuation follow the symbiotic phase, involving "a steady increase in awareness of the separateness of the self and the 'other' which coincides with the origins of a sense of self, of true object relationship, and of awareness of a reality in the outside world."[22] During the separation-individuation phase, in the second half of the first year and the second year of the infant's life, the child commences to construct his or her sense of identity, ego, or self. During this period the child is torn between separation anxiety and engulfment anxiety, which is often marked by "the rapidly alternating desire to push mother away and to cling to her."[23] While separation and individuation are intertwined developmental processes, they are not identical. As separation proceeds, the child develops its sense of self-identity.

According to Mahler, *"the drive for and toward individuation* in the normal human infant, *is an innate,* powerful *given,* which, although it may be muted by protracted interference, does manifest itself all along the separation-individuation process."[24] She also states, "It seems to be inherent in the human condition that not even the most normally endowed child, with the most optimally available mother, is able to weather the separation-individuation process without crises, come out unscathed . . . and enter the oedipal phase without developmental difficulty."[25] The tensions suffered during the period of oscillation between a longing to blissfully merge with the mother, and the fear of reengulfment by her and consequent loss of the nascent self identity, "[l]ike any intrapsychic process . . . reverberates throughout the life cycle [of the individual],"[26] and "together with inborn constitutional factors, determine every human individual's unique somatic and psychological make-up."[27]

Primary Narcissism and Recent Research on Infants

Some have claimed that recent research and clinical studies on infant development throw into question a number of fundamental assumptions of psychoanalytic theory.[28] In particular, it has been suggested that some of the recent literature reporting and summarizing this research is inconsistent with Freud's theory of the infantile state of primary narcissism.[29] Such a suggestion, however, is simply not accurate. There are no substantial findings, observations, or experiments which are inconsistent with the Freudian thesis of primary narcissism. The principal source of this suggestion, and the one most often cited as authority for the existence of a disparity between Freudian theory and contemporary research, are the writings of Emanuel Peterfreund, and in particular his paper, "Some Critical Comments on Psychoanalytic Conceptualizations of Infancy."[30]

The theory of the state of primary narcissism involves three assumptions. The first is that prior to and shortly after birth the infant's sensed experience is undifferentiated. The second and third assumption follow from the first. The second assumption is that the child does not differentiate itself from the external world or its mother. The third is that the psyche of the child is in a state of omnipotence because it recognizes no limits or any distinction between experiencing and bringing into creation. The state of primary narcissism is consciousness without a recognition of difference or limitations. These three assumptions are about the child's mental state before and shortly after birth, and not about the limitation of its sense organs such as its powers of sight or hearing.

Peterfreund correctly asserts that since infants are unable to describe their subjective mental states, as adults are able to do, the only way we can draw any conclusions as to what they are is by way of inference.[31] Peterfreund denies that newborn infants lack the power to differentiate, denies that the infant self and mother are merged for the infant, and denies that the infant senses itself as omnipotent. He relies on no empirical evidence for these assertions. Rather, he draws his conclusions as inferences from a thought experiment.[32] He goes on to suggest that the Freudian view stems from "two fallacies characteristic of psychoanalytic theories of infancy: the tendency to adultomorphize infancy and the tendency to label and characterize normal infant states with terms that apply to later psychopathological states."[33] What Peterfreund refers to as fallacies are essential aspects of the psychoanalytic methodology—viewing as a related continuum the relationship between infant and adult behavior, and the relationship between normal and pathological.

Peterfreund's position is representative of a split in psychoanalytic circles between the pure clinicians and those who add theory to clinical practice.[34] Theoretical concepts such as primary narcissism are referred to by the pure clinicians as metapsychology, upon which they frown because these concepts, being a matter of inference only, can neither be directly proven nor disproved. Peterfreund's critique is based on a confusion between the powers of perception and the powers of conception. He first makes the assumption that "[s]ome terms such as 'undifferentiated', presumably refer to subjective experiences as well as to behavior and biology and physiology. But it is not at all clear what such terms as 'omnipotence' or 'narcissism' are supposed to refer to."[35] He uses studies relating to the infant's powers of perception as a basis for inferences as to the infant's powers of conception. He seems to believe that because recent studies of infants indicate that they have greater powers of perception than previously thought, that they must also have greater powers of conception. It may not be clear to Peterfreund, but it is fairly clear in psychoanalytic literature that *undifferentiated, narcissism,* and *omnipotence* all refer to subjective experience and not to behavior and biology and physiology. Thus, the child studies which he cites in no way support his conclusions. The powers of perception which he refers to as being present in infants were in all probability well known to Mahler and her associates and to other psychoanalytic theorists who studied infant behavior, and whose work confirms the theory of primary narcissism.[36]

The distinction between self and other is not simply a matter of perception. It involves conception as well. The infant certainly does have some powers of perception present at birth. The powers of conception, however, develop slowly over time. A different kind of thought experiment than that proposed by Peterfreund will illustrate the difference between perception and conception. Imagine a person who has been blind from birth, and then has an operation which suddenly restores their sight. When the bandages are taken off will they immediately see trees, houses, or mountains? Probably not. The light rays which stimulate the retina will be similar to those received by anyone else looking at the same scene. It will not be processed by the brain in the same way, however, as it is likely that it would be an undifferentiated set of color sensations. How could such a person recognize shades of color without learning at the same time a conceptual structure of colors, shapes and objects? A person who had been deaf from birth and suddenly had their hearing restored, would not hear a Bach prelude, but only undifferentiated sounds. Those familiar with the process of meditation will have no problem in understanding the difference between perception and conception. Experienced meditators do not stop hearing sounds when meditating. The sounds simply become undifferentiated. What one loses in meditation is not the powers of perception, but the conceptual structure within which perceptions are differentiated.[37]

All of this has been clearly explained by Josephine Klein, who states, "By the time the simplest concept has been established, movement and behavior are already built in."[38] The theory of primary narcissism is about the infant's capacity of conception, not perception. No studies of infant behavior whether recent or otherwise, have proven that the assumptions about infant powers of conception entailed in the theory of primary narcissism are wrong. Psychoanalytic theorists have been studying infant behavior from the time of Anna Freud,[39] Melanie Klein,[40] and D. W. Winnicott,[41] to the contemporary studies of Mahler and her associates.[42] All have held firmly to the theory of primary narcissism.[43]

The limited conceptual power of infancy is an inference well recognized independently of psychoanalytic theory. Klein quotes Tennyson who wrote:[44]

The baby new to earth and sky,
What time his tender palm is prest
Against the circle of the breast,
Has never thought that "this is I".

But as he grows he gathers much,
And learns the use of "I" and "me",
And finds "I am not what I see
And other than the things I touch".

So rounds he to a separate mind
From when clear memory may begin,
As thro' the frame that binds him in
His isolation grows defined.

The distinction between the infant's capacity for sensual experience and its powers of conceptualization, and the relationship between them, is extensively canvassed by Klein in her study which fully takes into account contemporary research on early infancy. She writes:

The primitive self is a sensory experience, not a conceptual one. There is as yet no baby, only sensations registered in the cortex. There is as yet no (m)other, only sensations registered in the cortex. There are only neural effects. These effects make up a (m)other whom the baby experiences as part of its own body-imagery, the sensations being the baby's own bodily sensations. . . .

Sensory messages are streaming into the baby's cortex. The senses create cortical effects which gradually make shapes and patterns, and some of these, if all goes well, are increasingly accurately experienced as "me" while others are experienced as "not me but other." Messages about "not me but other" go to the cortex just as messages about "me" do. Where else? But some amount of cortical organization has to take place before these messages can find a place in the cortex *as* messages about "the (m)other." So at this time there is hardly any differentiation between the (m)other and the baby, or between the baby's various bodily parts, as far as the baby's experience goes. What the (m)other does is experienced in terms of those bodily zones which are just then in a state of excitement. Before differentiation, (m)other and baby are one in the baby's experience: both are embedded in the one stream of sensations. From the point of view of the baby's sensations, we might say that mother and baby are merged.[45]

In particular she finds the work of Frances Tustin on the autistic state in some children to be particularly revealing about the infant's powers of differentiation.[46]

The state of primary narcissism in newborn infants is the product of the complete lack of a conceptual structure which permits differentiation. This must be acquired gradually. The infant lacks a sense of self and other, and is unable to differentiate between its self and its (m)other because it has not as yet learned how to organize and structure its experience. It knows no limitations because a knowledge of limits requires conceptual powers of differentiation. This state of undifferentiated wholeness or pure undifferentiated consciousness is a continuum out of which the self and ego must be forged through often painful struggle. It remains as a counter pole to the pull of individuation. As perception is gradually organized around a conceptual framework, the separateness of the body requires the psyche to formulate a self and to recognize mental limitations which correspond to the physical limitations of the body. The original memory of the undifferentiated state is reshaped throughout one's lifetime as the polar opposite of the process of individuation. The more painful individuation becomes, the more attractive is its negation. The desire to recover that original undifferentiated state by merging the self in an external other remains throughout life, and leads people to surrender the self, in childhood by attempting to remerge with the mother, and in later life through intoxication, other drug-induced euphoria, sexual perversion such as masochism, meditation, religious or sexual ecstasy, romantic love, or even through consciously or unconsciously seeking death.

THE OEDIPAL STAGE

The Oedipal Passage of the Male Child

There is no sharp division between the Oedipal and pre-Oedipal stages. Rather, they are a continuity by which one process merges into the next. The final stages of separation are the initial stages of the Oedipus complex. The interrelationship between the Oedipal and pre-Oedipal stages in the development of the psyche are well recognized. Many psychoanalysts now believe that the nature of the passage through the Oedipus complex will largely be determined by the pre-Oedipal stages of separation from the mother and individuation of the self. The first steps the individual takes in forming her or his identity will affect all future social interaction.

The clinically-based studies and research centering on children and their parents in interaction carried out by psychoanalysts such as Mahler and her associates and Stoller, as well as studies by psychoanalytically-oriented feminists such as Dorothy Dinnerstein,[47] Nancy Chodorow,[48] and Jessica Benjamin[49] confirm that "biological factors are almost always too gentle to withstand the more powerful forces of environment in human development, the first and most profound of which is mothering."[50]

The male child enters the Oedipal passage by breaking his identification with his mother and forming an identification with his father. As the child starts to identify with the father, the mother, from whom the child is now fully separated, becomes his love object. At first these two relationships co-exist side by side without any tension or conflict. Prior to the appearance of Oedipal tensions, the child, rather than competing with the father for the attention of the mother, concentrates, on *"being loved by both parents at once, narcissistically and absolutely, without conflict and with all merging into one."*[51] At a mythic or archetypal level this state is, according to Grunberger, reflected in the *"narcissistic image of the Holy Child"* who appears "at the radiant center of the universe . . . attended by his parents, whose images merge with those of the domestic animals, asses and cattle, archaic images typical of dreams but also of certain collective daydreams that express man's continuing nostalgia for his paradise lost . . . a *megalomaniacal universal primal fantasy,* that of the one and only child at the peak of joy and exaltation."[52]

The object-cathexis toward the mother and the identification with the father "subsist side by side for a time without any mutual influence or interference."[53] What Grunberger calls the, "narcissistic triad" of child and parents eventually becomes spontaneously conflicted as a part of the process of normal mental development. As Freud described:[54]

> The little boy notices that his father stands in his way with his mother. His identification with his father then takes on a hostile colouring and becomes identical with the wish to replace his father in regard to his mother as well. Identification, in fact, is ambivalent from the very first; it can turn into an expression of tenderness as easily as into a wish for someone's removal.

The Oedipus complex, according to Freud, is the central phenomenon of the sexual period of early childhood.[55] Prior to the passage through the Oedipus complex, the boy "regards his mother as his own property."[56] Gradually, however, he realizes that he has a rival in the father for her love and affection. Contemporaneously with this stage, the young boy's interest begins to focus on his genital organs, and is manifested in the form of frequent handling. This produces a critical reaction in adults, generally his parents, sometimes involving express or latent threats of castration. Freud believed that two possibilities are open to the child, "He could put himself in his father's place in a masculine fashion and have intercourse with his mother as his father did . . . or he might want to take the place of his mother and be loved by his father."[57] Both alternatives, however, face him with the loss of his penis. The loss of the penis is a precondition for becoming a woman, and castration is the punishment which the child imagines awaits him if he attempts to take the place of the father. Thus, "a conflict is bound to arise between his narcissistic interest in that part of his body and the libidinal cathexis of his parental objects."[58] The fear of castration leads the boy to give up his object-cathexis centered on the mother, and is replaced by an identification with the father. As Freud explained, "The authority of the father or the parents is introjected into the ego, and there it forms the nucleus of the super-ego, which takes over the severity of the father and perpetuates his prohibition against incest, and so secures the ego from the return of a libidinal object-cathexis."[59] In this way the masculinity in a boy's character is consolidated by the dissolution of the Oedipus complex.[60] At this point the male child enters what Freud called a latency period.

It is a mistake to impute to the child in the course of the Oedipal passage the full attitudes, knowledge, and sexual feelings of the adult. The incest fantasy of the child often has more to do with the child's desire to return to and merge with and be exclusively loved by the mother than it does with sexual union and the desire to discharge sexual tension. On the other hand, one would be wrong to deny the sexual component of the child's desire to merge with the mother. Sexuality and unification are complexly interrelated and remain so throughout one's entire life. This point is well made by Chasseguet-Smirgel, where she writes:

> I would remind the reader here of Ferenczi's theory of genitality . . . in which he establishes that the wish to return to the mother's womb is the most fundamental human desire. Genital coitus allows this desire to be satisfied in three ways: "The whole organism attains this goal by purely hallucinatory means, somewhat as in sleep; the penis, with which the organism as a whole has identified itself, attains it partially or symbolically; while only the sexual secretion possesses the prerogative, as representative of the ego and its narcissistic double, the genital, of attaining *in reality* to the womb of the mother." (I would specify that for me—and in this I follow Freud's conception—the primary narcissistic state extends over a period of time which includes some time prior to the birth itself.) The pinnacle of human development thus contains within itself the promise of a return to the mother's womb or, in other words, to the most primitive phase of development. We are urged forwards by a sense of longing for a wondrous past (for a time when we were our own ideal). Between these two points in time, however, there lies the whole of man's psycho-sexual development.[61]

The Oedipal Passage of the Female Child

According to Shahla Chehrazi, "A psychobiological gender-related force is considered to be the primary factor characterizing entry into the oedipal phase."[62] Whereas the male and female infant both regard their mother as their first love object, the male child transfers his identification with the mother to an identification with the father. The female child, on the other hand, retains her identification with the mother and begins to take the father as a love-object.[63]

Freud seemed much less certain about the process of the Oedipus complex in girls than he was about its development in boys. However, he postulated that as little girls do not have a penis, they will not be propelled through the Oedipus complex by fear of castration. Castration is already an accomplished fact for them.[64] The female child either assumes that at an earlier date she had possessed a penis like the boys and has lost it, or she feels that her mother has deprived her of something which she should have had and, because she is lacking it, she is in some way inferior.[65] Suffering from penis envy rather than a fear of castration, the little girl envisions taking her mother's place and receiving a baby from her father.[66] Thus, she begins the process of adopting feminine attitudes toward her father. The Oedipus complex gradually recedes as the child realizes the impossibility of this wish.

Since the time of Freud, a substantial amount of clinical research, analysis and theoretical development have taken place concerning the nature of female psychology.[67] The increased attention placed on pre-Oedipal development in girls has led to the availability of much more information. Where Freud believed that girls only developed a vaginal awareness at puberty, recent research indicates the existence of an early pre-Oedipal genital awareness. J. A. Kleeman and others relate that little girls discover their external genitalia and vagina as a part of the normal process of body exploration and develop a genital awareness which is an integrated part of their body image.[68] Freud believed that little girls do not develop an early gender identity, but rather see themselves as being no different from little boys. As a result, girls suffer the shock of penis envy when they eventually learn of the anatomical differences. Contemporary research shows that little girls develop a core gender identity as female very early, and although penis envy is a common reaction to the discovery of the anatomical differences, the desire for a penis does not necessarily entail a desire to change gender. Often the penis is desired in addition to the girl's own genitals. Chasseguet-Smirgel writes, "My experience with women patients has shown me that penis envy is not an end in itself, but rather the expression of a desire to triumph over the omnipotent primal mother through the possession of the organ the mother lacks, i.e., the penis."[69] "The need to detach oneself from the primal omnipotent mother by denying her faculties, her organs and her specifically feminine features, and by investing in the father," she states, "seems to be a need both sexes share."[70] The entry of girls into the Oedipal phase, therefore, should no longer be considered as a reaction to a castration complex, but as the end process of a gradual development of female individuation and identity. In describing the Oedipal passage of the female child, Chasseguet-Smirgel writes:

> [T]he differences between the sexes impels the girl towards her father. Even if her eroticism runs counter to her wish to eliminate the gap between ego ideal and ego through a primary narcissistic fusion, it is nonetheless the case that for the girl motherhood is a solution that allows her to reconcile, in a sense, her erotic wishes which are directed towards her father with her wish to recapture the primitive state of fusion with her mother. The mother can reexperience with her child, admittedly on a much more evolved level, the sense of fusion which as a child she experienced with her own mother. It can be seen that, for obvious reasons, the girl is led to situate her wish in the future. And hence she is led to constitute for herself an ego-ideal that will include the project of becoming a mother—as mother, but also as the father's wife, who has been given a child by him. . . . I consider that the wish for a baby is something that appears very early, prior to penis envy. . . . I believe this desire also includes that of reconstituting the primary mother-infant unity.[71]

A further important difference between the contemporary view of female psychology and that held by Freud centers on the post-Oedipal stage of female development. The post-Oedipal female was seen by Freud as having an incomplete or faulty superego. The view of many current researchers is that the female superego is not defective but different, reflecting the change in emphasis from the early stages of psychoanalysis where female psychology was approached from the perspective of what it is not, rather than what it is. Carol Gilligan's work on the stages of moral development in females supports the contemporary psychoanalytic perspective in approaching the question of female psychology.[72]

Both boys and girls enter the Oedipus complex from a pre-Oedipal stage where they take their mothers as love objects. Both sexes must break this bond by replacing it with an attachment to the father. The contrast between the ways the male and female pass through the Oedipus complex lies in the nature which that attachment takes for each sex, and in the ways in which the fear of castration and penis envy function in the dissolution of the Oedipus complex. In the passage through the Oedipus complex the child must, "discover the anatomical difference, must recognize that it is a characteristic of maleness and femaleness, must see these characteristics as playing a role in the parents' relations with one another, must recognize its own potential role with the parents, must accept the incest taboo and finally become a sexual partner."[73]

What is truly amazing is not that Freud was wrong in certain aspects of his theories, but that he was consistently right about so many things, given the patriarchal bias of his age and the limitations of biological knowledge of that period. Freud himself was tentative and modest as to his conclusions about female sexuality. It was inevitable, and it was anticipated by Freud himself, that future research in psychoanalysis would require modifications in his theory.[74]

THE OEDIPAL PASSAGE AS A PROCESS OF GENDERIZATION

There is now a substantial body of psychoanalytic theory which has reconstructed Freud's theory of the Oedipal passage as a process of genderization. These views remain within the Freudian tradition. It would be a mistake to think of them as even being neo-Freudian, because they merely correct aspects of Freud where he was clearly wrong, and build on and advance Freud's work. Within this contemporary Freudian tradition, Freud's concepts and views are carefully shaped in terms of more recent research and experience.

Every infant, as soon as it is born, will be given a *sexual classification* as male or female, upon the basis of biologically determined physical properties which in turn are determined by whether the embryo has two X chromosomes, in which case it will develop as female, or one X and one Y chromosome, in which case it will develop as male. On the basis of the child's sex, it will be given a *gender assignment* as masculine or feminine. The child will be assumed to have an inherent propensity toward certain attitudes and abilities. The gender assignment will impose culturally determined sets of expectations as to what is proper or appropriate behavior. In fact most human characteristics will be bifurcated as masculine or feminine and will be expected to be manifested by the developing child according to its gender assignment. *Gender roles* in the form of expected and prohibited behavior will be imposed upon the child as a result of the gender assignment. As the child discovers its own biological sexuality, in the context of the way it is treated according to its gender assignment, and is socialized according to the gender roles, the child will develop a *core gender identity*.[75] The core gender identity will generally be established at about eighteen to twenty-four months, and thereafter is almost impossible to change.[76] A gender identity develops along with and as an integral part of the child's sense of self.

The gender roles which are assigned to the child entail roles in procreation, nurturing, and parenting. The parents of the child are the prime examples or patterns of appropriate gender roles. They thus learn from them both what they are and what they can anticipate becoming. At the same time as they learn about the sexual attraction and dynamics between their parents, they are developing a sense of their own sexuality which they see and project in terms of their relationship to their parents. The child thus develops its sense of self in terms of a gender identity and a generational identity, based first and primarily upon its relationships with its parents. The genderization process is an ongoing generational process in that the child's "emotional destiny" is the product of its parents' attitudes toward their own gender, forged in turn through the interaction with their own parents, and so on. "Awareness of gender identity thus provides an unconscious historical and dynamic generational link" which determines the Oedipal passage from one generation to the next.[77]

Freud's theory of genderization was colored by his belief that maleness and masculinity are the natural and primary states, and that the female and femininity are less valuable because they are incomplete. His views of women as incomplete males and of femininity as a pathological or defective state can no longer be taken seriously from either a biological or a psychological perspective. We now know that, "For mammals, the resting state of tissue is female, and male organs . . . are produced only if an androgen . . . is added."[78] The work of Stoller, who has spent over twenty-five years researching and treating gender identity disorders in biologically and genetically normal males, particularly children, is significant for a full understanding of the nature of the Oedipal passage of the male.[79] His work tends to focus on the later part of the pre-Oedipal and the Oedipal stages, while Mahler concentrated on the earlier part of the pre-Oedipal period. While Mahler focused on the problems of children in developing a separate identity, Stoller emphasized the development of that identity in terms of gender. Working from Mahler's conclusions, Stoller postulates that the primary gender state of the human psyche in both sexes is what he terms "protofeminine."[80] In the early stages of the pre-Oedipal period, the boy is *merged with the mother*. Consequently, "[s]ensing oneself a part of mother—a primeval and thus profound part of character structure (core gender identity)—lays the groundwork for an infant's sense of femininity."[81] Given this first stage of protofemininity, Stoller finds Freud's theory of gender development (as postulated in his theory of the Oedipus complex) to be accurate.[82]

The time in the pre-Oedipal stage when the individual starts to gain a sense of her-himself is the time when she or he starts to gain a sense of the other or others. To what extent does being an "I" mean being "I a girl" or "I a boy"? The process of individuation entails the self's separating from the (m)other. As separation takes place the child develops a sense of identity. Identity in humans entails gender, and thus, *"[s]exual differentiation proceeds in tandem with individuation."*[83] The gender ideal which the child must assimilate is to be found in the parent of the same sex. In forming her or his own identity, the child must introject the figure of the mother or the father as the ideal for her or his own development. Playing at being grown-up, a very common child occupation, is a reflection of this process of introjection.

We cannot understand the process of identity formation without understanding the process of gender formation, which has such important consequences for the future development of the individual. Stoller shows us that a person's identity as a self and his/her gender are inextricably intertwined. In our genderized world selves are either masculine or feminine, and gender ambiguity is a pathological, abnormal state. Core gender identity results from biological "force," including the effects of fetal androgens; sex assignment by parents and others on the basis of the external genitals; parental attitudes; biopsychic phenomena including the early postnatal effects caused by certain habitual patterns of handling the infant and other forms of conditioning which may even permanently modify the infant's brain; and finally, what Stoller terms "body ego"—"the myriad qualities and quantities of sensations, especially from the genitals, that define the physical and help define the psychic dimensions of one's sex."[84] According to Stoller, masculinity or femininity is not an incontrovertible fact, but rather is a mass of beliefs, "an algebraic sum of ifs, buts and ands" which one gets in childhood from one's parents and society at large.[85]

On the basis of his thesis that the earliest stage of development in both male and female children is one of protofemininity, Stoller makes the following adjustment to Freud's theory of the Oedipus complex:[86]

> If my theory [of protofemininity] is correct, femininity is not, as Freud thought, an inherently pathological state, for the girl is now seen to have

an advantage. From the start she is identifying with a person of the same sex. Though the potential homosexual nucleus is there, her first love object being female, the development of her femininity no longer seems so risk laden. Those conflict-free aspects of gender identity (for example, those that result from identifying with the gratifying aspects of being a woman) are present from earliest life. On the other hand, though the boy moves to heterosexuality early on, he must have already separated himself sufficiently from his mother so that he is an individual and knows his mother is a separate, different-sexed person. Then he will prefer to have, not to be, a woman.

Stoller concludes that "femininity in females is not just penis envy or denial or resigned acceptance of castration; a woman is not just a failed man. Masculinity in males is not simply a natural state that needs only to be defended."[87] Rather he offers a hypothesis (which he considers to be beyond proof) that protofemininity is "at its core a comfortable, primitive character structure that only after a time picks up its anxiety and conflict components."[88]

Stoller offers three bodies of evidence for his theory of original proto-femininity in the initial stages of the psychic development of infants.[89] First, he offers the results of his research with what he terms "primary transsexuals," defined as "boys who, without anatomic abnormality, have been feminine from the first year or so of life."[90] Each of the boys he studied, although anatomically normal, "was graceful, charming, and feminine in appearance and carriage."[91] Each wanted to dress in girls' clothing and to play exclusively with girls, and most important, each wanted his body changed to female. All the parents found that this behavior developed consistently from about the age of one, approximately the time when behavior could in any way be classified as masculine or feminine. Stoller finds, in nearly all such cases, the following pattern:[92]

1. "The mother's mother—the transsexual boy's grandmother—is a cold, harsh woman who has no love for the daughter who is to be the transsexual's mother. The girl, who is unquestionably female, is made to feel from birth on that being female is worthless."[93]

2. On the other hand, "her father loves her" and "they are close for a few years," but then "somewhere between age six and puberty he abandons her, by death, separation, divorce, or going into the service."[94]

3. After the father's desertion the girl begins acting like a boy, refusing to wear girl's clothes and playing exclusively with boys.
4. With the changes of puberty she, "stops waiting for maleness, becomes manifestly depressed, and puts on a feminine facade, giving up her boyish ways."[95]
5. She chooses to marry a distant and passive man who "is not involved with his family, not respected by his wife, and not physically present most of the time."[96]
6. This father is neither physically nor psychologically present during the childhood of the boy.
7. The mother is overjoyed at the birth of a son, and generally gives the boy a strongly masculine name. The boy, "becomes the beautiful phallus for which she has yearned since her sad, hopeless girlhood."[97]
8. When the mother holds the baby she feels "marvelous" and when he is out of her sight she feels anxious. Consequently she "keeps him unendingly in contact with her, skin to skin, day and night, with as little interruption as she can manage."[98]

Stoller concludes, "It is this passionate motherhood that produces the femininity or—to flip the coin over—that arrests the development of masculinity. Should another set of family factors arise that also leads to too much merging, it too, I predict, will lead to boyhood femininity *as long as mother and son are merged too well to long.*"[99] At the same time the father fails to interrupt the symbiotic relationship between mother and son, or to furnish a gender role model for the son to follow. Consequently the boy suffers no Oedipal conflict.[100]

The second body of evidence which Stoller offers for his thesis is his findings that female transsexuals and very masculine females "have suffered a premature and massive disruption of the mother-infant symbiosis, the opposite situation from the one that occurs in the too-feminine males."[101] Stoller points out that while the achievement of masculinity requires the male child to separate from the mother, "[f]emininity requires also that a girl separate from her mother, but not particularly from her mother's femininity."[102] Anni Bergman describes the difficulties of the girl's process of genderization and identity formation as follows:[103]

The little boy is aided in this process of differentiation from mother by identifying with father. The little girl has a more complex task. She, too, has to emerge from symbiosis with mother and attain realization of separateness. For her, too, the father is the important "other," but she has to identify with her mother to confirm her own identity as a girl while at the same time she has to dis-identify, differentiate from her to establish herself as a separate individual.

Stoller's third body of evidence is "the forms that masculinity typically takes in cultures everywhere—the macho belligerence that degrades women, makes many men fear tenderness and intimacy, and contributes . . . to the finding that the perversions are more common in men than women."[104] He states, "I attribute these sex differences not only to brain and hormones but to males' need for constant vigilance against their unacceptable yearning to return to the merging in the symbiosis."[105] This latter body of material suggests that people suffer engulfment anxiety or what Stoller refers to as "symbiosis anxiety"[106] throughout adulthood as well as throughout childhood. If so, this could account for the need in adults for a father figure to counteract the drive to lose the self, with all its conflicts and psychological tensions, and to recover the blissful Edenic state of symbiosis with the mother which ever beckons from the depths of the unconscious.

Stoller's work shows that the father plays an important role not only in the Oedipal stage, but in the post-Oedipal stage as well. If engulfment or symbiosis anxiety continue through the post-Oedipal period, and an examination of male perversions and behavior would certainly seem to confirm this hypothesis, the need for a father figure to counter the attraction of a return to the comfort and security of a symbiotic relationship with the mother or femininity, will also remain. By the time the child reaches adulthood, his/her aging father can no longer serve that function. A mythic father figure is required, whether projected onto the cosmos as creator or onto an individual male as a royal or societal father. Why else is there no passage out of kinship except through kingship?[107] What else can account for the near universality of kingship in those human societies which evolve beyond a kinship social structure? The need is not for an individual father, as the vast majority of children raised by a single female parent develop the same gender identities as those raised by two parents. The reason, no doubt, is because they are furnished with numerous father figures in the context of growing up.[108]

Another important study of the Oedipal passage as a process of genderization is that of Fast.[109] Fast suggests that while children learn very early their sexual identity as male or female by becoming aware of the nature of their own genitalia, they are unaware of gender differences. They become aware of their biological sex long before they understand or have assimilated the social meaning which is postulated upon the basis of the sexual bifurcation. Young infants, therefore commence life in a state of gender undifferentiation. In this state, children believe that they contain the entire range of human potential. Little boys believe that they can have babies just as girls can, and little girls see no difference between what they can do and what little boys can do. Fast gives the concept of castration anxiety a broader interpretation. As the child gradually assimilates a gender identity, it begins to realize its limitations. This produces a sense of loss of power or capacity.

Fast's theory of gender identity and differentiation is quite consistent with Stoller's view that the psyche of the young male commences in a state of protofemininity. She writes, "The growing body of literature that identifies an early feminine phase in boys, in which boys identify with their mothers in ways that include such female capacities as child-bearing, challenges both the notion of boys' exclusive masculinity and Freud's bisexuality theory."[110] It is because of the infant's close contact with the mother, and its early inability to distinguish between self and mother that the state of gender undifferentiation can still be viewed as a state of protofemininity. Fast succinctly states her thesis as follows:[111]

> [B]oys are biologically male, and girls female. Physiological factors probably contribute to sex difference in experience but are in the usual case overridden by social influences. From the time of sex ascription at birth, the caretaking environment treats girls and boys differently. Therefore boys' and girls' gender-related experience differs to some extent from the beginning, influenced by biological factors and differential handling by caretakers. With regard to gender awareness, it is proposed that girls' and boys' early experience is undifferentiated and overinclusive. That is, in the early processes of identification or establishment of self representations, the child has little sense that the characteristics of either femaleness or maleness, femininity or masculinity, are excluded for her or him respectively. Self representations or identifications are in this respect indiscriminate and over-inclusive (though due to the care-giving practices of this society probably occur more extensively in relation to the mother than the father). At a later time, probably around the second half of the second year, the child can identify self and others as to maleness or femaleness. However, while such positive identification as "girl" or "boy" has been learned, *delimitation* of the characteristics of each has not. This delimination occurs as part of the processes attendant on the child's recognition of sex difference. It involves renunciation of early gender-indiscriminate self representations and identi-

fications now found to be physically impossible or gender-inappropriate (to grow a baby in one's body, to have a penis, to be physically active, to be tender, to be aggressive, and so forth). It requires attributing sex and gender characteristics, renounced for oneself, to members of the other sex. It includes recognition of the sex- and gender-related limits of the other sex.

Freud recognized that humans of both sexes each have masculine and feminine characteristics. However, he erroneously concluded that boys and girls initially assume that possession of a penis is the norm. Consequently Freud misunderstood just how the process of genderization through the Oedipal passage proceeds. Young girls suffer not from the absence of a penis but from the narrowing of the range of possibilities. Correlatively, it is not just the possible loss of the penis which young boys fear, but the diminution of the range of human potential which follows from being categorized as nonmasculine.

Jung considered the Oedipal complex as "only a formula for childish desires in regard to the parents."[112] In some sense he recognized the process of genderization, in his conception of the male having to repress the feminine side of his nature into the unconscious where it forms a constellation which he called the *anima,* and the female repressing the masculine side of her personality into her unconscious where it coalesces as the *animus.*[113] This marks a fundamental difference between Freudian and Jungian theory. Explicitly or implicitly, the Freudian position is that there are essentially male psyches or selves and female psyches or selves. Even though Freud recognized that both sexes/genders can have qualities assigned as normal to the other, the process of individuation produces two different kinds of selves, male/masculine and female/feminine. Sexuality permeates the very process of the construction of the self. For Jung, however, there are only human selves, each of which has both masculine and feminine sides. A self in a male body will repress its feminine side into the unconscious as the *anima,* and a self in a female body will repress its masculine side into its unconscious as the *animus.* Full individuation for Jung entailed bringing the *anima* or *animus* out of the unconscious and into the conscious to achieve a state of androgyny.[114] All of this, again, reflects Jung's difficulty in accepting the primacy which Freud gave to the role of sexuality in the process of individuation.[115] Subsequent chapters will attempt to show that an analysis of history, culture, and institutions supports the Freudian rather than the Jungian position.

Fast's view presupposes the best of both Freud and Jung in postulating that the meaning of sex difference is not merely the presence or lack of a penis, but it is the loss of the "narcissistic assumption that all sex and gender characteristics are open" to the individual.[116] Castration anxiety is based upon the fear of the loss of maleness or of femaleness.[117] The mother or the father has what the child of the opposite sex must renounce. The boy must renounce the potential and possibilities which are defined as feminine, and the girl must face the loss of all the powers and capacities which appear to accompany and are symbolized by possession of a phallus.

There is now a body of psychoanalytic theory based on analysis and clinical research which, while remaining firmly within the Freudian tradition, reinterprets as a process of genderization the observations which Freud described within the framework of his theory of the Oedipus complex. The child forms a sense of personal identity in terms of a sexual and gender bifurcation patterned after parents so bifurcated. The genderization crisis of the Oedipal stage is a natural extension of the separation crisis of the pre-Oedipal stage. For the male child, retaining femininity entails not separating from the mother. The female child must separate but at the same time retain femininity.

THE POST-OEDIPAL STAGE AND THE ANIMALITY CRISIS

Just as the pre-Oedipal stage is a major determinant of the Oedipal stage, the Oedipal stage is a major determinant of the post-Oedipal stage. All analysis rests upon this presupposition. In the post-Oedipal stage, after the child has reached puberty and full sexual maturity, the adolescent starts to become fully cognizant of the bondage of human beings to the procreative cycle. It is only with the onset of the aging process that one becomes fully aware of one's mortality. The intermingling of sexuality with separation, individuation, engulfment anxiety, and genderization continues through the post-Oedipal stage. The child's relationship with its parents will inevitably shape the sexual patterns of the adult. Sexuality permeates mythic structure, and it is at the convergence of Eros and Thanatos that post-Oedipal male neurosis and pathology unfold.

While it is clearly recognized that the pre-Oedipal and Oedipal stages are major determinants of the post-Oedipal stage, the relationship between the Oedipal and the post-Oedipal is not nearly as well-developed in the literature as the relationship between the pre-Oedipal and the

Oedipal. One reason is that the pre-Oedipal and Oedipal stages are the subject matter of Freudian psychoanalysis, while those matters which fall into the post-Oedipal stage have been more the focus of attention of Jung and Rank, who departed from Freud's theory, in part because they discounted the theory of the Oedipal passage. These latter psychological systems are generally regarded as alternatives to Freud's work. While all, to varying degrees, pay tribute to Freud as the founding father, they work from the assumption (incorrect, in my opinion) that Freud placed far too much emphasis on sexuality and on Oedipal considerations. I find that all of the important insight of Jung and Rank can be fit within a Freudian framework as a part of the post-Oedipal stage, but not the reverse. When so viewed, the work of these men tends to corroborate Freud's position rather than negate it.[118]

Humans, in passing through the pre-Oedipal, Oedipal, and post-Oedipal stages, go through three corresponding crises, the separation crisis, the genderization crisis, and what I would term the animality crisis. The separation crisis entails the psychological birth of the self. The genderization crisis in the male consists of moving from a psychological state of protofemininity to full masculinity, and in the female, moving from a state of protofemininity to full femininity. The animality crisis arises at the post-Oedipal stage when the conscious mind begins to assimilate the almost unthinkable and unacceptable fact that humans are like all other animals in that we are biologically locked into the procreative cycle of sexual arousal, sexual frenzy, birth, and death.

Each of the crises produces psychic conflict. The separation crisis produces a psychic conflict between separation and engulfment anxiety, which not only affects the genderization and animality crises, but which continues on in its own right throughout our lives. The genderization crisis produces a conflict between the bipolarities of masculinity and femininity, which is intermingled with separation and engulfment anxiety and will also be a lasting source of tension. The animality crisis produces a third psychic conflict which is manifested in body-mind and nature-culture dualisms. These, in turn, are permeated with separation and engulfment anxiety, and are tinged with gender identification. By adulthood, these three crises have coalesced into the very structure of the psyche, and culture represents their coalescence at a societal level. Sexuality links the separation and the genderization crises to the animality crisis, as it is in some form or another the common factor in all three stages.

The link between Eros and Thanatos furnishes the link between separation, genderization, and death.

The ego ideal plays an important role in the animality crisis for it often represents a denial of and an escape from death. By merging or losing the fragile and impermanent ego with or in the object of the ego ideal one achieves the illusion of omnipotence lost when driven from the paradise of primary narcissism. Identification with the object of the ego ideal is one of the primary methods of repressing the reality of death.

The entire Oedipal passage of the human race, from the pre-Oedipal through the post-Oedipal, can be seen as a process of individuation which entails a denial and denigration of the feminine (m)other. Consequently culture is patriarchal. The male infant passes from a state of protofemininity to masculinity, and then develops both a superego and an object of the ego ideal which are masculinized. Females, while they are genderized as feminine, are also socialized to develop a superego and an object of the ego ideal which are masculine. This explains in part why so many women support and maintain patriarchal religions worshipping a father god.

6.

THE STRUCTURE OF
THE PSYCHE

THE FREUDIAN ANALYSIS

The Ego and the Id

Psychoanalysis is concerned with the analysis of the psyche, soul, or what we might call the mind. Freud used the term *geist*, the German term for the soul, but his English translators used *psyche* to avoid the religious connotations which the word *soul* might have for English readers.[1] The process of development of the psyche commences in infancy as the child starts to recognize its separateness from the mother. The first steps in the development of consciousness entail differentiating the self from the external world, including other persons. This process involves the development within the psyche of the agency which Freud called in German the *ich*. Its literal translation into English would be the *I,* but the translators of Freud have used instead, the Latin term for *I,* the *ego*.[2] According to Freud, while much of the ego resides in the conscious, part of it inhabits the unconscious.

As a child individuates, it develops an awareness of gender differentiation which it will later learn is culturally identified with its biological sex.[3] As the child separates itself from its mother, it begins to learn that it is a member of a family. While identifying him- or herself with the family, the child is differentiating itself from other persons, including its parents and siblings. In gender-polarized societies it is extremely difficult for any child to develop a sense of self without a distinct gender identification. Gender identification comes about through identification with the gender group- ings of male and female. The ego is thus genderized as either masculine or feminine, and occasionally may be somewhat androgynous.

The ego develops through processes of both differentiation and iden- tification which generally function in harmony with each other. Differen- tiation from others takes place in terms of the varying sets of group identities, and therefore inevitably involves identification. Our sex, family, extended family, tribe, language group, and nationality are all a part of our personal identity. The relationship between the "I" and the "we," therefore is not a dialectic between two conflicting poles in terms of which we must strike a balance. There can be no "I" without a "we," nor conversely, a "we" without a set of "I"s.

A strong sense of the "I" component is developed within people when they are allowed, encouraged, and taught to be autonomous individuals, freely making their own choices and taking responsibility for them. The Western tradition has always recognized the close link between freedom or liberty and responsibility.[4] Taking responsibility for one's actions, however, means choosing those actions in terms of their possible effect on other people. A strong sense of the "we" is developed when a person receives love and support within the family, and co-operation, fellowship, good feeling, and compassion from the group. At the same time, few people can develop a strong sense of the "I" without having a sense of appreciation and status within the group, since our evaluation of ourselves will generally reflect to some degree that of the group. It is, of course, possible to have a strong I-consciousness in conjunction with a very weak we-consciousness. Such persons will suffer from some form of pathology such as alienation. The psychopath or sociopath who is incapable of empathy for anyone else and who judges all action only in terms of his own immediate wants or desires is a classic example.

Analysis of the psyche must always start with the ego. It is the medium through which we formulate a picture of the other parts of the psyche such as the id, the superego, and the ego ideal.[5] Freud stated, "The ego is first and foremost a bodily ego."[6] The superego involves the internaliza- tion of the father or external social forces and moral and ethical standards and prohibitions. The ego ideal involves the merging of the self in an external other. The ego or the "I," on the other hand, is related to the external surface of the body. The link between the self contained within the body and the external world is through the ego.

The ego develops out of the id. Of the id Freud writes:[7]

> We now distinguish in our mental life (which we regard as an apparatus compounded of several agencies, districts or provinces) one region which we call the *ego* proper and another which we name the *id*. The id is the older of the two; the ego has developed out of it, like a cortical layer, through the influence of the external world. It is in the id that all our primary instincts are at work, all the processes in the id take place unconsciously. The ego . . . coincides with the region of the preconscious; it includes portions which normally remain unconscious. The course of events in the id, and their mutual interaction, are governed by quite other laws than those prevailing in the ego. . . . The *repressed* is to be counted as belonging to the id and is subject to the same mechanisms; it is distinguished from it only in respect to its genesis. The differentiation is accomplished in the earliest period of life, while the ego is developing out of the id. At that time a portion of the contents of the id is taken into the ego and raised to the preconscious state; another portion is not affected by this translation and remains behind in the id as the unconscious proper. In the further course of the formation of the ego, however, certain psychical impressions and processes in the ego are excluded [i.e., expelled] from it by a defensive process; the characteristic of being preconscious is withdrawn from them, so that they are once more reduced to being component portions of the id. Here then is the "repressed" in the id.

Impulses from the id must pass through the ego on their way to gratification. In so doing, "they are required to respect the demands of reality and, more than that, to conform to ethical and moral laws by which the superego seeks to control the behavior of the ego."[8] The instinctual impulses therefore produce tensions between the ego and the id.

The ego clashes with the id as the instinctual impulses try to "gain access to consciousness and to obtain gratification."[9] The ego defends itself by adopting defense mechanisms. Repression, sublimation, denial, illusion, and other defense mechanisms protect the ego from the incursions of instinctual material from the id which in their manifestation in consciousness threaten the ego.[10]

The Superego

There are two interrelated parts of the psyche which play a developmental role in the Oedipal passage. These are the superego and the ego.[11] It is a common truism in psychoanalytic theory that the superego is heir to the Oedipus complex.[12] Freud argued that neurosis and psychosis originate in the ego's conflicts with its various ruling agencies, including the super-ego. He used the term *superego* to describe the vehicle of conscience.[13] He wrote:[14]

> The super-ego is an agency which has been inferred by us, and conscience is a function which we ascribe, among other functions, to that agency. This function consists in keeping a watch over the actions and intentions of the ego and judging them, thus exercising a censorship. The sense of guilt, the harshness of the super-ego, is thus the same thing as the severity of the conscience. It is the perception which the ego has of being watched over in this way, the assessment of the tension between its own strivings and the demands of the super-ego. The fear of this critical agency (a fear which is at the bottom of the whole relationship), the need for punishment, is an instinctual manifestation on the part of the ego, which has become maso-chistic under the influence of a sadistic super-ego.

The super-ego comes into being during the latency period, a period characterized by the dissolution of the Oedipus complex and the resulting formation of ethical and aesthetic barriers in the ego.[15] At this time the relationship to the parents becomes desexualized in that it is diverted from its libidinal impulses. As the child develops and detaches itself from its parents, the role they play in the child's superego gradually decreases. Thus, the superego is the legitimate heir to the Oedipus complex in that it takes over the power, function, and methods of the parental agency. The metamorphosis of the parental relationship into the superego is brought about by "identification," "that is to say, the assimilation of one ego to another one, as a result of which the first ego behaves like the second in certain respects, imitates it and in a sense takes it up into itself."[16] As parents follow the precepts of their own superegos in educat-ing children, the child's superego becomes constructed on the model of the parent's superego.[17] The authority of the child's parents, particularly that of the father with its threatening power to punish, calls on the child to renounce his instinct and decides for him what is to be allowed and what forbidden.[18] This authority of the father is introjected into the ego, where it forms the nucleus of the superego which takes over the severity of the father and perpetuates his prohibition against incest.[19]

Freud pointed out that mental health depends on the normal develop-ment of the superego. This will occur when it has become sufficiently impersonal, "[a]nd that is precisely what it is not in neurotics, whose Oedipus complex has not passed through the correct process of transformation. Their super-ego still confronts their ego as a strict father confronts a child; and their morality operates in a primitive fashion in that the ego gets itself punished by the super-ego."[20]

The superego represents the ethical standards of mankind.[21]

> If civilization is a necessary course of development from the family to humanity as a whole, then—as a result of the inborn conflict arising from ambivalence, of the eternal struggle between the trends of love and death— there is inextricably bound up with it an increase of the sense of guilt, which will perhaps reach heights that the individual finds hard to tolerate.[22]

The cultural superego develops from this concept. It sets up its own demands. Those that deal with the relations among human beings are known as ethics. If the cultural superego issues a command which people cannot possibly obey, then just as such a situation will create a neurosis in an individual, so it will lead to a neurotic society.[23] Freud noted, "The past, the traditions of the race and of the people, lives on in the ideologies of the super-ego, and yields only slowly to the influences of the present and to new changes; and so long as it operates through the super-ego it plays a powerful part in human life, independently of economic conditions."[24]

The Ego Ideal

Freud introduced the term *ego ideal* in "On Narcissism: An Introduction," (1914),[25] but he demonstrated in *Totem and Taboo*, (1912),[26] the particular status he later accorded to the term. He placed it between infantile megalomania and object love, between the pleasure principle and the reality principle. In "On Narcissism," he put forward the notion that there may be a "special psychical agency" whose task it is to watch the actual ego and measure it by the ego ideal. In 1921, the distinction between the "ego ideal" and the "agency" concerned with its enforcement was dropped,[27] and in 1923 the concept was merged with the superego.[28] Janine Chasseguet-Smirgel argues that the critical agency, the superego, which is the heir of the Oedipus complex, has little in common with the ego ideal, which is the heir of primary narcissism[29]—the infantile illusion of omnipotence and the blissful feeling bound up with it.[30] Freud continued to see in narcissism a longing, which remains throughout a person's entire life, for the primal union, as he believed man is incapable of giving up such an intense satisfaction once enjoyed.[31] There is, therefore, a place in his theory for something like the ego ideal as separate from the superego.

Chasseguet-Smirgel asserts that if the child confronts its inferiority and helplessness the ensuing frustration will serve as an incentive to master its environment. If the ego ideal chooses to maintain these narcissistic illusions it will deny both gender and generational differences. She writes, "In its longing to recapture the experience of primal oneness and omnipotence, the ego ideal can follow either the short, direct, and regressive road marked out by the Nirvana principle or the long and difficult road of maturation and development."[32] She argues that one can "recapture the sense of oneness not by denying the fact of separation but by overcoming it in the pursuit of an ideal—erotic, aesthetic, or religious—of devotion and self-sacrifice."[33] Thus, her concept of the ego ideal is rooted in the biological side of man's nature: in the fear of death, the sense of helplessness and inferiority and the longing to reestablish a sense of primal unity with the natural order of things.[34]

According to Chasseguet-Smirgel, ideologies are "projective systems"[35] which create "the Illusion of the possibility of returning to the lost unity, a unity lost ever since the moment of primary separation."[36] She relates her account of ideology as the projection of the ego ideal[37] with Freud's theory of group mental phenomena in *Group Psychology and the Analysis of the Ego.*[38] Her description of how ideology dissolves the superego in the narcissistic elation of the meeting of ego and ideal[39] closely corresponds with Freud's description of the disappearance of the superego in group phenomena. Therefore, her separation of the ego ideal from the superego seems to be an important clarification rather than a modification of Freud's theory. We can conclude that in the post-Oedipal stage of psychological development, ideologies and religions often furnish the framework whereby the lost narcissistic unity is sought in various forms of group bonding.

Béla Grunberger, in his study of narcissism, places the concept of primary narcissism at the center of psychoanalytic theory by using it to tie together the pre-Oedipal, Oedipal, and post-Oedipal stages of the individuation into an integrated theory of mental development.[40] "The past . . . that man seeks to repeat," he writes, "is really his prenatal existence, a situation from which he was traumatically expelled and that he never ceases longing to recapture."[41] Grunberger concludes, "One could regard all the manifestations of civilization as a kaleidoscope of different attempts by man to restore *narcissistic omnipotence.*"[42] The restoration of narcissistic omnipotence is sought through the loss of the self by merging the self in the ego ideal.

The ego ideal is the link between the ego and the ideal other. Therefore, the ego ideal must develop in conjunction with the ego. In the state of primary narcissism there is no ego ideal because the self is not differentiated from the other or the nonself. Separation of the self from the (m)other produces the narcissistic wound and the desire to return to the blissful undifferentiated state by the ego reuniting with the ideal and regaining what Freud referred to as the oceanic feeling. In the pre-Oedipal stage the mother is thus the focus or object of the ego ideal. Chasseguet-Smirgel writes: [43]

> Thus narcissism, which is the stage of development in which the Ego furnishes itself with its own ideal, gives way to the object relation. The Ego is led to break with a part of its narcissism by projecting this form of an Ego Ideal. From this point onwards, there will be a gap, a rift between the Ego and its Ideal. The Ego will aim at stitching the two gaping sides of the wound which is henceforth its characteristic. Union with the first object in which the lost narcissistic perfection has been vested will become one way by which to retrieve its initial narcissism. As may be supposed, and clinical experience confirms this to some extent, the narcissistic state is fantasized as identical in nature to the fusion between the infant and its mother on the model of the intra-uterine situation (which Freud supposes is a primal phantasy). . . . Genital coitus, which is the apex of sexual development, contains and is an expression of the wish to return to the mother's womb, where, Ferenczi says, the rift between the Ego and the environment has not as yet taken place. . . . If the incestuous wish rests not only on a sexual drive but also on the desire to retrieve lost narcissistic unity, we can understand that in the course of his development the boy reaches a point at which he cathects the father's image with his Ego Ideal. He places his narcissism in his father who thus becomes his model, that is to say, his aim for identification.

Initially the object of the ego ideal is furnished by "[p]rojection of infantile narcissism onto the parents."[44] A successful Oedipal passage in the male child, at least, requires the object of the ego ideal to shift from the mother to the father, and thus from feminine to masculine. Just as the appearance of God in the collective psyche marks the separation of humans from nature, so the shift of the object of the ego ideal from mother to father marks the separation of the male child from the mother and the completion of the process of genderization.

At the Oedipal stage the father serves as the focal point of both the superego and the ego ideal. The role that the father figure plays in each agency, however, is different. The father is internalized in the form of the superego as an authority figure who proclaims what is right and wrong, permitted and prohibited. Thus, within the superego, the father figure functions as a critical agency. In the ego ideal, however, the father figure functions as an ideal of omnipotence with which the child wishes to identify, merge, or to become like. In this function the father figure is an ideal form for the ego to emulate, rather than a critical agency which judges the ego. Freud calls this function "identification." He writes, "Identification is known to psycho-analysis as the earliest expression of an emotional tie with another person. It plays a part in the early history of the Oedipus complex. A little boy will exhibit a special interest in his father; he would like to grow like him and be like him, and take his place everywhere. We may say simply that he takes his father as his ideal."[45] It was probably Freud's failure to distinguish this second function of the internalized father from the first function, which led to his eventual merger of superego and ego ideal.

Freud describes the young male as exhibiting "two psychologically distinct ties: a straightforward sexual object-cathexis towards his mother and an identification with his father which takes him as his model."[46] Thus, the father serves as an object of the ego ideal with which to identify, and the mother serves as an object of the ego ideal with which to merge. The Oedipus complex originates when the child realizes that the father stands in the way of his desire to merge with the mother.

In the post-Oedipal stage the superego develops as a function of differentiation while the object of the ego ideal functions as the link between the individual and the collective.[47] It seeks the healing of the narcissistic wound through reunification. The object of the ego ideal is initially genderized as feminine, and becomes masculine for the male if the Oedipal passage is successful. As far as the male is concerned, in the post-Oedipal stage the object of the ego ideal can remain masculine or return to the feminine. In a masculine form the ego ideal is identified with a union with and a loss of the self in some form of collective brotherhood. In a feminine form it is often identified with a particular woman with whom the male is in love.

In her study of the ego ideal, Chasseguet-Smirgel discusses both the feminine and masculine forms which the object of ego ideal can take in the male in the post-Oedipal stage of individuation. In the chapter which she entitles "The Ego Ideal, Being-in-Love and Genitality" she discusses a form which the object of the ego ideal can take which is obviously feminine.[48] In the next chapter, which she calls "The Ego Ideal and the Group," she describes a form which is clearly masculine.[49] When a beloved woman becomes the object of a male's ego ideal, union is sought through a surrender of the self or ego to her. However, this is not the only form which a union between a male and female may take. If the female is not identified with the ego ideal then the male seeks a union, not through a surrender of his self, but by incorporating the other into his own ego by seeing her as an object or objectifying her. In such a case the object of the ego ideal of the female would be masculine, as she surrenders herself to the male. The two alternative forms of male-female relationships are differentiated by Freud where, in describing romantic love, he writes:[50]

> It is now easy to define the difference between identification and such extreme developments of being in love as may be described as "fascination" or "bondage." In the former case the ego has enriched itself with the properties of the object, it has "introjected" the object into itself. . . . In the second case it is impoverished, it has surrendered itself to the object, it has substituted the object for its own most important constituent.

Women in a patriarchal culture are generally socialized to serve the needs of males—that is, to surrender themselves to an external other/father/ husband. Communities are male brotherhoods. The ideologies are male-oriented, reflecting male values, and the religious symbols and archetypes are masculine. Consequently, the object of the ego ideal of the female in patriarchal culture will generally be genderized as masculine.

The gender of the object of the ego ideal in the collective psyche of a people has important implications for social organization. If the object of the ego ideal of a male is feminine it is highly likely that he will tend to be more of an individualist. Freud wrote:[51]

> The last two remarks will have prepared us for finding that directly sexual impulses are unfavorable to the formation of groups. In the history of the development of the family . . . the more important sexual love became for the ego, and the more it developed the characteristics of being in love, the more urgently it required to be limited to two people. . . . Two people

coming together for the purpose of sexual satisfaction, in so far as they seek for solitude, are making a demonstration against the herd instinct, the group feeling. The more they are in love, the more completely they suffice for each other.

Thus love, as Chasseguet-Smirgel points out, "is a force that tends to fragment the collectivity. This is why it is attacked by all totalitarian regimes as 'egotistical,' 'possessive,' 'individualistic'."[52] If the object of the ego ideal is in a masculine form, it will be sought in a community or brotherhood. As Freud described, "A primary group of this kind is a number of individuals who have put one and the same object in the place of their ego ideal and have consequently identified themselves with one another in their ego."[53]

THE JUNGIAN ANALYSIS

Social theorists working within a psychoanalytic framework soon find themselves confronted with a serious dilemma. If they adopt a Freudian analytical structure, they are faced with the lack of a theory of the collective psyche. Freud, while asserting the necessity of the collective psyche, never developed a theory of its structure. Jung, on the other hand, wrote extensively about the collective unconscious and its archetypal structure. Yet the writers of Freudian psychoanalytic social theory have been much more prolific than their Jungian counterparts.[54] The Freudian emphasis on the importance of sexuality, including that of infants, and the Freudian concepts of primary narcissism and the Oedipal passage are, I would submit, essential for the development of a psychoanalytic social theory. What psychoanalytic social theory requires is a way of selecting those parts of Jungian theory which would be consistent with and enrich a Freudian perspective, from the more speculative and unfocused parts of Jung's theories.[55] This requires focal points in both Freud and Jung which can be interrelated or translated into each other.

While Jung recognized the importance of dreams in analysis, he believed, in contrast to Freud, that the key to unlocking the unconscious lies in the analysis of complexes.[56] The concept of the complex, important to both Freud and Jung, makes an ideal point for comparison. The other point of common reference is to be found between the Freudian concept of the ego ideal as developed by Chasseguet-Smirgel, and Jung's concept of the archetypes.

The most important contribution made by Jung to psychoanalytic theory is that of the collective unconscious and its archetypal structure, or his theory of archetypes.[57] These concepts are essential for the development of an adequate psychoanalytic social theory. It is unfortunate that the egos of both men prevented Jung's brilliant insights from enriching the theories of Freud. In seperating himself from Freud, Jung rejected some of Freud's fundamental ideas, which, in my opinion, has prevented Jungian psychology from ever being able to give a full and adequate explanation of mental life. It matters little who was most to blame, but there is no question that psychoanalytic social theory would have benefited if both men had continued as colleagues rather than becoming rivals. Freud's theories would have been richer because of the creative, imaginative, and intuitive genius of Jung. In particular, Freudian psychoanalysis would have produced a superior theory of the collective psyche. On the other side, the influence of Freud's disciplined mind might have prevented some of the more speculative flights of Jung's imagination, which have brought unwarranted discredit to his whole work.

Archetypes

The concept of the archetype is Jung's most important contribution to psychoanalytic theory, and in particular psychoanalytic social theory.[58] Nevertheless, it is not an easy concept to grasp. According to Jung, "[T]he concept of the archetype has given rise to the greatest misunderstanding and—if one may judge by the adverse criticisms—must be presumed to be very difficult to comprehend."[59] In the Jungian tradition a vast amount of literature is devoted to this subject.[60] Jung states, "The concept of the archetype, which is an indispensable correlate of the idea of the collective unconscious, indicates the existence of definite forms in the psyche which seem to be present always and everywhere."[61] Elsewhere he writes, "Archetypes may be considered the fundamental elements of the conscious mind, hidden in the depths of the psyche. . . . They are systems of readiness for action, and at the same time *images and emotions*. They are inherited with the brain structure—indeed they are its psychic aspect."[62] It is difficult to gain a clear idea of the nature of archetypes in Jung's system of thought from his own writings. The ambiguity surrounding this concept renders the collective unconscious unclear, since it is structured in terms of archetypes. Exponents of Jung have not succeeded in bringing further clarification. Jolande Jacobi writes that while "at first the notion of the archetype was applied by Jung primarily to psychic 'motifs' that could be expressed in images . . . in time it was extended to all sorts of patterns, configurations, happenings, etc." and eventually "came to cover all psychic manifestations of a biological, psychobiological, or ideational character, provided they were more or less universal and typical."[63] Jung is quite clear on one point, however, and that is the necessity to sharply distinguish between the archetype and its particular representation or "archetypal image."

In spite of the lack of clarity about the essential nature and source of archetypes in Jungian theory, they remain an essential concept for psychoanalytic social theory. Archetypes might be viewed as universal patterns of thought and structures of information to be found within human experience as recorded and expressed in culture. Their universal nature is derived from common experience which eventually rests upon the universality of the human genetic code, and the similarities to be found within the environments inhabited by humans. The two most common archetypes are that of the mother and the father. These archetypal forms are constructed from individuals' own experience with their respective parents, and the absorption from culture of the concept of the mother and father. The individual's own experience cannot be separated from the cultural context because individuals experience their own parents within the context of these cultural forms. The mother and father archetypes of the collective psyche consist of that which is common to human experience. The gods live and die in the collective psyche. The death of God or a particular god or the twilight of the gods, consist of the receding of a particular form of a representation of the father archetype within the collective psyche.

Complexes

In order to understand the nature and content of archetypes in Jungian psychology, one needs to understand Jung's view of the complex. Jacobi states, "A kinship appears between the concepts of the complex and of the archetype; the relation between the two proves to be complementary and reciprocal. The notion of the complex—if it is to be fully understood—calls, spontaneously as it were, for an attempt to clarify the concept of the archetype."[64] The converse is also true. The notion of the archetype, if it is to be fully understood, requires a clarification of the idea of the complex. In the next section it will be argued that we need to understand both complexes and archetypes if we are to clarify the concept and role of the ego ideal.

Jung defined complexes as "living units of unconscious psyche"[65] or "psychic agencies."[66] One of their most significant aspects is their autonomy. He writes:[67]

> What is not so well known, though far more important theoretically, is that complexes can *have us*. The existence of complexes throws serious doubt on the naive assumption of the unity of consciousness, which is equated with "psyche," and on the supremacy of the will. Every constellation of a complex postulates a disturbed state of consciousness. The unity of consciousness is disrupted and the intentions of the will are impeded or made impossible. Even memory is often noticeably affected, as we have seen. The complex must therefore be a psychic factor which, in terms of energy, possesses a value that sometimes exceeds that of our conscious intentions, otherwise such disruptions of the conscious order would not be possible at all. And in fact, an active complex puts us momentarily under a state of duress, of compulsive thinking and acting, for which under certain conditions the only appropriate term would be the judicial concept of diminished responsibility.

Jung also refers to complexes as "splinter psyches" which have their own freedom of action.[68] "Where the realm of complexes begins," he writes, "the freedom of the ego comes to an end."[69]

Complexes make up the structure of the unconscious, and therefore they are a normal phenomena of mental life.[70] Because all people have complexes, and complexes are the source of neurosis, the normal state of the human psyche is neurotic. The view of the normal psyche as fully rational or ever being able to achieve complete rationality is an illusion. All mental life is carried out on a continuum between a pole of rationality where the human ego is in complete control and decisions are made in terms of only conscious material (a pole which no human can achieve) to pathology and psychosis at the other extreme. Neurosis lies in between.[71] To the degree that our complexes are collective, they have their origin in the archetypes of the collective unconscious.[72]

A theory of the complex is much more developed in the writings of Jung than in the writings of Freud. Jung writes, "Freud became the real discoverer of the unconscious in psychology," because he was the first to examine the mental phenomena of the complex and to develop a theory of the unconscious which would explain it.[73] It was Freud's theories and thoughts about "the nature and effects of the psychic factors known as 'complexes'" which captured Jung's interest in Freud's work.[74] Freud believed that complexes arise from those aspects of one's private life and emotional experiences, generally arising in one's earliest years, which have been repressed into the unconscious because they are incompatible with the content of the ego. Jung, on the other hand, saw complexes as a combination of individual experiences framed within archetypal structures of the collective unconscious. The concept of the complex, therefore, plays a much greater role in Jungian theory than it does in Freudian theory.[75]

Jung believed that while complexes have their origins in archetypes, the archetypes can have superimposed upon them individual personal experience. According to Samuels:[76]

> The concept of a complex was Jung's way of linking the personal and the collective. Outer experiences in infancy and throughout life cluster round an archetypal core. Events in childhood, and particularly internal conflicts, provide this personal aspect. A complex is not just the clothing for one particular archetype (that would, more accurately, be an archetypal image) but an agglomerate of the actions of several archetypal patterns, imbued with personal experience and affect. . . . A complex is, therefore, not a simple entity; the "mother complex" contains emotions derived from the interaction of the ego position with numerous archetypal configurations: the individual, the mother, the individual and mother, mother and father, individual and father, individual and sibling, individual and sibling and mother, individual and family, etc., etc. To avoid the ramifications of such an endless list we need a concept like complex.

It might be said that archetypes shape personal experience. According to Jung, the archetypal material itself is a healthy component of the psyche, as the collective unconscious can never be pathological. A complex only becomes unhealthy or pathological when it undergoes a restructuring or transformation by being projected into an area of individual conflict through material from the personal unconscious. Thus, Jung distinguished between healthy and unhealthy complexes. For Freud, on the other hand, all complexes were unhealthy. The theory of the complex developed in the next few chapters will contain aspects of both Jungian and Freudian theory.

INTEGRATION

The first archetype in both mythic structure and in the structure of the psyche is what Erich Neumann describes as "original unity."[77] From a Freudian perspective, the parallel to this state would be the state of primary narcissism before the separation of the self from the mother. The unconscious memory of this state of undifferentiated and omnipotent bliss would be clearly archetypal, to use a Jungian term. The primal state of original unity, for which the cosmic egg and the uroboric serpent are archetypal symbols, are the analogue of Freud's oceanic feeling which he postulated has its origin in human thought as a conscious manifestation of the unconscious memory of primary narcissistic bliss. Freud thus provides a psychoanalytic explanation for the Eastern religious concept of the Buddhist nirvana, the Hindu Brahmin without difference or the Tao of Chinese Taoism. Neumann quotes Lao-tzu's description of the latter, which could equally be applied to the first stage of the life of the psyche:[78]

> There was something formless yet complete,
> That existed before heaven and earth;
> Without sound, without substance,
> Dependent on nothing, unchanging,
> All pervading, unfailing,
> One may think of it as the mother of all things under heaven.

While Jung never specifically refers to a Nirvana archetype, the concept appears to function archetypally in Jung's writings.[79] Jung does refer to the archetype of the "God-image."[80] He states that "one can never distinguish empirically between a symbol of the self and a God-image," as "the two ideas . . . always appear blended together."[81] He writes further that "[a]nything that a man postulates as being a greater totality than himself can become a symbol of the self."[82] Passages such as these lead me to believe that Jung's archetype of the God-image serves a remarkably similar function to that of Freud's ego ideal.

Other essential Jungian archetypes are a constellation which make up the Eternal Feminine or what Jung sometimes calls the *anima* archetype. Of this group the mother archetype is the most important. Jung explains that the mother archetype "appears under an almost infinite variety of aspects."[83] Of primary importance is the personal mother, then other personal mother figures such as the grandmother, stepmother, mother-in-law, or any woman having a special relationship of caregiving with the child. Then follow what Jung terms "mothers in a figurative sense."[84] These take the form of the mother of God or the Goddess, which in turn has three forms, the virgin, the nurturing mother, and the destroying crone. Jung goes on to point out that the archetype is also associated with things and places standing for fertility and fruitfulness such as a plowed field or a tree, a spring, or a cave.[85] He writes:[86]

> The word "mother," which sounds so familiar, apparently refers to the best-known, the individual mother—to "my mother." But the mother-symbol points to a darker background which eludes conceptual formulation and can only be vaguely apprehended as the hidden, nature-bound life of the body. Yet even this is too narrow and excludes too many vital subsidiary meanings. The underlying, primary psychic reality is so inconceivably complex that it can be grasped only at the farthest reach of intuition, and then but very dimly. That is why it needs symbols.

One of the primary symbols of the Goddess is the snake or serpent. The prevalence of the symbol of the serpent with goddess worship throughout the world furnishes an interesting confirmation of some of Jung's views on archetypes, symbols, and the collective unconscious.

A further series of archetypes are those of the masculine, which include the father, the Heavenly Father, the royal father or king, and the hero. Jung wrote only one essay on the father[87] but a great deal about the mother. Consequently the analysis of the father archetype is not nearly as well-developed in Jungian theory. Like the archetype of the mother, the father archetype also has numerous manifestations. That of the personal father is the most important. Then follow father figures such as grandfathers, uncles, or other males playing the role of the father. The father archetype also has its figurative forms such as God the father, or the king or monarch as the royal father. The father archetype in its figurative mold can also take the form of the hero, the loving and caring father, the destroying father or the wise old man. The father archetype is also associated with a variety of things such as law, a political order such as "the Father Land," or the plow. In one of the few places where Jung discusses the father archetype, he states:[88]

> The archetype of the mother is the most immediate one for the child. But with the development of consciousness the father also enters his field of

vision, and activates an archetype whose nature is in many respects opposed
to that of the mother. Just as the mother archetype corresponds to the
Chinese *yin,* so the father archetype corresponds to the *yang.* It determines
our relations to man, to the law and the state, to reason and the spirit and
the dynamism of nature. "Fatherland" implies boundaries, a definite locali-
zation in space, whereas the land itself is Mother Earth, quiescent and
fruitful. The Rhine is a father, as is the Nile, the wind and storm, thunder
and lightning. The father is the "auctor" and represents authority, hence
also law and the state. He is that which moves in the world, like the wind;
the guide and creator of invisible thoughts and airy images. He is the
creative wind-breath—the spirit, pneuma, *atman.*

Thus the father, too, is a powerful archetype dwelling in the psyche of
the child. At first he is *the* father, an all-encompassing God-image, a dynamic principle. In the course of life this authoritarian imago recedes into
the background: the father turns into a limited and often all-too-human
personality. The father-imago, on the other hand, develops to the full its
potential significance. Just as man was late in discovering nature, so he only
gradually discovered law, duty, responsibility, the state, the spirit.

There are two archetypes which are fundamental to Jungian theory,
but have no counterpart within a Freudian context. These are the *animus*
and the *anima.* Even among Jungians, a good deal of controversy sur-
rounds these two concepts.[89] At times Jung seems to apply them to sexual
differences, at other times to gender differences which have their foundation in biologically based sexual differences, and at other times to human
qualities which are independent of sexual differences but have been historically given a gender identification. In Jungian theory a series of dichotomies such as male/female, masculine/feminine, *logos*/eros, reason/feeling,
differentiated/undifferentiated are related to the animus/anima archetypal
dichotomy. In a Freudian framework of analysis, the animus and anima
must be rejected because they confuse biologically determined factors
with socially determined factors, and cannot be given a functional analysis
as separate agencies within the structure of the individual psyche.

Another archetype will be used throughout this book which is not
specifically mentioned as such by Jung, and that is the archetype of the
collective brotherhood. The proliferation of male fraternal organizations
throughout the world and throughout history reflects a male complex
which drives the male to band together into close-knit groups. Whether
these are sacred priesthoods, monastic orders, military orders, secret societies, fraternal orders, or merely private men's clubs, they are a product of
behavior which reflects a psychological basis. The drive of the male to
lose the self within brotherhoods is often counterposed against the con-

flicting drive to unite with a female. It will later be argued that this behavior is compulsive and reflects a complex which has archetypal foundations. There is a structure to the brotherhood archetype which can be found reflected within the myriad brotherhoods which males have formed and continue to form.

The ego ideal of Freudian psychoanalytic theory is analogous to the primary archetype of original unity in Jungian depth psychology. Objects of the ego ideal such as the mother, then the father, disembodied mind, the beloved, or the brotherhood of the collective can equally be viewed in terms of archetypes. Not all Jungian archetypes function as objects of the ego ideal, but all forms which the ego ideal may take are archetypal. We can greatly clarify the role of the ego ideal in the process of individuation when we examine the various objects which it takes in that process, as archetypes of a collective unconscious. In this way we can clarify the role of the collective psyche in the process of individual individuation, and conversely we can learn more about the evolution of the collective psyche when we compare it to the individual psyche and thus recognize the pattern of individuation in the collective psyche.

Since archetypes give rise to complexes, and mental life is framed within sets of complexes, and since the objects of the ego ideal are archetypal, the ego ideal can be seen as a major source of many of the complexes which govern our mental life. The primary value of integrating Freud and Jung at this point is that it provides a theoretical foundation for the function of the ego ideal, which in turn, is essential if we are to develop an adequate psychoanalytic social theory. We can now view the process of individuation in terms of not just the Oedipus complex, but a passage through a series of complexes.

THE PROCESS OF INDIVIDUATION

We can now interpret the process of individuation in terms of archetypal shifts. This process starts with the separation of the self from the (m)other. The separation creates the narcissistic wound, and the lost state of primary narcissistic wholeness and bliss becomes the ideal which the ego ever after will seek to regain. The first object of the ego ideal is the mother. The external physical mother is internalized as a part of the mother archetype within the unconscious. The separation crisis entails the shift from primary narcissistic unity which is the state of the ideal, to its replacement by the mother in her external form as a person and related inner arche-typal form. Both Freud's insistence on the actual mother and Jung's focus on the archetypal mother are an essential part of the mother as the object of the ego ideal.

The object of the ego ideal eventually switches from the mother to the father. This transition is marked by the Oedipus complex which reflects the genderization crisis. A male child who has an unsuccessful Oedipal passage is unable to replace the mother with the father as the object of the ego ideal. The process of individuation is blocked by a regression. The male child whose ego ideal continues to have the mother as its object can be said to suffer from a mother complex.

The next step in the process of individuation is for the child to replace the father as object of the ego ideal with other archetypal forms. Children who fail to make this shift can be said to suffer from a father complex. The anxieties generated by the process of individuation as the ego ideal shifts from one archetypal object to another are often mythically repre-sented in the form of the hero slaying a monster. The monster is often an archetypal representation of the devouring mother or the destroying fa-ther, while the hero is an archetypal representation of the self struggling to individuate. These themes are dealt with extensively in Jung and Neu-mann and other studies in the Jungian tradition.

In many myths of the heroic, the hero is a member of a brotherhood. Thus the hero knights of King Arthur are members of the Round Table. In the mythic theme of Mozart's opera, *The Magic Flute,* the father who struggles with the Queen of the Night (the Great Mother or Goddess) for the daughter, is a member of and leader of a sacred brotherhood or priesthood. The archetype of the hero marks a transition stage between the father and mother as objects of the ego ideal to the collective brother-hood. The process of individuation for the female is from the father to the hero, who takes her father's place as the object of her ego ideal. Her identification with the brotherhood is never that of an equal participant but is that of an auxiliary.

In the post-Oedipal stage of individuation when the ego must face the threat to its permanence in the form of impending death, pure mind, which is disembodied and consequently not subject to decay or death, becomes an object of the ego ideal. The illusion of immortality implicit in the idea of the soul or spirit encased with the body is a powerful defense against the fear of death. Thus, disembodied mind is a fundamental archetype which has its origin in the mind/body dualism implicit in human consciousness.

Viewing the objects of the ego ideal as archetypes of the collective unconscious helps us clarify the role of the collective psyche in the process of individuation of the individual. This process is generated by a movement and progression between different objects of the ego ideal. The psyche individuates by projecting the ego ideal onto the next archetype, drawn toward it and repelled by the old object of the ego ideal. Thus, the collective psyche furnishes the archetypal structure of the collective unconscious which generates the process of individuation. The process of individuation thus entails moving from one complex to another. Our psychic life unfolds within the framework of complexes. These complexes are generated by the archetypes of the collective psyche which take the form of parallel representations in the collective unconscious of the individual. Upon being given specific content from the personal unconscious and conscious wherein the individual interacts within the social framework of the family and society, these complexes form constellations or independent systems. The neurotic foundations of social order are to be found within the interaction of these complexes.

7.

TOWARD A THEORY
OF THE COLLECTIVE PSYCHE

Freud stated, "Without the assumption of a collective mind . . . social psychology in general cannot exist. . . . [I]f each generation were obliged to acquire its attitude to life anew, there would be no progress in this field and next to no development."[1] Not only did Freud argue for the necessity of a collective mind, he also asserted that "[e]ach individual is a component part of numerous groups," and, consequently, "has a share in numerous group minds—those of his race, of his class, of his creed, of his nationality, etc."[2] It is surprising that Freud could postulate the existence of the collective psyche, believe that its evolution followed that of the individual psyche, and yet, at the same time, find Jung's concept of the collective unconscious unhelpful.[3]

While Jung refers to the collective consciousness and the collective unconscious, he never refers to a collective mind or a collective psyche. However, he does refer to a "world soul."[4] Among Jungians, there is an underlying ambiguity on this point. It is never completely clear whether the collective unconscious is a part of the individual psyche or a part of a collective psyche, a parallel of Freud's collective mind. Marie-Louise von Franz, for example, seems to view the collective unconscious as having an existence independent of the individual psyche. She writes:[5] "From the point of view of cultural history the idea of the collective unconscious is . . . a new formulation of the archetypal conception of a 'world spirit,' as it was postulated by the Stoics, or of a 'world-soul' that animates the universe and flows from the divine or demonic 'in-fluences' (in-flowings)

132

into the human subject." If we make a clear separation between the individual psyche and the collective psyche or mind, it becomes obvious that there is no analogue to consciousness in the collective psyche. Thus, there can be no negation or contrast with consciousness, and consequently no collective unconscious. The presence of an unconscious assumes its counterpart, a consciousness. The collective unconscious, therefore, should be seen as a part of the individual psyche and I believe that this was Jung's view.[6] Since Freud did not adopt Jung's concept of the archetype, there would have been no necessity for him to divide the individual unconscious into the personal and the collective.

The concept of archetypes and the collective unconscious as parts of the individual psyche, however, are essential for an adequate theory of the collective psyche. It could be that Freud never developed a theory of the collective psyche because he would inevitably have been led to Jungian archetypes, and at this point in the careers of both men, Freud would have been reluctant to give this kind of recognition to what he perceived as a competing, rather than complementary, theory. Before the development of a theory of the collective psyche is undertaken, it will be helpful at this point to distinguish the collective unconscious from the collective psyche.

THE COLLECTIVE UNCONSCIOUS

The collective unconscious is a part of the psyche of each individual rather than the unconscious part of the collective psyche. It will be argued that the collective psyche can best be understood in terms of structures of information. Such a suggestion seems to imply that the term collective psyche is being used in a merely metaphorical sense since stored information does not entail a collective mind. However, a great many of the processes involved within the individual mind consist of the storage and processing of information. The collective psyche must be more than merely metaphor, but lacking consciousness, is not a complete analogue of the individual psyche.

A separation of the collective unconscious as a part of the individual psyche from the collective psyche can bring much clarity to the concept of archetypes. Archetypes are the essential link between the collective unconscious within the individual psyche, and the collective psyche. The same archetypal patterns will be found in both. The collective psyche is the source of archetypes. It may be the case, depending upon how the archetype itself differs from its representations and images, that archetypes are to be found only in the collective psyche, and these archetypes generate the representations and images which move from the collective psyche into the collective unconscious.

What Jung calls the collective consciousness, is equally a part of the individual psyche. Jung equates the collective consciousness with Freud's superego.[7] Jolande Jacobi defines the Jungian concept of "collective consciousness" as "the aggregate of the traditions, conventions, customs, prejudices, rules, and norms of human collectivity which give the consciousness of the group as a whole its direction, and by which the individuals of this group consciously but quite unreflectingly live."[8] Jung's collective consciousness, while it contains the superego, probably contains more.[9]

Jung was clear in his early writing on the definition of the collective unconscious. Some ambiguity arises in his later works, however, with the introduction of concepts such as "world soul" and synchronicity. Later he seems to vacillate between viewing the collective unconscious as some part of a universal mind which dwells within each individual psyche, and something which can be explained in terms of the biological structure of the brain, a common genetic code, or collected and structured information.[10] The physical expression of the genetic code in the organism represents the structure of the physical body of the human species, yet it has no existence outside of individual bodies. If all individual human beings disappear and no human cells are left, then the genetic code disappears. The collective psyche is like a cultural code. Its continued existence depends upon the existence of individual minds. The theory of the collective psyche to be later elaborated does not entail a universal mind, independent of individual minds, which can be divided between the conscious and the unconscious. There is no analogue to the individual brain, in the form of a collective brain.

This ambiguity stems from a deeper level ambiguity in Jung about the nature of mind itself. Jung is never clear as to whether and to what degree mind is atomistic or like a field. Are there only individual minds or are individual minds a manifestation of a universal mind? On this point Jung would probably retreat to an analogy with the particle-field view of the electron in modern physics, where the electron is recognized as having properties of both entities and waves. The mind is thus universal (a field) and individual (a particle). Jung was very much attracted by the

Eastern view of ultimate reality as a field of undifferentiated mind. He writes: [11]

> The Mind in which the irreconcilables—sumsara and nirvana—are united is ultimately our mind. Does this statement spring from profound modesty or from overweening hybris? Does it mean that the Mind is "nothing but" our mind? Or that our mind is the Mind? Assuredly it means the latter, and from the Eastern point of view there is no hybris in this; on the contrary, it is a perfectly acceptable truth, whereas with us it would amount to saying "I am God."

The necessity for this kind of mysticism can be avoided if the collective unconscious is separated from the collective psyche, and the collective psyche is explained in terms of the organization and structure of information.

A theory of the collective psyche in terms of structured information and informational agencies helps to clarify the relationship of myth to the collective unconscious. Myth is a product of the collective psyche. The structures of myths furnish an important key to the structure of the collective psyche. There is a mutual interrelationship between the collective psyche and the collective unconscious, in that the structure of the former underlies that of the latter. As personal experience follows collective patterns because of the similarity between the genetic codes of humans and the similarity of the natural environments which humans inhabit, the archetypal images of the collective unconscious feed back to alter the structure of the collective psyche. There is therefore a complex interrelationship between the personal part of the individual psyche, the collective part, and the collective psyche. Structured information moves in both directions between the collective psyche and the individual psyche. It is much easier to mark the parameters of the biological body than it is to define the parameters of the mind.

Nevertheless, the collective unconscious, while it exists only in individual psyches, reflects and entails the collective psyche. The universality of the collective unconscious, in that it is the same in all persons who make up the collective, entails that at least some information is universal in its content and structure. This is a sufficient foundation for the postulation of a collective psyche. To the degree that the collective unconscious is the same in individuals it makes sense to postulate the information, in whatever form it takes whether myth, symbol, or art, as an entity or agency independent of the minds which contain it. The collective unconscious is the manifestation in the individual psyche of the collective psyche. Since aspects of the collective psyche can be consciously manifested, it may well make sense to divide the conscious side of the individual psyche into a personal conscious and a collective conscious, depending upon whether the material has come from personal experience or through cultural learning. The collective consciousness and the collective unconscious are the manifestations of the collective psyche in the individual psyche. That part which comes from personal experience belongs to the personal consciousness and unconscious, and that which comes from the collective psyche belongs to the collective consciousness and unconscious of the individual psyche.

The similarities between Jungian depth psychology and Freudian psychoanalytic theory become evident when some of the more important insights of Jung are drawn together in the form of an integrated theory by Erich Neumann in his book, *The Origins and History of Consciousness.* That Jung approved of this work is made obvious by the short introduction which he wrote for it at Neumann's request. In it Jung bemoans the role of the pioneer (his own role), who "stumbles through unknown regions . . . is led astray by analogies . . . is overwhelmed by new impressions and new possibilities, and . . . knows afterwards what he should have known before." Of this book he states, "It begins just where I, too, if I were granted a second lease of life, would start to gather up the *disjecta membra* of my own writings, to sift out all those 'beginnings without continuations' and knead them into a whole. . . . Thus forewarned and forearmed, a representative of the second generation can spot the most distant connections; he can unravel problems and give a coherent account of the whole field of study, whose full extent the pioneer can only survey at the end of his life's work." [12]

The Origins and History of Consciousness comes closer to being a study of the evolution of the collective psyche than any other book in either the Jungian or Freudian tradition. Neumann finds it necessary to speak of consciousness separate from the collective consciousness or the collective unconscious. What Neumann refers to by the term *consciousness* is something very similar to what I mean by the term collective *psyche.* Neumann writes about "[t]he emergence of the collective human background as a transpersonal reality." [13] "The development of consciousness in archetypal stages," he writes, "is a transpersonal fact, a dynamic self-revelation of the psychic structure, which dominates the history of mankind and the individual." [14]

The thesis of Neumann's book is very Freudian in its orientation. He outlines his task as follows: [15]

[T]o show that a series of archetypes is a main constituent of mythology, that they stand in an organic relation to one another, and that their stadial succession determines the growth of consciousness. In the course of its ontogenetic development, the individual ego consciousness has to pass through the same archetypal stages which determined the evolution of consciousness in the life of humanity. The individual has in his own life to follow the road that humanity has trod before him, leaving traces of its journey in the archetypal sequence of the mythological images. . . .

The book is in two parts. Part 1, "The Mythological Stages in the Evolution of Consciousness," examines the stages in the mythic systems which reflect the archetypal images of the collective unconscious, and the second part of the book, "The Psychological Stages in the Development of Personality," traces the parallel stages in the development of the individual psyche. Both parts deal first with original unity, the separation and formation of the ego, and the process of individuation. The book concludes with a study of the psychology of groups, and what Neumann terms, "mass man." The process of individuation is viewed by Neumann in terms of archetypal shifts.

Thus, according to Neumann, the individual psyche passes through archetypal phases or stages of development which follow a pattern to be found in the evolution of human consciousness. The first stage, what he calls the *uroboric phase,* correlates the period of primary narcissism before the child separates itself from its mother, with the period of human history before humans separated themselves from nature. The uroboros, the snake that bites its own tail, "is a representation, not of childhood, or infancy as a whole, but of the state of consciousness characteristic of that time. The uroboros is an image which captures in one bound the essence of infantile omnipotence, solipsism and relative lack of conscious differentiation." [16] The second phase, which Neumann calls the *matriarchal phase* "is ruled by the image of the Mother Goddess with the Divine Child. It emphasizes the necessitous and helpless nature of the child and the protective side of the mother." [17] The final stage or the *patriarchal phase,* is marked by the shift from the archetypal mother to the archetypal father reflected in the decline of Goddess worship and the rise of patriarchal father god religions. Neumann sees the struggle of the individual to separate itself from the mother as a struggle of the hero against the dragon-monster. The hero must then in turn slay the tyrant king, which reflects the individual ego's struggle to escape from the authority of the father. While Neumann disassociates himself from Freud's view of sexual rivalry between father and son for the affections of the mother, it nevertheless follows very closely the pattern of the Oedipal passage.[18]

THE COLLECTIVE PSYCHE—REALITY OR METAPHOR?

We do not as yet have a satisfactory theory of the mind. Without it, we cannot have a satisfactory theory of the collective psyche or collective mind. The very use of the term "collective" in conjunction with the mind, psyche, or unconscious is somewhat problematic. Mind is not a thing as it does not occupy space through time as a brain does. We often speak of several people being of one mind. "Collective" and "individual" are terms more appropriate for things. The concreteness which is implicit in a reference to an individual mind is possible because we refer to the mind in relation to a particular material body. So far as the logical character of mind is concerned, "I" and "you" are ideas, and an idea is not a physical entity.

The relationship between one person's thoughts and another's, when symbolized by the same word, is one of intentionality rather than identity. The problem of thinking about mind in terms of individual and collective underlies the philosophical issues surrounding the problem of the nature of universals. It is doubtful that we will be able to develop a satisfactory theory of archetypes until we have solved the issue of whether universals exist only at the level of language or whether they have some form of existence independent of language. The difficulties with which we are faced, however, should not prevent us from attempting to gain further clarification. Each new paradigm helps us to see the issues a little more clearly. Psychoanalysis has profoundly advanced our understanding of the nature of mind. Cognitive science and the related disciplines of computer science and artificial intelligence may help to take us another step forward.

The collective psyche is the product of the ability to accumulate information and convey it from generation to generation. To draw an analogy with computers, an analogy which will be expanded upon later in this chapter, human brains are the hardware and the collective psyche is the software. Every isolated tribe would have its own collective psyche. Only with the storage and interchange of information which modern technology has made possible, does it become meaningful to postulate a collective psyche for the entire human race. Such a single collective psyche would include systems of information which could be considered to make up collective psyches in their own right to the degree to which they constitute separate cultures.

Even in ancient times there were major centers of civilization from which collected and stored information was shared between many different tribes and races of people. Alexander the Great connected the Mediterranean world, which formed a common cultural pool, with the culture emanating from the Indus valley of India. The ancient world consisted of at least three collective psyches, one emanating from the cultural centers of China, one emanating from the cultural centers of India, and the Mediterranean basin cultural center which the Romans carried throughout most of southern and central Europe, including the British Isles.

The collective psyche of the culture is inherited or "programmed into" each individual born into a particular society. Thus, people do not have to rediscover knowledge from generation to generation. It is the collective psyche which gives humans a past and a future. What we call progress consists of the development and expansion of the collective psyche.

A reader may well ask, Why call culture a collective psyche? Why use a metaphor for mind in regard to something which is not mental, but merely consists of stored information which is passed from generation to generation? My response would be to point out that a great deal of what we would call mind or at least mental activity consists of the processing of stored information. With the development of writing it becomes difficult to separate the individual psyche from that of the collective in that information can be passed back and forth between the two. It is no longer possible for any human mind to acquire, store in memory, and assimilate all known information. What information we need individually, we extract from the memory (stored information) of the collective.

The development of computers as extensions of the human brain or of the mind also lend support for a conception of a collective psyche. Very few people, if any, fully understand a simple desktop computer, from the solid-state physics required for comprehending the function of the microchips, through the electronic theory of the design of the hardware, into machine language, and finally the programming languages which allow interface with the ordinary language of the user. The use of the computer entails using information which is not stored in or comprehended by the user's own mind. Computers in which we store our own information thus become extensions of our memory.

The essence of psychoanalytic social theory is the thesis that the collective psyche has gone through and continues in a process of individuation which closely parallels that of the individual psyche in that we can find a close correspondence between a pre-Oedipal period, an Oedipal period, and a post-Oedipal period. Through participating in the collective psyche, the individual psyche is able to accelerate the process of and go farther in the direction of individuation than it could without such participation. If this is so then individuals who are a part of isolated tribal societies will be less individuated than those who are a part of a society sharing a post-Oedipal collective psyche. The distinction between the pre-Oedipal, the Oedipal, and the post-Oedipal stages of mental development in a person is a matter of degree of individuation. At the Oedipal stage the psyche of a child is more differentiated than it is at the pre-Oedipal, and at the post-Oedipal stage, the psyche is more individuated than at the Oedipal stage. The fact that people generally are more individuated at a later stage of history than they are at an earlier stage should not be startling. The fact that members of contemporary Western cultures are more individualistic than many of those in Eastern or Third World societies, and that family and community are more valued outside of the West, has often been noted.

The past lives on in us. We inherit it in the process of enculturization. It is a part of the cultural code. Pan lives on in phrases like "horny old goat." We are historical animals. We inherit a past. We do not live only in the here and now. Our history lives in us, and we live in and through our history. To explore further the appropriateness of the concept of a collective psyche as an important analytical tool for both psychoanalysis and social theory we must first look more closely at the nature of mind itself.

MIND AS THE EMBODIMENT OF INFORMATION

Warren S. McCulloch, one of the pioneers of cognitive science, in the title to a paper posed the question, "What Is a Number, That a Man May Know It, and a Man, That He May Know a Number?"[19] There is no problem in defining what a member of the human species is in biological terms, nor does explaining the meaning of the concept of number in terms of number theory present any particular difficulty. McCulloch, however, by joining the two questions into a single conjunctive, was seeking a definition for both a man and a number in terms of the framework of a single theory. Neither number theory nor biology can answer both questions in terms of a common set of assumptions or concepts. Cognitive science, a new discipline which has come into being to develop a common framework to study both humans and their artifact the computer, can respond to questions of this nature. Needless to say, the article which followed the title, did not fully answer the question posed, as the answer would require a solution to the body-mind problem. An answer to McCulloch's question requires a common framework of analysis for both conceiver and concept, and thus must be able to bridge the body-mind duality. In spite of some of the more inflated claims of some of the leading scientists in artificial intelligence, an adequate operational method of explaining mind simply does not exist.[20]

We can operationally define the concept of yellow in terms of a machine which will recognize the light wave with the frequency which we have named yellow. However, we cannot build a machine which will have an experience of yellowness, or experience yellow in the way a seeing person does when light waves of that frequency are reflected by objects. A solution to the body-mind problem will require an explanation of what is entailed in seeing yellow, or any other sensual experience. From a philosophical point of view the explanations which reduce all phenomena to mind are still much more persuasive than those which reduce it all into material operational terms. Understanding and defining mind raises particular epistemological problems because we have no outside frame of reference. It requires mind turning in on itself.

While failing to furnish us with a definitive solution to the body-mind problem, both psychoanalytic theory and cognitive science shed a great deal of light on the nature of mind. They both present us with new frameworks of analysis. Sherry Turkle, a sociologist at the Massachusetts Institute of Technology, has shown that there are some astounding similarities in the theories of mind entailed in cognitive science and psychoanalytic theory.[21] She writes:[22]

> Despite their differences, psychoanalysis and AI have always shared theoretical affinities—among these . . . the challenge to the idea of the autonomous, intentional actor, the need for self-reference in theory building, and the need for objects such as censors to deal with internal conflict. But the affinity became something stronger when the cluster of issues about objects

came to occupy center stage for both. This new orientation has made the old common elements more common: agent theories in AI highlight theoretical concerns that echo psychoanalytic ones. These include conflict, internal inconsistency, and perhaps most dramatically, the subversion of the subject, the "decentered" self.

At first glance, one would think that artificial intelligence would support a behaviorist psychology rather than a psychoanalytic one. In fact, Turkle has shown that artificial intelligence shares many assumptions about the nature and structure of mind which are implicit in psychoanalytic theory, and contradict the behaviorist model.

Freud discovered that the unconscious was a dynamic part of the mind which profoundly influenced the conscious. He denied the reality of a unified self, and showed it to be an illusion. He viewed the mind as being made up of a collection of what in some places he refers to as "agencies," such as the ego, the id, and the superego.[23] These agencies function with a relative degree of independence and are often in conflict or opposed to each other.

The similarities between the way minds and computers function is the foundation of cognitive science, a new discipline which focuses on the processing of information. The obvious parallels between computer hardware and the brain, and computer software and the mind, have produced a new way for people to see themselves. Turkle refers to this perspective as the computational model of the mind. She has extensively studied how the phenomenon of computers has impacted on human psychology whereby people think of themselves in computational terms. Central to this is the view of the mind as program.[24] In presenting us with a new way of looking at and thinking about the mind, the new paradigms of cognitive science, according to Turkle, furnish us with new ways to think about Freud and psychoanalysis which allow us to replace Freudian metaphors about mental mechanisms in terms of hydraulic pressures,[25] with the idea of programs or structures of information.[26] A computer program is a system of information, and to view mind in these terms is to see it as being made up of systems of information which form parts of larger systems. One view of mind which has developed within the artificial intelligence community is best represented by Marvin Minsky in his book, *The Society of Mind*. Minsky adopts the term *agency*, the same term used by Freud, to refer to the individual systems which constitute the mind. Needless to say, the whole will always be greater than its parts. One need not accept this view of mind as having entirely solved the body-mind problem to have a powerful mythic framework for learning more about ourselves.

"AI scientists," states Turkle, "believe that the most important thing about people is that we are intelligent and as such closer than anything else in nature to pure program."[27] "[W]hat remained a strong metaphor within the AI world was the idea of a society of limited agents whose intelligence is emergent from their interaction, the idea that a computer system as a whole will be significantly, qualitatively different than the sum of its parts."[28] The old view of mind was that of a single unified agent. Freud's view of the psyche as being made up of conflicting agencies, often in opposition and tension with each other, shattered the monolithic view of the mind. Likewise, the concept of mind as structures of information furnishes a model of the psyche made up of particular agencies which may be in internal conflict and contradiction, but from which a coherent behavior can emerge.[29]

The most important study to date of the relationship between these disciplines devoted to the study of the mind is that of Kenneth Mark Colby and Robert J. Stoller in their book *Cognitive Science and Psychoanalysis*.[30] They state that the analogy which they draw "between poorly understood human mental systems and better understood computing systems," involves "an equivalence assumption."[31] They write, "We assume the human mental system . . . has an innate, species-specific, capacity for symbol-processing, a basic software resource (e.g., the capacity to acquire natural language) that comes with the wetware of our neural system. Supervenient on these two biologic levels is a semantic level, termed the 'intentional' in philosophical psychology."[32] "Our initial analogy," they state, "asserts that mental systems and modern computer systems are instances of computational systems that take in, manipulate, transform, and produce symbolic expressions."[33] "The question is not whether the mind 'is' a computational system, but whether it can be adequately modeled by a computational system."[34] They even go so far as to suggest that Freud himself foreshadowed the shift in psychoanalytic theory.

Information is central to thought, and thinking consists at least in part of the processing of information.[35] We have programming languages for computers, and we may view human languages as programs which are fed into young children. We speak of both humans and computers as having memories, as both store information which can be subject to recall. Inputting information is essential to programming computers and educating human beings. The view of the psyche as a society of interacting and often conflicting programs conforms closely to Freud's view of the psyche and furnishes us with conceptual tools for a better analysis of the collective psyche.

There are many disputes within and without the artificial intelligence community about the nature of artificial intelligence.[36] There is not even a consensus on what is meant by the term *artificial*. Does it mean not true intelligence like an artificial flower is not a true flower, or does it mean that it is true intelligence but it is artificial because it is nonhuman?[37] Whatever position one takes on these issues, however, does not affect the validity of a view of mind as structures of information.

There are serious conceptual problems with the use of a mind-computer metaphor. George Lakoff calls the metaphor "the mind-as-machine paradigm." He writes:[38]

> The mind-as-machine view shares the traditional mind-body distinction, according to which the mind is disembodied, abstract, and independent of bodily functioning. According to this view, the mind is a computer with biological hardware and runs using programs essentially like those used in computers today. It may take input from the body and provide output to the body, but there is nonetheless a purely mental sphere of symbolic manipulation that can be characterized in terms of algorithms of the sort used in computer programs.

Lakoff points out that "the mind-as-machine paradigm has nothing to do with a physical computer. It is an abstract position having to do with the character of mind."[39] Since "algorithms concern the manipulation of meaningless disembodied symbols," the mind-as-machine paradigm is clearly inadequate since there is more to mind than the mere manipulation of symbols.[40] The problem is we are not fully aware of what the "more" is. If we were, we would probably be in a position to fully describe the relationship between mind and body.

There are obvious limitations in whatever model we use for the mind. Nevertheless, mind and thought entail a flow of information and meaning. This flow is not free, but rather is structured. Structure is entailed in meaning. Therefore a view of mind in terms of structures of information is about the best and most useful model we can presently find. In using it, however, one must keep its limitations in mind. Furthermore, we must not lose sight of the fact that body and mind are a part of a single system.

Psychoanalytic theory has probably done more than any other branch of psychology to uncover the interrelationship between mind and biology.

AGENCIES OF THE COLLECTIVE PSYCHE

Since a good deal of the processing of information by the brain goes on at an unconscious or preconscious level, the view of mind as being embodied in programs of information is a useful analogy. Continuing the analogy, the collective psyche can be viewed as sets of programs of structured information embodied in systems of intercommunicating brains. The individual psyche cannot be fully understood in isolation because each is a part of larger systems. Without such contact the individual psyche would be like that of Helen Keller before communication, or the occasional child who survives in a purely animal environment. If individual psyches are part of larger systems, then it will not be possible to have an adequate theory of mind which refers only to the part and has no place for the whole. One cannot have an adequate theory of the individual psyche without a theory of the collective psyche.

In culture, we can find collective manifestations of the id, the ego, the superego and the ego ideal. To the degree that the superego represents an introjection of the father in terms of a cultural authority figure, and a father god and his teachings, the superego of the individual is a pattern of a program in the collective psyche. The father-god archetype as manifest in the forms of the paterfamilias, the monarch, and God the father, (as long as there is God the father, the father will be god), is the analogue in the collective psyche of the superego of the individual psyche. Freud gives the following description of what he calls the community or cultural superego: [41]

> The analogy between the process of civilization and the path of individual development may be extended in an important respect. It can be asserted that the community, too, evolves a super-ego under whose influence cultural development proceeds. . . . The super-ego of an epoch of civilization has an origin similar to that of an individual. It is based on the impression left behind by the personalities of great leaders—men of overwhelming force of mind or men in whom one of the human impulses has found its strongest and purest, and therefore often its most one-sided, expression. . . . Another point of agreement between the cultural and the individual super-ego is that the former, just like the latter, sets up strict ideal demands,

disobedience to which is visited with "fear of conscience." Here, indeed, we come across the remarkable circumstance that the mental processes concerned are actually more familiar to us and more accessible to consciousness as they are seen in the group than they can be in the individual man. In him, when tension arises, it is only the aggressiveness of the super-ego which, in the form of reproaches, makes itself noisily heard; its actual demands often remain unconscious in the background. If we bring them to conscious knowledge, we find that they coincide with the precepts of the prevailing cultural super-ego. At this point the two processes, that of the cultural development of the group and that of the cultural development of the individual, are, as it were, always interlocked. For that reason some of the manifestations and properties of the super-ego can be more easily detected in its behavior in the cultural community than in the separate individual.

According to Freud, the ego is the agency which connects the self to reality. One's sense of identity is formulated within the ego. The ego, in the nature of its identifications, relates the individual self to the collective. At the same time, the ego as the focal connection between reality and the mind, forms its identity in terms of the physical limits of the particular body within which it is embodied as a part of the mind. There are also parallel physical limitations within the collective, with which the ego identifies. The "I" of the ego is formulated in terms of the "we" of the various collectives. We identify ourselves as humans, separate and distinct from animals. Each race has its own form of the human genetic code in terms of which we identify ourselves as Caucasians, Africans, or Asians. The boundaries of the nation state give the ego a further identity in terms of "we English," "we Germans," "we Japanese," or "we Americans." The different languages and cultures of the collective psyches furnish the terms of identity for the individual ego. We often give them an ego-like identification such as Germany, England, Russia, America, the Party, the Church. We say things such as "Germany shall rise from the ashes," or "England shall never be conquered." Thus, we have a parallel of the ego of the individual psyche in the form of the community or cultural ego in the various collective psyches.

ARCHETYPES, THE COLLECTIVE PSYCHE, AND THE FORMATION OF THE SELF

Archetypes are structural aspects of information, which are stored in the unconscious but shape information at the conscious level. They are the analogues of higher level programs. The masculine and feminine and the father and mother sets of archetypes arise out of the sexual and reproductive bifurcation of the human species. While it is the biological determined sex of the infant which dictates the appropriate archetypal structure, that structure is not directly biologically determined. Masculinity and femininity do not arise from within the individual. Rather, humans are born into archetypal gender structures. Thus, it is not the presence or absence of a penis which is important, but the social significance of this fact, which comes from the collective psyche.

The question as to what creates the differences between the sexes is central to psychoanalytic theory.[42] Juliet Mitchell states:[43] "[N]o human being can become a subject outside the division into two sexes. One must take up a position as either a man or a woman. Such a position is by no means identical with one's biological sexual characteristics, nor is it a position of which one can be very confident—as the psychoanalytical experience demonstrates." There are no pre-existent selves which adopt masculine or feminine characteristics. Freud, and Lacan as well, reject "any theory of the difference between the sexes in terms of pre-given male or female entities."[44] There are only male and female selves according to the orthodox Freudian position. Selves do not acquire sexuality, rather, sexuality (in the broad Freudian sense of the word) gives rise to two different kind of selves. This implicitly requires something like a collective psyche having an archetypal structure, since it is the archetypal structure which forms the self thereby permitting the little human animal to become a person.

There has been much criticism of Jung's concept of the archetype. We must concede that the concept is not all that clear. Nevertheless there appears to be ample evidence that at least a part of the unconscious is structured. It is also clear that the structure is shared as between more than one individual, and to that degree the structure is collective. However, the nature and source of this structure and exactly what it is that is shared are subject to a good deal of controversy. We know that much of animal behavior is instinctual or innate, and therefore collective. We also know that just as DNA can produce regularity and pattern in animal behavior, some human behavior will be determined by the genetic code. We know that the brain has a neurological structure which determines in part how we think and perceive the world.[45] The language abilities of humans, for example, are probably determined by the neurological structure of the brain. Work in psycholinguistics, such as that of Noam Chomsky, deals with patterns of language acquisition, and what Chomsky refers to as "formal" and "substantive" universals suggest collective structure which seems to be linked at one pole in the neurological structure of the brain, and at the other, in unique but shared human languages. A wide spectrum of studies ranging from child psychology to anthropology attest to structure in human thought and culture. Much of human behavior which can be called shared or collective results in action which arises from the unconscious rather than from the conscious part of the psyche. There seems ample reason for postulating the existence of part of the unconscious as collective.

It is not clear to what degree archetypes are rooted in DNA and the neurological structure of the brain, and to what degree the collectivity is to be found merely in the structure of the information which makes up culture. The concept of the archetype probably spans both. While this may be the main weakness in using such a concept, given our present lack of knowledge about the neurological structure of the brain, it may be in part its strength. It is useful to have a concept like archetype which spans the range from biological and neurological structure to the structure of information, when we have good reasons for believing that the two are related, but are not certain as to how. We know that there is at least one important relationship between biological structure and the structure of information, and that is the relationship of meaning. We give meaning to biological differences such as that between the sexes. We give meaning to birth and death. This meaning is often shared or collective. The concept of the archetype allows us to link culture with nature at the level of the collective.

Samuels has pointed out some of the striking parallels between the work of Lacan and that of Jung. Lacan is clearly the most structuralist of the Freudian psychoanalytic tradition. Lacan, like Jung, postulates that the unconscious is structured.[46] Samuels argues, "A case can be made for regarding Lacan's theory as compatible with that of Jung."[47] According to Samuels, "Lacan divides the phenomena with which psychoanalysis deals into three 'orders': 1) the Symbolic, which structures the unconscious by a fundamental and universal set of laws; 2) the Imaginary, which approximates to psychological reality, inner world processes (such as fantasy, projection, introjection), attitudes and images derived from, but not the equivalent of, external life . . . ; 3) the Real, corresponding . . . to external reality."[48] He writes: [49]

[S]ymbolic and Imaginary orders may be aligned with Jung's archetypal theory (collective unconscious) and personal unconscious respectively. The Symbolic order patterns the contents of the Imaginary in the same way that archetypal structures predispose humans towards certain sorts of experience. If we take the example of parents, archetypal structures and the Symbolic order predispose our recognition of, and relation to them. Images of parents in the personal unconscious are indirectly connected to actual parents, being coloured by the archetypal structure or the Symbolic order. The resultant images of parents are both subjective, in the sense of personal, and objective, i.e. phylogenetic. . . . Although the language is quite different, Jung would probably have agreed with Lacan that the unconscious is organized in an intricate network governed by association, above all "metaphoric associations." The existence of the network is shown by analysis of the unconscious products: dreams, symptoms, and so on.

Mitchell concisely sets out one of the primary tasks which Lacan set for himself. She writes: [50]

Lacan dedicated himself to reorienting psychoanalysis to its task of deciphering the ways in which the human subject is constructed—how it comes into being—out of the small human animal. It is because of this aim that Lacan offered psychoanalytic theory the new science of linguistics which he developed and altered in relation to the concept of subjectivity. The human animal is born into language and it is within the terms of language that the human subject is constructed. Language does not arise from within the individual, it is always out there in the world outside, lying in wait for the neonate. Language always "belongs" to another person. The human subject is created from a general law that comes to it from outside itself and through the speech of other people, though this speech in its turn must relate to the general law.

Any language is obviously a collective phenomenon. Language is an essential and fundamental part of the information which makes up the collective psyche. We can paraphrase Mitchell's description of one of Lacan's basic themes by substituting "the collective psyche" in place of "language." The human animal is born into the collective psyche, and it is within its structure that the human subject is constructed. Thus, Lacan's denial of the human subject at the center of his own history is consistent with the view argued for in this book, that the individual is a product of the collective psyche, is born into it, and the self is structured by it. We have no sense of self outside of or transcending male and female, because our sense of self is provided to us through the collective psyche, and the collective psyche only provides us with male and female selves. The self (as a psychic phenomenon) is not male or female because it is biologically determined, but rather because it has been archetypally structured by the collective psyche as male or female. The collective psyche lies between the biological world of bimorphic sexuality and the gender world of male and female selves. Thus, the existence of a collective psyche seems implicit in Lacan's view of the unconscious.[51]

Lacan's belief that the unconscious is structured symbolically and linguistically[52] parallels Jung's belief that the unconscious is archetypally structured. These two views are not mutually exclusive. Linguistics focuses on the structure of language, and archetypes focus on the structure of concepts. Concepts, however, are learned and communicated not only through language, but also through other forms of signs and images. The linguistic structure of the unconscious is interwoven with the archetypal structure. These two structures, while not identical, are closely interrelated.

The archetypal structure of maleness has implications for the archetypal structure of femaleness, as does the archetypal structure of femaleness for maleness. Sex/gender has never been a classification of two equal but different poles like a yin/yang opposition or two equal complementary independent axes. Rather, each is defined in terms of the presence or absence of a characteristic or property of the other. This is because the foundation of the sex/gender bifurcation is desire, which "persists as an effect of a primordial absence."[53] Freud stated, "[W]e must reckon with the possibility that something in the nature of the sexual instinct itself is unfavorable to the realization of complete satisfaction."[54]

A matriarchal consciousness would see the feminine/female as the norm, and the male as diminished and secondary. His breasts are undeveloped and his penis and testicles are appendages or growths. The paradigm of creativity would be giving birth and the symbols would be of vessels or caves which creatively give forth new life. The archetypal structure would be of Goddess and consort. The male is he who fertilizes, but the female is she who brings forth into existence. Reproduction is primary and production is secondary. A patriarchal consciousness would see the male/masculine as the norm, and the female as diminished, inferior, and secondary. She is viewed as an incomplete or castrated male. The paradigm of creativity would be creating as an act of the will. The penis becomes the phallus. Impregnation becomes primary, and the female is seen as a mere receptacle for the male's child. Concepts are primary and conception is secondary.

Each gender/sex is defined in terms of what it is and what the other is not. One is a base line and the other is defined in relation to it. One cannot be a male without a phallus. J. Money records that the Psychohormonal Research Unit at Johns Hopkins University Hospital has files on forty-five genetically normal males who were born with diminutive or no penis, or they had suffered complete ablation of the penis as a result of a circumcision accident. In all cases, the decision was made that "it is possible, with surgery and hormonal therapy, to habilitate a baby with a grossly defective penis more effectively as a girl than a boy."[55] It would appear that the possession of a phallus is a necessary condition for maleness, whatever the make up of the genetic code or the otherwise normal structure of the body. It is for this reason that the Jungian concepts of the anima and animus and androgyny are not particularly helpful.

An adequate psychoanalytic theory of the nature of female and male sexuality requires the postulation of a collective psyche and a collective or structured part of the unconscious of the individual psyche. The self is not a separate psyche into which language, culture, and socialization are poured. The self is in part a product of the collective psyche. The collective psyche furnishes two paradigms of the self, male/masculine and female/feminine. These two patterns are not independent of each other but are interrelated. The self is either one or the other. It may be useful to view the collective psyche as made up of a male/masculine collective psyche and a female/feminine collective psyche.

The critical issue for psychoanalytic theory is whether or not the sex/gender archetypal and language structures of the collective psyche have always been and must necessarily remain phallocentric. Freud and Lacan believed that it must necessarily have been and remain male-phallic and female-castrated. It is on this issue that feminist psychoanalytic theory takes issue. The existence of an earlier age of matriarchal consciousness is important to this question. Even if such an age did not exist historically, however, the existence of the Goddess-consort and related archetypal structures suggest that phallocentricity is neither necessary nor permanent.

If any part of the unconscious is structured it must exist in some sense, at least, independently of the individuals who are born into it and assimilate it at the unconscious level. It follows that if this structure changes through time, and if the changes parallel the process of individuation of the individual psyche, then the concept of a collective psyche or mind will be useful not only for psychoanalytic social theory, but for clinical psychoanalysis.

Individuals construct the self within an archetypal bifurcated framework of male/masculine and female/feminine. These archetypes shape the self through being the objects of the ego ideal. They furnish the structure of human sexuality. They function as an ideal pattern which the ego seeks to emulate, and they function as the internal representation of an external other with which the ego desires to merge. Sexuality is not a need because the sexual drive can never be satisfied in the way that needs can. The sexual drive is much more complex than merely a need to release sexual tension. It generally involves the desire to merge the self in the external other, usually of the opposite sex/gender to that of the self. The object of the ego ideal is often projected upon another person. Since the source of the desire is to heal the narcissistic wound by recovering the lost state of primary narcissistic bliss, and this is never possible, desire can never be fully satisfied. Biologically based sexual tension, release, and pleasure can never be fully separated from the archetypal structures of the objects of the ego ideal.

Within a framework of archetypal analysis, Lacan's views about the nature of desire, and the nature of sexual identity, can be integrated and made consistent with Chasseguet-Smirgel's view of the importance of and function of the ego ideal. At the same time, Jung's important insights into the nature of the collective unconscious can be brought within a Freudian framework by substituting the ego ideal taking male/masculine and female/feminine archetypal objects in place of the anima and the animus. While Freud recognized the fact that each person, irrespective of his or her sex, has characteristics of the opposite sex,[56] he retained the critical element of sexual difference which becomes blurred in Jungian androgyny.

8.

MISOGYNY AND INDIVIDUATION

THE FUNCTION OF MYTH AS CONSTELLATIONS OF COLLECTIVE DEFENSE MECHANISMS

Psychoanalytic social theory postulates that the "determinants of neurosis," which can be identified in individual analysis and clinical studies, can also be "translated into social terms as determinants of social organization," and "represent the essential substance of external as well as internal reality."[1] If this is the case then it should follow that the defense mechanisms adopted to protect the ego in its conflicts with the id through the crises and tensions of the pre-Oedipal, Oedipal, and post-Oedipal periods of individuation, should also be incorporated into the "essential substance" of both internal and external reality. Therefore, defense mechanisms against shared psychic conflicts will take the form of constellations which will form a part of the mythic systems which furnish the cultural heritage. The world view which any child inherits will furnish defense mechanisms which protect the ego in the process of individuation.

The first crisis of individuation is that of separation from the mother, and the anxieties which are produced are those of engulfment on the one hand, and separation on the other. The nascent ego must be protected against the separation anxiety which drives it to remerge with the mother. The world view functions as a set of mythic systems which impel the child away from the mother toward the father. The mythic systems facilitate the individuation process by making the mother a negative pole which

153

will repel the child, and the father a positive pole which will attract the child. In the process, the object of the child's ego ideal must switch from mother to father, from feminine to masculine.

The process of individuation, while impelling the child to separate from the mother, would not be well served by hostility toward the mother. Such hostility would produce counterproductive psychic conflict. The mythic system must generate negativity toward the properties which the mother has which attract the child and thus hinder separation, while at the same time maintaining a positive attitude in the child toward the mother as an individual person. The mythic system will inevitably contain a good deal of ambivalence in the way in which women are portrayed. The ambivalence felt toward the mother-female has its origins in the ambivalence of separation. The child requires love and nurture to assuage separation anxiety, and on the other hand feels resentment when too much nurture leads to engulfment anxiety. Children's fairy tales which have stories about wicked mothers and good mothers, children lost in the woods or abandoned, furnish mythic focal points for children to focus their anxieties.[2]

To facilitate females individuating as feminine, the negativity toward the feminine must not be so strong as to drive them to adopt masculine gender identities. Femininity, while it must remain secondary for both male and female children, must still maintain a positive value for females. One of the ways in which the mythic systems maintain the ambivalence without too great an amount of contradiction is to separate sexuality from femininity and gender roles. The mythic systems maintain this separation by desexualizing motherhood. The archetypal image of the Virgin Mary and the baby Jesus is a mythic form of desexualized motherhood. The high value placed on female virginity and the double sexual moral standard for males and females further perpetuates this separation in the mythic systems.

This polarity of attraction and repulsion is reinforced in the mythic system by creating a sexual and gender hierarchy in terms of negative and positive values. The polarity of values is created in terms of an ordering of male and female and masculine and feminine by the attribution of superiority and inferiority. Superiority and inferiority are attributed first at a biological and psychological level and from that, judgments of political and moral superiority and inferiority are drawn.

THE FUNCTION OF MYTH IN SOCIALIZATION
FOR SERVICE

The process of individuation entails the object of the ego ideal which is initially feminine, having its source in the mother, changing to masculine, having its focal point in the father. At this stage, the father is both internalized as the superego and adopted as the ideal of the ego. At the beginning of the Oedipal passage the young male child wishes to merge with the mother (sexually or otherwise, depending on factors unique to each child), and sees the father as a rival whom he wishes to displace. If the object of the ego ideal of the male child fails to switch from feminine to masculine it is unlikely that the child will successfully adopt an appropriate gender identity. No such danger lurks for the female child, however, as she would develop an appropriate gender identity even if the object of her ego ideal remained and developed as feminine.

The transition of the object of the ego ideal from feminine to masculine produces a particular problem for males. The narcissistic wound is the result of a separation from the feminine. The original primary narcissistic state is one of protofemininity. The narcissistic wound cannot be healed by merger with a masculine object of the ego ideal. Separation from the feminine can only be healed by merging with the feminine. The solution which has evolved for males is to incorporate the female into their own selves, thus maintaining a masculine object of the ego ideal while at the same time feeding the need created by the narcissistic wound. In this way, the drive to individuate and the assuaging of the narcissistic wound can both be accomplished.

The method by which the object of the ego ideal can remain masculine and at the same time the drive for reunification with the feminine can be achieved is through the socialization of females to serve male needs. Females must be socialized to limit their own process of individuation by sacrificing themselves through incorporation into the psyche of the male. The female must shift the object of her ego ideal from feminine to masculine and it must remain masculine. She must heal her own narcissistic wound by merging with and giving herself to a male.

How do you socialize over fifty percent or more of the human race to sacrifice their selves and limit their own free agency for the benefit of the other less than fifty percent? They must be made to want to give themselves voluntarily to something or someone greater than themselves. They must adopt a masculine object of their ego ideal. This is exactly what the set of mythic systems which we call patriarchy accomplishes. Patriarchy, in whatever form or shape it may take throughout the world, must achieve three things in the process of socialization of women. First, it must transform the object of the ego ideal from feminine to masculine. This is accomplished by negating the feminine and placing positive value on the masculine through myths of female inferiority and male superiority. Second, patriarchy must proclaim that the biologically determined destiny of females is to serve males, and that they can only achieve fulfillment and happiness by conforming to their true nature through this service. This is accomplished by myths which project maleness and male values on ultimate reality. Third, patriarchy must proclaim the diminished agency of women. Women can best be persuaded to sacrifice their own selves for the benefit of others by being convinced that they are incomplete without a male. Autonomous agents are individuals with their own set of goals and ordered set of priorities, who act in order to achieve their own ends. Persons who are not autonomous are in subjugation and therefore act for the goals of others rather than for their own. They are not ends in and of themselves, but are means toward the achievement of someone else's ends. Therefore, they are the extension of someone else's agency. The myths of the diminished agency of women often proclaim that they lack full rationality. This incompleteness prevents them from being fully autonomous agents.

The myths of female inferiority, determined biological destiny, and limited agency function together to reinforce each other. They form the very structure of patriarchal world views. Humans are born into a mental world of mythic systems. They share in the collective psyche. They are furnished with gender roles which they must internalize and weave into their very identity. Women are socialized from birth to be eventually entered, penetrated, occupied, and possessed, and to serve the will of a masculine other. If they conform to the archetypal role furnished them they are given positive reinforcement. If they fail to conform, they are made to suffer. They are socialized in mythic systems which proclaim an orderly world of men and a gentle world of womanly love.

They are socialized to believe that their true value lies in their attractiveness for males, that is, their potential for meeting male needs. Yet at every turn they are faced with the ambivalence which underlies these mythic systems. They are socialized to believe that their value lies in their sexual attractiveness, but are condemned if they demonstrate sexuality.

Motherhood is praised within a context of female inferiority. Generally, misogyny functions within individuals at an unconscious level. It is ingested from the mythic structure, and underlies the praise of motherhood and romantic love, and the idealization of little girls. Individual women can be loved and prized as mothers, wives, or lovers, while at the same time the mythic systems maintain the structure of domination and subservience, superiority and inferiority, and the misogyny which energizes and drives the process of individuation. In this way, "the determinants of neurosis" are "translated into social terms as determinants of social organization."[3] While the forms that patriarchal structures take vary from age to age and place to place, they all attempt to achieve voluntary subjugation by diminishing women's sense of their selves. In *The Fear of Women*, a study of many patriarchal mythic systems, Wolfgang Lederer states:[4]

> In the course of history man has, since those first heroic victories, attempted many a defense against woman: during the Dark Ages, he tried to banish femininity; during the Middle Ages, through the inquisition, he sought himself to devour the all-devouring Kali; since then, woman has been the toy of the Rococo, the doll (Ibsen's Nora) of the bourgeoisie. The proletariat, out of brotherly love, mass produced denim-blue female comrades shorn of all feminine appeal. Each social system, in its own way, tried to limit her magic.

THE MYTH OF FEMALE INFERIORITY

The Oedipal passage for both sexes requires the child to separate from the mother at the psychological level. This is a far more difficult and dangerous process for the male than for the female, as the female moves from a state of protofemininity to full femininity while the male must tear away from protofemininity to masculinity. "In mammalian species the function of cells is female in both sexes until androgens are added in fetal life. In fact, except for the chromosomes, one cannot talk about two sexes until the androgens have been added; there is only femaleness."[5] Misogyny is the analogue of androgens in the psychic passage from protofemininity to masculinity. Infants of both sexes share the natural drive toward individuation—the evolving of a separate self. However, the self can be either masculine or feminine for either biological sex. True transsexuals—feminine males—can have fully individuated selves. Something further is

required to drive individuation in the male in the direction of masculinity.

For both male and female children, the drive toward individuation is
often insufficient to counter the force of separation anxiety and the desire
to heal the narcissistic wound by uniting with and losing the self in the
mother. Engulfment anxiety, or what Stoller calls "symbiosis anxiety," is
a counter force to separation anxiety and the desire to merge. Hostility
toward the mother and toward the feminine can strengthen the desire to
separate. Stoller writes:

> The argument begins with the observation that the ever-present memory of
> oneness with mother acts like a magnet, drawing one back toward repeating
> the blissful experience against mother's body. . . . A vital part of the process
> of separating from mother, then, is release from her female body and
> feminine psyche.
>
> The ubiquitous fear that one's sense of maleness and masculinity are in
> danger and that one must build into character structure ever-vigilant de-
> fenses against succumbing to the pull of merging again with mother, I shall
> call symbiosis anxiety. While ostensibly set up to protect us from outer
> threats and insults, it must ultimately be established against our own inner,
> primitive yearning for oneness with mother. . . . This is to suggest that
> masculinity as we observe it in boys and men does not exist without the
> component of continuous pushing away from mother . . . and psychologi-
> cally in the development of character structure that forces the inner mother
> down and out of awareness. . . . [M]other, in her representation as an evil,
> hated creature, may also lend herself to the task of permitting the symbiosis-
> mother to be repressed; one would hardly wish to merge with a witch. One
> can wonder if at its most primitive level, perversion is that ultimate in
> separations, mother murder (more than, as Freud may have felt, father
> murder).[6]

He concludes, "Here is a proposition that can in time be tested empirically: our culture, as do most others, defines masculinity—for better or
worse—by how completely one demonstrates that one is rid of the need
for symbiosis with mother."[7] This proposition is not difficult to demonstrate. The natural hostility and resentment which any child feels when
the mother fails to satisfy all of its demands or places limits on its behavior
are insufficient to push the male child toward masculinity. Society and
culture, through myth and ritual, furnish a structure which imbues children of both sexes with misogyny. An examination of the mythic structures of any society will confirm Stoller's hypothesis. For example, a great
many tribal societies put a male child through a painful process of coming

of age or coming into manhood. In many, the young boys stay exclusively with the women and then after the transition ceremony, are required to stay exclusively with the males. The male child's body is often marked in some way to force him to internalize the new status, and break the emotional unity with the feminine.

It is not just in the Oedipal passage that misogyny is used as a cultural tool to drive the male toward masculinity. Masculinity itself in the post-Oedipal stage remains fragile at best, since it is a state reached through repression of aspects of the human psyche. Childhood anxieties do not simply disappear, but take pathological forms in the adult ranging from neurosis to perversion. Adult males constantly need to insist on their masculinity and fear any attack upon it. The irrational hatred of homosexuals is merely one way in which this fear is expressed.

Misogyny is a necessary condition for the creation and maintenance of masculinity as we know it. A mythic foundation is a necessary condition for the maintenance of misogyny. These mythic systems are two-pronged, involving the assertion of differences between male and female (the biological foundation) and the cultural meaning given to these biological differences (the inferiority of the female). The social expression of misogyny becomes legitimized through the mythic systems. Male domination of the female is the ultimate method for the maintenance of masculinity. Patriarchy rests ultimately on misogyny, and the sustaining myths of patriarchy are the same as those which furnish the driving forces of misogyny. The myths of the Greeks, for example, reek with misogyny.[8] No better example of a mythic source of misogyny can be found than the interlocking versions of the theft of fire and the creation of woman to be found in Hesiod's *Theogony* and *Works and Days*. The different parts of the story, found in the two books, form an interrelated whole.[9] When the gods and men were still united, Zeus furnished men with the gift of fire. Prometheus offers Zeus, the King of the gods, a fraudulent present which Zeus accepts. The trick gift or *dolos* is the bones of a sacrificed ox, dressed up to look like the flesh or the best part, which Prometheus gave to men instead as their share. In anger, Zeus denies mankind the celestial fire. Prometheus then steals the fire. In order to punish mankind, Zeus in turn gives them a *dolos,* a trick present or gift which looks attractive on the outside but is actually worthless, or even worse, a curse. Up to this time only men exist. The evil gift which Zeus gives to punish men is Pandora or women. In the *Works and Days* Hesiod writes: [10]

"The price for the stolen fire will be a gift of evil
to charm the hearts of all men as they hug their own doom."
This said, the father of gods and men roared with laughter.
Then he ordered widely acclaimed Hephaistos to mix earth with water
with all haste and place in them human voice
and strength. His orders were to make a face
such as goddesses have and the shape of a lovely maiden;
Athena was to teach her skills and intricate weaving,
and golden Aphrodite should pour grace round the maiden's head,
and stinging desire and limb-gnawing passion.
Then he ordered Hermes the path-breaker and slayer of Argos
to put in her the mind of a bitch and a thievish nature.

In the *Theogony* the story unfolds: [11]

Once he had finished—not something good but a mixture of good
and bad—he took the maiden before gods and men,
and she delighted in the finery given her by gray-eyed Athena,
daughter of a mighty father. Immortal gods and mortal men
were amazed when they saw this tempting snare
from which men cannot escape. From her comes the fair sex;
yes, wicked womenfolk are her descendants.
They live among mortal men as a nagging burden
and are no good sharers of abject want, but only of wealth.
Men are like swarms of bees clinging to cave roofs
to feed drones that contribute only to malicious deeds;
the bees themselves all day long until sundown
are busy carrying and storing the white wax,
but the drones stay inside in their roofed hives
and cram their bellies full of what others harvest.
So, too, Zeus who roars on high made women
to be an evil for mortal men, helpmates in deeds of harshness.
And he bestowed another gift, evil in place of good;
whoever does not wish to marry, fleeing the malice of women,
reaches harsh old age with no one to care for him;
then even if he is well-provided,
he dies at the end only to have his livelihood shared
by distant kin. And even the man who does marry
and has a wife of sound and prudent mind
spends his life ever trying to balance
the bad and the good in her. But he who marries into a foul brood
lives plagued by unabating trouble in his heart
and in his mind, and there is not cure for his plight.

Religion forms an essential part of the network of mythic systems
which make up patriarchy. Monotheism entails two basic bifurcations,

the polarity of good and evil, and the polarity of masculine and feminine. God is good and masculine. Women are not masculine and not good. This is clearly reflected in one of the fundamental myths of the Western cultural tradition, the Genesis story of Adam and Eve. In the garden of Eden, Adam and Eve are in a state of innocence. They are unaware of sexuality and death, and are unified with nature. The eating of the forbidden fruit brings an awareness of sexuality, reflected in a sense of nakedness and an awareness of impending death, thus providing for the convergence of Eros and Thanatos in the structure of the myth. With this knowledge, the Edenic state is no longer possible, so they are cast out into the harsh world. It is Eve who brings Adam the forbidden fruit and tempts him with it. Thus, Eve is made to carry the burden of animality.[12] There is an interesting parallel between the structure of the Adam and Eve myth, and the three states of the pre-Oedipal separation process. The Garden of Eden is a state of symbiosis between male and female, and humans and nature. The Fall marks a state of separation, and the departure from the Garden marks the beginning of individuation. Like the Pandora myth of the Greeks, women are again held responsible for the evil men suffer. It is the female of the species who draws the male into copulation, into the world of the physical, into nature, into an awareness of his animality. The male response to this dependency on the female, with its resulting psychological effects, is to declare the female inferior.

The Myth of Creation for Subordination

The supreme myth of creation for subordination is found in Genesis, and underlies the mythic structure of all Christian, Islamic, and Jewish culture. According to Genesis, God first created the man Adam and placed him in the Garden of Eden. "And the Lord God said, It is not good that the man should be alone; I will make . . . an help meet for him," and so God created Eve out of a rib of Adam. The exercise of male power is made legitimate in the words of Jehovah to Eve, "[A]nd thy desire shall be to thy husband, and he shall rule over thee."[13] This statement, and not the Ten Commandments, is the fountainhead of law in one of the oldest of Western legal traditions. The theme of male authority and female submission is carried throughout the scriptures and theology of these three Semitic religious traditions. Religious doctrine is filled with descriptions of the proper role of women as servants of men and bearers of children.

According to Saint Paul, "The head of every man is Christ; and the head of the woman is the man."[14] He admonishes women to "submit yourselves unto your own husbands, as unto the Lord."[15] He proclaims the predetermined destiny of women to serve man in the words "Neither was the man created for the woman; but the woman for the man."[16] Paul elaborates on the above theme, stating:[17]

> Let the woman learn in silence with all subjection.
> But I suffer not a woman to teach, nor to usurp authority
> over the man, but to be in silence.
> For Adam was first formed, then Eve.
> And Adam was not deceived, but the woman being deceived
> was in the transgression.
> Notwithstanding she shall be saved in childbearing, if they
> continue in faith and charity and holiness with sobriety.

The mythic structures which proclaim males as ends and females as means, or in other words, males are full agents and women as incomplete agents created to serve males, are the foundations for male authority. God—Father—authority are three concepts which are necessarily linked and can only be defined in terms of each other. They are in turn correlated with the three interrelated concepts wife—mother—submission. This set is defined in terms of its subordinate relationship with the first set. It has been said that when God is the Father, the father is god. This holds true for every patriarchal mythic system whether the god is Zeus,[18] Jehovah,[19] or Bhagavan.[20] Wife and mother are archetypal structures of the collective psyche which are embodied in the mythic systems of patriarchy whereby women are socialized to accept that they have been created for the purpose of serving males.

Parallel to the theme that women are created to serve male needs, is the mythic theme that the very earth itself and all of nature exist for the enjoyment of the male.[21] Genesis proclaims that in the beginning God created the heaven and the earth and filled it with living creatures and then created man in his own image and gave him dominion over all his other creation. Thus man is proclaimed as the center and purpose of creation, and all else, including woman, every creature, and the very earth itself, are merely means in the service of man's agency. Genesis relates:[22] "And God blessed them, and God said unto them, Be fruitful, and multiply, and replenish the earth, and subdue it: and have dominion over the fish of the sea, and over the fowl of the air, and over every living thing that moveth upon the earth." In the Book of Psalms (Psalm 8:3–8) the theme of homocentricity is again poetically expressed:

> When I consider thy heavens, the work of thy fingers, the moon and the stars, which thou hast ordained;
> What is man, that thou art mindful of him? and the son of man, that thou visitest him?
> For thou hast made him a little lower than the angels, and hast crowned him with glory and honour.
> Thou madest him to have dominion over the works of thy hands; thou hast put all things under his feet:
> All sheep and oxen, yea, and the beasts of the field;
> The fowl of the air, and the fish of the sea, and whatsoever passeth through the paths of the seas.

The right of men to exploit and the duty of women to submit are a fundamental theme in all patriarchal mythic systems.

THE MYTHS OF PATRIARCHAL SCIENCE AND DIMINISHED AGENCY

The archetypal structure of the collective psyche is reproduced in the collective unconscious of the individual through mythic structures. To the degree that philosophy and science entail or presuppose archetypal structures, they will contain a mythic dimension. The shift from *mythos* to *logos* among the Greeks, in the middle of the sixth century B.C., was a sudden and "explosive event" which has been described by Sambursky as "a historical phenomenon bordering on the miraculous."[23] Sambursky points out, however, that "the suddenness of the transition from *mythos* to *logos,* measured against the time-span of human history, should not be allowed to obscure the fact that the transformation of mythological concepts into their scientific counterparts was still a gradual process."[24] An examination of the philosophical and scientific views of women, from the time of the birth of philosophy and science with the Greeks down to the present, will show that the archetypal images of women did not radically change in the shift from *mythos* to *logos.* Consequently, when philosophy and science have had to deal with women, they have remained primarily mythic. Philosophy and science have retained the myth of female inferiority which underlies patriarchal religion by continuing the archetypal structure of female inferiority. Thus, they serve to perpetuate and legitimize male domination.

How can philosophy remain philosophical and science remain scientific while maintaining this mythic dimension? It does so by furnishing the archetypal structure which is projected onto reality. Thus, illusion becomes fact by the observation of that which we project. The Jungian analyst James Hillman describes this process: [25]

Fantasy especially intervenes where exact knowledge is lacking; and when fantasy does intervene, it becomes especially difficult to gain exact knowledge. Thus a vicious circle forms, and the mythical usurps theory-forming; furthermore, the mythic is given fantastic witness in observation. Seeing is believing, but believing is seeing. We see what we believe and prove our beliefs with what we see.

Hillman cites many examples of the projection of illusion onto our view of reality, and then using that illusory reality as a scientific observation to verify the illusion. One of his most striking examples is that of the early seventeenth-century scientists who reported seeing minute forms of men inside of the spermatozoa when they examined it under the microscope. [26]

In political philosophy, Aristotle's view of women as inferior or diminished agents remained a fundamental presupposition of Western political theory for many centuries. Aristotle wrote: [27]

In the first place there must be a union of those who cannot exist without each other; namely, of male and female, that the race may continue . . . and of natural ruler and subject, that both may be preserved. For that which can foresee by the exercise of mind is by nature lord and master, and that which can with its body give effect to such foresight is a subject, and by nature a slave; hence master and slave have the same interest. Now nature has distinguished between the female and the slave. For she is not niggardly, like the smith who fashions the Delphian knife for many uses; she makes each thing for a single use, and every instrument is best made when intended for one and not for many uses. But among barbarians no distinction is made between women and slaves, because there is no natural ruler among them: they are a community of slaves, male and female. . . .

Out of these two relationships [between man and woman, master and slave] the first thing to arise is the family, and Hesiod is right when he says, *First house and wife and an ox for the plough,* for the ox is the poor man's slave.

Hegel, who helped to lay the foundations of modern political theory, maintained a view of women which differed very little from that of Aristotle. He wrote: [28]

> Hence the husband has his real essential life in the state, the sciences, and the like, in battle and in struggle with the outer world and with himself. . . . In the family the wife has her full substantive place, and in the feeling of family piety realizes her ethical disposition.
>
> Hence piety is in the "Antigone" of Sophocles most superbly presented as the law of the woman, the law of the nature, which realizes itself subjectively and intuitively, the law of an inner life, which has not yet attained complete realization, the law of the ancient gods, and of the underworld, the eternal law, of whose origin no one knows, in opposition to the public law of the state. This opposition is in the highest sense ethical, and hence also tragic; it is individualized in the opposing natures of man and woman.
>
> Women can, of course, be educated, but their minds are not adapted to the higher sciences, philosophy, or certain of the arts. These demand a universal faculty. Women may have happy inspirations, taste, elegance, but they have not the ideal. The difference between man and woman is the same as that between animal and plant. The animal corresponds more closely to the character of the man, the plant to that of the woman. In woman there is a more peaceful unfolding of nature, a process, whose principle is the less clearly determined unity of feeling. If women were to control the government, the state would be in danger, for they do not act according to the dictates of universality, but are influenced by accidental inclinations and opinions. The education of woman goes on one hardly knows how, in the atmosphere of picture-thinking, as it were, more through life than through the acquisition of knowledge.

Philosophical and scientific explanations of female inferiority are based on biological and psychological differences between the sexes. Biological justifications of hierarchical social ordering between races and classes are now generally considered not only ill-founded but repugnant. Scholarly attempts to find any distinction as to mental abilities between races are not tolerated within the academic community. Given the inadequacy of biological explanations for almost all patterns of dominance and servience, it is surprising to see the degree to which a biological explanation for the domination by the male of the female is still considered by many to be creditable. The very fact of its limited application and inability to account for other patterns of domination ought to make it highly suspect as an explanation of male domination.

There is a literature, much more modest than would justify the extent to which its thesis is taken seriously, which argues that males have inherited certain biological properties, principally greater strength and a higher degree of aggression, that explain and account for the male domination of the female. The argument runs something like this:

> Aggressive and strong people can satisfy their needs at the expense of weaker and submissive people,
> Males are stronger and more aggressive than females.
> Therefore males are able to satisfy their needs at the expense of females.

We are told by some social theorists that aggression is a positive quality, important for the evolution of the human species.[29] Reference is often made to animal studies showing a hierarchy of domination, such as the pecking order of hens in a barn yard.[30] The argument would be that aggression is a natural human instinct which produces a hierarchical public order in terms of the natural relationships of domination and subjection. Since men are more naturally aggressive than women, and women are physically smaller and weaker than men, and since it is natural for the stronger and more aggressive to dominate the weaker and more submissive, it is only natural that males should dominate females, and what is natural must be right.[31]

A classic example of such a social Darwinian scientific/mythic explanation is to be found in the book *Human Aggression* by Anthony Storr.[32] It is worth examining because it is representative of a whole range of literature in this field, and sets out assumptions held to be true by a great many males and well-socialized females. Aggressive behavior in humans, according to Storr, is instinctive, natural or innate.[33] Aggression is "a positive drive which is an essential part of human equipment"[34] "an essential ingredient in the structure of society."[35] "In most of the higher species of animals, including ourselves, the male is habitually more aggressive than the female."[36] "Male sexuality, because of the primitive necessity of pursuit and penetration, does contain an important element of aggressiveness; an element which is both recognized and responded to by the female who yields and submits."[37] "In the relation between the sexes, the spermatozoon swims actively, whilst the ovum passively awaits its penetration. The anatomy of the sexual organs itself attests the differentiation of the sexual role."[38]

And it is highly probable that the undoubted superiority of the male sex in intellectual and creative achievement is related to their greater endowment of aggression. It is true that women have often been badly treated by men, deprived of opportunities of education, denigrated, or forced to be unnecessarily subservient. But, even when women have been given the opportunity to cultivate the arts and sciences, remarkably few have produced original work of outstanding quality, and there have been no women of genius comparable to Michelangelo, Beethoven, or Goethe. The hypothesis that women, if only given the opportunity and encouragement, would equal or surpass the creative achievements of men is hardly defensible."[39]

The greater aggression of the male insures the survival of the fittest. Aggression is a normal component of male sexuality. It is natural for males to wish to dominate and for females to wish to be dominated.[40] "The idea of being seized and borne off by a ruthless male who will wreak his sexual will upon his helpless victim has a universal appeal to the female sex."[41] (The idea that women like "the idea of being seized and borne off by a ruthless male who will wreak his sexual will upon his helpless victim" appears to have a universal appeal to the male sex.) "Men and women are only fully themselves when related to each other."[42] Bachelors often become fussy, soft and old maidish, while spinsters become mannish.[43]

"Aggression between members of the same species is necessary if the strongest are to be selected and to flourish."[44] "[T]he aggressive drive may well have had the same function which it performs in other social animals; that of creating a stable society based on dominance."[45] "[E]very society recognizes the need for some kind of leadership."[46] "The aggressive potential of the group is disposed hierarchically in such a way that each man dominates the next below him in rank until the lowliest peasant is reached."[47] "There has to be some method of either re-directing aggression, or else ritualizing the aggressive drive in such a way that it serves the function of uniting rather than separating individuals."[48]

There is some evidence that males are more aggressive than females, possibly because of the effects of the male hormone testosterone.[49] Even if this were the case it would explain only how it is possible for males to dominate females; it would not explain why they do so. The male domination of the female certainly has nothing to do with the survival of the species, nor does aggression lead to superiority or to greater creativity. Storr's book presents one of the modern myths of male superiority which has evolved to replace the Judaeo-Christian mythic structure that viewed woman as inferior to man, created by God to serve man and to be ruled by him. While the myth has become secularized and framed in the language of scientific inquiry, it is still a projection of the male psyche where "nature" or the natural evolutionary process has been substituted for a heavenly creating father.[50] Hillman, after an extensive examination of "scientific" versions of the myth of female inferiority writes:[51]

> We have been examining the fantasies of female inferiority through the historical changes in consciousness. We have seen the inferiority, but where is the change in consciousness? The same view of female inferiority, based on one or another physiological argument, runs with undeviating fidelity from antiquity to psychoanalysis. History evidently has no effect on the permanent structure of the archetype. Changes have been in detail only; the substance of the arguments remains the same.

Further on, he states:[52]

> The image of female inferiority has not changed, because it remains the image in the masculine psyche. Theories of the female body are preponderantly based on the observations and fantasies of men. These theories are statements of masculine consciousness confronted with its sexual opposite. No wonder archetypal levels of unconsciousness intervene in theory-forming. We must bear in mind that the evidence in anatomy, as in all fields of science, is gathered mainly by men and is a part of their philosophy. We know next to nothing about how feminine consciousness or a consciousness which has an integrated feminine aspect regards the same data.

Anything which attempts to explain or justify the male domination of the female in the human species in terms of either the greater strength or the extra aggressiveness of the male, as compared to the female, will be inadequate as it cannot explain the role of patriarchal institutions as the modality of domination. While violence against women has always been prevalent and widespread, it tends, more often than not, to be the result of spontaneous anger or frustration rather than a manifestation of a sustained effort to maintain dominance through brute force. The truth is that in general, throughout much of the recorded history of the human race, women have submitted to the domination of the male because they have believed that it is right and proper to do so. It has been the function of patriarchal institutions such as the traditional family, law, religion, and monarchy to create and sustain those beliefs which legitimize not only the domination of females by males, but domination as between males.

Many of the studies of dominance and social structure among primates are suspect because, consciously or unconsciously, humans have sought to establish the legitimacy of male domination in terms of the natural order of which the animal kingdom is a part.[53] Thus, culture is projected onto nature and our view of nature becomes a part of our mythic structure. Recent studies of primates no longer support a view of consistent and clear domination by males of female primates. The violence which a male primate vents on a smaller female may parallel a beating of a wife by a husband, but it in no way compares to the cultural institutions which justify the use of violence by a husband on a wife, or which leave her no choice but to tolerate it.

MYTHIC FOUNDATIONS OF MISOGYNY IN THE COLLECTIVE PSYCHE

Myths reflect the stage of societal psychic development within which they were produced. Pre-Oedipal myths reflect separation and engulfment anxieties. They often portray the mother or mother figure as fearful people or monsters. Many fairy tales have such a dimension, and the myths of heroes fighting monsters and dragons have been interpreted as reflecting engulfment fears, while myths of the hero being abandoned as an infant reflect separation anxiety.[54] Myths of sons killing fathers, such as those surrounding Uranus, the Titans, Cronus, and Zeus, reflect Oedipal anxieties, as do myths containing themes of fathers killing or sacrificing sons such as the Abraham and Isaac myth.[55] The Oresteia is replete with themes of parent-child hostility and misogyny.[56] The Oedipal mythic cycle itself contains many themes, but the theme selected by Freud, "contains the realization of two intimate childhood dream phantasies: The phantasy of the death of the father and of the love relationship with the mother."[57] The fixation on sexuality and death which pervades the post-Oedipal period of the development of the psyche permeates almost all mythic systems.

Since different cultures have entered these stages at different times, and since there has always been a degree of cultural borrowing and interchange, pre-Oedipal, Oedipal, and post-Oedipal mythic systems will often be found functioning within a specific society at the same time. One should, however, be able to identify the primary stage of the society by seeing if the major mythic system which justifies and legitimizes the social order is pre-Oedipal, Oedipal, or post-Oedipal. The mythic systems of traditional societies are Oedipal, while those of most Westernized nation states tend to be post-Oedipal. Thus, most current political ideologies serve post-Oedipal functions.

If societies and the mythic justifications of their social orders can be meaningfully classified as pre-Oedipal, Oedipal and post-Oedipal, then the mythic structures of kinship tribal societies should furnish us with a rich body of mythic material for the study of the Oedipal passage at the societal level. Two recent studies by anthropologists who are sensitive to the importance of psychoanalytic theory to social theory, contain excellent examples of Oedipal myths and the related rituals. These are the Papua New Guinea studies of Gilbert H. Herdt,[58] and Thomas Gregor's study of the Mehinaku, a small Amazonian tribe.[59] Both Herdt and Gregor found it necessary to understand the gender structure of the tribe before a comprehensive picture could be formed of these cultures.

One of the myths of the Mehinaku, the parallel of which can be found in the mythic structure of almost every tribal society, is related as follows:

> In ancient times, a long time ago, the men lived by themselves, a long way off. The women had left the men. The men had no women at all. Alas for the men, they had sex with their hands. The men were not happy at all in their village; they had no bows, no arrows, no cotton arm bands. They walked about without even belts. They had no hammocks, so they slept on the ground, like animals. They hunted fish by diving in the water and catching them with their teeth, like otters. To cook the fish, they heated them under their arms. They had nothing—no possessions at all.
>
> The women's village was very different; it was a real village. The women had built the village for their chief, Iripyulakumaneju. They made houses; they wore belts and arm bands, knee ligatures and feather headdresses. . . . Oh, they were smart, those round-headed women of ancient times.
>
> The men saw what the women were doing. . . . "Ah" said the men, "this is not good. The women have stolen our lives!" The next day, the chief addressed the men: "The women are not good. Let's go to them." . . . The men came close to the village. . . . They leaped up at the women like wild Indians. . . . They raced into the village and chased the women until they had caught every one, until there was not one left. . . . The men ripped off the belts and clothes and rubbed the women's bodies with earth and soapy leaves to wash off the designs.
>
> The men lectured the women: "You don't wear the shell yamaquimpi belt. Here, you wear a twine belt. We paint up, not you. We stand up and make speeches, not you. You don't play the sacred flutes. We do that. We are men." . . . "You are just women," they shouted. "You make cotton. You weave hammocks." . . . Later that night, when it was dark, the men came to the women and raped them.

This myth, like almost all within which gender differences are a major theme, is rich in Oedipal meaning. The suppression of the powerful women represents the repression of the drive to return to the mother. Masculinity requires the repression of femininity. Women are perceived as superior, so they must be controlled. The resurgence of the feminine is a constant threat to masculinity.[60] "[T]he castration complex overlays the ruins of a destroyed empire over which the Mother-Goddess once reigned."[61]

Males have been able to dominate females because they have dominated the world view. The mythic structures and related institutions, including language, reflect the projections of the male psyche. This kind of domination cannot be adequately explained in terms of aggression and physical strength. The very existence of patriarchal institutions of moral, legal, and political authority bespeaks the inadequacy of aggression to maintain male domination. It does so because their function is to retain male dominance through voluntary acceptance on the part of the female. If aggression is sufficient, then why the need for authority? According to Janet Radcliffe Richards, if women had acquiesced willingly, there would have been no need for a superstructure of law and convention to keep them in their place. She writes, "[I]f it was just that men *were* stronger, what was the point of the colossal superstructure of law and convention which kept women in their weaker position? . . . If men needed laws to keep women in their power, it must have been the case that without such laws they could not have got whatever it was they wanted from women."[62]

The domination of the female by the male is a product of male authority. It is, therefore, authority which must be explained. How does aggression explain authority? If male domination is the product of authority, then explanations which simply link aggression and greater strength to the fact of domination or the physical potential for domination will have little to do with the reality of the human condition. The source of the domination by males of females must be sought in the etiology of authority. Studies of animal behavior have little relevance to this question.

Since the larger and more complex forms of society have evolved from and reflect the structure of the patriarchal family, it is likely that mythically justified social hierarchy and authority first evolved in the relationship of male to female before it evolved to include males dominating other males. Once the pattern is set for the justification or legitimization of the domination of women and children, it can be applied by analogy to other groups of males.

While one of the important functions which law has served is that of minimizing violence between males in order to preserve the cohesiveness of the community, it has also served the purpose of leaving the male free to possess and control females, and to exercise a wide latitude in the use of violence upon them. While the peaceful resolution of conflict can account for the adjudicative function of law, it cannot account for the regulative function, one of the most important aspects of which in almost every legal system is the regulation and control of sexuality. Therefore, explanations of the evolution of law in terms of minimizing violence are totally inadequate to explain patriarchy. Equally, explanations of patriarchy in terms of economic analysis or the needs which are served by social organization may justify a need for social order, but can furnish no justification for that order being patriarchal. Economics itself is a patriarchal science as it recognizes as valuable only the contributions to production of wage labor. It ignores the costs of the "shadow work" and labor which takes place within the home, and is thus generally performed by women, but which is necessary to place the worker at the scene of production.[63]

If patriarchy is not innate, and cannot be justified in terms of economic or social analysis, and since it is universal and derives its legitimacy from mythic structures, we can infer the existence of a need on the part of males to dominate females. Since that need is powerful, persistent, and almost universal, and has been terribly destructive of the welfare of women in general, and since that need has produced institutions and practices which are antilife and violent, it is reasonable to view that state of mind as pathological. Consequently, parallels or analogies drawn between domination relations between animals or the pecking order appear to have little relevance to an understanding of the evolution of law and social hierarchy.

The pathological need of males to dominate females stems from a deep-seated unconscious hostility toward women which ranges from a mere resentment or fear of the feminine to hatred.[64] An unconscious misogyny and gynophobia appears to be a part of the psyche of the male of the species. The inferiority of the female is a presupposition of the collective psyche which is expressed throughout its archetypal structure.[65] It generates misogyny which drives the process of individuation. This archetypal structure links to the collective unconscious of the individual, which produces the individual misogyny within the male and the assimilation of inferiority within the female. When we consider that so many of our institutions and social practices are gender-bifurcated, and that gender has its origins in human sexuality, and when we study the cultural origins of social order in patriarchal mythic systems, the material cries out for some psychoanalytic explanation.

Cultures and societies which have moved beyond the Oedipal to the post-Oedipal will be more secure in their masculinity, and can tolerate a greater mixing of the sexes without masculinity being threatened. Gender bifurcation and the separation of the sexes is the societal analogue of the separation of the male child from the mother, and its passage from protofemininity to masculinity. Societies in a post-Oedipal stage where individuals have well-developed egos require less separation. Nevertheless, gender bifurcation remains necessary for males to achieve masculinity, and misogyny remains essential to fuel the Oedipal passage. Today we take equality to be a fundamental postulate of legal and political theory which needs no justification and is beyond question. Those who would challenge it are immediately branded as sexist. Yet at the same time we maintain male domination in almost every aspect of life.

9.

THE QUADRANT OF COLLECTIVE DEFENSE MECHANISMS

SEXUALITY, DEATH, AND REPRESSION

When we appreciate the fact that repression is the foundation of the entire theoretical structure of psychoanalysis, and that repression produces neurosis, then we can understand why Freud's startling vision of culture as neurosis has to be the central perspective of psychoanalytic social theory. The psychic conflicts which are the source of repression are numerous and varied. Some we all share as a part of the human condition, some may be common only to a particular society or culture, while others arise out of experience unique to particular individuals. Yet these different conflicts reflect common patterns, as nearly all those which have their source in experiences unique to particular individuals are rooted in psychic conflicts which are common to the members of particular societies or cultures. Similarly, those which are common to the members of particular societies or cultures originate in the psychic conflicts which are an inevitable part of the human condition.

These psychic conflicts are common because they arise from an aspect of the human condition which is biologically determined. All humans are born of mothers from whom they must separate. Everyone must eventually die and must face their impending death at the conscious level. The dualistic nature of human sexuality is also biologically determined, and consequently, repression relating to psychic conflict arising out of our sexuality is common to every human. Yet because males and females are biologically different, the psychic conflicts take somewhat different form, and consequently the neuroses of the male are different from those of the female. Gender is an example of a universal archetypal structure which permeates all culture. Little of what we call gender is biologically determined or necessary. Yet, it arises out of psychic conflict which has its roots in biologically determined sexuality. To the degree that gender entails hierarchy, it reflects repression, and to the degree that it reflects repression, it is a manifestation of neurosis. The particular details of the genderization process within any society and at any particular time or place will, of course, differ. While gender roles are not universal, their hierarchical patterning appears to be so.

People living and cooperating together and sharing a common language experience their psychic conflict in similar ways, and adopt similar defense mechanisms which have their roots in repression. Collective defense mechanisms are responses to collective complexes. They take the form of social structures, institutions and practices and represent the collective neuroses of a society. Within particular cultures, individuals live out their own unique lives, suffer their own individual psychic conflict, and develop their own neuroses. Just as particular cultural neuroses may take many different forms but still reflect universal patterns, so the neuroses of individuals may take a wide variety of forms yet reflect particular cultural neuroses. Thus, an individual may develop a particular bizarre fetish as a result of a sexually-oriented psychic conflict which had its origins in a unique experience within the context of a sexually-repressed society. Even our individual neuroses and pathologies, which arise out of our unique existential experience, reflect common cultural and universal psychic conflict and neuroses, so that they can be generically classified into types such as fetishes and perversions, each subdividable into kinds such as exhibitionism and voyeurism.

The major sources of all psychic conflict (repression and its consequent neuroses) are separation from the mother, the frustrations of emotional and sexual dependency, and the fear of death. Separation and engulfment anxieties, sex, and death are the fountainheads of culture and consequently of social order. The human condition entails being consciously aware of our animality. We are bound by the reproductive process and we will die. Our minds are chained to our bodies, and in our own human way we are as sexually driven as rutting dogs in the street. More so, perhaps, because with the cyclicality of estrus other animals at least have periods of respite from the sexual drive. The source of the psychic conflict which underlies the neuroses common to all persons is what Ernest Becker calls, "the condition of individuality within finitude," and refers to as "an existential paradox," which he describes as follows:

> Man has a symbolic identity that brings him sharply out of nature. He is a symbolic self, a creature with a name, a life history. He is a creator with a mind that soars out to speculate about atoms and infinity, who can place himself imaginatively at a point in space and contemplate bemusedly his own planet. This immense expansion, this dexterity, this ethereality, this self-consciousness gives to man literally the status of a small god in nature, as the Renaissance thinkers knew.
>
> Yet, at the same time, as the Eastern sages also knew, man is a worm and food for worms. This is the paradox: he is out of nature and hopelessly in it; he is dual, up in the stars and yet housed in a heart-pumping, breath-gasping body that once belonged to a fish and still carries the gill-marks to prove it. His body is a material fleshy casing that is alien to him in many ways—the strangest and most repugnant way being that it aches and bleeds and will decay and die. Man is literally split in two: he has an awareness of his own splendid uniqueness in that he sticks out of nature with a towering majesty, and yet he goes back to the ground a few feet in order blindly and dumbly to rot and disappear forever. It is a terrifying dilemma to be in and to have to live with. The lower animals are, of course, spared this painful contradiction, as they lack a symbolic identity and the self-consciousness that goes with it. They merely act and move reflexively as they are driven by their instincts. ... But to live a whole lifetime with the fate of death haunting one's dreams and even the most sun-filled days—that's something else.[1]

Jung, Rank, and Becker are directly or indirectly critical of Freud in that they believe that he overemphasized the importance of sexuality and underemphasized the role that the fear of death plays in repression and neurosis. Becker even goes so far as to argue that this reverse emphasis stems from Freud's repression of his own fear of death.[2] The dispute over whether death or sexuality is primary underlies the issue of whether the Oedipal complex should be central to psychoanalytic theory, and thus is one of the central issues which separate the many of the dissidents in the psychoanalytic movement from the more traditional Freudians.

Two responses can be made to this criticism. First, an examination of social institutions, the genderization of culture, the nature of perversion, law, art, and literature, will reflect a much greater concern with sexuality than with death. Arguably, this is because our repression mechanisms are more effective against death. The knowledge of impending death remains cerebral so long as we are in good health. We can often forget it for long periods of time. Sexuality, on the other hand, is constantly present. There is an obvious interrelationship between sexuality and death in our mythic systems, art, religious symbolism and many aspects of human experience[3] such as the heightened sexuality of men at war,[4] the common phenomenon of erotic arousal in people witnessing executions or torture, and sexual assaults ending in murder.[5] It is only when age or illness cause a deterioration of the body that the fear of death becomes primary and sexuality secondary.

The second response is that psychic conflict first takes place in infancy during the separation crisis, and this conflict becomes sexualized as it progresses from the pre-Oedipal to the Oedipal stage. The structure of the psyche and of its neuroses are already set long before the idea of death as a threat to its own ego can enter the consciousness of the child. Subsequent neuroses will always be shaped and colored by separation and engulfment anxieties.

THE GENIUS AND LIMITS OF FREUD

Freud understood the importance of the function of bifurcation in human thought, and recognized the process of repression which is often entailed therein. He realized that the pole to which we consciously give a positive evaluation is often the least important, and the negative evaluation which we give to the opposite pole entails an unconscious repression of its true importance. After successfully reversing the order of hierarchical oppositions between many of our basic dualities such as normal/pathological, real/imaginary, conscious/unconscious, and life/death,[6] Freud left intact the central and most critical of all human hierarchical bifurcations, that of gender. Rather than reverse the order of importance as he did with most dualities, Freud took the male psyche as the norm, interpreting the psyche of the female in terms of a pathological reaction to masculinity. He thereby left untouched much of the repression mechanism underlying human culture. Using Freud's basic methodology, we note that the positive evaluations always fall on the masculine side and the negative on the feminine. This seems to be strong evidence that massive repression underlies the world views of most societies, and that the mythic structures upon which their legitimacy rests are principally a projection of the male psyche.

The literature of psychoanalysis and depth psychology suggests two possibilities regarding human sexuality: that male and female sexuality are either symmetrical or that they are asymmetrical. Jung took the former position while Freud viewed them as dimorphic, by explaining female sexuality as a pathological reaction to masculinity. There is a third position which can be opposed to those of Freud and Jung: that human sexuality is dimorphic but rather than the masculine, the feminine should be taken as the norm.

Females should be taken as the norm because males have a stronger need to satisfy their sexual dependency and hence are less "complete" in themselves than females are. This results in the male need to control females, which results in much pathology. However, this notion of psychological normalcy is complicated somewhat because, as will be later shown, males are unwilling to admit their dependency. Thus, although the feminine is the psychological norm, the masculine is presented as the norm in social mythology. It was precisely this paradigm of male normalcy which guided Freud to his views on male and female sexuality.

From the perspective of the law, we can find a great deal of aberrant male sexual behavior of legal significance, such as multicide, rape, incest, child molestation, wife beating, prostitution, pornography, sexual harassment, sex discrimination, and exhibitionism. When we consider such problems in the context of other common misogynous and gynophobic attitudes and practices, it seems highly likely that there is some relationship between male sexuality and our patriarchal social institutions. The only way adequately to present this relationship is by deconstructing these mythic structures.

The theories of Darwin and Freud are inextricably linked: survival of the fittest (in terms of the passing on of genes to future generations) and sexual selection, both explain why biologically we exist as sexual creatures. The evolution of the upright posture, the lengthy period of gestation and infant dependency, the shift in the human female from estrus to constant sexual receptivity, with the corresponding shift to a more visual sexual arousal mechanism, has produced a sexually dimorphic, mutually dependent species. The female, during pregnancy and the period of infancy of her children, has needed the male as protector and food-gatherer; the male has evolved greater body size and strength to serve these functions. The male requires the female for sexual and emotional satisfaction.[7]

It is inevitable that with the evolution of human consciousness these dimorphic, biologically-determined dependencies would profoundly affect the evolution of culture as well as the development of the individual psyche. Sex/gender is the fundamental categorical distinction of culture, as it defines our identity as individuals, and thus underlies our entire psychological development. Since the male represents the norm in social mythology, and females are defined in terms of the absence of properties which define the male,[8] our biological evolution has resulted in a cultural evolutionary process which has produced a genderized, male-defined and -dominated world. The sexual dependency of the male on the female, however, is distressing to the male psyche; thus, our patriarchal culture has evolved elaborate taboos which surround sexual matters.

Freud stripped away the mechanisms of repression and faced us with what most haunts our unconscious—sexuality and death. He forced us to assimilate intellectually the cultural implications of Darwin. Freud's genius lay in forging new links between biology and culture, between the natural order and the social order. Even so, he was unable to transcend the predominant cultural patriarchal paradigms which haunted his own unconscious. His analysis of female sexuality perpetuates and rationalizes the world views and mythic systems which are predominantly a product of the male psyche or what might be called "the male collective unconscious." An adequate psychoanalytic social theory must transcend the prevailing paradigms to uncover the complexes which have produced the genderized, male-dominated world within which we live.

MALE DEPENDENCY AND REPRESSION

There is no consensus as to what degree and in which ways male and female sexualities differ, and whether the differences are to be explained in terms of biological or cultural causation. Since, in the past, the differences between males and females have been used to argue for both the legitimacy and the inevitability of patriarchy,[9] it is understandable why recent literature tends to minimize differences in sexuality. Nevertheless, it is biologically determined that females give birth and males impregnate. It is also an almost universal pattern of human sexual behavior that the male plays the role of supplicant for sexual satisfaction.[10] In general, it is the male who is the pursuer, pleader, wooer, purchaser, or rapist. The female may invite, tease, or entice, but it is she who will deny, receive, acquiesce, or be forced. From this near universal pattern we can infer a nonreciprocal dependency of the male upon the female, since in even mutually beneficial relationships the person who is the most driven by need must play the role of supplicant, and consequently is in the dependent position.[11]

While the physiological and psychological responses of males and females are similar at a coital or orgasmic level, there are many differences in precoital behavior that would indicate that there are differences in sexual arousal. Males appear to have less control over their sexual arousal, and less ability to tolerate sexual abstinence.[12] The wide distribution and demand for pornography, the greater propensity to resort to masturbation,[13] for which pornography itself is an aid, the prevalence of prostitution,[14] of sexual assaults on nonconsenting females whether in the form of incest, pedophilia, or rape within or outside the home, the higher degree of marital infidelity, and the greater prevalence of perversion, would indicate that the male's dependency, which forces him to the role of supplicant, stems from a difference between male and female sexuality.[15]

While there is little evidence of any difference between males and females in the intensity of the sexual response, there is persuasive evidence that there is a difference in triggering mechanisms between the two sexes. Females tend to become sexually excited more by tactile stimuli and thought processes, while males are more likely to be aroused by visual stimuli.[16] The male proclivity for pictorial pornography would seem to support this conclusion. While this difference may seem to be insignificant at first glance, it may be of great psychological importance in the following sense. One can exercise a great deal of choice over the body contact one experiences with others, and over what one thinks about, listens to, or reads. One has much less control, however, over the visual stimuli with which one is bombarded. If nature has programmed the male to be sexually excited by the sight of the contours of female breasts and buttocks, then it follows that females are able to exercise a great deal more control over their own sexual arousal, or absence of it, than males. Therefore, males are frequently in the position of being involuntarily aroused, and at the same time are dependent on some other person or persons for satisfaction of their sexual drive. It should not surprise us that this could result in frustration and both conscious and unconscious hostility against women, who both trigger the arousal and control the means of satisfaction. The biological imperatives of reproduction function differently for males than for females. The emotional and sexual attraction that the female holds for the male has resulted in a sense of dependency and bondage of the male to the female which contributes to misogyny and gynophobia.

The process of separation from the mother is different for the male than for the female. The male has to make the transition from protofemininity to masculinity. The female merely moves from protofemininity to full femininity. It is the crisis in the process of genderization, and the fear of a castrated state as a result of failure, which under certain conditions produce the much higher incidence of perversion in the male than in the female.[17]

In addition, we have the almost universal pattern of social behavior of male domination. Male sexual dependency serves reproduction. Patriarchy is the product of the male reaction to sexual dependency and motherhood. If this is so, pscyhoanalysis might well be better served by focusing more on dependency than on aggression.[18] Aggression can then be viewed as one kind of response to need and dependency.[19]

Dependency relationships can be viewed and analyzed in terms of a quadrant. That upon which one is truly and critically dependent can:

Control	Nourish
Deny	Destroy

A child's first sense of dependency arises in relation to its mother. The mother nourishes the child physically and emotionally. Since child rearing is almost exclusively the domain of the female, it is the mother who tells the child what to do, who limits the child's freedom of action, and who judges the child or punishes it. Even when a father disciplines a small child, it is often at the instigation of the mother. Since the mother can seldom fully satisfy the child's emotional demands, the child often feels a sense of having been denied when love and affection is also given to siblings and to the father.[20] It is the mother who the child sees as most threatening to the development of its individual ego. The child suffers the ambivalence of wishing both to regain the former unity with the mother and to achieve independence. The mother threatens ego destruction both by her attraction to the child and her own desire not to lose the child.[21]

The sexual dependency of the male upon the female which we can infer from the almost universal role of supplicant which males must play, reaches its apex in the relationship between the lover and the beloved.[22] The beloved can emotionally nourish and sexually satisfy the lover. Where biologically and/or culturally determined patterns of behavior dictate the role of supplicant for the male, the female's capacity to meet the emotional and sexual needs of the lover places her in a position of control. The beloved may also deny, and if the emotional need is sufficiently intense she may "break the heart" or destroy the soul of the lover.

Our mind-body dualism also takes the form of a dependency relationship. The body nourishes the mind or soul with sexual satisfaction and the sensual pleasures of musical harmony, smell, taste, aesthetic beauty, and warmth. At the same time the body controls the mind by limiting it in time and space, and making demands which the mind must continue to see are met. The body denies the mind the sensual pleasures and sexual satisfaction as it begins to fail through age. Eventually, through accident, disease, and finally death the body destroys the mind through its own failure.[23]

For the male, if not for all human beings, the most powerful physical drives are those of hunger and sex. Hunger is generally easier to satisfy than sex, and thus sexuality predominates as a psychic and cultural determinant.[24] For the male the primary source of satisfaction of the sex drive is the physical body of the female. The dependency of the lover on the beloved parallels the dependency of the mind on the body, such that culturally mind-body dualism has become genderized with the mind classified as masculine and the body as feminine.

The dependence of the mind on the body which is implicit in mind-body dualism is paralleled by a dependency of humans upon the earth. The earth nourishes us with the physical requirements of existence such as food, water, air, and materials for shelter and clothing, as well as delighting our senses. Yet we are under its control, being subjugated to the laws of nature and destined to labor for our sustenance. The earth denies us with drought and infertility, and destroys us with floods, fires, earthquakes, and other natural disasters.

The culture-nature bifurcation is an analogue of mind-body dualism and it too has been genderized with culture as masculine and nature as feminine.[25] The equating of human reproduction with the productivity of the earth is reflected in phrases such as *mother earth* or *mother nature*. We speak of the motherland if we mean the earth itself, as in *mother Russia*,[26] but when we talk of the "fatherland" the reference is generally to the state and political power.

The process of individuation, which commences with the separation of the child from the mother, is also paralleled in the separation of humans from nature. In most kinship societies people recognize a closeness between humans and nature. Humans consider themselves to be a part of nature, fellow creatures with the animal world. The evolution of culture involves a separation between man and nature. As consciousness evolves, the gap between humans and nature widens until unity becomes polarity —opposites to be known by way of contrast.

In our genderized world patriarchy is counterposited to motherhood, the lover is generally conceived to be male, and the beloved, female. Males are conceived to be more cerebral, females more emotional and in touch with their bodies. Culture is the domain of the male while the role of the female is to serve the reproductive and male-servicing functions which is ostensibly dictated by their "nature." Thus the quadrant of dependency converges on the feminine to produce the archetypal patterns within which women are viewed, defined, and stereotyped by males—that is, as nourishing, controlling, denying, or destroying.

The hostility and resentment which generally accompany dependency account for the ambivalence which males often feel toward females, as reflected in so many misogynous or gynophobic practices. The fact of this dependency and the misogyny which it engenders is distressing and painful to the male, so it is repressed. Freud has shown us that that which is repressed is not spoken or obvious. Ironically, the Oedipus complex, in focusing upon antagonisms between male (son) and male (father) and female (daughter) and female (mother), masks the unconscious resentment toward the female which is generated by the male's sense of dependency.

Not only is the sense of dependency repressed, but the ambivalence arising from dependency leads to the repression of that which can be identified with the feminine within the psyche of the male. Even the range of human qualities, skills, abilities, and emotions become genderized, such that those which are characterized as female must be repressed in the male, and those classified as male must be repressed in the female. Thus, it is likely that in dependency we will find the etiology of genderized human culture.

MALE DEFENSE MECHANISMS

In response males have culturally evolved four different kinds of defense mechanisms which corresponds with the quadrant of dependency.

Dominate and Control	Deify and Submit
Deny and Transcend	Destroy and Exclude

One can willingly submit to, and even worship or deify, that upon which one is dependent, thus losing the sense of enslavement in voluntary surrender. One can escape the enslavement of dependency if one can dominate and control that upon which one is dependent. One can also escape dependency by denying and transcending that upon which one has been dependent. Finally, one can escape dependency by destroying or eliminating its source through excluding it from one's presence or leaving its presence. One must then live without it or find a substitute.

Whatever the causes of misogyny and gynophobia, and whatever cultural responses have been spawned as defense mechanisms, it is clear that mankind suffers from five destructive bipolar projections:

1. The split between good and evil, as projected in the form of a deity and devil, an evil stereotype projected onto an enemy, or the repression into the unconscious of the "bad side" of our own natures;
2. Masculinity and femininity projected as stereotypes onto the male and female, such that those aspects of the psyche which have been identified with feminine stereotypes are feared and repressed within the male psyche, just as those traits identified with the masculine must be repressed in the female;
3. Adultness and childishness projected onto the young and full-grown, such that the mature of years must suppress and fear characteristics such as spontaneity, playfulness, and wonder;
4. Mind and body, such that we view ourselves as spirits or souls inside a material shell;
5. Culture and nature, such that we see ourselves and our activities

COLLECTIVE DEFENSE MECHANISMS

as humans separate, apart from, and above nature rather than as an aspect or part of it.

The female of the human species is not only often identified with evil, childishness, the body and bodily functions, but with nature itself. All of these are viewed as negative identifications, so that the male, in preserving his "masculinity," must suppress not only the female, but children as well. Male children must be turned into masculine adults, and childish behavior is again tolerated only when a person is very old. Nature is something to be dominated and subjugated, the body must be mastered, and physical drives such as the sexual must be either suppressed or controlled.

Males fear that which threatens their masculinity. Even to admit the fear is to expose weakness and unmanliness. The identification of the fear entails an admission that males are not what they claim and have within themselves that which they fear. Since the nonmasculine within the male psyche must be repressed, males must constantly engage in behavior which is identified with masculine stereotypes, such as hunting, military operations, and violent forms of sports, in order to reinforce their sense of masculinity. While males seek power and vigilantly maintain a masculine persona, they are often secretly driven by perversions which reflect a longing to surrender the hard-won masculine self. Professional prostitute dominatrixes and female-sadist/male-masochist pornography, with its various forms of leather/high heels/bondage scenarios, reflect and serve these unconscious drives.

The result is a set of patriarchal world views which, although they may differ in detail from place to place and time to time, reflect the linkage between man, mind, and culture, and women, body, and nature in these systems of myth. An analysis of these systems will reveal both the quadrant of dependency and the quadrant of defense mechanisms. Social order is a product of these systems. Women are considered to be, by their very nature, inferior to males. This difference is used to justify the imposition of the will of the male upon the female. The exercise of the will is conceived to be "law." Law, being a part of a set of these mythic structures, is thus a product of the projection of the male pscyhe onto the cosmos, thereby producing institutions of social hierarchy from which any extensive input of the female psyche has been excluded.

Since there is a close interrelatedness between birth and sexuality (from a male perspective) with women, it is not surprising to find women related to death in mythic systems and symbols. There is a close parallel between engulfment anxiety and death anxiety in that each entails the loss of the self. Since it is the mother who is seen as threatening to engulf the individuality or self of her children, the mother is often viewed as a destroyer. This identification is particularly marked in the symbols and myths related to the Triple Goddess. The central archetypes of the Triple Goddess are the sexually appealing young woman, the birth-giving matron, and the death-bringing old crone. The old woman, or crone, is identified with the bringer of death, the devouring mother, or the terrible mother, such as Kali in Indian mythology.[27]

At the heart of the fear of death is the threat of the loss of the self. Consciousness, and the dread of its loss, underlies the dualisms of the body and mind, of nature and culture, and of the self and the other. Culture is a manifestation of the mind and the body is a manifestation of nature. The self is always mental and internal, while the other, even in the form of other "selves," is always external and physical, as it cannot be known by direct mental introspection.

Humans have developed four different kinds of defense mechanisms to deal with the fear of death. These defense mechanisms are the product of the repression of that fear. The first is by incorporating the self into the other. The other always remains after the self is gone. Therefore, if the self can be incorporated into the other, it can partake of the permanency of the other. The Eastern spiritual, religious, and philosophical traditions such as Buddhism, Hinduism, and Taoism, where salvation consists of eventually losing the self into nirvana, the Brahmin without differences, the Tao, or ultimate reality, is a response to the fear of death by achieving the permanency of ultimate reality. In this Eastern tradition, ultimate reality is undifferentiated. If you become a part of ultimate reality, and there are no differences, then you become ultimate reality. This ideal represents the ultimate in permanency. Thus, the response to death of the Eastern tradition consists of identifying the central core of the self with the other.

Another form which this kind of defense mechanism can take is to attempt to lose or sacrifice the self to an organization or cause which will outlast the self. By becoming a part of it, the self has some kind of survival after death. This kind of neurosis can often take the form of a wish to be dominated by another person who is perceived to be greater and stronger. By being so dominated, the self can be incorporated into the other and thus share in its power and strength. This drive toward submission can explain in part the need which people have for leaders. We project onto a human being mythic and superhuman powers, then surrender our selves to that person allowing us to identify with him by being incorporated as means toward his ends. In its most pathological form, this drive takes the form of masochism.

The second kind of defense mechanism consists of attaining a continuity with the other by incorporating the other into the self, thus creating the illusion of permanency and omnipotence. These kinds of neuroses and pathologies result in narcissism and the inflation of the self. The more a person can use others by incorporating them as means into their own ends, the more a person can feel superhuman and godlike. In its more pathological form, this escape mechanism is manifested in sadism whereby the self is aggrandized by denying the self in another. Attempting to achieve continuity with the other through incorporating the other, and obtaining continuity with the other through losing the self in the other, can function simultaneously within the same person. Thus, fathers need kings to feel a part of something larger than themselves, and they inflate a particular man to superhuman or mythic status, while at the same time they incorporate their wives and families into their own inflated selves through the domination and authority they exercise over them, thereby duplicating the role of the king on a small scale.

The domination and control of nature is also a form of gaining continuity with the other through incorporating it into the self. The more humans can control the forces of nature, the less animal they feel and the more they feel that they are gods. The very concept of gods and goddesses who are immortal and have control over nature, are a projection of our wishes.

A third kind of defense mechanism to repress the fear of death is to seek a form of immortality by the self transcending the other. The postulation of a spirit or soul which inhabits the body and which will remain after the body disintegrates is a paradigm example. The Christian belief in a life after death, based on the immortality of the soul, is an express denial of the reality of death. Saint Paul asks, "O death, where is thy sting? O grave, where is thy victory?"[28] Elsewhere he admits, "If in this life only we have hope . . . we are of all men most miserable."[29]

There are other methods of seeking a form of immortality for the self, through incorporating the self into a work which will last beyond the death of the body. Thus, a part of the self can live on in works of music, art, literature, or philosophy. Even a statue or monument preserves a little of the self beyond death, and monuments to the self can take many different forms. The desire to create such monuments or have them created in one's image is a common neurosis which is one of the driving forces behind culture.

The fourth kind of defense mechanism against the fear of death is by negating and excluding the other, thus creating the illusion that the self is greater than the other. This neurosis often takes a very destructive form. This pathology is manifested in the variety of attempts to destroy nature, whether hunting for sport or exploiting for profit. The killing and destruction of war, is another form of this pathology. The Nazis, in turning the Jews into the other and then slaughtering them, reflect a deep fear of death. To become the destroyer, the bringer of death, to have the power of life and death over others—all create the illusion that one is beyond the power of death, above death so to speak, or has become death incarnate. The words of Robert Oppenheimer when he saw the explosion of his first atomic bomb, "I am become ... the destroyer," and his willingness to suspend his normal humanitarian sentiments to achieve his place in history, reflect both the third and fourth kinds of defense mechanism against death.

The inflation of the self, and the four kinds of defense mechanisms against the fear of death, are reflected in the role which the concept of the hero and the heroic stance play in almost all aspects of human culture. The hero is the archetypal image of the inflated self. We tend to identify with heroes and view ourselves as playing a heroic role. One need only recall one's early childish daydreams and even our adult contemporary fantasies, and note the role of the hero in literature, drama, movies and television, to realize the importance of the role of the heroic in human psychology.

Jung and Neumann have analyzed the role of the hero image in the process of individuation of the self.[30] They explain the structure of the heroic myths where the hero struggles against a monster, such as Saint George slaying the dragon or Perseus killing the Medusa, in terms of the self struggling to individuate and separate from the mother. The monstrous fear is the fear of engulfment, that is, the loss of the self.

Joseph Campbell in *The Hero with a Thousand Faces* sets out the structure of the archetypal journey of the hero.[31] The first stage is where the hero is in the peaceful comfort of his home. This represents the initial stage of warm and peaceful symbiosis with the mother. Then comes the call to adventure, followed by an initial refusal. The call to adventure is the drive toward individuation which Mahler recognized as existing in all infants, and the refusal is the expression of separation anxiety. Then follows the call of a supernatural being or force, which can be seen as the intervention of the father, drawing the child away from the mother. The hero next crosses a threshold, which represents individuation, and enters the world of chaos, which will be the Oedipal struggle completing the process of genderization and the passage from protofemininity to masculinity. Within the world of chaos the struggle takes place, where the Hero battles the monster—struggles between the opposing forces of separation and engulfment anxiety in the development of the ego. Eventually the hero triumphs, the ego has formed, full maleness is achieved, and the father is now internalized as the superego. The hero can then return in triumph to his home to claim the hand of the fair maiden. The male self is now prepared to assume the role of the father by taking a wife and having children of his own.

Otto Rank and Ernest Becker analyze the hero and the heroic state in terms of a defense mechanism against death.[32] The heroic image constitutes an inflation of the self and a denial of death. The interpretations of Rank and Becker are not inconsistent with those of Jung and Neumann, in that the basic theme of the heroic is the struggle against engulfment, whether against engulfment and the consequential loss of self by symbiotic merger with the mother/the feminine, or by death.

The four different kinds of defense mechanisms against death:

Incorporating the Other into the Self	Incorporating the Self into the Other
Transcending the Other	Excluding and/or destroying the Other

correspond with four different kinds of heroes. That is, each kind of defense mechanism against death has a heroic mode or archetypal aspect. These are:

The Conquering Hero	The Sacrificing Hero
The Transcending Hero	The Destroying Hero

This quadrant of the heroic can be found in practically all versions of the hero. The hero as soldier takes the form of the soldier dying for his country or to save his fellow soldiers, the victorious soldier, the soldier who transcends all odds and never surrenders, and the soldier as destroyer. The hero as saint takes the form of martyr, conqueror, ascetic, and holy destroyer or crusader. The hero as king takes the form of the ritually sacrificed or sacral king whose death guarantees the fertility of the land and the prosperity of the people, the king as conqueror and ruler, the king as cultural hero, and the king as destroyer. The hero as a god takes the form of dying saviour god, ruling father god, transcendent god or the *Logos,* and the devil god or demon.

The psyche carries with it its history. The post-Oedipal psyche is the product of the pre-Oedipal separation and the Oedipal passage and process of genderization. How the post-Oedipal psyche deals with the animality crisis will depend upon what has happened in the separation and genderization crises. The scars of these two passages will be the sources of tension in the animality crisis. The tensions between separation anxiety and engulfment anxiety will form the basis for adult alienation and attitudes toward groups. Whether an adult is libertarian or communitarian in political orientation could well depend more upon the resolutions to the tensions between separation and engulfment anxiety than upon persuasive political argument.

The process of the development of the psyche from pre-Oedipal, through the Oedipal to the post-Oedipal involves the receding of the id, the development of the superego and finally of the ego. As Freud said, "Where id was, there ego shall be."[33] Separation anxiety produces the desire to return to and merge with the mother. This would entail the id re-engulfing the nascent ego. The superego and the prohibition against incest enforced through castration anxiety drives the individual through the Oedipal passage, at the end of which the ego is strong enough to resist the "return to the mother." The narcissistic wound, however, still remains. Separation anxiety does not disappear. The genderization process ensures that the ego cannot return to lose itself in the feminine other.

The ego consequently attempts to merge itself in the substitute other—
the masculine other—the brotherhood of man. The object of the ego
ideal shifts from the original mother symbiosis to a masculine other from
which the feminine is excluded.

The shift in development and emphasis of the psyche then follows the
path from the archetypal mother to the archetypal father, to disembodied
mind, to the brotherhood of the collective as object of the ego ideal.

Archetypal Father	Archetypal Mother
Disembodied Mind	Brotherhood of the Collective

The four pathologies which make up the post-Oedipal stage of the
development of the psyche:

Dominate and Control	Deify and Submit
Deny and Transcend	Destroy and Exclude

parallel the Oedipal passage and represent the assimilation of its four
states as measured in terms of the objects which the ego ideal takes in
moving from the pre-Oedipal through the Oedipal to the post-Oedipal.

10.

THE QUADRANT OF COMPLEXES

One of the most basic intellectual needs which leads to the creation of myth is the need for interrelationships and wholeness in our symbolic systems of thought. It manifests itself in many different intellectual and psychological activities. The desire to systematize, to worship, and to formulate a world view, are but a few of the forms which it takes. This need represents an intellectual drive toward unification, and is reflected in mythic systems of thought, religion, and science, and other cultural achievements.

Our psychological complexes, such as the Oedipus complex, are a focal point of unification of many different drives, experiences, psychic conflict, and repressions. Like the Oedipal genderization crisis, the animality crisis also becomes a unifying focal point. Male dependency on the mother and on females in general, the dependency of the mind on the body, and our dependency on the earth interrelate around a common quadrant of vulnerability:

Control	Nourish
Deny	Destroy

This quadrant of dependency produces in turn a quadrant of defense mechanisms:

Dominate and Control	Deify and Submit
Deny and Transcend	Destroy and Exclude

Our fear of death produces a parallel set of defense mechanisms:

Incorporating the Other into the Self	Incorporating the Self into the Other
Transcending the Other	Excluding and/or destroying the Other

These two sets of defense mechanisms converge in the mythic structure and neurosis of heroism, which takes a corresponding form:

The Conquering Hero	The Sacrificing Hero
The Transcending Hero	The Destroying Hero

In the pre-Oedipal stage the infant suffers psychic conflict between separation anxiety and engulfment anxiety as it passes through four stages:

Separation	Symbiosis
Individuation	Gender Unification

The male child recognizes that it belongs to the male gender long before it has fully separated emotionally and psychologically from the mother. At this point the process of masculinization has not yet been completed. It only becomes complete after the child passes through the Oedipal complex and has internalized the idea of the female and the feminine as other. This is often marked by the rejection of female children as friends. The male psyche eventually develops to the stage where it seeks to possess a woman or women to replace the mother as a source of gratification, and strives to become a member of the brotherhood of the male. At this point, gender unification is complete.

The maternal, sexual, body, and nature dependencies which coalesce in the four pathological stages as a defense against the dependency on the female and the urge to lose oneself in a reunification with the mother, converge with the defense mechanisms against death in the neurosis of heroism, to produce four different kinds of complexes in the psyche of the male, which can be named:

To Dominate and Control **The Persean Complex** To Incorporate the Other into the Self	*To Deify and Worship* **The Dionysian Complex** To Incorporate the Self into the Other
Transcend the Other **The Apollonian Complex** *To Deny and Transcend*	To Destroy and Exclude the Other **The Heraclean Complex** *To Destroy and Exclude*

These four complexes have their focal point in four archetypal objects of the ego ideal:

The Persean Complex The Archetypal Father	**The Dionysian Complex** The Archetypal Mother
The Archetype of Disembodied Mind **The Apollonian Complex**	The Archetype of the Brotherhood of the Collective **The Heraclean Complex**

COMPLEXES AND THE DEFENSE OF THE EGO

The infant commences life, "lying inert in the unconscious, merely being there in the inexhaustible twilit world, all needs effortlessly supplied by

the great nourisher . . . the refuge for all suffering, the goal of all desire."[1]
As the young infant male grows and develops, "he discovers that his first
love is both an inferior and unlike himself. The price of his initiation into
the privileged masculine world is the ruthless suppression of all things
feminine in himself."[2] The process of genderization must be carried out
both internally and externally. The mother is "the home we come from,
she is nature, soil, the ocean; father does not represent any such natural
home . . . he represents the other pole of human existence; the world of
thought, of man-made things, of law and order, of discipline, of travel
and adventure."[3] Freud's Oedipal complex highlights an important crisis
in the evolution of the psyche of the child, and that is the painful process
of assimilating sexual and gender differentiation. The denying of the
mother and identification with the father, which is entailed in the separation of ego from id and the development of the superego, creates a
longing to return to the mother. Separation anxiety and the memories of
the warmth and security of the symbiotic union with the mother maintain
the desire to lose the burden of masculinity and to reunite with the
feminine.

I call this the Dionysian complex because Dionysus was a god particularly identified with Goddess and nature worship.[4] The essence of the
Dionysian experience lies in the loss of the self in some greater whole.
This loss of self through union with the other can be achieved in many
different ways such as meditation, sexual ecstasy, or intoxication. According to one writer:[5]

> The God Dionysus is represented by the goat below and the god above:
> man is crucified between animal and the divine instinct; the Dionysian
> condition signifies a breaking loose of all that is animal, yet at the same
> time, something which is divine is released. Man is filled with horror at the
> annihilation of his individuality, but he also feels a rapturous delight at its
> destruction; in his condition, when individuality is suspended, man again
> finds man, and every man feels himself one with his neighbor.

Dionysus is unlike all the other gods of the Olympian pantheon. He is
the oldest of all, going back to the horned god of matriarchal paganism.
Compared to all of the other gods, he is an anomaly in that he is a true
friend of women, and is not misogynous. Regarding Dionysus, the classicist Walter F. Otto writes:[6] "He, himself has something feminine in his
nature. To be sure, he is in no way a weakling but a warrior and a hero
who triumphs . . . But his manhood celebrates its sublimest victory in the

arms of the perfect woman. This is why heroism *per se* is foreign to him in spite of his warlike character."

Elsewhere, Otto states:[7]

> We should never forget that the Dionysiac world is, above all, a world of women. Women awaken Dionysus and bring him up. Women accompany him wherever he is. Women await him and are the first ones to be overcome by his madness. And this explains why the genuinely erotic is found only on the periphery of the passion and wantonness which make their appearance with such boldness on the well-known sculptures. Much more important than the sexual act are the act of birth and the feeding of the child. But more will be said about this later. The terrible trauma of childbirth, the wildness which belongs to motherliness in its primal form, a wildness which can break loose in an alarming way not only in animals—all these reveal the innermost nature of the Dionysiac madness: the churning up of the essence of life surrounded by the storms of death. Since such tumult lies waiting in the bottom-most depths and makes itself known, all of life's ecstasy is stirred up by Dionysiac madness and is ready to go beyond the bounds of rapture into a dangerous wildness. The Dionysiac condition is a primal phenomenon of life in which even man must participate in all the moments of birth in his creative existence.

According to Helene Deutsch, Dionysus "appears as a great social revolutionary—the first feminist in the history of mankind—in order to free the enslaved women."[8]

The fear of the surrender to the feminine which is linked with the fear of the ego being overwhelmed by the id is reflected in the Bacchae myths as dramatized by Aeschylus (only two lines survive) or Euripides. "Bacchus" is the Roman name for Dionysus. The unconscious inner drive to reunite with the feminine is also reflected in the poem from *The Carmina of Catullus,*[9] in which Catullus writes concerning the Dionysian god-hero figure, Attis, "Carried across deep seas in a fast ship, quick-footed Attis entered the forests of Phrygia and eagerly hurried to the dark tree-circled place of the goddess. And there, his mind bewildered, driven by violent madness, he castrated himself with a sharp stone." After the self-immolation/emolliation Catullus uses the pronoun "she" rather than "he" for Attis. "Then Attis, her fanaticism quieted after sleep, reviewed in her mind what she had done, and clearly saw what she had lost . . . cried piteously to her homeland . . . [n]ever to see the forum again, or palaestra, or stadium or gymnasium." Catullus ends the poem with the plea, "Goddess, great goddess . . . keep your anger far from my house. Goad others, mighty lady, with your fury and your madness."[10]

As the male child matures, his dependency on the mother is replaced by a sexual and emotional dependency on other women. The emergence of his ego which dictates that he individuate himself from the mother, now dictates that he satisfy his new dependency by incorporating the woman or women into himself as an extension of himself. Thus, the patriarchal family is an extension of the father and requires a surrender of the mother's autonomy. The free, independent woman is a threat to the dependent male ego. She is the Medusa which must be tamed, castrated —beheaded. The term *Persean complex* therefore seems an appropriate name for the drive to seek independence by making the woman dependent.

Perseus was the son of Zeus by a mortal mother.[11] He was an archetypal figure of monarchy in that he was mortal but descended from the patriarchal father god, and was thus patriarchy incarnate. He assumed the task of slaying Medusa, one of three sisters called the Gorgons. The number of Gorgons corresponds with the facets of the Great Mother, the triple goddess. Medusa was terrible to look upon and her head was full of writhing snakes rather than hair. The serpent or snake has always been an important symbol in Goddess worship. The Medusa is one of several mythic horrible female creatures that the Great Mother or goddess figures were reduced to in the shift from matriarchal consciousness to patriarchy. Those who looked at Medusa would be turned to stone.

According to one form of the myth Medusa had been a beautiful maiden who had been transformed by Athene. It was Athene who showed Perseus the face of Medusa in the mirror side of her shield, and gave him the shield so that he could look into it and see the image of Medusa without being turned to stone as he slew her. It is said in another version of the myth that Athene guided the hand of Perseus when he struck the fatal blow with his sword, and it was to Athene that he presented the head of Medusa on his return. The sculptures and paintings of Athene portray her holding a shield with the head of Medusa emblazoned in the center.

Athene is the archetypal embodiment of the woman who adopts and internalizes male values and becomes a defender of patriarchy. She was not born of a female but sprang from the head of Zeus. An example of her mythic role is furnished by Aeschylus in the *Oresteia*. Clytaemnestra, Orestes' mother, killed his father and her husband, Agamemnon, because of his deceitful sacrifice of their daughter Iphigenia in order to obtain favorable wind conditions to reach Troy. Orestes, in turn, killed his mother. At his trial before the gods, it was Athene who cast the deciding vote for acquittal. She justifies her vote for patriarchy in the following words:[12]

> It is my task to render final judgment here. This is a ballot for Orestes I shall cast. There is no mother anywhere who gave me birth, and, but for marriage, I am always for the male with all my heart, and strongly on my father's side. So, in a case where the wife has killed her husband, lord of the house, her death shall not mean most to me. And if the other votes are even, then Orestes wins. You of the jurymen who have this duty assigned, shake out the ballots from the vessels, with all speed.

Women who take on roles of power and influence in the defense of patriarchy are the daughters of Athene. The archetypal father is the object of their ego ideal. Female activists in the pro-life movement, women who had led the fight against the ERA (Equal Rights Amendment), the leaders of the various women's groups which supported the Nazis and helped to bring them to power,[13] are all in the grip of an Athene complex.

Medusa—the free woman, the virgin owned by no man—is the converse of Athene. She is the spirit of the feminine, undistorted, unrepressed, and untrampled—the angry woman, the witch in the pathological society. It is her face which turns a man into stone. *The terror of Medusa is the terror of castration,*[14] but not just the loss of phallic potency, but the loss of the power for which it stands.

Men see women as but a reflection in the mirror of Athene. The mirror of Athene is the patriarchal definition of the feminine, the female stereotype constructed and projected by the male psyche. And the sword of Perseus which is used to cut off the head of Medusa is the law. The slain Medusa is the patriarchally subjugated female: an object without an identity of her own, to be used by the male for his purposes and pleasure. She is the "total woman" of Marabel Morgan,[15] the "fascinating woman" of Helen Andelin,[16] the androids of Ira Levin's *The Stepford Wives.*[17]

The Oedipal pain of separation from the mother and the Dionysian desire for wholeness can never be fully satisfied by the incorporation of women as extensions of the male self, nor can the emotional and sexual dependency be escaped through forcing women to be the servants of male needs. Despite male domination women are and remain separate persons with their own desires and objectives. The male therefore seeks escape from his sexual bondage through the denial of sexuality by abstinence, and the diversion of libido into the kinds of activities which can be disassociated from sexuality, women, and reproduction. The term "Apollonian" seems apt for this kind of complex since Apollo was the god who absolved Orestes of the crime of killing his mother, and became the symbol of the male patriarchal world of wisdom, culture, and learning.[18] By these means, the male ego seeks to compensate for its comparative irrelevance in the reproductive processes of birth and nurture.[19]

At the center of the Apollonian complex is the denial of our animality. The Apollonian complex results from the repression of the fact that we are mere animals who are born, copulate, and die like the rest of the animal kingdom. It is too painful to accept the fact that our individuality, our sense of our unique selves, is irrelevant to nature. In nature, all that really counts is the perpetuation of the species. This repression is reflected in almost all human activity which can be called culture. Our heroism, our religions, our art, our science, our politics, and our mythic systems are attempts to deny this by creating the myth that humans are important —that we have a unique destiny in the plan of nature. In some mythic structures, this belief goes so far as to assume that the universe was created for the sake of man. We are the supreme achievement of God's creation for which all else exists, and may be used, shaped for our own purposes, or destroyed. In its secular form, the myth postulates an evolutionary process whereby man evolves toward perfection, or a unique and special destiny. The perpetuation of the species is not an end in itself for the Apollonians, it is only a necessary condition to achieve these higher ends.

By placing concepts over conception (females conceive, but males have concepts), mind over body, culture over nature, and above all, man over woman, the male denies his true identity as a biped primate which has evolved a brain big enough to store and process information in unique ways. He views himself as god, hero, king, and patriarch. Women are devalued because their unique role in the reproductive process is devalued. We wish to devalue and deny reproduction with its entailment of enslavement to sexual desire, and its inevitable consequence—death.

The Apollonian complex lies behind industry and the accompanying destruction of the environment, whether organized by private capital or through state enterprise. It lies behind the pathological destruction of many animal and plant species, and the striving to leave the earth behind and travel into the vast reaches of space. It lies behind the world of science and academia where we search for any kind of meaning other than what is obvious on the entire face of nature.

The Dionysian complex seeks wholeness through losing one's self in the other, the Persean complex by incorporating the other into one's self, and the Apollonian complex by making one's self sufficient to itself. The Heraclean complex "aims not at active or passive symbiosis but at elimination of its object. . . . I can escape the feeling of my own powerlessness in comparison with the world outside myself by destroying it."[20] Heracles was the greatest of the Greek heroes, and was the only hero to achieve godhood.[21] He was the son of Zeus and Alcmene, and the great-grandson of Perseus. While he had several wives, he was no friend of women and was often in conflict with them. He began life by crushing a pair of serpents with his bare hands while still in the crib. (The snake or serpent is one of the symbols of the Goddess, and artistic depictions of Heracles holding a snake in each hand call to mind the goddess figurines found at the palace of Knossos in Crete.) In a fit of madness, he killed his wife and children. He was a member of the brotherhood of heroes that made up the Argonauts, the crew of the ship *Argo*. As the archetypal hero, he seems an appropriate mythical figure to give his name to the destructive misogynous drives in males which generate such activities as rape and multicide, and exclude women from the various brotherhoods, whether military, scholastic, or religious.

THE QUADRANT OF PORNOGRAPHY

The explanatory power of a psychology of dependency can be demonstrated by analyzing male sexuality in terms of these four complexes. In analysis, the psychoanalyst will often use the analysand's dreams as a key to unlocking the material repressed into the unconscious. Word association, Freudian slips, and jokes often are useful tools in uncovering unconscious structures and patterns. Another tool very useful to the psychoanalyst are the daydreams and fantasies of the analysand as these generally arise spontaneously from the unconscious realm.[22] Pornography represents readymade fantasies. Stoller calls fantasy, "that vehicle of hope, healer of trauma, protector from reality, concealer of truth, fixer of identity, restorer of tranquility, enemy of fear and sadness, cleanser of the soul. And creator of perversion."[23] He writes:[24]

> Just as every human group has its myth, perhaps for every person there is *the* sexual fantasy (perversion?). In it is summarized one's sexual life history —the development of his or her erotism and of masculinity and femininity.

In the manifest content of the fantasy are imbedded clues to the traumas and frustrations inflicted on sexual desires in childhood by the outside world, the mechanisms created to assuage the resultant tension, and the character structure used to get satisfaction from one's body and the outside world (one's objects). The analyst has the opportunity to study this sexual fantasy and uncover these origins. And the findings of the single analysis, I have suggested, may be confirmed en masse: by pornography. Pornography is the communicated sexual fantasy of a dynamically related group of people. Rarely, the fantasy may not take a cognitive form at all but may be manifested consciously only in the ritual used for masturbation.

The nature and structure of pornography, therefore, should reveal a good deal about the nature and structure of the male psyche. The form that pornography takes is shaped by the market which represents the demands of the purchaser, in turn reflecting the kinds of fantasies which they find erotically stimulating, and thereby meeting or reflecting an unconscious need or neurosis. Stoller points out that the pornographer, since he wishes to make money, must develop fantasies which are not idiosyncratic, but contain features shared in common. Consequently, "pornography is for the researcher a sort of statistical study of psychodynamics."[25] Analysis of male pornography and male reactions to pornography reflects the four complexes, and furnishes some evidence of the validity of the theory of the quadrant of complexes. By analyzing an individual's sexual fantasies and the kinds of pornography which he finds erotically stimulating, it can be ascertained where he fits within the quadrant.

A major kind of pornography is made up of pictures and descriptions of males being spanked or disciplined by women. This kind of pornography was particularly popular in the Victorian period. Bondage and domination pornography, with titles such as *Bitch Goddesses, Rubber Domination, Mistress,* and *Female Supremacy,* filled with ads for bondage paraphernalia and the services of professional dominatrixes, still makes up a substantial portion of today's pornography market. The prevalence of pictorial and verbal imagery relating to spanking and enemas illustrates how aspects of pre-Oedipal and Oedipal development help shape the forms which the animality crisis takes in adulthood. This type of pathology often involves a good deal of fetishism in the form of leather, whips, and bondage paraphernalia, the sales of which enjoy a wide market as is evidenced by the number of catalogues and advertisements in pornographic magazines. A number of such advertised instruments are gadgets for restraining and causing pain to the penis. Descriptions and pictures of the foreskin or penis being pierced by sterilized needles reflect a desire to lose the burden of masculinity and return to the conflict-free and blissful state of protofemininity. It is not all that uncommon for the emergency wards of hospitals to receive men who have cut off their own penises.

In a study of the phenomenon of male masochism, the sociologist Gini Graham Scott writes, "The commercial world of sex . . . shows a growing interest in female dominance. About 100 sexually oriented magazines feature this theme, and each has a circulation of about 10,000 to 20,000. Also, perhaps 100,000 to 150,000 males each year visit a professional dominant or mistress for erotic satisfaction."[26] The psychological drive for one person to lose himself or to be incorporated into another, which is so characteristic of masochism, permeates this kind of pornography. This kind of masochism often takes the form of seeking to be humiliated. Where males have the will and the money to actualize their fantasies, they hire professional dominatrixes to do such things as urinate on them (euphemistically called "the Golden Shower") or urinate in their mouths, sit on their heads, ride them, or stand on them in high-heeled shoes. The desire to escape the enslavement of sexuality in the deification and worship of women and the desire to lose the self in the other, which underlie the psychology of male masochism, thus coalesce in this pathological form. The Dionysian nature of this pathology is graphically illustrated by a church of Goddess worship where domination by women and the accompanying bondage and discipline are ritualized. Needless to say, this church is run by men and the organizing force is male.[27] Males whose pathologies and neuroses take this form have great difficulty in finding willing female participants, which is why the market for dominatrix prostitutes is so lucrative. According to experts in this field, the stronger and driving force in sadomasochistic relationship lies with the masochist, with the other partner playing the role of sadist reluctantly.[28] This is not the case where the male is sadistic. It is true where the male is masochistic.

Other kinds of pornography, such as that which shows naked women lying flat or in some kind of sitting position with their legs spread apart, reflect the Persean Complex. This kind of pornography is an expression of the male desire or fantasy of women as willing and ready receptacles to receive the thrusting male. The wishful fantasy of women as objects rather than persons in their own right, with their own needs and goals, acting to achieve their own objectives, is even more strongly reflected in the pornography which portrays women tied into these positions, often with gags in their mouths, thus making them voiceless. Male sadistic pornography showing women tied, tortured, and raped, reflects a more pathological Persean complex in that the greater the woman's suffering and humiliation, the more she is incorporated into the extension of the male self. A common pornographic image, and frequent request made of prostitutes (and often of wives as well), involves fellatio, with the woman on her knees servicing the man.

One of the most common ways in which the Persean Complex is reflected is in the ways by which males wish to turn women into or see them as children. The bondage and discipline pornography with males in the dominating position is a reflection of the process by which males deny the individuality or agency of women by infantizing them. This complex takes a more pathological form in the male desire for children as sexual objects rather than fully developed women with strong personalities in their own right, as is evidenced by an extensive underground child pornography industry. Porn shops carry a wide range of pornography which feeds this pathology without the use of actual children. Books containing vivid descriptions of incest and sexual relations with children, and pictorial depictions of young adult models dressed as children or teenagers, with titles such as *Teen Cupcakes, Baby Dolls, Young Buns,* or *Peach Fuzz Pussies,* reflect the male desire for willing personalityless receptacles for the male penis. Another kind of pornography which serves this need is the sets of magazines showing women with their pubic areas shaved, thus giving their genitals a childlike or pre-pubescent look. The high rate of incest and male sexual molestation of children gives testimony to how often the strength of this pathology moves men from fantasy to action.[29]

The Apollonian complex is reflected in the way that male-dominated society comes to terms with or deals with pornography. Rather than viewing it as wrong because it denigrates women and perpetuates a false male stereotype of the female, pornography is suppressed, to the degree that it is suppressed at all, as "obscene." It is categorized as obscenity because it has to do with sex. The repression of sexuality, particularly characteristic of the Judaeo-Christian tradition, is the product of the psychic conflict between the sexual nature which is a part of our animality, and our desire to be pure of mind, free of the biological dictates of the body. The Christian clergy who rail against pornography and its use are as pathological in their own way as the consumers of pornography. In fact, the repression entailed in the Apollonian complex often exacerbates the Persean or Heraclean complexes. For example, the renowned Protestant theologian Paul Tillich was an avid user of pornography portraying naked women tied and exposed in various positions. Crosses and whips were also central images in his sexual fantasies.[30] Recent revelations about the hidden sexual lives of television evangelists and the sexual molestation of children by clergymen and priests, furnish further evidence of the pathology which the Apollonian entails.

The Heraclean complex is reflected in the demand for extreme sadistic pornography which goes beyond mere bondage and discipline to the torture of female breasts and the external genital organs. Magazines carrying titles such as *Tit Torture, Big Tits in Bondage, Enslave* or *Submit,* and snuff movies portraying torture to the point of death and even the dismembering of the woman's body, are evidence of the destructive fantasies so characteristic of the Heraclean complex. The kind of paraphernalia advertised in the sado-masochistic catalogues, such as "tit-clamps," reflect a pathological misogyny that focuses on the external organs which mark the state of being female. This pathology moves from fantasy to reality in the rape-murders and multicides by the Rippers and Bundys of the world who represent the more extreme examples of the Heraclean complex. Often these rape-murders include torture and mutilation of the victims' breasts and female organs, the full details of which are seldom published in the public media.[31] Macho male homosexuality and its pornography is an example of another form which the Heraclean complex can take.[32] Motorcycle and leather homosexuality, whether in clubs or a subgroup within Rohm's Nazi Brownshirts, is an example of the ultimate in the brotherhoods of man.

THE QUADRANT OF PATHOLOGY

There is a close interrelationship between pornography and perversion. Stoller defines perversion as "a *fantasy* put into action."[33] In a fuller definition he writes:[34]

> *Perversion,* the erotic form of hatred, is a fantasy, usually acted out but occasionally restricted to a daydream (either self-produced or packaged by others, that is, pornography). It is a habitual, preferred aberration necessary for one's full satisfaction, primarily motivated by hostility. . . . The hostility in perversion takes form in a fantasy of revenge hidden in the actions that make up the perversion and serves to convert childhood trauma to adult

triumph. To create the greatest excitement, the perversion must also portray itself as an act of risk-taking.

Perversion can enter into the very fabric of the mythic systems which generate, via misogyny, the counterforce to the desire to return to the mother and the narcissistic wound by closing the gender gap. Perversion, according to Stoller, is an erotic form of hatred which entails an element of revenge against the mother (woman) for trauma suffered in the process of separation and genderization.[35] We generally conceive of perversion as an abnormality, a variant, or a departure from the norm. Yet according to Freud, "No healthy person . . . can fail to make some addition that might be called perverse to the normal sexual aim. . . ."[36] The difference between normality and perversion is one only of degree.[37]

One of the criteria of perversion is that it is a departure from the norm. However, it is possible to have collective perversions, where the perversion is the norm in a culture or a society. The erotically based practice of foot-binding in traditional China, adult males taking young female children as brides in many traditional societies, and pederasty in ancient Greece [38] are but a few examples. Even here, we can use groups of cultures and societies to provide a norm. What is or is not perversion should be measured in terms of an analysis of psychic processes rather than in terms of comparison between groups, one taken to be the norm and the other as perverse.

In China, for example, foot-binding was the norm. At an early age, little girls had their toes bent back and tightly bound until their feet became stunted stumps. This practice was not only legitimate, but for nearly two thousand years was a necessary condition for marriage for all but peasant girls. The process was agonizing and its only function was to serve as a source of erotic stimulation for the husband.[39] The unconscious connection between the crippling of a woman by the binding of her feet and sexual stimulation is revealing of the structure of the male psyche. This practice evidences hostility against the female. The crippling is a constant act of revenge having a highly erotic motivation. It meets in every way the elements of perversion, except that it was the norm for century after century throughout an entire culture. It is a classic example of a collective perversion reflecting the Persean complex.

In India, the traditional practice of suttee, whereby the wife was expected to throw herself on her husband's funeral pyre, is another example of a collective perversion. The wife was seen as having no value or personhood in her own right. She was merely an extension of her husband, and upon his death she had no more value. The social pressures on the widow were such that she had practically no choice other than to commit suttee. Enforced suicide is little different than murder, but it became duty within the patriarchal framework of legitimacy.[40] One might argue that the practice of suttee lacked the erotic element, but those who witnessed this self-immolation might well have experienced perverse sexual excitement at the event.[41]

One of the worst forms of perversion which the Persean complex can take is the rape or sexual molestation of children.[42] Yet in many societies this was a legitimate practice. Forcing little girls to marry older men, as was done in many traditional societies, is nothing more than child molestation and rape. The marriage ceremony merely legitimizes it, without in any way changing its perverse nature. Sexual intercourse in these marriages often resulted in serious injury to the child. Katherine Mayo in her book, *Mother India*, gives a list of injuries to young child brides, first compiled in 1891 by a group of women doctors then practicing in India, and presented to the Viceroy with a petition for intervention. The new brides ranged in age from "about seven" to twelve, and the list includes, "pelvis crushed out of shape," "bleeding profusely," "bleeding to death from the rectum," "so completely ravished as to be almost beyond surgical repair," "lower limbs completely paralyzed,"and "died in great agony after three days."[43] What is child molestation and rape becomes a husband's right, and therefore legitimate, when patriarchally institutionalized.

A common pattern in many brutal sexual assaults is the torture and mutilation of the genitalia of the female victim. How does this differ from the genital mutilation of young girls still practiced in many African and Islamic countries?[44] Girls at approximately the age of seven have either the clitoris or the clitoris plus the labia removed, and the vagina sewn up to be cut open on marriage. The procedure is carried out under unsanitary conditions without anesthetic except where the child is a member of the upper class. A recent study in Egypt, one of the most advanced of the Islamic countries, showed that 75 percent of the young girls in the city still suffer some form of this mutilation, as do 100 percent of the female children in rural areas.[45] Clitoridectomies were even performed in the late nineteenth and early twentieth centuries in Europe[46] and America.[47] Dr. A. J. Block, a visiting surgeon at the Charity Hospital in New Orleans, in his paper, "Sexual Perversion in the Female," described how he successfully treated a case of masturbation in a two-and-a-half-year-old girl by the excision of her clitoris.[48] Dr. Alvin Eyer, a surgeon at St. John's Hospital in Cleveland reported in his paper, "Clitoridectomy for the Cure of Certain Cases of Masturbation in Young Girls," that after the failure to stop a seven-year-old girl from masturbating by blistering and severe cauterization of the clitoris and vagina, he successfully treated the condition by a clitoridectomy, "care being taken that the entire organ, with a considerable portion of its two crura, was removed."[49] It is highly likely that the unconscious motivation for a late-nineteenth-century doctor to mutilate a little girl's genitals is similar to that which motivates some rapists to mutilate the genitals and breasts of his victim. However, male pathology becomes legitimized when placed within a mythic patriarchal framework. A less serious example of the same Heraclean misogyny is the entertainment popular in a number of Michigan bars, where scantily dressed females stand with legs apart while male customers shoot them in the breasts and crotch with streams of water from mock Uzi submachine guns.[50]

Forcing a woman into sexual intercourse without her consent constitutes rape. Yet a husband cannot rape his wife. For a husband to force his wife to have intercourse is not rape, because he is only doing what he has a right to do. Marriage thereby legitimizes what would otherwise be rape. Recently a number of jurisdictions have amended the law of rape so that a marriage relationship between the victim and the accused no longer precludes a conviction. Traditionally, husbands were allowed to beat their wives. Not only was this a right, but the mythic structure of legitimacy encouraged it as a duty where it was necessary in order to ensure a wife's obedience. Legitimacy does not remove the hostility entailed in these practices. However, it does reduce the element of risk, and to that extent Stoller's definition of perversion may not be fully met.

An examination of male fantasies, pornography, perversions, and sexually related social practices, show that they fall easily into the quadrant of male complexes, as the following chart will show:

A Quadrant Analysis of Male Sexual Pathology	
Persean Complex	**Dionysian Complex**
Pornography	*Pornography*
—child	—male masochistic-female
—exposed female genitalia	sadistic (female
—discipline of females	disciplining males)

Mild Pathology –spanking of females –humiliation of females	*Mild Pathology* –wearing of women's under- garments –humiliation by prostitutes
Extreme Pathology –wife beating –incest –paedophilia	*Extreme Pathology* –transsexualism –transvestism –some forms of homosexuality

Pornography
–erotica
 	
Mild Pathology
–some forms of psychological
    impotency
–guilt arising from sexual
    feeling
 	
Extreme Pathology
–celibacy
–self flagellation
	Pornography
	–extremely sadistic
	–snuff movies
	–homosexual
	
	Mild Pathology
	–avoidance of contact
	    with women by
	    membership in male
	    macho societies,
	    e.g., army
	
	Extreme Pathology
	–use of life size inflatable
	    or foam dolls
	–rape
	–multicide
	–macho homosexuality

Apollonian Complex	**Heraclean Complex**

THE PSYCHE OF THE POST-OEDIPAL MALE

To varying degrees, most males adopt all four defense mechanisms since they experience all four modes of dependencies. As some males mature, certain complexes come to predominate according to the nature of individual experience. A male child who is overly caressed and mildly disciplined by a strong-willed mother could develop as a Dionysian, while a child raised in an all-male atmosphere, such as that of a private school where sports and military activities are stressed, may develop a pronounced Heraclean complex. However, most males oscillate between two or more poles of the quadrant. We can place well-known figures or types of male persons on the quadrant as paradigm examples.

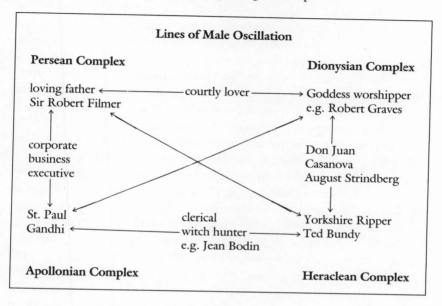

Males can also oscillate across the diagonals. A celibate Virgin Mary worshipper could oscillate between the Apollonian and the Dionysian, while a Nazi death camp commandant who goes home at night to his wife and children would oscillate between the Persean and the Heraclean. The knight who managed an estate with wife and family while worshipping his courtly lover, and at the same time periodically raping peasant women, would oscillate between the Persean, Dionysian, and Heraclean.

There is an exhilaration in exercising power over another person. The drive for power is one of the most fundamental in human experience. When power is exercised by males over females it clearly takes on a sexual dimension. This interrelationship is reflected in the widespread use of phallic imagery within the symbolism of power. The most common form of male profanity, in the English language at least, is "fuck you" or "screw you." Women are called "cunts" and to have sexual intercourse with a woman is often referred to as "poking" a woman. Underneath all this terminology and imagery is a deep pathology wherein male sexuality and male power are closely interrelated.[51]

There is a close interrelationship between transcendence as a defense against sexual dependency and transcendence as a repression mechanism against the fear of death. Transcendency as a repression of the fear of death entails the denial of the body, and a denial of the body entails a denial of sexuality. This is why the ascetic religious tradition always entails celibacy and sexual repression. As we would expect, one can also find a close interrelationship between the psychological release derived from destructive activity and the destructive drive in its sexual form. Rape, wife beating, the psychopathic murder of women are but a few examples. It is no accident that rape accompanies war almost as a natural incident.[52] In rare moments of intellectual and psychological honesty, males have testified to the intensification of the sexual drive during conflict.[53]

The practices, institutions, and systems of belief which make up the defense mechanisms against dependency and the fear of death converge in the neuroses and pathologies of heroism. Becker notes the role of heroism in the repression of the fear of death but ignores the sexual dimensions of the heroic.[54] The fight against death is heroic because it is hopeless. Because it is hopeless we are prepared to admit our fear. The facing of the fear of death is the very essence of courage. Male dependency on women is not heroic, but rather is seen as demeaning. Males generally repress it and deny it at all costs. It is difficult to be heroic with regard to an erection, and the fact that masturbation takes place in secret is indicative of something of which one is not proud. The role of seducer is far from noble, and pleading or purchasing sexual satisfaction is simply not heroic. The convergence of our defense mechanisms against sexual and emotional dependency with those against the fear of death, allows the former to surreptitiously take on the heroism of the latter.

The convergence of *Eros* and *Thanatos* within the quadrant of the heroic, and the pathology of heroism, is manifested in the life and works of the great Japanese writer, Yukio Mishima, who became himself a mythic figure in his own lifetime.[55] Mishima was born in 1925, the son of a middle-class government official and his twenty-year-old wife. His parents lived in the home of his paternal grandmother who dominated and despised her ineffectual husband, and who was disappointed by her son's lack of achievement. Less than two months after his birth, Mishima was taken from his mother by his grandmother and was reared beside her sickbed. He was raised and treated by his grandmother as if he was a girl rather than a boy. He was overprotected and seldom allowed out of his grandmother's presence, and developed into a fragile and sickly child. Thus, Mishima had difficulties in the separation-individuation stage, and in the Oedipal process. During this period of his childhood he developed a fascination with death which remained with him during his entire life, and ended with his theatrically committing *seppuku* after haranguing the Japanese National Defence Forces. The semi-autobiographical novel *Confessions of a Mask* reveals his problems relating to individuation and genderization.[56]

His death, through which he hoped he would be able to reawaken the army and the nation to the values of traditional Japanese culture, allowed him to play the role of the sacrificing hero, and was presaged in his writing by the death of several young heroes, such as Isao in *Runaway Horses* who committed *seppuku* for the benefit or welfare of the nation. His obsession with martyrdom and the death and symbolism surrounding Saint Sebastian, his Buddhism, and his fascination with the entire Japanese tradition surrounding *seppuku* all indicate a neurotic "drive" to meet the fear of death by surrendering to death. The sexual dimensions of his neurotic desire to lose the self in the deification and surrender to death is evidenced in his masochism, as reflected in the character Osamu, one of the heroes in his novel *Kyoko's House*. Osamu's mistress periodically tortures him—eventually, with his consent and complicity, to death.[57]

Although as a young man Mishima avoided war service, he was fascinated with the military and the militaristic values and spirit of the Samurai tradition. He became an ardent nationalist. He organized and was the leader of a paramilitary group which he called the *Tatenokai* or Shield Society. The soldier and samurai as conquering hero was an archetypal role which he played during the latter part of his life with his own private army. While all this was more theatrical than real, it was obviously feeding a neurotic need within Mishima. Militarism and patriotism formed the theme of several of his works.[58]

In spite of his homosexuality Mishima married and fathered two children. He married to please his mother before she died of cancer, and sought a wife through formal arrangement, setting out the stipulations that "She should be no taller than her husband, even in high heels," and that she must be pretty.[59] Another stipulation was that she would not discuss or in any way show any interest in his work.

The heroic struggle of the conqueror against death is again made manifest in Mishima's concern with his body. In 1955 he began taking intensive physical training and bodybuilding, until he eventually developed a splendid physique. Again, the passion with which he undertook this physical transition is neurotic, to say the least, and the nature of this neurosis becomes clear in his statement:[60] "But the body is doomed to decay, just like the complicated motor of a car. I for one do not, will not, accept such a doom. This means that I do not accept the course of Nature. I know I am going against Nature; I know I have forced my body onto the most destructive path of all." In his last two novels of his quartet, *The Sea of Fertility*,[61] and particularly in the last novel of that series, *Decay of the Angels*,[62] Mishima reflects his abhorrence of bodily decay and aging through the mouth of the central figure, Honda.

As artist, Mishima was a classic example of the transcending hero. In art he could have a limited success in achieving a kind of immortality. Yet because this immortality was not complete, his feeling toward it was ambivalent. In his novel *The Temple of the Golden Pavilion,* this ambivalence is expressed through the figure of Mizoguchi, who burns the golden pavilion through envy of a beauty which would outlive him.[63] The function of art as neurosis is dealt with in depth by Rank and Becker,[64] and Mishima, as a writer, fits so closely to their descriptions that one would almost think they specifically had him in mind.

Mishima's life is fertile soil for psychoanalytic speculation. He is the neurotic's "man for all seasons." The combination of a childhood which made severe neurosis almost inevitable with a natural artistic brilliance produced a paradigmatic example of the pathology of heroism, and a classic combination of all four complexes within one man.

Yukio Mishima was an individual who was more or less evenly pathological on all four points of the quadrant. Gandhi was strongly Apollonian in his asceticism. He slept with young teen-aged girls such as his niece in order to conquer all sexual desire,[65] and on the odd occasion when he "suffered" an erection he also suffered intense guilt.[66] The political philosopher Jean Bodin oscillated between the Persean, Apollonian, and Heraclean. From a philosophical perspective, Bodin is described as one of the "great political philosophers of all time," and "one of the most representative spirits of the Renaissance."[67] His list of publications in political and legal theory rarely include his infamous *De la Demonomanie des Sorciers* [Demonomania of Witches], in which he instructs how to torture, interrogate, condemn and execute witches.[68] His misogyny is reflected in numerous passages, such as "the more women, the more witches," and his instructions in the use of torture. He presided as a judge in many witch trials where he put his recommendations into practice. His misogyny and his membership in the Carmelite order of friars suggest an integration of strong Persean, Apollonian, and Heraclean complexes.

Women develop a different set of complexes according to which archetype is serving as the object of their ego ideal. The archetypal objects of the ego ideal are the same as in the male—the Mother, the Father, disembodied mind (*Logos* or Atman), and the collective. If the object of the ego ideal is the Mother-Goddess archetype serving an identification function, the ideal which the ego will seek to emulate will be that of the powerful feminine. We can refer to this as the Demeter complex.[69] If the object of the ego ideal is the archetypal father-God-king-hero serving a merger function, the female will seek to surrender her identity and objectify herself as an extension of the masculine ideal. We can call this the Eve Complex.[70] The object of the ego ideal will also be masculine if the female adopts differentiated disembodied mind (the *Logos*) as the ideal with which to identify. Body, reproduction, nature, and feminine values will be secondary, while mind, culture, and masculine pursuits will be primary. We might refer to this as the Athene complex.[71] Women may also adopt undifferentiated disembodied mind (the Atman) as the archetypal ideal with which their ego seeks to merge. Again, the object of the ego ideal will be masculine, and denial and transcendency of the body will be sought in a monastic life patterned after that of the Apollonian male. Finally, women may seek to merge their ego in the collective. However, since most collectives are brotherhoods, the object of the ego ideal would also tend to be masculine. In this way, the archetypal objects of the ego ideal which are furnished by the collective psyche to females sustain patriarchy and guarantee that the process of individuation in women prepares them for exploitation.

The complexes of the female are not parallels of the complexes of the male. Women are not pathologically driven to deny the feminine. They are much less dependent on the male for sexual and emotional satisfaction than is the male on the female. The female role in reproduction links them to life, and their animality crisis is much more benign. The quadrant of archetypal objects of the ideal as diagrammed below is not linked to collective defense mechanisms to the same degree as they are in the male.

Quadrant of Archetypal Objects of the Ego Ideal	
The Archetypal Father **The Eve Complex**	*The Archetypal Mother* **The Demeter Complex**
The Athene Complex *Disembodied Mind*	*The Collective*

A classic paradigm of the Perseus (Adam) complex is Sir Robert Filmer's *Patriarcha* which proclaims the divine right of kingship of each father over his own wife and posterity.[72] Helen R. Andelin's *Fascinating Womanhood* and Marabel Morgan's *The Total Woman* are paradigmatic examples of the Eve complex, declaring that true happiness and fulfillment for women can only be found in worship of and obedience to their husbands.[73] While several hundred years separate *Patriarcha* from these two books, they are almost perfect correlates with each other.

When it serves male purposes, women who are prepared to adopt patriarchal values and male modes of behavior are allowed to play the role of Athene in a male environment. Convents parallel monasteries, daughters who have no brothers reign as queens in order to preserve the continuity of the male blood line, and women who deny their femininity are tolerated in male-dominated professions, particularly when lip-service must be paid to an ideological demand for equality.

Ayn Rand, the passionate exponent of rugged individualism, was a paradigm example of a woman in the grips of an Athene complex. On the one hand, she was able to proclaim that "women are not inferior to men in ability or intelligence," and "may reach the ranks of Congresswomen, Senators, Judges, or any similar rank they choose."[74] On the other hand, she felt that while a woman could often do a better job as the president of the United States, no woman should become president, nor would Rand vote for a woman to be president no matter how well she was qualified.[75] She even went so far as to say, "I do not think that a rational woman can want to be President [sic],"[76] explaining:[77]

The issue is primarily psychological. It involves a woman's fundamental view of life, of herself and of her basic values. For a woman *qua* woman, the essence of femininity is hero-worship—the desire to look up to man. "To look up" does not mean dependence, obedience or anything implying inferiority. It means an intense kind of admiration; and admiration is an emotion that can be experienced only by a person of strong character and independent value-judgments. . . . Hero-worship is a demanding virtue: a woman has to be worthy of it and of the hero she worships. Intellectually and morally, i.e., as a human being, she has to be his equal; then the object of her worship is specifically his *masculinity,* not any human virtue she might lack. . . .

Now consider the meaning of the Presidency: in all his professional relationships, within the entire sphere of his work, the President is the *highest authority;* he is the "Chief Executive," the "Commander-in-Chief." . . . [A] President is the final authority who sets the terms, the goals, the policies of every job in the executive branch of the government. In the performance of his duties, a President does not deal with equals, but only with inferiors (not inferiors as persons, but in respect to the hierarchy of their positions, their work and their responsibilities).

This, for a rational woman, would be an unbearable situation. (And if she is *not* rational, she is unfit for the Presidency.

Rand's writing, her advocacy of independence for women, her belief that women do most things better than men, and her own individual influence and power, indicate that the object of her ego ideal was masculine, differentiated, disembodied mind, or the *Logos.*

It is not difficult to find examples of women who seek to merge their ego in brotherhoods of the collective, though they are generally marginalized in "auxiliary" functions. Women are the mainstay of most Christian churches. Several powerful women's movements supported and helped bring the Nazis to power in Germany.[78] Nevertheless, the drive to lose the self in the collective is not strong in women. Where it exists, it reflects an aspect of a masculine object of the ego ideal serving a merger function. It will generally be found in conjunction with a stronger Eve or Athene complex.

The two sets of quadrants can be used to represent the basic dimensions of post-Oedipal complexes in a patriarchal world. Not only do males and females oscillate along the axes of the masculine and feminine quadrants, but persons can move into the opposite quadrant or oscillate between the male and female quadrants. The tensions created in the psyches of those who function in the quadrant opposite to their biological sex can be so great that they may be driven to have their bodies surgically and hormonally altered in order to physically correspond with the gender of their psyche.

A graphic example of how the male and female quadrants can blend is furnished by the sado-masochistic practices of certain lesbian women. The book, *Coming to Power,* a collection of writings by members of a group called SAMOIS, furnishes examples of their fantasies, descriptions of their sadomasochistic practices, justifications of why they do what they do, and explanations of what they feel while doing it.[79] The most striking feature of this phenomenon is its masculinity. What the women playing the dominant role do to the women playing the submissive role is identical to what male sadists do or fantasize about doing to females, using the very same equipment such as whips, chains, handcuffs, nipple clamps, and so on. The name of the organization is taken from a pornographic novel, *Story of O,*[80] and it is clear from the title *Coming to Power* and the experiences described therein that these women experience the link between pain, power and eroticism which underlies male sadomasochism.

There are various ways in which unities can be bifurcated and bifurcations unified. The possibilities for quadrants, in turn, become multitudinous. Nevertheless, for reasons best explored through the medium of historical and psychological perspectives, certain bifurcations predominate and combine. The quadrants of complexes reflect not just the quadrants of the four male defense mechanisms (dominate and control, deify and submit, deny and transcend, and destroy and exclude), but also quadrants of archetypal objects of the ego ideal (archetypal mother, archetypal father, disembodied mind, and brotherhood of the collective). This confirms the Freudian view that human sexuality overlaps or colors nearly all human activity.

11.

THE QUADRANT OF CULTURE

POLITICAL POWER AND PERVERSION

An examination of the origins and history of social order reveals that it is a product of the Persean complex. It has its origins in the male-dominated patriarchal family. The legal paradigm is the will of the father. Monarchy, with its law as the will of the Royal Father, and religion or the combined church and state, with its law as the will of the Heavenly Father, served to legitimize patriarchy and male domination.[1] The voice of Jehovah to Eve, "and thy desire shall be to thy husband, and he shall rule over thee"[2] has taken many different forms in a variety of mythic systems. It is the voice of the male collective unconscious speaking out of its pathology which wells up out of need and dependency. It will continue to speak in the name of God's law, the law of nature, the law of the state, so long as Eve is willing to listen and obey.

Historically, there has been a clear interrelationship between patriarchal social order and male sexuality, which reflects the archetypal structure of the four complexes. Does that same relationship exist today in modern enlightened democracies where women have the vote? Do the complexes still structure modern society in the same way? One way to answer these questions would be to examine the network of complexes structuring the psyches of men in power, as reflected in the kinds of pornography they use, how they treat women in their personal lives, their sexual fantasies, and their perversions.

Pornography and perversion are the manifestations of complexes. These complexes are normal for males because they have their origins in archetypal structures of the male collective unconscious which all males share and which arise from being born of women and being biologically male. The degree of pathology, the particular combination of complexes, the degree of control, and the particular images which the archetypes take, will differ from male to male. Perversion is a matter of degree, but the archetypal structure is the same for the perverse and those not so pathological.

One could accept the above but still question its relevancy for social order. An important study carried out by Dr. Sam Janus, a professor of clinical psychiatry and a psychoanalyst, and Dr. Barbara Bess, also a professor of clinical psychiatry, show that there is a correlation between male pathology and the desire to achieve and exercise political power.[3] These two researchers had spent a number of years in the study of sexual deviance. Their private practices consisted mainly in treating young adults between the ages of twenty and thirty, most of whom were college students, and many of whom were suffering from drug addiction. As their research progressed, they discovered that many of the young women who were suffering from substance dependencies were supporting their habit through prostitution, and formed a subculture within the drug-user community. This led to a parallel study of the psychodynamic patterns of the prostitutes who ranged from street walkers with little education to high-priced call girls, a number of whom were also university students. These studies eventually led to the realization that there was a special class of "elite prostitutes" who "catered to an entirely different type of client" and "that the social and psychological dynamics of their lives could not be understood without reference to this clientele."[4] Through their interviews with these women they discovered that the majority of their clients were men with a political background. They concluded, "What these women were implying about the relationship of illicit sex to the political power structure in America encouraged us in our idea that the client was the missing link in understanding the function of the prostitute in contemporary society."[5]

This research led to the development of the project which was eventually reported in the book which they wrote with Carol Saltus, *A Sexual Profile of Men in Power*. Extensive interviews with eighty of these high-priced call girls became the source of information for the profile. Of the 7,645 clients, 60 percent, or 4,587 exercised some form of political power. The other 40 percent who were mainly wealthy businessmen, were used as a control group. On the basis of this study they reached the following conclusions:[6]

1. Men in politics are much more sexually active than the average man, and this activity continues undiminished to an advanced age.
2. Politicians are much more likely than the average man to frequent prostitutes, and they do so much more often.
3. In a high percentage of cases, politicians seek out prostitutes in order to satisfy compulsive needs for "kinky" (deviant) sex (that is, sexual acts in which neither coitus nor oral-genital sex is the primary source of gratification . . .); that the form of deviance preferred was mainly sadomasochistic in nature; and that the types of sexual release politicians most frequently request from these girls involve bondage, "discipline," humiliation, and pain.
4. In the pursuit of these pleasures, politicians on the whole spend much more money than the average man does for the satisfaction of his sexual needs.

From this study they formulated the tentative hypothesis that "men who achieve success within our political system . . . possess a sexual drive which is different both in quantity and kind from that of the average citizen . . ."[7] and that "the force of this sex drive is related directly, indeed is indistinguishable from, the power drive."[8]

To test these conclusions, a further research project was established during which sexual profiles were prepared on approximately fifteen hundred men who were active in politics at a fairly high level. The research material was obtained from extensive interviews from the call girls who were cooperating with the project, and the authors report that, "We sought confirmation from at least two other sources for each report on the sexual demands of their politician clients before we would include it as reliable data. . . ."[9] One conclusion is rather startling. They discovered that "Very seldom (only about 8 to 10 percent of the time) does a politician ask a call girl for straight intercourse." Rather, they requested practices related to "games of humiliation and dominance."[10] They go on to report that:[11]

[T]he women whom we interviewed reported that their clients went much further than that, often demanding them to act out complicated scenes of torture and mortification of the flesh, involving floggings, lacerations, mock crucifixions, and mutilation of their genitals. A few men—those who were rich enough to afford the fees (and the hospital bills) and powerful enough to suppress the media—needed to do some of these things to the women; such men were in the minority, but they included several who were at or near the top of the American political power structure.

The second study fully confirmed the thesis formulated upon the basis of the first. At the end of the second study the authors drew the following conclusion:[12]

> To understand why so many politicians are not merely promiscuous but are addicted to sadomasochistic practices for which they need the expensive services of a "paraprofessional sex therapist" requires a deeper look into the psychodynamics of the power seeker.
>
> These are characterized by a strong need to dominate which co-exists in precarious equilibrium with an equally intense need for submission. This psychological pattern is manifested outwardly by a drive to subjugate and control others (but always in obedience to some higher ideal), and in private by imperious demands for violently aggressive sex which upon orgasm abruptly become transformed into an equally sharp regression to a state of infantile dependence.

If their conclusion that the power drive is closely interrelated with the sex drive is correct, then it follows that the male need to dominate others is closely interrelated with their need to dominate women. These needs or drives are the manifestations of complexes which originate from archetypal focal points in the collective unconscious. An analysis based on the quadrant of complexes indicates that these politicians have a combination of powerful Persean, Heraclean, and Apollonian complexes, often in tension with a powerul counter Dionysian complex.

The desire to dominate is the expression in behavior of the neurotic need to inflate the self in the unconscious drive to recover the state of primary narcissistic omnipotence. Political domination, however is only one kind of self inflation. Domination is the product of power, and power can take many forms. The acquisition and exercise of economic power is another major expression of the neurotic need to inflate the self. Robert L. Heilbroner, in his book *The Nature and Logic of Capitalism*,[13] defines wealth as "a social category inseparable from power."[14] Political power can be applied physically to the body, wherein the essence of economic power lies in the capacity to make available to or deprive persons of the use and access to capital. Marx viewed capitalism as a continuing process of transformation whereby capital-as-money is changed into capital-as-commodities which in turn is changed into capital-as-more-money. In answer to the question of "What is the rationale of this endless process?"[15] Heilbroner postulates, "If we have gone beyond [Adam] Smith or Marx in this regard, it is only insofar as we can link the need for preeminence to the unconscious levels of the personality, and to the degree that we recognize the universal human capacity to treat things as extensions of the person."[16] He concludes that "the drive to amass wealth is inextricable from power, and incomprehensible except as a form of power."[17]

Both males and females may attempt to recover the lost omnipotence of primary narcissism through the inflation of the self by the acquisition and exercise of power. Males, however, are much more pathologically driven because the neurotic needs which lead them to seek and exercise political and economic power are much more interrelated with their sexuality. Political and economic power take on a sexual dimension in the male as they become functions of the Persean, Apollonian, and Heraclean complexes. Political and economic power serve the Persean complex when the power is used to dominate women. They serve the Apollonian complex when they are used to deny and transcend our mortality and the primacy of reproduction in the cycle of life. They serve the Heraclean complex when they are used to create corporate structures from which women are excluded.

Chasseguet-Smirgel has argued that "many forms of group psychology originate in the same illusion that underlies the ideology of sexual perversion."[18] Chasseguet-Smirgel and Grunberger have developed a theoretical analysis of perversion in terms of the ego ideal as the heir to primary narcissism. The ego ideal becomes the substitute of primary narcissistic perfection. Normal development of the child takes place when the maternal bond is gradually weakened. This happens in the Oedipal passage when the child shifts the object of his ego ideal from the mother to the father.[19] One of the principal causes of sexual perversion is the failure to make this shift, which marks the internalization of the difference between the sexes and the difference between the generations. Part of the process of a child becoming genderized is the acceptance of the limitations which are entailed in the differences between the sexes. Internalizing the differences between the generations entails the acceptance of the limitations of immaturity. The child cannot replace the father. His little penis cannot satisfy the mother. Perversion is the result of the child failing to internalize these differences. Reality fails to replace illusion. According to Chasseguet-Smirgel, "The necessity to maintain the illusion of the lack of difference between the sexes, which corresponds to a denial of the difference between the generations, the one governing the other, which is common to all perversions, would explain why fetishism can be found in all the perversions."[20] If the conclusions of the authors of *A Sexual Profile of Men in Power* are valid, there is a correlation between male sexual perversion and patriarchal political power. If Chasseguet-Smirgel is right about the relationship of perversion to the functions of the ego ideal, then an analysis of the role of the ego ideal in the process of individuation should help us understand the relationship between male sexuality and social order. It should then be possible to show that the structure of the collective psyche is reflected in culture.

THE FUNCTIONS OF THE EGO IDEAL

The physical separation of the child's body from that of its mother is the biological foundation for the separation of the self from the other and the start of the process of individuation. "[T]he conscious ego," Freud has stated, "is first and foremost a body-ego."[21] The separation of the child's body from that of the mother in conjunction with the original mental unity is the source of the narcissistic wound. What is lost is wholeness and connectedness, the feeling and experience of omnipotence, and the feeling of being fulfilled and without need. This loss constitutes the narcissistic wound. The wound creates a need to feel whole and connected, to feel omnipotent, fulfilled, loved, embraced, and encompassed. However, the needs of the emerging ego are inconsistent with these needs. The emergence of the ego requires separation, which negates wholeness. The ego is the link which allows the psyche to relate with reality. Reality entails a realization of limitations which deny omnipotence and completeness. Thus, the needs generated by the narcissistic wound, the inevitable result of separation, are inconsistent with the need of the emerging ego to separate.

If these needs simply pulled against each other they would cancel each other out, and the process of individuation could not take place or would be seriously hampered. Individuation is possible only when the needs generated by the narcissistic wound and the needs of the ego to individuate pull in the same direction rather than against each other. In order for the drive to heal the narcissistic wound to pull in the same direction as the drive to separate from the mother, the mother, as the ideal object with which merger is sought, must be replaced by a substitute ideal. Thus, in the process of individuation, the child requires both an ideal which it can emulate and an ideal with which it can seek to merge—a substitute for the mother. The parent of the child's own sex often serves the first function. The male child will adopt the archetype of the father as the ideal of identification, and the female child will adopt that of the mother.

One can postulate a single ego ideal which serves two different functions, an identification function and a merger function, by taking different archetypal objects, or one can postulate an agency for each function, an ideal ego and an ego ideal. Chasseguet-Smirgel points out that some French authorities draw this distinction. However, she states that for her part, she has "not judged it necessary to distinguish between ego ideal and ideal ego, in as much as any study of the ego ideal implies a study of the different forms that the attempt to recapture lost narcissism may take."[22] This book will adopt her approach in order to remain as much as possible within the Freudian tradition and avoid the proliferation of the agencies of the psyche.

Thus, the self will be viewed as consisting of the ego, which is individual, and the ego ideal, which takes at least two archetypal objects. One object serves the function of a role model, providing an ideal pattern for the ego to emulate, while the other furnishes an ideal state of being with which merger is sought. As the ego ideal embodies illusion, any contradiction between the archetypal objects serving these two different functions does not matter. The object of the ego ideal is an archetype of omnipotence, whether it is serving the identification or merger function. When the object of the ego ideal serves the identification function, it invites the ego to incorporate the other (whether persons or nature) into it as objects, and thus achieve the illusion of omnipotence, wholeness and completeness. The ego is inflated through incorporation. The merger function meets the needs of the narcissistic wound through ego surrender. Losing the differentiations and limitations of the self in a merger with the external other creates the illusion of wholeness and omnipotence. The fact that the merger and identification functions both serve to assuage the narcissistic wound further justifies the postulation of a single ego ideal as heir to primary narcissism.

There are at least four major archetypal objects of the ego ideal. They are the archetypal mother, the archetypal father, disembodied mind, and the brotherhood of the collective. All can serve either or both the identification function and the merger function. The archetypes of the mother and the father have their origins in the biological division between male and female and their respective roles in the process of procreation. The archetype of disembodied mind has its origin in mind-body dualism. This archetype manifests itself in terms of concepts such as the spirit or soul. We conceive of ourselves as owning our own bodies so that the body is not a part of the self, but is a receptacle within which the self, soul, or spirit lives. The archetype of disembodied mind serves the identification function as ideal differentiated mind in the form of the archetypal *Logos* or God. It serves the merger function as undifferentiated mind in the form of the archetypal Atman or Nirvana. Individuals relate to the divine in two ways, through identification or becoming godlike (as in the Christian tradition), or by merger, thus becoming one with God (as in the East). The archetype of the brotherhood of the collective is a manifestation of male bonding on the basis of identification and similarity. The first brotherhoods of the collective arose from the biological relatedness of sons of a common father within a family, cousins within a kin lineage, and common ancestry within a tribe.

The first object of any child's ego ideal is the mother. In this state the mother serves a merging function in that the child is drawn to her and suffers separation anxiety. For the female child, the archetype of the mother initially serves both the identification and the merger function. Like the boy, the girl must separate from the mother. In her Oedipal passage, she must substitute the archetypal father for the mother as the ideal object with which to merge. In making the Oedipal passage male children adopt the father as the object of their ego ideal serving the identification function. As described by Freud, "A little boy will exhibit a special interest in his father; he would like to grow like him and be like him, and take his place everywhere. We may simply say that he takes his father as his ideal."[23] In the development of the male ego in the normal process of individuation, the object of the ego ideal must shift away from the father or else the child cannot develop the necessary independence which individuation requires. At this stage the archetype of differentiated disembodied mind (the *Logos*) serves the identification function, and the archetype of the brotherhood of the collective serves the merger function. Thus, both archetypes pull in the same direction and toward further individuation by moving the ego away from the mother and father.

THE QUADRANT OF COMPLEXES AND THE EGO IDEAL

Complexes are the result of archetypal activity in the unconscious. The four complexes which are the heir of the Oedipal passage in the post-Oedipal male, have as their dynamic source the four archetypal objects which the ego ideal may take. The energizing force of the Persean complex is the archetypal father serving the identification function as object of the ego ideal. The essence of fatherhood is authority and control over wives and children. In emulating this pattern by identifying the ego with such an ideal monarchal father figure, the individual male will in turn be driven to exercise authority over women and children and thus inflate his own ego. The illusion of omnipotence is a fundamental characteristic of primary narcissism. Males in the grip of the Persean complex assume that they are all-powerful in relation to the women they own and possess, and to their children. Thus, the Persean complex reflects an illusion of omnipotence which suggests the internalization of an archetypal godlike father figure in the form of the object of the ego ideal.

The object of the ego ideal of women in the grip of the Eve complex is that of the omnipotent father, serving a merger function. The woman in patriarchal society is socialized to surrender herself to the father-husband and merge her life in his. The male in the grip of the Persean complex is driven to dominate and objectify the woman and incorporate her into himself, thus feeding his illusion of omnipotence. The fact that women are some of the most ardent supporters of monotheistic patriarchal father-god religions is likely due to their socialization to project their ego ideal onto the father and away from the mother. However, individual male human beings could not function alone as objects of the ego ideal for either males or females. What is being internalized is the archetypal figure of the father. It is with this that omnipotence is identified and then projected onto a particular male.

The source of psychic energy for the Apollonian complex is the archetype of disembodied mind. Chasseguet-Smirgel writes, "It is understandable that on the road back to primary narcissistic fusion the subject experiences his body as a worthless garment to be cast off in order to go beyond the bounds imposed by embodiment."[24] She refers to this as the gnostic way of thinking, and points out that, "the avatars of this are timeless."[25] The drive to "free himself from matter, from his earthly trappings," and become "an ethereal body and finally a pure luminous and spiritual essence" in a "union with the divine," which is found in a variety of forms throughout culture both in the East and West, according to Chasseguet-Smirgel "clearly represents a return to the union of ego and ideal, to the primary undifferentiated state."[26] The drive to transcend the body can be by way of identification or by way of merger of the ego with omnipotent and omnipresent mind, whether the Christian neo-Platonic *Logos,* the Atman or the Brahman without difference of Hinduism, the nirvana of Buddhism, or the Tao.

The Apollonian is much more a male complex than a complex found in females. The capacity to bear children is a natural part of being a female. The breasts and womb are essential parts of the body. Bearing children has been one of the few things for which women have been valued. It is one of the few functions which males have not as yet been able to take from them. Furthermore, in a world where females have been socialized to see their own value in terms of their physical sexual appeal to men, the drive to transcend the body will be less strong and probably will not be as pathological as it often is in males.

The brotherhood of the collective is the archetypal object of the ego ideal which energized the Heraclean complex. In *Group Psychology and the Analysis of the Ego,* Freud described the psychological processes whereby an individual would surrender the self, and the individual ego would merge into a group identity. "This extension of the ego to the group," Chasseguet-Smirgel states by way of elaboration, "allows the individuals who constitute it to taste in anticipation (or rather through a sort of hallucinatory wish fulfilment) the joy of the reunification of the ego and the ego ideal. The group is at one and the same time ego, primary object, and ego ideal finally intermingled."[27] There is an extensive psychoanalytic literature describing the psychology of group phenomena which, as has been shown by Chasseguet-Smirgel, indicates that the group becomes a very common form which the ego ideal may take. These groups are almost always brotherhoods of the male. Freud defined man as a *horde animal.*[28] Thus, for Freud, this drive to lose the self by merging in a union in the collective brotherhood substitutes the group for the omnipotent mother. The group illusion of omnipotence is projected in the form of the group ideology.

Another form of projection the ego ideal may take is that of a love object. According to Chasseguet-Smirgel, Freud saw the focal point of being in love as the projection of the ego ideal on to the love object. She quotes him as saying.[29]

> We see that the object is being treated in the same way as our own ego so that when we are in love a considerable amount of narcissistic libido over-flows on to the object. It is even obvious, in many forms of love-choice, that the object serves as a substitute for some unattained ego ideal of our own. . . . The whole situation can be completely summarized in a formula: *The object has been put in the place of the ego ideal.*

Given that the objects of the ego ideal are substitutes for the mother, the original object of the ego ideal, one can see that the beloved can be a substitute for the mother. The essential element of the Dionysian complex is the surrender of the self to a feminine object, whether the mother, the beloved, nature, or the earth.

The ego ideal can take different forms at the same time. It is not at all inconsistent for a male to take as the object of his ego ideal a god-king archetype in relationship to women, while at the same time attempting to merge his ego in a collective brotherhood. A person who enters a monastic order seeks to merge his soul (ego) with the pure mind which is God by transcending his body through sexual abstinence and fasting, while at the same time merging his ego in a collective brotherhood of the monastic order.

ARCHETYPES OF NEGATION

In the state of primary narcissism there is no split between ego and ideal, but only a blissful wholeness. This state of primary narcissism is a state of protofemininity. The first object which the ego ideal takes is the mother. While the ego ideal may later take masculine archetypes as its object, these are only substitutes for the state of primary narcissism and the original object of the ego ideal. While these masculine substitutes may serve identification and merger functions, they can never fully heal the narcissistic wound. The wound will always bleed from the unconscious because a masculine archetypal object can never fully match the structure of the ideal.

The primary object of the ego ideal will always be the archetypal mother, or the Great Mother or Goddess. Consequently, there will always be a drive within women to identify with it in terms of the role model function of their ego ideal. There is within the collective unconscious of all women a drive toward individuation in terms of power and strength. No matter how much women have been socialized by patriarchal culture the manifestation of the archetype still emerges. Often this very power and strength is co-opted by males in furtherance of patriarchy.[30]

Correspondingly the primary object of the ego ideal within the male is also the archetypal mother, Great Mother, or Goddess. Being feminine, however, the mother archetype cannot serve the identification function for the male, but only the merger function. As such, however, the drive to merge pulls the ego in the contrary direction to the drive to individuate. The power of the archetypal mother must, therefore, be negated. Negation entails driving it back into the unconscious. This is accomplished by two interrelated processes. The first is to replace the archetypal mother with the archetypal father as the object of the ego ideal. This replacement serves to pull the ego of the male toward individuation by furnishing the father archetype for the identification role of the ego ideal. The second process involves repressing the archetypal mother with negative archetypes of the female which negate the Goddess archetype.

In this manner the Goddess archetype is repressed into the unconscious from whence it activates the Dionysian complex. The power of patriarchy and the strength of the patriarchal mythic systems and archetypes attest to the power and strength of the mother-Goddess archetype and the force of the Dionysian complex. The archetypal Dionysus lurks in the unconscious of every male driving toward the surrender of the self to the female. When repressed it can produce bizarre masochistic sexual perversion in the male. The repression of the Dionysian also produces in part the equally bizarre and far more dangerous sexual perversions in which the Persean, Apollonian, and Heraclean complexes manifest themselves.

The pull of the primal mother archetype is never lost. It must be continually negated if its psychic force is to be minimized or limited. This negation is accomplished at the cultural level with a set of negative feminine archetypes which are interrelated with the mythic systems which embody, support, and maintain the Persean, Apollonian, and Heraclean complexes. One of the more powerful archetypes of negation is that of the castrating bitch. The Goddess is negated and women are offered the archetypal sacrificing Eve to serve the identification function. The archetypal structure of the Persean complex, therefore, is that of the father-king-God, and the sacrificing Eve who gives herself to the male, becomes incorporated into his life and inflates his ego. The castrating bitch generates the misogyny which drives both male and female toward the father archetype. The father archetype serves the identification function for the male and the merger function for the female.

The next step in the process of individuation for the male requires that he break away from his own father and become a father in his own right. The son replaces the archetypal father with the archetypal hero as the object of his ego ideal. This is facilitated by the adoption of a negative father archetype in the form of the destroying father who kills or eats his own sons. When the son becomes a hero, and thus free of his father, the archetype of the parental father serving the identification function is replaced by the archetype of the *Logos,* the spirit, the soul, the rational agent—the mind in its own body, acting for its own self.

At the stage of individuation in the male when the archetype of disembodied mind creates the illusion of our true selves as separate from our bodies, and merely inhabiting them, the feminine nature of the primary archetype draws us away from mind and back to the body. The dependence of the male on the female for sexual satisfaction, which is dictated by the very nature of male sexuality, continues to pull counter to the direction of individuation. A second negative archetype of the feminine continues the generation of misogyny by negating body, earth, nature, and sexuality. The Goddess archetype is replaced with the polluting siren, the bloodsucking vampire, the temptress and destroyer who kills the spirituality (pure mind) of the male, dragging him down to the earth to copulate like a dog in the mud. A more positive archetypal image of the feminine, also negating and repressing the Goddess archetype and reinforcing the archetype of disembodied mind, is that of the sexless virgin, the dutiful daughter, the servant of patriarchy. Athene and the Virgin Mary are just two of the mythic representations which this archetype can take.

The archetypal object as disembodied mind, spirit, soul, or the rational agent inside the body, generally serves only an identification function. The need to merge the ego in the ideal (m)other remains. The pull of the primary mother-Goddess archetype, though repressed, remains active in the unconscious. To serve the merger function without a return to the Goddess, the archetype of the brotherhood of the collective is adopted as the object of the ego ideal. To continue the negation of the Goddess and the repulsion of misogyny a further negative archetype of the feminine functions in the collective unconscious, that of the inferior, flawed, and weaker vessel. It can take many different forms, from that of the child-woman to that of the sexually voracious whore. Each and every form of the archetype, however, provides a reason in terms of some kind of weakness or inferiority for the exclusion of women from the collective.

The images of women which arise from these basic negative archetypes, the castrating bitch, the polluting siren, and the inferior or flawed vessel, can take many different forms. Bram Dijkstra, in a study entitled, *Idols of Perversity,* prepared an analysis of male fantasies about women during the latter half of the nineteenth century, as reflected in art and literature.[31] He refers to this period as constituting a war against women "fought on the battlefield of words and images," which had "a fundamental influence on twentieth-century modes of thinking about sex, race, and class" and which in part "permitted the implementation of the genocidal race theories of Nazi Germany."[32] The very titles of the chapters suggest the appropriate archetypal images reflected in the subject matter. The chapter entitled "Raptures of Submission" reflects the prevalence of the Eve archetype. "Poison Flowers; Maenads of the Decadence and the Torrid Wail of the Sirens" clearly suggests the archetype of the polluting siren, as does "Metamorphoses of the Vampire; Dracula and His Daughters." "Gold and the Virgin Whores of Babylon; Judith and Salome: The Priestesses of Man's Severed Head" furnishes clear examples of the archetype of the castrating bitch. These archetypal images of art and literature were rein-forced by both religion and science.[33]

Another study from a different time and place illustrates the same kind of archetypal framework. Klaus Theweleit carried out a very detailed study of the fantasies of the members of the German Freikorps which was made up of men who were hired by the Socialist Chancellor Ebert to suppress the left wing of the Socialist party and to prevent revolution.[34] Many of these men went on to become members of Hitler's Brown Shirts and the SS. In the foreword of the first volume of Theweleit's book, *Male Fantasies,* Barbara Ehrenreich writes, "The Freikorps-men hate women, specifically women's bodies and sexuality. It would not be going too far to say that their perpetual war was undertaken to escape women."[35] She states:[36]

> This hatred—or dread—of women cannot be explained with Freud's all-purpose Oedipal triangulation. . . . The dread arises in the pre-Oedipal struggle of the fledgling self, before there is even an ego to sort out the objects of desire and the odds of getting them: It is a dread, ultimately, of dissolution—of being swallowed, engulfed, annihilated. Women's bodies are the holes, swamps, pits of muck that can engulf.

As this dread lies in the hearts of all men and is "implicit in the daily relationships of men and women," Ehrenreich points out that "Theweleit refused to draw a line between the fantasies of the Freikorpsmen and the psychic ramblings of the 'normal' man."[37] She writes:[38]

> [T]he male ego will be formed by, and bounded by, hideous dread. For that which they loved first—woman and mother—is that which they must learn to despise in others and suppress within themselves. Under these conditions, which are all we know, so far, as the human condition, men will continue to see the world divided into "them" and "us," male and female, hard and soft, solid and liquid—and they will, in every way possible, fight and flee the threat of submersion. They will build dykes against the "streaming" of their own desire. They will level the forests and pave the earth. They will turn viciously against every revolution from below—and every revolution starts with a disorderly bubbling over of passion and need. They will make their bodies into hard instruments. They will confuse, in some mad revery, love and death, sex and murder. They may finally produce the perfect uniformity, the smooth, hard certainty that transcends anything that fascism aspired to: a dead planet.

In the foreword to the second volume of *Male Fantasies,* Jessica Benjamin and Anson Rabinbach comment, "He [Theweleit] shows that in this world of war the repudiation of one's own body, of femininity, becomes a psychic compulsion which associates masculinity with hardness, destruction, and self-denial."[39] They go on to comment, "The key to the fantasy of destructive violence and rage against women is the conflict between the longing for fusion and simultaneous terror at the destructive implications for the self that such merger entails. Women represent the splitting of masculine desire into the opposites of fusion/autonomy and erotic merging/armored self."[40]

The quotes above help us to understand the threat of castration (loss of the phallus) implicit in the archetype of the castrating bitch. The archetype of the Goddess is not feared by the male because she will disempower him against his will. Rather, the basis of the fear is an unconscious drive within the self to be "castrated"—to give up the burden of masculinity and merge the self in the (m)other. The Goddess is feared because of her power to activate the Dionysian archetype which will produce the Dionysian complex and lead to voluntary castration. The fear is of activating the primary archetypal object of the ego ideal, which is the Goddess. Powerful women who embody the Goddess archetype by letting it serve the identification function of their ego ideal, trigger within the male the Dionysian desire to surrender the phallus. The fear of castration coalesces the other three complexes against the Dionysian.

COLLECTIVE COMPLEXES AND THE ARCHETYPAL OBJECTS OF THE EGO IDEAL

The various forms which the object of the ego ideal can take through projection and introjection are to be found within the collective psyche as aspects of mythic structure. Myth embodies the archetypes which serve as the objects of the ego ideal. Myth not only embodies these archetypes, but embodies the entire structure of the complexes. The four basic complexes of the post-Oedipal male unite the collective defense mechanisms against animality with the archetypal objects of the ego ideal into a common mythic structure. Thus, the objects and functions of the ego ideal have a psychosexual dynamic and a relationship with the psychological dimensions of death. Sexuality, death, dependency, identification, and merger all come together in the Dionysian, Persean, Apollonian, and Heraclean complexes of the male in the post-Oedipal period. The archetypal images which the objects of the ego ideal take are framed within the context of these complexes. The mythic structure of culture is built up of the experience of vast numbers of peoples in the grip of these complexes. In turn, these complexes become an integral part of the collective psyche. They furnish the very framework for its informational organization. By sharing a common archetypal structure, the collective unconscious of the individual and the collective psyche enforce each other. Individual complexes become collective complexes and collective complexes create complexes in the individual.

The four complexes of the male psyche, which generate the pathology which we call culture and the neurotic behavior which constitutes history, are structures of the collective psyche which arise out of the pathology of individual males. As the collective psyche is internalized in the process of individuation of the male, the complexes of the individual are magnified and fortified by the complexes of the collective. Human institutions, ideologies and mythic systems map neatly onto the quadrant of male complexes:

Persean Complex	Dionysian Complex
Institutions —family —Church —state —law	*Institutions* —fertility cults and mystery religions
Ideologies —theology —political theory —social Darwinian theory —traditional psycho- analytic theory	*Ideologies* —matriarchal paganism *Myths and Mythic Figures* —the great Mother Goddesses —Dionysus —Shiva —Pan
Myths and Mythic Figures —Adam and Eve Creation Myth —Hesiod's Prometheus —Perseus —The Oresteia	
Institutions —monastic orders —universities —industry	*Institutions* —male brotherhoods —military —coming of age rituals —police forces

Ideologies
—asceticism
—monasticism
—scholasticism
	Ideologies
	—Nazism
	—militarism
	—15th through 17th century
	   Christian doctrine on
	   witchcraft and demonology

Myths and Mythic Figures —Athene (positive) —Virgin Mary (positive)	

−Lorelei (negative) −Sirens (negative)	*Myths and Mythic Figures* −Kali −Medusa −witches and related demons
Apollonian Complex	**Heraclean Complex**

The passage of the individual male psyche from birth through to adulthood can be usefully viewed as a process of individuation marked by transition from one object of the ego ideal to another. We can diagram the passage as follows:

OEDIPAL	PRE-OEDIPAL
Object of ego ideal −archetypal Father	*Object of ego ideal* −archetypal Mother
Function −identification and ego inflation	*Function* −merger
Object of ego ideal −Logos	*Object of ego ideal* −Brotherhood of the Collective
Function −identification	*Function* −merger
Object of ego ideal −Atman	*Object of ego ideal* −Hero
Function −merger	*Function* −identification
POST-OEDIPAL	POST-OEDIPAL

The four complexes of the post-Oedipal stage can be diagrammed in relationship to the archetypal objects of the ego ideal which are their focal points, in a corresponding pattern to that of the process of individuation:

Complexes of the Post-Oedipal Male	
Persian Complex	**Dionysian Complex**
Focal archetype Father-King-God	*Focal archetype* Great Mother or Goddess
Focal archetype Logos Atman	*Focal archetype* Brotherhood of the Collective Hero
Apollonian Complex	**Heraclean Complex**

The Dionysian, Persean, Apollonian, and Heraclean Complexes are not merely complexes of the psyche of individual males, but are also complexes of the collective psyche. They are reflected in the very structure of institution, mythic systems, and world views. The psychic life of each individual is played out within the following archetypal framework:

The Fundamental Archetypal Structure of the Collective Psyche in the Post-Oedipal Age of History	
The Persean Complex	**The Dionysian Complex**
Focal Archetype Father-King-God	*Focal Archetype* Great Mother or Goddess
Correlative archetype *of the female* Sacrificing wife/mother	*Correlative archetype* *of the male* The consort Dionysus-Shiva The Horned God
Negative Archetype *of the Female* The castrating bitch	

Focal Archetypes
Differentiated Disembodied
   Mind—The Logos
	Focal Archetypes
	The Brotherhood of the
	   Collective
	The Hero

Undifferentiated Disembodied Mind —The Atman	
Correlative Archetype of *the Female* The sexless virgin –Mary –Athene	*Correlative and Negative* *Archetype of the Female* The helpless child-woman The inferior or flawed vessel
Negative Archetype *of the Female* The polluting siren	–prostitute –slut –witch
The Apollonian Complex	**The Heraclean Complex**

Monotheistic father-god religions, the ideology of the divine right of kings, the patriarchal family, and male political ideology furnish an object of the ego ideal in terms of the father archetype. They provide a model with which the individual male may identify in the inflation of his ego. At the same time they legitimize the sexual and economic exploitation of women by providing them with an ideal with which they can merge. The very nature of our institutions provides the structure of the Persean complex. The glorification of nonreproduction-related activities within the institutions and mythic ideological systems of the academic world and the marketplace wherein the male seeks immortal fame reflects the Apollonian complex. Religious ideologies such as neo-Platonic Christianity, Buddhism, Hinduism, or Taoism furnish an object of the ego ideal in terms of universal disembodied mind. Political ideologies furnish an object of the ego ideal in terms of collective brotherhoods. The numbers and kinds of organizations from which women are excluded in whole or in part attest to the force of the Heraclean complex and the strength of the brotherhood of the collective as object of the ego ideal. The analysis of the archetypal structure of the male collective unconscious confirms Freud's dark vision of culture as neurosis. As Norman O. Brown states, "The doctrine of the universal neurosis of mankind, if we take it seriously, therefore compels us to entertain the hypothesis that the pattern of history exhibits a dialectic not hitherto recognized by historians, the dialectic of neurosis. . . . A reinterpretation of human history is not an appendage to psychoanalysis but an integral part of it."[41]

12.

HISTORY AS
THE EXTERNALIZATION
OF THE OEDIPAL PASSAGE

The passage of the individual psyche from birth through to adulthood can be usefully viewed as a process of individuation starting with a pre-Oedipal state of symbiotic union with the mother, passing through an Oedipal stage of separation and genderization, and progressing to a post-Oedipal stage where the individual is in the grips of archetypally-based complexes through which a healing of the narcissistic wound is sought. The premise which underlies psychoanalytic social theory is that the evolution of society follows the pattern of the evolution of the individual psyche. If this assumption is true, then history could be viewed as the externalization of the Oedipal passage. Each stage in the process would be a stage in history, and each important aspect of the psyche and the structure of the family would have its social counterpart. History, from this perspective, could be said to begin with the externalization of the pre-Oedipal stage and end when the post-Oedipal stage has been fully externalized.

The concept of a beginning of history entails the postulation of a period prior to history when human life and culture would be conceived of as nonhistorical. According to the Freudian theory of history being developed here, the beginning of history would be measured in terms of the development of a mythic structure and world view which is a projection of the pre-Oedipal stage of human existence. If we use the externali-

238

zation of the Oedipal passage as the measure of history, then we may be able to use our knowledge of isolated tribes such as the aborigines of Australia or Papua New Guinea as examples of "non-historical" peoples, in a Hegelian like sense of history. The classification of cultures into historical and nonhistorical is not meant to entail any judgment about superiority or inferiority. In the first place, this book views history as arising from neurosis and pathology. Secondly, the fact that the evidence suggests that history begins at localities where there is a great deal of interchange between diverse cultures, would suggest that history arises as a result of interchange and accumulation of mythic structures and world views rather than from any genetic difference which may have existed between various peoples.

From what we know of the lives and culture of non-historical peoples in the eighteenth, nineteenth, and twentieth centuries, we may safely conclude that male domination was the norm. Generalizing from this fact, it could well be the case that male domination of the female was common before the beginning of the first stage of history, the age of matriarchal paganism. If so, the domination of the male rested more on his greater bodily strength and on the possibly greater degree of aggression, rather than on institutions of male authority. If male domination was characteristic of nonhistorical peoples, it was very different from that of the age of patriarchy, because it did not rest upon powerful mythic systems of legitimacy. Again, generalizing from the remnants of nonhistorical peoples in the last three centuries, they are socially structured along kinship lines. Therefore, it is likely that there was less control by individual males over individual females, with kinship groupings having more control over the individual members making up the kin.

THE HEGELIAN VIEW OF HISTORY

In order to be able to view history as the externalization of the Oedipal passage, it is useful to have a theory or perspective of history which can be related to the idea of a collective psyche. A theory of history which can be linked to the theory of myth developed in chapters 3 and 4 could serve the purpose since myth would furnish the common link. The theory of history which has had the most profound effect on social theory has been the dialectical theory of Hegel, that history unfolds following a pattern of thesis, antithesis, and synthesis. This structural analysis of history was adopted by Marx in constructing the theory of history which underlies Communism. There was another equally important aspect of Hegel's theory of history which Marx did not adopt. This was Hegel's analysis of history in terms of the evolution of human consciousness or mind. This was rejected by Marx, who instead, substituted an economic-based theory of class struggle in terms of control over the means of production. There is, however, a close interrelationship between the dialectical and psychological aspects of Hegel's theory of history. It is the structure of the human mind which dictates the dialectical structure of social change. If a Hegelian theory of history is adopted, both the view of history as the unfolding of human consciousness and the dialectical structure of social change must be retained. One entails the other.

A Hegelian perspective of history seems to fit naturally with a Freudian view. Given that Freud comes out of a Germanic tradition, it would be surprising if he had not been influenced by Hegel's pioneering work on the nature of mind.[1] The interpretation of Hegel which best fits with the psychoanalytic perspective is that of Alexandre Kojève. Kojève, a young Soviet political theorist, left the Soviet Union in order to study philosophy in Germany and France. In his search for an answer as to what had gone wrong with Communism, he came to the conclusion that Marx made a fundamental error in his application of Hegel's theory of history, an error which could only be corrected by returning to the study of Hegel. Kojève became one of the world's leading Hegelian scholars, and his *Introduction to the Reading of Hegel*[2] furnishes an interpretation that makes Hegel relevant to the twentieth century.[3]

For Hegel, history ended with the establishment of the universalistic homogeneous European states following the French Revolution. According to Barry Cooper in his book, *The End of History: An Essay on Modern Hegelianism,*[4] "the content of Kojève's interpretation expresses the self-understanding of modernity. It presents the aims and premises of the modern world."[5] Cooper argues that Kojève's interpretation of Hegel is the most comprehensive and coherent account of contemporary modern political life and that Kojève has provided an exhaustive account of our own post-historical existence. In the introduction to his book, Cooper writes:[6]

Scholars have disputed Kojève's interpretation. It is not balanced. It is not fair. It is a wilful distortion of Hegel's meaning, a cunning reading that finds in the text what the commentator put there. None of that concerns us directly. The Hegel scholars are probably correct to say that Kojève has vulgarized Hegel. So far as political science is concerned, that is not necessarily a fault, nor does it detract from the value of his argument. Perhaps, however, the scholarly detraction of Kojève's interpretation is but the reflection of self-righteous anger at the desecration of a mystery. . . . The thesis is that Kojève's account of Hegel is coherent and comprehensive. What it accounts for is modern self-consciousness. That is, the content of Kojève's interpretation expresses the self-understanding of modernity. It presents the aims and premises of the modern world. . . . One should ask, therefore, not whether Kojève has got his Hegel right, but whether contemporary modern life, especially political life, is post-historical in Kojève's sense.

I will not attempt to draw a distinction between what Hegel is considered to have said and what Kojève might have added to Hegel. Rather, throughout this chapter, the Hegelian perspective will be that of Hegel as interpreted by Kojève. I am relying a good deal on Cooper's interpretation of Hegel/Kojève, as I have found it both accurate and enlightening.

Cooper himself reinterprets the Hegel-Kojèvian thesis in terms of the postmodern world of the late twentieth century. The end of history thesis remains the same, but what changes in the interpretation is the nature of the state. Cooper outlines the structure of the state in terms of the world of the post-Holocaust, the *Gulag Archipelago,* and the totalitarian regimes of the late twentieth century. Relying a good deal on Hannah Arendt's book, *The Origins of Totalitarianism,*[7] Cooper argues that "there was a connection between the emancipation of bourgeois spirituality from the constraints of medieval life, experience, and symbolism, and the eventual creation of a novel political regime, totalitarianism."[8] He concludes:

> If, as I contend, power and knowledge are constituent elements of an ensemble, the argument of Hegel, Kojève, Hobbes, or anybody else has a component of power to it. Usually this is called truth and is meant to be persuasive because it is rational. But certainly since the early days of modernity, truth has been linked to power. . . . The endpoint of this opinion, which I do not for the moment question, is the conjunction of the political science of Hobbes, Hegel, and Kojève with a political regime that has been described in various ways as totalitarian, bureaucratic, technocratic, tyrannical, and so on.[9]

There are, as Arendt has pointed out, factors in twentieth-century society which lead to totalitarianism. Well over one hundred million people have died in the twentieth century as a direct or indirect result of governmental action.[10] According to Richard Rubenstein, "The Holocaust was an expression of some of the most significant political, moral, religious and demographic tendencies of Western civilization in the twentieth century."[11] He concurs with Arendt in concluding, "Twentieth-century bureaucratized violence in all of its manifestations is an expression of contemporary Western civilization rather than a rebellion against it."[12] Social structure at the end of the twentieth century is corporate, whether in the form of multinational corporations or corporate states.[13] Corporate structure is nondemocratic because it is bureaucratic.[14] It becomes an end in itself, and as such is a mythic structure wherein personhood, or agency, and teleology are projected onto an abstract entity. The autonomous agency imputed to the corporate structure absorbs and replaces the autonomy of the individual agents.

A psychoanalytic social theory does not in any way depend upon a Hegelian view of history. A comparison of Freud with the Hegelian-Kojèvian thesis, however, allows psychoanalytic social theory to be linked with a rich and fertile theory of the evolution of history in terms of the development of mind. In particular, Hegel's concept of the universal mind has much in common with Freud's notion of the collective mind. While there are a good many differences between the two concepts, both views appear to share common presuppositions. While at times Hegel's view of the world or universal mind seems to go beyond the mere totality of culture and would appear to have an existence independent of human minds, as some form of spirit or geist, at other times his discussion appears to be closer to Freud's view.[15] In his *Philosophy of Right,* Hegel writes:

> History is mind clothing itself with the form of events or the immediate actuality of nature. The stages of its development are therefore presented as immediate natural principles. These, because they are natural, are a plurality external to one another, and they are present therefore in such a way that each of them is assigned to one nation in the external form of its geographical and anthropological conditions.
>
> The nation to which is ascribed a moment of the Idea in the form of a natural principle is entrusted with giving complete effect to it in the advance of the self-developing self-consciousness of the world mind. This nation is dominant in world history during this one epoch, and it is only once that it can make its hour strike.[16]

Charles Taylor describes Hegel's "objective spirit" as follows: [17]

[W]e can think of the institutions and practices of a society as a kind of language in which its fundamental ideas are expressed. But what is "said" in this language [are] not ideas which could be in the minds of certain individuals only; they are rather common to a society, because embedded in its collective life, in practices and institutions which are of the society indivisibly. In these the spirit of the society is in a sense objectified. They are, to use Hegel's term, "objective spirit."

According to Hegel, the stages of history are matched by dialectical shifts in world views or mythic systems which take place at a particular time and place, that is to say at a particular historical moment.

The Hegelian-Kojèvian view of the nature of history is that history ends when man fully understands "the phenomenological, metaphysical, and ontological meaning of his essential finiteness,"[18] or, in other words, his mortality. Kojève states:

Man's definitive satisfaction, which completes History, necessarily implies *consciousness* of individuality that has been realized (by universal recognition of particularity). And this consciousness necessarily implies consciousness of death. If, then, Man's complete satisfaction is the goal and the natural end of history, it can be said that history completes itself by Man's perfect understanding of his death.[19]

According to Kojève's interpretation of Hegel, death is a dialectical negation of being. Man is essentially different from the world of animals because he is conscious of his impending death, which is a dialectical and total end. Man remains free to face death voluntarily as a calculated risk, to take his own life, to negate his death by a delusion of immortality, or he can transcend death by going beyond his given existence through participating in work and action that survive him. He asserts, "It is thus that History is possible, and that is why it can be realized in spite of, or rather because of death."[20] "Thus, by (actively) negating the real natural World, Man can create a historical or human ('technical') World, which is just as real, although real in a different way."[21]

History began with the appearance of masters and slaves, and "stops at the moment when the difference, the opposition, between Master and Slave disappears." The posthistorical society will be homogeneous and universal, in that the equality of the individual will be the underlying presupposition of social order. It will be without war, in that the military will be replaced by the police. It will be based on technology, where nature is controlled and managed to serve production and consumption.

Hegel's theory of history, however, is based on a pre-Freudian view of the mind. It assumes a kind of rationality unaffected by the unconscious. This does not invalidate it as a theory of history, but it does presuppose a particularly limited view of what it means for humans to understand their death. A "perfect understanding" of one's death would entail an acceptance of one's animality as well.

Individuals accept and comprehend their mortality when they no longer repress the knowledge of their animality (which includes not only the acceptance of one's death, but the acceptance of one's sexual and emotional dependencies on others) and their physical dependencies on the body and on nature. Individuals transcend their Oedipal passage when they have fully accepted their animality and assimilated it into their psyches. Their animality is, of course, their true humanity. Similarly, the collective psyche would transcend its historical Oedipal passage when the nature of human animality has been assimilated into the mythic structures and world views of humanity, so that a knowledge and an acceptance of the human condition is assimilated by the individual as a part of his or her cultural heritage. This would entail the elimination of hierarchical mind-body, culture-nature, and gender bifurcations. While symbols and myth would remain, a high degree of illusion would be replaced by a more accurate view of reality.

THE DIALECTICS OF HISTORY

Hegel's dialectical methodology furnishes a useful tool for psychoanalytic social theory. The thesis describes the real when it is taken as a given; the negation of the given is the antithesis which describes the aspect of negativity which is now seen in the real; and the synthesis comes to describe the real in a new totality which in turn can become a new thesis.[22] All mythic systems contain both truth and illusion. The antithesis denies the illusion in the thesis and substitutes a new illusion. The synthesis denies or negates the illusion in the antithesis and integrates the truth left in the thesis with that in the antithesis, although the synthesis itself may incorporate new illusion.

The parallels of the Hegelian-Kojèvian view of history to psychoanalytic social theory are fairly obvious. The need for recognition can be explained in terms of the repression of the fear of death. The Oedipal passage is dialectic in its nature in that the separation from the mother entails a negation of the mother through identification with the father. The resolution of the tensions between separation and engulfment anxieties is structured dialectically. The process of individuation whereby the self separates from the mother entails a negation of the mother as other. Full individuation requires a concept of our identity as a synthesis in which we recognize both our singularity and our commonality. The acceptance of our animality requires a synthesis in which we recognize both our identification with nature, and our uniqueness as the creature with mind—the biped primate which developed a cortex.

Hegel and Kojève give a masculine view of history and its ending, and of the dynamics of the master-slave conflict which constitutes the unfolding of history. According to the Hegelian-Kojèvian view, the need for the recognition of the self leads to master-slave relationships. The master enhances his sense of self by turning the slave into an object to serve the master's needs. The slave seeks freedom by negating his slavish nature. "[A]ll of History," according to Kojève, "is nothing but the progressive negation of Slavery by the Slave, the series of his successive 'conversions' to Freedom. . . ."[23] Underlying all class struggles, however, lies the struggle of males to dominate females, and of females to assert their independence.[24] The split and antagonisms between the sexes is the basic and fundamental division of humankind. It is this which has produced the genderization of society and culture. It represents a class struggle more far-reaching than that between capital and labor, master and slave, caste, color, or race. It was the first to appear at the beginning of history, and if the end of history is to be marked by the resolution of class struggle, it will be the last to disappear. If so, then an end to history, arising from a perfect understanding of our animality, would mark the end of patriarchy.

A PSYCHOANALYTIC VIEW OF HISTORY

For at least a hundred thousand years, *homo sapiens* have lived throughout the world in small groups, gathering food, hunting, and fishing. We know little of human social organization in early times, but if it resembled that of primates and many other mammals, it was what Marilyn French terms *matrifocal* or *matricentric*—the mother-child relationship being the strongest social bond.[25] While it is quite conceivable that there was some form of male dominance based on the superior size and possibly greater aggressiveness of the male, there is neither any evidence, nor good reason to believe, that anything like the idea of "male authority" existed. Patriarchal culture arose just a few thousand years ago as a negation of the human identity with nature.

In the pre-Oedipal stage the child seeks a close connection with the mother while it gradually develops a sense of her or his own self. The male child wishes to possess the mother and often sees the father as a rival. In the pre-Oedipal stage of history the collective psyche projects the mother onto the earth, or the cosmos, thus externalizing the archetypal figure of the mother as Goddess. The collective wish is that the earth and/ or nature is nourishing and benign, and that even when we are taken by death, we are taken back into the womb of the earth-mother. The wish leads to the illusion that the earth is as we wish it to be. What is repressed is the general harshness of the environment and the constant need for struggle to survive. Myth serves this twofold function of maintaining the illusion and repressing the reality by identifying the category of the social with the natural, thus anthropomorphizing nature, and presenting "facts belonging to one category in the idioms appropriate to another."[26] The mythic structure, by relating the mother to *the* mother (Goddess), women to the earth, the earth to mother, thus transforms the first stages of history into nature. From the perspective of the law, the pre-Oedipal stage of history was one of custom and social practices within which women played a major role.

In the Oedipal stage of the child's development, the child assimilates the incest taboo imposed through the authority of the father. The male child identifies with the father and hopes to be like him and possess a mother-wife of his own. The female child internalizes the nurturing role which she sees her mother play. The father, for the child of either sex, becomes an external figure which the child uses as an opposite pole to draw it away from the mother in its own process of individuation. In the Oedipal stage of history the projection of the collective psyche shifts from the earth to the sun or to the heavens, with the archetype of the father as god or the Heavenly Father. The process of collective individuation of the human race from earth and nature leads to a view of humanity as a unique creation, separate from and master of earth, animals, and nature. This entails a negation of the feminine in the mythic proclamation of the superiority and mastery of the male over women, earth, and nature. In this sense, the age of matriarchal consciousness was the thesis, and patriarchy, its negation, the antithesis.

In the post-Oedipal stage of development of the individual psyche, when the process of individuation has produced a strong ego, the male develops toward and becomes a father in his own right, and an equal among other fathers. In the post-Oedipal stage of history the nature of human hierarchy changes. Oedipal hierarchy is based on the biological properties of progenitorship and order of birth—father over progeny, first-born over later-born, and highborn over lowborn. In the post-Oedipal stage of history all males are equal in the brotherhoods of man. Hierarchy takes the form of corporate structures such as the state, in which any of the brotherhood who succeed in climbing the corporate ladders can achieve power. The struggle is open to all members of the brotherhood. The post-Oedipal stage of history is the state of corporatism or "fraternal patriarchy."[27]

If the development of the individual psyche is a process of individuation which starts with the separation of the self from the mother, and continues to a state of individual independence, and if the development of the collective psyche follows a similar pattern, then we should find, at the beginning of history, a close identification between humans and their natural environment. Humans would view themselves as a part of the earth, at one with the trees and animals of the forest, and not as unique creatures. The path of individuation for the collective psyche would be one of a gradual recognition of the uniqueness of humankind, with rationality separating humans from everything else.

The end of history must entail an acceptance of reality through a synthesis in which all people become free by recognizing their individuality. This must be defined in terms of each person's particular uniqueness and the agency which all humans have in common with each other, and our animality which we have in common with all life on the planet. The trans-Oedipal stage of human existence, which would correspond with the Hegelian end of history, would be reached when there is a synthesis of individuality and community within the individual self. This could become possible when both the recognition of our animality-mortality and our individual uniqueness as autonomous agents is externalized into the mythic structure of culture. Each child would assimilate through the process of enculturization an identity as an autonomous agent, but also a part of the whole; a part of nature rather than a god above nature using and manipulating it; a biped primate with a cortex sharing the earth with other creatures. In such a world all would be free and would have a sufficiently strong sense of the self that we would not require recognition through the master-slave relationship to reinforce identity. Thus, class and gender struggles would be ended, and so in a Hegelian sense, history would end.

THE DIALECTICS OF PATRIARCHY

Patriarchy has a dialectic of its own. The age of patriarchy falls into three periods. The first, the Oedipal stage of history, is the age of patriarchal monarchy. Authority is vested in the Heavenly Father, the royal fathers, and the monarchal fathers of the individual and extended families, the paterfamilias. The family is the community, and communities are families, and there is little place for individuality.[28] The second stage of patriarchy is the age of liberalism and individualism. The various ideologies of equality and the rule of law negate the authority of the fathers and kings, and proclaim the antithesis or negation of parental authority, the autonomy of the individual. In the last, post-Oedipal, stage the antithesis of autonomous individuality is negated by the synthesis of the egalitarian corporate state, where both community and individuality are recognized in the corporate structures of late patriarchy.[29] The corporate structures of the post-Oedipal stage of history are sufficiently powerful that under a democratic, egalitarian guise, the mythic structure could be frozen, thus blocking further development of both the individual and the collective psyches.[30]

Totem and Taboo is generally considered to be one of the weaker of Freud's great essays on psychoanalytic social theory.[31] In this work, Freud postulated a prehistoric traumatic event where at the dawn of civilization the primal violent and jealous father drove away his sons and kept all the females for himself. "One day the brothers who had been driven out came together, killed and devoured their father and so made an end of the patriarchal horde."[32] Then in their guilt they form the brotherhood of man who divide up and take possession of the women.

Freud appeared to believe that this was an actual historical event, the aftermath of which lived on within the collective psyche, fueled by the ambivalence within each male toward his own father. Most people discount the possibility that at a particular period of time an actual primal murder took place which lives on in the collective memory. Freud has recognized an archetypal pattern which, rather than lying at the beginning of history, is a pattern for the unfolding of history itself. The killing of the father represents the rebellions and revolutions which overthrow monarchy. Thus, it is the pattern of the shift from the Oedipal stage of history to the post-Oedipal stage characterized by the brotherhood of the collective.

There was an actual and historical parricide which took place within the collective psyche. The father has truly been murdered by the collective brotherhood. Freud's mistake, however, was to place the murder prior to history rather than within history. The killing of the father has occurred historically in the beheading of Charles I, the guillotining of Louis XVI, and the shooting of Nicholas II. The death of the father is the death of the paterfamilias, the royal father (monarchy), and the death of God (the Heavenly Father), with the rise of the brotherhood of man. With the triumph of the brotherhood, the women are divided among the brethren within a social contract that recognizes each individual's authority over his wife and children.[33] Each individual male, in a symbolic sense, murders his own father by achieving independence. When the ego takes over from the superego, the internalized father dies. To "murder" one's father by achieving independence is a normal part of individual development in the male. This desire, no doubt, is fed by Oedipal hostility and jealousy.

Freud was right in putting great stress on the theme of parricide.[34] The archetypal murder that he postulated in *Totem and Taboo* can be illustrated in many ways. To reject the religion or values of one's father is a way of killing the father within (freeing the ego from the superego). The rejection of the paterfamilias or patriarchal extended family head, the death of kings by the revolutionary brotherhood, the rejection and denial of the father Gods whether Zeus or Jehovah, are all part of the process of individuation of the collective mind which parallels the pattern of individuation of the individual psyche by first internalizing the father within the psyche as the superego, and then rebelling by taking responsibility for one's actions.

There is very little historical evidence for an era in human prehistory of Freud's primal horde. The primitive form of human social organization is that of kinship, and not "that of a horde ruled over despotically by a powerful male."[35] Kinship societies are generally highly structured, consisting of nuclear families, extended families, minor and major lineages, and tribes. The appearance of a strong leader such as a chieftain appears to be a later development.[36] Freud describes a group or horde as consisting of "many equals" who can identify themselves with one another, held together by a leader.[37] The kind of equality that the group entails, according to Freud's own definition, is a late rather than early development in the evolution of social order.

Freud recognized the identification between the group and the ego ideal, in that the ego ideal was projected onto the group, and in particular onto its leader.[38] He describes the need of the ego to lose itself by uniting with the ego ideal and the "feeling of triumph when something in the ego coincides with the ego ideal."[39] The problem stems from Freud's convergence of the superego and the ego ideal. When these two agencies are differentiated along the lines argued for by Janine Chasseguet-Smirgel,[40] Freud's intuitions of a historical and collective parricide can be reconstructed to conform with and help explain the evolution of social order.

A psychoanalytic social theory rooted in a Hegelian view of history reveals a possible (but not necessarily probable) way out of the pessimistic vision we are left with in the Hegel-Kojève-Cooper view of history ending with the totalitarian-egalitarian corporate state. At the beginning of history humans viewed themselves as a part of nature. History is the process of the development of mind. The development of mind takes place by negating body and nature. In the process of negating nature in the evolution of human consciousness, the Oedipal passage of individuals becomes projected onto the developing mind of the collective with the result being that humans are dichotomized through genderization on the mind-body and culture-nature bifurcations.[41] Females become identified with nature and body, and males with mind and culture. The negation of nature entailed in the development of mind is internalized as gender bifurcation between male and female. Patriarchy is the negation of women. Just as the thesis was negated in the parallels of body-nature-female and mind-culture-male, the synthesis, which is the negation of the negation, must also be paralleled by a healing of these bifurcations. For humans, there can be no synthesis of mind and body, nature and culture, individual and community, without the synthesis of male and female.

The path to this synthesis does not lie in a balance between fundamental rights and social equality, as this is only a synthesis within the dialectics of patriarchy. It cannot lie in some type of Jungian androgyny because androgyny is not a negation,[42] nor can it lie along the path of either liberal feminism or socialist feminism. Only radical feminism is a negation of patriarchy. Patriarchy itself is only an antithesis of a larger dialectic. The synthesis of this larger dialectic would deny patriarchy and would lead to the acceptance and internalization of our animality in bringing together mind and body, culture and nature, self and other, and male and female. The end of history, therefore, must entail the end of misogyny. If misogyny does not end, neither will history, and there will be no synthesis, no acceptance and internalization of the knowledge of our animality.

The end of history should take place when the Oedipal passage of the collective psyche has been fully externalized and then transcended. The collective psyche can transcend the Oedipal passage only when individuals are able to transcend it. The post-history stage of human existence must commence with the emergence of trans-Oedipal individuals. Trans-Oedipal persons will be those who have faced, accepted, and internalized their animality; who while recognizing their unique individuality also accept themselves as a part of the whole; who if male have purged themselves of misogyny, and if female have rejected the patriarchal image of diminished self and reclaimed their power by transferring their ego ideal from a masculine to a feminine archetypal object.

The trans-Oedipal collective psyche will be the totality of a culture and of a world view which does not pathologically bifurcate or hierarchicalize body and mind, culture and nature, or male and female. A dialectical tension may still be present as in a yin and yang balance, but integration will co-exist alongside of playful and nonpathological swings. In such a world neither fathers nor authority would be necessary for individuation. Humans will always individuate and struggle with the burden of the consciousness of animality. Consequently, as a species we will continue to dream, and neurosis will be the norm. However, in such a future state we may have rid ourselves of widespread pathology.

SHIFTS IN MYTHIC PARADIGMS AND SOCIAL CHANGE

The dynamic force of history derives from the mythic structures produced by the collective psyches. The mythic structures arise from the psychological forces or "drives" of the individuals as they are collectively projected or externalized, and the paradigms of reality or nature which peoples create or choose. History moves from one state to another as the result of the right combination of projected psychological drives in conjunction with a paradigmatic shift in the collective view of nature or reality.

These paradigmatic shifts appear to take place where there is cross-fertilization of ideas between peoples. Thus, civilization appears to arise only where different peoples come into contact with each other through travel and trade along major routes of traffic such as roads, rivers, or ocean coasts. Tribes which are isolated in valleys between high mountains and/or are isolated by oceans, appear to remain culturally stable over long periods of time. The cultures of the aborigines of Australia or the mountain tribes of Papua New Guinea, for example, have probably changed very little in the past ten, twenty, or even thirty thousand years.

The individual psyche from birth onward is driven to separate from the mother and to individuate by establishing its own identity. The collective psyche follows the same pattern in terms of separating from mother earth and nature, and individuating as a species by developing a sense of the uniqueness of mankind. At the same time, there is also a drive to give up the burden of individuality by losing the self in the other. In ego psychology, these drives are conceptually dealt with in terms of object relationship, ego functioning, and narcissism. Psychoanalytic social theory lacks a vocabulary and tight theoretical analysis to elucidate this process in the collective psyche.

The process of individuation within the individual psyche is characterized by crises, complexes, and stages, rather than an even and gradual evolution. The process of individuation of the collective psyche appears to follow a similar pattern. Rather than a gradual evolutionary process, change appears to take place in terms of paradigmatic shifts brought about by changes in the collective view of nature when new facts are uncovered or discoveries are made. The shift from matriarchal consciousness to patriarchy, that is to say from the pre-Oedipal to the Oedipal stage of history, appears to have been triggered by the eventual recognition of the uniqueness of human consciousness. The discovery of the role of the male in procreation produced the archetype of the horned God, the consort to the Goddess who was essential to her fertility. The development of science in ancient Greece, which has been described as the shift from *mythos* to *logos,* marks the beginning of the post-Oedipal stage of history in the West.

13.

THE PRE-OEDIPAL STAGE
OF HISTORY

THE ARCHETYPAL MOTHER AS OBJECT OF
THE EGO IDEAL

The mother archetype is a partial aspect of the archetypal feminine.[1] The archetypal feminine and the archetypal masculine are the manifestations within the collective psyche of the experience of being born and living as a female or a male. They reflect the structure of what is universal in those kinds of encounters of the self with others of the same and opposite sex within and between the generations. The most complete study of the mother archetype is that of Erich Neumann in his book, *The Great Mother*. He writes:[2]

> When analytical psychology speaks of the primordial image or archetype of the Great Mother, it is referring, not to any concrete image existing in space and time, but to an inward image at work in the human psyche. The symbolic expression of this psychic phenomenon is to be found in the figures of the Great Goddess represented in the myths and artistic creations of mankind.
> The effect of this archetype may be followed through the whole of history, for we can demonstrate its workings in the rites, myths, symbols of early man and also in the dreams, fantasies, and creative works of the sound as well as the sick man of our own day.

This archetype furnishes the first object of the ego ideal in the developing child, and furnished the first object of the ego ideal in the evolution and development of the collective psyche. This archetypal structure has been built up from projections of the unconscious onto the cosmos whereby the earth is viewed or experienced as feminine and as a life-giving mother, and introjection whereby women are identified with the unconscious. These interrelations form the foundation of mythic structures whereby the natural world is differentiated from, contrasted with, and identified with the social. These contrasts and identifications have their origin in the similarities and differences we attribute through meaning. The reproductive power of women is linked with the fertility of the earth. The loss of the boundaries of the self entailed in sexual ecstasy, meditation, euphoric drug experience, or death, is linked in terms of understanding and meaning with the original state of narcissistic union with the mother.

As discussed in chapter 11, the archetypal object of the ego ideal can serve either an identification or a merger function When the gender of the archetypal object of the ego ideal matches the gender of the self, the object of the ego ideal functions as a pattern to be followed or assimilated. The ego seeks to be like its ideal. When the gender of the ego ideal is the opposite of the gender of the self, then the self seeks to lose its unique identity by merging with the object of the ego ideal. When the mother archetype is the object of the ego ideal of a woman, she identifies with it and becomes a goddess in herself. When the gender of the object of the ego ideal of the woman is masculine, she seeks to merge with it by giving herself up to it. In an earlier chapter this constellation was referred to as the Eve complex. When the self is male and the object of the ego ideal is masculine, the male seeks to emulate the ideal by becoming heroic, monarchical or godlike. When the self is male and the gender of the object of the ego ideal is female, the self seeks to surrender to and merge with the feminine ego ideal. This constellation was referred to as the Dionysian complex.

In this century many people (primarily females, but some males as well), have shifted the object of their ego ideal from masculine to feminine. This shift has taken different forms in different persons. Some have revived fertility cult paganism and some actually worship a literal Goddess.[3] Most, however, regard the Goddess as "the focal point of religious and spiritual feelings."[4] Many have sought all they can learn about this ancient and first world religion[5] and have reinvented and designed rituals and beliefs where what went before has been lost.[6] Most of the groups practicing fertility cult paganism sprang up in the early sixties. It is difficult to form a judgment about the size of the movement since most groups are small and relatively unstructured. The practicing groups alone, however, number in the thousands.[7] Many women have entered into the practice through feminism.[8] Newsletters and journals keep people of similar interests in touch with each other.

Others who wish to keep some relationship to traditional theology, and who identify the Divine with ultimate reality, seek to view the Divine as androgynous.[9] Still others choose to conceive of the Divine as Goddess or Mother rather than as Heavenly Father.[10] The changing of the gender of the Divine from masculine to feminine changes the mythic structure of ultimate reality from a teleological mind to nature struggling to produce life. Such a shift avoids the problem of evil which haunts patriarchal monotheism—why would an all-powerful Divine being create anything less than perfection? The Divine as Mother, like any mother, has no direct control over the sex or physical well-being of her child, but unconsciously struggles to bring forth life.

Some women "regard the image of the Goddess purely as metaphor, a symbol of women's reclamation of personal power and the right to determine the path of our own lives."[11] Still others use the concept of the goddess as an archetypal image which they internalize and with which they identify.[12] They infuse the power and strength of the Goddess images into their own sense of their selves. For women who have had a masculine object of their ego ideal, and consequently a negative image of their own selves, use of the Goddess image can be a powerful tool for inner change. Feminists are powerful and strong persons. The very essence of feminism is a positive view of women and mothers. The process of politically changing from a liberal, conservative, or a socialist to a feminist requires an inner psychological transformation of the object of the ego ideal from the masculine archetype to the feminine. This changes the process of relating the ego to the ego ideal from one of losing or surrendering the ego to the object of the ideal, to one of identification with the ideal. As one feminist stated, "The Goddess is everywoman without exception throughout the world. When they ask us 'Who is the Goddess?' you can always tell them 'I am.'"[13]

The male who replaces the father-king-hero masculine archetype as object of his ego ideal with that of the mother-Goddess feminine archetype seeks to merge with or surrender the ego to the ego ideal. The complex is well expressed in the song of a male Hindu Goddess *bhakta* (devotee):[14]

O Mother, make me mad with Thy love!
What need have I of knowledge or reason?
Make me drunk with Thy love's Wine:
O Thou who stealest Thy bhakta's hearts,
Drown me deep in the sea of Thy love!

The adoption of the female archetype as object of the ego ideal also brings with it a transformation in one's views about and attitude toward nature and the earth. Many feminists are actively engaged in the struggle to protect the environment, or at least are sympathetic to that cause.[15] They recognize that there is a direct relationship between the exploitation by males of females, and the exploitation of the environment and of nature.[16]

THE AGE OF MATRIARCHAL CONSCIOUSNESS

In almost every culture, nature and the earth are characterized as feminine or female.[17] In most languages where nouns are genderized, nature and the earth are classified as feminine, and in nearly all languages the feminine pronoun is used in reference to the earth or to nature. Languages abound with analogies between the earth and women or mothers, such as "mother nature," "virgin resources," "rape of the earth," and "fertile land." The following passionate *cri de coeur* made by Smohalla, a late nineteenth-century American Indian prophet of the Umatilla tribe, furnishes a paradigmatic example of the identification of mother and earth: [18]

> You ask me to plough the ground? Shall I take a knife and tear my mother's bosom? Then when I die she will not take me to her bosom to rest. You ask me to dig for stone? Shall I dig under her skin for her bones? Then when I die I cannot enter her body to be born again. You ask me to cut grass and make hay and sell it, and be rich like white men! But how dare I cut off my mother's hair?

The state of symbiotic union of the child and mother would have its correspondence with the symbiotic union between people and nature. There is a good deal of anthropological evidence that within the mythic structures of so-called primitive or primal peoples there is a close identity between people and animals and plants such as trees. Such peoples also have a close identity between themselves and the lands which they have traditionally occupied and traversed. They see themselves as belonging to or related to the land rather than owning it. There is little question that the concept of ownership of land brought by the European invaders was very different and quite alien to that of the aboriginal peoples whom they were displacing in the colonized parts of the world. If this is true of aboriginal societies, how much more is it likely to be true of that period of early history when throughout the centers of nascent civilization nature and the world were anthropomorphized as a nurturing mother.

Archaeological evidence, the analysis of ancient mythic structures, and an examination of humankind's earliest written records, are pointing more and more to the conclusion that long before the monotheism of the Hebrews or the pantheons of gods of the Greeks, Norse and Germanic peoples, or Aryan-Indians, a common form of religion, matriarchal paganism, existed throughout almost all of Europe, the Mediterranean basin, and much of Asia. This religion was the first expression of human spirituality within a cultural context. There is little question that it was passed from tribe to tribe and thus spread widely. Whether it had a single source of origin or not is not known. It likely had several. Its origins may go back as far as 10,000 B.C. or even earlier, but it was in full bloom by the sixth millennium B.C., and during the Neolithic Age.

Throughout much of Europe, the Middle East, India, and China, (as well as many other parts of the world) are to be found numerous female figurines and sculptures, dating from the Upper Paleolithic period through into the Bronze Age, and even beyond, which suggest an age of matriarchal consciousness when a Goddess was worshiped. Archaeological evidence conclusively establishes Çatal Hüyük in Anatolia, the Minoan culture of Crete, ancient Sumeria, and the pre-Aryan Dravidian culture of the Indus valley as having similar well-developed religions sharing many of the same kinds of rituals and symbols. In the very earliest mythologies, the mother parent was exalted in her procreative powers which were identified with the Earth. It is likely that this religion was fairly monotheistic, in that the various forms which the Goddess took were manifestations of the same being. The Babylonians knew the Goddess as Ishtar, the Phoenecians as Astarte, the Celts as Cybille, and the Egyptians as Isis. Given the diversity of cultures, the structure of this ancient religion remains remarkably similar.

The Goddess is a projection of the archetypal image of the mother onto the cosmos. The holy earth itself was conceived as feminine and as the mother of all life.[19] The focus of worship was the creative power of life embodied in the form of the mother. The Goddess figure formed a common link and unifying theme between women and the earth. The creative powers of the earth were embodied in women, and femaleness was embodied in the earth. Given the power of this archetype, it is surprising how little influence it would appear to have on our contemporary world view.

The age of matriarchal consciousness is not a part of our standard historical chronologies. There is no reference to it in high school or college history texts, and a general disbelief prevails that such an age could even be possible.[20] There are few university courses which deal with it, and it simply does not enter in to our perceptions about our past. Yet, this absence is not due to a lack of evidence nor even of scholarly neglect. There are numerous books about the age of Goddess worship. Some are works of classical scholarship such as Robert Briffault's *The Mothers: A Study of the Origins of Sentiments and Institutions*,[21] first published in 1927, or E. O. James's *The Cult of the Mother Goddess*.[22] Many others are careful scholarly works by female academics which would meet all the standards by which males measure the objectivity and methodology of scholarship. These include books such as *The Goddesses and Gods of Old Europe*,[23] by Marija Gimbutas, or *The Creation of Patriarchy*,[24] by Gerda Lerner. The Jungian scholar, Erich Neumann's book, *The Great Mother*,[25] is an important contribution from a psychological perspective to the scholarly literature. There are many other important books which approach this history from a feminist perspective.

What is significant, however, given all of the books written about the age of Goddess worship, is that there have been no serious attempts to discredit the thesis or respond to the evidence by giving an alternative explanation. It is not difficult to see why the world of male scholarship has ignored the age of matriarchal consciousness. It would totally undermine the implicit or express premise of patriarchal history and institutions that women are inferior and that male domination is natural. Nevertheless, given the evidence from myth and archeology of the existence of an age of matriarchal consciousness in many early societies, it is unusual that there would not be more reference to it in our earliest writings. This lack of reference in recorded history, however, can be accounted for by conscious suppression and unconscious repression.

If the history of the Semitic peoples is at all typical, then we have an answer to this problem. Much of the Old Testament is concerned with the suppression by the Israelites of the Goddess-worshiping fertility cults which prevailed amongst their neighbors, and often pervaded their own society.[26] Part of the attack on matriarchal paganism consisted of negating it by seldom mentioning the Goddess and instead placing the attack against the male consort.[27] Thus, the Old Testament refers many times to the worship of Baal (the lord), who was merely the consort to the Goddess Astarte, but not the Goddess herself. There are a few indirect references to her as the Whore of Babylon. Yet, much of the entire Old Testament is a record of a fierce and often bloody struggle between the Goddess-worshiping fertility cults and the patriarchal monotheism of the Hebrews. There are many references to Israel "whoring" after other gods, rather than goddesses.[28] The identification of whoring with pagan worship, and the abhorrence against fornication which permeates the Old Testament, are easily explained in light of the prevalence of the performance of the sexual act as a magical ritual to achieve the fertility of flocks and crops which was characteristic of much of matriarchal pagan worship.[29] God commands the Israelites to cut down the sacred groves and destroy the phallic symbols associated with Goddess worship.[30] Castrated males were not permitted to worship in the congregation of the faithful.[31] The ruthless extermination of conquered peoples proclaimed in the name of Jehovah was for the express purpose of wiping out Goddess worship, and preventing it from spreading amongst themselves.[32] The prevalence of Goddess worship amongst the Hebrews is referred to in several places in the Old Testament, but none is as clear as the response of the Jews to Jeremiah: [33]

> As for the word that thou hast spoken unto us in the name of the Lord [Jehovah], we will not hearken unto thee.
> But we will certainly do whatsoever thing goeth forth out of our own mouth, to burn incense unto the queen of heaven, and to pour out drink offerings unto her, as we have done, we, and our fathers, our kings, and our princes, in the cities of Judah, and in the streets of Jerusalem: for then had we plenty of victuals, and were well, and saw no evil.
> But since we left off to burn incense to the queen of heaven, and to pour out drink offering unto her, we have wanted all things, and have been consumed by the sword and by the famine.
> And when we burned incense to the queen of heaven, and poured out drink offerings unto her, did we make her cakes to worship her, and pour out drink offerings unto her, without our men?

Throughout the Old Testament, the description of pagan worship referred to sacred groves of trees and high places, which were the standard places of worship in matriarchal paganism.[34]

There is a problem, however, with the thesis of the existence of a period of prehistorical matriarchal consciousness which is more difficult to deal with, and that is the argument which was raised by anthropologists in their attack on Bachofen. There simply is little or no evidence of matriarchal consciousness in kinship and tribal societies.[35] If humans progress through a stage of matriarchal consciousness at some point in their societal development, then, so the argument goes, we should have discovered some aboriginal people who were at this stage, whether in Africa, North or South America, New Zealand, New Guinea, or Australia, yet no such peoples have been found. Kinship in nearly all these societies ranges from weak to strong male domination.

I have suggested earlier that in the age prior to the rise of civilization, some kind of male dominance might have existed among humans, based on the superior strength and greater degree of aggressiveness of the male. This could account for the lack of evidence of matriarchal consciousness among isolated tribal and kinship societies. Whatever the explanation is, it would appear to be the case that matriarchal consciousness appeared at the centers from which what we call civilization developed and spread. It formed the basis of a world view and religious and spiritual mythic structure which spread throughout most of Europe and much of Asia. It lasted for several thousands of years and then disappeared. The age of matriarchal consciousness and the spread of Goddess worship mark the beginnings of a collective psyche which transcends the collective psyches of individual tribes. The pattern of history is for smaller collective psyches to become immersed in larger structures, as humans move toward a single collective psyche and pattern of individuation. What should strike us as truly strange is the present universality of phallocentric and patriarchal culture, given that women make up more than fifty percent of the human race. The astounding fact requiring explanation should be the suppression of women, and their exclusion from the construction of mythic systems and world views.

THE DIONYSIAN COMPLEX IN THE
PRE-OEDIPAL AGE

It would appear that in the earlier stages of Goddess worship, only a Goddess was recognized. Later, a son or consort appeared in conjunction with the Goddess, whose function it was to fertilize Her. It seems reasonable to speculate that the discovery of the role of the male in procreation was the event which triggered the appearance of the consort and of the phallus in a variety of forms and images as an important symbol in matriarchal paganism.

The archetypal images of the female and male of any culture are linked. They are not formed in isolation, but in relationship to each other. There is an archetypal pattern for the male, and it is similar throughout all matriarchal pagan cultures. It is that of the horned god, consort to the Goddess, whose principal role is to fertilize the Goddess. The archetypal dominating father figure of later patriarchal paganism and Semitic monotheism is simply not to be found in the earliest mythic structures and their artifacts. The nature of the horned god depended upon which animal played the most important part in serving the material needs of the people. In some parts of the Mediterranean basin the horns were those of a goat, while in other parts they were those of a bull. In northern Europe the horns are those of a stag, as is so graphically illustrated by the two-thousand-year-old Danish carving of Cernunnos on the Gunderstrup Caldron. These gods were often referred to as Lords of the Animals.

Some of the most impressive evidence for the existence of what Jung called the collective unconscious is furnished by the symbols which are to be found throughout matriarchal paganism anywhere in the world. The most common symbol in relationship to the Goddess is that of the serpent or snake. The sacred tree or tree of life was also a widespread Goddess symbol. Very often the snake and the tree are found in conjunction with each other. Another important symbol related to Goddess worship is that of the hill or mountain. Sometimes the Goddess is known as the Lady of the Mountain. The principal name of the Goddess in India, for example, is Parvati which means "she of the mountain." The home of the Goddess was often thought to be on the top of a mountain, and the ceremonies related to Goddess worship were often carried out in high places.

The principal symbol of the horned god consort to the Goddess was the phallus. Phallic symbols are found along with Goddess figurines throughout the areas where matriarchal paganism was practiced. Where there were priests who served the Goddess, they were generally castrated, and there is evidence that human sacrifice played an important role in many areas. However, this sacrifice was generally of young adult males.[36] In later matriarchal paganism animals such as bulls or rams were substituted. The sacrifice of children and females only became prevalent after paganism had become highly patriarchalized.

The symbols, rituals, and practices of matriarchal paganism are an important source for understanding the mythic world view of humans at the dawn of culture and history.[37] In particular, they are important for understanding the archetypal gender structure of that period. The fundamental theme is unity between humans and nature. Creative motherhood joins females to the earth and nature to humans. Fertility and the ongoing cycle of life is the highest value which is reflected. A common form which the horned god consort to the Goddess often took was that of half human and half animal, such as Pan or the Minotaur. Thus, man is both animal and human, and animals are seen to have humanity. Harmony and interdependency between humans and nature, and the oneness of all life is reflected in the symbolism and rituals of matriarchal paganism.

Castration and male sacrifice also reflect a deep religious meaning which is an essential theme in matriarchal paganism. The essence of true sacrifice is that it is voluntary. Certainly the entering of the priesthood of the Goddess would be voluntary and thus also the castration which would follow. According to many of the traditions of the sacrifice of the sacred king, voluntariness was assumed in that to take on the role was to accept the end. An important truth must have dawned upon humans at the beginning of culture and history. Domestication of animals, the development of agriculture, and the origin of permanent residency in villages, towns, and cities brought about a radical change in human lifestyle. To put it in terms of our own understanding, human males for several hundred thousand years had been genetically coded for a life of struggle competing with other animals for food on the plains of Africa. Millennia of evolution produced a male with a greater body weight, a higher degree of aggression, and a strong sexuality which is easily triggered. Before culture, this genetic coding helped ensure the survival of the species. With the birth of culture, evolution took a new direction. In addition to the genetic code, a cultural code developed which could be passed from generation to generation. When we look at the cultural code, we realize that humans are evolving at a dizzyingly rapid rate, and that the genetic code is now often in conflict with the cultural code in that it threatens the existence of the species. The only answer is for males to voluntarily sacrifice for the sake of mothers and children and the ongoing cycle of life. Hence the deeper meaning behind voluntary castration and sacrifice of the sacred king is the necessity for males to surrender themselves by making the interests of the mother primary. This can be seen as a form of castration.[38] One of the most powerful images relating to this period and mythic structure is that of the Ephesian version of the Goddess Artemis. Hanging from her neck are strings of testicles from castrated bulls,[39] and around her head and over her dress from the waist down are the carved heads of horned bulls. The power and meaning of this figure are obvious.

Human sexuality played an important role in the symbols and rituals of matriarchal paganism, and gave it a strong erotic element. The figure and symbolism of the Goddess, the Great Mother, would inevitably relate to the unconscious memory of narcissistic bliss when infant and mother were one, and would reinforce the drive to lose the self in the (m)other. In this first stage of history the object of the ego ideal would remain feminine. There would be functioning in the collective psyche of the male, a strong drive to merge with the female-goddess-mother by the surrender of the self. The archetypal gender pattern would be that of Goddess and consort. The psychological dynamic would be that of the Dionysian complex. The structure of the collective psyche would reinforce the drive to deify and worship women. In such a society, male domination, if it existed at all, would be incidental and unsupported by institutions of authority. Males and females would have power and respect in their own spheres. Female values related to reproduction, however, would be primary.

In later matriarchal paganism, as humans gradually realized their uniqueness in the animal world in terms of consciousness, the figure of the consort lost his horns. In the Mediterranean world he became known as Dionysus, and in India he became known as Shiva. The comparison of the mythic structure of Dionysus and Shiva leaves little doubt that they are the same archetypal god figure.[40] Both have their origin in the horned god who was lord of the animals. Both have early horned versions. For Dionysus it is Pan, and for Shiva it is the horned Shiva or bull-Shiva.[41] There are a great many similarities in the myths surrounding both gods, and it is possible that one is a derivative of the other. If so, it is likely that Shiva is the older form. Behind both, however, lies the ancient horned god, consort of the Goddess.

Both Shiva and Dionysus belong to mythic systems involving Goddess worship. Women play a major role in the cults of both deities. The central theme in both cults is that of the surrender of the boundaries of the self, thus dissolving the distinction between the self and other. Both have an early history involving the sacrifice of males.[42] Dionysus is the God of wine and loss of the self through intoxication. In this form he is often known by the Roman name of Bacchus. Both Dionysus and Shiva are gods of the surrender of the self in sexual ecstasy.[43] Both are gods of the dance and of the theatre.[44] The mask is one of the symbols used for both gods, which is another representation of the erosion of the boundaries of the self. Thus, at the first stages of culture and history there appears to have been a common religious mythic system structured around the archetypal figures of the Goddess and consort as patterns for female and male development. It would follow from this that the sex/gender archetypes structuring religion in the earliest stage of history and culture were that of powerful fecundant women and phallically oriented males.

While both Dionysus and Shiva are gods of ecstatic sexuality, they remain fundamentally monogamous. Dionysus saves Ariadne after she has been abandoned and betrayed by Theseus, and myths depict his complete devotion to her and her alone. Similarly, Shiva marries and is devoted to Parvati only. When the Goddess is embodied in every woman, then each woman is the Goddess. The central essence of the Dionysian-Shiva archetype is the male sacrifice of the self to the Goddess.[45] Once the self is given, it can't be taken back and re-given. The Don Juan complex is opposite to the Dionysian, and is misogynous at its core.

SOCIAL ORDER IN THE PRE-OEDIPAL AGE

There is no historical evidence that there was anywhere or at any time a matriarchy in the sense of a converse of patriarchy. We have no record of any society where females had dominance in a social hierarchy of political power. However, it is inconceivable to think that female children raised in a Goddess-worshiping culture would be socialized as inferior to males. It would seem highly improbable that females would be politically dominated by males, while at the same time the Divine as the sacred was given a female form. If political hierarchy reflects archetypal ideals, one would not expect to find males dominating females when the archetypal structure of the Divine is that of a primary female figure (Goddess) and a secondary male figure (consort). Such contradictions would be inconsistent with the kind of structural unity which a mythic system or world view requires. While it is not clear what political power women exercised in the age of matriarchal paganism, there is strong evidence that women were held in high esteem and played an important, if not leading, cultural and societal role. As Thompson states, "It is a question not of masculine political power, but of feminine cultural authority."[46] A mythic system is patriarchal when the projection onto the cosmos is primarily the product of the male psyche. There is a great deal of evidence that during the age of matriarchal consciousness, the psychic content projected onto the cosmos had a powerful female component and the mythic structure reflects a strong input from the psyche of females.[47]

The archetypal images of the female as portrayed in the figurines, carvings, and statues of the Goddess show powerful women. One of the earliest and most striking figurines is that of the Goddess found at Çatal Hüyük. The figure is that of a large-breasted, heavy-bellied (probably showing pregnancy) woman sitting on a throne between two lionesses. Another example is the Goddess of the Minoans, with an owl sitting on her head and her hands upraised with a serpent in each. Even the figures of the Goddess from the era of the Greeks, showing Demeter or Artemis the huntress are forceful and dynamic portrayals.

The matriarchal vision of life was oriented to a cyclical flow of nature dominated by woman through her life-giving forces rather than by man through acts of will connected to legal structures. One of the most intriguing aspects of the matriarchal framework was that there was nothing that could be termed a law. Certainly there were rules of some sort, customs and taboos. There is no reason to assume that social practices such as property, trading, and forms of marriage were absent. The significant point is that whatever regulations did exist were carried out as part of an integrated mythos, as an undifferentiated, unconscious part of living. There was no consciousness of law in the abstract or lawmaking as a social practice, nor of a formal set of rules to govern social activity.

A particularly striking illustration of the non-legalistic view of life characteristic of matriarchal society is provided by the oldest reference to freedom which exists in any written text, in a Sumerian document dated *circa* 2350 B.C.. The word which the Sumerians used to refer to the concept of freedom was *amargi*, which means literally, "return to the mother."[48] The experts on ancient Sumerian culture admit that they have absolutely no idea why when "we find the word 'freedom' used for the first time in man's recorded history," this particular figure of speech came to be used.[49] To understand why and how "return to the mother" came to mean freedom we would need to know what one was turning away from in "the return." This first appearance of the word *amargi* was in a Sumerian document which, "records a sweeping reform of a whole series of prevalent abuses, most of which could be traced to a ubiquitous and obnoxious bureaucracy consisting of the ruler and his palace coterie," and which also "provides a grim and ominous picture of man's cruelty toward man on all levels—social, economic, political, and psychological."[50] What the turning was from, therefore, is revealed by the context within which the word *amargi* or freedom appears; it was a turning from law and the authority of kingship. But what did the "return to the mother" consist of, and why was this state equated with freedom? An examination of the preliterate history of this area, as reconstructed through archaeological evidence and the earliest recorded myths, suggests an answer. The earliest Sumerians worshipped the Goddess Inanna.[51] There is much evidence to suggest that women held a high status which was gradually lost with the development of patriarchy in the form of a transition to the worship of male gods, kingship, and the rise of law. Lineage was traced through the mother, and property was inherited accordingly. This was the age of "mother right" and "mother-kinship." Freedom as "the return to the mother" would mean, therefore, a return to *the* mother, that is, to matriarchal consciousness, which would mean a return from kingship to collective social order, from law to custom, and from "masculine political power" to "feminine cultural authority."[52]

The institution of law is incompatible with the archetype of the mother and a society where the mother is the object of the ego ideal of the collective psyche. So long as our images of the mother are formed in early childhood, and given that they are generally positive for most children, the associations with the mother will be those of nurture, love, and comfort. There is an essential opposition between law and justice on the one hand, and love, mercy, and other related forms of emotion on the other. Law is a product of the will and is associated with the father. Love, mercy, and reconciliation are related to the mother and the feminine. Justice requires a penalty and mercy requires forgiveness.

Freud believed that since women do not experience castration anxiety, they maintain a pre-Oedipal attachment to their mothers and consequently lack fully-developed superegos. "I cannot evade the notion," wrote Freud, "that for women the level of what is ethically normal is different from what it is in men. . . . [T]hey show less sense of justice . . . [and] are more often influenced in their judgments by feelings."[53] The Swiss child psychologist Jean Piaget noted that boys displayed an inclination to follow rules, and a facility in their application, while girls tended to be more pragmatic and less inclined to slavishly follow and apply rules in their games and behaviour.[54] The Harvard psychologist, Lawrence Kohlberg, devised a scale of levels of moral development in terms of facility in the use of rules and logical consistency in reaching moral judgments, upon which he tested males and females, and concluded that females fell substantially lower on the scale.[55]

Carol Gilligan, a Harvard colleague of Kohlberg, confirms that there is a difference between the way boys and girls, and men and women approach moral disputes and rules. However, in her study *In A Different Voice,* she strips away the aura of superiority which has been given to the masculine mode.[56] Her studies show that boys and girls approach rules and dispute settlement differently. She concludes that there are different approaches to social order and disputes which are interrelated with and differ according to gender. She discusses a typical reaction of a boy, Jake, and a girl, Amy, to a moral dilemma which Kohlberg posed to a group of eleven-year-olds to measure their moral development. The dilemma was whether a man who requires a drug to save his wife's life, and can't afford to purchase it, should steal it. Jake was clear that the man should steal the drug because a life was more valuable than property. Amy, on the other hand, considered neither property nor law, but was more concerned about the various human relationships which were involved in the situation. She responded, "If he stole the drug, he might save his wife then, but if he did, he might have to go to jail, and then his wife might get sicker again, and he couldn't get more of the drug, and it might not be good. So, they should really just talk it out and find some other way to make the money." Gilligan comments, "Seeing in the dilemma not a math problem with humans but a narrative of relationships that extends over time, Amy envisions the wife's continuing need for her husband and the husband's continuing concern for his wife and seeks to respond to the druggist's need in a way that would sustain rather than sever connection."[57]

There would appear to be a fundamental difference between the approach and attitude which humans can take toward dispute settlement and transgression which depends upon the archetypal framework within which they are functioning. Some have referred to a difference between what they call the "maternal principle" and the "paternal principle."[58] The paternal principle dictates the obedience of an inferior in a hierarchical social order to a superior who has the authority to lay down rules for which obedience can be demanded as a duty. The maternal principle reflects the relationship of nurture whereby a dependent person can rely upon the love or emotionally based goodwill of another for the satisfaction of a need. The paternal principle encourages individuals to define themselves in terms of their place in a hierarchy, while the maternal principle seeks a definition of the self in terms of a network or relationships.

The difference between these two approaches reflects a fundamental contradiction in Western legal consciousness between legal justice on the one hand, and mercy, love, emotion or what has been called prophetic justice in the Judaeo-Christian tradition, on the other. It has its origins, in part at least, in gender bifurcation. Thus, we can conclude that there is a fundamental relationship between legal consciousness and the Oedipus complex. The identification of law with authority, authority with the father, and the father with the state, while at the same time identifying love, mercy, and emotion with the mother, while excluding her from power, helps ensure the separation of law and human emotion which is so characteristic of the legal tradition.

Within patriarchal consciousness, including the views of both Freud and Kohlberg, justice according to rules is a higher form of mental development, and following one's emotions is considered a reflection of a desire to revert to the mother, and is thus an impediment to the development of the self. Freud viewed it as a form of wish fulfillment which left one within the grips of the Oedipus complex, never fully able to transcend it. This, in part, accounts for his positive evaluation of the masculine and his negative evaluation of the feminine.[59]

This difference between the nonlaw "feminine" approach and the law-related, rule-governed "masculine" approach is a dichotomy which runs throughout the Western legal tradition, and which is reflected not only in the symbolism of the traditional figures of justice which adorn so many of the courtrooms of the Western world, but also in Western religion, morality, philosophy, art and literature.[60] These assumptions reflect a bifurcated view of justice and mercy. Mercy must function extralegally, that is to say outside the legal system. Judges cannot pardon, as the prerogative of mercy belonged at common law to the Crown and is now exercised by the executive, its successor. When the Chancellor was delegated by the English Kings, the power to override the common law, a strong element of mercy functioned in correlation with but externally to the law. When, however, the office of the Chancellor evolved into the Courts of Chancery administering the law of equity, this element of mercy disappeared, so that by the mid-nineteenth century Dickens picked the Court of Chancery to unleash his savage attack in *Bleak House,* on the mercilessness of the legal system.

There are many references in literature to the tension between justice and mercy. A famous example is furnished by William Shakespeare in *The Merchant of Venice:* [61]

> The quality of mercy is not strained,
> It droppeth as the gentle rain from heaven
> Upon the place beneath. It is twice blest:
> It blesseth him that gives, and him that takes.
> 'Tis mightiest in the mightiest, it becomes
> The throned monarch better than his crown.
> His sceptre shows the force of temporal power,
> The attribute to awe and majesty,
> Wherein doth sit the dread and fear of kings;
> But mercy is above this sceptred sway.
> It is enthroned in the hearts of kings,
> It is an attribute to God himself,
> And earthly power doth then show likest God's
> When mercy seasons justice. Therefore, Jew,
> Though justice be thy plea, consider this:
> That in the course of justice, none of us
> Should see salvation. We do pray for mercy,
> And that same prayer doth teach us all to render
> The deeds of mercy.

In the novel *Billy Budd,* Herman Melville has clearly touched a chord in the Western collective psyche, and provides us with an example of the consequence of this bifurcation.[62] The story is set aboard a British warship at sea in 1797, when England was at war with revolutionary France. The plot contains three main characters: Billy Budd, first mate Clegg, and Captain Devere. Billy Budd is a Christlike figure who embodies goodness. Clegg is basically an evil man, and Captain Devere is a kind and compassionate officer who runs his ship efficiently but humanely. The plot is simple, as befits these archetypal figures. Clegg, who is disturbed by Budd's inherent innocence and goodness, attempts to destroy him by accusing him of fomenting a mutiny. When confronted with this accusation in the presence of Clegg, Budd, whose only defect is that he is a stutterer, is unable to articulate his outraged denial. In frustration, he strikes Clegg with his fist. Clegg hits his head when he falls, and dies.

Striking an officer was at this time in the British Navy a capital offense, as was the killing of an officer. Yet, as Melville is at pains to point out, Billy Budd's moral guilt is minimal. He was accused of a crime which could cost him his life, and, given his stutter, was defending himself the only way he could. Thus, Captain Devere is on the horns of an excruciating dilemma; he loves the beautiful and innocent Billy Budd as a son, but knows that if the law is not followed he will lose control of the crew. In the end Captain Devere obeys the law, and his "duty," and hangs the boy. Although he is a good man, he cannot save Billy; he cannot show mercy and still remain Captain. By having the officers of the court martial consider and eventually reject the various arguments which they themselves raise in attempting to save Budd, Melville reveals two related fundamental contradictions in the Judaeo-Christian tradition: one pertains to God, the other pertains to law. God can be just, or He can be loving and merciful, but He cannot be both. Reflecting this dichotomy, the law can be either just or merciful, but not both.

This contradiction between a God of justice and law and a God of love and mercy, is reflected in the Judaic religious tradition in the dichotomy of "The Law and the Prophets." The law was administered by priests who taught duty to strict rules of obedience. The prophets were the voice of compassion and righteousness, and were often critics of the law.[63] The very strength of the Judaic tradition lay in the dialectical process which kept the contradictions in balance. There is always the danger that emotions can readily change. Love can turn to hatred and compassion to cruelty. The ties to the legal tradition of the priests kept the prophetic tradition from the excesses which often accompany charismatic leadership, and kept the prophetic tradition within a consistent and logical structure. The prophets, on the other hand, when acting as critics of the priests and the law, produced in ancient Israel one of the most humane systems of law that the world has ever seen.[64]

This dialectical tension is vividly reflected in the teachings of Jesus of Nazareth, the last and greatest in the line of prophets who constituted the prophetic tradition of Judaism. On the one hand he bitterly denounced the priests and lawyers, the servants of the law, while on the other he asserted that the law was not to pass away, but was to be fulfilled.[65] When Christianity was no longer a Jewish sect but had become a world religion in its own right, the belief in the reconcilability of prophetic justice with the law facilitated the move toward a unification of the church and state, which witnessed the end of the prophetic tradition.[66]

The religion of the Old Testament had no place for priestesses. There were no female priests. This meant that law was a male preserve. This was not so within the prophetic tradition. Even though ancient Israel was a highly patriarchal society there were prophetesses. In the early stages of the nation of Israel, before the institution of kingship had become clearly established, there was a period when Israel was governed by judges who were prophets and prophetesses. According to the Book of Judges:

> And Deborah, a prophetess . . . judged Israel at that time. And she dwelt under the palm tree of Deborah between Ramah and Bethel in mount Ephraim: and the children of Israel came up to her for judgment.[67]
> In those days there was no king in Israel: every man did that which was right in his own eyes.[68]

In several other places within the Old Testament, prophetesses are referred to,[69] but priests, the custodians of the law, had to be male.[70]

In the suppression of matriarchal consciousness, the nurturing framework surrounding the mother archetype and the closely interrelated concepts of love and mercy are stripped from the female and attached to a new kind of masculine archetype, the Christ. Jesus represents the masculine form of the mother figure. In the book *Jesus as Mother,* Caroline Walker Bynum documents the maternal image that was projected onto Jesus by the medieval world. The "Mother Jesus" references and imagery strip the feminine from the female.[71] The logic of patriarchal culture has been that if there is something of value within the mother archetype which it wishes to retain, it must be removed from a female archetypal framework and attached to a male one. On the other hand, if a female archetypal image is absolutely necessary, such as the mother required by the God made flesh, then Mary must be severed from the female by the Immaculate Conception.[72] It must be the male figure of Jesus who is the epitome of love and calls the little children unto himself.[73]

Law is the product of a collective complex having its origins within the archetypal structure of the collective psyche. The most central concept to law is that of the will. The archetypal paradigm of law is the command of the monarchal father, whether God, king, or paterfamilias. The archetypal figure of the mother is one of nurture, encouraging the development and well-being of children. It is inconsistent with a legal framework. This does not mean that an age of matriarchal consciousness is inconsistent with rules or rule-governed activities or practices, nor does it entail the absence of disputes and public dispute resolution. Even within highly law-regulated patriarchal cultures, many social practices take place outside of the legal framework and disputes are often settled in a nonlegal manner, such as by mediation.[74]

As explained in earlier chapters, law requires legitimacy which is obtained by a conformity of the social order with what is conceived to be the natural order. Given that the social order reflects the view which the culture takes of the natural order, we should be able to trace the parallels between the two. A holistic world view, where an interconnectedness is seen to relate all forms of life, is inconsistent with the institution of law which historically has been based on the presupposition of the superiority of male over female and the uniqueness of the human species.

14.

THE OEDIPAL STAGE OF HISTORY

GENDER AND THE OBJECT OF THE EGO IDEAL

Just as the mother archetype is a partial aspect of the archetypal feminine, the father archetype is a partial aspect of the archetypal masculine.[1] Like the archetypal feminine, the archetypal masculine takes several different forms, the most important of which are those of God, the king or monarch, the father, the paterfamilias (head of the family), the hero, and the brother. The father archetype extends to related mythic structures such as religion, law, and scholarship, just as the hero archetype extends to war, hunting, and many forms which characterize the struggle of the male against powerful odds or opposition. In the mythic structure energized by this archetype, the archetypal father and masculinity are interrelated with individuation and separation, just as the mother archetype is interrelated with wholeness and integration.

The masculine and feminine archetypes underlie the entire structure of gender. Gender is essential to identity. Children do not simply grow up and mentally evolve into adult men and women through some process of natural evolution. As their bodies develop and mature, archetypal role models derived from the collective psyche are imposed on their minds. Their psyches are poured into these molds. They become individual instances of archetypal patterns.

Gender structures are higher level "programs" that run through or impact on most other structures of knowledge. Religion, politics, produc-

273

tion, and child rearing are some of the systems of information which direct human behaviour in terms of gender. At almost every point of communication with other people, children receive information and messages concerning gender roles. Many are blatant, such as "boys don't do that," and others can be as subtle as a difference in the way a child is touched, or the tone of a voice. The sexual bifurcation of the human species, the fact that humans are born of the female, and our conscious and unconscious assimilation of these factors into the mind, are the foundations of gender bifurcation. The gender archetypal structures are the social counterpart of biological bimorphic sexuality. Normal humans are either female or male. They are subsequently programmed to become masculine or feminine. The programmable nature of gender is shown most sharply in genetically normal males who have become possessed with the archetypal gender structures normally found in females.[2]

The archetypes which serve the identification function as objects of the ego ideal generally correspond to the sex of the individual. If not, that individual will have a mismatch between mind and body which will result in serious social and psychological problems. The archetypal object of the ego ideal which serves the merger function, however, need not and often does not correspond with the sex of the individual. The particular gender structure, whether male or female, will be affected by the gender of the object of the ego ideal serving the merger function. Thus, if a male has the archetypal mother as the object of his ego ideal, his gender structure will be Dionysian. His defining gender archetype will be that of the consort. If a woman has the archetypal father as the object of her ego ideal, her gender structure will be defined by the Eve archetype.[3]

The archetypal structures which define gender are interrelated. Each archetype has a correlation with another archetype of the opposite gender. Within the mythic structure of gender, the archetypal father is correlated with the archetypal Eve figure, and the archetypal mother is correlated with the Dionysian or consort figure. Thus, there are two different archetypal gender structures available to each sex. For the male, there is the God-monarch-father-hero on the one hand, and the Dionysus-Shiva consort on the other. The latter is far from effeminate. It is highly masculine, often erotic, and can be very powerful. In myth, Dionysus is a god to be feared, and is often linked with the panther or the bull. For the female, the alternatives are the subordinate Eve and the Goddess. The archetypal combination of objects of the ego ideal serving the merger and identification functions furnishes the energizing force of the related complexes.

James Hillman points out, "The psychological history of the male-female relationship in our civilization may be seen as a series of footnotes to the tale of Adam and Eve."[4] One can find a paradigm example of women who have the father archetype as the object of the ego ideal serving the merger function in Marabel Morgan and Helen B. Andelin. In her book, *The Total Woman*, Morgan writes under the subtitle "Oh King, Live Forever": [5]

> I have been asked if this process of adapting places a woman on a slave-master basis with her husband. A Total Woman is not a slave. She graciously chooses to adapt to her husband's way, even though at times she desperately may not want to. . . . Marriage has also been likened to a monarchy, where the husband is king, and his wife is queen. In a royal marriage, the king's decision is the final word, for his country and his queen alike.

In a similar vein Andelin writes: [6]

> The meaning of the word *submissive* is to be yielding, compliant, obedient, to yield to power or authority, or to leave matters to the opinions, discretion or judgment of another or others. . . . Since we expect men to be our leaders and therefore dominant and aggressive, we should be the opposite in order to be the most feminine. We should be yielding and submissive to their rule, their opinions and their judgment.

Both Morgan and Andelin argue that women can find happiness and fulfillment only in surrendering themselves to males, and their books are filled with descriptions of how to make males happy. The neurosis manifested in their writings is that of a strong Eve complex, activated by a powerful masculine object within which they wish to merge their egos.

In some very interesting cases a male will have the archetypal father as the object of the ego ideal serving not only an identification but also a merger function. What is particularly fascinating is that the male adopts a feminine archetypal role. Males who seek a mystical union with God adopt a feminine archetypal definition to define their relationship with Him. The archetypal structure which is adopted is that of the groom and the bride in the union of marriage. In the Old Testament Israel is often referred to as the bride of God. "For thy Maker is thine husband; the Lord of hosts is his name."[7] "And I will betroth thee unto me for ever."[8] The longing to lose the self by uniting with God is often expressed in Jewish poetry. Eleazar Ben Kallir expresses the sense of alienation from

God as an abandonment by a husband of his wife. In *The Dialogue of Zion and God,* he has Israel complain as the abandoned wife: [9]

> The mother of children moans like a
> dove; she mourns in her heart and
> complains out loud; she cries bitterly,
> calls out desperately; she sheds tears,
> she is silent and stunned:
>
> "My husband has abandoned me and
> turned away, and has not remembered
> my love as a bride; he has scattered
> and dispersed me far from my land; he
> has let all my tormentors rejoice at my downfall."

And he has God respond in the words of a lover:

> "O my dove, O plant of delight in my
> garden bed, why do you cry out against
> me? I have already answered your
> prayer, as I did in days of old, when I
> dwelt crowned in your midst."

The same analogy is carried on in the New Testament to portray the relationship between Christ and His church. [10] The longing to merge with God is expressed in the writings of the Christian mystics in terms of a woman seeking her lover. Thus the Spanish Christian mystic, Luis De Granada proclaims: [11]

> May I love Thee, then, O Lord, with the straitest and most fervent love. May I stretch out mine arms—that is, all my affections and desires, to embrace Thee, sweetest Spouse of my soul, from Whom I hope for all good. The ivy clings so closely to its tree that the whole of it seems to be throwing out arms wherewith to grasp the tree more closely, for by means of this support it mounts on high and attains what to it is perfection. And to what other tree must I cling than to Thyself, that I may grow and attain what I lack? This plant clinging to the trees grows not more, nor throws more widely its lively branches than the soul grows in virtues and graces when it clings to Thee. Then why shall I not love Thee with all my soul, and strength and powers? Help me, my God and my Saviour, and raise me on high in quest of Thyself, for the grievous weight of this mortal life drags me downward. Thou, Lord, Who didst mount the tree of the Cross to draw all things unto Thee; Thou Who with so vast a love didst unite two

such different natures in one Person, to make Thyself one with us: do Thou be pleased to unite our hearts with Thyself by so strong a bond of love that they may at last become one with Thee, since Thou didst unite Thyself with us that we might be united with Thyself.

THE ARCHETYPAL FATHER AS OBJECT OF THE EGO IDEAL

The father stands at the head of the patriarchal family. Headship entails domination, domination requires authority, and to be a father is to have authority. The concepts of fatherhood and authority are inextricably entwined. God is conceived of as the Heavenly Father, His subjects as His children. The state is often called the fatherland. Kings are deemed to be the fathers of their people. The term *sovereign* is used to describe the power of the father over children and wife or wives, and that of the monarch over his subjects. The classic definition of law of traditional English positivism is the command of the sovereign backed by a sanction.[12]

The concept of fatherhood is an archetypal structure which encompasses the family, the state, and the divine. Fatherhood entails the right to rule and to be obeyed. Only when the ruler wore the mantle of the father was his domination legitimate. As the king was the father of his people, he had the right to command, and they in turn were subject to his authority, as are the children of any father. This pattern of the patriarch of the family was projected onto the body politic in the form of monarchy, and onto the divine in the form of father gods or heavenly fathers.[13] Conversely, the powers of the king and of the gods are projected onto the family head. As the father is to his children, so is the king to his subjects, and God to his people, and similarly the father is God and king to his children. Law has its origins in this interrelated mythic structure.

J. W. Perry wrote, "In archaic times it was typical for a society to establish a powerful focal point where the world of myth met and entered the world of human community."[14] This focal point was the sacral king. In the mythic structure of most archaic cultures, the king was "the embodiment of or the son of the First Ancestor-Founding King, living in the world of the dead, the earth, or the underworld,"[15] and was generally identified as the son by adoption, descendant of, or a special representative of the sky, sun, or heavenly father-god.[16] Perry writes:[17]

The king as the Royal Father was the acme of all father figures. In these days of prevalence of psychoanalytic thinking, we might be inclined to think of him as a surrogate father, created out of the reminiscences of the parents of individuals' childhood, and engendering the same emotions as those of early life. However, there is a larger sense of the term "father figure" than that which implies a re-creation of the father of one's youngest years. This Royal Father in history was not only shepherd of the people, but also center of the realm, a functionary endowed with a magical or numinous potency concentrating in his person the properties of the masculine principle. This constellation of attributes involved emotions that reached far beyond the limits of childhood and family into the more awesome plane of spiritual and cosmic and timeless issues. The king was mediator of the life force itself, giving fertility and virility; carrier of the power of authority, giving order and integrity; and bearer of the aggressive might of the executive function, giving chastisement to disorder and encouragement to obedience. He thus embodied male qualities so intensely valued that they were experienced by the people as divine.

The mythic structure of patriarchy achieved its ultimate form in monotheism. Judaeo-Christian monotheism became the mythic structure which led a good part of the Western world into the Oedipal period of history. The ultimate expression of this mythic structure was the "Divine Right of Kings" of Christian Europe in its age of monarchy.[18] James I, in his speech to Parliament on 21 March 1610, proclaimed, "The state of monarchy is the supremest thing upon earth; for kings are not only God's lieutenants upon earth, and sit upon God's throne, but even by God himself they are called gods," because "they exercise a manner or resemblance of divine power upon earth."[19] "Kings," he also stated, "are also compared to fathers of families, for the king is truly *parens patriae*, the political father of his people."[20]

The classic statement of patriarchal authority within the Judaeo-Christian context is to be found in Sir Robert Filmer's *Patriarcha*.[21] In this book, philosophy and myth coalesce. In his introduction to *Patriarcha and Other Political Works of Sir Robert Filmer*, Peter Laslett, the editor, writes:[22]

[T]he writings of Filmer have a significance in the history of European social thinking which is quite independent of the relation they bear to Locke's theory of obligation and of the position of the English Tories in later Stuart times. The value of *Patriarcha* as a historical document consists primarily in its revelation of the strength and persistence in European culture of the patriarchal family form and the patriarchal attitude to political problems. It was because of patriarchalism that Sir Robert Filmer was read, not because of his literary or philosophical ability. It was because of patriarchalism that Locke and Sidney had to answer him, for in appealing to the power of the father and the relevance of the family to the state he touched the assumptions of all his own readers and of most of Locke's. . . . [T]he social anthropologist classifies European culture of all periods, even in the present era of self-conscious rationalism, as markedly patriarchal. It is patriarchal in its family forms, it is patriarchal in its emotional attitudes: it is even patriarchal in its politics and economics.

According to Filmer, God "made man Prince of his posterity,"[23] and "Patriarchs had, by right of fatherhood, royal authority over their children."[24] The right of kings to rule is inherited from the original patriarchs, and they rule as fathers of their people. He continues, "If we compare the natural duties of a Father with those of a King, we find them to be all one, without any difference at all but only in the latitude or extent of them."[25]

A profound, far-reaching change took place in human culture with the shift from matriarchal consciousness to patriarchy, where the male became dominant and mother-right died out. The god-king-father archetype succeeded in replacing the mother-earth-nature ideal of the ego of the collective psyche in the shift from the pre-Oedipal to the Oedipal stage of history. Since there is a god there can be a king in his image; because there is a king, there can be a paterfamilias in his image; and because there are fathers there can be kings and gods. The father archetype functions as the ideal of the ego in order to shift the ego ideal away from the mother. The archetypal transition of the ego ideal of the collective psyche from female to male marked a process of individuation in the separating of the collective mind from matter and nature. A corresponding change took place in the mythic structure as the archetypal figure of the consort gradually evolved into a husband and eventually into a Father God, with the Goddess becoming subservient as a wife. The mother who was viewed as the source of life now became viewed as a mere receptacle in which the male placed the essence of the new life. Bachofen, who first discovered the ancient prehistoric age of matriarchy, described this move as an evolution in human consciousness. Neumann, who has written in the tradition of Bachofen and Jung, went on to describe the matriarchate as the infantile phase of ego-consciousness, "the stage when ego consciousness is undeveloped and still embedded in nature and the world."[26] Neumann observed that matriarchy carried with it man's total dependence on the Earth as mother, which is reflected in the preoccupation of matriar-chal cultures with fertility. This has been linked to the speculation that the male's relationship to human reproduction was simply not under-stood. The prevalence of phallic symbols associated with Goddess wor-ship makes this assumption somewhat doubtful.

The transition from matriarchy to patriarchy entailed a radical transfor-mation in man's view of the nature of creation, and the origins of the male monopoly over the formulation of mythic structures can be seen in the shift in creation myths from the paradigm of birth to that of creation by an act of will.[27] In the matriarchal perspective, the earth-Mother-Goddess was the source of all life; the creative process was not causal, but magical, mystical and fundamental. Creation in matriarchy was fertility and procreation, and procreation was a matter of essence and being rather than cause-effect. In the shift to the Sky-Father-Gods, earth and nature had to be accounted for by "acts" of creation. Creation was no longer the flow of nature, but an intervening act which was the exercise of "will," whereby order was brought out of chaos, or the world out of nothing.[28] The order of the world was consequently reflected in Divine will, which was indistinguishable from the law of nature. The will of the god was divine law. The authority of the king was derived from his relationship to the god, and his right to rule was based on the belief that he was a god incarnate or that he descended from the gods.[29] The father was sovereign within the family, and for his family his will was law. Thus the will of the sovereign, whether family, royal, or heavenly father, is the paradigm of law. In this scheme, the patriarchal family became the archetype of social order.

The projection of the Sky-Father-Gods onto the cosmos was accompa-nied by a denial of personhood to the earth. The earth became an object or a resource for men's exploitation. As said by the Psalmists, "Thou madest him [man] to have dominion over the works of thy hands; thou hast put all things under his feet: All sheep and oxen, yea, and the beasts of the field; The fowl of the air, and the fish of the sea. . . ."[30] With the denial of the personhood of the earth, and its objectification, came the objectification and denial of personhood to women.[31]

It is difficult to discover whether the shift from matriarchal to patriar-chal consciousness was a gradual change and to what degree it was the product of the patriarchal Aryan invaders. The transition from matriarchal to patriarchal paganism and patriarchal monotheism corresponds with the invasion of the male-dominated Aryan tribes. They probably, however, accelerated a process which had already begun. There are many indications of a gradual shift to patriarchy in the latter stages of matriarchal paganism. It is probable that the male-dominated Aryan tribes adopted these patriarchal strains to formulate new patriarchal mythical systems, and at the same time their domination of females fed the emerging patriarchal strains of paganism.

In the world of the Mediterranean basin, a noticeable change took place in sculpture, the carving on friezes and various other forms of artistic imagery. We see the appearance of the hero. Goddess figures begin to be replaced by figures of the athletic male body. Many of these images are of males killing bulls or minotaurs. The Goddess is transformed into female monsters which are killed by the heroes. The Goddess and her symbol, the serpent, become the Medusa whose look turns men into stone. Another common pattern on friezes and murals is that of the hero killing figures of powerful women called Amazons. The myth of the Amazons is a residual carryover of the archetypal female gender pattern of the age of matriarchal paganism.[32] The memory of the women of the age of matriarchal paganism lived for centuries in the collective psyche in the form of the archetype of the Amazon.[33]

We then have the gradual appearance of Greek pornographic images of women. Eva Keuls, in her book, *The Reign of the Phallus,* has reproduced a large number of paintings from plates and vases which show men beating female prostitutes, or forcing them to perform fellatio or submit to anal sex. At the same time, similar portrayals of pederastic sex appear. When one lays out photographs of these various images of women, from the lion Goddess of Çatal Hüyük through slaughtered Amazons to sodomized prostitutes, one can see evidence of a profound change in the collective psyche. The object of the ego ideal has switched from the mother archetype to the father archetype. The prevailing collective complex has, at the same time, shifted from the Dionysian to the Jehovah-Persean in the male and from the Demeter to the Eve complex in the female. Paralleling this transition, a radical change appears to have taken place in the lives of women and their role in society. At the height of Greek patriarchal culture, women (other than slaves or prostitutes) were imprisoned within the confines of the home. Their activities were limited to procreation, menial labor, and providing sexual satisfaction to males.[34]

In the first stage of the age of patriarchy, which corresponds with the Oedipal stage of history, the price to be paid for being a paterfamilias and owning and possessing women and children, was to be subject to a king in turn. Law in the Oedipal stage preserved the absolute rule of the father within his own home. He was god, king, and high priest over his own family.

LAW AS THE WILL OF THE FATHER

The object of the ego ideal as mother invites a merger in which the individual ego seeks to lose its boundaries in a return to the blissful state of primary narcissism. The archetypal object of the ego ideal as mother/earth/nature, furnished to the individual by the collective psyche, invites a merger of the self into the external other. The father as object of the ego ideal represents the expression of individual will. To emulate the father by being like the father means that the nascent self identifies with the father's will, and develops and expresses a will of its own. The will lies at the center of the ego. The development of the individual will is the essence of the process of individuation. The object of the ego ideal of the collective psyche as father-god is the embodiment of will. God willed the universe into existence—creation was an act of will. The Lord's Prayer affirms, "Thy will be done." God is separate from and above nature because nature is merely an expression of His will. Man is created in God's image and finds his essential existence in the expression of his own will. By his will he takes dominion over the earth and nature and objectifies it for his own purposes. Thus, the power of the old object of the ego ideal (the archetypal mother) is broken. The emergence of the new object of the ego ideal (the archetypal father) marks the triumph of the will. This shift in the object of the ego ideal left women subject to the will of the male which is legitimized as "law." The right to make law by expressing the will is legitimized as "authority." Males identified their own egos with the archetypal hero/father/king/god. Females, in adopting the same archetype as the object of the ego ideal, sought to unite ego with its ideal through surrendering the ego, and merging the self with the ideal. Fathers and husbands became the living representations of the archetype.

Law as a social institution and a conceptual structure originated within the framework of the archetypal father. As Lacan wrote, "It is in the *name of the father* that we must recognize the support of the symbolic function which, from the dawn of history, has identified his person with the figure of the law."[35] The Freudian psychoanalyst Antoine Mooij elaborates on the relationships between the Oedipus complex, the father archetype, and law. He writes: [36]

> Following on along the same lines, we can distinguish three forms of fatherhood. First, there is the symbolic father, the name of the father, or the law, who forbids the child to take the mother as sexual object, and who deprives the child of its position as being mother's phallus or having a phallus.
>
> Secondly, there is the imaginary father figure, which is described in the "Totem and Taboo"-myth as the archetypical father, in as far as he possesses the women and also possesses *that* which enables him to possess all women: the phallus (the all-powerful penis). Like the symbolic father, the law, who is potentially present in the life of every individual, thus the imaginary father too can potentially be seen in every person. It is the father with whom the child has an ambivalent, hate-love, or idealizing relation of the dual type; he is the one who is big and strong and with whom the child enters into an aggressive and also mirroring relation.
>
> Finally, the real father is the biological father, the father of the primal scene in which the child is conceived in the mother, which constitutes a barrier behind which we cannot go.
>
> And the actual father? He is a *mixtum compositum* of these three elements. He is, if he is the biological father, the real father. He functions also as an imaginary father (as rival and as identification figure), with whom the child is involved in a constantly ambivalent relation, a relation in which the father should offer himself to the child as target. Finally, he has to play an intermediary role towards the law, which he will to some extent impersonate or represent, simply by existing as a father.

Fatherhood entailed lawgiving, and lawgiving entailed fatherhood. Law was the expression of the will of the father, and the will of the father was law. The royal father, through his will, regulated social order between the paterfamilias, and the paterfamilias through the expression of their will regulated their own families. While a number of ancient legal codes evolved, such as the Laws of Hammurabi or the Laws of Manu, they were only a part of the law. They maintained a stability of expectations and a continuity, but seldom limited the power of the royal will. Such codes sometimes functioned to prevent the will of the king from becoming completely arbitrary. More often, however, they expedited the royal will by leaving a codified form for consultation by judicial bureaucrats and administrators which made it unnecessary for the king to become directly involved in minor matters. The monarch seldom had to bother with the appropriate penalty for a man of a lower caste assaulting a man of a higher caste. Such disputes could be handled by a code.

The authority of ancient law rested on its divine origin as the will of the supreme Father-God. The laws of Manu, Hammurabi, Moses, and the Greek and Moslem worlds were all connected to divine law-giving acts.[37] Authority was derived from the right to rule as a Father-God incarnate or a descendant of such a God. The king's will was law because it reflected the will of a god figure. Therefore, the right to govern carried with it an irreproachable aura.

As discussed, the model of autocratic male leadership is most clearly reflected in the family, where for almost 3,000 years both in the West and East, the male has been the declared lawgiver of households. The history of Western political and legal theory is full of images of the family, with the male cast as the source of power and the recipient of effective authority. In all patriarchal systems, the family unifies religion, law, and morality under the dominion of the male head. The consequence of such a well-defined universe, with its attendant hierarchy of status-bound family members, is that conflict is resolved according to the place of the various members in the system, with the male in charge of sanctions and rewards. In tight patriarchal structures the woman established jurisdictions within the home, but in order to be efficacious, her control had to be self-limiting in the light of the deference due to the male head. Patriarchal systems from the Hebraic to the Chinese bear witness to this history.

Within the patriarchal family the will of the father is law. In ancient and traditional societies where there is a state, the state regulates relations between families, but seldom interferes within the family. The power of the state could often be used by the father to enforce his will against his children. Occasionally, some legal systems placed a few rules of restraint against cruel and excessive abuses of patriarchal power, but the government, when it did function within the family, did so as the agent of the father to enforce the father's will.[38]

Within the family, disputes are settled by the family head. Disputes between members of different families are generally settled by mediation. There are, of course, vast differences between the legal orders of different cultures and societies, but all traditional non-Western and tribal societies, without exception, are hierarchically ordered to some degree along genealogical lines.[39] Where such societies developed legal codes, the codes provided penalties according to the status of the victim and offender as well as the seriousness of the offence. Thus, the penalty differed according to the status of the parties involved. If a lowborn person committed an offence against a highborn person, the penalty was much more severe than if the situation had been reversed.[40] The basic aim of dispute settlement was the restoration of harmony within the community. Compensation and retribution were secondary, and mainly served as mechanisms to restore harmony. While a dispute might have its origin in the acts of individuals, it had to be settled by the heads of the families of which the individuals were members. Since the nature of the wrong and the corresponding remedy depended upon the relative status of victim and perpetrator, harmony could not be restored without following the dictates of status.

Some regard traditional China as the paradigmatic patriarchy. In Chinese culture, the family constituted a self-contained universe, wherein each participant had a deep understanding of and sensitivity to familial continuity. In short, the family was a mini-state.[41] The citizens possessed a sense of the importance of the history of the institution and its justification for being. Authority went totally without question, and the natural ingredients of punishment and mercy flowed from an acceptance of the wisdom of the male elder. Nepotism and status-by-birth did not cause disturbances in such a framework. The fact that peasant revolts occurred and that Western influences were felt at various stages does not alter the reality that traditional Chinese patriarchy remained remarkably intact until the twentieth century.

There is a negative and a positive aspect to the patriarchal archetype which is important to note if we are to appreciate the dialectical variations within patriarchal law. On the positive side, there is the all-wise and protecting father—the fountain of justice and the source of wisdom and guidance. The negative aspect is that of the terrible father—the administrator of punishment and retribution. Both features of the patriarchal archetype can generally be found to function in most cultures. Jehovah appears in the Old Testament both as a God of vengeance, sowing destruction among those who break his law, and as a protector, a God of justice and a refuge to those who obey his will. These two sides of the patriarchal archetype are reflected in the mythologies of gods and kings as well as in psychological reactions to one's own father. The dualistic nature of the patriarchal archetype is reflected in the mechanisms used to obtain compliance with the patriarchal will. Obedience may be sought through moral education or severe punishment. The 143d Psalm entreating, "Teach me to do thy will for thou art my God," stresses the Eternal Father as moralist, while threats of the fires of hell reflect the Father of judgment and damnation. Again, traditional China furnishes us with an example.

Within the Confucian system, the father played the role of moral guide and teacher, but the law also recognized the father's right to punish members of his family and acted as his agent in administering extremely harsh penalties for unfilial conduct. Professor T'ung-Tsu Ch'u, in his book *Law and Society in Traditional China,* discusses the extent of parental control: [42]

> The above facts indicate the almost absolute power of the parent over his child. The government merely acted as agent, framed the regulations and saw to it that they were carried out. But the will of the parents was decisive, and, generally speaking, a child's freedom or lack of it depended on that will. The law was the chief instrument through which the parental will was recognized and implemented. . . .
>
> Obviously, whether he was to be beaten or banished depended entirely on the will of his parents. The authorities merely acted as punishing agents.
>
> As noted above, when parents asked to have an unfilial son prosecuted, the authorities demanded no evidence, nor did they raise any objections to the punishment asked. The law states clearly: "When a father or mother prosecutes a son, the authorities will acquiesce without question or trial." "No parents in the world are wrong" is a very popular adage in China.

Thus, the terrible father imposing his will and exacting obedience by a harsh and cruel law was a powerful archetypal image in the legalist tradition in China. Concurrently, however, Confucian ethics stressed the positive side of the patriarchal archetype by teaching obedience through education and example.

A view of patriarchy in terms of pure domination and the naked exercise of power is a gross oversimplification which ignores the dual aspect of the father archetype. The will of the father was not perceived as arbitrary; age represented experience and wisdom. This was not an assumption that the will of the father was reasonable in the sense of the Platonic identification of goodness with truth, but rather that the will of the father embodied understanding and virtue. The various forms of patriarchy had in common a system of reciprocal rights and duties. The father had rights to obedience but also duties of protection and supervision. His subjects had duties of obedience but also rights dependent on their status. Confucius believed that orders were not necessary if children were properly taught. Just as the father had learned virtue as a filial son, he in turn taught his offspring by precept and example. The will of the virtuous father functions within moral parameters and a set of norms related to the status of each person. For Confucius, the virtuous ruler was like the North Star around which the lesser stars are placed, each in its proper position. Yet, at the same time, it was improper to question the will of the father. The patriarchal system required unquestioning obedience. "It was all a question of filial piety. Right and wrong were a matter of position: I am wrong because I am my father's son; what he says or does is right because he is my father."[43] The Judaeo-Christian paradigm of the virtuous son is Isaac, who lay himself obediently on the altar of sacrifice, as well as Abraham, who was willing to sacrifice his own beloved son without question if it was the will of his Father-God.

LAW AND SOCIAL ORDER AS MANIFESTATIONS OF THE PERSEAN COMPLEX

Within the male, the archetypal father as object of the ego ideal triggers the Persean complex. The male seeks to objectify the female and incorporate her into his own self. She becomes a part of him, like a rib. He is the justification for her existence. When the female adopts the father as the object of her ego ideal, the archetype is manifested in the form of the Eve complex. The surrender of herself to her husband becomes a noble sacrifice, and in its more pathological form can become masochistic. The result of the conjunction of the Persean complex in the male with the Eve complex in the female is the ownership of the woman by the man. If she is merged with him she is an extension of him, and as such she belongs to him.

There is a clear link between property and authority. The principal difference between the two lies in the fact that property legitimizes control over things while authority legitimizes control over people. The conceptual interrelationship between property and authority can be demonstrated in the language and concepts of the Bible. God is the Father and has the authority of a father because He is the Creator and the source of all life. In other references Christ is spoken of as purchasing or ransoming His people. For one person to exercise authority over others is to conceive of them and treat them like objects. This is why patriarchy conceives of and treats women as things. It is inherent in the entire conceptual apparatus. To the degree that a person is conceived of as an object or treated as such, their own autonomy is denied.

The objectification and exploitation of children is an integral aspect of patriarchy. The denigration of women entails the denigration of reproduction, and this in turn entails the denigration of children. The neglect and abuse of children, when seen on a global scale, is one of the most serious problems which humankind faces. Since damaged children produce damaged adults, the costs are passed on from generation to generation. Roger Sawyer's recent study of child abuse throughout the world, *Children Enslaved,* documents that children are objectified like women in patriarchal culture. The ownership of women entails the ownership of children.

The relationship of the mother to her child needs no mythic legitimization. The child comes from her womb and she has nurtured it with her body. Men have no similar relationship to children. The mere fact of fertilization bears no comparison. The father's authority must be culturally created. The mother has a natural link to the children of her body for which there is no counterpart for the male. In order for the father to have authority over the children he must make them his own by owning their mother. She must become his wife. Thus, the ownership of the women is fundamental to all patriarchal hierarchical social order.[44] Freud fully understood what fatherhood entailed. He wrote, "A father is one who possesses a mother sexually (and the children as property). The fact of having been engendered by a father has, after all, no psychological significance for a child."[45]

The central role of the female in procreation must be denigrated by viewing the female as an empty vessel in which the male places his seed, the real source of life. The mythic view of male dominance is then carried on through tracing the bloodline through the male—the family carrying the male surname. If the father owns the child through owning the mother, then the father will own the children of his children. The husband owns the wife because he has purchased her or been given her by her father who owned her. When in the traditional Christian marriage ceremony the cleric asks "Who gives this bride in marriage?" and the father steps forward (after bringing his daughter to the altar), an appeal is being made to psychologically deep-seated principles of property. Here, "give" is used in its proprietorial sense.

Two concepts are essential for both authority and property, and consequently for the maintenance of the patriarchal family. These are the principle of inheritance and the principle of primogeniture. According to the principle of inheritance, children have a greater claim or right to the property of their dead parents than do any nonmembers of the family. The principle of primogeniture specifies that the first-born male has a better claim than the female or younger male children. Authority is inherited along similar lines. Thus, control of property generally follows the lines of authority. In highly patriarchal societies the oldest son takes control over his mother on his father's death, and primogeniture dictates that he also inherits control over his younger brothers and sisters, and their progeny. The whole theory of monarchy rests on the assumption that the king is the oldest son of the oldest son, going back to the founding patriarch of the tribe or nation.

An analysis of ancient and traditional legal codes and treatises will reveal that there is very little discussion of the position of women under the law. The reason is quite clear. If women "belong" to men, they have little or no autonomy and are to be treated as objects rather than actors. Law holds between men and applies to men giving them protection and freedom from interference while they use and enjoy what is theirs, whether land, cattle, women, or children. Very little of the law of archaic, ancient, and traditional societies furnished protection for women and children. What little protection the law did furnish was not given to them in their own right, but as property of husbands and fathers, the true subjects of the law. They were rarely, if at all, protected against their husbands and fathers. Rather than giving protection to women and children, law tended to legitimize their exploitation. Thus, law has furnished a mythic framework which has legitimized the acting out of male pathology against women by denying the personhood or agency of women and making them male property.

The Lacanian method of text analysis entails, in part, reading between the lines of the text, and looking at what is not said, as well as what is said. Often, what is not said is of more significance from a psychoanalytic perspective than what is said. This certainly holds true for the law. The law is relatively silent regarding social order within the family and in regard to male authority over women. An examination of legal texts, from those of ancient law through to those of contemporary Western legal systems, will show that they deal almost entirely with the regulation of conduct between males. The supreme command of the law, however, is that the female shall be subject to the authority of the male. The fundamental commands of the law are those which are not articulated, because they include every command which the male (father) wishes to impose on the females subject to his authority. The substance of law, therefore, is in its silence, and not in its voice. The essence of the law is not to be found in the words of its text. The heart of the law remains unwritten so that it remains limitless. The words are only its periphery. They merely regulate, protect and enforce phallic authority. The law is the will of the father, whatever that will may be, and includes every authoritative command of a father. It is the right to command and the duty to obey. Phallic will is the substance of the law, and it can command all things. If the constitution, whether written or unwritten, establishes the monarch as absolute, then his every decree is law. Thus, the view of a public sphere of law and a private sphere which remains unregulated is an illusion. The idea that law has no place in the bedrooms of the nation is false. The bedrooms of the nation are the halls of lawmaking for phallic authority. All political authority is phallic by nature.

There is no legal tradition anywhere in the world, to my knowledge, which has not at one time presupposed the subjugation of the female to her father and then to her husband. Many make the mother subject to her son upon her husband's death. The Laws of Manu of ancient India, for example, are a paradigm of a patriarchal social order. They begin with an account of their mythological origin. "Then the divine Self-existent . . . shone forth of his own will . . . to produce beings of many kind from his own body, first with a thought created the waters, and placed his seed in them." Next follows an account of the creation of the various castes, and a declaration by Manu of his origin by springing from the Self-existent, thus giving a divine origin to the law which he then proclaimed. The regulations which constitute the laws of Manu deal mainly with events which occur between males. An English translation will fill a single volume, while Laws 147, 148, and 151 state simply: [46]

> By a girl, by a young woman, or even by an aged one, nothing must be done independently, even in her own house.
>
> In childhood a female must be subject to her father, in youth to her husband, when her lord is dead to her sons; a woman must never be independent.
>
> Him to whom her father may give her, or her brother with the father's permission, she shall obey as long as he lives, and when he is dead, she must not insult (his memory).

Laws such as these are not unique to India. In *Law and Society in Traditional China*, Professor T'ung-Tsu Ch'u states: [47]

> Under the principle of the "three dependencies" a woman could never act autonomously. On her wedding day her parents gave her their final instruc-

tions, saying, "Be respectful and cautious, do not disobey your husband."
The husband's authority replaced the father's, and "the husband was a
leader to his wife" in much the same way as the ruler was a leader to his
minister, the father to his son.

The law of the Israelite people of biblical times is found in the Pentateuch,
the first five books of the Old Testament. It includes the *Decalogue* (Exod.
20:2–17), the *Code of the Covenant* (Exod. 20:22–23:33), *Deuteronomy*
(Deut. 12–26), *The Law of Holiness*, (Lev. 17–26), *The Priestly Code* (Lev.
1–7).[48] However, this vast legal text is merely the framework for the law
which provides that *Thy desire shall be to thy husband, and he shall rule over
thee*.[49]

Even contemporary Western legal systems such as the common law,
which expressly or implicitly proclaim the equality of all persons, differ
little in this regard. The Married Women's Property Acts of most common law jurisdictions, which expressly recognize the power of married
women over their own property, usually also provide that no husband or
wife is entitled to sue the other for a tort.[50] This means in effect that
women cannot invoke the protection of the civil law against their husbands. They cannot obtain an injunction to prevent an assault or an
imprisonment, nor can they recover damages for injury to their person.
All common law jurisdictions, with a very few recent exceptions, provide
a definition of rape which excludes anything which a husband might do
to his wife.[51] The effect of this is that no women can invoke the protection of the criminal law against any sexual act which her husband may
wish to commit on her body. Until recently, a woman was unable to get
the protection of the criminal law against any form of physical assault
because of the longstanding common law principle that a husband was
entitled to physically discipline his wife.[52] In effect, a woman under the
common law has had a right against everyone in the legal system for
wrongful interference with her person, except against her husband. She
has been in the position of a serf, since a serf was a person who had rights
against everyone in the legal system for wrongful interference, except
against his lord.[53] Thus, the law makes the husband a lord and the wife a
serf. It is that law which structures patriarchal society, and furnishes the
paradigm for all other hierarchical relationships in the social order.

The degree to which the law incorporates patriarchy and the methods
by which it does so differ from culture to culture. However, there is
sufficient conformity in pattern that certain generalizations can be made.

Although they do not fit all cultures, they fit a good many, and while not all cultures will reflect all of the possible generalizations, every culture will reflect at least some. The following are some of the ways whereby law has been used to structure societies along patriarchal lines:

1. Women are viewed as a particular kind of property and the proprietary practices and institutions include women as objects of value to be given for exchange or other forms of benefit.
2. Women are denied full legal capacity to hold or convey property.
3. Women are denied the capacity to make commercial agreements.
4. Women are denied the capacity to choose to marry or not to marry, and to arrange or terminate their own marriages.
5. The law generally provides no or very little protection against the violence of their fathers or husbands.
6. Women are often restricted in their freedom of movement and in their choice of actions.
7. Women are considered to be magically dangerous or unclean; therefore, the law provides a special set of rules enforcing taboos which isolate and limit their contact with males under certain conditions.

Thus, law is the institutional representation of the Jehovah/Persean-Eve set of complexes of the collective psyche.

15.

THE SELF IN THE POST-OEDIPAL STAGE OF HISTORY

MYTHIC SHIFTS AND SOCIAL CHANGE

The shift from the pre-Oedipal stage of history to the Oedipal was marked by the discovery of the uniqueness of human consciousness. The discovery that only the human species had a mind brought about the separation in human awareness and perception between culture and nature. Human-kind began to look upon itself as a unique creation for whom animals and the world existed as other and as objects. The culture-nature bifurcation corresponded with the shift in the object of the ego ideal of the collective psyche from the archetypal mother to the archetypal father. The shift from the Oedipal to the post-Oedipal stage of history also began with a paradigmatic shift in conceptual structure, originating in a changing view of the nature of reality, which brought with it a revolutionary change in the mythic structure. The shift started with the recognition that the common-sense world of the sensations of touch, sight, and sound, is not real since it is subjective to each experiencer. The view that the sensed properties of objects are a part of the objects themselves and define their reality—that the red sweater is still red in the dark, or that the tree makes a sound when it falls in the forest even though there is no ear to hear it— is often called *naive realism.*[1] As the empirically known world is to some extent illusionary and secondary to mind, mind now achieves a unique status over matter. Mind becomes the measure of reality, and matter its product. As the shift from the pre-Oedipal to the Oedipal stage of history was marked by a radical culture/nature bifurcation, so the shift from the Oedipal to the post-Oedipal is marked by mind/body dualism. The object of the ego ideal of the collective psyche shifts from the archetypal father to the archetype of disembodied mind.

Naive realism was spontaneously rejected by the learned in at least two places on earth, ancient India and ancient Greece. In both places a radical paradigmatic shift in world view took place. While the philosophers or sages of both India and Greece came to the realization that sensed experience was relative to the experiencer, and therefore could not furnish a basis for ultimate reality, they took their new reconstructions of reality in entirely opposite directions. The scientific world view had its origins in the physical theories of nature of Thales, Anaximander, Anaximenes, and Heraclitus, the founders of the Milesian School. They began one of the most revolutionary and profound paradigmatic shifts in human thought, a shift that is still in progress.[2] While the subjective nature of empirically known reality was realized by the ancient thinkers of India, and such knowledge was incorporated into Hinduism and Buddhism, Eastern thought continued to maintain a substantial mythic dimension. The Greeks, on the other hand, rejected myth as a reliable or useful form of knowledge and attempted to understand nature and the cosmos in ways which were independent of the knower and would therefore give meaning to an objective external reality.[3] Xenophanes, in his poem *Of Nature,* said "If oxen, horses, and lions had hands and could paint pictures and carve statues, they would represent the gods under the guise of oxen, horses, and lions, in the manner of men who represented them in their own image."[4] This statement reflects a clear understanding of the mental process of projection which is involved in mythic thought. With the rejection of naive mythic thought, the Greeks established the foundations of the scientific approach to knowledge.[5] The basic paradigms of scientific thought, such as mathematical laws of physical nature and theoretical constructs such as the concept of the atom of Democritus and the concept of the continuum of Stoic physics,[6] remain the foundations of modern science.

The result was a totally new and different view of nature and the cosmos. The universe was no longer conceived as a product of the will of the gods or of magical and mystical forces. Given that man legitimizes his social order in terms of the natural order, the shift from myth to science in ancient Greece had profound and far-reaching repercussions for social order. The implications of this new view of nature for ethics and law were revolutionary and shattering.[7] Nature was no longer to be viewed as the creation by act of will of a male deity or mythic heroic king figure, but rather in terms of universal physical laws, which ideally could be given a precise mathematical formulation.

There are two fundamental presuppositions of the Greek scientific view of nature. The first is that nature is physical. This is to say that nature is stuff. This presupposition was implicit in the teachings of Thales. The second presupposition, proclaimed by Heraclitus, was that the essence of nature is change. It was the genius of Parmenides to recognize that these two presuppositions are incompatible, if nothing else is assumed. If reality is stuff then it is both physical and permanent since the real is being, "where being means that the real does not change its properties."[8] It follows on this view that reality is eternal in and of itself. It cannot be created, therefore no creator is required. Permanence is a very part of its nature. Parmenides argued that change, as Heraclitus must have emphasized it, must be due to generation or motion. It cannot be due to generation, for that would mean that the 'real' changes its properties, and that would be incompatible with the principle of being. Change cannot be due to motion, for motion requires that a thing move from where it is to where it is not, while remaining the thing. But if nature is nothing but the stuff that moves, there is no 'where-it-is-not', and hence motion is impossible. Parmenides therefore concluded that reality consisted of nothing but unchanging, unmoving, undifferentiated material.[9] Reality is either stuff, or it is change or flux, but it cannot be both unless something further is presupposed. The something further was furnished by Leucippus and Democritus postulating the existence of absolute space within which stuff as microscopic atoms could move. Democritus concluded that "sweet and bitter, cold and warm as well as all the colors, all these things exist but in opinion and not in reality; what really exists are unchangeable particles, atoms, and their motions in empty space."[10]

While a monistic worldview was accepted in the East, monism was rejected in Greece, probably because it was presented in a powerful but nonpersuasive form. At the stage when it is discovered that "all the choir of heaven and furniture of the earth, in a word, all those bodies which compose the mighty frame of the world, have not any subsistence without a mind"[11] and that the sensed qualities like color, taste, smell, and sound, "can no more be ascribed to the external objects than can the tickling or the pain caused sometimes by touching such objects,"[12] one can take either a mental or material view of reality. The mind or matter can be either differentiated or undifferentiated. While ancient India adopted mental monism,[13] Greece embraced atomistic materialism. Consequently, the only form of monism that was seriously considered by the Greeks was the logically elegant but unpersuasive material monism of Parmenides.

While Thales recognized the significance of mathematics for an understanding of nature, its importance was not fully appreciated until the Greeks produced a mathematical formulation of the laws of musical harmony and of the movement of heavenly bodies. These successes led the Pythagoreans to postulate that reality is of the nature of number. The mathematical theory of nature required no reference to physical objects. This led the later Greeks to conclude that the real is rational rather than physical. If ultimate reality is rational rather than physical, then two things follow. As postulated by Plato, behind the apparent physical world lies a real world of forms, which are known only by reason. The existence of these rational forms presupposes an ultimate reality as a universal mind. This shift brought about the death of science. Attention shifted from the material world to that of thought and speculation. God, or the gods, as absolute mind behind the material world, replaced science. The result was the turning from science back to myth and the foundation was laid for the worldview of the Middle Ages. Both East and West now identified ultimate reality with mind. For the East, ultimate mind was undifferentiated. For the West, it was differentiated. In each tradition, however, physical reality was considered unreal and secondary. Science was reborn with Galileo, and with the rebirth of science a fundamental dualism was enshrined in the Western worldview.

The dialectical tensions between science and religion parallel the dialectics of body\mind dualism. The presuppositions upon which science rests are in contradiction to the presuppositions underlying the religious worldview of both the East and the West. Science is based on the presupposition that the real is stuff. As such it is uncreated, and whatever ultimate description we can give it, its being includes time and space. Whether before or after the big bang, and whether expanding or contracting, there is no outside of the universe. The universe does not float within some external empty space. There is no outside to stuff nor any place for it not to be, as space itself is subsumed in its being. There is no before, since the space/time continuum lies within and not outside. There is no higher ultimate reality behind it. It, therefore, causes mind, and not the converse. On the scientific view the particle\wave\matter\energy\space\time continuum is the cause and mind is the effect. It cannot be directly known, and any descriptions we give of it, whether mathematical or otherwise, are not to be confused with its being. The real, if it is stuff, is neither logical nor rational. Knowledge about it may be so, but knowledge itself is merely an incomplete isomorphic representation at best. Religion, on the other hand, is based on the presupposition that the real is mind, and stuff is caused or created by it. As such, stuff is secondary, not eternal and not ultimate. On the religious view the ultimate Mind\God, whether differentiated as the Logos, Jehovah, or Allah, or undifferentiated as Brahman, Nirvana, or Tao, is the cause, and all else is effect.

THE DENIGRATION OF THE BODY AND THE GLORIFICATION OF MIND

A distinction between the mind or spirit and the body was likely made very early in the development of human thought. It is implicit in almost any view of an afterlife. A radical mind/body dualism, along with the premise of the primacy of mind over matter and the subjective nature of material sense experience, leads to a rejection of the body as an integral part of the self. Mind and body are seen as being in opposition. To give in to the dictates and needs of the body is to deny the primacy of the mind. The archetype of disembodied mind lies at the core of the Apollonian complex which seeks to deny and transcend the body. Hillman writes: [14]

> The Apollonic fantasy of reproduction [i.e., that life originates in the male] and female inferiority recurs faithfully in the Western scientific tradition. We call it "Apollonic" because, unlike "Adamic," with its overtones of the natural *Urmensch*, mystical man, and androgynous man, "Apollonic" evokes the purified objectivity and the scientific clarity of masculine consciousness. The Apollonic view of the feminine appears to be inherent in the same structure of consciousness as the methods by which the fantasy is supposedly proven.

The powerful, body-centered sexual drive is the most threatening to the primacy of mind. The denial and transcending of the sex drive becomes one of the central fixations of the Apollonian complex. Since it is women who trigger sexual arousal in the male, women furnish the opposition to disembodied mind as the object of the ego ideal. The negation of the body which is implicit in adopting disembodied mind as an object of the ego ideal entails the negation of women. Males see themselves as mind and women as bodies.

Body-mind dualism lies at the very foundation of patriarchal religion. Misogyny is an integral part of any religion which, as a mythic system, offers disembodied mind as the object of the ego ideal. In this regard the difference between Eastern and Western religions is purely one of degree. In *Women in Buddhism,* Diana Paul presents a wide variety of texts from Buddhist scriptures and literature which are replete with misogyny. She concludes: [15]

> Traditional Buddhist attitudes toward woman as inferior reflect a view of woman as temptress or evil incarnate. The lustful woman is seen with unrestrained sensuality, perhaps irrevocably so. She has an animalistic nature associated with innate sexual drives not found in the nature of the male. Buddhist literature implies that woman is biologically determined to be sexually uncontrollable. By despising her own nature, woman can perhaps deny her biological destiny of depravity.

The monastic and ascetic tradition of Eastern religions and Christianity reflect the same basic formula—body is identified with female and contrasted with mind which is identified with male, and female is identified with evil and the pollution of mind. Negative archetypal images which deny the archetypal feminine as object of the ego ideal are abundant in their mythic structures.

The creation myth of Genesis reduces the Goddess to the figure of Eve, a secondary creation out of the rib of Adam, created for his benefit. The sacred tree of Goddess worship becomes the tree of the forbidden fruit, and the serpent, the symbol of the Goddess, becomes the devil/tempter. William Blake's illustrations for Milton's *Paradise Lost,* for example, furnish graphic evidence of the negation of the Goddess archetype implicit in Judaeo-Christianity.[16] In *The Temptation of Eve,* Eve is shown naked and entwined in a large serpent which holds out the forbidden fruit to her in its mouth.[17] In the illustration *Satan, Sin, and Death,* Blake portrays Eve with serpents curled around her legs and feet with two male demonic figures on either side.[18] Thus, the symbols of life and fertility of the Goddess and consort become the symbols of evil and death in the new mythic structure. At the same time a new archetype of the male appears as father god, king, and hero. In the gender structure which underlies and permeates Christianity, the figure of the consort is split into two, the

Devil and Christ. One of the most important symbols of Dionysus is that of the grape. Joseph Campbell writes of Dionysus as "the deified grape," and compares a mural of Dionysus clothed with grapes with a carved Church door portraying Jesus hanging on the cross surrounded by clusters of grapes.[19]

Christianity is the grand synthesis of the ancient world. It was the funnel which carried ancient culture through the dark ages of the medieval period into the modern. The story of the formulation of Christianity is one of struggle between conflicting archetypal structures, and the integration of Hellenism and Judaeo-Christianity into a grand synthesis. The cultural streams which survived through inclusion were Greek philosophy, including Plato, Aristotle, and Stoicism; monotheistic Judaism (which survived independently as well as through its incorporation into Christianity); and Greek political theory.[20]

The early Christian Church itself was a product of a struggle between conflicting archetypal mythic structures. Judaeo-Christianity embodied Judaism within the framework of a belief centered in Jesus as the Jewish Messiah.[21] Pagano-Christianity, which was the product of the teachings of Paul of Tarsus, turned matriarchal paganism on its head.[22] The dying-reborn son sacrificed for the fertility of the earth in the name of the mother now becomes the Christ dying in the name and according to the will of the Heavenly Father. Gnostic Christianity was pagan Gnosticism restructured within a Christian framework of symbols and figures.[23] Pagano-Christianity won the struggle against the other two competing forms.

The Epistles of Paul are the earliest among the writings which make up the New Testament.[24] The four Gospels, the book of Acts, the Book of Revelation, and the remaining Epistles were all written later. Paul never met the historical Jesus. He refers very seldom, if at all, to the events of his life, other than his death and purported resurrection. He never quotes Jesus or refers directly to his teachings as authority for the Pauline version of Christianity. Unlike all of the other disciples of Jesus, Paul was not born and raised in Judaea but was a Jew of the dispersion, born, raised, and educated in the Greek city of Tarsus. Many have noted the similarities between the Christ of the teachings of Paul, and the dying and resurrected savior gods of paganism, all having their origin in the Dionysian archetype of the consort to the Goddess.[25] These pagan prototypes for the Pauline Christ, the doctrine of salvation through rebirth, the sacrament of the eating of the flesh and blood of the sacrificial figure (generally a bull), all became woven into the framework of Pagano-Christianity.

The early Christians were well aware of the similarities between Dionysus and Christ. The classicist, Walter F. Otto, cites a passage from Plutarch's *De Oraculorum defectu* where Plutarch relates the story of a ship which, while passing by the Echinades island, was hailed from the shore by someone calling to the pilot, Thamus. The hailer told him, "When you come opposite to Palodes, announce that Great Pan is dead." All on the ship, according to Plutarch, were astounded, and Thamus made up his mind that if there was a breeze, he would sail by the island without delivering the message, but if there was no wind and the seas were smooth he would do as he had been bid. On reaching Palodes, the seas became smooth and the wind dropped. Thamus called out the message as he had been instructed, and cried out to the shore, "Great Pan is dead." There followed, according to Plutarch, "a great cry of lamentation, not of one person, but of many, mingled with exclamations of amazement." According to Otto this event was supposed to have taken place in the first century A.D. during the reign of Tiberius. Otto goes on to relate that "Later, . . . Christian legend was to suggest that Pan had died on the very day when Christ had mounted the cross."[26]

The transition in the ancient Mediterranean basin from Dionysus-Bacchus-Pan to Christ presents an outstanding example of an archetypal structure within a religious framework replacing an older structure by taking over the symbols, archetypal figures and images, and reversing their meanings. The sacred king-saviour now voluntarily sacrifices himself for the heavenly father god rather than the Goddess. Body is replaced by Spirit, female values by male values, the focus on life by a focus on death. The earth is secularized and the heavens are made sacred. In this shift the image of woman is even robbed of its ultimate positive characteristic, that of love and sacrifice of the mother for the child. It is now Jesus who says, "Suffer the little children to come unto me."[27] It is the love of Jesus which now becomes the ultimate example of unselfish love. The archetype of the Mother is transformed within Christianity from that of the powerful Goddess figure to that of the grieving Mary, who is to be cared for by John, a disciple whom Jesus loved. A real woman could not be the mother of a Christ, so her entire material body and sexuality were denied in the myths of the Immaculate Conception of Mary, the virgin birth of Jesus, and the Assumption of Mary into Heaven.[28]

The archetype of the Christ eventually lost all its physicality by its identification with the Greek *Logos* (word, order, structure). The opening verses of the Gospel of John proclaim:

1. In the beginning was the Word *[Logos]*, and the Word *[Logos]* was with God, and the Word *[Logos]* was God.
2. The same was in the beginning with God.
14. And the Word *[Logos]* was made flesh, and dwelt among us, (and we beheld his glory, the glory as of the only begotten of the Father,) full of grace and truth.

At the same time, the other, older half of the Dionysian archetype, the ancient horned God, is turned into the Devil, thus shattering the mind-body unity implicit in the figures of Dionysus and Pan. Throughout the later history of Christianity the devil is portrayed as horned, with a tail, and with cloven hoofs in place of feet.

The crucifixion of Dionysus on the cross of mind/body, good/evil, heaven/hell (earth) dualism was the culminating archetypal shift in the collective psyche of Western man from a more unified to a radical dualistic structure. This bifurcation underlies the whole monastic tradition in the West as well the East. Brother Giles, the companion of St. Francis, proclaimed:[29] "Our wretched and weak human flesh is like the pig that ever delighteth to wallow and befoul itself in the mud, deeming mud its great delight. Our flesh is the devil's knight; for it resists and fights against all those things that are of God and for our salvation." This bifurcation moved the sacred from earth to the heavens. According to Richard Rubinstein, "[t]he process of secularization . . . led to the bureaucratic objectivity required for the death camps," which, he suggests, "was an essential and perhaps inevitable outcome of the *religious* traditions of the Judaeo-Christian west."[30] This bifurcation also underlies the pathological destruction of the environment being carried out by industrial societies.

The splitting of Dionysus into the fleshless *Logos*-Christ and the Devil in the mythic system we call Christianity laid the foundations for a holocaust against the remnants of matriarchal paganism, and women who had the audacity to adopt the archetype of the Goddess as object of their ego ideal and express their own inner selves. No one knows exactly how many women were massacred as witches. Figures range from hundreds of thousands into the millions. Fertility cult paganism was transformed into the dark, reverse side of Christianity.[31] Not only practicing pagans were eliminated, however, but also midwifes, healers—any woman who refused to adopt the Eve complex. The pathology with which witches were hunted, questioned, tortured, and then executed, clearly reflects the fact that deep, unconscious forces from the male psyche were at work in the mind of the collective.[32]

In this modern age of the death of God, while the old mythic structures are not taken literally by the more enlightened, they retain their hold over the general masses. These structures continue to function at an unconscious level in the minds of even the educated elites who reject a literal intepretation of the myths. In the mythic structure of Christianity as reflected in the Book of Revelation, the Father is to let loose the devil, the evil one, who will finally be conquered with the second coming of Christ. The old horned God, however, arises from drives in the collective psyche committed to life and the perpetuation of the species through children, while Christ is the god of death, denial of the body and of the earth. Lucifer or the devil and Christ are archetypal representations of body-mind dualism implicit in the archetype of disembodied mind. So after the "twenty centuries of stony sleep . . . what rough beast, its hour come round at last, Slouches towards Bethlehem to be born?"[33] In the Second Coming, who is the real saviour and who is the real devil? Which archetypal figure will usher in the millenium, the horned god uniting body and mind, male and female, earth and nature, or the *Logos,* the embodiment of mind and masculine spirituality?

The religious history of the West should not be viewed as merely a set of disparate cults and religions which develop and disappear. Rather, it should be seen as a process which follows a pattern which can be recognized and understood within a psychoanalytic framework. The history of the sacred begins with matriarchal paganism. The mother archetype is gradually replaced by the father archetype in the shift to patriarchal paganism. In the West, patriarchal paganism developed into monotheism with the supremacy of Jehovah worship. Jehovah, the Father God, is gradually transformed into the *Logos,* under the impact of Greek philosophy and the recognition that the universe can, at least in part, be described in mathematical terms. While it is true that cults appear and disappear, those which survive to become integrated into the collective psyche are those which best reflect the internal struggles of the individual and collective psyches in the Oedipal passage.

THE ARCHETYPES OF DISEMBODIED MIND

The difference between "the Western mind" and "the Eastern mind" reflects a different view of the nature of mind itself as between the two cultural traditions. In the East a monistic view of the mind developed, while in the West an atomistic view emerged. Thus, the object of the ego ideal of the collective psyche of Eastern culture was an archetype of undifferentiated disembodied mind, while that of the Western collective psyche was differentiated disembodied mind. To the degree that mind was viewed differently in the East, that difference will be echoed in the networks of institutions and conceptual structures which developed. The difference between the two kinds of archetypes of disembodied mind produced very different kinds of social order. These differences indicate that there is a close interrelationship between a people's view of reality, their mythic structures, their social order, their view of the self, and the process of individuation at both the individual and the collective level.

In India, philosophers and sages concluded that since sensed experience was relative to the percipient, and therefore illusory, the only reality was an undifferentiated field of consciousness which was called Brahman or Atman,[34] nirvana,[35] or Tao.[36] Thus, the East adopted mental monism. Monism, however, is inconsistent with individuation, as individuation entails the accentuation of differences while monism denies difference. A monistic point of view would coalesce with the drive toward the loss of self in the whole, and would reinforce separation anxiety. Salvation in the Eastern religious and philosophical tradition lies in losing the differentiations which make each individual self unique, thus merging the self with the field of undifferentiated consciousness. The archetype of undifferentiated disembodied mind functions as an object of the ego ideal through which primary narcissistic bliss is sought to be recovered.

According to Jung the concept of the self is an archetypal idea,[37] which "expresses the unity of the personality as a whole."[38] He writes that "the self appears in dreams, myths, and fairytales in the figure of the 'superordinate personality' . . . such as a king, hero, prophet, saviour, etc., or in the form of a totality symbol, such as the circle, square, *quadratura circuli,* cross, etc."[39] It is clear from Jung's discussions of the self that it includes both the ego and the ego ideal. Jung appears to use the term *self* as equivalent to the Freudian term *psyche* as he speaks of the self as "psychic totality."[40] "The self," writes Jung, ". . . is both ego and non-ego, subjective and objective, individual and collective. It is the 'uniting symbol' which epitomizes the total union of opposites."[41] For Jung, Christ and the *Logos,* both of which he refers to as the *principium individuationis,*[42] and the Atman of Hinduism,[43] are archetypal representations of the self. It may be somewhat confusing to view an archetypal representation like the *Logos* (which was used by the Greeks to refer to reason, relation, idea, the faculty of speech, concept, and mind, and thus represents individuation and differentiation) and an archetypal representation like the Atman (which represents undifferentiated wholeness) as different forms of the same archetype. I prefer to use the Freudian term *psyche* to refer to the totality of the individual mind. The idea of the self can be more clearly explained in terms of the ego and the ego ideal. The ego ideal can take different archetypal objects, the most important of which, in relationship to the self, is that of disembodied mind. The idea of the homunculus is implicit in the idea of the self.[44] Self-examination often entails the separation of the self into a more limited rational agency which examines the more comprehensive self. The use of the concept of the "false self" in psychoanalysis entails the concept of what could be considered a "true self."[45] In such ways we conceive of more than one self in the same body, illustrating that we conceive of the self as disembodied in the sense of being separate from our body. This is implicit in a phrase such as "my body."[46]

The archetype of differentiated disembodied mind has one of its clearest manifestations in the philosophical concept of the rational autonomous agent. This archetype is implicit in Greek and Roman Stoicism, and since the time of Kant has been fundamental in Western political thought. Philosophically, the concept of the agent is part of the philosophy of the mind since agency is conceived independently of the body, with the body being the primary tool of an agent. The archetype of differentiated disembodied mind is also the foundation for all religious beliefs that postulate that man has a soul or spirit which survives death. It takes a variety of representative forms ranging from God himself through lesser spirits such as angels or other heavenly forms, to the soul which resides in the body, to ghosts and demons. Just as it underlies all mind/body dualism, it also underlies the bifurcation between the spiritual and the material.

When disembodied mind as object of the ego ideal serves the identification function, we conceive of it as differentiated. The form which this archetype takes is that of the *Logos,* or God as pure mind, complete rationality and omniscience. When disembodied mind serves the merger function, we conceive of it as undifferentiated. The form which this archetype takes is that of the Atman or Brahman without difference, nirvana or the Tao. The Divine, in both East and West, is conceived of in terms of disembodied mind. In Western religions God is said to be Spirit, or a spirit. He is all-knowing and the essence of knowledge is differentiation. In Eastern religion, the material is considered to be illusionary. Only mind is real. Since differentiations are illusionary by nature, the Divine is undifferentiated. Thus the Divine, or God, in East or West, is an ideal— the ideal mind—the archetypal ideal with which the ego seeks either to identify or to merge.

Shakespeare's famous lines from *Hamlet* furnish a paradigm description of the ego ideal as disembodied and differentiated mind: [47]

> What a piece of work is a man!
> How noble in reason, how infinite
> in faculties, in form and moving
> how express and admirable,
> in action how like an angel, in
> apprehension how like a god!
> The beauty of the world. . . .

In the West, another archetypal figure of disembodied differentiated mind is that of Apollo. The contrast between the Apollonian and the Dionysian was made famous by Nietzsche,[48] and further developed by Freudians and Jungians alike.[49] Apollo, according to Jung, is another "divine image of the *principium individuationis.*"[50] In his contrast of the Apollonian with the Dionysian he identifies Apollo with illusion and Dionysus with intoxication.[51] He writes: [52]

> He [Apollo] signifies measure, number, limitation and subjugation of everything wild and untamed. . . . The Dionysian impulse, on the other hand, means the liberation of unbounded instinct, the breaking loose of the unbridled dynamism of animal and divine nature; hence in the Dionysian rout man appears as a satyr, god above and goat below. The Dionysian is the horror of the annihilation of the *principium individuationis* and at the same time "rapturous delight" in its destruction. It is therefore comparable to intoxication, which dissolves the individual into his collective instincts and components—an explosion of the isolated ego through the world.

The Dionysian merger is very different from that of the merger of the ego in disembodied mind. The Dionysian is a merger of the masculine with the feminine, mind with the body, and humans with the earth. The object of the ego ideal is the Goddess. The merger with disembodied mind entails a denial of the body and earth.

In Western religions during the Oedipal stage of history the central figure of worship was an anthropomorphic father. With the beginning of the shift from the Oedipal to the post-Oedipal stage, the concept of God changes from that of a physical being to pure mind. Thus, in Greece Zeus gives way to the *Logos*-like God of the Stoics and the Neo-Platonists. The Greeks achieved monotheism through philosophy. Among the Jews, Jehovah gradually is transformed from an anthropomorphic being to pure spirit. Because of this transition, the convergence of both Judaism and Christianity with Greek philosophy was not difficult.

THE SELF AND SOCIAL ORDER IN WESTERN MYTHIC STRUCTURE

The revolution against domination, in its various forms of monarchy, aristocracy, slavery, racism, and sexism, did not start with an oppressed class seeking freedom. It was not a product of class struggle, nor of the unfolding of economic forces. It arose out of the birth of science, out of speculative thought, but more as an afterthought in the working out of implications of one area of knowledge for another.[53] For reasons totally unrelated to economic forces, morality, or other social issues, a radical paradigmatic shift took place in ancient Greece with the evolution of philosophy and science and the development of deductive and abstract mathematics. The nature of that shift was such that it invalidated the mythic structure of legitimacy upon which all social order up to that time rested, and it led to or permitted a new set of inferences regarding social order which furnished no meaning for hierarchy or domination. The history of legal and political thought from that time until the present has been an attempt to avoid this implication, resist it, and find new ways of justifying hierarchy and domination. None of this has proven successful. The scientific view of nature cannot provide a paradigm for social hierarchy. All forms of legitimization of social hierarchy in terms of conformity with nature inevitably turn out to support the autonomy of the individual instead. The scientific view of nature furnishes a clear justification for a social order without hierarchy. In light of this fact, contemporary justifications for hierarchy tend to be pragmatic. Practical arguments, however, cannot furnish a ground for its legitimacy.

In theory, the scientific paradigm of nature brought with it the implied invalidity of all patriarchal legal systems. The change in man's view of nature required a change in legal archetype, since the nature to which man was now to appeal was a universe of natural laws.[54] The laws of nature became the paradigm for the laws of social order. The Greeks were conscious that they were appealing to nature as a source of legitimacy of their laws. This process, in itself, became the subject of analysis and thought, and gave rise to the first legal philosophy, natural law. Ernest Cassirer explains, in *The Myth of the State:*[55] "Before studying politics they [the Greeks] had studied nature. In this domain they had made their first great discoveries. Without this preliminary step it would not have been possible for them to challenge the power of mythical thought. The new conception of nature became the common ground for a new conception of man's individual and social life."

The new paradigm of natural law to which the social law had to conform in order to acquire legitimacy was that of the physical laws of nature. The most critical property of the laws of physical nature is their universality. A single persistent counter-example is sufficient to reject the validity of a purported law. The Greeks originated the scientific culture which became the foundation of Western civilization by taking the mathematics of Babylonia and Egypt and changing it from an empirical practical discipline into a deductive, theoretical, abstract system. Pre-Greek mathematics consisted of "a collection of empirical conclusions."[56] The great genius of the Greeks was to convert mathematics "from an empirical science into a deductive system of thought."[57] They "eliminated the physical substance from mathematical concepts and left mere husks."[58] This is equivalent to saying that they eliminated the naive realistic conception of scientific objects as directly-sensed material substances.

Another great contribution of the Greeks was that "they realized that mathematical constructs could be used symbolically for a rational description of both celestial and terrestrial phenomena."[59] The realization that the movement of the stars could be described and predicted mathematically, and the formulation of the laws of harmony through mathematical ratios, had a momentous impact on the Greek world view. Thereafter, in every sphere of human knowledge, the Greeks sought universal laws, universals or mathematical relations. Balanced proportions were explored in architecture, and the perfect figure became the goal of the sculptor. In the area of human conduct, moral philosophers sought universal laws for such conduct.

Through the creation of a limited number of logical constructs the Greeks were able to deal with a maximum amount of empirical phenomena.[60] The existence of universal laws in the natural science is based on the uniformity of causation. It is because like causes have like effects that causal relations between changes or states can be expressed in the form of universal laws. Although the Greek comprehension of cause and effect was limited, they did recognize that the necessity of causation was at the very root of the laws of nature. Sambursky has observed, "[T]he Stoic statement, which simply reads 'every time A is restored B must follow again', is the first statement on causality on record which introduces the element of recurrence and the idea of reproductability of a situation B from a situation A."[61]

The assumption of the uniformity of cause is as much the basis of universality in law as in the natural sciences. It is the fact that similar actions produce like effects that permits us to frame laws to control human behavior. Because cause-effect functions uniformly even for human actions, what is a good reason for any one person to do a particular act is equally a good reason for other persons in relevantly similar circumstances. This is why judgments of what we ought to do, whether prudential, moral, or legal, are said to be universalizable.[62] The universalizability of legal judgments is the foundation of the doctrine of precedent that like cases ought to be decided alike. The universalizability of legal rules over the class of all persons is the basis of fundamental principles of liberty and human rights traditionally associated with natural law, such as equality before the law and the rule of law.[63]

To be universal, a law had to have as its subject or domain the whole of a class or species to which it would apply.[64] Since the characteristics which races share are far more numerous than the differences, and since the capacity for rational thought was assumed to be the necessary and sufficient condition for humanity, a universal law of human conduct was defined as one which would be applicable to all persons. From this it followed that the law should deal with the individual citizen and not with families, and that each citizen had to be equal with every other before the law. The practice was attributed to both Socrates and Diogenes of answering, "Of the universe," when asked the question "Of what city are you?"[65] Marcus Aurelius proclaimed, "But my nature is rational and social; and my city and country, so far as I am Antoninus, is Rome, but so far as I am a man, it is the world."[66] Statements such as these reflect the unity in Greco-Roman universalism. Perhaps the clearest expression of this paradigm in recorded history is the inscription believed to have been written above Plato's Academy, "Nobody ignorant of geometry should enter my roof/ That is, no unjust person should pass these portals/ Because geometry is equality and justice."[67] In this tradition, Aristotle defined natural justice as that which "has the same validity everywhere and is unaffected by any view we may take about the justice of it. . . . The rules of law and justice are in each case related to the actions performed in conformity with them as is universal to particular, for the actions are many, the law governing them only one, being universal."[68]

All humans have agency or rationality in common, and therefore a law which conforms to the natural law paradigm will be one which applies universally to any agent whatsoever, regardless of sex, order of birth, family or race. There is no natural basis for treating people as unequal before the law. The specific conditions imposed in the law cannot function to deny its universality.[69] No political ideology has yet been found which has been able to remain consistent with the scientific paradigm of the laws of nature, and reduce the range over which the laws of social order are universalizable to a particular class of persons.

The paradigm of universal laws, the entities of which are variables, require that the law be universalizable over the entire universe of discourse which defines the variable. If the law applies to a particular entity variable under particular conditions, then it must also apply, under relevantly similar conditions, to any other instance of the variable. If a law of social ordering is patterned after the scientific pattern of the laws of nature, then that law will be universalizable. This means that the laws of social ordering must conform to a principle of formal justice. That principle can be stated as follows:[70] "If it is the case that in any judgment made in regard to a particular situation, that a particular person is or is not legally obligated to do a particular act, then it logically follows that anyone in a relevantly similar situation is or is not legally obligated to do the same act." Thus, each case or judgment which holds that a particular person has a legal obligation to do a particular act, instances a rule of law which applies to all other persons in a relevantly similar situation.

The mythic world view in which the object of the ego ideal was the archetypal god/king/paterfamilias could not withstand the contradictions which the scientific world view introduced. The verification of the Greek scientific world view in terms of the mathematical properties of music, and the mathematical laws which permitted the prediction of the movement of celestial bodies, prevented the scientific world view from being repressed or denied by the collective psyche. The mathematical model of equality and the concept of the variable became the paradigmatic form within nature which would be the analogue of the equality of citizens. Any one citizen can be substituted for any other. The convergence of the new paradigm of nature with the drive to individuate away from the old object of the ego ideal, the archetypal father, furnished the conditions for a revolutionary change in social order which has spread throughout the world.

The natural law paradigm of social order presumes a society of free agents, any one of which can be substituted for any other as the subject of a law when the circumstances or conditions of the law are applicable or similar. The most fundamental assumptions of natural law, therefore, are first that man is born free, and second that he is born equal. These are not empirical assertions but moral, legal, and political presuppositions. They are simply a denial of the patriarchal social order based on biological properties determined by birth. They reflect the shift from a mythological to a rational-scientific view of nature. The postulate that man is born free means only that he comes into the world without rights and duties attached to him on the basis of his sex, family, color, race, or order of birth.

If the laws of the social order are to comply with the scientific paradigm of the laws of nature, they must recognize the equal agency of females, and may not discriminate on the basis of sex. Any and all forms of patriarchy are inconsistent with the scientific natural law paradigm. Patriarchal social order simply cannot be legitimized in terms of a scientific view of the natural order. The Greeks, when they found themselves in the intellectual predicament of being unable to deny the scientific world view and, at the same time, being unable to justify or legitimize either the domination of women or slavery, resolved the problem by denying rationality to women and slaves. They dehumanized them in order to exclude them from the universe of discourse of the laws of social order.

The Stoics integrated science and the humanities in their view of human knowledge as a triangle, the three points being physics, logic, and ethics.[71] Consequently Stoic political theory proclaimed the equality of all rational beings; the universality of law and social order; the equality of women; that slavery was contrary to the law of nature; and that the moral order is to be derived from the natural order. There was one science which the Greeks were unable to formalize, or fit within the mathematical model of universal laws, and that was biology. Plato, who remained committed to the mathematical model, was forced to concede the equality of women. In *The Republic* he envisaged women rulers as philosopher kings. Aristotle, on the other hand, made biology the primary science, developed a class logic rather than a propositional logic, and continued to maintain the inferiority of women and slaves by denying them equal rationality. Aristotle, more than any other Greek philosopher, has remained a central figure in Western political theory. It has been the naturalistic directly sensed world of the biological sciences, rather than the conceptual and theoretical world of mathematical physics, which has furnished the "natural" for natural law. The biological differences between the sexes and between races have furnished the paradigms for the mythic projection of superiority and inferiority onto people. The formal structures of the law have been filled with patriarchal content, and legal judgments are consequently universalizable only over the community of the brotherhood. Law has protected the authority of the male over the female and has until only very recently left the father as monarch within the home.

WESTERN LAW AND THE CONCEPT OF THE SELF

All Western law, whether the codified variety of the civil law or the common law, has its origins in classical Roman law. It is recognized that the creation of classical Roman law was a unique achievement and one of the most important Roman contributions to the world. Roman law, compared to all other systems of its time, according to Pringsheim, "rises like a mountain above the common level of the others."[72] It is also widely recognized that the unique factor in the development of Roman law was the presence, for the first time in any legal system, of legal constructs. This factor has been described in many different ways by different authorities in this field. According to Pringsheim, "simplicity is the striking feature of classical law. It was reached by abstraction."[73] Lawson states, "The Romans taught the world—including even the world of the common law—the possibility of forming a legal framework for society, composed of the smallest possible number of elements."[74] Wolff describes the same characteristics when he speaks of "that great, scientific treatment of the law which enabled Roman law, in a manner unique in ancient times, to combine consistency, theoretical refinement, and a high degree of practical elasticity. . . ."[75] Schulz writes, "Often the jurists' statements almost give the impression of a mathematical treatise."[76] Savigny, in similar terms declared:[77]

> The conceptions and rules of their science do not seem to them to be products of their own creation—they are real beings, with whose existence and genealogy they have become acquainted through long and intimate association. That is why their whole procedure is tinged with an assurance not found elsewhere except in mathematics, and it is no exaggeration to say that they make calculations with their conceptions.

From these writers we learn that the factors which makes classical Roman law unique is the economy of terms and principles whereby a large body of phenomena can be dealt with by use of a minimum of concepts. This is possible because Roman law contains concepts which are theoretical, having "image-less" logical rather than "image-ful" naive realistic properties. The development of such concepts, enabling the transformation of a typical archaic legal system into a legal science, must have corresponded to a revolutionary paradigmatic change in the world view of Roman lawyers. There can be little question that such a change took place and resulted from the impact of Greek philosophy.[78]

In order to understand the relationship between Roman law and Greek philosophy we must keep in mind how different the philosophy of Greece was from that of other cultures.[79] One of the principal channels through which the influence of Greek philosophy, science, and mathematics reached Roman lawyers was Stoicism.[80] Classical Roman law was the creation of a small group of juri-consults, most of whom were Stoics. The most influential of this group was probably Q. Mucius Scaevola, who wrote a classic treatise of the law, remaining today only in a few scattered fragments.[81] The creation of classical Roman law was not just the result of the introduction of the dialectical method of organizing a body of knowledge into a scientific system by dividing it into genera and species and then ascertaining the principles "governing the kinds and explaining individual cases."[82] Not only were the Roman jurists familiar with Stoic propositional logic, but in their legal treatises they entered into complex discussions of its finer points as it applied to law and legal reasoning.[83] The writings of jurists such as Proculus, Julianus, and Scaevola show that the creators of classical Roman law thought axiomatically and deductively.

Through conceiving law as abstract relations between "legal persons", Western legal systems built universality into the very structure of the law.[84] As Lawson stated, "A well-marked and well-known characteristic of Roman law is its tendency to become steadily more universal."[85] "There is little or nothing that is purely national in the Roman Law contained in Justinian's *Corpus Juris*. It was ready for reception by any people that had reached a state of civilization which demanded it and was capable of using it."[86] Western law is universalistic, theoretical, and abstract, and it was the adoption of the paradigm of the laws of physical nature which gave it this quality.

The concept of the self as autonomous agent is fundamental to Western law and political and moral theory.[87] All autonomous agents are equal before the law. Since the subject of a law is "any person", or the citizen, we can ignore personal identity. Indeed, the legal person is the basic unit of mature Western legal systems. One jurist has remarked, "For the logic of the system it [the legal person] is just as much a pure 'concept' as 'one' is in arithmetic. It is just as independent from a human being as one is from an 'apple'."[88] Another legal theorist has written,

> Legal personality and legal persons are, as it were, mathematical creations devised for the purpose of simplifying legal calculations. Just as unknown quantities denoted by algebraical symbols such as X are used to simplify problems which could, with a great expenditure of time and labor, be solved by purely arithmetical methods, so legal problems which ultimately concern human beings and physical objects are often more easily solved by interpolating an artificial legal person between the human being or beings and their relation to another person or thing.[89]

That is, legal relations can be applied to anyone under the specific condition or conditions of the rules. Contracts, for example, are empty forms into which we fit persons and patterns of behavior. In other words, they are relations, the entities of which are variables.

Aside from its universality, Roman law had another fundamental characteristic which marked it as radically different from any other legal system in the world up to that time. All law elsewhere in the world, even that of Athens, legitimized domination. Roman law did just the opposite —it established the autonomy of the individual. It was a law of liberty. The spirit of Roman law was reflected in Cicero's proclamation, "We are all servants of the law for the very purpose of being able to be freemen."[90] This unique characteristic of Roman law had its roots in classical Roman private law. The essential part of Roman private law was made up of three divisions, the law of delict or what is called in the common law the law of torts, the law of property, and the law of contracts. These three divisions lie at the heart of the private law component of any Western legal system, whether common law or civil law. The law of torts and property are concerned with the protection of the individual from wrongful interference with his person or property by others, and the law of contract is concerned with allowing people to obtain the beneficial action of others for their own objectives. Thus, the function of Western law is the protection of human action from interference, and the extension of autonomy or agency.

Both the common law and the civil law are the direct descendents of classical Roman law just as modern mathematics, logic, and science are direct descendents of those of the ancient Greeks.[91] The entire law of civil obligations, whether in the form of a civilian code or in the reported cases which make up the common law, guarantees the necessary conditions for autonomous agency to function.[92] Thus, there is an archetypal relationship in terms of the conceptual structure of the rule of law and the state of political liberty. There is, as well, an archetypal relationship in Western societies between the conceptual structure of moral, legal, and political theory based on the assumption of the autonomy of the individual, and the archetypal structure in terms of which people develop their sense of their selves. Implicit in this structure is mind/body, culture/nature dualism.

THE SELF AND SOCIAL ORDER IN EASTERN MYTHIC SYSTEMS

The Eastern mythic tradition is to be found in three principle forms, Hinduism, Buddhism, and Taoism. Each has at its foundation the same view of ultimate reality, that of undifferentiated disembodied mind. In Hinduism it is known as the Brahman without differences or Atman, in Buddhism it is known as nirvana, and in the Chinese tradition as the Tao. These all refer to the Universal Soul. It is undescribable because description entails differentiation and it contains no differences. It is monistic throughout. Consequently, you can only say what it is not and it is not anything which you can say. This archetypal structure developed first in India before the Aryan invasions. It survived on within Hinduism and was carried into Buddhism and Taoism.

The idea of the soul, or the true inner self, is very different in the Eastern tradition than that of the West. In the East, the soul in each individual is a mere manifestation of a single infinite Divine soul, while in the Western religious tradition every individual possesses an immortal soul unique to them. In the Eastern tradition, therefore, the true inner self of every person is not only equal but identical. The fundamental archetypal structure of Eastern mythical systems can provide no meaning for hierarchical social ordering, nor for any form of male domination, since the true inner self of both male and female is the same.

Within the Eastern tradition, Buddhism has produced the most articulated doctrine of the self. The tradition of Buddhism recognizes the temporal, passing, impermanent, changing nature of personal identity, and by so doing is led to find the true self through identification with universal oneness. According to the Lama Anagarika Govinda:[93]

> He who wants to follow the Path of the Buddha must give up all thoughts of "I" and "mine." But this giving up does not make us poorer; it actually makes us richer, because what we renounce and destroy are the walls that kept us imprisoned; and what we gain is that supreme freedom, according to which every individual is essentially connected with all that exists, thus embracing all living beings in his own mind, taking part in their deepest experience, sharing sorrow and joy.

Govinda further states that "all individuals . . . have the whole universe as their common ground, and this universality becomes conscious in the experience of enlightenment, in which the individual awakens into his true all-embracing nature."[94] T. P. Kasulis writes, "then rejection of the self as an independent agent separate from the web of interconnected conditioned causes—is called in Sanskrit the doctrine of *anatman* ('no-ego'; . . . *muga* in Japanese)."[95] The great Zen teacher Rinzai is reported to have related, "In this clump of raw flesh there is a true person of no status continually entering and exiting your [sense organs]."[96] It is not surprising, therefore, that Eastern culture is not as individualistic as Western culture, as the concept of an individual self is considered to be an illusion.

Without question, Buddhism has had a profound impact on the development of the Japanese psyche,[97] as is reflected in the Zen aphorism, "true person of no status."[98] A typical Buddhist text provides, "I am not a Brahmin, rajah's son or merchant; nor am I any what; I fare in the world a sage, of no-thing, homeless, self completely gone out—it is inept to ask me of my lineage."[99] This passage calls to mind similar Stoic aphorisms of universality. The archetypal structure of disembodied mind as object of the ego ideal, and the related perspectives of ultimate reality, provide no basis for legitimizing hierarchy. Rather, they legitimize equality.

Eastern philosophy and religion have always had to have a patriarchal component to legitimize hierarchical social order. Thus, Buddhism in Japan coexists with Shintoism. Japanese marry in Shinto ceremonies performed in Shinto temples, but the ceremonies relating to death take place in Buddhist temples. In India the caste system forms an integral part of Hinduism, and the Brahman or Atman is of significance only at a philosophical level. Hindus, like Jews, Christians or Moslems, worship a "genuine, monotheistic, personal God"[100] or heavenly father generally referred to as Bhagavan. In China, Taoism and Buddhism have coexisted with Confucianism which has provided the structure for social order. All of south and east Asia based social order either on the Laws of Manu of ancient India (which "is not so much a set of laws, in the sense of Western codes, as a book of forms for how the king should act"[101] to maintain the social order according to caste), or on the Confucian model.[102] The archetypal structure of undifferentiated disembodied mind, which underlies almost all Eastern philosophical and religious mythical systems and provides the structure for what is considered to be ultimate reality, can provide no meaning for nor legitimization of male domination of the female. In order to justify the domination of the female demanded by the neurotic and pathological needs of the male psyche, it is necessary that the collective psyche of both Eastern and Western man retain the archetypal structure of the paterfamilias-king-god. This requires the naive realistic view of the nature of reality to remain alongside a philosophical view in the East which maintains that sensed properties are subjective and therefore illusory, and alongside the scientific view of nature in the West.

Domination and hierarchical social order cannot be legitimized in either the East or the West because it cannot be justified in terms of the view of the natural order implicit in either the scientific world view or the Eastern religious and philosophical world view. Authority, therefore, in the sense of the right to command and a duty to obey is simply nonexistent. To achieve the myth of legitimacy, Oedipal archetypal structures of the self must be maintained in the collective psyche within the post-Oedipal stage of history. The struggle for liberation from domination takes place within the conceptual and psychological framework of conflicting mythic systems in both the East and the West.

16.

BROTHERHOODS OF THE COLLECTIVE IN THE POST-OEDIPAL STAGE OF HISTORY

THE COLLECTIVE AS AN ARCHETYPAL OBJECT OF THE EGO IDEAL

Social order is legitimated by mythic systems, which give a construction of reality such that the social order is seen to reflect or be derived from the natural order. The world views and mythic structures that underlie social order entail a view of the nature of the self, and a view of the nature of the collective or community. These in turn are, as a part of the myths of legitimacy, derived from or reflect the particular view of the natural order. The view of the self and of the community are interrelated, as collectives or communities are made up of individuals. A paradigmatic shift in one will, by necessity, entail a related shift in the other. The paradigmatic shifts in world view in both the East and the West that mark the beginning of the passage of the collective psyche from the Oedipal to the post-Oedipal stage of history, entailed a radically new view as to the nature of what reality was believed to be, and a corresponding shift in the view of the self and of the collective. Just as the law, and the legal and political institutions of the Oedipal stage of history reflect particular archetypes of the self and the collective, so the law and legal and political institutions of the post-Oedipal stage reflect a different set of archetypes of the self and the collective. Chapter 15 examined archetypal structures of

318

the post-Oedipal self. This chapter will explore the nature and structure of the archetypes of the collective that underlie contemporary post-Oedipal social order. Chapter 17 will then investigate the theoretical tensions between the presuppositions that underlie the idea of individual citizenship, and those that underlie political authority and the sovereign power of the state in post-Oedipal legal and political theory, as these are but the manifestations of the dialectics of the archetypal configurations of the self and the collective that structure our identity and social order.

Freud defined a group as "a number of individuals who have put one and the same object in the place of their ego ideal and have consequently identified themselves with one another in their ego."[1] When individuals form into a group they develop "a sort of collective mind which makes them feel, think, and act in a manner quite different from that in which each individual of them would feel, think, and act were he in a state of isolation."[2] Freud goes on to state:[3]

> A group is impulsive, changeable and irritable. It is led almost exclusively by the unconscious. The impulses which a group obeys may according to circumstances be generous or cruel, heroic or cowardly, but they are always so imperious that no personal interest, not even that of self-preservation, can make itself felt. Nothing about it is premeditated. Though it may desire things passionately, yet this is never so for long, for it is incapable of perseverance. It cannot tolerate any delay between its desire and the fulfilment of what it desires. It has a sense of omnipotence; the notion of impossibility disappears for the individual in a group.

Another important attribute of the group mind, according to Freud is that, "In groups the most contradictory ideas can exist side by side and tolerate each other, without any conflict arising from the logical contradiction between them."[4] Freud, in listing the features of the group mind, goes on to point out that the group mind seeks illusions rather than truth.[5] A further property is "the individual's lack of freedom in a group."[6]

Freud sets out a number of characteristics which constitute the psychology of the group. Some of these are:

1. The "blotting out of individual personalities"[7] which allows the members of the group to merge in a common identification.
2. The suspension of the superego and individual rational judgment, adopting instead a common "hallucinatory wish fulfillment."[8]

In obedience to the new authority (that of the group) he may put his former "conscience" out of action, and so surrender to the attraction of the *increased pleasure* that is certainly obtained from the removal of inhibitions. On the whole, therefore, it is not so remarkable that we should see an individual in a group doing or approving things which he would have avoided in the normal conditions of life.[9]

3. The development of a common will which is substituted for the individual will.

The will of the individual was too weak; he did not venture upon action. No impulses whatever came into existence except collective ones; there was only a common will, there were no single ones. An idea did not dare to turn itself into an act of will unless it felt itself reinforced by a perception of its general diffusion.[10]

4. All members of the group must be equal to each other.[11]
5. A leader is required who serves as the common focus of the projections of the members of the group.[12]
6. The leader must be the bearer or carrier of the ideology which is the manifestation of the collective illusion.[13]
7. A drive to eliminate from the group those who are different, and thus threaten the solidarity and unity of the collective.[14]
8. A desire to proselytize and convert individuals who share similarities with the group but are not members, and to attack as enemies those who fall outside the group.[15]

Most of these characteristics apply to all kinds of groups, whether they are formed as a spontaneous crowd or whether they are what Freud refers to as "stable" or "artificial" groups, in which external force is employed to prevent disintegration.[16] Freud gives the Catholic Church and the army as two examples of the latter. He also recognized the intellectually creative genius of the group mind to create a wide variety of rule-governed social practices such as language, games, trading, and markets, and mythic structures such as law, politics, and religion.[17] These are not consciously invented but rather develop gradually and spontaneously.

Just as the self is an archetypal structure, there are also archetypal structures of the group. The foundational form is that of the family. This archetype underlies the structure of other archetypal forms such as the kin, the tribe, and the kingdom. Humankind form themselves into a wide variety of groupings, not all of which are archetypal. Those kinds of collectives which are enduring and are similar from one culture to another are manifestations of universal archetypes. The classical archetypal representations of collectives are generally structures along gender lines. The archetypal structure of the patriarchal family is made up of a set of component archetypes including that of the father, the mother, and the brotherhood. Any group which is structured according to the family archetype contains within itself a brotherhood or set of brotherhoods. This archetypal structure takes many different forms such as bands of warriors, priesthoods, monastic orders, guilds, or fraternal orders.

One of the most important contributions in recent years to the psychoanalytic theory of group phenomena is to be found in the writings of the French psychoanalyst, Janine Chasseguet-Smirgel. She explains the phenomenon of individuals losing their individuality within the group as an attempt to heal the narcissistic wound or regain the state of primary narcissistic bliss.[18] The group therefore functions as an object of the ego ideal. She explains:[19]

(The primary narcissistic state extends over a period of time which includes some time prior to the birth itself.) The pinnacle of human development thus contains within itself the promise of a return to the mother's womb or, in other words, to the most primitive phase of development. *We are urged forwards by a sense of longing for a wonderous past (for a time when we were our own ideal)* [my italics]. Between these two points in time, however, there lies the whole of man's psycho-sexual development.

She describes the need of the corporate brotherhood "to reduce the citizens to a single entity, a single body."[20] In describing this state she writes:[21]

The will of the individual no longer exists. All private interests fuse into the general will, according to the social consensus, for the sake of Common Good, to mention some of the expressions dear to writers of utopias.

It is obvious that here we have an excellent description of totalitarianism. . . . If there exists, as I believe from my clinical experience, a fantasy of reintegrating the mother's smooth belly, emptied of its contents, it follows that the complete realization of this fantasy applied to nature would end in an eradication of the human species to the benefit of the single Self.

In her analysis of group psychology she finds the work of Didier Anzieu particularly insightful.[22] Anzieu establishes an analogy between the group and the dream arguing that "Any group situation will be experienced as hallucinatory wish fulfillment."[23] She gives the following summary of Anzieu's thesis:[24]

> According to the author, in the group as in the dream, the psychic apparatus undergoes a triple regression. Temporally the group has a tendency to regress to primary narcissism; topographically, the ego and the superego can no longer exercise their control. The id takes possession of the psychic apparatus with the ideal ego which *"seeks to realize a fusion with the omnipotent mother and the introjective restoration of the lost primary love object.* The group becomes, for the members, the substitute for this lost object."

There are, according to both Chasseguet-Smirgel and Anzieu, three characteristics of group phenomena: the "setting up of an egalitarian theory,"[25] the banishment of the father figure, and the adoption of a leader. These three are closely interrelated in that the equality of the male denies the superiority of the father over the sons, and the leader, who is always a member of the brotherhood, replaces the father. The egalitarian ideology of the group functions to deny difference and to achieve homogeneity. The denial of difference requires the exclusion or marginalization within the group of those with obvious biological differences. Ideological equality requires sameness, and consequently one often finds racism and sexism co-existing comfortably with an ideology of equality. It is an equality of the brethren. The archetype of the group is that of the brotherhood of the collective. Women are not physically the same as men, and they will therefore be excluded from the brotherhood. Since women will never be fully accepted as the same as men by the brotherhood, they will never achieve equal status with the brethren. Obvious biological racial differences function to deny full membership within the brotherhoods in a somewhat similar fashion.[26] Nazi Germany furnishes the paradigm example of the group functioning as object of the ego ideal. The Nazis began by imposing homogeneity upon themselves and eliminating those who were different. They first destroyed their own handicapped, mentally defective and insane, homosexuals, and political dissidents.[27]

An ideology of equality is inconsistent with the authority of the father. "The father figure is in fact chased away, excluded from the group, as is the superego."[28] By excluding the father and denying the superego, by rejecting individuality and pursuing a common will, and by replacing reality with illusion, individuals will do things as members of a group that they would never do by themselves. Regardless of how high, rational, and fine the ideals of a group ideology may be, the most horrendous crimes can be committed by people in the grip of a group illusion. Thus, the horrors of the Inquisition could be carried out in the name of Jesus. The terrors of the French revolution were done in the name of freedom, equality, and fraternity. The massive slaughters of Marxist-Leninist revolutions have been carried out in the name of social justice. The illusionary ideological heavens of utopias lead inevitably to the most hellish of realities.[29] As Djilas stated, "ideology is predominantly irrational and ideal."[30] "[B]elief is stronger than fact, the needs of life *(I would say the needs of the psyche)* more decisive than truth."[31]

The leader is "the promoter of Illusion."[32] He is "the intermediary between the masses and the ideological illusion."[33] According to Chasseguet-Smirgel, "there can be no idealization of the ego without projection,"[34] and consequently a focal point of the projection is required. The leader serves this function. The absolute power of the leader lies in his ability to grasp the essential structures of group illusion, and to restructure it in the form of an ideology. Therefore, the leader, while displacing the Oedipal father, is a replacement for the omnipotent mother.[35] As described by Chasseguet-Smirgel:[36]

> The regression seems . . . to be closely linked to the Illusion whose arrival is promised by the leader. If one considers that this promise stimulates the wish for the fusion of ego and ideal by way of regression and induces the ego to melt into the omnipotent primary object, to encompass the entire universe . . . one can understand, in a general way, that the propensity to a loss of the ego's boundaries makes the individual particularly liable to identify himself not only with each member of the group but with the group formation as a whole. His megalomania finds its expression in this, each person's ego being extended to the whole group. The members of the group lose their individuality and begin to resemble ants or termites. This loss of personal characteristics is all the more necessary, because it contributes to the homogenization of the group as a whole. It thus allows each member to feel himself to be, not a minute, undifferentiated particle of a vast whole, but, on the contrary, identified with the totality of the group, thereby conferring on himself an omnipotent ego, a colossal body.

In pluralistic societies such as those of North America, there is a diversity of groups which to varying degrees serve as archetypal objects of the ego ideal. Nevertheless, the sexism, racism, and intolerance of difference to be found in contemporary America still reflect much of the group phenomena described in the psychoanalytic theory of group psychology.

A homogeneous society such as that of Japan furnishes an even clearer example of the group as object of the ego ideal. Dr. Takeo Doi, in *The Anatomy of Dependence,*[37] provides an analysis of the collective Japanese psyche which reveals a great deal about the archetypal structure of the brotherhood of the collective as object of the ego ideal. According to Dr. Doi, "the chief characteristic of the Japanese" is best expressed by the concept *amae*. As Dr. Doi put it, *amae* "is a thread that runs through all the various activities of Japanese society," and is the foundation of "the spiritual culture of Japan."[38]

"*Amae*," according to the foreword of *The Anatomy of Dependence,* "refers initially, to the feelings that all normal infants at the breast harbor toward the mother."[39] It is the noun form of the verb *amaeru* which is defined in the foreword as follows:[40]

> It is the behavior of the child who desires spiritually to "snuggle up" to the mother, to be enveloped in an indulgent love, that is referred to in Japanese as *amaeru* (the verb; *amae* is the noun). By extension, it refers to the same behavior, whether unconscious or deliberately adopted, in the adult. And by extension again, it refers to any situation in which a person assumes that he has another's goodwill, or takes a—possibly unjustifiably—optimistic view of a particular situation in order to gratify his need to feel at one with, or indulged by, his surroundings.

The term *amae* is used to describe the feeling people have when they wish to be dependent upon and seek another's indulgence.[41] Dr. Doi points out that there is no similar term to be found in European languages, but that *amae* means the same thing as was meant by Michael Balint when he coined the phrase "passive object-love."[42] According to Balint, "all the European languages fail to distinguish between active love and passive love."[43] "I believe," writes Dr. Doi, "that *amae* was traditionally the Japanese ideology—not in its original sense of 'the study of ideas' but in its modern sense of a set of ideas, or leading concept, that forms the actual or potential basis for a whole social system—and still is to a considerable extent today."[44] Dr. Doi goes on to state that he has become increasingly convinced, "that what has traditionally been referred to vaguely as the 'Japanese spirit' or the 'soul of Yamato,' as well as more specific 'ideologies' such as emperor worship and respect for the emperor system can be interpreted in terms of *amae*."[45] "When the infant is left by its mother," he writes, "it feels an uneasiness, a threat to its very life; and it seems likely that it is precisely this feeling that lies at the heart of what is described by modern man as 'human alienation.' "[46]

There are two aspects of the Japanese psyche which are not brought out and discussed by Dr. Doi. One is that it is highly patriarchal, and the other is that the exclusion of those who are different is severe. One need only look at the position of women, ethnic Koreans, and the aboriginal Ainu, as well as the history of the treatment of the mentally ill and the *Burakumin,* a class of more or less "untouchables", to realize that the world of *amae* described by Dr. Doi, applies only to the Japanese male.[47] Not only equality but biological sameness is required for membership in the brotherhood of the collective.

In Ian Buruma's book, *A Japanese Mirror,*[48] the images presented of aspects of Japanese culture reflect the exact same archetypes of the female as are to be found in Bram Dijkstra's *Idols of Perversity*[49] and Klaus Theweleit's *Male Fantasies.*[50] The archetypes behind the images suggest the presence of the same four complexes of the post-Oedipal male psyche as are to be found in the West—the Dionysian, the Persean, the Apollonian, and the Heraclean. An examination of Japanese pornography also reflects the same patterns. What is interesting about Dr. Doi's study, however, is that the conceptual framework in terms of concepts is derived from the archetypal structure of the mother. The entire description of *amae* found throughout the book reflects the desire and drive to recover the state of primary narcissism. This furnishes one of the most striking examples that verifies that archetypal objects of the ego ideal such as the brotherhood of the collective function as substitutes for primary narcissism and the first object of the ego ideal, the archetypal mother.

CLASS STRUCTURE AND POWER ELITES

Hobbes stated, "I put for a generall inclination of all mankind, a perpetuall and restlesse desire of Power after power, that ceaseth onely in Death."[51] History confirms Hobbes's astute observation. His explanation for the power drive was that a man "cannot assure the power and means to live well, which he hath present, without the acquisition of more."[52] Psychoanalytic theory would explain the drive for power as an attempt to recover the state of primary narcissism. "The development of the ego," Freud wrote, "consists in a departure from primary narcissism and gives rise to a vigorous attempt to recover that state. This departure is brought about by means of the displacement of libido on to an ego imposed from without; and satisfaction is brought about from fulfilling this ideal."[53] A Jungian explanation of the power drive would view it as a complex. Jung defined the power-complex as "the whole complex of ideas and strivings which seek to subordinate all other influences to the *ego,* no matter whether these influences have their source in people and objective conditions or in the subject's own impulses, thoughts, and feelings."[54] A Freudian and a Jungian conception of the power drive are reconcilable when one realizes that mankind's primary complexes can best be explained as attempts to recover the state of primary narcissism. Jung stated, "Complexes are in truth the living units of the unconscious psyche,"[55] and Freud stated, "What he [man] projects before him as his ideal is the substitute for the lost narcissism of his childhood in which he was his own ideal,"[56] and both are correct. The brotherhoods of the collective, as representations of the brotherhood as archetypal object of the ego ideal, furnish the institutional frameworks within which the power-drive-complex is expressed.

The foundation of class structure is the drive for power, which seems to characterize the ruling class in every society.[57] The drive for power is the common factor which links sexual domination with class domination. The function of power is to regain the lost feeling of primary narcissistic omnipotence by objectifying others and nature and treating them as extensions of the self, or as means. Thus, the group functions in two different ways to heal the narcissistic wound and to recover the original narcissistic state. First, it functions as an object of the ego ideal into which the self can be merged, and second, it functions as an instrument of power. Individuals seek both to merge the self into the group and to merge the group into the self. As a person becomes a part of the group, the group becomes a part of him. Group and individual merge so that the power of the group is felt and enjoyed by its individual members. Outside of the group the individual is naked and alone. The self is miniscule. Within the group each self takes on the power of the group and shares the sense of omnipotence. Brotherhoods tend to coalesce around and become centers of power. Thus, men seek membership in brotherhoods to recover the lost narcissistic bliss through both merger and inflation of the self. The pursuit of power through and within the brotherhoods becomes the ideal of action by which mortality and animality are denied. The will to power helps to repress and suppress our knowledge of the human condition. The reality of the human condition is poetically expressed by Yeats: [58]

> sick with desire
> And fastened to a dying animal
> It knows not what it is.

Within the group this reality is repressed and illusion flourishes.

There are three basic kinds of power: physical power, economic power, and ideological power. Physical power entails the capacity to use brute force on other persons. Economic power entails the capacity to grant or withhold economic benefits, whether in terms of money, property, or resources.[59] Ideological power consists of the capacity to affect other people's actions by persuasion. The use of violence, wealth, and authority, by groups are closely interrelated. Economic power is difficult to exercise and enjoy unless it can be protected through the use of physical power. Physical power alone is valued only by bullies and sadists. It is a rather empty exercise unless it can bring with it economic power. The principle use of physical power is to acquire, enjoy, and protect the use of wealth. It is extremely difficult to maintain a monopoly on physical power without the legitimation of acquisition and use. Physical power must be backed by authority and authority comes from ideology. The effective exercise of physical power requires the use of ideological power. Equally economic power must be legitimized if it is to be efficient and effective. In turn the brotherhoods which have a monopoly on ideology must have some economic power, and often seek physical power to keep the monopoly or to make it effective. The use of physical, economic, and ideological power, are closely interrelated. They must be used in tandem.

Monopoly is the essence of power. It is difficult for any brotherhood to control any more than one kind of power at any one time. In the past no single brotherhood has been able to maintain a monopoly on all three kinds of power at the same time. The occasions when a brotherhood had a monopoly on two kinds of power are few and limited in duration. Cooperation and mutual tolerance between brotherhoods has nearly always been essential. Each brotherhood has at its apex a power elite with a leader at the top of the hierarchy. The exercise of power, therefore, requires a ruling class made up of the elites of the brotherhoods of the three kinds of power.

The ruling class is able to dominate other classes through the possession of a combination of physical, economic and ideological power. Each kind of power is essential. No ruling class can maintain its hierarchical position without the use of violence. The power to apply physical force is exercised through the control of a military or policelike body. Equally the control of wealth must lie with the ruling class. The control of property is essential to maintain a monopoly over violence and to enjoy the fruits of domination. Otherwise a group would not be preeminent as a class. No ruling class can control wealth and maintain its dominant position for very long by force alone. The control of wealth and the exercise of force must be legitimized. According to Heilbroner, "It is precisely the presence or absence of . . . a sense of deeply-felt and universal authority—an authority that needs neither apology nor defense—that separates the idea of class from that of estates, elites, power groups, and the like."[60] It is essential for any ruling class to control the ideology of a society. The foundations of class structure rest, therefore, on enforcement (military power), wealth (economic power), and authority (ideological power). Each is a necessary condition and none alone is a sufficient condition for class rule.

Societies became structured along class lines with the rise of monarchy. Social order during the age of matriarchal consciousness was probably along nonpatriarchal kinship lines. Class structure appears only in complex societies during and after the shift from kinship to kingship.[61] The first ruling class is the aristocracy. In order to have an aristocracy there must exist a royal bloodline and a royal family. Until the rise of a capitalist class, the only kind of ruling class to be found is that of aristocracy. If the monarchy is not overly powerful and the ruling bloodline has not been long established, the ruling class will tend to be feudal. The mythic structure which provides the authority or ideological foundation for the ruling class is that of the archetypal father (heavenly, royal, and paterfamilias) and the patriarchal family. Until the rise of capitalism, the ideological foundation of class domination was the same as the ideological foundation of sex domination—patriarchy. The same mythic system and kind of authority underlay both. Military and economic power could not be effectively and efficiently exercised until it could be ideologically legitimized. The ruling family had to become the royal family, and the ruling class had to become viewed as "high-born" or "noble". Patriarchy formed the ideological underpinning of the ruling class, and ideological power was exercised through religious and legal institutions. The control of ideology made the monopoly over violence "lawful" and the enjoyment of wealth a matter of right. Class structure is the very hallmark of the Oedipal stage of history, and an inevitable aspect of patriarchal social order.

A variety of brotherhoods function within class-structured society. These brotherhoods are the medium through which the various kinds of power are organized and exercised. Thus there are military brotherhoods, ideological brotherhoods, and economic brotherhoods. The military make up the primary set of brotherhoods which organize and control the monopoly on violence. The Church is made up of a set of brotherhoods which control and exercise ideological power. Brotherhoods of producers, merchants, and bankers organize and control economic power. The elite of the brotherhoods are often members of the ruling class and it is through them that the ruling class is able to exercise physical, ideological, and economic power. In class-structured societies there will inevitably be struggle within and between the brotherhoods for power. By rising to positions of power and control within the brotherhoods people can enter the ruling class. Struggles, for example, between church and state were not struggles between classes so much as they were struggles between brotherhood elites for membership and influence in the ruling class, each elite having a monopoly on different forms of power.

An analysis of the corporate brotherhoods of the collective which make up the social structure of "fraternal patriarchy" entails the clarification of the role of the corporate structures in the formation of and maintenance of the ruling class at any point in history. The domination of social classes requires a different kind of analysis from that of the domination of women by men. Nevertheless, the two forms of domination are not unrelated. Robert Heilbroner's intuition that "the same general aspects of the human psyche would apply to the case of patriarchy as to that of class rule" is sound.[62] Since class domination takes place within the framework of patriarchy and was a product of patriarchal social order, an analysis of the neurotic foundations of class rule should come out of an analysis of patriarchy rather than an analysis of patriarchy from that of class struggle.

While there are many different kinds of brotherhoods, there is a fundamental structural difference between those of the Oedipal and those of the post-Oedipal stages of history. The latter are corporate structures and the former are not. The family, the extended family, or the tribe are led by patriarchs while corporate brotherhoods have leaders. There are fundamental differences between the archetypal figure of the father and that of the leader. The leader is in many ways opposite to the father. The father rules because he has authority which is derived from the superiority of his biologically determined position. The leader is not above the brotherhood but a member of it and its ultimate personification. The structure of the patriarchal family and that of the group are radically different. The essence of the structure of the family, whether the individual family, the extended family, tribal family, or nation family, is that the place of each individual in the group is different. The difference may be determined by paternity, sex, order of birth, family, caste, or class. Within the group, however, everyone is equal, and if biological differences are so pronounced that equality is considered to be precluded, then such persons must be excluded from the group.

Although the concept of the equality of members is essential to the conceptual structure of the kind of group which substitutes for the omnipotent mother as object of the ego ideal, such groups contain hierarchical structures, as well as a leader who must himself be a member of the group and, as such, an equal. The key to understanding how the equality of the members is reconcilable with an all-powerful leader, power elites, and other hierarchical structure to be found within groups, lies in understanding the nature of the corporation. Corporate structures are entities in and of themselves. They have an identity separate and apart from the individuals who make them up. The whole is always greater than its parts. A corporate structure is viewed as an agent, capable of acting, albeit through its members, but having its own goals and their ordering. It has, in other words, a will, which constitutes the common will of its membership. Corporate structures are groups personified. Personhood is projected onto the group. The corporate structure is able to reconcile the equality of its members with a pyramidical hierarchy with a leader at the top because the positions of the hierarchy are variables into which any member of the group may fit. Anyone can rise to be the leader, or climb up the hierarchy as far as they are able. Corporate structures require a view of the individual which would not have been conceptually possible without the development of the concept of the variable in Greek mathematics, science, and logic. Individual members can come and go, and leaders may die and new ones replace them, but the corporate structure lives on. The paradigm examples of the corporate structure are the state, the church, and the political party. Business enterprises which adopt the corporate structure are a relatively new form of this kind of group.

It is the equality of the members of the corporate group, which assumes their interchangeability and which makes a corporate structure a brotherhood. It is the personification (the projection of personhood) onto the corporate structure which makes possible the illusion of a common will. Corporate structures as brotherhoods of the male become the ideal into which the individual can merge his ego. While the corporate structure is hierarchical, the individual does not sense that he is subjugated because he has merged his will with the common will. Conformity is expected from all alike. Even the leader is trapped within the conceptual structure of the group, and must serve the group illusion to survive. He must be the very embodiment of the general will. His will is absolute because it is the general will. The more inclusive the corporate structure is, the better it can serve as the focus of the ego ideal. Corporate structures tend to grow by submerging other corporate structures. Thus, church and state have struggled to incorporate each other, and political corporate entities seek to expand control into every possible field. Conformity is achieved through the elimination of diversity.

The brotherhoods of collective power must function within an institutional framework if the monopolies on the various kinds of power are to effectively support each other. The brotherhood elites which make up the ruling class must be members of a common corporate structure or overriding brotherhood which integrates the brotherhoods of power and gives a common identity to the ruling class. The corporate nation-state serves this function. The transition from the Oedipal to the post-Oedipal state of history is marked by the transition from the kingdom to the republic, from the family state to the corporate state.

THE IDEOLOGICAL FOUNDATIONS OF THE RULING CLASS

The decline of the aristocracy as a ruling class and the rise of the capitalist class also marks the shift from the Oedipal to the post-Oedipal stage of history. Capitalism has been defined as "the use of wealth in various concrete forms, not as an end in itself, but as a means for gathering more wealth."[63] The capitalist class exercises primarily economic power through the withholding or granting access to capital.[64] The drive to accumulate wealth for the sake of power is the motivating psychological force behind capitalism. Economic power becomes a means of indirectly controlling physical and ideological power. Physical and ideological power are exercised by the capitalist class through their control of political parties, the law, the church, and the state.

The ideological foundations of capitalism are threefold: legal, political, and religious. The archetypal structure of the rule of laws is essential to capitalism. It furnishes the conceptual foundation for negating the ideological basis of aristocracy and monarchy by proclaiming the autonomy and equality of the individual citizen. The shift from biologically determined hierarchical social order to a social order which presupposes the recognition of individual autonomy and equality requires a negation of the archetypal paterfamilias-king-God, or the replacement of the archetypal father as object of the ego ideal with that of the archetype of the self as disembodied mind. In this shift the old form of law, law as the will of the father, had to be replaced by a new form of law. The conceptual structure of Greek mathematics and science furnished its paradigm. The presupposition of this kind of law is that all men are born equal. The function of this new form of law is to deny the authority of the father and proclaim the equality of the brethren. Each individual agent is equal to every other individual agent. The function of this kind of law was to protect the agency of each man from wrongful interference. This new kind of law received its first scientific treatment in the body of writing of Roman legal scholars known as the Digests or the Pandects of the *corpus juris*. Its contemporary form is the law of the Civilian Codes such as those based on the Napoleonic code or the Germanic code, and the common law of the English speaking world. This kind of law constitutes the framework for individual freedom since it maintains the necessary conditions for individual autonomy and action. It is a law of individual rights.

The rule of law guarantees the necessary liberty for the process of wealth accumulation which underlies capitalism. It furnishes a common framework of rules for the international movement of capital and resources, and has furnished an ideological basis for the universalism entailed in such movements. It also functions as an ideological and institutional basis for the restriction of the power of the state. The civil law is made up of sets of legal obligations which are multitermed relations holding between the person who has the right and the person who has the duty, and which always is in regard to particular patterns of behavior. Any obligation can be reduced to a duty to do an act, a duty to not do it, no duty to do it, and no duty to not do it.[65] Legal relations may contain more than three terms. Property relations are four-termed in that they always relate to an object of ownership. Legal relations exist in sets, often called "interests." An interest may be contractual or proprietal.

A bundle of legal relations which constitutes an interest can itself be the subject of ownership of another bundle of relations. The right or duty holder in a legal relationship can itself be a set of relations which we call a corporation. These bundles of legal relations can be combined in an almost infinite number of different combinations by one bundle acting as an entity in another. By this technique all human beings are reduced to common entities which are interchangeable, and all or any part of nature can be made the material constant of a variable, and thus made subject to ownership and control. In the *Legal Foundations of Capitalism*, John R. Commons describes the process in this way: [66]

> Thus the meaning of property has spread over from visible things to invisible things. The invisible things are encumbrances and opportunities. Encumbrances are the duties that other people owe to me, and opportunities are their liberties, their absence of duties to me. Yet both are valuable to me and valuable to third parties who buy them of me, and are therefore property in the sense of exchange-values, or assets.
>
> These two kinds of property are rightly described as intangible, incorporeal, invisible. They cannot be seen by the naked eye like physical things, and they are not always even symbolized by words written out on paper as evidences of ownership. They may be created by word of mouth. They may even be implied from the conduct of the parties. Their intangibility is the invisibility of the promised and expected behavior of people, which is felt, not seen, by the inner eye of confidence.
>
> These intangible and incorporeal properties are more valuable than all physical things, in a land whose government and people are stable, for upon them are built both the credit system and the business initiative that have displaced feudalism by capitalism.

Common's convoluted description of the properties of legal relations can be explained in a straightforward way in terms of the formal properties of relations, the entities of which are variables. [67]

Capitalism has always required the help of the state and has used the state, as "capitalism only triumphs when it becomes identified with the state, when it is the state." [68] Through control of the state the monopoly on violence is maintained for the protection of capital, and to guarantee access to markets and resources. A further important function of the state is to maintain the infrastructure within which the economic realm can function. Heilbroner describes this function as follows: [69]

What seems to be only a "public" duty of government has, however, another masked aspect. It is the manner in which inputs needed for the accumulation of capital, but unprofitable to produce within the market framework, can be provided to the economic realm. From this viewpoint the state does not merely add "public" works to private ones. Rather, it accepts from the economic realm whatever necessary undertakings cannot remain in it. In these cases, the state foists upon the public the costs of those activities that would result in monetary "losses" if they were carried out by the economic sphere, while recognizing as inviolable the right of private enterprise to benefit from its profitable undertakings. This socialization of losses applies to much of the network of canals, railways, highways, and airways that have played an indispensable part in capitalist growth, as well as the provision of literate and socialized work forces through public education programs, the protection of public health, and the like.

"What the economic realm can do, the government is generally enjoined from doing," writes Heilbroner. "That which business cannot do, but which requires to be done, becomes the business of the public sector."[70] Capitalism must be able to keep the state sufficiently weak that it can both control and use it, while at the same time keep it sufficiently strong that it can maintain internal control of dissident and criminal elements and give external protection in the international sphere. It preserves this delicate balance through maintaining the ideology of the rule of law in conjunction with the contradictory ideology of the sovereignty of the state.

Capitalism also requires the ideology of paternal rule. It serves two functions. The first is to legitimize the exploitation of women within the economic sphere. In recent years, women's research on women's work has revealed the degree to which such work has contributed to the economic sphere in ways which cannot be measured in terms of traditional economic analysis.[71] Not only have women been exploited in the economic sphere through unequal wages, but the very nature of women's work within the home has been transformed with the formation of the class of wage earner.[72] Ivan Illich refers to "shadow work" and "the nether economy" in regard to necessary labor performed by women for the function of the economic sphere, but yet not fully recognized, measured, or rewarded within that sphere.[73]

The second function of patriarchal religion is to desacralize nature. "Capitalism would be impossible in a sacralized world to which men would relate with awe and veneration. . . . The culture of capitalism thus expresses a voracious, even rapacious, attitude toward the material world —a point of view that would be impossible if that world were portrayed as 'mother' Nature."[74] Capitalism requires an ideology which legitimizes the exploitation of both women and nature. Patriarchal religion in conjunction with science as ideology serves this purpose.

The ideological foundations of capitalism thus entail conflicting presuppositions, as well as three inconsistent legal paradigms: the rule of law or law as reason, law as the common will or the will of the sovereign state, and law as the will of the divine father and the paterfamilias. While self-contradictory, they make sense within the framework of capitalism. We see the ruling capitalist class manipulating the ideology of liberty and the rule of law to limit the power of the state, professing a strong nationalistic ideology centered on the flag and the country and seeking a strong state in the international sphere. At the same time it supports the patriarchal family structure and an ideology of Christian fundamentalism. The various brotherhoods, whether of the police and the military which exercise the monopoly on violence, the legal and judicial professions which administer the rule of law, the politicians and bureaucrats who manage the state, the professional corporate managers, bankers, and developers who manage the economic sphere, and the clergy and educators who control ideology, are used and manipulated by the ruling class to maintain the process whereby money is turned into commodities which are transformed again into money in the ongoing process of capital accumulation.

THE LOGIC OF PATRIARCHY

The dialectics of patriarchy are reflected in three kinds of law or legal paradigms. The first stage of patriarchy (thesis) is the age of monarchy. Monarchy with its law as the expression of the will of the royal father, is negated by law as the protection of the rights of the individual agent—the law of civil obligations—which is fundamental to classical liberalism (the antithesis). The third kind of law is law as the expression of the will of the collective brotherhood, or, in other words, law as the expression of the common will, which negates the individualism which underlies the law of civil obligations. The law which expresses the collective or common will is a synthesis because it combines the equality of the individual agent, which is an essential presupposition of the law of civil obligations, with the collectivity of law by fiat or legislation. Law as the expression of the common will is not made by judges or legal technicians, as was the case with the civil law or the common law. It is the law created by the sovereign power of the corporate state. This kind of law is manifested in whatever form the expression of the common will of the collective brotherhood may take. It may be the proclamation or fiat of the leader, or it may be the proclamation of some body which expresses the common will such as a legislature.

Behind these three kinds of law lie three different archetypes, each of which can serve as the object of the ego ideal. The archetypal father underlies traditional law as the will of the paterfamilias, king, or God. The archetype of differentiated disembodied mind underlies the systems of law which have their origin in classical Roman law and make up the civil side of the law of all Western legal systems. The archetype of the brotherhood underlies law as legislation or the will of the collective. These three forms of law are the embodiment of the three kinds of complexes of the psyche of the post-Oedipal male. Law having its origin in the archetype of the father embodies the Persean complex. Law having its origin in the archetype of differentiated disembodied mind embodies the Apollonian complex, while law having its origin in the archetype of the brotherhood of the collective embodies the Heraclean complex. These archetypal structures, because they are a product of a dialectical development of the collective psyche, are contradictory. The legal structures reflect the same contradictions. Thus, the system of law which guarantees the necessary conditions for individual autonomy and action contradicts law as the will of the father. The authority of the father is in direct contradiction to individual autonomy. The law which embodies the will of the collective is in contradiction to the law which guarantees the fundamental rights to the autonomy of the individual. This contradiction underlies all of the legal and political debates between legal positivism and various rights theories. An Apollonian male will be driven to favour libertarianism and individual autonomy. A male suffering from alienation will be driven toward a communitarian view of law as reflecting the will of the collective.

The way these three kinds of law are integrated and related reflects the coalescing of the three complexes, Persean, Apollonian, and Heraclean, in the continued suppression of women. It works in this way. Social order is divided into three spheres, and each sphere is regulated by one kind of law and archetypal structure. The first sphere is that of the family. The state does not intrude within the family, though this does not mean that the family is not regulated by law. It is very much so. The law, however, is that of the will of the father. The second sphere is that of private and commercial action, which is regulated by the civil law, with the third sphere being that of governmental regulation. The distinction between private law and public law marks the division between social order left up to the individual and that regulated by the collective. To this day neither private nor public law has recognized, protected, or guaranteed the full equality of the female with the male. Consequently, females are excluded from full participation in the collective. As far as women are concerned their exclusion is the same whether the collective is on the left or the right of the political spectrum. The collectives, whether the proletariat of Marxism-Leninism, we the people of American politics or the *Volk* of the Nazis, are all brotherhoods from which women are excluded from full participation.

The conundrum of post-Oedipal males is how to maintain the claim of their own individual autonomy and equality while at the same time denying autonomy and equality to females. The conundrum arises in this way. Any theory of the natural order which can be used to legitimate the equality of the male can equally be used to justify the equality of the female with the male. This holds true for Eastern mythic systems as well as Western. Consequently, any political theory which justifies the individual autonomy and equality of the male, equally justifies the autonomy and equality of the female with the male. Since males are neurotically and pathologically driven to dominate females, they are driven to hold two contradictory mythic systems at the same time. The inherent contradiction within male political theory confirms the thesis that political life is primarily a product of the unconscious, manifested in a collective mind within which contradictory ideas can exist side by side. In this manner, the collective mind continues to maintain the equality of the self and the inferiority of the female. The actual position of women within any society will reflect to what degree individual rationality has counted, and to what degree neurosis has prevailed. The need to be rational, consistent, and logical is a troubling matter for the male. The logical structure of private law and its ideological implications have probably been the most powerful archetypal tool which women have had in their struggle for equality.

Even when the equality of the sexes is proclaimed at an ideological level, as in Marxism, male authority is still retained. In spite of its claim that it is scientific and egalitarian, Marxism is as patriarchal as any other

male-created political theory.[75] It is sexist in principle as well as in practice. Women's role in procreation has been given a lesser value than
production in Marxist economic analysis.[76] When one reads a work such
as *Woman and Socialism* by August Bebel, where the thesis is set out that
"when all who are able to work shall be obliged to perform a certain
amount of *socially necessary* labor . . . [w]oman shall become a useful
member of human society enjoying full equality with man" [emphasis
added],[77] or Lenin's statement that women will not be emancipated and
become coequal with men until they participate in "general *productive*
labour," [emphasis added][78] it becomes clear that Marxism places a very
low value on the work women do in the home. Reproduction and child
rearing do not count as production and, therefore, have a lesser value.
Consequently, women's rights have never been an important issue in
Marxism.[79] Marxist political parties do not share power with women any
more than other political systems or parties. Marxism has not freed the
woman, but has merely brought her into the work force to do inferior,
low-valued, or ill-paid work, expecting her to continue to carry out all the
functions of homemaking and childrearing in her "spare" time.[80]

There are two elements which are integral to Marxism. One is utopianism—the achievement of the ultimate society when the state has finally
withered away. Since Marx did not really develop this concept, there is
no clear outline or perspective of what the role of women would be in
such a society. The other aspect of Marxism is the revolutionary interval
when one has to divide labor and make distinctions. It is here that sexism
raises its head. Women, who are weaker, must play a subordinate role.
Some form of hierarchy is required. How do we avoid the means becoming the ends? Here, Marxist theory is incomplete and leaves an ominous
gap which was left to Lenin and Stalin to fill. The failure of Marxist
theory to provide for how we are to get from where we are to where we
want to go leaves room for the reemergence of the oppression of women.
Yet, Marxism is no more sexist than any other political ideology. All of
"the great tradition of political philosophy consists, generally speaking, of
writings by men, for men, and about men."[81] Nearly all the major political theorists of the past speak of a division of labor between the male and
female based on the role of the female in reproduction, undervaluing that
role and then advocating distinctions in the political roles of the sexes on
that basis.

The rule of law is a necessary condition for freedom. So long as it
endures women will increasingly demand liberation and equality and, all

other things being equal, will eventually reject the mythic systems of patriarchy. However, males have often shown that they would prefer to sacrifice their own freedom and accept domination by other males, rather than see women liberated. Thus, they continue to maintain an ambivalence toward liberty and the rule of law.

17.

THE LIMITS OF TRADITIONAL LEGAL AND POLITICAL THEORY

RATIONALITY AND SOCIAL ORDER

The thesis of this book is that the most critical determining factor of social order is neurosis. If this thesis is correct, it would follow that political principles do not count in and of themselves for any particular intrinsic truth which they contain. These principles are allowed to function only when they meet psychological needs. If a political principle runs contrary to psychological needs it will be denied and ignored. Rationality, in other words, is not primary. There is an interrelationship between reality and political principles in that if the political principles directly or implicitly entail factual assumptions which are false, they will be less stable. Nevertheless, if these principles serve neurotic needs well, we will change our view of reality to conform to the false assumptions. Consider how long the view of women as inferior has lasted in spite of the fact that it is contrary to reality. The principles which will be incorporated into the ideological fabric of the collective psyche are those which will function to legitimize a state of the social order which will serve prevailing neurotic needs. If they happen to reflect the true state of affairs in nature, so much the better.

If we examine the history of social order in the West in terms of the history of ideas, we will build up a picture of a gradual breakdown of the structure of the extended family, and the decline of monarchy with the rise of classical liberalism. Such portrayals will trace political theory from

Plato and Aristotle through Hobbes, Locke, and Rousseau, Kant and Hegel, into Marx, and finally contemporary political theory with theorists such as Rawls and Nozick. Classical liberalism will be contrasted with socialism as reflecting the tension between individualism and communitarianism, and legislative sovereignty will be contrasted with a doctrine of fundamental rights. Within the political arena, people argue about political ideology as if it were a question of rationality. It is assumed that people follow political principles because they are convinced that they are true, rather then because they justify a particular state of the psyche. If Freud is correct in that it is the unconscious rather than conscious rationality that determines group behavior, then most of the conventional views about the development and history of political change are misconceived since they assume a gradual progress dictated by increasing rationality. What progress has been made in social order is due to the fact that our neurotic needs proceed in the direction of individuation of the collective psyche. Change in social order, therefore, comes about as a result of a complex matrix of neurotic needs, including the drive to individuate, and the necessity dictated by the very nature of mythic thought to hold a unified world view by making our social order conform to our view of the natural order. The principle of political equality has been necessary to meet the neurotic needs of males, and the progress which has been made in the status of women has come about because of the difficulty males have had in finding a good reason to exclude females from its ambit.

There is one overwhelming and tragic fact about social order which lends substantial support to the Freudian view as against the more conventional perspective of the nature of social change. The political principles which justify male domination of the female were discredited well over two thousand years ago in both the East and the West, yet male domination continues in both parts of the world. If the driving force of political change and social order was conscious rationality, and if political principles counted in and of themselves, patriarchy would have disappeared centuries ago. This is not to say that political principles do not count in the political process. Their main value, however, lies in their use as a tool to point out the inconsistencies in the legitimization of power. Political principles are more valuable to deny the legitimacy of the use of political power than they are for legitimizing or rationalizing it. No one really takes political rights seriously (as a matter of principle) who does not at the same time take the rights of women seriously.

Again, I must reiterate, I am not suggesting that political and legal philosophy are not important, but that they are important for reasons other than those which are normally given. The importance of legal and political theory lies in turning political principles back upon those who wish to use them to legitimize present patriarchal social order. The principles underlying democracy can be turned back on those who use those principles to legitimize social orders where ninety-five percent of the elected officials are male, or who use fundamental rights to maintain male control over female bodies. The importance of political principles is to use those principles which legitimize social order to show that no form of patriarchal social order, no form of male political power over females, can be legitimated in the terms of those principles, whatever they may be. This leads to the inevitable conclusion that if the concept of political and legal obligation is to have any *normative* meaning, in the sense that "obligation" implies "ought", women have very few legal and political obligations within existing social orders. This is so because the male domination of women simply cannot be justified nor legitimized by any set of political principles used to justify the equality of the members of the brotherhoods of the collective. This is to say no more than that political principles serve a primarily mythic function.

THE PARADOX OF WESTERN LEGAL AND POLITICAL THEORY

In the last few chapters the evolution of social order was examined in terms of a process of individuation in the collective psyche which paralleled that of the individual psyche. Two basic drives appear to govern this process whether in the individual or in the collective. The first is the drive to separate the self from the (m)other. The second is the drive to heal the narcissistic wound, which may take the form of the ego attempting to merge with its ideal or identify with the ideal. The process of individuation of the self thus involves both differentiation and identification, and it reflects engulfment anxiety and separation anxiety.

Individuation takes place when the processes of differentiation and identification both pull the self or psyche in the same direction. The ego ideal is the focal point of repulsion and attraction. The process of individuation takes place by shifting the ego from one ideal to another. The self undergoes individuation when the old object of the ego ideal no longer attracts but instead repels the ego, while at the same time the ego is attracted by a new object. If the power of an object of the ego ideal is so great that the ego is never repulsed and a new object is unable to draw it away, then individuation is retarded. Examples include a male child who is unable to make a successful Oedipal passage because it cannot separate from the mother, or a child who is never able to escape the influence and domination of his father and develop a strong ego of his own.

If this psychoanalytic analysis has validity for the individuation of the collective psyche, then we should be able to find some correspondence with the patterns of historical change. One of the principal objectives of the last few chapters was to explore this correspondence. This chapter will attempt to trace a similar correspondence in legal and political theory. It will be argued that the concept of individual autonomy or liberty is the articulation in terms of legal and political theory of the drive to differentiate the self from the earlier object of the ego ideal as the archetypal father, and the concept of the general will in political theory is the articulation of the drive to merge the ego in a new object of the ego ideal in the form of the corporate collective brotherhood.

The central concern of nearly all legal and political theory is freedom. The concept of freedom is central because it receives its historical articulation as a negation of existing kinds of authoritarian political structures or the ideologies which provide their legitimization. Freedom is the norm against which domination and authority must be justified as legitimate limitations. Freedom is assumed to be the primary state of affairs out of which the political structure must develop. The autonomy of the individual agent is the underlying presupposition of nearly all western legal and political thought.

Because autonomy is a presupposition of law[1] and politics, a fundamental dilemma arises—how to reconcile autonomy and authority. The most elegant statement of the problem is to be found in Robert Paul Wolff's *In Defense of Anarchism*.[2] Wolff effectively argues that authority and autonomy simply cannot be reconciled. To the degree that we recognize authority (the right to command and the correlative duty to obey), we sacrifice autonomy (the taking of full moral responsibility for one's own actions). Wolff takes one by one the various philosophical strategies for reconciling autonomy and authority, such as representative government, or the social contract, and shows that none will work. All require a surrender of autonomy. His conclusion is that there is no such thing as legitimate authority, and that anarchy is the only state consistent with autonomy. The idea of a legitimate state is, therefore, self-contradictory.[3]

Since there is no way in which limitations on autonomy can be justified or legitimized, there can be only one form of social order which is consistent with it, and that is unanimous direct democracy—"that is, a political community in which every person votes on every issue—governed by a rule of unanimity."[4]

If one assumes that a particular social order is legitimate, then one must assume that everyone agrees to every aspect of it. Everyone, therefore, wills the same thing. The assumption of the legitimacy of social order must consequently postulate the existence of a "general will" in order to be reconcilable with the assumption of individual autonomy. Charles Taylor clearly spells out to what extent individual autonomy is reconcilable with the general will, and what assumptions are necessary for that reconciliation:[5]

> Complete freedom would require that the whole outcome be decided by me. But of course, since the whole outcome is a social one, it cannot be decided by me alone. Or rather, if I decide it alone, then no one else who lives under this outcome is free. If we are all to be free, we must all take the decision. But this means that we must all take the whole decision, we must all participate in a decision about the nature of the total outcome. There must be universal and total participation. Participation must be not only universal, that is, involving everybody, but in this sense total, that all have a say in the whole decision. Of course, even this is not enough. If there are irreconcilable differences of view, so that some of us are voted down and forced to knuckle under, then we will be unfree, coerced. The theory of absolute freedom thus requires some notion of the unanimity of our real will; and this is what we have in the theory of the general will.

Taylor then argues that "[t]he aspiration to absolute freedom cannot consort with any articulated differentiation of the society."[6] If all are to take the decision, all must be homogeneous. The homogeneity of society is therefore an underlying presupposition of the existence of the general will, and is a necessary condition for absolute freedom. Thus, we have the paradox of Western legal and political theory. The autonomy of the individual is a presupposition which cannot be denied. We cannot, however, live in isolation. Some form of society is necessary. The only form of society which would be consistent with autonomy is one which is the product of the general will. The general will must be homogeneous. Homogeneity can only be achieved by excluding that which is different. The homogenization of society requires the kind of totalitarian force which ends up negating the autonomy of the individual.

lation of the existence of a general will. Such an assumption, therefore, is essential to any political theory which tries to preserve an objective good. As well, the existence of a general will presupposes the autonomy of individual wills, limited only by the preservation of the necessary restrictions on interference, which makes free individual action possible.

If we assume that the general will is rational, then any individual whose will does not conform to the general will is not rational. If the individual agent is not a rational agent, then she or he is not a full agent, and consequently can be excluded or forced to be rational—conform to the general will. Thus, the combined presuppositions of autonomy and the objective good lead to totalitarianism since almost total political power is necessary to achieve homogeneity.

While this dichotomy probably reaches back in the history of human thought to the Greeks, the philosopher who saw the opposition most clearly and stated the dilemma most sharply was Hegel. Kant, on the one hand, and the French Revolution, on the other, formed the crucible out of which Hegel forged his political theory. Kant restated, in its purest and most analytic philosophical form, the case for the autonomy of the individual which was implicit in the Western legal tradition having its origins in classical Roman law, as formulated in the Digests and in the thought of the Roman Stoics such as Cicero. The French Revolution represented the first attempt to radically reconstruct society according to the general will. Taylor, in his book *Hegel and Modern Society*, writes that "Hegel . . . sees the French Revolution as the culminating attempt to realize the dictates of human reason in the world."[7] Hegel saw the political predicament of his time as the problem of reconciling the freedom of personal autonomy with an ethical framework derived from the necessary conditions for mankind to live in harmony with and reconciled with nature. The freedom of individual autonomy is empty of ethical content, and guarantees only the prerequisites for action itself.[8] Autonomy in a Kantian sense entails self-determination as a free moral will independent of any natural considerations and inclinations.

"How to unite radical autonomy with the fullness of expressive unity with nature," was, according to Taylor, the essential task which Hegel set for himself in developing his political theory. Hegel rejected absolute freedom and unanimous direct democracy as empty of any ethical content and unworkable, leading inevitably to a reign of terror such as that which followed the French Revolution.[9] It can tear down an old society, but can build nothing new. The revolutionary force consequently becomes self-destructive. Elaborating on Hegel's position, Taylor writes: [10]

> The Terror also has a characteristic attitude towards its enemies and their liquidation. The essence of humanity is to be found in the general will; man's real self is there, the content of his freedom. What opposes the general will can only be the irrational, whatever there is in man of deformed misanthropy or perverse caprice. In doing away with such enemies one is not killing really autonomous men, whose opposition is rooted in their own independent identity, but empty, refractory, punctual selves which have no more human content.

Hegel's solution to the problem was to speculate that men in society were different as they belonged by nature to different estates. This necessary specialization allowed for an autonomous life within each estate, which in turn was relatable to the whole.[11] Hegel believed that when man is able to live in harmony with nature and his own nature "[t]he opposition between social necessity and individual freedom disappears," and "objective and subjective will are then reconciled and form one and the same untroubled whole."[12] It is at this point that men reach the end of history. Hegel's solution is no longer persuasive nor tenable for modern society. Modern society has continued from the time of Hegel toward greater homogeneity rather than diversity.

Taylor shows us that while Hegel's "view of the polity based on the ontology of Spirit,"[13] is unhelpful, his analysis of the problems surrounding autonomy is of great relevance to twentieth-century political thought. Taylor describes the "modern dilemma" in this way: [14]

> Disentangled from Hegel's particular theory of social differentiation, the basic point of this critique is this: absolute freedom requires homogeneity. It cannot brook differences which would prevent everyone participating totally in the decisions of the society. And what is even more, it requires some near unanimity of will to emerge from this deliberation, for otherwise the majority would just be imposing its will on the minority, and freedom would not be universal. But differentiation of some fairly essential kinds are ineradicable. . . . Moreover they are recognized in our post-Romantic climate as essential to human identity. Men cannot simply identify themselves as men, but they define themselves more immediately by their partial community, cultural, linguistic, confessional and so on. Modern democracy is therefore in a bind. . . .
>
> Thus Hegel's dilemma for modern democracy, put at its simplest, is this:

Psychoanalytic social theory could furnish us with an alternative conception of freedom as a state of full individuation. The process of individuation proceeds in a dialectical fashion commencing in a state of nondifferentiation of self and other (thesis), a denial of other and an affirmation of self (antithesis), and a reintegration of self with other, thus healing the mind/body, culture/nature, masculine/feminine bifurcations (synthesis). To be free as an individual in this psychological sense is to be conscious of one's own psyche as being both self and other. In a psychoanalytic legal and political theory the individual member of society would be the individuated agent rather than the autonomous agent. To be free as a collective would require a culture which embodies in its manifestations such as art, literature, philosophy, institutions, a conscious awareness of humans as being both body and mind, sentient beings and a natural animal species, and masculine and feminine. The collective psyche must transcend the animality crisis.

The political and legal concept of freedom is merely a synthesis within the dialectics of patriarchy reconciling individualism (antithesis) with community based on biological status (thesis). Since modern political theory is only a synthesis within patriarchy, which itself is merely an antithesis of a larger dialectic as a denial of other-body-nature-feminine, it cannot possibly provide the synthesis for reconciling self with other, body with mind, culture with nature, or masculine with feminine. One side of these bifurcations is entirely outside the patriachal political dialectic. The post-Oedipal stage of patriarchy is what Carole Pateman has called *fraternal patriarchy*, wherein women are excluded from the social contract.[20] Women can never achieve freedom within the patriarchal political framework of liberalism because they will always remain as other.

PSYCHOANALYTIC SOCIAL THEORY AND LIBERALISM

Like Marxism, which represents a general theory of history, psychoanalysis as a social theory is radical and deconstructive of widely-held belief systems. This shared deconstructionist perspective has led some to attempt a synthesis of Marxist and Freudian thought[21]—a merger, however, which was disclaimed by Freud. The basic presuppositions of psychoanalysis and Marxism are inconsistent.[22] Freud wrote, "[A]lthough practical Marxism has mercilessly cleared away all idealistic systems and illusions, it has itself developed illusions which are no less questionable and unprovable than the earlier ones."[23]

Freud, one could assume, would be suspicious of any attempt to use psychoanalytic theory to lend support to any particular political ideology, as explanations of social phenomena in terms of concepts such as repression and neurosis would deflate rather than strengthen transcendental ideological claims. Nevertheless, there are some of Freud's writings which can be shown to clearly buttress liberalism.[24] Various of Freud's texts, such as *Totem and Taboo*, suggest that Freud was a liberal at heart. While Freud explodes religion's claim to transcendental authority, he does not do the same thing for law.[25] However, even if certain parts of Freud's writings support liberalism, Freud's system of thought and methodology as a whole do not.[26] Their application will not only show that law is as much the product of repression and neurosis as religion is, but that its "contingent and rational authority" is equally suspect. There are two aspects of Freud's theory which he himself, toward the end of his life, recognized as weak and needing further development. These are, as pointed out earlier, his views on the importance of the relationship of the child to the mother in the pre-Oedipal stage, and his views on women, their sexuality and passage though the Oedipus complex. Contemporary psychoanalytic research and theory has made remarkable progress in these two areas.[27] When this current literature, which is completely consistent with Freud's methodology, is taken into account, little comfort is to be found for contemporary liberalism.

Freud's failure to apply his deconstructive methodology to gender bifurcation produced an ambivalence in his writings which haunted him all his life. It commenced with his agonizing over whether to believe, or to treat as illusionary, the accounts of his female patients as to their sexual molestation in early childhood.[28] If he had taken their memories as factual, he would have been forced to focus his attention on "normal" males, the nature of their sexuality, and the repressed content of the male psyche, all of which account for the male treatment of the female. Instead, Freud talked and wrote about "human sexual perversions" while describing practices carried out almost exclusively by males.[29]

In his later writings this ambivalence is reflected in the tension between his views of civilization as neurosis and civilization as necessary to human enlightenment and progress. Nowhere is this inconsistency more evident then in *Civilization and Its Discontents*, in which he writes:[30] "We are threatened with suffering from three directions: from our own body,

Thus, traditional Freudian psychoanalysis, in itself, contains a paradigm example of the justification of male domination on the grounds of female inferiority.[37]

The appeal of liberalism for Freud comes in part from his view of what constitutes a successful Oedipal passage. He stresses separation, individuation, and a strong ego, all of which are consistent with the individualistic orientation of liberalism. Community is to be achieved through the voluntary empathetic relationship between members of the brotherhood of man (whether male or female), rather than through political processes as advocated by both Marxists and conservatives. The autonomous, individuated male, striving to be rational against the forces of his own unconscious, is seen to be the norm. Nonperverse male sexuality is seen to be normal so long as it is kept in control with societal laws and inhibitions. According to this measure women are inferior, and consequently male domination is natural and legitimate. He states: [38]

> I cannot evade the notion (though I hesitate to give it expression) that for women the level of what is ethically normal is different from what it is in men. Their super-ego is never so inexorable, so impersonal, so independent of its emotional origins as we require it to be in men. Character-traits which critics of every epoch have brought up against women—that they show less sense of justice than men, that they are less ready to submit to the great exigencies of life, that they are more often influenced in their judgements by feelings of affection or hostility—all these would be amply accounted for by the modification in the formation of their super-ego which we have inferred above. We must not allow ourselves to be deflected from such conclusions by the denials of the feminists, who are anxious to force us to regard the two sexes as completely equal in position and worth; but we shall, of course, willingly agree that the majority of men are also far behind the masculine ideal.

Freud accepts uncritically the entire structure of gender bifurcation implicit in patriarchal culture. Gender bifurcation is a paradigm example of myth. In the Barthesian sense, the biological distinctions of sexual difference are used to justify the contingent history of male domination.[39] The categories of masculine and feminine are applied to objects, actions, and attributes, in such a way that the kind of categorical errors which Ryle saw as the essence of mythic thought are committed.[40] In Tucker's sense of myth,[41] gender is a projection of the male psyche onto the external world. The projection is an illusion which masks a reality, painful to males, which is repressed into the unconscious. While it is true that support for liberalism can be found in Freud, it is to be found at those limits which he failed to break through. We should not, however, minimize Freud's greatness or his contribution to human thought because he was stopped by the boundaries of his historical cradle. Few people in the history of human thought have pushed those boundaries so far.

If we use Freud's methodology to reverse the hierarchy of gender bifurcation, females would be seen as the norm and males, in comparison, as pathological. The thesis of the Oedipal passage would still be maintainable, but its norms and description would be altered. Such a perspective, while seeming to be anti-Freudian at a surface level, would be true to the spirit of Freud and Freud's own view of himself as a scientist. To remain true to Freud requires us to struggle with the legacy of his thought. Nothing has been more damaging to that legacy than the obsequious and unquestioning rigidity of many of the practitioners of psychoanalysis, who have turned his legacy into a religiouslike doctrine rather than a living, changing, expanding area of human knowledge.

PSYCHOANALYTIC SOCIAL THEORY AND RADICAL FEMINISM

Freud introduced the idea of culture as neurosis. His analysis of religion is the paradigm example of psychoanalytic social theory. However, he failed to apply the same kind of analysis to social order in general. In marked contrast to most of his views which were often shocking and radically different from commonly held ideas (e.g., infant sexuality and religion as neurosis), Freud notes that his theory about the origin and nature of civilization differs little from that commonly held by most people. He writes in *Civilization and Its Discontents:*[42] "In none of my previous writings have I had so strong a feeling as now that what I am describing is common knowledge and that I am using up paper and ink and, in due course, the compositor's and printer's work and material in order to expound things which are, if fact, self-evident." Freud's failure to deconstruct gender prevented him from deconstructing culture. Even later Freudians such as Norman Brown[43] and Ernest Becker,[44] who have developed theories of culture as neurosis in repression of the fear of death, fail to come to terms with the fact that culture is patriarchal and patriarchy is our culture. Thus, this culture is the product of male misogyny and gynophobia, and the fear of death is only a part of this larger neurosis.

and accept our own animality and place in nature. Each step of separation should be accompanied with a new integration.

Feminism has its roots in, and important ties with, liberalism, Marxism, and psychoanalytic theory. It does not deny the importance of reason and rational patterns of thought such as universalizability,[51] which are entailed in the very concepts of justice and the rule of law implicit in liberalism. Rather, it uses those very tools to expose the abuses of patriarchal ideology. It uses the liberal ideology of the autonomy of the individual male to demand an equal recognition of the autonomy of every female agent. It turns Marxism on its head in terms of a class analysis based on gender to reveal the sexism in Marxist ideology and practice.[52] As Catharine MacKinnon states, "Feminism stands in relation to marxism as marxism does to classical political economy: its final conclusion and ultimate critique."[53] "Sexuality is to feminism what work is to marxism: that which is most one's own, yet most taken away."[54] Feminism uses the tools of psychoanalysis to reveal what psychoanalysis itself has repressed. Thus, it is liberal, Marxist, and psychoanalytic methodologies, not their mythic ideologies, which have helped nourish feminism. While there are basic contradictions between classical liberalism and Marxism as political ideologies, no such conflict appears as between methodologies with the broader radical feminist perspective. If women take control of their own sexuality, they will in the process take control of reproduction, and in taking control of sexuality and reproduction they take control of their own bodies and lives. By taking control of their bodies and lives as of right, their autonomous agency becomes recognized and achieves legal protection.

While feminism is more strongly rooted in the liberal and the Marxist tradition than it is in the Freudian, many feminists such as Dorothy Dinnerstein,[55] Nancy Chodorow,[56] and Jessica Benjamin,[57] have used his legacy in the development of feminist theory, and feminist legal theorists such as Ann Scales have used it in the development of feminist jurisprudence.[58] Indeed, Juliet Mitchell argues that "a rejection of psychoanalysis and of Freud's work is fatal for feminism."[59] As radical feminism has roots in the post-Oedipal mythic structures of patriarchy, which is the antithesis which negated matriarchal consciousness, it can be viewed as the synthesis which produces the new view of reality. It is a synthesis which expands human consciousness because it brings the other half of the human race into the process of defining reality. Radical feminism represents a paradigmatic shift in human consciousness which could take humankind from a post-Oedipal to a trans-Oedipal state.

While the conjunction of radical feminism with a contemporary deconstructed psychoanalytic social theory furnishes a persuasive answer to a good many questions, it also raises a new series of important issues which need exploration. Is genderization necessary for the process of individuation? Can genderization take place without misogyny? Will a failure to genderize lead to sexual perversion in the male? Will a social meaning inevitably be given to the biological differences between the sexes? If so, will not such a social meaning, when freed from the repression and illusion which produces misogyny, lead to a recognition of the primacy of the ongoing cycle of life, and to the recognition of the dominant and paramount role of the female in that process? If so, will males be able to psychologically accept social meaning which gives preeminence to children and females? Has the evolution of the collective psyche reached a stage where we can develop an alternative world view which will be life supportive?

Such questions as these lead to other questions in the context of law and politics. Do we really select our legal and political theories or ideologies because we are led to them by a process of reasoning, or do we select them on the basis of our psychological needs? Do we adopt liberalism when our egos are seeking separation because we are suffering from engulfment anxiety, and adopt some form of communitarian legal or political theory because we seek the healing of the narcissistic wound when separation anxiety is stronger than engulfment anxiety? Is there still a role to be played in the evolution of the collective psyche for a depatriarchalized paradigm of the rule of law? Can liberalism be used by women to demand the equal recognition of their own agency? Can the communitarian legal and political ideologies which have historically legitimized the brotherhoods of the male, still serve a foundation for nonmisogynous nonsexist communities? [60] Can nonvoluntary community be reconciled with liberty and freedom? Does state intervention, nominally on behalf of the interests of women, lead to their autonomy or does it tend to maintain and legitimize the corporate brotherhood structures which perpetuate male dominance? The answer to questions such as these must, in the final analysis, remain with women. They must have voice and power. The decision should be theirs. After centuries of exploitation by males, it is the right of women to determine what the structure of society should be.

The existence of a death instinct was first suggested by Sabina Spiel-rein, a brilliant young analyst who had been a pupil of both Jung and Freud.[4] Jung never accepted the death instinct, but recognized only "a general life instinct" to which he applied Freud's term *libido*. Freud, on the other hand, did accept the existence of a death instinct, although he did so only reluctantly and gradually.[5] Part of his difficulty lay in unravell-ing the relationship between the erotic or sexual instincts, ego instincts, and the life and death instincts.[6] At an earlier period Freud equated ego-instincts with death instincts and sexual instincts with life instincts. He finally concluded, however that the basic opposition was between life instincts and death instincts,[7] and that the sex drive can be interlinked with both in that each can take on an erotic component.[8]

Neither Freud nor Jung clearly distinguish between the concepts of *drive* and *instinct*. Jung developed a theoretical analysis of the relationship of the instincts with archetypes and the collective unconscious, which is important for the understanding of how instincts manifest themselves within the psyche. In his paper, "Instinct and the Unconscious," Jung suggests that human behavior is influenced by instinct to a much greater degree than most people realize. "Instincts," he writes, "are typical modes of action, and wherever we meet with uniform and regularly recurring modes of action and reaction we are dealing with instinct, no matter whether it is associated with a conscious motive or not."[9] "Archetypes," he writes, "are typical modes of apprehension, and wherever we meet with uniform and regularly recurring modes of apprehension we are dealing with an archetype, no matter whether its mythological character is recognized or not."[10] "The instincts and the archetypes together form the 'collective unconscious,'" Jung concludes.[11] "[U]nconscious appre-hension through the archetype determines the form and direction of instinct."[12]

One problem in dealing with both Freud and Jung on these matters is that both wrote in German, and we are dealing with English equivalents which probably do not have the exact same meaning as the original German terms. Part of the difficulty lies in finding good analogies for dealing with mental phenomena. The terms *drive* and *psychic energy* reflect a hydraulics model of mind where something flows from one compart-ment to another. Instinct, on the other had, suggests a kind of "hard wired" genetic programming more related to animal behavior.

Since archetypal activity produces "uniform and regularly recurring modes of action and reaction" manifested in the form of "uniform and regularly recurring modes of apprehension," it will be highly likely that when instincts or drives effect behavior we will have in process a psychological phenomena which meets Jung's criteria for the presence of a complex. Psychoanalytic theory often identifies uniform and regularly recurring action which is expressed and perceived in archetypal forms as manifestations of Eros or Thanatos, or life and death drives. Thus, we may conclude that mental phenomena exist which we can properly call a life complex and a death complex. We will find that these complexes are expressed or manifested in a variety of representations of a few basic and fundamental archetypes. Perhaps we can avoid some of the theoretical problems which lie behind the terms *instinct* and *drive* by referring to an Eros and a Thanatos complex without having to decide whether the source of psychic energy fueling the complex is an instinct or a drive, and whether or not it makes a difference. Furthermore, I seriously doubt whether or not there is a life instinct or drive separate from the sex drive, and I find no evidence of the existence of a death instinct or drive. What can be found, however, is ample evidence of mental phenomena which reflect the presence of Eros and Thanatos-like complexes.

The Dionysian complex, for example, appears to be a particular kind of Eros complex. The drive to merge the self in the other to recover primary narcissism may be an expression of either an Eros complex or a Thanatos complex, depending upon what instinct and archetypal structure underlie it. The drive to lose oneself in the brotherhood of the collective has underlying it a psychic energy which often appears to drive its members to seek death. The theme of death literally permeates many of the mythic structures and archetypal representations associated with various kinds of brotherhoods. We may integrate the ideas of Jung which are essential for psychoanalytic social theory with Freud's postulate that "the evolution of civilization may . . . be simply described as the struggle for life of the human species" between Eros and Thanatos, by suggesting that the struggle is between the Eros complex and the Thanatos complex. These complexes lie within the collective psyche as well as the individual psyche.

The three complexes of the post-Oedipal male are able to coalesce into a single archetypal framework even though the three underlying archetypal sources are inconsistent and contradictory because they each serve a different but complementary function. The common underlying themes are patriarchy and misogyny. The Persean complex based on the archetype of the father produces the drive of the male to dominate the female. The

THE PARADOX OF THE FREUDIAN METHOD

An examination of the struggle between Eros and Thanatos reveals a fundamental paradox in Freudian methodology. In traditional psychoanalytic theory patriarchy is identified with individuation and progress, yet patriarchy is a denial of Eros and an affirmation of Thanatos. If this is so, then the end product of the process of individuation of the individual psyche is the death drive or complex. If the collective psyche follows the path of the individual psyche, then the process of individuation of the collective psyche leads to Thanatos and not to Eros.

Implicit in the orthodox Freudian view of individuation is the assumption that patriarchy is necessary for separation from the mother. Unless the object of the ego ideal transfers from the mother to the father, the child will not have a successful Oedipal passage. According to Chasseguet-Smirgel, "The need to detach oneself from the primal omnipotent mother by denying her faculties, her organs and her specifically feminine features, and by investing in the father, seems to be a need both sexes share."[16] She writes:[17]

> If the incestuous wish rests not only on a sexual drive but also on the desire to retrieve lost narcissistic unity, we can understand that in the course of his development the boy reaches a point at which he cathects the father's image with his Ego Ideal. He places his narcissism in his father who thus becomes his model, that is to say, his aim for identification.

She states elsewhere:[18]

> The mother's attitude of seduction may . . . destroy in her child this wish to be big and grown up and prevent him from experiencing this admiration for his father who becomes his model for identification, the bearer of the child's Ego Ideal. . . .
>
> Thus the long path which leads the subject to the Oedipus Complex and genitality must be seen as opposed to the short path which maintains the subject fixed in pregenitality. These two paths define two different forms of Ego Ideal.

All of the attributes which mark successful individuation appear to be masculine related, and those which appear to lead to narcissistic forms of perversion are related to the feminine. Penis envy in the female is dictated by the biology of reproduction. Chasseguet-Smirgel writes:[19]

It is noteworthy that Athene, a woman, and Apollo, a man, band together to deny the maternal prerogatives.

The girl's penis envy seems to me not to rest upon her ignorance of the vagina and her subsequent feelings of castration . . . but on her need to beat back the maternal power. . . . My experience with women patients has shown me that penis envy is not an end in itself, but rather the expression of a desire to triumph over the omnipotent primal mother through the possession of the organ the mother lacks, i.e., the penis. Penis envy seems to be as proportionately intense as the maternal imago is powerful.

It goes without saying that the narcissistic decathexis of the maternal organs and qualities which then follow makes identification with the mother and the acceptance of femininity rather difficult.

Not only is the replacement of the mother as the object of the ego ideal essential for individuation in both the male and the female, but, according to the orthodox Freudian position, "Destruction of the paternal universe is, in fact, a consequence of the desire to merge with the mother," and thus trade reality for illusion.[20] The father represents reason and law.[21] "Thus, we see that *separation is the foundation upon which law is built,* or to put it in other words, separation and Law (in the moral as well as in the juridical sense of the word) are one and the same thing. Anything bringing about a separation is to be considered as a representation of the father who prevents the infant from returning to the mother's womb."[22] Given that thought and reason are the manifestation of the reality principle, and that both thought and reason are linked to the paternal universe, the denial of patriarchy would constitute the substituting of illusion for reality. As Chasseguet-Smirgel states, "The fact is that the place of the father, and thence of Reason, is fundamental to the Freudian venture and to the psychoanalytic method."[23] Thus, orthodox Freudian theory appears to assume that an archetypal shift between the mother and the father is a necessary condition for the individuation of the individual psyche, and at the level of the collective psyche, patriarchy is a necessary condition for the evolution of human culture by permitting mankind to break free of nature. Thus, patriarchy is equated with progress, reality, and the proper course of individuation.

The paternal universe itself, however, is also an illusion and a denial of reality. It denies the primacy of the perpetuation of the species as the underlying direction of biological evolution by implicitly projecting onto the evolutionary process an anthropocentric teleology according to which the evolution of mind is somehow the goal of the evolutionary process of life. It denies the primacy of the female in the process of evolution by

its view of what constitutes the completion of the process of individuation. Individuation is viewed as complete if the Oedipal passage has been successful, and the individual has developed a strong ego. Both Freudian and Jungian theory represent the struggle of the psyche to individuate and transcend the pull backward into the womb of primary narcissism as the struggle of the hero which ends in the victory of breaking free. The end of the struggle is marked by transcending illusion and accepting reality. However, individuation must entail more than separation. The Freudian paradox exists because what is taken as the end of the process of individuation, is only a step, and not the final objective. The process of individuation is dialectical. The thesis, oneness with the (m)other, is denied by the separateness of the self implicit in the paternal universe, the antithesis. A true Hegelian dialectic, however, is completed with a synthesis. The synthesis denies the antithesis by a new perspective which transcends both thesis and antithesis in a union of the truth (reality) with a rejection of the false in the two former positions. The synthesis of the process of individuation is a return to the (m)other, thus uniting the maternal and paternal universes, bringing together and healing the breach between male and female, body and mind, culture and nature. The return to the mother is not a return to the state of primary narcissism by losing the self in the other. The self holds onto its center and reintegrates back into the (m)other. In the truly individuated self, (m)other and ego are the poles between which the individual psyche plays.

There is a final stage in the process of individuation which lies at the end of the post-Oedipal age of history. Humankind is at the end of the age of the paternal universe, the stage of the antithesis in the dialectical process of individuation of the collective psyche. It has not, as yet, entered into the final stage, the stage of the union of the maternal and paternal universes. The end of such a synthesis would mark the transcending of the Oedipal passage of history. The emergence of a trans-Oedipal collective psyche would mark the end of history in the Hegelian sense.

Before there can be a synthesis of the maternal and the paternal universes into a new world view, there must be a negation of the paternal universe. It was the paternal universe which negated the maternal universe. Only a negation of the paternal universe can restore the maternal universe, enabling a synthesis to take place. The negation of the paternal universe does not mean its elimination. The negation is of the illusion of its primacy. The synthesis can only follow after the negation. Equally, the restoration of the maternal universe is not a return to the past, but a restoration of that which was true or valid in the maternal world view. The illusionary aspect which was negated by the paternal universe will remain negated. What is united in the synthesis are the parts of the maternal and paternal universes (world views) which remain valid after the two processes of negation.

The paternal universe required the sacrifice of the female. The Eve complex marked the acceptance of that sacrifice by the woman. Whether or not there was another way for the collective psyche to individuate which did not require this sacrifice, is beyond the ambit of this book. The reality is that the sacrifice was made, and is still being made. The negation of the paternal universe requires the sacrifice of the male. There is simply no other way. The sacrifice of the male for the sake of ongoing life is the essence of the Dionysian complex in its most positive form. A Jungian analyst who fully understands the nature and structure of the Dionysian archetype is M. Esther Harding. She recognizes that the essence of the Dionysian lies in sacrifice. There is no sacrifice involved in androgyny. Dionysus has to be placed within the archetypal framework of matriarchal paganism, with the emphasis on the sacrifice of the sacred king or the consort of the Goddess. For the female, the sacrifice means that she must give up the Eve complex of living for the male. For the male, it entails that he must sacrifice his use of the woman as an object. This, she points out, is the meaning behind the archetype of castration. She writes:[31]

It is no accident that the sacrifice of the son is represented by a castration, for the most fundamental demand for satisfaction that man makes upon woman is the demand for the satisfaction of his sexuality. It is in this realm that he feels himself most helpless to cope with his own need, except by demanding that the woman serve him. This childish demand on his part and the equally undeveloped maternal wish to give on hers, may serve on a low level of psychological development to produce an alliance between a man and a woman which passes for relationship. But when a necessity arises for something more mature in the situation between them this demand has to be replaced by a greater submission to the laws of Eros. The man may be compelled to recognize that the woman is something more than the reciprocal of his need, something other than the counterpart of his conscious personality. When she refuses any longer to mother him, no longer repressing her own needs in her determination to fulfill his, he will find himself faced with the necessity of meeting the reality of the situation, which shows itself as different from what he had thought it. This involves the sacrifice of

Thanatos to Eros entails moving away from a dangerous to a more benign complex. The pathology of the Dionysian complex can be minimized and controlled, and possibly transcended, through the analytic process whereby content in the unconscious is integrated into consciousness.

The Dionysian individual is able to move from self to other and back to self. The boundaries of the self can be given up because the process of individuation has left the self strong enough that the center will hold when the boundaries disappear. There are a few Dionysian males who to a large degree have transcended misogyny. There is a growing interest in the Dionysian and the archetype of Dionysus-Shiva. The appearance of Dionysian males is related in many ways to the women's movement. Powerful women call forth the Dionysian in males. It is the Goddess which calls forth the consort. In addition, women who consciously or unconsciously have rejected the Eve complex and have internalized the Goddess archetype will generally ensure that their children are genderized with as little misogyny as possible. People are able to transcend the gender crisis when they are able to transcend misogyny and move freely between and incorporate into themselves any of the full range of human possibilities and potentials. The process of genderization within a patriarchal framework entails the loss of potential. Transcending the gender crisis means regaining some of that potential. This does not necessarily imply androgyny. Dionysus and Shiva are not androgynous figures. They are archetypal masculine figures which display a full range of powers, although a few of their archetypal representations show androgynous characteristics.

Transcending the animality crisis requires an internalization and acceptance of one's dependence on the body and on nature, and the acceptance by the male of his dependency on women. An acceptance of that dependency means the surrender of defense mechanisms. There is an essential truth in the teachings of Jesus that one can only find one's soul (self) through surrendering it for the benefit of others. In its Christian form, however, the other is male or a male brotherhood. In the Dionysian surrender the self is found or saved by its surrender to the female other. For the male to transcend the animality crisis he must accept his identity as a part of nature. The last stage of the post-Oedipal period of individuation requires the male to shift from the Persean, Apollonian, and Heraclean complexes to the Dionysian.

History has been examined, throughout this book, in terms of the externalization of the stages of the Oedipal passage. History is the Oedipal passage of the collective psyche. Some individuals must always precede the stage of individuation of the collective psyche for it to be incorporated into the collective mind. Nothing can exist in the collective psyche which has not been developed first in at least some individual minds. The present age is that of the externalization of the object of the ego ideal in the form of the corporate brotherhoods of the male. The next stage should be the externalization of the return to the mother. This would entail a shift in the archetypal structures of the collective psyche from Thanatos to Eros, which would in turn entail a shift from a Thanatos complex to an Eros complex. In a trans-Oedipal world the psyche of the male would fluctuate playfully between Apollo and Dionysus, and the psyche of the female would follow the call of either or both Athene and Demeter as her free spirit chooses. The archetypal structure of the collective psyche would be a dialectical synthesis of what have been called the maternal and paternal universes. In such a world, the limitations of the rigid structure of gender would be diminished. The biological differences between the sexes would continue to be given social meaning, but free of unconscious misogyny.

When the Oedipal passage has been fully externalized in the collective psyche, individuals will no longer have to struggle to the same degree through the separation, genderization, and animality crises. It will all be externalized in the collective psyche. The archetypal structure of the collective psyche will lead the individual through these passages and crises. The next stage of human individuation, the trans-Oedipal, would follow when the collective psyche has fully completed the Oedipal cycle by transcending the post-Oedipal stage of history. In a trans-Oedipal world pathology would be replaced with mere neurosis. Infants would still be born of mothers, would separate, and would have to internalize the biologically determined differences between the sexes and the generations. Humans would still struggle and dream. A trans-Oedipal world would not be a utopia. Class struggles, whether based on wealth, family, race, or sex, would have ended because the collective brotherhoods would have disappeared as objects of the ego ideal. In a trans-Oedipal world, communities would be less structured, and freely entered into and abandoned. Freedom would be guaranteed through a sense of the highly individuated self, and community would be ensured through a recognition that our very sense of self is constituted in large part by group identifications. In the trans-Oedipal world made up of the synthesis of the old maternal and paternal universes, the welfare of children would be the highest value. When the interest of children are placed by humanity above all others,

simply settle it by choosing death," Mishima describes suicide as "the ultimate expression of free will."[37] Mishima extensively discussed the importance of what he called the death impulse. He wrote:[38]

> We do not like to extract from death its beneficial elements and try to put them to work for us. We always try to direct our gaze toward the bright landmark, the forward-facing landmark, the landmark of life. And we try our best not to refer to the power by which death gradually eats away our lives. This outlook indicates a process by which our rational humanism, while constantly performing the function of turning the eyes of modern man toward the brightness of freedom and progress, wipes the problem of death from the level of consciousness, pushing it deeper and deeper into the subconscious, turning the death impulse by this repression to an ever more dangerous, explosive, ever more concentrated, inner-directed impulse. . . . But death alone exists unchanged and regulates our lives now as in the era of *Hagakure*.

Mishima, anticipating his act of ritual *seppuku* on 25 November 1970, at the headquarters of the Ground Self-Defense Forces, wrote, "But the body is doomed to decay. . . . I for one do not, will not, accept such a doom. This means that I do not accept the course of Nature."[39] His suicide was an act of rebellion against nature. This act was the ultimate mind-body bifurcation. Mind was freed from nature and body by a supreme act of will, even if it meant the dissolution of mind.

Aligned with the repression of death is the repression of the male's vulnerability to the sex drive. The stance of the hero and the triumph of the will, reason and logic drift away under the hot sun of sexual passion. The Thanatos complex is a mixture of rage, rebellion, separation, and destruction marking a determination not to surrender the mind-will of man to that which has been biologically determined by nature. Thus it is a negation of life. It is a surrender to death as an act of defiance toward life. It is an illusion because life and death are a part of the same process. In its more pathological form, the death drive or complex seeks not merely to extinguish consciousness, but to destroy as much of life and nature as possible in revenge for being cursed with sentience and mortality. Like the blinded Samson, the desire is not just to die, but to pull down the temple as well.

Euripides' play, *The Bacchae*, is rich in psychoanalytic meaning for the late twentieth century. We see it acted out at an individual level with Christian evangelists such as Jim Bakker and Jimmy Swaggart, who like

Pentheus reject Dionysus when he comes to them in disguise. And like Pentheus, they both suffer the revenge of Dionysus which is delivered at the hands of women. In *The Bacchae,* Dionysus brings a temporary madness to women, including Pentheus's own mother, which leads them to believe that he is a wild animal whom they then proceed to tear apart. In the madness of the late twentieth century the various competing corporate states see the wild and evil beast in each other. The revenge of Dionysus will be the madness of nations seeing other nations as the beast. Already the mythic structures of right-wing Christian America, Marxist-Leninist ideology and Fundamentalist Islam see the enemy as the beast and the beast in the enemy. To recognize our uniqueness as conscious, sentient beings, and at the same time to recognize and accept our animality—that we are biped primates—is to become as Pan. In rejecting Dionysus, the collective psyche rejects both the body and Eros, and consequently must embrace Thanatos. There is simply no other alternative.

Our very idea of consciousness itself is a product of the Thanatos complex. The Jungian analyst, James Hillman, after an extensive discussion of male fantasies of female inferiority, states: [40]

> This structure [misogynous fantasies of female inferiority] produces these theories of the human body as part of a philosophy which guarantees the superiority of male consciousness and the inferiority of any opposite with which it will be conjoined. And there is no way out of the dilemma as long as this Jahwistic or Apollonic structure informs not only scientific thought but *the very notion of consciousness itself* . . . . There must be recurrent misogyny presented with scientific justification because the positivism of the scientific approach is informed by Apollo. Until the structure of the consciousness itself and *what we consider to be "conscious"* change into another archetypal vision or way of being-in-the-world, man's image of female inferiority and a disbalanced *coniunctio* in every sphere of action will continue.

Hillman concludes, "[T]he termination of analysis in both Freud and Jung coincides with the termination of misogyny,"[41] and he affirms that there is no escape from misogyny except through Dionysian possession.[42]

Hillman, however, conceives of the path to the Dionysian through androgyny. On this point he is an orthodox Jungian. He recognizes that "[t]he end of analysis coincides with the acceptance of femininity."[43] However, he does not see that the acceptance of the feminine must mean much more than the acceptance of the feminine side of the male psyche.

It must mean the full acceptance of women in and of themselves. The real danger of androgyny prior to the termination of patriarchy is that men will enrich their personalities by incorporating the feminine while at the same time continuing to exploit women. Mary Daly describes such androgyny as "a unisex model, whose sex is male," and as "male femininity incarnate."[44] In another book, she describes it as "cannibalistic, androgynous maleness."[45] Adrienne Rich, in pointing out the dangers of androgyny within patriarchy, writes, "The urge to leap across feminism to 'human liberation' is a tragic and dangerous mistake. It deflects us from our real sources of vision, recycles us back into old definitions and structures, and continues to serve the purposes of patriarchy, which will use 'women's lib', as it contemptuously phrases it, only to buy more time for itself—as both capitalism and socialism are now doing."[46] Jung himself furnishes us with a paradigm example of the androgynous patriarch in his treatment of the women in his life, such as Sabina Spielrein,[47] and his cruelty toward his wife Emma Jung in his adulterous relationship with Antonia Wolff. Jung, in a letter to Freud, refers to the "polygamous components" of his psyche.[48] In another letter, Jung writes, "The prerequisite for a good marriage, it seem to me, is the license to be unfaithful."[49] Elemire Zolla, in *The Androgyne: Reconciliation of Male and Female,* confirms Daly's and Rich's analyses in the statement, "One has Buddha's example of a femininity developed beyond that of any female."[50] This description of the Buddha as more feminine than the female, corresponds to the description of the Christ as "my mother and more than my mother."[51] There is a movement in contemporary theology toward an androgynous God, or a concept of the divine beyond gender.[52] However, so long as the divine is conceived of as mind, or the *Logos,* it will remain inevitably and essentially male. An androgynous God is simply a male with some positive feminine attributes.

Jungian androgyny confuses identity of the self, which is biologically determined as male or female, with the limits and potential of human attributes and actions which are culturally determined as masculine or feminine. Sandra Lipsitz Bem highlights this confusion when she states:[53]

[T]he concept of androgyny is problematic from the perspective of gender schema theory because it is based on the presupposition that there is a feminine and a masculine within us all, that is, that "femininity" and "masculinity" have an independent and palpable reality and are not cognitive constructs derived from gender-schematic processing. Focusing on androgyny thus fails to prompt serious examination of the extent to which gender organizes both our perceptions and our social world. . . . . Thus, if gender schema theory has a political message, it is not that the individual should be androgynous. Rather, it is that the network of associations constituting the gender schema ought to become more limited in scope and that society ought to temper its insistence on the ubiquitous functional importance of the gender dichotomy. In short, human behaviors and personality attributes should no longer be linked with gender, and society should stop projecting gender into situations irrelevant to genitalia.

Patriarchy is so much a part of the conceptual structure of orthodox Freudianism that Freud even viewed Eros in terms of love between men, rather than love between men and women. When Albert Einstein in 1932 wrote to Freud, seeking some solution, solace, or hope in the face of his knowledge of the potential for the release of atomic energy, and the threat of impending war in Europe,[54] Freud responded:[55]

> Our mythological theory of instincts makes it easy for us to find a formula for *indirect* methods of combating war. If willingness to engage in war is an effect of the destructive instinct, the most obvious plan will be to bring Eros, its antagonist, into play against it. Anything that encourages the growth of emotional ties between men must operate against war. These ties may be of two kinds. In the first place they may be relations resembling those towards a loved object, though without having a sexual aim. There is no need for psycho-analysis to be ashamed to speak of love in this connection, for religion itself uses the same words: 'Thou shalt love thy neighbour as thyself.' This, however, is more easily said than done. The second kind of emotional tie is by means of identification. Whatever leads men to share important interests produces this community of feeling, these identifications. And the structure of human society is to a large extent based on them.

The paradigm example of the misogyny entailed in male Eros is that of Count Leo Tolstoy. In *Intercourse,* Andrea Dworkin analyzes the views of women held by this great man of peace and Christlike love, as reflected in his relationship with his wife and in his writings.[56] In *The Kreutzer Sonata* Tolstoy tells the story of a man driven to kill his wife, as this was the only way he could free himself from his sexual dependency on her.

There is no shortcut to the trans-Oedipal stage of individuation nor to a trans-Oedipal stage of history. The necessary condition for the full individuation of the psyche is the elimination of misogyny. Misogyny is a product of the archetypal structure of the objects of the ego ideal. There must be a shift in the object of the ego ideal from that of the father-disembodied-mind/collective brotherhood archetypal mythic framework to that of the archetypal mother/earth/nature. For the female this means the adoption of the Goddess archetype as the object of her ego ideal serving the identification function, and for the male it means the adoption of the Goddess archetype as the object of the ego ideal serving the merger function. As a correlative it means adopting a Dionysian-consort object of the ego ideal for the identification function. Only in this way can the pathology of the narcissistic wound be healed.

This passage cannot be achieved through Freudian heroic struggle, liberal equality, or Jungian androgyny. The Thanatos complex is far too powerful. It takes an archetype to replace an archetype. It takes a complex to transcend a complex. There is no other way than a return to the mother. The road to liberty lies as much today in *Amargi* (return to the Mother) as it did at the time of the Sumerians.[57]

This is the necessary condition for humankind to reach a trans-Oedipal stage, and this is also the reason why history will probably end with the triumph of the corporate brotherhood. Males will not make the necessary sacrifice without a major shift in the archetypal structure of the collective psyche, and there appears to be no evidence that such a shift is taking place. The New Age movement is filled with far too much mysticism and is still patriarchally dominated. The only kind of movement which could produce such an archetypal shift would be a massive explosion of radical feminism. It is the only social movement that has the required archetypal structure.

BEYOND HOPE AND DESPAIR

The unisexual primitive single cell organism, which reproduces by splitting, has shown itself to be an inefficient form of life so far as evolutionary change is concerned. Such a life form can remain stable for literally millions of years. Evolution, in the sense of evolving life forms of ever increasing complexity, requires a multiplicity of forms so that those that are the most fit can survive. Reproduction through splitting tends to replicate the same life form. A species that can slightly modify itself in reproduction is able to evolve new life forms. Bimorphic sexuality, by mixing genes into a new form, is much more effective in producing variations in life forms. When a further complexity in genetic structure increases the chances of survival of the particular species, the complexity will be perpetuated.

If, as the result of a variety of natural contingencies, a species of mammal reaches the point in the evolutionary process where it evolves a "mind" as the result of the complexity of its brain, then it will, in addition to the relatively slow process of biological evolution, commence a new kind of evolution, the evolution of consciousness. The species will produce a collective mind, which in and of itself will evolve. As the collective mind programs the individual minds of the members of the species, the species will change. If the species is typical of most mammals its sexuality will be such that the males will be hormonally driven to struggle with each other for access to the females. If the female of the species is in continuing state of sexual receptivity, and the means of sexual arousal has shifted from an olfactorial to a visual mechanism whereby the mere presence of the female can trigger a sexual response, then the males of the species will be subject to constant sexual arousal. If the contingencies of evolution happen to produce such a sexually driven mammal that also has evolved a brain with a cortex capable of producing consciousness, then there will be a very close interrelationship between its genetically and hormonally determined sexual structure and the world view that the collective psyche constructs.

Early homo sapiens, while biologically similar, are very different creatures from modern humans having minds derived from the collective psyche of the contemporary human race. A process of individuation, with something like the Oedipal passage, would be an inevitable development in any species or form of mammal that evolved a brain sufficiently complex as to produce a psyche divided into the conscious and the unconscious. The bimorphic sexuality of biological evolution, while at first a powerful force in the evolution of the mind (probably the most powerful force), will eventually, as the mind evolves, lead to a conscious awareness of its own death, its genetically determined procreation, and an unconscious memory of its prenatal narcissistic state. This in turn will produce repression, neuroses, pathology, and illusion, which in their turn will produce the struggles that constitute a history. Sentient forms of life, wherever they exist throughout the universe, in their evolutionary process may face some form of the Thanatos barrier, which must be crossed before history can end.

The psychoanalytic analysis of history, in conjunction with radical feminist methodology, uncovers a fundamental problem in the Hegelian analysis of history. The end of history in the Hegelian analysis has at least three necessary conditions. The first is a perfect understanding of death, which assumes that the reality of death and its dialectical negation of being is fully accepted and integrated into the psyche. The second is the emergence of the universal and homogeneous technological state, and the third is the absence of masters and slaves. The psychoanalytic analysis reveals that the universal and homogeneous technological state is in part a result of the attempt to transcend death. It is the product of the Thanatos complex, which represses the fear of death, thus producing illusion and neuroses. The radical feminist analysis of the subordinate position of women in the universal, homogeneous, technological state reveals that males are masters and females are slaves within the Hegelian meaning of these terms. The industrial technological state is a product of the Apollonian and Heraclean complexes, which elevate production over reproduction, marginalize women and their contributions and experiences, and deny the intrinsic value of nature. The male is subject, agent, and actor. All else is objectified. The Hegelian end of history is identical with the state of post-Oedipal patriarchy. It represents the triumph of the brotherhoods of the collective. The first and third conditions of the Hegelian end of history are inconsistent with the second. Only in the trans-Oedipal stage of history can there be a perfect understanding of death, and a true equality of the sexes. A perfect understanding of death and the abolition of subjugation with the emergence of true equality are both necessary conditions for the end of history. The social order that would emerge from their fulfillment, however, would have to be very different from that envisaged by Hegel, Kojève, or Cooper. It would be one in which there were room for both a playful technology and a respect for nature and where the welfare of children would be primary. Sex/gender would be radically reconstructed and, with it, the entire justification for social order. Such a world would be both beyond history and post-modern.

The modern age began with Rousseau and the French Revolution, when the belief that man could change human nature by changing the material conditions of life became a principle of political action. The horrendous misery produced by twentieth-century revolutionary governments, whether of the left or right, has dissipated this hope. Freud and the psychoanalytic method should leave us with no illusions about the possibility of changing the human condition. The causes of human misery lie in the realm of what Freud called "psychic reality,"[58] which is rooted in biology and material conditions. That reality is represented through mental processes that are both "constructive and significational," and that historicize the present through the process by which representations of the past are woven into the very fabric of the representations of new experience.[59] Humans cannot consciously change psychic reality through acts of the will because they operate within it. There is no neat dividing line between subject and object.

In the post-Oedipal stage of history many individuals in their own process of individuation will be able to transcend the Oedipal passage. Radical feminists who reject the patriarchal objects of their ego ideal and shift to that of a powerful Goddess archetype are trans-Oedipal individuals. Those few Dionysian males who are able to look directly into the face of the Medusa, without the distorting mirror of the patriarchal misogynous images of women, approach the possibility of moving beyond the post-Oedipal to a trans-Oedipal state.

In order to produce a significant shift in the collective psyche, it would require a great many more people than are at present able to integrate their animality into their conscious mind. At present, powerful women who reject the Eve complex, and males who are ridding themselves of misogyny tend to trigger or inflame the misogyny of those caught in the Thanatos complex. There is simply not a powerful enough female or feminine object of the ego ideal to pull women away from the patriarchal archetypal structures that maintain misogyny, let alone pull men away. The next movement in the evolution of the collective psyche has to be a spiral return to the archetypal mother. In the past, the process of individuation was marked by a convergence of the drive away from the archetypal mother and the pull toward merger with a new object of the ego ideal. Now misogyny pulls in the opposite direction from that required to move from the brotherhood of the collective to a new feminine object of the ego ideal. This is the Thanatos barrier, which must be crossed before the human race can move from the post-Oedipal to the trans-Oedipal state.

The post-Oedipal stage of history, wherein the collective psyche remains frozen in the Thanatos complex, fixated on the masculine objects of the ego ideal, may last a very long time. No alternative mythic structure may be powerful enough to break males away from the convergence of the Persean, Apollonian, and Heraclean complexes, which fuel the energy and furnish the misogyny behind the Thanatos complex. Consequently corporate, technological, male-dominated society will likely remain far into the future. The tools of science, in the hands of pathological male corporate elites, may be able to control the mythic structures so that no archetypal counterobject of the ego ideal will be able to arise to challenge the brotherhoods. Apollonian technological industry is likely to triumph throughout the world. Its requirements will determine the nature of future social orders. While the brotherhoods may wear liberal democratic masks, the degree of true freedom and diversity that they will tolerate will depend upon what best serves economic needs.

This conclusion is not based on an ability to predict the future, but rather on the realization that the evolution of history is beyond the control of the human will. Given the present direction, *there is no particular reason for having hope.* Hope assumes that something can be done about the human condition. Hope perpetuates the illusions that human suffering has external causes and that human nature can be changed by altering material conditions. These two illusions form the very essence of ideology. The reality is that the causes of human suffering lie within the psyche. Hope maintains the illusion that we are rational by nature, and that reason will eventually prevail. We should realize, however, that we are controlled by the archetypal structure of the collective unconscious. Individual action occasionally makes a difference, but only when it works in conjunction with the forces of the collective psyche.

Hope is the delusion of the collective brotherhoods. It invites the pathological to pursue their pathology. The worst pathological and psychotic actions of which men have shown themselves capable have always been carried out in the name of the highest ideals. As Chasseguet-Smirgel states, "The end (the coming together of ego and ideal) justifies the means (annihilates the superego)."[60] Evil in the name of evil is tolerable because it is direct and does not hide behind illusion. The most dangerous kind of evil is that which appears wearing the mantle of hope.

Hope for social change is the method that the corporate brotherhoods and their male elites use to channel the support and energy of women. Hope is what keeps women supporting patriarchy. We need look only at the way hope was offered to women by the socialist movement throughout its history, and how that hope was then betrayed.[61] It was the hope that National Socialism offered for the improvement of the position of women that brought the massive support that many German women gave Nazism, in spite of its expressed and implicit misogyny.[62] It is hope that the fundamentalist Christian movement and the Right offer to the women of America. By offering hope of social change to women, the corporate structure is able to suck the energy from the women's movement parasitically and strengthen itself at the small price of allowing a few Athene-possessed women into the corporate hierarchies, where they generally remain marginalized.

Seeking to change society through rational planning and organized enforcement invites pathology. Thus, hope for social change leads eventually to despair, and despair to inertia. The surrender of hope frees us from the pathology of purpose. We escape despair by rejecting hope. We are neither hopeful nor hopeless because we have moved beyond and outside the context of hope. To move beyond hope for social change is not to reject social action or politics. Rather, political action should become its own end. This is the politics that Henry Kariel describes in his book *The Desperate Politics of Post-modernism*.[63] From the political perspective, postmodernism commences with the realization that conscious acts of the human will cannot produce the kind of radical change that is required to alter the substantial course of history. Radical change in the course of history requires radical change in the structure of the collective psyche. By accepting the human condition and rejecting the hope that through male-dominated political, education, or ideological institutions we can radically alter society, we free ourselves as actors and protect ourselves from the danger of being co-opted. We can still change ourselves, not in order to change the world, but for the sake of the change itself. We can influence people around us, not to change the world but for the sake of the interaction. We can, through social action, accomplish limited set tasks such as preserving park land, founding day care centers, alleviating specific distress, or saving an endangered animal species, not because any of this will make a substantive difference to the world, but because it is what we want to do at the time. This is action as play rather than action as pathology.

What does one do when faced with the realization that there is no point to hope or to despair? What is left for the individual is nonpathological life-affirming action. What lies beyond hope and despair is play in the midst of tragedy and comedy. One can act and change one's own psyche, but not that of the collective. Human destiny is literally in the hands of the Goddesses and Gods—the archetypes and complexes of the collective psyche. We can alter our own psychic reality only to the degree that we can energize and de-energize the archetypes of our own collective unconscious. The only chance for males to escape the pathology of the Thanatos complex is through Dionysian possession. Only an Eros complex driven by the pathology of the Dionysian complex can energize an archetype which can shift the object of the ego ideal away from a male or masculine form to that of the female or feminine.

The Great Mother, Goddess of the Earth, is as dead as the Sky-Father-God, but "the struggle between Eros and Death, between the instinct of life and the instinct of destruction, as it works itself out in the human species" still continues.[64] History cannot repeat itself, and we can never return to the pre-Oedipal stage of matriarchal paganism. A return to the Goddess must be made by way of a spiral and not a closed circle. The Goddess must be located within the psyche of living women, and Dionysus must return out of the individual unconscious of the male.

Beyond hope and despair lie the spinning of the Goddess[65] and the dance of Dionysus-Shiva.

NOTES

Preface

1. Fraser, "Social Criticism without Philosophy," 19.
2. Kariel, *Desperate Politics of Post-Modernism,* 151.
3. Fraser, *supra* note 1, at 22.

Chapter 1: Law, Society, and Psychoanalysis

1. Kojève, *Introduction to the Reading of Hegel.* There is some debate as to what degree Kojève remained a Marxist. See Riley, "Introduction," 5–48. It is clear from a reading of Kojève that he is not a dialectical materialist.
2. Hegel never actually presented his dialectics in the form of the triad of thesis, antithesis, and synthesis. According to Hall's discussion of "Dialectic" in the *Encyclopedia of Philosophy,* vol. 2, at 388, the word *antithesis* was introduced into translations of Hegel where it was not required. The underlying relationship of the two parts of a Hegelian dialectic is that of contradiction or negation. The idea of the synthesis, however, is implicit in Hegel in that the German term which he uses to mean "cancel," *aufheben,* has a dual meaning, in that it also means to preserve. According to Acton, "The concept of view that is *aufgehoben* is transcended without being wholly discarded" (*Encyclopedia of Philosophy,* vol. 3, at 436).
3. Not all forms of Marxian socialism are rooted in dialectical materialism, but that form which takes the name *Marxism-Leninism* certainly is. Both Marx and Engels were strict materialists, following the philosophy of Ludwig Feuerbach. Feuerbach argued that there are two possible fundamental epistemological foundations for philosophy. The one is materialism which is founded on the premise that all knowledge comes from sensed experience, and the other, idealism, which asserts the primacy of mind. The primary issue is whether mind is dominant and

matter subordinate, or whether matter is dominant and mind subordinate. Both Marx and Engels were naive realists in the sense that they believed that the world we know through sensed experience is real (objective). Feuerbach's view of the nature of reality, while it may have looked reasonable in the light of nineteenth-century science, certainly is totally inadequate in terms of twentieth-century physics. The theory of dialectical materialism was fully developed by Engels in *Anti-Duhring*. The theory of history which comes out of dialectical materialism is often referred to as *historical materialism*.

4. Djilas, *New Class*.

5. Djilas, *Unperfect Society*, 69–114.

6. By a theory of history I mean a structuralist view of history. Structuralism entails "that surface events and phenomena are to be explained by structures, data, and phenomena below the surface." de George and de George, introduction to *Structuralists from Marx to Lévi-Strauss*, xii. One can, of course, hold as a theory of history that there is no structure which underlies history.

7. See for example, Hartsock, *Money, Sex, and Power;* MacKinnon, *Toward a Feminist Theory of the State;* Jaggar, *Feminist Politics and Human Nature;* Guettel, *Marxism and Feminism*.

8. See for example, Hartsock, *supra* note 7; Jaggar, *supra* note 7; Lerner, *Creation of Patriarchy;* French, *Beyond Power;* Sanday, *Female Power and Male Dominance*.

9. Since psychoanalytic social theory is based on a mentalist view of historical development, and Marxism is based on a materialist theory, there can be no true integration of Marx and Freud. Some have attempted such a synthesis. See for example, Reich, *Dialectical Materialism and Psychoanalysis;* Marcuse, *Eros and Civilization;* Fromm, *Beyond the Chains of Illusion*. All such amalgams contain fundamental contradictions. Either Freudian or Marxian theory is inevitably distorted. For discussion of these contradictions see Chasseguet-Smirgel and Grunberger, *Freud or Reich?*

10. I am adopting the usage of *(m)other* as equivalent to *other-mother*. For an analysis of this interrelationship see Garner, Kahane, and Sprengnether, eds. *(M)other Tongue*.

11. The figures for the United States, Great Britain, and France are taken from the *Christian Science Monitor*, 23 May 1988.

12. See for example Kairys, ed., *Politics of Law*.

13. Hayek, *Constitution of Liberty*.

14. S. Freud, *Moses and Monotheism, Standard Edition* (hereafter *S.E.*), vol. 23, at 3; *id., Totem and Taboo, S.E.*, vol. 13; *id., Group Psychology and the Analysis of the Ego, S.E.*, vol. 18; *id., The Future of an Illusion; id., Civilization and Its Discontents, S.E.*, vol. 21. In general, see Gay, *Freud for Historians;* Roth, *Psychoanalysis as History;* Badcock, *Psychoanalysis of Culture;* Endleman, *Psyche and Society*.

15. See for example Stoller, *Presentations of Gender;* Chasseguet-Smirgel and Grunberger, *supra* note 9.

16. See for example Spiro, *Oedipus in the Trobriands;* Roheim, *Psychoanalysis and Anthropology;* Gregor, *Anxious Pleasures*. See in general Wallace, *Freud and*

Anthropology; Kardiner et al., *Psychological Frontiers of Society;* Harris, "Culture and Personality: Freudian," in *Rise of Anthropological Theory,* chap. 16, 422–48.

17. See Samuels, *Jung and the Post-Jungians.*

18. For a general discussion of the value of feminist theory for psychoanalytic theory, see Robert Seidenberg, "Psychoanalysis and the Feminist Movement," in Nelson and Ikenberry, eds., *Psychosexual Imperatives,* chap. 10, 307–23.

19. Brown, *Life against Death,* 3; E. Becker, *Denial of Death,* 178.

20. See S. Freud., "Repression," in *Papers on Metapsychology, S.E.,* vol. 14, at 141–58; *id.,* "Resistance and Repression," in *Introductory Lectures on Psychoanalysis,* lecture 19, *S.E.,* vol. 16, at 286–302.

21. Grunberger, *Narcissism,* 78.

22. Chasseguet-Smirgel, *Ego Ideal,* 4.

23. S. Freud, *Group Psychology, supra* note 14, at 140–41.

24. *Ibid.* at 58.

25. For a discussion of what constitutes perversion and for a defense of the continued use of the term, see Stoller, "Perversion and the Desire to Harm." See also Chasseguet-Smirgel, *Creativity and Perversion.*

26. Dr. Robert Pos, Clinical Director of Psychiatry at the University of British Columbia, uses the term *the We-unconscious* instead of the term *collective unconscious.* He contrasts this with the *I-unconscious.*

27. S. Freud, *Totem and Taboo, supra* note 14, at 157–59.

28. The only references to the collective mind are in S. Freud, *Totem and Taboo, supra* note 14, at 158–59, and *id., Group Psychology, supra* note 14, at 79–87.

29. Freud found the concept of a collective unconscious to be unhelpful. See *Moses and Monotheism, supra* note 14, at 132.

30. S. Freud, *Totem and Taboo, supra* note 14.

31. West, "Law, Rights."

32. Elliot, *Twentieth Century Book of the Dead,* 1.

Chapter 2: Struggling with Freud's Legacy

1. S. Freud, "Obsessive Actions and Religious Practices," *S.E.,* vol. 9, at 126–27.

2. Brown, *Life Against Death,* 12.

3. See Chasseguet-Smirgel and Grunberger, *Freud or Reich?,* 30–48; Gabriel, *Freud and Society;* Jacoby, *Repression of Psychoanalysis.*

4. S. Freud, "On the History of the Psychoanalytic Movement," *S.E.,* vol. 14, at 57.

5. S. Freud, "Claims of Psycho-analysis to the Interest of the Non-psychological Sciences," *S.E.,* vol. 13, at 185–86.

6. Chasseguet-Smirgel and Grunberger, *supra* note 3, at 30–48.

7. S. Freud, *Group Psychology and the Analysis of the Ego, S.E.,* vol. 18, at 117.

8. S. Freud, "Postscript" to "An Autobiographical Study," *S.E.*, vol. 20, at 72.

9. Sagan, in *At the Dawn of Tyranny*, represents the structure of psychoanalytic theory as a triangle with double arrows running in both directions between the three points (at 348).

10. *Ibid.* at 383.

11. S. Freud, "On the Universal Tendency to Debasement in the Sphere of Love," *S.E.*, vol. 11, at 189. Freud used the same paraphrase of Napoleon's saying in "The Dissolution of the Oedipus Complex," *S.E.*, vol. 19, at 178. He also postulated that biology is destiny, in "The Economic Problem of Masochism," *S.E.*, vol. 19, at 168–69.

12. S. Freud, See "Instincts and Their Vicissitudes," in *Papers on Metapsychology*, *S.E.*, vol. 14, at 105–215. Regarding metapsychology, Freud writes (at 181):

> It will not be unreasonable to give a special name to this whole way of regarding our subject-matter, for it is the consummation of psycho-analytic research. I propose that when we have succeeded in describing a psychical process in its dynamic, topographical and economic aspects, we should speak of it as a *metapsychological* presentation. We must say at once that in the present state of our knowledge there are only a few points at which we shall succeed in this.

See also *id.*, "A Metapsychological Supplement to the Theory of Dreams," *S.E.*, vol. 14, at 217–35. One of Freud's missing papers on metapsychology was recently discovered, *A Phylogenetic Fantasy*, edit. Ilse Grubich-Simitis. Included in the volume is an essay by Grubich-Simitis, "Metapsychology and Metabiology."

13. See S. Freud, "Overview of the Transference Neuroses," in *A Phylogenetic Fantasy*, at 13.

14. S. Freud, *Civilization and its Discontents*, *S.E.*, vol. 21.

15. Marcuse, *Eros and Civilization*. See also Gabriel, *supra* note 3, at 197–205.

16. Brown, *supra* note 2. See also Gabriel, *supra* note 3, at 205–13; Lewin, *Sexual Self-destruct*, 124–28.

17. Brown, *Love's Body*.

18. Becker, *Denial of Death*. See also Gabriel, *supra* note 3 at 239–45.

19. Fine, *Psychoanalytic Vision*.

20. Chasseguet-Smirgel and Grunberger, *supra* note 3, at 50.

21. Eysenck, *Decline and Fall*, 208.

22. *Ibid.* at 34.

23. See for example Thornton, *Freud and Cocaine*.

24. See for example Bakan, *Sigmund Freud*. Gay, in *The Godless Jew*, persuasively argues that Freud's philosophical position as an atheist was essential for the development of psychoanalytic theory but his Jewish cultural heritage was of minimal consequence.

25. See for example Balmary, *Psychoanalyzing Psychoanalysis*.

26. This view was also held by Lacan. See *Four Fundamental Concepts of Psycho-analysis*.

27. Ernst Federn, addressing the symposium "Struggling with Freud's Legacy" at the University of British Columbia in May 1986. Federn said that Popper,

as a Viennese native German speaker, should have known better than to make the criticism which he did. One of the best discussions of the status of psychoanalysis as a science is to be found in Barratt, *Psychic Reality and Psychoanalytic Knowing*. He states at 86–87:

> Freud repeatedly insists that psychoanalytic discourse is *scientific*, yet it is worth noting an ambiguity in this insistence, especially because it has caused certain confusions among his successors. Freud seems sure that his discourse is scientific, *wissenschaftlich*, but, despite his personal enthusiasm for the neo-positivism of the "unified science" movement, he admits doubt about whether the discipline of psychoanalysis is natural-scientific, *naturwissenschaftlich*. In his posthumously published *Abriss der Psychoanalyse*, for example, Freud writes of his psychology as "a natural science like any other." Yet a few years earlier, he refers, with somewhat neo-Kantian undertones, to the existence of "two sciences, psychology . . . and natural science." For Freud's commentators who do not read the German original, this ambiguity is exacerbated in part by James Strachey's routine translation of Wissenschaft as "science." Whereas in English "science" commonly implies objectivistic investigations of the natural world within the framework of logical empiricism, the German *Wissenschaft* has a broader connotation that includes any disciplined, scholarly pursuit.

28. S. Freud, *Gesammelte Werke*, vol. 10, (1946), 62, 142, and 210; translated in *S.E.*, vol. 14, at 24, 77, and 117.

29. Popper, *Conjectures and Refutations*.

30. Grunbaum, *Foundations of Psychoanalysis*, 97–104.

31. See for example, Eysenck, *supra* note 21; Grunbaum, *supra* note 30; Rachman, ed., *Critical Essays on Psychoanalysis*; Pinckney and Pinckney, *Fallacy of Freud and Psychoanalysis*; Jurjevich, *Hoax of Freudism*; P. Kline, *Fact and Fantasy in Freudian Theory*; Eysenck and Wilson, *Experimental Study of Freudian Theories*; Farrell, *Standing of Psychoanalysis*; Stevens, *Freud and Psychoanalysis*; C. S. Hall, *Meaning of Dreams*; G. H. Pollock, "Freud as Scientist"; Nagel, "Methodological Issues in Psychoanalytic Theory"; Edelson, "Psychoanalysis as Science"; Rubinstein, "Problem of Confirmation in Clinical Psychoanalysis." P. Kline, the author of *Fact and Fantasy in Freudian Theory*, concludes that while some parts have been confirmed, some have neither been proven nor refuted, and that "there are few good experiments which actually refute the theory" (at 438). He writes (at 437–38), "[I]t seems clear that far too much that is distinctively Freudian has been verified for the rejection of the whole psychoanalytic theory to be possible."

32. Colby and Stoller, *Cognitive Science and Psychoanalysis*.

33. *Ibid.* at 35–37.

34. *Ibid.* at 1.

35. *Ibid.* at 48.

36. *Ibid.* at 38.

37. *Ibid.* at 38–39, 153.

38. Kuhn, *Structure of Scientific Revolutions*. For a discussion of the value of using the concept of paradigmatic shift in the context of the social sciences, see Gutting, ed., *Paradigms and Revolutions*.

39. See Dilman, *Freud and the Mind*; Gabriel, *supra* note 3, at 9–26.

40. Turkle, "Artificial Intelligence and Psychoanalysis."

41. Samuels, *Jung and the Post-Jungians,* 6–8; Schafer, *New Language for Psychoanalysis.*

42. See for example, Stannard, *Shrinking History.* For a superb defense of the value of Freud for historians see Gay, *Freud for Historians.* See also Roth, *Psychoanalysis as History.*

43. Harris, *Cannibals and Kings; id., Cultural Materialism,* 258–86. Harris discusses the value of psychoanalytic theory for anthropology in "Culture and Personality: Freudian," in *Rise of Anthropological Theory,* chap. 16, at 422–48.

44. Malinowski, *Sex and Repression in Savage Society.*

45. See for example Boyer and Grolnick, eds., *Psychoanalytic Study of Society,* vol. 11; Badcock, *Psychoanalysis of Culture.*

46. Roheim, *Psychoanalysis and Anthropology.*

47. See for example Herdt, *Guardians of the Flutes; id.,* ed., *Ritualized Homosexuality in Melanesia; id., Rituals of Manhood.* Gregor, *Anxious Pleasures.*

48. S. Freud, "Question of Lay Analysis," *S.E.,* vol. 20, at 248.

49. See Jacoby, *Repression of Psychoanalysis.*

50. Turkle, *Psychoanalytic Politics.*

51. Ellenberger, *Discovery of the Unconscious;* Whyte, *Unconscious before Freud.*

52. Whyte, *supra* note 51, at 177.

53. Masson, *Assault on Truth.* Masson's critics, in general, have been more interested in attacking him personally than in responding to his arguments. See Malcolm, *In the Freud Archives.* For a response to this kind of criticism, see Masson, "Persecution and Expulsion of Jeffrey Masson"; Goldman, "Playing with a Bad Boy."

54. S. Freud, "Aetiology of Hysteria," *S.E.,* vol. 3, at 203.

55. S. Freud, *Complete Letters,* letter dated 26 April 1896, at 184.

56. *Ibid.* See letters of 8 October 1895, at 140; 28 April 1897, at 236; 22 June 1897, at 253.

57. S. Freud, "Femininity," in *New Introductory Lectures on Psycho-analysis,* Lecture 33, *S.E.,* vol. 22, at 112.

58. S. Freud, *supra* note 55, letter dated 21 September 1897, at 264.

59. *Ibid.*

60. See Wolff, *Postcards from the End of the World.*

61. Herman, *Father-daughter Incest;* Rush, *Best-kept Secret.*

62. Balmary, *supra* note 25.

63. See *Assault on Truth, supra* note 53.

64. *Ibid.* at 100–102.

65. *Ibid.* at 113.

66. *Ibid.* at 114–17. In his letter to Fliess dated 22 December 1897, Freud writes concerning a recent case, "The father belongs to the category of *men who stab women,* for whom bloody injuries are an erotic need. When she was two years old, he brutally deflowered her and infected her with his gonorrhea, as a consequence of which she became ill and her life was endangered by the loss of blood and vaginitis. . . . A new motto: 'What has been done to you, you poor child?' " S. Freud, *supra* note 55, at 288–89.

67. Sandor Ferenczi, "Confusion of Tongues between Adults and the Child," in Masson, *supra* note 53, at 288. Ferenczi writes:

> Above all, my previously communicated assumption, that trauma, specifically sexual trauma, cannot be stressed enough as a pathogenic agent, was confirmed anew. Even children of respected, high-minded puritanical families fall victim to real rape much more frequently than one had dared to suspect. Either the parents themselves seek substitution for their lack of [sexual] satisfaction in this pathological manner, or else trusted persons such as relatives (uncles, aunts, grandparents), tutors, servants, abuse the ignorance and innocence of children. The obvious objection that we are dealing with sexual fantasies of the child himself, that is, with hysterical lies, unfortunately is weakened by the multitude of confessions of this kind, on the part of patients in analysis, to assaults on children.

68. Krull, in *Freud and His Father,* presents an analysis of the seduction theory which falls between Masson's and Balmary's explanations.

69. S. Freud, *supra* note 55, at 255.

70. Gay, *Freud,* 95. In fact, Gay views the abandonment of the seduction theory as a progressive step in the development of Freud's thought. He writes (at 91), "The seduction theory in all its uncompromising sweep seems inherently implausible; only a fantasist like Fliess could have accepted and applauded it. What is astonishing is not that Freud eventually abandoned the idea, but that he adopted it in the first place."

71. Lothane, "Love, Seduction, and Trauma."

72. Wigmore, *Evidence,* sect. 924a.

73. J. H. Fisher, "Obtaining and Presenting Evidence in Sex Cases," 156.

74. See S. Freud, *Three Essays on the Theory of Sexuality, S.E.,* vol. 7.

75. See S. Freud, "Some Psychological Consequences of the Anatomical Differences between the Sexes," *S.E.,* vol. 19.

76. Mitchell, *Psycho-analysis and Feminism.*

77. Brown, *supra* note 2, at 126.

78. Chasseguet-Smirgel, *Sexuality and Mind,* 25.

79. See in general Steele, *Freud and Jung;* Kaufmann, *Discovering the Mind,* vol. 3: *Freud versus Adler and Jung,* 289–433. See also Jung, *Freud and Psychoanalysis, C.W.,* vol. 4; William McGuire, ed., *Freud/Jung Letters.*

80. Rank, *Myth of the Birth of the Hero.* See in general James Lieberman, *Acts of Will.*

81. Jacoby, *Repression of Psychoanalysis,* ix.

82. *Ibid.* at xi.

83. Culler, *On Deconstruction,* 85–86.

84. See for example, Jung, "Symbols of Transformation," *C.W.,* vol. 5; *id.,* "Battle for Deliverance from the Mother," 274–305; and *id.,* "Dual Mother," 306–93; *id.,* "Psychological Aspects of the Mother Archetype," *C.W.,* vol. 9i, at 75–110. See in general Roazen, *Freud and His Followers,* 224–96.

85. Groddeck, *Book of the It; id., Meaning of Illness.* See in general Roazen, *supra* note 84, at 331–35.

86. Rank, *supra* note 80; *id.*, *Double*. See in general Roazen, *supra* note 84, at 391–418.

87. Ferenczi, *Sex in Psychoanalysis; id., Final Contributions; id., First Contributions;* and *id., Further Contributions*. See in general Roazen, *supra* note 84, at 363–71.

88. Brunswick, "Preoedipal Phase," 293–319. See in general Roazen, *supra* note 84, at 420–36.

89. M. Klein, *Psycho-analysis of Children*, Klein, Heimann and Money-Kyrle, eds., *New Directions in Psycho-analysis*. See in general Roazen, *supra* note 84, at 478–88.

90. Sullivan, *Collected Works*.

91. Winnicott, *Mother and Child; id., Collected Papers*.

92. Erikson, *Childhood and Society; id., Identity and the Life Cycle*.

93. Mahler, Pine, and Bergman, *Psychological Birth of the Human Infant*. See also Mahler, *Memoirs of Margaret S. Mahler*.

94. Mahler, Pine, and Bergman, *supra* note 93.

95. Stoller, *Presentations of Gender*.

96. Chasseguet-Smirgel, *Ego Ideal*.

97. Fast, *Gender Identity*.

98. There are, of course, many other recent developments in Freudian psychoanalytic theory. Much of it deals with analysis itself. See for example, Eagle, *Recent Developments in Psychoanalysis*.

99. See for example Sagan, *supra* note 9.

100. See for example, Chodorow, *Reproduction of Mothering*, 58–62; Benjamin, "Bonds of Love," 42 and 49.

101. See in particular, Mitchell and Rose, eds., *Feminine Sexuality;* Mitchell, *supra* note 76; Gallop, *Reading Lacan;* Irigaray, *Speculum of the Other Woman; id., This Sex Which Is Not One;* Jardine, *Gynesis*.

102. See in general Clement, *Lives and Legends of Jacques Lacan;* Schneiderman, *Jacques Lacan;* Turkle, *Psychoanalytic Politics*.

103. See in general Archard, *Conscious and the Unconscious;* Felman, *Jacques Lacan and the Adventure of Insight;* Gallop, *supra* note 101; Lemaire, *Jacques Lacan;* MacCabe, ed., *Talking Cure;* MacCannell, *Figuring Lacan;* Ragland-Sullivan, *Jacques Lacan and the Philosophy of Psychoanalysis;* Schneiderman, *Returning to Freud;* Stanton, *Outside the Dream*.

104. Honey and Broughton, "Feminine Sexuality," 543–44.

105. Gallop, *supra* note 101.

106. Mitchell, *supra* note 76.

107. See Lacan, *Speech and Language in Psychoanalysis; id.*, "Unconscious and Repetition," in *Four Fundamental Concepts of Psycho-analysis*, 17–64. See also *id., Écrits*, chap. 3, 30–113 and chap. 5, 146–78.

108. See Samuels, *supra* note 41, at 40–41.

109. See Lacan, "Subversion of the Subject and the Dialectic of Desire in the Freudian Unconscious," in *Écrits, supra* note 107, at 292–325; *id.*, "Feminine Sexuality in Psychoanalytic Doctrine," in Mitchell and Rose, *supra* note 101, at 123–36.

110. See Lacan, "Meaning of the Phallus" and "Feminine Sexuality in Psychoanalytic Doctrine," in Mitchell and Rose, *supra* note 101, at 74–136.

111. Chasseguet-Smirgel, *supra* note 78; Honey and Broughton, *supra* note 104, at 527.

112. See Alpert, ed., *Psychoanalysis and Women;* Horney, *Feminine Psychology;* Chasseguet-Smirgel, *supra* note 78; Chasseguet-Smirgel, "Freud and Female Sexuality," 275; Honey and Broughton, *supra* note 104; Nelson Garner, Kahane, and Sprengnether, eds., *(M)other Tongue;* Chodorow, *supra* note 100; *id.,* "Feminism and Difference"; *id., Feminism and Psychoanalytic Theory;* Benjamin, *Bonds of Love,* Sayers, *Sexual Contradictions;* Dinnerstein, *Mermaid and the Minotaur;* Mitchell, *supra* note 76; Gallop, *Daughter's Seduction;* Irigaray, *Speculum of the Other Woman;* Irigaray, *This Sex Which Is Not One;* Strouse, ed., *Women and Analysis;* Kofman, *Enigma of Woman;* Moore, "Freud and Female Sexuality"; Gilman, "Freud and the Prostitute"; Montgrain, "On the Vicissitudes of Female Sexuality"; Crowell, "Feminism and Modern Psychoanalysis."

113. Stoller, *Perversion,* 215.

114. *Ibid.* at 216.

115. *Ibid.* at 218.

116. Benjamin, *supra* note 112.

117. *Ibid.* at 181.

118. *Ibid.*

119. *Ibid.* at 134–35.

120. *Ibid.* at 177.

121. *Ibid.*

122. *Ibid.*

123. *Ibid.* at 147–58.

124. Law is not a necessary condition for social practices. Property, bargaining, selling, promising, and language are all social practices which can be found to exist outside of legal frameworks.

125. Jaggar, *Feminist Politics and Human Nature.*

126. MacKinnon, *Toward a Feminist Theory of the State.*

127. Culler, *supra* note 83, at 160.

128. MacKinnon, *supra* note 126.

129. *Ibid.* at 117.

130. *Ibid.* at 83.

131. *Ibid.* at 127.

132. *Ibid.*

133. Chodorow, *Feminism and Psychoanalytic Theory.*

134. *Ibid.* at 169.

135. MacKinnon, *supra* note 126 at 124.

136. *Ibid.* at 121.

137. Barratt, *Psychic Reality and Psychoanalytic Knowing.*

138. MacKinnon, *supra* note 126 at 104.

Chapter 3: The Mythological Dimensions of Culture

1. Frankl, *Unheard Cry of Meaning*, 31.
2. Hopper, "Myth, Dream and Imagination," in *Myths, Dreams and Religion*, ed., Campbell, 115–16, writes:

> Myth today has gone underground. We have lost the notion of myth as the "story about a god," and are thrust back upon primordial images of the unconscious—upon dream, upon primary anecdote, upon radical metaphor which functions inwardly as the means of correlating our inner and outer experience—or even (since we inherit the time of the "in between") the means of correlating our "depth" psyches with our still operative 'Cartesian' egos.

3. Barthes, *Mythologies*, 129.
4. Barthes, *supra* note 3, at 142.
5. For discussions of the interrelationship between myth and philosophy see, Richard A. Underwood, "Myth, Dream, and the Vocation of Contemporary Philosophy," in Campbell, *supra* note 2, at 225. See also the writings of Cassirer, in particular, *Philosophy of Symbolic Forms*, vol. 2; *id., Language and Myth; id., Myth of the State*. Cassirer notes that historically we find no great culture that is not dominated by and pervaded with mythical elements. While myth pervades and governs the whole of man's social feeling and social life, it reaches its full force when man has to face an unusual and dangerous situation. The powers of myth are checked and subdued by superior forces. As long as these forces, intellectual, ethical, and artistic, are full-strength, myth is tamed and subdued. But once they begin to lose their strength chaos again comes. Mythical thought then starts to rise anew and to pervade the whole of man's cultural and social life.
6. See Eliade, *Myth and Reality; id., Sacred and the Profane; id., Myths, Dreams, and Mysteries; id., Images and Symbols*; Lévi-Strauss, *Myth and Meaning; id., Anthropology and Myth*. Berger and Luckmann, *Social Construction of Reality*; Malinowski, *Magic, Science and Religion*; Douglas, *Natural Symbols*; Luckmann, *Invisible Religion*.
7. For examples see Hillman, "On Psychological Feminity," part 3 of *The Myth of Analysis*. A more recent example would be the purported projection by Mead of Franz Boas's cultural determination on Samoan society in her book, *Coming of Age in Samoa*. See Freeman, *Margaret Mead and Samoa*.
8. Smith and Weisstub, *Western Idea of Law*. See the discussion of mythology as method in the review by Barton in *Legal Studies Forum*, vol. 10, 137.
9. For examples of where science and myth merge, see Capra, *Tao of Physics*; Zukav, *Dancing Wu Li Masters*; De Riencourt, *Eye of Shiva*; Talbot, *Mysticism and the New Physics*; Yukawa, *Creativity and Intuition*.
10. Ryle, *Concept of Mind*, 8.
11. "[O]nce religion and scientific thought attempt to escape from the implicit ambiguities of an unself-conscious mythic involvement such thought must either destroy itself at the reflective level of mythic meaning, or else find itself at what in

effect becomes an irreducibly tensional level of metaphorical significance." Berggren, "From Myth to Metaphor," 530.

12. See Joseph Campbell, "Mythological Themes," in Campbell, *supra* note 2; Thompson, *Time Falling Bodies Take to Light*, 5–7.

13. Frye, *Great Code*.

14. Tucker, *Philosophy and Myth in Karl Marx*, 219.

15. For a discussion of the psychoanalytic uses of myth, see Eisner, *Road to Daulis*.

16. S. Freud, *Psychopathology of Everyday Life*, S.E., vol. 6, at 258–59. For a discussion of what Freud meant by the term *metapsychology*, see his newly discovered manuscript, *A Phylogenetic Fantasy*. See also Grubich-Simitis's essay, "Metaphyschology and Metabiology," published in the same volume.

17. E. Becker, *Denial of Death*, 178.

18. Cox, in "Place of Mythology in the Study of Culture," (at 86) writes, "Myths, then, are largely projections with greater or lesser elements of wish fulfillment. They become institutionalized because they give type answers to type problems. Thus, they come to take on the nature of an anxiety allaying device."

19. Abraham, *Dreams and Myths*, 18.

20. The theory of myth favored by Lévi-Strauss is a revised form of the "symbolic analysis" which he calls structural. He does not oppose sociology to psychology, he contraposes psychology and structure. See for example *Structural Anthropology*, chap. 4.

21. For a discussion of political ideology as myth see Barthes, *supra* note 3 at 109–59.

22. Arlow wrote dreams "are made to be forgotten" but myths are made to be remembered and repeated. They express "communally acceptable versions of wishes" ("Ego Psychology and the Study of Mythology," 379).

23. Stoller, *Sexual Excitement*, xiv.

24. The reality principle functions to trigger paradigmatic shifts in our mythic systems. S. Freud, *Civilization and Its Discontents*, S.E., vol. 21, at 67–80; *id.*, *Beyond the Pleasure Principle*, S.E., vol. 18, at 10.

25. S. Freud, *Future of an Illusion*, S.E., vol. 21, at 31.

26. Chasseguet-Smirgel and Grunberger, *Freud or Reich?*

27. *Ibid.* at 15–16.

28. Engels, "Engels to Mehring; London, 14 July 1893," *Selected Correspondence, 1846–1895*, 511.

29. S. Freud, "The Question of *Weltanschauung*," in *id.*, *New Introductory Lectures on Psycho-analysis*, S.E., vol. 22, at 180.

30. See for example Fromm, *Beyond the Chains of Illusion*. Fromm believed that his combination of Marxism with psychoanalytic theory had taken him beyond illusion. Yet when he found a conflict between the thought of Marx and Freud, it is Freud whom Fromm sacrificed. He writes (at 12) "that Marx is a figure of world historical significance with whom Freud cannot even be compared in this respect hardly needs to be said. . . . I consider Marx, the thinker, as being of much greater depth and scope than Freud." See also Schneider, *Neurosis and Civilization*.

31. Chasseguet-Smirgel and Grunberger, *supra* note 26, at 207.

32. *Ibid.* at 209.

33. *Ibid.* at 212–13. The authors are severely critical of any kind of Freudian-Marxist synthesis on the grounds that the ends of each are radically different and even diametrically opposed, such that any attempt to synthesize Marxism and psychoanalysis will inevitably end up denying essential elements in each system of thought.

34. Djilas, *New Class.*

35. Kuhn, *Structure of Scientific Revolutions.*

36. Chasseguet-Smirgel and Grunberger, *supra* note 26, at 50.

37. Djilas, *supra* note 34.

38. Chasseguet-Smirgel and Grunberger, *supra* note 26.

39. See Becker, *supra* note 17.

40. Frankl, *Man's Search for Meaning,* 121.

41. Einstein, *Ideas and Opinions,* at 272, states that the "concepts and fundamental principles" of physics "are free inventions of the human intellect, which cannot be justified either by the nature of that intellect or in any other fashion *a priori.*"

42. Cowan, *Masochism.*

43. A. Freud, *Ego and the Mechanisms of Defence.*

44. Becker, *supra* note 17.

Chapter 4: The Mythic Foundations of Social Order

1. Barthes, *Mythologies,* 129 and 142.

2. Ryle, *Concept of Mind,* 8.

3. Hume, *Treatise of Human Nature,* book 3, part 1, sect. 1.

4. I use the word "reality" as a postulate, since it cannot be directly known free from illusion. We come closer to it by stripping away a set of illusions, but the new paradigm will contain its own illusory content. While each step in conscious awareness may take us closer to "reality," the best we can achieve, within a lifetime, is the awareness that whatever view of "reality" we hold, we cannot entirely escape illusion.

5. Eliot, *Sweeney Agonistes.*

6. Sherfey, *Nature and Evolution of Female Sexuality;* Montagu, *Natural Superiority of Women;* Cherfas and Gribbin, *Redundant Male;* Durden-Smith and deSimone, *Sex and the Brain.*

7. Stoller, *Perversion,* 16.

8. See chap. 8, *infra.*

9. Pleck, *Myth of Masculinity.*

10. See Stoller, *supra* note 7, at 99; Stoller, *Observing the Erotic Imagination,* 34. Most descriptions of the various forms of perversion apply only to males. See for example, Chasseguet-Smirgel, *Creativity and Perversion;* Stoller, "Perversion and the Desire to Harm."

11. For analyses of the interrelationship of biological factors and cultural

factors in the formation of gender, see Fast, "Developments in Gender Identity," 443; *id., Gender Identity;* Archer and Lloyd, *Sex and Gender;* Pleck, *supra* note 9; Friedman, Richart, and Vande Wiele, eds., *Sex Differences in Behavior;* Mitchell, *Human Sex Differences;* Moberly, *Psychogenesis;* Hyde and Linn, eds., *Psychology of Gender.*

12. Rousseau, *Social Contract,* 6.
13. Bentham, *Principles of Morals and Legislation,* chap. 1, para. 1.
14. Northrop, "Comparative Philosophy of Comparative Law," 617.
15. Hart, *Concept of Law,* 18–19.
16. See J. C. Smith, *Legal Obligation,* chaps. 2–5.
17. H. J. Wolff, *Roman Law.*
18. Maine, *Ancient Law,* 114.
19. Tylor, *Anthropology,* 405.
20. Coker, *Family Property among the Yorubas,* 5.
21. Redfield, "Maine's Ancient Law in the Light of Primitive Societies."
22. Coker, *supra* note 20, at 4.
23. Sagan, *Dawn of Tyranny.*
24. Maine, *supra* note 18.
25. *Ibid.* at 229.
26. Barkun, *Law without Sanctions,* 127.
27. *Ibid.* at 129.
28. R. P. Wolff, *In Defense of Anarchism.*
29. Maine, *supra* note 18, at 151.

Chapter 5: The Course of Individuation

1. S. Freud, "Creative Writers and Day-dreaming," *S.E.,* vol. 9, at 152.
2. Rank, *Myth of the Birth of the Hero.*
3. Abraham, *Dreams and Myths,* 72.
4. Neumann, *Origins and History of Consciousness,* 197.
5. Jung, *Psychological Types, C.W.,* vol. 6, par. 757.
6. Mahler, Pine, and Bergman, *Psychological Birth of the Human Infant,* 4.
7. Grunberger, *Narcissism,* 10–17.
8. Lewin, *Sexual Self-destruct,* 64.
9. Fast, *Gender Identity.*
10. *Ibid.* at 111.
11. *Ibid.* at 115.
12. Grunberger, *supra* note 7, at 22.
13. Fast, *supra* note 9, at 117–18.
14. *Ibid.* at 135.
15. While theorists such as Janine Chasseguet-Smirgel and Béla Grunberger use the term *narcissistic wound* to deal with the child's sudden awareness of utter dependency and helplessness, and the blow to primary narcissism which this entails, I shall be using the term more broadly to refer to any effect of the separation from the mother.

16. S. Freud, *Civilization and Its Discontents,* S.E., vol. 21, at 65 and 72; see also Grunberger, *supra* note 7.

17. Grunberger, *supra* note 7, at 69.

18. Mahler, Pine, and Bergman, *supra* note 6, at 3.

19. *Ibid.* at 4.

20. *Ibid.* at 44.

21. *Ibid.* at 44.

22. *Ibid.* at 48.

23. *Ibid.* at 95.

24. *Ibid.* at 206.

25. *Ibid.* at 227.

26. *Ibid.* at 3.

27. *Ibid.* at 197.

28. One such set is that which pertains to how the ego and the sense of the self evolve in babies and young children. These challenges are not serious and require only minor adjustments to psychoanalytic theory. Fast, in *Event Theory,* proposes a strategy for integrating psychoanalytic and Piagetian psychologies for dealing with the problem of self-nonself differentiation in the process of individuation, which is consistent with contemporary research on the development of the self in infants.

29. Stern, in *Interpersonal World of the Infant,* writes at 10: "Infants begin to experience a sense of an emergent self from birth. They are predesigned to be aware of self-organizing processes. They never experience a period of total self/other undifferentiation. There is no confusion between self and other in the beginning or at any point during infancy." See also Peterfreund, "Some Critical Comments"; Stechler and Kaplan, "Development of the Self"; Lichtenberg, *Psychoanalysis and Infant Research.*

30. Peterfreund, *supra* note 29. See also Peterfreund, *Information, Systems, and Psychoanalysis; id.,* "Need." Stern, *supra* note 29, cites Peterfreund at 19; Stechler and Kaplan, *supra* note 29, cite Peterfreund at 86.

31. Peterfreund, *supra* note 29, at 430.

32. *Ibid.* at 431–32.

33. *Ibid.* at 440.

34. Stechler and Kaplan, *supra* note 29. See also Apfelbaum, "Ego Psychology." Gill and Holzman, eds., *Psychology versus Metapsychology.* Holt, "Freud's Mechanistic and Humanistic Images of Man." Rubinstein, "Psychoanalytic Theory"; *id.,* "Explanation and Mere Description." G. S. Klein, *Perception, Motives, and Personality; id., Psychoanalytic Theory.*

35. Peterfreund, *supra* note 29, at 430.

36. Mahler, Pine, and Bergman, *supra* note 6.

37. This state of perception without conception, which is sought through meditation, is particularly well described by Kasulis in *Zen Action/Zen Person,* 43–51. In Japanese it is called *mu,* meaning a state of "no-mind." Kasulis summarizes by stating (at 47): "[N]o-mind or no-thought is a state of consciousness in which the dichotomy between subject and object, experiencer and experienced, is overcome."

38. J. Klein, *Our Need for Others*, 30.

39. A. Freud, "Discussion"; *id.*, "Problems of Infantile Neurosis"; *id.*, "Some Remarks on Infant Observation."

40. M. Klein, "Infant Analysis"; *id.*, "On Observing Behavior"; *id.*, "Our Adult World and Its Roots in Infancy"; *id.*, *Psychoanalysis of Children.*

41. Winnicott, "Observation of Infants in a Set Situation"; *id.*, "Baby as a Person"; *id.*, "Birth Memories"; *id.*, "Innate Morality of the Baby"; *id.*, *Mother and Child; id.*, "Ordinary Devoted Mother and Her Baby"; *id.*, "Theory of the Parent-infant Relationship"; *id.*, *Child, the Family, and the Outside World; id.*, *Maturational Processes and the Facilitating Environment.*

42. Mahler, Pine, and Bergman, *supra* note 6.

43. See also Hamilton, *Narcissus and Oedipus.*

44. Tennyson, "In Memoriam A. H.," xlv, quoted in Klein, *supra* note 38, at 4.

45. *Ibid.* at 76.

46. See Tustin, *Autism and Childhood Psychosis; id.*, *Autistic States in Children.*

47. Dinnerstein, *Mermaid and the Minotaur.*

48. Chodorow, *Reproduction of Mothering.*

49. Benjamin, *Bonds of Love*, 133–81.

50. Moore, "Freud and Female Sexuality," 289.

51. Grunberger, *supra* note 7, at 170.

52. *Ibid.* at 171–72.

53. S. Freud, *Group Psychology and the Analysis of the Ego, S.E.*, vol. 18, at 105.

54. *Ibid.*

55. S. Freud, "Dissolution of the Oedipus Complex," *S.E.*, vol. 19, at 173; *id.*, "The Development of the Libido and the Sexual Organizations" vol. 16 at 320–38. For a general discussion of the Oedipus complex, see Rudnytsky, *Freud and Oedipus.* For a critical analysis, see Deleuze and Guattari, *Anti-Oedipus.*

56. S. Freud, "Dissolution of the Oedipus Complex," *supra* note 55, at 173.

57. *Ibid.* at 176.

58. *Ibid.*

59. *Ibid.* at 176–77.

60. S. Freud, *Ego and the Id, S.E.*, vol. 19, at 32.

61. Chasseguet-Smirgel, *Ego Ideal*, 27.

62. Chehrazi, "Female Psychology," 27.

63. S. Freud, "Female Sexuality," *S.E.*, vol. 21, at 227–35.

64. S. Freud, "Dissolution of the Oedipus Complex," *supra* note 55, at 178.

65. *Ibid.* at 179. See also S. Freud, *Outline of Psycho-analysis, S.E.*, vol. 23, at 193–94.

66. S. Freud, "Dissolution of the Oedipus Complex," *supra* note 55, at 178.

67. See for example Mendell, ed., *Early Female Development.*

68. Kleeman, "Establishment of Core Gender Identity;" *id.*, "Freud's Views." See also references cited in note 111 of chap. 2.

69. Chasseguet-Smirgel, *Sexuality and Mind*, 27–28.

70. *Ibid.* at 25.

71. Chasseguet-Smirgel, *supra* note 61, at 35.

72. Gilligan, *In a Different Voice.*

73. Grossman, "Discussion," 303.

74. Moore, *supra* note 50, concludes (at 297–98):

> Biological bisexuality is a factor, but apparently of less importance than he [Freud] assumed; it has been replaced by a more useful psychoanalytic concept, based on the identification of the child with both parents. . . . In the main the emphasis Freud attached to drive development and the psychosexual stages was well placed. It is apparent that he underemphasized the prephallic phase and confused some pre-oedipal and oedipal phenomena. It appears, however, that he was correct in the importance he attached to the castration complex in the little girl and penis envy as factors determining progression to the positive Oedipus complex. . . . The evidence for superego differences seems to be at least partially substantiated as well. Freud's mistake was to describe them in terms that implied value judgements. As a result the strongest objections to his theories have been couched in terms of a patriarchal bias, a phallocentric attitude attributed to the male-dominated period in which he lived. . . . As one example of this bias, he failed to give adequate and explicit recognition to the role of motherhood in femininity despite the fact that it is implicit in his work.

75. Formanek, "On the Origins of Gender Identity," in Mendell, ed., *supra* note 67, at 2.

76. *Ibid.*

77. Bergmann, "Female Oedipus Complex," in Mendell, *supra* note 67, at 175.

78. Stoller, *Presentations of Gender,* 12.

79. *Ibid.*

80. *Ibid.* at 16–17.

81. *Ibid.* at 16.

82. *Ibid.* at 17.

83. Grunberger, *supra* note 7, at 289.

84. Stoller, *supra* note 78, at 11–13.

85. *Ibid.* at 11.

86. *Ibid.* at 17.

87. *Ibid.* at 18.

88. *Ibid.* at 26.

89. *Ibid.* at 16–17.

90. *Ibid.* at 16.

91. *Ibid.* at 28.

92. *Ibid.* at 28–33.

93. *Ibid.* at 29.

94. *Ibid.*

95. *Ibid.*

96. *Ibid.*

97. *Ibid.* at 30.

98. *Ibid.*

99. *Ibid.*

100. *Ibid.* at 33.

101. *Ibid.* at 17.

102. *Ibid.* at 16.

103. Bergmann, *supra* note 77, at 66.

104. Stoller, *supra* note 78, at 17.

105. *Ibid.*

106. *Ibid.* at 183.

107. See Sagan, *At the Dawn of Tyranny.*

108. Formanek, *supra* note 75, at 15–16.

109. Fast, *supra* note 9.

110. *Ibid.* at 2.

111. *Ibid.* at 12.

112. Jung, *Theory of Psychoanalysis, C.W.,* vol. 4, par 344.

113. Jung, "Anima and Animus," in *Relations between the Ego and the Unconscious, C.W.,* vol. 7, 188–211; *id.,* "The Syzgy," in *C.W.,* vol. 9ii, 11–22; *id.,* "Concerning the Archetypes," *C.W.,* vol. 9i, at 54–72.

114. For a general discussion of Jungian androgyny, see Singer, *Androgyny.* See also Zolla, *Androgyne.*

115. See Frey-Rohn, *Freud to Jung,* 135–83.

116. Fast, *supra* note 9, at 52.

117. *Ibid.* at 63.

118. See Frey-Rohn, *supra* note 115; Steele, *Freud and Jung;* Becker, *Denial of Death;* Roazen, *Freud and His Followers.*

Chapter 6: The Structure of the Psyche

1. Bettelheim, *Freud and Man's Soul,* 70–78.

2. *Ibid.* at 53–56.

3. See for example Bem, "Gender Schema Theory," at 354–64; Mahler, Pine, and Bergman, *Psychological Birth of the Human Infant;* Money and Ehrhardt, *Man and Woman, Boy and Girl;* Oakley, *Sex, Gender, and Society;* Stoller, *Sex and Gender;* Duberman, *Gender and Sex in Society.*

4. Coval and Smith, *Law and Its Presuppositions,* chaps. 1–3. R. P. Wolff, *In Defence of Anarchism.*

5. A. Freud, *Ego and the Mechanisms of Defence,* 6.

6. S. Freud, *Ego and the Id, S.E.,* vol. 19, at 26.

7. S. Freud, *Moses and Monotheism, S.E.,* vol. 23, at 96.

8. A. Freud, *supra* note 5, at 7.

9. *Ibid.* at 33.

10. See in general A. Freud, *supra* note 5. See also Lewin, *Sexual Self-destruct,* 50.

11. See Bettelheim, *supra* note 1. We should never lose sight of the fact that Freud, writing in German, used the German pronoun "Ich" or the "I". For some reason the English translators preferred to use the Latin, "ego" rather than translating the terms directly into English as the "I"-Ideal, the super "I" or the "I".

12. S. Freud, *supra* note 6, at 10, 34–36, 38–39, 48–49; *id.,* "Economic

Problem of Masochism," *S.E.*, vol. 19, at 167–69; *id.*, "Dissolution of the Oedipus Complex," *S.E.*, vol. 19, at 179, 257.

13. S. Freud, *Question of Lay Analysis*, *S.E.*, vol. 20 at 223. See also, *id.*, *supra* note 7, at 116–20; *id.*, *An Outline of Psycho-analysis*, *S.E.*, vol. 23, at 146, and 205–7.

14. S. Freud, *Civilization and Its Discontents*, *S.E.*, vol. 21, at 136.

15. S. Freud, *Inhibitions, Symptoms and Anxiety*, *S.E.*, vol. 20, at 114.

16. S. Freud, *New Introductory Lectures on Psycho-analysis*, *S.E.*, vol. 22, at 63.

17. *Ibid.* at 62–67.

18. *Ibid.* at 118–20.

19. S. Freud, "Dissolution of the Oedipus Complex," *supra* note 12, at 176–77.

20. S. Freud, *Question of Lay Analysis*, *supra* note 13, at 223.

21. S. Freud, *Autobiographical Study*, *S.E.*, vol. 20, at 59. For a discussion of the relationship between the superego and conscience, see Lewin, *supra* note 10.

22. S. Freud, *supra* note 14, at 133.

23. *Ibid.* at 142–44.

24. S. Freud, *supra* note 16, at 67.

25. S. Freud, "On Narcissism," *S.E.*, vol. 14, at 67.

26. S. Freud, *Totem and Taboo*, *S.E.*, vol. 13, at 1.

27. S. Freud, *Group Psychology and the Analysis of the Ego*, *S.E.*, vol. 18, at 65.

28. S. Freud, *supra* note 6, at 1.

29. Chasseguet-Smirgel, *Ego Ideal*, 241; see also Benjamin, *Bonds of Love*, 148–56.

30. Chasseguet-Smirgel, *supra* note 29, at x.

31. S. Freud, *supra* note 25, at 94: "[H]e seeks to recover it [this early perfection that has been taken from him] in the new form of an ego ideal. What he projects before him as his ideal is the substitute for the lost narcissism of his childhood in which he was his own ideal."

32. Chasseguet-Smirgel, *supra* note 29, at xii.

33. *Ibid.* at xii.

34. *Ibid.* at xvi.

35. Chasseguet-Smirgel and Grunberger, *Freud or Reich?* 208. Chasseguet-Smirgel and Grunberger (at 15) give a definition of ideology: "[I]t is a system of thought which claims to be total, it is a historical and political interpretation whose (unconscious) aim is the actualization of an illusion, of illusion *par excellence,* that the ego and its ideal can be reunited by a short-cut, via the pleasure principle."

36. *Ibid.* at 14.

37. Chasseguet-Smirgel, *supra* note 29, at 76–93.

38. S. Freud, *supra* note 27.

39. Chasseguet-Smirgel, *supra* note 29, at 78.

40. Grunberger, *Narcissism*.

41. *Ibid.* at 10.

42. *Ibid.* at 78.

43. Chasseguet-Smirgel, *Creativity and Perversion*, 27.

44. *Ibid.* at 28.

45. S. Freud, *supra* note 27, at 105.

46. *Ibid.*

47. Chasseguet-Smirgel, *supra* note 29.

48. *Ibid.* at 46–75.

49. *Ibid.* at 76–93.

50. S. Freud, *supra* note 27, at 113.

51. *Ibid.* at 140.

52. Chasseguet-Smirgel, *supra* note 29.

53. S. Freud, *supra* note 27, at 116.

54. Efforts at creating a Jungian psychoanalytic (depth psychology) social theory have been markedly unsuccessful. Other than Neumann's *Origins and History of Consciousness,* there are no books in the Jungian tradition which are the equivalent of Brown's *Life against Death;* Marcuse's *Eros and Civilization;* or E. Becker's *Denial of Death.* For examples of Jungian social theory see Progoff, *Jung's Psychology and Its Social Meaning;* Odajnyk, *Jung and Politics;* Mattoon, "Politics and Individuation," 77.

55. For a general discussion of the differences between Freud and Jung, see Frey-Rohn, *From Freud to Jung;* R. S. Steele, *Freud and Jung.*

56. Frey-Rohn, *supra* note 55, at 225–53.

57. Edinger, *Ego and Archetype.*

58. See in general Jung, *Archetypes and the Collective Unconscious,* C.W., vol. 9i.

59. Foreword by Jung to Jacobi, *Complex/Archetype/Symbol in the Psychology of C. G. Jung,* x.

60. Jacobi, *supra* note 59; Edinger, *supra* note 57; A. Stevens, *Archetypes;* Whitmont, *Symbolic Quest;* M. A. Jacoby, *Longing for Paradise;* N. Hall, *Moon and the Virgin;* M. E. Harding, *Parental Image;* Neumann, *Great Mother;* Ulanov and Ulanov, *Witch and the Clown;* Redfearn, "Nature of Archetypal Activity," 127.

61. Jung, "Concepts of Collective Unconscious," *C.W.,* vol. 9i, par. 89.

62. Jung, "Mind and Earth," *C.W.,* vol. 10, par. 53.

63. Jacobi, *supra* note 59, at 34.

64. *Ibid.* at 30.

65. Jung, "Review of the Complex Theory," *C.W.,* vol. 8, par. 210.

66. *Ibid.,* par. 216.

67. *Ibid.,* par. 200.

68. *Ibid.,* par. 204.

69. *Ibid.,* par. 216.

70. *Ibid.,* par. 218.

71. Jacobi, *supra* note 59, at 28.

72. See in general Jacobi, *supra* note 59.

73. Jung, *supra* note 65, par. 210.

74. Jacobi, *supra* note 59, at 19.

75. Frey-Rohn, *supra* note 55, at 13–40.

76. Samuels, *Jung and the Post-Jungians,* 47.

77. Neumann, *supra* note 54, at 264–65.

78. *Ibid.* at 9.

79. See for example Jung, "On 'Tibetan Book of the Great Liberation,' " *C.W.*, vol. 11, paras. 791–830.

80. See for example, Jung, *Symbols of Transformation, C.W.*, vol. 5, pars. 89, 129, 497; *id., Psychology and Religion, C.W.*, vol. 11, par. 102; *id.*, "A Psychological Approach to the Dogma of the Trinity," *C.W.*, vol. 11, par. 238.

81. Jung, "Psychological Approach," *supra* note 80, par. 231.

82. *Ibid.* par. 232.

83. Jung, "Psychological Aspects of the Mother Archetype," *C.W.*, vol. 9i, par. 156.

84. *Ibid.*

85. *Ibid.*

86. Jung, "Practical Use of Dream-analysis," *C.W.*, vol. 16, par. 345.

87. Jung, "Significance of the Father in the Destiny of the Individual," *C.W.*, vol. 4, at 301–23.

88. Jung, *supra* note 62, paras. 65–66.

89. Samuels, *supra* note 76, at 207–40.

Chapter 7: Toward a Theory of the Collective Psyche

1. S. Freud, *Totem and Taboo, S.E.*, vol. 13, at 158.

2. S. Freud, *Group Psychology and the Analysis of the Ego, S.E.*, vol. 18, at 129.

3. In *Moses and Monotheism, S.E.*, vol. 23, Freud writes (at 132), "It is not easy for us to carry over the concepts of individual psychology into group psychology; and I do not think we gain anything by introducing the concept of a 'collective' unconscious. The content of the unconscious, indeed, is in any case a collective, universal property of mankind."

4. Jung, "On the Nature of the Psyche," *C.W.*, vol. 8, par. 393; *id.*, "Synchronicity," in *ibid.*, vol. 8, par. 931; *id.*, "On 'The Tibetan Book of the Great Liberation,' " in *ibid.*, vol. 11, par. 759; *id.*, "The Conjunction," in *ibid.*, vol. 14, par. 700; *id.*, "Forward to Schleich," in *ibid.*, vol. 18, par. 1116.

5. von Franz, *Projection and Re-collection in Jungian Psychology*, 78.

6. See Jung, *C.W.*, vol. 9i, par. 88–90.

7. Jung, "Archetypes of the Collective Unconscious," *C.W.*, vol. 9i, 3–41, note 2, at 3. Discussing Freudian concepts, Jung states, "He called the instinctual psyche the 'id', and his 'super-ego' denotes the collective consciousness, of which the individual is partly conscious and partly unconscious."

8. Jacobi, *Psychology of C. G. Jung*, note 2, at 29–30.

9. Jacobi continues:

This concept coincides in part with the Freudian concept of the "superego," but differs from it in so far as for Jung it includes not only the "introjected" dos and don'ts of the environment, operating from within the psyche, but also those which pour in uninterruptedly from outside to influence the individual in his commissions and omissions, his feeling and his thinking. (*Ibid.* at 30)

10. Jung, "On 'The Tibetan Book of the Great Liberation,' " *C.W.*, vol. 11, paras. 793–805.

11. *Ibid.* at par. 800.

12. Jung, foreword to Neumann, *Origins and History of Consciousness*, xiii.

13. *Ibid.* at xviii.

14. *Ibid.* at xxii.

15. *Ibid.* at xvi.

16. Samuels, *Jung and the Post-Jungians*, 70.

17. Neumann, *supra* note 12, at 43.

18. Samuels, *supra* note 16, at 72.

19. McColloch, *Embodiments of Mind*, 1–18.

20. Minsky, *Society of Mind*.

21. Turkle, *Second Self; id.*, "Artificial Intelligence and Psychoanalysis."

22. Turkle, "Artificial Intelligence," 261.

23. S. Freud, *Interpretation of Dreams, S.E.*, vol. 4, at 144–46, 177, 235–36, 260; *ibid.*, vol. 5, at 479; *id., On Dreams, S.E.*, vol. 5, at 676–80.

24. Turkle, *The Second Self, supra* note 21, at 243.

25. Colby, *Energy and Structure in Psychoanalysis*.

26. *Ibid.* at 247–50; see also Turkle, "Artificial Intelligence."

27. Turkle, *Second Self*, 256.

28. *Ibid.* at 281.

29. *Ibid.* at 258.

30. Colby and Stoller, *Cognitive Science and Psychoanalysis*.

31. *Ibid.* at 15.

32. *Ibid.*

33. *Ibid.* at 16.

34. *Ibid.* at 17. See also Colby, "Computer Simulation of a Neurotic Process"; *id.*, "Simulation of Belief Systems"; *id., Artificial Paranoia; id.*, "Mind Models," 159–85; *id.*, "Modeling a Paranoid Mind," 515–60; *id.*, "Ethics of Computer-assisted Psychotherapy," 414–15; Colby and Spar, *Fundamental Crisis in Psychiatry;* Colby and Parkinson, "Linguistic Conceptual Patterns," 181–94.

35. Turkle, "Artificial Intelligence," 264.

36. See for example, Searle, *Minds, Brains and Science;* Dreyfus and Dreyfus, "Making a Mind"; Sokolowski, "Natural and Artificial Intelligence."

37. Sokolowski, *supra* note 36.

38. Lakoff, *Women, Fire, and Dangerous Things*, 338.

39. *Ibid.* at 340.

40. *Ibid.*

41. S. Freud, *Civilization and Its Discontents, S.E.*, vol. 21, at 141–42.

42. Juliet Mitchell, introduction 1, in Mitchell and Rose, eds., *Feminine Sexuality*, 6.

43. *Ibid.*

44. *Ibid.*

45. See MacLean, "Brain Roots of the Will-to-power"; *id.*, "Triangular Brief"; *id.*, "Editorial"; *id.*, "A Mind of Three Minds."

46. Samuels, *supra* note 16, at 40.

47. *Ibid.*

48. *Ibid.*

49. *Ibid.* at 40–41.

50. Mitchell, *supra* note 42, at 5.

51. MacCannell refers to the Lacanian "cultural unconscious." See *Figuring Lacan.*

52. Lacan, *Speech and language in Psychoanalysis.* See also Ragland-Sullivan, *Jacques Lacan and the Philosophy of Psychoanalysis,* 130–266.

53. Mitchell, *supra* note 42, at 6.

54. S. Freud, "On the Universal Tendency to Debasement in the Sphere of Love," *S.E.,* vol. 11, at 188–89.

55. Money, "Ablatio Penis," 66.

56. See the discussion of "constitutional bisexuality" in *S. Freud, Ego and the Id, S.E.,* vol. 19, at 31–33.

Chapter 8: Misogyny and Individuation

1. Weinstein and Platt, *Psychoanalytic Sociology,* 2.

2. Bettelheim, *Uses of Enchantment.*

3. Weinstein and Platt, *supra* note 1.

4. Lederer, *Fear of Women,* 284.

5. Stoller, *Perversion,* 29.

6. *Ibid.* at 149–50.

7. *Ibid.* at 162.

8. See Slater, *Glory of Hera.*

9. Vernant, *Myth and Society in Ancient Greece,* 168.

10. Hesiod, *Theogony, Works and Days, Shield,* 68, lines 58–69.

11. *Ibid.* at 27–28, lines 585–613.

12. For discussion of the Eve myth, see Naomi Goodman, "Eve, Child Bride of Adam," in Nelson and Ikenberry, eds., *Psychosexual Imperatives,* 33–60.

13. Gn 2:18, 3:16.

14. 1 Cor 11:3.

15. Eph 5:22.

16. 1 Cor 11:9.

17. 1 Tm 2:11–15. These themes are elaborated upon extensively in later Christian theology. See for example St. Augustine, *City of God;* St. Thomas Aquinas, *Summa Theologica.*

18. Lloyd-Jones, *Justice of Zeus.*

19. de Vaux, *Ancient Israel.*

20. Chaudhuri, *Hinduism,* 149.

21. Gray, *Green Paradise Lost.*

22. Gn 1:28–31.

23. Sambursky, *Physical Thought,* 4.

24. *Ibid.* at 3.

25. Hillman, *Myth of Analysis,* 220–22.

26. *Ibid.* at 221.

27. Aristotle, *Politics,* 1, chap. 2, part 2.

28. In Hegel, *Philosophy of Right,* 3d part, sect. 166 at 171–72. For similar views of women held by political theorists, see Clark and Lange, eds., *Sexism of Social and Political Theory;* Agonito, *History of Ideas on Woman.*

29. See for example, Montagu, *Man and Aggression;* Lorenz, *On Aggression;* Eibl-Eibesfeldt, *Biology of Peace and War;* Ardrey, *Territorial Imperative.*

30. See for example, Wynne-Edwards, *Animal Dispersion,* 134–38; de Waal, *Chimpanzee Politics.*

31. For a counterview from a feminist perspective see Hrdy, *Woman That Never Evolved;* Sayers, *Biological Politics.*

32. Storr, *Human Aggression.*

33. *Ibid.* at 11.

34. *Ibid.* at 21.

35. *Ibid.*

36. *Ibid.* at 59.

37. *Ibid.* at 63.

38. *Ibid.* at 62.

39. *Ibid.*

40. *Ibid.* at 64.

41. *Ibid.*

42. *Ibid.* at 66.

43. *Ibid.*

44. *Ibid.* at 31.

45. *Ibid.* at 26.

46. *Ibid.*

47. *Ibid.* at 26–26.

48. *Ibid.* at 36.

49. Holliday, *Violent Sex.* Lips and Colwill in *Psychology of Sex Differences,* argue persuasively that the evidence does not support the conclusion that testosterone is a cause of aggression in males.

50. See as examples Goldberg, *Inevitability of Patriarchy;* A. Stevens, *Archetypes,* 180–93. For feminist critiques of this kind of abuse of science, see Birke, *Women, Feminism, and Biology;* Bleier, *Science and Gender;* Keller, *Reflections on Gender and Science;* S. Harding, *Science Question in Feminism.*

51. Hillman, *supra* note 25, at 246–47.

52. *Ibid.* at 249.

53. See Power, "Foraging Adaptation of Chimpanzees"; *id., Mutual Dependence;* M. F. Small, ed., *Female Primates;* G. D. Mitchell, *Human Sex Differences;* Hrdy, *supra* note 31.

54. See for example Neumann, *Origins and History of Consciousness,* 131–91; Rank, *Myth of the Birth of the Hero.*

55. Abraham, *Dreams and Myths,* 10–11.

56. Aeschylus, *Oresteia.*

57. Abraham, *supra* note 55, at 10.

58. Herdt, *Guardians of the Flutes.*

59. Gregor, *Anxious Pleasures*.

60. On the one hand, there are images of women as weak, inferior, polluting and seductive. See Dijkstra, *Idols of Perversity*. On the other hand, there are also images of women as powerful, castrating, and aggressive. See for example the discussion of the myth of the Amazon in Kleinbaum, *War against the Amazons*. These two images are sometimes combined in the same myth. Myths of heroes killing female monsters reflect this ambivalence of the male psyche. Thus, in the myth of Perseus killing the Medusa there is the powerful Amazonian image that can turn a man to stone which the conquering hero turns into a beheaded lifeless body.

61. Chasseguet-Smirgel, "Transexuality, Paranoia, Repudiated Femininity," in Nelson and Ikenberry, *supra* note 12, at 201.

62. Richards, *Sceptical Feminist*, 140.

63. Illich, *Gender*, 45–57.

64. Lederer, *supra* note 4; O'Faolain and Martines, eds., *Not in God's Image*.

65. See Stevens, *supra* note 50, at 174–209.

Chapter 9: The Quadrant of Collective Defense Mechanisms

1. Becker, *Denial of Death*, 26–27.

2. "The Problem of Freud's Character, Noch Einmal," in *ibid.*, 93–124.

3. See Bataille, *Eroticism*.

4. See for example, Broyles, "Why Men Love War," 62–63.

5. See Brownmiller, *Against Our Will*.

6. Culler, *On Deconstruction*, 165.

7. H. E. Fisher, *Sex Contract*. For an interesting but somewhat different view, see Hrdy, *Woman That Never Evolved*. See also Holliday, *Violent Sex*.

8.

Boys will be boys, and girls will not. These two phrases together form the basis for the everyday understanding of the meaning of gender. They are understood . . . as both a description of what is and as a prescription of how it must be. . . . males are defined by what they are, while females are defined by what they lack by comparison to males. The male sex is seen by most people as a baseline against which the female sex is seen as an incomplete version of the male. . . . Concomitant with this is the belief that there are two and only two genders (girls/women and boys/men), and that whatever a woman does will somehow have the stamp of femininity on it, while whatever a man does will likewise bear the imprint of masculinity. (Devor, *Gender Blending*, vii.)

See also Money, "Ablatio Penis," 65. The paradigm statement of the definition of masculinity as the norm and femininity in terms of the negation of masculinity is to be found in Weininger, *Sex and Character*.

9. See for example S. Goldberg, *Inevitability of Patriarchy*; A. Stevens, *Archetypes*.

10. Symons, "Copulation as a Female Service," in *Evolution of Human Sexuality,* chap. 8.

11. Hite, in *Hite Report on Male Sexuality,* writes:

Most men said that women did not seem to want sex as much or as often as they did. When asked what they would like to change about sex, the most common answer by far was: no change, just *more.* This complaint was somewhat more pronounced in men in longer marriages, but in fact, throughout all the answers to all the questions, from men of every age and situation—married, single, or living with a woman—this was the complaint heard most frequently: I want sex more than she does, I never get enough sex.

12. For discussion of the relevant literature see Symons, *supra* note 10, at 170–84 and 265.

13. Hite, *supra* note 11, writes: "When asked, 'How often do you masturbate?' almost all men, whether married or single, with or without an otherwise active sex life, said they made masturbation a regular part of their lives" (at 485).

14. See Bullough and Bullough, *Women and Prostitution.* Hite, *supra* note 11, notes about the response to the question "How did you feel about paying for sex?" "This question brought out a surprising assumption about the relationship between men and women; the most common reaction was 'You always pay anyway' " (at 759).

15. One of the more easily documented differences between male and female sexuality is the greater desire among males for sexual variety. For a discussion of the relevant literature see Symons, "The Desire for Sexual Variety," in Symons, *supra* note 10.

16. *Ibid.* at 170–84. See also Faust, *Women, Sex, and Pornography,* 26–30. There is a substantial literature on male/female differences in sexual behavior. Not all of this literature, by any means, supports a difference in male and female arousal patterns. Some of this literature is based on empirical testing, but the results are inconclusive. See for example Hatfield, Sprecher, and Traupmann, "Men's and Women's Reactions to Sexually Explicit Films"; Schmidt, "Male-Female Differences"; Steele and Walker, "Male and Female Differences in Reaction." The authors of "A Comparison of Male and Female Patterns of Sexual Arousal," Steinman, et al., conclude (at 530), "Although the studies cited above were not designed to look specifically at gender differences, taken together, the results provide preliminary support for the hypothesis of gender-specific differences in terms of differential sexual responsivity to varying erotic content." The kind of clinical experiment described in much of this literature is of questionable value because it does not distinguish between the arousal caused by the visual stimuli in and of itself and that caused by the imagination responding in terms of fantasies triggered by the visual stimuli. In any case, there is little in this literature to cause one to question the conclusions reached by Symons.

17. Stoller, *Perversion,* 99; *id., Observing the Erotic Imagination,* 34.

18. There is very little literature on the psychology of dependency. One of the few studies is Memmi, *Dependence.* See also Lederer, *Fear of Women.* Lederer writes (at vii):

Man, confronted by woman, does seem to feel, variously, frightened, revolted, dominated, bewildered and even, at times, superfluous. . . . Nor is any of this incompatible with what he also feels, and feels no less: the love, the devotion and the dependence. Rather is it so that, in a complicated interaction and feedback, the positive and the negative feelings keep reinforcing each other.

19. Valzelli, *Psychobiology of Aggression and Violence*. Dr. Valzelli points out (at 75) that aggression is no longer considered to be a unitary behavioral concept "but rather a series of different specialized behaviors . . . that animals have available for achieving different goals." He lists the following major kinds of aggressive behavior: predatory aggression, territorial aggression, maternal protective aggression, female social aggression, sex-related aggression, and instrumental aggression. It is clear from these categories that aggression is a particular kind of response to or in aid of basic needs. See also Dollard et al., *Frustration and Aggression*.

20. For an analysis of the impact on the psyche of the child of predominantly female child-rearing see Dinnerstein, *Mermaid and the Minotaur*, and Rich, *Of Woman Born*.

21. Neumann, *Origins and History of Consciousness*.

22. S. Freud, "A Special Type of Choice of Object Made by Men," *S.E.*, vol. 11; *id.*, "On the Universal Tendency to Debasement in the Sphere of Love," *S.E.*, vol. 11.

23. Lowen, *Betrayal of the Body*.

24. In a society where there is a continual shortage of food and constant hunger, the psychological development of the people will switch from being sex-driven to food-driven. Then food rather than sex will become the cultural determinant. See C. Turnbull, *Mountain People*.

25. Griffin, *Woman and Nature; id., Pornography and Silence; id., Made from This Earth*. Merchant, *Death of Nature*; Kolodny, *Lay of the Land*; Ortner, "Is Female to Male as Nature Is to Culture?"; Gray, *Green Paradise Lost*; Lovelock, *Gaia*. See also Becker, *supra* note 1, at 39–42.

26. Hubbs, *Mother Russia*.

27. See Neumann, *Great Mother*. See also B. G. Walker, *Skeptical Feminist*, 191–97.

28. 1 Cor 15:55.

29. 1 Cor 15:19.

30. Jung, *Symbols of Transformation, C.W.*, vol. 5, at 171–206, 274–305; Neumann, *supra* note 21, at 131–91.

31. Campbell, *Hero with a Thousand Faces*.

32. See Rank, *Myth of the Birth of a Hero*; Becker, *supra* note 1.

33. S. Freud, *New Introductory Lectures on Psycho-analysis, S.E.*, vol. 22, at 80.

Chapter 10: The Quadrant of Complexes

1. Neumann, *Origins and History of Consciousness*, 15.

2. Herman, *Father-Daughter Incest*, 55.

3. Fromm, *Art of Loving,* 42.
4. Graves, *Greek Myths,* vol. 1, 103–11; Otto, *Dionysus;* Deutsch, *Psychoanalytic Study;* Nietzsche, "Birth of Tragedy"; Eisner, *Road to Daulis;* Detienne, *Dionysos Slain;* Brun, *Le Retour de Dionysos;* Jung, "Apollonian and the Dionysian," *C.W.,* vol. 6, par. 223; Needles, "Orgastic Loss of Consciousness," 54, 315; Hillman, "Dionysus in Jung's Writings"; Cowan, "Dionysus," in *Masochism,* chap. 6; Evans, *God of Ecstacy;* N. Hall, *Those Women;* Fierz-David, *Women's Dionysian Initiation;* Houser, *Dionysos and His Circle;* A. Danielou, *Shiva and Dionysus;* Kerenyi, *Dionysus.*
5. Eckstein, "Third Reich and Goethe," 58.
6. Otto, *supra* note 4, at 175.
7. *Ibid.* at 142.
8. Deutsch, *supra* note 4, at 27.
9. Catullus, *Carmina of Catullus,* 101–5.
10. *Ibid.*
11. Schwab, *Gods and Heroes,* 66–72; Graves, *supra* note 4, at 237–45; Napier, "Perseus and the Gorgon Head," in *Masks, Transformation, and Paradox,* 83–134.
12. Aeschylus, *The Eumenides,* in *Oresteia,* 161.
13. See Koonz, *Mothers in the Fatherland.*
14. S. Freud, "Medusa's Head," *S.E.,* vol. 18, at 273.
15. Morgan, *Total Woman.*
16. Andelin, *Fascinating Womanhood.*
17. Levin, *Stepford Wives.*
18. Graves, *supra* note 4, at 76–82.
19. The psychological roots of the Apollonian complex are well expressed by Ray Bradbury in a passage from *Something Wicked This Way Comes,* 42:

His wife smiled in her sleep. Why? She's immortal. She has a son. Your son, too! But what father ever really believes it? He carries no burden, he feels no pain. What man, like woman, lies down in darkness and gets up with child? The gentle, smiling ones own the good secret. Oh, what strange wonderful clocks women are. They nest in Time. They make the flesh that holds fast and binds eternity. They live inside the gift, know power, accept, and need not mention it. Why speak of Time when you *are* Time, and shape the universal moments, as they pass, into warmth and action?

20. Fromm, *Escape from Freedom,* 154.
21. Graves, *Greek Myths,* vol. 2, 84–210; Schwab, *supra* note 11, at 156–201; Fraser, "Heracles."
22. Wilson, *Secrets of Sexual Fantasy.* Watkins, *Waking Dreams* (1976); Symposium on Fantasy, *International Journal of Psychoanalysis* 45 (April–July 1964): parts 2–3; Laplanche and Pontalis, "Fantasy and the Origins of Sexuality."
23. Stoller, *Perversion,* 55.
24. *Ibid.* at 115.
25. *Ibid.* at 83.
26. Scott, *Dominant Women, Submissive Men,* xi.

27. *Ibid.* at 123.

28. *Ibid.* See also Moser, "An Exploratory-Descriptive Study"; Weinberg, Williams, and Moser, "Social Constituents of Sadomasochism," 379–89.

29. See Rush, *Best-kept Secret;* Herman, *supra* note 2.

30. Tillich, *From Time to Time.* See also Daly, *Gyn/ecology,* 94–95.

31. An exception is Heather Robertson, in "Portrait of a Sex Killer," where she publishes excerpts from the confession of a seventeen-year-old rapist and murderer who after describing the rape stated (at 272):

> I took her to the other side of the car where I told her I had a present. I reached through the window under the seat and produced a small brick. She said, "Oh no," terrified-like. I said she wouldn't get pregnant this way. I hit her in the head with it, and she didn't fall to the ground, so I pushed her to the ground. I covered her mouth while she screamed. I kept saying, "Shh." She quietened. She said not to strangle her, so I picked up a brick and proceeded in hitting her head. It made a knocking noise. I then dropped it [the brick] on her face. She started choking on blood, so I picked up a piece of wood and put it to her throat to strangle her. . . . When I released, air was sucked in, and she started quivering. Neat, eh?
>
> So I bashed her head a couple more times and . . . I picked up a brick that you found on top of her head. There she was also quivering so I picked up a piece of board with a nail, [with] which I punctured her heart-lung area approximately five times on top and two or three times on the side, one time to the back of her neck where you guys probably found it. I dropped the brick on her stomach to break her ribs. I then disrobed her [and had oral sex]. By this time, it was 11:20 P.M.
>
> I found a lighter had dropped out of her lumber jacket. I picked it up and singed the hair on her clitoris. Then I pushed up her top [and burned her right nipple]. The left one I put her safety pin through, which also fell from her pocket.

32. For an extensive study of homosexuality, see Socarides, *Homosexuality.*

33. Stoller, *supra* note 23, at xiv.

34. *Ibid.* at 4.

35. See Stoller, "Perversion and the Desire to Harm."

36. S. Freud, "Sexual Abberations," in *Three Essays on the Theory of Sexuality, S.E.,* vol. 7, at 160.

37. S. Freud, *Introductory Lectures on Psycho-analysis, S.E.,* vol. 16, at 322.

38. Keuls, *Reign of the Phallus,* 274–99.

39. H. S. Levy, *Chinese Foot-binding;* Dworkin, "Gynocide," in *Woman Hating,* chap. 6; Daly, "Chinese Foot-binding," in Daly, *supra* note 30.

40. Daly, "Indian Suttee," in Daly, *supra* note 30.

41. Although suttee has been forbidden by law in India since 1829, it still occasionally occurs. The last incident reported in the public media was on 4 September 1988, when Roop Kunwar died on her husband's funeral pyre before an audience of 250,000 witnesses.

42. See Groth and Birnbaum, "Adult Sexual Orientation," 175–81; *Sexual Offences against Children,* Report of the Committee on Sexual Offences against Children and Youths appointed by the Minister of Justice and Attorney General of Canada, (1984); Miller, *Thou Shalt Not Be Aware;* Herman, *supra* note 2; Rush, *supra* note 29.

43. Mayo, *Mother India,* 365. The list is taken from the Legislative Assembly Debates of 1922, vol. 3, Part 1, 919, Appendix.

44. Daly, "African Genital Mutiliation," in Daly, *supra* note 30; Janssen-Jurreit, *Sexism,* chap. 22.

45. Berthiaume, in "Des Millions de Femmes Mutilées," gives the following description of an occurrence of the practice (at 39):

On the bedroom floor a pretty seven-year-old girl lies, legs apart, in the arms of a woman. In front of her, a midwife using a razor blade and without the help of any anaesthetics, cuts her minora labium and clitoris. The child's horrible cries fill the room. They violently increase when the midwife pours alcohol directly onto the wound in order to disinfect it. . . . The dangers of infection are by no means eliminated since the midwife proceeds to use old unsterilized pieces of linen to sponge the blood and dress the wound. Put to bed in all her misery, the little girl forcefully hits the wall with her fists as if this would help easing her pain. Her tears, cries and noise barely cover her mother's scolding, telling her to keep quiet.

Contrast this with Gustave Flaubert's cavalier comments on the practice in one of his letters describing his sexual use of Arab women provided for him while living in the Near East. In *The Letters of Gustave Flaubert 1830–1857,* 181:

The oriental woman is no more than a machine: she makes no distinction between one man and another. Smoking, going to the baths, painting her eyelids and drinking coffee—such is the circle of occupations within which her existence is confined. As for physical pleasure, it must be very slight, since the famous button, the seat thereof, is sliced off at an early age. What makes this woman, in a sense, so poetic, is that she relapses into the state of nature.

See also Hosken, *Hosken Report;* El Saadawi, *Hidden Face of Eve,* chap. 6; Boulware-Miller, "Female Circumcision."

46. Masson, in *Dark Science,* provides a collection of late nineteenth-century medical literature in which the mutilation and torture of very young females, purportedly for the purpose of curing masturbation, is described in graphic detail.

47. Barker-Benfield, *Horrors of the Half-known Life;* Daly, "American Gynecology," in Daly, *supra* note 30.

48. A. J. Block, "Sexual Perversion in the Female."

49. Eyer, "Clitoridectomy," 261.

50. Greene, "Bar Wars," 61–62.

51. See Dworkin, *Intercourse.*

52. Brownmiller, *Against Our Will.*

53. See for example, Broyles, "Why Men Love War," 62–63.

54. Becker, *Denial of Death.*

55. See H. S. Stokes, *Life and Death of Yukio Mishima.*

56. Mishima, *Confessions of a Mask.*

57. Mishima, *Kyoko No Ie* [Kyoko's House], in *Mishima Yukio Zenshu* [Complete Works of Yukio Mishima], vol. 11.

58. See for example Mishima, "Patriotism," in *Death in Midsummer and Other Stories; id., On Hugakure; id., Runaway Horses.*

59. Stokes, *supra* note 55, at 130.

60. *Ibid.* at 184.

61. Mishima, *Sea of Fertility.*

62. *Ibid.*

63. Mishima, *Temple of the Golden Pavilion.*

64. Rank, *Art and Artist;* Becker, *supra* note 54, chap. 8, at 159–75.

65. See Bose, *My Days with Gandhi,* 170–207, in particular 174–88; Collins and LaPierre, *Freedom at Midnight,* 64–69; Mehta, "Profiles, Part 3," at 41; Daly, *Pure Lust,* 39–41.

66. See Collins and LaPierre, *supra* note 65, at 66–67.

67. *Encyclopedia of Philosophy,* vol. 1, at 327.

68. Bodin, *De la Démonomanie des Sorciers.*

69. "Demeter" is one of the names for the Goddess. Greek *meter* is "mother" and *De* is the delta or triangle, "a female-genital sign known as 'the letter of the vulva' in the Greek sacred alphabet." B. G. Walker, *Woman's Encyclopedia of Myths and Secrets,* 218.

70. According to ancient Hebrew myth, Lilith was the first wife of Adam, created as his equal. She refused to lie under Adam in intercourse and left him, and became a Kali-like or terrible mother figure. Eve was then created by God, out of the rib of Adam to ensure her servient position. In traditional psychoanalytic literature, femininity has been associated with masochism. In Freud, see for example, "A Child Is Being Beaten," *S.E.,* vol 17, at 179–204; *id.,* "Economic Problem of Masochism," *S.E.,* vol. 19, at 159–72. See also Bonaparte, *Female Sexuality;* Deutsch, *Psychology of Women,* vols. 1 and 2; *id.,* "Significance of Masochism in the Mental Life of Women." The Eve complex furnishes an alternative explanation to the above. For a recent and balanced examination of the subject, see Benjamin, "Alienation of Desire," 113–38.

71. Athene, not being born of woman, but springing from the forehead of Zeus, was a goddess of patriarchy.

72. Laslett, ed., *Patriarcha.*

73. Andelin, *Fascinating Womanhood,* and *Fascinating Girl;* Morgan, *Total Woman.*

74. Rand, "An Answer to Readers," 1.

75. *Ibid.*

76. *Ibid.*

77. *Ibid.* at 1–2.

78. Koonz, *supra* note 13.

79. SAMOIS, *Coming to Power.* See also Linden, et al., eds., *Against Sadomasochism.*

80. Réage, *Story of O.* For a discussion of this book, see Griffin, *Pornography and Silence,* 218–32; *id.,* "Sadomasochism and the Erosion of Self," in Linden et al., *supra* note 79, at 184–201.

Chapter 11: The Quadrant of Culture

1. "Mythological Origins of Law," in Smith and Wiesstub, *Western Idea of Law*, chap. 2, 147–94.
2. Gn 3:16.
3. Janus, Bess, and Saltus, *Sexual Profile*.
4. *Ibid.* at x.
5. *Ibid.* at xi.
6. *Ibid.* at xix.
7. *Ibid.* at xxi.
8. *Ibid.* at xx.
9. *Ibid.* at xx.
10. *Ibid.* at 68.
11. *Ibid.* at 170.
12. *Ibid.* at 171–72.
13. Heilbroner, *Nature and Logic*.
14. *Ibid.* at 45.
15. *Ibid.* at 42.
16. *Ibid.* at 44.
17. *Ibid.* at 52.
18. Chasseguet-Smirgel, *Ego Ideal*, xv.
19. *Ibid.* at 11.
20. *Ibid.* at 17–18.
21. S. Freud, *Ego and the Id.* (1923), S.E., vol. 19, at 27.
22. Chasseguet-Smirgel, *supra* note 18, at 245.
23. S. Freud, *Group Psychology and the Analysis of the Ego*, S.E., vol. 18, at 105. See also Chasseguet-Smirgel, *supra* note 18, at 98.
24. *Ibid.* at 58.
25. *Ibid.* at 59. Chasseguet-Smirgel cites Pasche, "Freud et l'Orthodoxie Judéo-Chrétienne," in *À Partir de Freud*, 129–56.
26. *Ibid.* at 59.
27. *Ibid.* at 86.
28. *Ibid.* at 81.
29. *Ibid.* at 54, from S. Freud, *Group Psychology*, *supra* note 23, at 112–13.
30. Koonz, *Mothers in the Fatherland*.
31. Dijkstra, *Idols of Perversity*.
32. *Ibid.* at vii.
33. Masson, *Dark Science*.
34. Theweleit, *Male Fantasies*, vol. 1.
35. *Ibid.* at xiii.
36. *Ibid.*
37. *Ibid.* at xv.
38. *Ibid.* at xvi–xvii.
39. Benjamin and Rabinbach, in foreword to Theweleit, *Male Fantasies*, vol. 2, at xiii.

40. *Ibid.* at xix–xx.
41. Brown, *Life against Death,* 12.

Chapter 12: History as the Externalization of the Oedipal Passage

1. Hegel, *Phenomenology of Spirit.* For a summary of Hegel's contribution to theory of the mind, see W. Kaufman, *Discovering the Mind,* vol. 1, 199–269.
2. Kojève, *Introduction of the Reading of Hegel.*
3. For an explanation of Kojève's relationship to Hegel, see the editor's introduction to Kojève, *supra* note 2. See also Riley, "Introduction to the Reading of Alexandre Kojève." The best explanation by far of the relationship is found in Cooper, *End of History.* For a more traditional view of Hegel, see Taylor, *Hegel; id., Hegel and Modern Society.*
4. Cooper, *supra* note 3.
5. *Ibid.* at 4.
6. *Ibid.* at 3–4.
7. Arendt, *Origins of Totalitarianism.*
8. Cooper, *supra* note 3, at 329.
9. *Ibid.*
10. Elliot, *Twentieth Century Book of the Dead.*
11. Rubenstein, *Cunning of History,* 6.
12. *Ibid.* at 94.
13. Hegel, *Philosophy of Right,* 189–93. See also Cooper, *supra* note 3, at 249–50.
14. See Arendt, *supra* note 7, at 244–45; Rubenstein, "Bureaucratic Domination," in Rubenstein, *supra* note 11; Cooper, *supra* note 3, at 265–72.
15. Compare Freud's concept of the collective mind with Hegel's discussion of the world or universal mind in *Philosophy of Right, supra* note 13, at 216–20, and in *id., Lectures on the History of Philosophy,* 3.
16. Hegel, *supra* note 13, at 217.
17. Taylor, *Hegel and Modern Society,* 89.
18. Kojève, *supra* note 2, at 258.
19. *Ibid.*
20. *Ibid.* at 257.
21. *Ibid.* at 256.
22. *Ibid.* at 206–7.
23. *Ibid.* at 225.
24. The feminist scholar Jessica Benjamin adopts the Hegelian concept of history and places it within a psychoanalytic framework in developing her analysis of patriarchy. See Benjamin, "Bonds of Love"; *id.,* "Oedipal Riddle"; *id.,* "Shame and Sexual Politics," 155; *id.,* "Authority and the Family Revisited," 33; *id.,* "Internalization and Instrumental Culture." See also Mills, "Hegel and 'The Woman Question.' "
25. French, *Beyond Power,* 27.
26. Ryle, *Concept of Mind,* 8.

27. Pateman, *Sexual Contract,* 3.

28. Redfield, "Maine's Ancient Law," 586–89; also in Smith and Weisstub, *Western Idea of Law,* 81–83. Maine states: "But Ancient Law, it must again be repeated, knows next to nothing of Individuals. It is concerned not with Individuals, but with Families, not with single human beings, but groups" (Maine, *Ancient Law,* 229; also in Smith and Weisstub, *Western Idea of Law,* 194).

29. In *Hegel and Modern Society,* Taylor describes the drive for homogeneity in the modern state as an attempt to reconcile individual autonomy with the demands of community (100–125).

30. See for example the kind of world envisioned by Atwood in her futuristic novel, *Handmaid's Tale.*

31. See Girard, *Violence and the Sacred,* 193. For a contrary view, see Badcock, *Psychoanalysis of Culture.*

32. S. Freud, *Totem and Taboo, S.E.,* vol. 13, at 141.

33. See Pateman, *supra* note 27.

34. S. Freud, *supra* note 32, at 1. See also S. Freud, "Dostoevsky and Parricide," *S.E.,* vol. 21, at 177.

35. S. Freud, *Group Psychology and the Analysis of the Ego, S.E.,* vol. 18, at 122.

36. Sagan, *Dawn of Tyranny.*

37. S. Freud, *supra* note 35, at 121.

38. *Ibid.* at 134.

39. *Ibid.* at 131.

40. Chasseguet-Smirgel, *Ego Ideal.*

41. See Griffin, *Woman and Nature;* Merchant, *Death of Nature;* Kolodny, *Lay of the Land;* Ortner, "Is Female to Male as Nature Is to Culture?"; Lovelock, *Gaia.* See also Becker, *supra* note 22, at 39–42.

42. Daly, in *Gyn/ecology,* 88; *id., Pure Lust,* 207. Rich, "Towards a Woman-Centred University," in *On Lies, Secrets, and Silence,* 134, note 11, cited and discussed by Scales in "Emergence of Feminist Jurisprudence," note 60.

Chapter 13: The Pre-Oedipal Stage of History

1. Neumann, *Great Mother,* 10.

2. *Ibid.* at 3.

3. See Adler, *Drawing Down the Moon.*

4. Canadian Broadcasting Corporation (CBC) Transcripts, "Return of the Goddess," 23.

5. See for example, Bord and Bord, *Earth Rites.*

6. See Starhawk (Miriam Simos), *Spiral Dance.*

7. Adler, *supra* note 3.

8. See for example, Starhawk, *supra* note 6.

9. See for example, Ochs, *Behind the Sex of God.*

10. See for example Christ, *Laughter of Aphrodite.*

11. CBC, *supra* note 4, at 23. See also Goldenberg, *Changing of the Gods.*

12. See for example, Perera, *Descent to the Goddess;* M. E. Harding, *Woman's*

Mysteries; M. Stone, *Ancient Mirrors of Womanhood;* Bolen, *Goddesses in Every-woman.*

    13. CBC, *supra* note 4, at 22.

    14. Whitmont, *Return of the Goddess,* 59.

    15. Starhawk, *Truth or Dare.*

    16. See for example, Gray, *Green Paradise Lost;* Ortner, "Is Female to Male as Nature Is to Culture?"; Merchant, *Death of Nature.*

    17. See for example, Hubbs, *Mother Russia.*

    18. Mooney, "Ghost-Dance Religion."

    19. See in general, Ashe, *Virgin;* Bachofen, *Myth, Religion and Mother-right;* Bakan, *And They Took Themselves Wives;* Berger, *Goddess Obscured;* Briffault, *Mothers;* Burkert, *Structure and History,* 99–142; von Cles-Reden, *Realm of the Great Goddess;* Dames, *Avebury Cycle;* Davis, *First Sex;* Diner, *Mothers and Amazons;* Eisler, *Chalice and the Blade;* Fisher, *Woman's Creation;* French, *Beyond Power;* 27–104. Gimbutas, *Goddesses and Gods;* Graves, *White Goddess;* Hawkes, *Dawn of the Gods;* James, *Cult of the Mother Goddess;* Johnson, *Lady of the Beasts;* Lerner, *Creation of Patriarchy,* 141–60; Levy, *Gate of Horn;* Markale, *Women of the Celts;* Monaghan, *Book of the Goddess and Heroines;* Neumann, *Great Mother;* Ochshorn, *Female Experience;* Olson, ed., *Book of the Goddess;* Patai, *Hebrew Goddess;* Pomeroy, *Women in Hellenistic Egypt;* Preston, ed., *Mother Worship;* Showerman, *Great Mother of the Gods;* Sjöö and Mor, *Great Cosmic Mother;* Spretnak, *Lost Goddesses of Early Greece;* Stone, *When God Was a Woman; id., Ancient Mirrors of Womanhood;* Teubal, *Sarah;* B. G. Walker, *Woman's Encyclopedia of Myths and Secrets; id., Crone;* Whitmont, *Return of the Goddess;* Wolkstein and Kramer, *Inanna.*

    See also Iida, ed., *Nihon Shoki Shinko* (New Lectures on Japanese Tales), vol. 1, 29–69, which shows that many of the ancient Japanese myths suggest that Japanese society was originally matriarchal. Chinese Literature on Japan shows that the country was ruled by a female called Himiko. See for example Sanson, *Short Cultural History of Japan,* at 28; Murdoch, *History of Japan,* vol. 1, at 36. In *Bokeisei No Kenkyu,* a study of matrimonial systems in ancient Japan, Itsue Takamure came to the conclusion that early Japan was matriarchal and matrilineal. For a discussion of goddess worship in India, see Avalon, *Shakti and Shakta.*

    The archaeological evidence uncovered at the site of the ancient town of Çatal Hüyük, in Anatolia, for example, which covered approximately thirty-two acres and had a population of several thousand people, furnishes evidence of a period when women were afforded a high status of such a nature as to be inconsistent with a patriarchal culture. Women and children were buried under the large central platforms of the houses while men were buried in smaller corner spaces along with their hunting weapons. See J. Mellaart, *Çatal Hüyük.* For a critique of Mellaart see Todd, *Çatal Hüyük in Perspective.* See also French, *Beyond Power,* 46; Thompson, *Time Falling Bodies Take to Light,* 138–50; Lerner, *Creation of Patriarchy,* 32–35.

    20. See for example, Goldberg, *Inevitability of Patriarchy,* 54–61.

    21. Briffault, *supra* note 19.

    22. James, *supra* note 19.

    23. Gimbutas, *supra* note 19.

24. Lerner, *supra* note 19.

25. Neumann, *supra* note 19.

26. See Bakan, *supra* note 19; Teubal, *supra* note 19; Patai, *supra* note 19; Cobley, "Evolution to Patriarchy," 86. In *Zondervan Pictorial Encyclopedia of the Bible*, vol. 1, in the article on the ancient goddess Ashtoreth (Astarthe, Inanna, Queen of Heaven), W. White states (at 361):

> Throughout history the Jews were constantly tempted to worship this pagan goddess and attend her rituals, and it was this forbidden practice which finally led to Israel's captivity and the seventy years in Babylon. There is no doubt, from the nude statuettes with exaggerated breasts and pudenda and the frequent association of sexual licence mentioned by both Biblical and classical authors in connection with Ashtoreth, that her rituals were offensive to the Jews at many points. Her cult was kept alive well into the Christian era.

27. For example, see the Old Testament, Judg. 6:25–35; 1 Kings 16:31, 18:20–40; 2 Kings 10:18–29, 11:18, 17:16, 21:3, 23:4–5; Numbers 22:41. In Judg. 2:13 and in 1 Sam. 12:10 Baal and Ashtaroth are mentioned together.

28. See for example, Exod. 34:12–16; Ezek. 23:1–49.

29. See Briffault, *supra* note 19, vol. 3, at 196–232. White, *supra* note 26, states, "This sexual aspect of the worship of the mother goddess appears to have carried over into every culture of the Near E[ast] where her cult was practiced" (at 360). Sacred prostitution generally formed an integral part of goddess worship in the ancient Near East: See *New Larousse Encyclopedia of Mythology*, "Assyro-Babylonian Mythology," 58.

30. Deut. 12:2–3; 2 Kings 17:9–11.

31. Deut. 23:1.

32. See Deut. 12:2–3; Josh. 6:21, 10:38–40.

33. Jer. 44:16–19. See also Jer. 7:16–20. It is anomalous that an earth goddess is referred to as the Queen of Heaven. This is probably explained by the relationship of the earth goddess to the moon. The parallel between women's menstrual cycle and the lunar phases, and the use of the crescent moon as a symbol for both women and the horns of a bull in fertility cult worship, probably account for the importance of the moon in goddess worship.

34. See for example Exod. 34:13; Deut. 12:2–3; 2 Kings 17:9–11.

35. See for example, Bamberger, "Myth of Matriarchy."

36. See Frazer, *Golden Bough;* and *id. Adonis, Attis, Osiris;* Burkert, *supra* note 19, at 99–101; *id., Ancient Mystery Cults,* 111–12.

37. The written descriptions of fertility cult paganism which have survived relate to an era when paganism had already shifted from a matriarchal to a patriarchal consciousness. For general descriptions of the religious practices of the Mediterranean world before the triumph of Christianity, see J. Harrison, *Prolegomena to the Study of Greek Religion;* Frazer, *Golden Bough,* vols. 1–4. Frazer's *Golden Bough* has received a good deal of academic criticism. For a balanced view of the reliability of Frazer's work see the introduction by Mary Douglas to *Illustrated Golden Bough.* For a more contemporary description, see Reitzenstein,

Hellenistic Mystery-Religions; Burkert, *supra* note 36; and *id., Structure and History;* J. Ferguson, *Religions of the Roman Empire.* For a description of fertility cult paganism in early Britain, see Bord and Bord, *supra* note 5.

38. See M. E. Harding, *Woman's Mysteries,* 195–96.

39. At one point these were thought to be breasts, but the shape is not breastlike nor are there nipples in what is otherwise carved to a very fine detail. See Attenborough, *First Eden,* 106–8.

40. A. Danielou, *Shiva and Dionysus.*

41. *Ibid.* at 24.

42. *Ibid.* at 168–69.

43. *Ibid.* at 56.

44. *Ibid.* at 199.

45. *Ibid.* at 168–72.

46. Thompson, *supra* note 19, at 150.

47. Thompson, *supra* note 19; Neumann, *supra* note 19; Stone, *supra* note 19; de Reincourt, *Sex and Power in History,* chap. 3; Davis, *supra* note 19; Diner, *supra* note 19; Reed, *Woman's Evolution.* For a contrary view, see Bamberger, *supra* note 35; Beauvoir, *Second Sex,* 70–71.

48. Kramer, *Sumerians,* 79.

49. *Ibid.*

50. *Ibid.*

51. Teubal, *supra* note 19, at 77–131; E. Fisher, *Woman's Creation,* 267–80; Thompson, *supra* note 19, at 159–208.

52. Thompson, *supra* note 19, at 149–50.

53. S. Freud, "Some Psychical Consequences of the Anatomical Distinction between the Sexes," *S.E.,* vol. 19, at 257–58.

54. Piaget, *Moral Judgment of the Child; id., Six Psychological Studies; id., Structuralism.*

55. Kohlberg, *Philosophy of Moral Development.* See also *id.,* "A Cognitive-Developmental Analysis of Children's Sex-Role Concepts and Attitudes."

56. Gilligan, *In a Different Voice.*

57. *Ibid.* at 25–32.

58. Kawashima, "Status of the Individual."

59. See Van Herik, *Freud on Femininity and Faith.* Van Herik argues that Freud's theories of gender, religion, and the Oedipus complex are all interrelated and inseparable. Because females are already castrated, since they lack a penis, there can be no fear of castration which will drive them through the complex. Rather they remain in a pre-Oedipal state which Freud equates with wish fulfillment. Judaism is a more advanced religion because it renounces wish fulfillment and is thus closer to the reality principle, while Christianity, on the other hand, remains an expression of wish fulfillment. Thus the assymmetry which Freud finds between male and female, he finds also reflected in the contrast between Judaism and Christianity.

60. See Ripa, *Baroque and Roccoco Pictorial Imagery,* no. 120.

61. Shakespeare, *The Merchant of Venice,* Act IV, Scene I, lines 180–98.

62. Hayford and Sealts, eds. *Billy Budd.* Billy Budd has been discussed from

several standpoints. See for example, Stafford, *Billy Budd and the Critics*, and Franklin, "From Empire to Empire," 199. The structure of the narrative of *Billy Budd* would seem to indicate that Melville's primary artistic aim was to reveal the social mythology which masks the inability of law to combine justice with compassion.

63. See Heschel, *Prophets*.

64. See de Vaux, *Ancient Israel*, 143–52; Y. Kaufmann, *Religion of Israel*, 316–40.

65. See Matt., chaps. 5 and 23.

66. See J. Danielou, "Christianity as a Jewish Sect"; and Randall, *Hellenistic Ways*, 137–55.

67. Judg. 4:4–5.

68. Judg. 21:25.

69. Exod. 15:20; 2 Kings 22:14–17; Neh. 6:14; Isa. 8:3; Luke 2:36.

70. Exod. 28:1, 38–43; Num. 3:40–41.

71. Bynum, *Jesus as Mother*, 167–68.

72. Ashe, *Virgin*.

73. Mark 10:14.

74. Barkun, *Law without Sanctions*.

Chapter 14: The Oedipal Stage of History

1. Greenfield, "Archetypal Masculine"; Vitale, "Saturn"; Stein, "Devouring Father"; von der Heydt, "On the Father in Psychotherapy," 128.

2. Stoller, *Presentations of Gender*.

3. For an analysis of the Eve myth in Western religious history, see Phillips, *Eve*.

4. Hillman, *Myth of Analysis*, 218.

5. Morgan, *Total Woman*, 82.

6. Andelin, *Fascinating Girl*, 161.

7. Isa. 54:5.

8. Hos. 2:19. For similar images, see Ezek. 16:8–14; Jer. 3:20, 31:32.

9. Carmi, ed. and trans., *Penguin Book of Hebrew Verse*, 223–24.

10. See for example Eph. 5:22–25. See also Rev. 21:9.

11. Luis De Granada, *Consideration of the Divine Perfections*, Part 5, chap. I, in Peers, *Mystics of Spain*, 78–79.

12. Austin, *Lectures on Jurisprudence*, I.

13. Frankfort, *Kingship and the Gods*; Baynes, "On the Psychological Origins of Divine Kingship," in *Analytical Psychology*, 180–203.

14. Perry, *Lord of the Four Quarters*, 3. See also Perry, "Reflections."

15. Perry, *Lord of the Four Quarters*, 18.

16. *Ibid*.

17. *Ibid*. at 4.

18. Kern, *Kingship and Law in the Middle Ages*; Kantorowicz, *King's Two Bodies*.

19. Kenyon, ed., "James I on Monarchy," in *The Stuart Constitution,* 12–13.

20. *Ibid.*

21. Laslett, ed., *Patriarcha.*

22. *Ibid.* at 21–23.

23. *Ibid.* at 57.

24. *Ibid.*

25. *Ibid.* at 63.

26. Neumann, *Origins and History of Consciousness,* 42.

27. Sanday, *Female Power and Male Dominance,* chaps. 1 and 2.

28. See Gen. 1:1–2.

29. Frankfort, *supra* note 13, and Perry, *Lord of the Four Quarters.*

30. Psalms 8:6–8.

31. Gray, *Green Paradise Lost.*

32. See Tyrrell, *Amazons.*

33. See Kleinbaum, *War against the Amazons.*

34. Lefkowitz and Fant, *Women's Life in Greece and Rome,* Part 1; Keuls, *Reign of the Phallus;* Slater, *Glory of Hera;* Pomeroy, *Goddesses, Whores, Wives, and Slaves;* Arthur, "Early Greece."

35. Lacan, *Ecrits,* 67.

36. Mooij, "Symbolic Father," 217–18.

37. See Smith and Weisstub, *Western Idea of Law,* 147–73; Lloyd-Jones, *Justice of Zeus.*

38. Ch'u, *Law and Society in Traditional China,* 28–29; Westrup, "Patria Potestas," in *Introduction to Early Roman Law,* vol. 3, book 2; Fustel de Coulanges, *Ancient City,* book 2, chap. 8.

39. Redfield, "Maine's Ancient Law in the Light of Primitive Societies."

40. See, for example, "Laws of Manu," in Muller, ed., *Sacred Books of the East,* 25, 301–4; "Laws of Hammurabi," in Edwards, trans., *Hammurabi Code,* 61–63.

41. Ch'u, *supra* note 38.

42. *Ibid.* at 27–29.

43. *Ibid.* at 29.

44. See in general Hirschon, ed., *Women and Property—Women as Property.*

45. Letter to Jung no. 314, May 1912, in McGuire, ed. *Freud/Jung Letters.*

46. "Laws of Manu," *supra* note 40, laws 147–66, at 195–97.

47. Ch'u, *supra* note 38, at 102–3.

48. de Vaux, *Ancient Israel,* 143–52.

49. Gen. 3:16.

50. Holcombe, *Wives and Property.*

51. D. E. H. Russell, *Rape in Marriage;* Estrich, *Real Rape.*

52. Walker, *Battered Woman;* U.S. Commission on Civil Rights, *Under the Rule of Thumb;* Hilberman, "Overview"; Breines and Gordon, "New Scholarship on Family Violence"; O'Faolain and Marines, eds., *Not in God's Image,* 175–78.

53. In his famous speech in defense of the Petition of Right before the House of Lords, Sir Edward Coke argued:

An imprisoned man upon will and pleasure is,
1. A Bondman.
2. Worse than a Bondman.
3. Not so much as a man; for "mortuus homo non est homo," a prisoner is a dead man.

1. No man can be imprisoned upon will and pleasure of any, but he that is a Bondman and Villein, for that imprisonment and bondage are "propria quarto modo" to villeins. Now "propria quarto modo," and the species, are convertible; whosoever is a Bondman, may be imprisoned upon will and pleasure, and whosoever may be imprisoned upon will and pleasure is a Bondman.

2. If a Freeman of England might be imprisoned at the will and pleasure of the king or his commandment, then were they in worse case than Bondmen or Villeins; for the lord of a villein cannot command another to imprison his villein without cause, as of disobedience, or as refusing to serve, as it is agreed in the Year books. ([1628], 3 Howell State Trials 128)

The villein, under English law, had all the rights of any other person in the legal system, and against everyone in the system, except one single person, his lord; and this one exception left him little better than a slave. Coke reasons from this that if even just one person, the king, is not bound by these duties, the members of the legal system are no better than villeins; and therefore in order that these liberties be preserved the duty must rest equally upon everyone including the king.

Chapter 15: The Self in the Post-Oedipal Stage of History

1. For a general discussion of realism and the epistemological problems surrounding it, see Northrop, *Logic of the Sciences and the Humanities*.

2. Cassirer, *Myth of the State*, 53–60.

3. *Ibid.;* Bonnard, *Greek Civilization*, 54–73; Sambursky, *Physical World of the Greeks*, 18–21.

4. Robinson, *An Introduction to Early Greek Philosophy*, 52. See also Kirk and Raven, *Presocratic Philosophers*, chap. 5; Bonnard, *supra* note 3, at 66.

5. In *Ideas and Opinions*, Einstein stated (at 271):

We reverence ancient Greece as the cradle of western science. Here for the first time the world witnessed the miracle of a logical system which proceeded from step to step with such precision that every single one of its propositions was absolutely indubitable—I refer to Euclid's geometry. This admirable triumph of reasoning gave the human intellect the necessary confidence in itself for its subsequent achievements.

See Sambursky, *supra* note 3; *id., Physics of the Stoics; id.,* "Structural and Dynamic Elements"; Sambursky, ed., *Physical Thought*, 37–119. Bonnard, *supra* note 3, at 54–75; Northrop, "Mathematical Background"; Kline, *Mathematics in Western*

Culture, 24–34; Turnbull, "The Great Mathematicians"; Thomas, "Greek Mathematics."

6. Sambursky, ed., *Physical Thought,* 55–57; *id., Physics of the Stoics,* at 1–20. See also Boorse and Motz, eds., *World of the Atom,* 1–21.

7. Northrop, "Comparative Philosophy of Comparative Law," also Smith and Weisstub, *Western Idea of Law,* 106–118. Smith, "Theoretical Constructs of Western Contractual Law," *id.,* Unique Nature of the Concepts of Western Law."

8. Northrop, *Science and First Principles,* 6. See in general pp. 1–16.

9. Parmenides, *A Text;* Burnet, "Parmenides of Elea," in *Early Greek Philosophy,* 180–82; Van Melsen, in *From Atomos to Atom,* states Parmenides' argument as follows (at 15–16):

> All that *is,* together forms the being . . . that which is must be *one,* i.e. it must possess unity, for if it were manifold there would have to be something which divides it. But outside being, nothing is. Therefore, there is nothing which can divide being, and, therefore, being is *one.* This one being is also unchangeable. For what could be the meaning of change? It could mean either the transition from one kind of being to another . . . or the transition from non-being to being. . . . The transition from one kind of being to another kind of being . . . really amounts to being remaining what it is. . . . [B]ecause non-being *is not;* . . . it cannot become anything.

10. Democritus, quoted in Barnett, *Universe and Dr. Einstein,* at 20.

11. Berkeley, *Treatise,* 25–6.

12. Galileo, quoted in Barnett, *supra* note 10, at 20.

13. See Tigunait, "Vedanta," in *id., Seven Systems of Indian Philosophy,* 213–49.

14. Hillman, *Myth of Analysis,* 225.

15. Paul, *Women in Buddhism,* 3.

16. Blake, illustrations for Milton's *Paradise Lost,* reproduced in Phillips, *Eve.* The volume contains a large number of similar representations.

17. *Ibid.* at 66.

18. *Ibid.* at 9.

19. Campbell, *Mythic Image,* 248–53.

20. Randall, *Hellenistic Ways of Deliverance.*

21. Danielou, "Christianity as a Jewish Sect."

22. Randall, *supra* note 20; Danielou, *supra* note 21; Armstrong, *First Christian.*

23. Pagels, *Gnostic Gospels.*

24. Armstrong, *supra* note 22, at 25.

25. The degree of similarity is a matter of controversy. See for example Metzger, "Considerations of Methodology"; Nock, "Hellenistic Mysteries and Christian Sacraments"; Angus, *The Mystery Religions and Christianity;* Kennedy, *St. Paul and the Mystery Religions;* Wedderburn, "Paul and the Hellenistic Mystery Cults"; Wiens, "Mystery Concepts". See in general Burkert, *Ancient Mystery Cults,* 3.

26. Otto, *Dionysus,* x.

27. Mark 10:14.

28. Ashe, *Virgin*.

29. Workman, *Evolution of the Monastic Ideal*, 64.

30. Rubenstein, *Cunning of History*, 30.

31. See Bord and Bord, *Earth Rites*, 214–15.

32. See Bodin, *De la Démonomanie des Sorciers*. Summers, ed. and trans. *Malleus Maleficarum of Heinrich Kramer and James Sprenger*; Boguet, *Examen of Witches*. Harrison, ed., *Daemonlogogie*. See also Robbins, *Encyclopedia of Witchcraft and Demonology*; Wedeck, *Treasury of Witchcraft*.

33. Yeats, "The Second Coming."

34. See Tigunait, *supra* note 11, at 218–22.

35. Sangharakshita, *Survey of Buddhism*, 50–58. See also Jacobson, *Understanding Buddhism*, 1–2, 24–25, 37–45, 51–52.

36. The problem of explaining the undifferentiated is reflected in Lao Tsu's descriptions of the Tao in the *Tao Te Ching*. See chap. 14:

> Look, it cannot be seen—it is beyond form.
> Listen, it cannot be heard—it is beyond sound.
> Grasp, it cannot be held—it is intangible.
> These three are indefinable;
> Therefore they are joined in one.

and chap. 48:

> In the pursuit of learning, every day something is acquired.
> In the pursuit of Tao, every day something is dropped.

37. Jung, *Psychological Types*, C.W., vol. 6, par. 791.

38. *Ibid.*, par. 789.

39. *Ibid.*, par. 790.

40. *Ibid.*

41. Jung, "Psychology of the Transference," C.W., vol. 16, par. 474.

42. Jung, "Transformation Symbolism in the Mass," C.W., vol. 11, par. 400; *id.*, "Christ," in *Aion*, C.W., vol. 9ii, par. 118, Jung, *supra* note 37, par. 226.

43. Jung, "Relations between the Ego and the Unconscious," C.W., vol. 7, par. 303; Jung, *supra* note 37, paras. 330, 189.

44. The idea of the mind and the body is referred to by Gilbert Ryle as "the dogma of the ghost in the machine." For a critique of this view, see his book *Concept of Mind*.

45. Winnicott, "Ego Distortion in Terms of True and False Self," in *Maturational Processes*, 140–52.

46. McCulloch, *Embodiments of the Mind*.

47. William Shakespeare, *Hamlet*, act 2, sce. 2, line 286.

48. First described by Nietzsche in "The Birth of Tragedy."

49. See for example, "Apollo and Dionysus," in Brown, *Life against Death*;

Jung, "The Apollonian and the Dionysian," in Jung, *supra* note 37, at 136–46. Hillman, "Dionysus in Jung's Writings"; *id.*, *Myth of Analysis.*

50. Jung, "Apollonian and the Dionysian," *supra* note 49, par. 226.

51. *Ibid.*

52. *Ibid.*, paras. 226 and 227.

53. Northrop, *supra* note 8; *id.*, *Complexity of Legal and Ethical Experience,* 216–29. Smith and Weisstub, "Evolution of Western Legal Consciousness." J. C. Smith, "Theoretical Constructs."

54. Smith and Weisstub, *supra* note 53.

55. Cassirer, *supra* note 2, at 53.

56. Kline, *supra* note 5, at 24.

57. *Ibid.* at 30.

58. *Ibid.* at 31.

59. Sambursky, "Structural and Dynamic Elements," at 243.

60. Sambursky, *supra* note 3, at 21.

61. *Physics of the Stoics, supra* note 5, at 54.

62. Hare, *Freedom and Reason; id., Language of Morals.*

63. See J. C. Smith, *Legal Obligation,* chaps. 6, 7, 12. The assumption of the uniformity of cause may be expressed by the following principle: If a particular state X under condition S causes state Y, then any state X in conditions like S in all relevant aspects, will cause state Y.

The principle of the universalizability of ought judgments can be stated as: If it is the case that a particular person under condition S ought to do X, then it is the case that any person in conditions like S in all relevant aspects, ought to do X. Moral and legal judgments are particular species of "ought" judgments. The principle of universalizability of ought judgments can be made more specific by applying it to morality or law in the form of a principle of formal justice such as: Any judgment made in regard to a particular situation, that a particular person is or is not legally (or morally) obligated to do a particular act, logically entails that the judgment instances of rule of law (or morality) such that anyone in a relevantly similar situation is or is not legally (or morally) obligated to do the same act.

64. *Ibid.* at 109–30.

65. Arnold, *Roman Stoicism,* 273.

66. Marcus Aurelius, *Meditations* 6, 44.

67. Sambursky, "Structural and Dynamic Elements," at 239.

68. Aristotle, *Ethics of Aristotle* [Nicomachean Ethics], book 5, chap. 7.

69. Smith, *supra* note 63, at 109–30.

70. *Ibid.* at 89.

71. For Stoic physics see Sambursky, *Physics of the Stoics.* For Stoic logic see Mates, *Stoic Logic.* For Stoic ethics see Arnold, *supra* note 65.

72. Pringsheim, "Unique Character of Classical Roman Law," 60.

73. *Ibid.*

74. Lawson, *Common Law Lawyer,* 67.

75. H. J. Wolff, *Roman Law,* 91.

76. Schulz, *Principles of Roman Law,* 35.

77. Quoted in *ibid.* at 36.

78. Northrop, *supra* note 8, at 643–57; Schulz, *History of Roman Legal Science,* 60–98.

79. Kline, *supra* note 5, at 24–39; Sambursky, "Structural and Dynamic Elements," at 237; R. W. Harris, *Science, Mind and Method,* vol. 1; Hutten, *Origins of Science,* 14–20, 126–27; Einstein, *World as I See It,* 31.

80. Wright, "Stoic Midwives." See also Maine, *Ancient Law,* 48–50; Arnold, *supra* note 65, at 384.

81. Schulz, *supra* note 78, at 41.

82. *Ibid.* at 62.

83. Miquel, "Stoic Logic and Roman Jurisprudence," 333. Miquel furnishes as examples passages from the *Digest* such as Proculus's discussion of disjunction at *Digest* 50, 16, 124, Proculus, Epistles, book 2:

> The following words, "So-and-So or So-and-So," are not only disjunctive, but subdisjunctive in their signification. They are disjunctive; for example, when we say "It is either day or night," for having suggested one of two things, it is necessary to cancel the other, since to suppose one disposes of the other. Therefore, by a similar form of words, an expression can be subdisjunctive. There are, however, two kinds of subdisjunctives; one where in a molecular proposition both atomic propositions cannot be true, and neither of them may be; as, for instance, when we say, "He is either sitting or walking," for as no one can do both these things at the same time, neither of them may be true, for example, if the person should be lying down.
>
> The other kind of disjunctive occurs in a statement where of two things neither may be true, but both of them can happen to be; for instance, when we say "Every animal either acts or suffers," for there is no animal which neither acts nor suffers, but an animal may act and suffer at the same time.

See also *Code of Justinian,* book 6, Title 37, 4, vol. 14, and The *Digests* or *Pandects,* book 45, title 1, 129, vol. 10, both in Scott, trans., *Civil Law.*

84. Contrast the universality of Western law with the biologically determined status provisions of the ancient codes of Hammurabi and Manu, which are characteristic of non-Western legal systems:

Laws of Hammurabi

202. If a man strike the body of a man who is great above him, he shall publicly receive sixty lashes with a cowhide whip.

203. If a man strike the body of the son of a free man of like condition, he shall pay one mina of silver.

204. If a plebian strike the body of a plebian, he shall pay ten shekels of silver.

205. If a man's slave strike the body of the son of a free man, his ear shall be cut off. (Edwards, *Hammurabi Code,* 62–63)

Laws of Manu

277. A Vaisya and a Sudra must be punished exactly in the same manner according to their respective castes, but the tongue (of the Sudra) shall not be cut out; that is the decision.

279. With whatever limb a man of a low cast does hurt to (a man of the three) highest (castes), even that limb shall be cut off; that is the teaching of Manu.

> 281. A low-caste man who tries to place himself on the same seat with a man of a high caste, shall be branded on his hip and be banished, or (the king) shall cause his buttock to be gashed. (Muller, *Sacred Books of the East*, 303)

The contrast between a universal morality and the restricted morality of kinship is illustrated by the following incident related by the anthropologist Maude in a paper, "Evolution of the Gilbertese 'Boti.' " In describing the Gilbertese concept of *utu* or kindred he writes:

> On one occasion, a man mentioned in my presence that on crossing the lagoon an hour before he had passed a woman endeavouring to swim for the shore with a baby (evidently her canoe had sunk) and he expressed the opinion that she would never make it. When asked why he had not stopped to pick her up his reply was, to all except me, perfectly reasonable: *tikai kain au utu* (she was not a member of my *utu*).

85. Lawson, *supra* note 74, at 91.
86. *Ibid.* at 96.
87. Coval and Smith, *Law and Its Presuppositions*.
88. Derham, "Theories of Legal Personality," 5.
89. Lawson, "Creative Use of Legal Concepts," 915.
90. Cicero, *For Cluentius*, bk. 53, at 164.
91. The development of legal constructs in the English common law was primarily due to the influence of Roman law. See generally Sherman, *Roman Law in the Modern World*, vol. 1; Vinogradoff, *Roman Law in Medieval Europe*, 97–118; Scrutton, *Influence of the Roman Law*; Holdsworth, *History of English Law* vol. 2, at 133–49, 176–78, 202–6; Pollock and Maitland, *History of the English Law*; Spence, *Equitable Jurisdiction of the Courts of Chancery*, vols. 1 and 2. During the twelfth and thirteenth centuries an important revival of Roman law took place in Northern Italy which was marked by the founding of a number of universities, the first and most important at Bologna. Pollock and Maitland, in describing this period, write (vol. 1 at 111):

> From every corner of Western Europe students flocked to Italy. It was as if a new gospel had been revealed. Before the end of the century complaints were loud that theology was neglected, that the liberal arts were despised, that Seius and Titius had driven Aristotle and Plato from the schools, that men would learn law and nothing but law.

In the thirteenth century Roman law was introduced into Cambridge, and both Cambridge and Oxford taught only Roman law down to the seventeenth century. This subject next to theology was the most important study at these two universities. From the school of Bologna, the Lombard jurist Vacarius was brought by Archbishop Theobald and his clerk, Thomas Becket, who had himself studied law there. Vacarius was appointed professor at Oxford and was "the first teacher and the real founder of the study both of the civil and of the canon law," in England (Holdsworth, *supra* at 147).

At the same time that the civil law was entering England, Roman law also was brought through the medium of Canon law. See generally Pollock and Maitland, *supra,* at 11–135; Holdsworth, *supra,* at 137–42; Sherman, *supra,* at 217–22. Mention need only be made of some of the important chancellors and advisors such as Guala Bicchieri, Ricardus Anglicus, William of Drogheda, who taught Roman law at Oxford, Henry of Susa, and Franciscus Accursii, all of whom were ecclesiastics, to show that the effects of Canon law were not limited to ecclesiastical matters.

In regard to the strict common law itself in contrast to Equity, Admiralty, and the Ecclesiastical Courts, there can be no question but that the most important channel of Roman law was through Bracton. Bracton's most important work was his *On the Laws and Customs of England,* which was a summa similar to those of the Bolognese. Like Justinian's *Institutes,* the work is divided into three parts, the law of persons, the law of things, and the law of actions and obligations; although eight times longer than the *Institutes,* the work was still uncompleted. This book was the first scientific exposition of English law and no English jurist again attempted such a mammoth task until Sir Edward Coke. As to the amount of Roman law in Bracton's momentous work, the authorities are in conflict. For this problem, see generally Guterbock, *Bracton;* Maitland, ed., *Select Passages,* vol. 8; Richardson, *Bracton;* Plucknett, *Early English Legal Literature,* 42–79; Kantorowicz, *Bractonian Problems;* Vinogradoff, *Roman Law,* 101–18; Woodbine, "Roman Element"; Holdsworth, *supra,* at 267–86; Main, *Ancient Law,* at 67–68.

Opinions have ranged from that of Sir Henry Maine who considered the borrowing to be extensive, to that of Professor Maitland who suggests that the Roman influence was not very great. The better view appears to be that Bracton used "Roman terms, Roman maxims, and Roman doctrines to construct upon native foundations a reasonable system" (Holdsworth, *supra,* at 286). To rephrase, what Bracton did was to introduce the legal constructs of Roman law into the common law, and reinterpret it in these new terms.

The principal source of Bracton's Roman law was the "Summa Institution" of Azo, one of the greatest teachers produced by the University of Bologna. Guterbock states (*supra,* at 52): "Throughout nearly the whole of Bracton's book, we can distinctly trace the scientific influence of Azo's views and doctrines, especially in the definitions and divisions of legal notions and conceptions, which are generally clothed in Azo's words." Bracton, however, did not rely upon Azo alone, but also went directly to Justinian's *Institutes.* For the next hundred years the English lawyers "were steeped in Bracton," but during the fourteenth and fifteenth centuries his influence began to wane, only to revive again to achieve its greatest influence during the sixteenth and seventeenth centuries (Holdsworth, *supra,* at 288). The influence of Roman law during the twelfth to the fourteenth century is summarized by Professor Sherman as follows:

From the coming of Vacarius to Oxford in the middle of the 12th century to the end of the reign of Edward I over 150 years later, the influence of Roman law on the formation of English law was so great that this whole period should be styled the "Roman epoch of English legal history". During this period, and even as late as the reign of Edward II in the first quarter of the 14th century, Roman law authorities were habitually cited in the Common Law courts, and relied upon by legal writers, not as illustrative and secondary testimonies as at present, but as primary and as practically conclusive. Throughout the entire history of the development of the English legal system there was a continual borrowing from Roman law, sometimes directly and sometimes indirectly. (Sherman, *supra,* at 360)

92. See Coval and Smith, *supra* note 87.
93. Cited by Jacobson, *Buddhism and the Contemporary World,* 84.
94. Govinda, *Creative Meditation and Multi-dimensional Consciousness,* 10.
95. Kasulis, *Zen Action/Zen Person,* 44.
96. "Mu i shin jin," in *ibid.* at 51. See also Suzuki, Fromm, and de Martino, eds., *Zen Buddhism and Psychoanalysis,* 32.
97. See for example Picken, *Buddhism;* Shinsho, "Buddhism of One Great Vehicle"; Yoshifumi, "Status of the Individual in Mahayana Buddhist Philosophy"; Ando, *Zen and American Transcendentalism,* 7–52; Suzuki, Fromm, and Martino, *supra* note 96, at 24–43.
98. "Mu i shin jin," *supra* note 95, at 51.
99. "Suttanipata," 455–56, reproduced in Edward Conze et al., eds., *Buddhist Texts through the Ages,* 105.
100. Chaudhuri, *Hinduism,* 148.
101. Lee, *Legal and Moral Systems in Asian Customary Law,* 27.
102. *Ibid.* at 8.

Chapter 16: Brotherhoods of the Collective in the Post-Oedipal Stage of History

1. S. Freud, *Group Psychology and the Analysis of the Ego,* S.E., vol. 18, at 116.
2. *Ibid.* at 73.
3. *Ibid.* at 77.
4. *Ibid.* at 79.
5. *Ibid.* at 80.
6. *Ibid.* at 95.
7. Freud, quoted in Chasseguet-Smirgel, *Ego Ideal,* 80.
8. *Ibid.* at 81.
9. *Ibid.* at 79.
10. *Ibid.* at 80.
11. S. Freud, *supra* note 1, at 122.
12. *Ibid.* at 94.
13. *Ibid.* at 82.
14. *Ibid.* at 81–87. Chasseguet-Smirgel, *Creativity and Perversion,* 58–65.
15. Chasseguet-Smirgel, *supra* note 7, at 87. Chasseguet-Smirgel and Grunberger, *Freud or Reich?* 18.
16. S. Freud, *supra* note 1, at 93.
17. *Ibid.* at 83.
18. Chasseguet-Smirgel, *supra* note 7, chap. 4. See also Chasseguet-Smirgel and Grunberger, *supra* note 15.

19. Chasseguet-Smirgel, *supra* note 7, at 27.

20. Chasseguet-Smirgel, *Sexuality and Mind,* 100.

21. *Ibid.*

22. D. Anzieu, "L'Etude Psychanalytique des Groupes Réels"; *id.,* "L'Illusion Groupale"; Anzieu and Martin, *Dynamique des Groupes Restreints.*

23. Chasseguet-Smirgel, *supra* note 7, at 81.

24. *Ibid.*

25. *Ibid.*

26. Braxton, *Women, Sex, and Race;* Bock, "Racism and Sexism in Nazi Germany."

27. Aly and Roth, "Legislation of Mercy Killings."

28. Chasseguet-Smirgel, *supra* note 7, at 82.

29. *Ibid.* at 84, Chasseguet-Smirgel writes:

> The principle of political machiavellism that "the end justifies the means" is indeed an idealist principle that is applied each time the Illusion is reactivated. The end (the coming together of ego and ideal) justifies the means (annihilates the superego). "Liberty, how many crimes are committed in your name!" is a cry that still resounds. (One has only to think of substitutes for "liberty" such as Purity, Happiness, Greatness, Justice, Equality, Revolution, etc.)

30. Djilas, *Unperfect Society,* 91.

31. *Ibid.* at 101.

32. Chasseguet-Smirgel, *supra* note 7, at 82.

33. *Ibid.*

34. *Ibid.* at 84.

35. *Ibid.* at 83.

36. *Ibid.* at 85.

37. Doi, *Anatomy of Dependence.* See also Doi, *Anatomy of Self.*

38. Doi, *Anatomy of Dependence,* 26. While some writers and commentators have taken issue with Dr. Doi on various points, I have been unable to find any serious challenge to his book and its thesis. See for example Lebra, *Japanese Patterns of Behavior,* 54, where the author states:

> The role of expressing *amae,* called *amaeru,* must be complemented and supported by the role that accepts another's *amae.* The latter role is called *amayakasu.* Doi did not take into consideration the necessity of role complementarity between *amaeru* and *amayakasu,* perhaps because of the role asymmetry in the therapeutic relationship, where the therapist is inhibited from indulging the *amae* wish of the patient.

Points such as these are matters of expansion rather than refutation. D. D. Mitchell, in *Amaeru,* uses Dr. Doi's thesis to explain "The Expression of Reciprocal Dependency Needs in Japanese Politics and Law." While some have attacked this book for being simplistic or superficial, the criticism has generally not been of Doi's thesis, but of Mitchell's particular application of it. See for example H. Wagatsuma's review of *Amaeru* in *Journal of Asian Studies* 39 (1979/80): 173; and E. P. Tsurumi's review in *Pacific Affairs* 51 (1978/79): 310. Of interest to

Japanese readers will be the as-yet-untranslated *'Amae' to Shakai Kaguku* ('Amae' and Social Science), by Otsuka, Doi, and Kawashima.

39. Doi, *supra*, note 38, at 7.

40. *Ibid.* at 8.

41. *Ibid.*

42. Balint, *Primary Love and Psychoanalytic Technique*, 56, 105, 108, 233. Balint points out that it was Sandor Ferenczi who first coined the phrase and developed the idea of "passive object-love." For a comparison of the psychology of dependency in Western culture see for example, Gurian and Gurian, *Dependency Tendency;* Memmi, *Dependence;* Parens and Saul, *Dependence in Man.*

43. Balint states, "In one respect, however, all European languages are the same—again as far as I know them. They are all so poor that they cannot distinguish between the two kinds of object-love, active and passive" (*supra* note 42, at 56).

44. Doi, *supra* note 38, at 57.

45. *Ibid.*

46. *Ibid.* at 150.

47. International Commission of Jurists, "Report on Human Rights"; and Kamiya, "Women in Japan"; "Japanese Women." *The Economist.*

48. Buruma, *A Japanese Mirror.*

49. Dijkstra, *Idols of Perversity.*

50. Theweleit, *Male Fantasies,* vol. 1.

51. Hobbes, *Leviathan,* 79.

52. *Ibid.* at 80.

53. S. Freud, "On Narcissism," *S.E.,* vol. 14, at 100.

54. June, *Psychological Types, C.W.,* vol. 6, par. 782.

55. Jung, "A Review of the Complex Theory,'" *C.W.,* vol. 8, par. 210.

56. S. Freud, *supra* note 53, at 94.

57. S. Freud, "Why War?" *S.E.,* vol. 22, at 200.

58. Yeats, "Sailing to Byzantine," 3d stanza; quoted in Colby and Stoller, *Cognitive Science and Psychoanalysis,* 18.

59. Heilbroner, *Nature and Logic of Capitalism.*

60. *Ibid.* at 130.

61. Sagan, *At the Dawn of Tyranny.*

62. Heilbroner, *supra* note 59, at 49.

63. *Ibid.* at 34–35. See also Braudel, *Afterthoughts,* 47.

64. Heilbroner, *supra* note 59, at 46.

65. Robinson, Coval, and Smith, "Logic of Rights."

66. Commons, *Legal Foundations of Capitalism,* 23–24.

67. See Robinson, Coval, and Smith, *supra* note 65; J. C. Smith, *Legal Obligation,* 190–232. See also Coval and Smith, *Law and Its Presuppositions.*

68. Braudel, *supra* note 63, at 64.

69. Heilbroner, *supra* note 59, at 101–2.

70. *Ibid.* at 105. For a counterargument to the thesis that capitalism does not pay its proper share of the infrastructure, see Block, "Public Goods and Externalities."

71. See Maroney and Luxton, eds., *Feminism and Political Economy*.

72. Illich, *Gender*.

73. *Ibid.* at 45–60.

74. Heilbroner, *supra* note 59, at 135. See also Rubenstein, *Cunning of History*.

75. For a general discussion, see Coward, *Patriarchal Precedents,* 130–87.

76. Clark, "Politics and Law," 42–49; O'Brien, "Reproducing Marxist Man," 99; *id., Politics of Reproduction*.

77. Bebel, *Woman and Socialism,* 232.

78. Lenin, "Women and Society," in *Woman Question,* 52.

79. Janssen-Jurreit, *Sexism,* 103–27.

80. H. Smith, *Russians,* 176–87; Scott, *Does Socialism Liberate Women?;* Wolf, *Revolution Postponed;* Tay, "Status of Women"; Stacey, *Patriarchy*.

81. Okin, *Women in Western Political Thought,* 5.

Chapter 17: The Limits of Traditional Legal and Political Theory

1. Coval and Smith, *Law and Its Presuppositions*.

2. Wolff, *In Defence of Anarchism*.

3. *Ibid.* at 71.

4. *Ibid.* at 23.

5. Taylor, *Hegel and Modern Society,* 106.

6. *Ibid.*

7. *Ibid.* at 103.

8. Coval and Smith, *supra* note 1.

9. Taylor, *supra* note 5, at 100–111.

10. *Ibid.* at 120.

11. Hegel, *Philosophy of Right,* 122–55.

12. Quoted in Taylor, *supra* note 5, at 90.

13. *Ibid.* at 111. Taylor describes Hegel's

way of formulating and answering the yearning of his age to unite somehow the radical moral autonomy of Kant and the expressive unity of the Greek *polis*. Hegel's answer to this conundrum was . . . an extraordinary and original combination of the ultra-modern aspiration to autonomy, and a renewed vision of cosmic order from the idea of radical autonomy itself, via a displacement of its centre of gravity from man to *Geist*. This synthesis he saw as the goal of history. (at 95)

14. *Ibid.* at 114.

15. *Ibid.* at 116.

16. *Ibid.* at 115.

17. Hegel, *supra* note 11, part 3, sect. 166, at 172.

18. James Andersen framed the paradox in this way.

19. S. Freud, *Group Psychology and the Analysis of the Ego, S.E.,* vol. 18, at 140–41.

20. Pateman, *Sexual Contract*, 3.

21. See for example, Fromm, *Beyond the Chains of Illusion;* Marcuse, *Eros and Civilization;* Fenichel, "Psychoanalysis."

22. See S. Freud, *Civilization and Its Discontents, S.E.,* vol. 21, at 112–14. See also Chasseguet-Smirgel and Grunberger, *Freud or Reich?*

23. S. Freud, "The Question of *Weltanschauung,*" in *New Introductory Lectures on Psycho-analysis,* Lecture 35, *S.E.,* vol. 22, at 180.

24. West, "Law, Rights, and Other Totemic Illusions." Freud hoped that someday there would be a major rapprochement between psychoanalysis and law. See letter from Anna Freud to Dr. Alan A. Stone, referred to by Stone in "Psychoanalysis and Jurisprudence Revisited," 357.

25. West, *supra* note 24, at 822.

26. West argues that only an appeal to a higher moral authority will assure obedience, so the law, to be legitimate, must be grounded in moral imperatives. She points out that while legal liberals assert that moral rights and principles emerge from human history and community, they do not explain how this apolitical legal system came about.

27. See for example, Mahler, Pine, and Bergman, *Psychological Birth of the Human Infant;* Stoller, *Perversion; id., Sexual Excitement;* Chasseguet-Smirgel, *Ego Ideal; id., Creativity and Perversion; id., Sexuality and Mind.* For a general overview, see Eagle, *Recent Developments in Psychoanalysis.*

28. See discussion of Freud and the seduction theory in chap. 2, of Chasseguet-Smirgel, *Sexuality and Mind,* at 9–15.

29. S. Freud, "Sexual Aberrations," in *Three Essays on the Theory of Sexuality, S.E.,* vol. 7, at 135–72.

30. S. Freud, *supra* note 22, at 77.

31. *Ibid.* at 95.

32. *Ibid.* at 90.

33. *Ibid.* at 82.

34. *Ibid.* at 101–2.

35. *Ibid.* at 122.

36. *Ibid.* at 103–4.

37. See for example, S. Freud, *supra* note 29, at 151; *id.,* "Femininity," Lecture 33, in *New Introductory Lectures on Psycho-analysis, supra* note 23, at 116–35; *id.,* " 'Civilized' Sexual Morality and Modern Nervous Illness," *S.E.,* vol. 9, at 199; *id.,* "Some Psychical Consequences of the Anatomical Distinction between the Sexes," *S.E.,* vol 19, at 252.

38. S. Freud, "Some Psychical Consequences," *supra* note 37, at 257–58.

39. Barthes, *Mythologies,* 129.

40. Ryle, *Concept of Mind,* 10.

41. Tucker, *Philosophy and Myth in Karl Marx,* 219.

42. S. Freud, *supra* note 22, at 117.

43. Brown, *Life against Death.*

44. Becker, *Denial of Death.*

45. MacKinnon, *Toward a Feminist Theory,* 116–17.

46. Alice Jardine, "Men in Feminism," in Jardine and Smith, eds., *Men in Feminism*, 61.

47. *Ibid.* at 60.

48. See for example, French, *Beyond Power*, 25–122; Lerner, *Creation of Patriarchy*.

49. MacKinnon, in the introduction to her book, *Feminism Unmodified*, describes the two themes of her book as follows (at 3):

> My arguments and meditations to this end provide the themes that unify this volume. The first theme is the analysis that the social relation between the sexes is organized so that men may dominate and women must submit and this relation is sexual—in fact, is sex. Men in particular, if not men alone, sexualize inequality, especially the inequality of the sexes. The second theme is a critique of the notion that gender is basically a difference rather than a hierarchy. To treat gender as a difference (with or without a French accent) means to treat it as a bipolar distinction, each pole of which is defined in contrast to the other by opposed intrinsic attributes. Beloved of left and right alike, construing gender as a difference, termed simply the gender difference, obscures and legitimizes the way gender is imposed by force. It hides that force behind a static description of gender as a biological or social or mythic or semantic partition, engraved or inscribed or inculcated by god, nature, society (agents unspecified), the unconscious, or the cosmos. The idea of gender difference helps keep the reality of male dominance in place.

Chasseguet-Smirgel, in *Ego Ideal*, points out that she considers "the bed-rock of reality is not only the difference between the sexes, but that which corresponds absolutely to this, like the two faces of a coin: namely, the difference between the generations. The reality is not that the mother has been castrated; the reality is that she has a vagina that the little boy's penis cannot satisfy" (at 15). Biology/reality has to be separated from myth/hierarchy. The hierarchy to which MacKinnon refers arises not from reality but from the mythic dimension of gender difference. Within patriarchal culture it has become almost impossible, because of the pervasiveness of that dimension, to separate reality from myth. Therefore, MacKinnon is right in her assertion that gender difference leads to gender hierarchy.

50. For a general discussion of gender difference see: Eisenstein and Jardine, eds., *Future of Difference;* Stoller, *Sex and Gender;* Birke, *Women, Feminism, and Biology;* Bleier, *Science and Gender;* Keller, *Reflections on Gender and Science;* Gilligan, *In a Different Voice;* Illich, *Gender*.

51. J. C. Smith, *Legal Obligation*, chap. 6.

52. See MacKinnon, *supra* note 45.

53. *Ibid.* at 125.

54. *Ibid.* at 3.

55. Dinnerstein, *Mermaid and the Minotaur*.

56. Chodorow, *Reproduction of Mothering*.

57. Benjamin, "Bonds of Love" *id.,* "Oedipal Riddle"; *id.,* "Shame and Sexual Politics," 155; *id.,* "Authority and the Family Revisited," 33.

58. Scales, "Towards a Feminist Jurisprudence"; *id.*, "Emergence of Feminist Jurisprudence."

59. J. Mitchell, *Psychoanalysis and Feminism*, introduction at xiii. See also Crowell, "Feminism and Modern Psychoanalysis," 221–35; Donovan, "Feminism and Freudianism," in *Feminist Theory*, chap. 4, 91–116; Sayers, *Sexual Contradictions*; Gallop, *Daughter's Seduction*; Garner, Kahane, and Sprengnether, eds., *(M)other Tongue*; Irigaray, *Speculum of the Other Woman*; *id.*, *This Sex Which Is Not One.*

60. For a general discussion, see West, "Jurisprudence and Gender"; Ferguson, *Feminist Case against Bureaucracy*; McElroy, ed., *Freedom, Feminism, and the State.*

Chapter 18: The End of History

1. S. Freud, *Civilization and Its Discontents*, S.E., vol. 21, at 122.

2. Gay, *Freud*, 553.

3. S. Freud, *supra* note 1, at 145.

4. Spielrein, "Die Destruktion als Ursache des Werdens" (Destruction as the Cause of Becoming). See Gay, *supra* note 2, at 396; Carotenuto, *Secret Symmetry*, 143–52.

5. Gay, *supra* note 2, at 396–97, suggests reasons as to why it took Freud so long to accept the death instinct.

6. S. Freud, *supra* note 1, at 117–22.

7. See Brown, *Life against Death*; Marcuse, *Eros and Civlization.*

8. S. Freud, *Group Psychology and the Analysis of the Ego*, S.E., vol. 18, at 52–61. For further analysis of the kinds of links which the mind can forge between sex and death see Georges Bataille, *Eroticism.*

9. Jung, "Instinct and the Unconscious," *C.W.*, vol. 8, par. 273.

10. *Ibid.*, par. 280.

11. *Ibid.*, par. 270.

12. *Ibid.*, par. 277.

13. Arendt, *Origins of Totalitarianism*, xxx.

14. *Ibid.* at 438.

15. *Ibid.* at 467.

16. Chasseguet-Smirgel, *Sexuality and Mind*, 25.

17. Chasseguet-Smirgel, *Creativity and Perversion*, 27.

18. *Ibid.* at 29.

19. Chasseguet-Smirgel, *supra* note, 16, at 26–28.

20. *Ibid.* at 143.

21. *Ibid.* at 142.

22. *Ibid.* at 138.

23. *Ibid.* at 134.

24. *Ibid.* at 129, 128.

25. I have borrowed this title from an unpublished paper by Cal Deedman.

26. See Otto, *Dionysus*; Deutsch, *A Psychoanalytic Study*; Friedrich Nietzsche, "Birth of Tragedy," in W. Kaufmann, ed. and trans. *Basic Writings of Nietzsche*;

Eisner, *Road to Daulis;* Detienne, *Dionysos Slain;* Brun, *Le Retour de Dionysos;* Jung, "Apollonian and the Dionysian," *C.W.,* vol. 6, par. 223; Needles, "Orgastic Loss of Consciousness"; Hillman, "Dionysus in Jung's Writing"; Cowan, "Dionysus," in *Masochism,* chap. 6, 95–114; Evans, *God of Ecstasy;* N. Hall, *Those Women;* Fierz-David, *Women's Dionysian Initiation;* Houser, *Dionysos and His Circle;* Danielou, *Shiva and Dionysus;* Kerenyi, *Dionysus.*

27. Chasseguet-Smirgel, *supra* note 16, at 142.

28. *Ibid.* at 144.

29. *Ibid.* at 37.

30. *Ibid.* at 40.

31. M. E. Harding, *Woman's Mysteries,* 195–96.

32. Chasseguet-Smirgel, *supra* note 16, at 104.

33. S. Freud, *New Introductory Lectures on Psycho-analysis, S.E.,* vol. 22, at 80.

34. Kojève, *Introduction to the Reading of Hegel,* 258.

35. See Stokes, *Life and Death of Yukio Mishima.* Mishima's novel *Confessions of a Mask,* is semi-autobiographical of his youth.

36. Mishima, *On Hagakure,* 99–100.

37. *Ibid.* at 103.

38. *Ibid.* at 29.

39. Stokes, *supra* note 35, at 184.

40. Hillman, *Myth of Analysis,* 250–51. For discussion of Apollonian patriarchal aspects of science and the scientific approach, see Bleier, *Science and Gender;* Keller, *Reflections on Gender and Science;* Birke, *Women, Feminism, and Biology;* Corea, *Mother Machine;* S. Harding, *Science Question in Feminism.*

41. Hillman, *supra* note 40, at 293.

42. *Ibid.* at 258–98.

43. *Ibid.* at 292.

44. Daly, *Gyn/ecology,* 88. For a discussion of androgyny within a Jungian framework see Singer, *Androgyny.*

45. Daly, *Pure Lust,* 207–8.

46. Andrienne Rich writes, "Feminism is a criticism and subversion of *all* patriarchal thought and institutions—not merely those currently seen as reactionary and tyrannical" ("Toward a Woman-Centered University," in *On Lies, Secrets, and Silence,* 134, note 11, cited and discussed by Scales in "The Emergence of Feminist Jurisprudence," at note 60). In that article, Scales writes (at 1383–84):

> By trying to make everything too nice, incorporationism represses contradictions. It usurps women's language in order to further define the world in the male image; it thus deprives women of the power of naming. Incorporationism means to give over the world, because it means to say to those in power: "We will use your language and we will let you interpret it."

47. See Carotenuto, *supra* note 4.

48. McGuire, ed., *Freud/Jung Letters,* 207.

49. *Ibid.* at 289.

50. Zolla, *Androgyne,* 6.

51. Bynum, *Jesus as Mother,* 153.

52. See Daly, *Church and the Second Sex.* In the 1985 edition Mary Daly adds a "Feminist Postchristian Introduction," in which she shows why an androgynous God will always remain essential patriarchal, and in which she disassociates herself from her earlier views. See also Ochs, *Behind the Sex of God;* Ochshorn, *Female Experience;* Armstrong, *Gospel According to Woman;* Ulanov, *Receiving Woman;* Plaskow and Romero, eds., *Women and Religion;* Christ and Plaskow, eds., *Womanspirit Rising;* Christ, *Laughter of Aphrodite.* For a criticism of these attempts, see Daly *Beyond God the Father;* Goldenberg, *Changing of the Gods.*

53. "Gender Schema Theory and Child Development," 245.

54. Letter of 30 July 1932 from Einstein to Freud, in "Why War?" *S.E.,* vol. 22, at 199.

55. *Ibid.* at 212. See also S. Freud, *supra* note 1, chap. 5, at 101 and 108–16.

56. Dworkin, *Intercourse.*

57. Kramer, *Sumerians,* 79.

58. Barratt, *Psychic Reality and Psychoanalytic Knowing,* 3.

59. *Ibid.* at 8–9.

60. Chasseguet-Smirgel, *The Ego Ideal,* 84.

61. Janssen-Jurreit, "Feminism and Socialism," in *Sexism,* 114–27.

62. See Koonz, *Mothers in the Fatherland.*

63. Kariel, *The Desperate Politics of Post-modernism.*

64. S. Freud, *supra* note 1.

65. Daly, *Gyn/ecology.*

BIBLIOGRAPHY

Abraham, Karl. *Dreams and Myths*. Trans. William A. White. New York: Journal of Nervous and Mental Disease, 1913.

Adler, Margot. *Drawing Down the Moon*. Rev. ed. Boston: Beacon Press, 1986.

Aeschylus. *Oresteia*. Trans. Richmond Lattimore. Chicago: University of Chicago Press, 1953.

Agonito, Rosemary. *History of Ideas on Woman: A Source Book*. New York: Perigee Books, 1977.

Alpert, Judith L., ed. *Psychoanalysis and Women*. Hillsdale, N.J.: Analytic Press, 1986.

Aly, Gotz, and Karl Heinz Roth. "The Legalization of Mercy Killings in Medical and Nursing Institutions in Nazi Germany from 1938 until 1941." *International Journal of Law and Psychiatry* 7 (1984): 145–63.

Andelin, Helen B. *The Fascinating Girl*. Santa Barbara, Calif.: Pacific Press, 1975.

———. *Fascinating Womanhood*. Rev. ed. New York: Bantam Books, 1980.

Ando, Shôei. *Zen and American Transcendentalism: An Investigation of One's Self*. Tokyo: Hokusei do Press, 1970.

Angus, S. *The Mystery Religions and Christianity*. New York: Scribner's, 1925.

Anzieu, Didier. "L'Etude Psychanalytique des Groupes Réels." *Les Tempes Modernes* 242 (1966).

———. "L'Illusion Groupale." *Nouvelle Revue de Psychanalyse* 4 (1971).

Anzieu, Didier, and Jacques-Yves Martin. *La Dynamique des Groupes Restreints*. Paris: Presses Universitaires de France, 1969.

Apfelbaum, B. "Ego Psychology, Psychic Energy, and the Hazards of Quantitive Explanation in Psychoanalytic Theory." *International Journal of Psycho-analysis* 46 (1965): 168–82.

Aquinas, St. Thomas. *Summa Theologica*. London: R. & T. Washbourne, 1912.

Archard, David. *Consciousness and the Unconscious*. Problems of Modern European Thought, vol. 1. London: Hutchinson, 1984.

Archer, John, and Barbara Lloyd. *Sex and Gender*. Harmondsworth, Middlesex: Penguin, 1982.

Ardrey, Robert. *The Territorial Imperative*. New York: Atheneum, 1967.

Arendt, Hannah. *On Revolution*. New York: Viking Press, 1963.

———. *The Origins of Totalitarianism*. 5th ed. New York: Harcourt Brace Jovanovich, 1973.

Aristotle. *The Ethics of Aristotle*. [The Nicomachean Ethics] Trans. J. A. K. Thomson. London: Allen & Unwin, 1953.

———. *The Politics*. Ed. Stephen Everson. Cambridge: Cambridge University Press, 1988.

Arlow, Jacob. "Ego Psychology and the Study of Mythology." *Journal of American Psychoanalytic Association* 9 (1961): 379.

Armstrong, Karen. *The First Christian: Saint Paul's Impact on Christianity*. London: Pan Books, 1983.

———. *The Gospel According to Woman*. London: Pan Books, 1986.

Arnold, E. Vernon. *Roman Stoicism*. Oxford: Clarendon Press, 1936.

Arthur, Marylin B. "Early Greece: The Origins of the Western Attitude toward Women." In *Women in the Ancient World,* ed. John Peradotto and J. P. Sullivan. Albany, State University of New York Press, 1984.

Ashe, Geoffrey. *The Virgin*. London: Routledge & Kegan Paul, 1976.

Attenborough, David. *The First Eden*. London: Collins/BBC Books, 1987.

Atwood Margaret. *The Handmaid's Tale*. Toronto: McClelland & Stewart, 1985.

Augustine, St. *The City of God*. Trans. Marcus Dods. Edinburgh: T. & T. Clark, 1871.

Aurelius, Marcus. *Meditations* 6, 44. In *The Stoic and the Epicurean Philosophers,* ed. Whitney J. Oates. New York: Random House, 1940.

Austin, John. *Lectures on Jurisprudence,* I. 5th ed, London: J. Murray, 1885.

Avalon, Arthur. *Shakti and Shakta*. New York: Dover Publications, 1978.

Bachofen, J. J. *Myth, Religion, and Mother Right*. Trans. Ralph Manheim. New Jersey: Princeton University Press, 1967.

Badcock, C. R. *The Psychoanalysis of Culture.* Oxford: Basil Blackwell, 1980.

Bakan, David. *And They Took Themselves Wives: The Emergence of Patriarchy in Western Civilization.* New York: Harper & Row, 1979.

———. *Sigmund Freud and the Jewish Mystical Tradition.* New York: Schocken Books, 1958.

Balint, Michael. *Primary Love and Psycho-analytic Technique.* New York: Liveright, 1965.

Balmary, Marie. *Psychoanalyzing Psychoanalysis: Freud and the Hidden Fault of the Father.* Trans. Ned Lukacher. Baltimore: John Hopkins University Press, 1982.

Bamberger, Joan. "The Myth of Matriarchy: Why Men Rule in Primitive Society." In *Woman, Culture, and Society,* ed. Michelle Zimbalist Rosaldo and Louise Lamphere. Stanford: Stanford University Press, 1974.

Barker-Benfield, G. J. *The Horrors of the Half-Known Life: Male Attitudes toward Women and Sexuality in Nineteenth-Century America.* New York: Harper Colophon Books, 1976.

Barkun, Michael. *Law without Sanctions.* New Haven: Yale University Press, 1968.

Barnett, Lincoln. *The Universe and Dr. Einstein.* New York: New American Library, 1953.

Barratt, Barnaby B. *Psychic Reality and Psychoanalytic Knowing.* Advances in Psychoanalysis: Theory, Research, and Practice, vol. 3. Hillsdale, N.J: Analytic Press, 1984.

Barthes, Roland. *Mythologies.* Trans. Annette Lavers. New York: Hill and Wang, 1972.

Barton, Thomas B. Review of *The Western Idea of Law,* by J. C. Smith and David N. Weisstub.

Bataille, Georges. *Erotism: Death and Sensuality.* Trans. Mary Dalwood. San Francisco: City Lights Books, 1986.

Baynes, H. G. *Analytical Psychology and the English Mind, and Other Papers.* Ed. Anne Baynes. London: Methuen, 1950.

Bebel, August. *Woman and Socialism.* Trans. Meta L. Stern. New York: Socialist Literature, 1910.

Becker, Ernest. *The Denial of Death.* New York: Free Press, 1973.

Becker, J. E. *The Sexual Life of Japan.* New York: American Anthropological Society, 1934.

Bem, Sandra Lipsitz. "Gender Schema Theory: A Cognitive Account of Sex Typing." *Psychological Review* 88 (1981): 354–64.

———. "Gender Schema Theory and Its Implications for Child Development: Raising Gender-aschematic Children in a Gender-schematic

Society." In *The Psychology of Women,* Ed. Mary Roth Walsh. New Haven: Yale University Press, 1987.

Benjamin, Jessica. "Internalization and Instrumental Culture: A Reinterpretation of Psychoanalysis and Social Theory," Ph.D. diss., New York University, 1978.

———. "Authority and the Family Revisited; or, A World without Fathers?" *New German Critique* 13 (1978): 1.

———. "The Oedipal Riddle: Authority, Autonomy, and the New Narcissism." In *The Problem of Authority in America,* eds., John P. Diggins and Mark E. Kann. Philadelphia: Temple University Press, 1981.

———. "Shame and Sexual Politics." *New German Critique* 27 (1982): 151.

———. "The Bonds of Love: Rational Violence and Erotic Domination." In *The Future of Difference,* eds. Hester Eisenstein and Alice Jardine. New Brunswick: Rutgers University Press, 1985.

———. "The Alienation of Desire: Women's Masochism and Ideal Love." In *Psychoanalysis and Women,* ed. Judith L. Alpert, 113–38. Hillsdale, N.J.: Analytic Press, 1986.

———. *The Bonds of Love: Psychoanalysis, Feminism, and the Problem of Domination.* New York: Pantheon Books, 1988.

Bentham, Jeremy. *The Principles of Morals and Legislation,* New York: Hafner, 1948.

Benvenuto, Bice, and Roger Kennedy. *The Works of Jacques Lacan: An Introduction.* London: Free Association Books, 1986.

Berger, Pamela. *The Goddess Obscured: Transformation of the Grain Protectress from Goddess to Saint.* Boston: Beacon Press, 1985.

Berger, Peter L., and Thomas Luckmann. *The Social Construction of Reality.* Garden City, N.Y.: Doubleday, 1966.

Berggren, Douglas. "From Myth to Metaphor." *The Monist* 50 (1966): 530.

Bergmann, Maria V. "The Female Oedipus Complex: Its Antecedents and Evolution." In *Early Female Development,* ed. Dale Mendell. New York: Spectrum Publications, 1982.

Berkeley, George. *A Treatise Concerning the Principles of Human Knowledge.* New York: Liberal Arts Press, 1957.

Berthiaume, Christiane. "Des Millions de Femmes Mutilées." *Chantelaine* (January 1982): 39.

Bettelheim, Bruno. *The Uses of Enchantment.* New York: Alfred A. Knopf, 1976.

———. *Freud and Man's Soul.* New York: Alfred A. Knopf, 1983.

Birke, Lynda. *Women, Feminism, and Biology.* New York: Methuen, 1986.

Bleier, Ruth. *Science and Gender*. Oxford: Pergamon Press, 1984.

Block, A. J. "Sexual Perversion in the Female." *New Orleans Medical Surgical Journal* 22 (July 1984): 4.

Block, Walter. "Public Goods and Externalities: The Case of Roads." *Journal of Libertarian Studies* 7 (1983): 1–34.

Bock, Gisela. "Racism and Sexism in Nazi Germany: Motherhood, Compulsory Sterilization, and the State." *Signs* 8 (1983): 400–421.

Bodin, Jean. *De la Démonomanie des Sorciers*. Paris: Du Puys, 1580.

Boguet, Henry. *An Examen of Witches (Discours des Sorciers)*. Trans., E. Allen Ashwin. Ed. Montague Summers. New York: Barnes & Noble, 1971. First pub. London: John Rodker, 1929.

Bolen, Jean Shinoda. *Goddesses in Everywomen*. New York: Harper & Row, 1984.

Bonaparte, Marie. *Female Sexuality*. New York: International Universities Press, 1953.

Bonnard, Andre. *Greek Civilization*. London: George Allen & Unwin, 1959.

Boorse, Henry A., and Lloyd Motz, eds. *The World of the Atom*. New York: Basic Books, 1966.

Bord, Janet and Colin Bord. *Earth Rites: Fertility Practices in Pre-Industrial Britain*. London: Granada, 1982.

Boulware-Miller, Kay. "Female Circumcision: Challenges to the Practice as a Human Rights Violation." *Harvard Women's Law Journal* 8 (1985): 155–77.

Boyer, L. Bruce, and Simon A. Grolnick, eds. *The Psychoanalytic Study of Society* 11 (1985). New York: International Universities Press.

Bracton, Henry de. *On the Laws and Customs of England*. Vols. 1–4, Trans. Samuel E. Thorne. Cambridge: Harvard University Press, 1968.

Bradbury, Ray. *Something Wicked This Way Comes*. Toronto: Bantam Pathfinder Editions, 1962.

Braudel, Fernand. *Afterthoughts on Material Civilization and Capitalism*. Trans. Patricia M. Ranum. Baltimore and London: Johns Hopkins University Press, 1977.

Braxton, Bernard. *Women, Sex, and Race*. Washington, D.C.: Verta Press, 1973.

Breines, Wini, and Linda Gordon. "The New Scholarship on Family Violence." *Signs* 8 (1983): 490.

Briffault, Robert. *The Mothers: A Study of the Origins of Sentiments and Institutions*. New York: Macmillan, 1927.

Brown, Norman O. *Life against Death*. Middletown, Conn.: Wesleyan University Press, 1959.

————. *Love's Body*. New York: Random House, 1966.

Brownmiller, Susan. *Against Our Will: Men, Women, and Rape*. New York: Simon & Schuster, 1973.

Broyles, William, Jr. "Why Men Love War." *Esquire* (November 1984): 55–65.

Brun, Jean. *Le Retour de Dionysos*. Paris: Desclee et Cie, 1969.

Brunswick, Ruth Mack. "The Preoedipal Phase of the Libido Development." *Psychoanalytic Quarterly* 9 (1940): 293–319.

Bullough, Vern, and Bonnie Bullough. *Women and Prostitution: A Social History*. Buffalo, N.Y.: Prometheus Books, 1987.

Burgin, Victor, James Donald, and Cora Kaplan, eds. *Formations of Fantasy*. London: Methuen, 1986.

Burkert, Walter. *Structure and History in Greek Mythology and Ritual*. Berkeley: University of California Press, 1979.

————. *Ancient Mystery Cults*. Cambridge: Harvard University Press, 1987.

Burnet, John. *Early Greek Philosophy*. London: A. & C. Black, 1892.

Buruma, Ian. *A Japanese Mirror*. Harmondsworth, Middlesex: Penguin, 1984.

Bynum, Caroline Walker. *Jesus as Mother*. Berkeley: University of California Press, 1982.

Campbell, Joseph. *The Hero with a Thousand Faces*. New York: Pantheon, 1949.

————. *The Masks of God*. 4 vols. New York: Viking Press, 1959–1968.

Campbell, Joseph, ed. *Myth, Dreams, and Religion*. New York: E. P. Dutton, 1970.

————. *The Mythic Image*. Princeton: Princeton University Press, 1974.

Canadian Broadcasting Corporation (CBC) Transcripts, "Return of the Goddess." January 1986.

Capra, Fritjof. *The Tao of Physics*. Berkeley: Shambhala Publications, 1975.

Carmi, T., ed. and trans. *The Penquin Book of Hebrew Verse*. New York: Penguin Books, 1981.

Carotenuto, Aldo. *A Secret Symmetry*. Trans. Arno Pomerans, John Shepley, and Krishna Winston. New York: Pantheon Books, 1982.

Cassirer, Ernst. *Languag and Myth*. Trans. Susanne K. Langer. New York: Dover Publications, 1946.

————. *The Myth of the State*. New Haven: Yale University Press, 1946.

————. *The Philosophy of Symbolic Forms*. 3 vols. New Haven: Yale University Press, 1953–1957.

Catullus. *The Carmina of Catullus*. Trans. Barriss Mills. West Lafayette, Ind.: Purdue University Studies, 1965.

Chasseguet-Smirgel, Janine. *The Ego Ideal: A Psychoanalytic Essay on the Malady of the Ideal.* Trans. Paul Barrows. London: W. W. Norton, 1975.

————. "Freud and Female Sexuality." *International Journal of Psycho-Analysis* 57 (1976):275.

————. "Transsexuality, Paranoia, and the Repudiation of Femininity." In *Psychosexual Imperatives,* ed. Marie Coleman Nelson and Jean Ikenberry. New York: Human Sciences Press, 1979.

————. *Creative and Perversion.* London: W. W. Norton, 1985.

————. *Sexuality and Mind: The Role of the Father and the Mother in the Psyche.* New York: New York University Press, 1986.

Chasseguet-Smirgel, Janine, and Béla Grunberger. *Freud or Reich? Psychoanalysis and Illusion.* New Haven: Yale University Press, 1986.

Chaudhuri, Nirad C. *Hinduism, a Religion to Live By.* New York: Oxford University Press, 1979.

Chehrazi, Shahla. "Female Psychology: A Review." *Journal of the American Psychoanalytic Association* 34 (1986): 111–62. Reprinted in *The Psychology of Women,* ed. Mary Roth Walsh. New Haven and London: Yale University Press, 1987.

Cherfas, Jeremy, and John Gribbin. *The Redundant Male.* New York: Pantheon Books, 1984.

Chodorow, Nancy. "Feminism and Difference: Gender, Relation, and Difference in Psychoanalytic Perspective." *Socialist Review* 9 (1976):51.

————. *The Reproduction of Mothering: Psychoanalysis and the Sociology of Gender.* Berkeley: University of California Press, 1978.

————. *Feminism and Psychoanalytic Theory.* New Haven: Yale University Press, 1989.

Christ, Carol P. *Laughter of Aphrodite.* San Francisco: Harper & Row, 1987.

Christ, Carol P., and Judith Plaskow, eds. *Womanspirit Rising: A Feminist Reader in Religion.* San Francisco: Harper & Row, 1979.

Christensen, Johnny. *An Essay on the Unity of Stoic Philosophy.* Copenhagen: Munksgaard, 1962.

Ch'u, T'ung-Tsu. *Law and Society in Traditional China.* The Hauge: Mouton & Co., 1961.

Cicero. "Speech in Defence of Aulus Quentius Avitus." Book 53. In *The Orations of Marcus Tillus Cicero.* Vol. 2. London: G. Bell, 1917.

Clark, Lorenne M. G. "Politics and Law: The Theory and Practice of the Ideology of Male Supremacy; or, It Wasn't God Who Made Honky Tonk Angels." In *Law and Policy;* ed. David N. Weisstub. Toronto: York University, 1976.

Clark, Lorenne M. G., and Lynda Lange, eds. *The Sexism of Social and Political Theory: Women and Reproduction from Plato to Nietzsche.* Toronto: University of Toronto Press, 1979.

Clement, Catherine. *The Lives and Legends of Jacques Lacan.* Trans. Arthur Goldhammer. New York: Columbia University Press, 1983.

Clissold, Stephen. *Djilas, The Progress of a Revolutionary.* Hounslow, Middlesex: Maurice Temple Smith, 1983.

Cobley, John. "Evolution to Patriarchy: The Subjugation of Woman in the Old Testament." *Perspectives* (1972): 86.

Coker, G. B. A. *Family Property among the Yorubas.* 2d ed. London: Sweet and Maxwell, 1966.

Colby, Kenneth Mark. *Energy and Structure in Psychoanalysis.* New York: Ronald Press, 1955.

————. "Computer Simulation of a Neurotic Process." In *Computer Simulation of Personality,* eds. S. Tomkins and S. Messick. New York: Wiley, 1963.

————. "Simulation of Belief Systems." In *Computer Models of Thought and Language,* eds. R. C. Schank and K. M. Colby. San Francisco: W. H. Freeman, 1973.

————. *Artificial Paranoia: A Computer Simulation of Paranoid Processes.* New York: Pergamon Press, 1975.

————. "Mind Models: An Overview of Current Work." *Mathematical Biosciences* 39 (1978): 159–85.

————. "Molding a Paranoid Mind." *Behavioral and Brain Sciences* 4 (1981): 515–60.

————. "Ethics of Computer-Assisted Psychotherapy." *Psychiatric Annals* 16 (1986): 414–15.

Colby, Kenneth Mark, and R. C. Parkinson. "Linguistic Conceptual Patterns and Key-Idea Profiles as a New Kind of Property for a Taxonomy of Neurotic Patients." *Computers and Human Behavior* 1 (1985): 181–94.

Colby, Kenneth Mark, and James E. Spar. *The Fundamental Crisis in Psychiatry: Unreliability of Diagnosis.* Springfield, Ill.: Charles C. Thomas, 1983.

Colby, Kenneth Mark, and Robert J. Stoller. *Cognitive Science and Psychoanalysis.* Hillsdale, N.J.: Lawrence Erlbaum, 1988.

Collins, Larry, and Dominique Lapierre. *Freedom at Midnight.* New Delhi: Vikas Publishing House, 1975.

Commons, John R. *Legal Foundations of Capitalism.* Madison: University of Wisconsin Press, 1924.

Conze, Edward, L. B. Horner, D. Snellgrove, and A. Waley, eds. *Buddhist Texts through the Ages.* New York: Harper & Row, 1964.

Cooper, Barry. *The End of History: An Essay on Modern Hegelianism.* Toronto: University of Toronto Press, 1984.

Corea, Gena. *The Mother Machine.* New York: Harper & Row, 1985.

Coval, S. C. and J. C. Smith. *Law and Its Presuppositions.* London: Routledge & Kegan Paul, 1986.

Cowan, Lyn. *Masochism: A Jungian View.* Dallas: Spring Publications, 1982.

Coward, Rosalind. *Patriarchal Precedents.* London: Routledge & Kegan Paul, 1983.

Cox, Howard L. "The Place of Mythology in the Study of Culture." *American Image* 5 (1948): 86.

Crowell, Mimi Grand-Jean. "Feminism and Modern Psychoanalysis: A Response to Feminist Critics of Psychoanalysis." *Modern Psychoanalysis* 6 (1981): 221–35.

Culler, Jonathan. *On Deconstruction.* Ithaca: Cornell University Press, 1983.

Daly, Mary. *The Church and the Second Sex.* With the Feminist Postchristian Introduction. Boston: Beacon Press, 1985. First pub. Harper & Row, 1968.

———. *Beyond God the Father: Toward a Philosophy of Women's Liberation.* Boston: Beacon Press, 1973.

———. *Gyn/ecology: The Metaethics of Radical Feminism.* Boston: Beacon Press, 1978.

———. *Pure Lust.* Boston: Beacon Press, 1984.

Dames, Michael. *The Avebury Cycle.* London: Thames & Hudson, 1977.

Danielou, Alain. *Shiva and Dionysus.* Trans. K. F. Hurry. London and The Hague: East-West Publications, 1982.

Danielou, Jean. "Christianity as a Jewish Sect." In *The Crucible of Christianity,* ed. Arnold Toynbee. New York: World Publishing, 1969.

Davis, Elizabeth G. *The First Sex.* New York: G. P. Putnam's Sons, 1971.

de Beauvoir, Simone. *The Second Sex.* Trans. H. M. Parshley. New York: Alfred A. Knopf, 1953.

de George, Richard T., and Fernande M. de George, eds. *The Structuralists from Marx to Levi-Strauss.* Garden City, N.Y.: Anchor Books, 1972.

de Riencourt, Amaury. *Sex and Power in History.* New York: Dell, 1974.

———. *The Eye of Shiva.* New York: William Morrow & Co., 1980.

de Vaux, Roland, *Ancient Israel.* New York: McGraw-Hill, 1961.

de Waal, Frans. *Chimpanzee Politics: Power and Sex among Apes.* New York: Harper & Row, 1982.

Deleuze, Gilles, and Felix Guattari. *Anti-Oedipus: Capitalism and Schizo-*

phrenia. Trans. Robert Hurley, Mark Seem, and Helen R. Lane. New York: Viking Press, 1977.

Derham, David P. "Theories of Legal Personality." In *Legal Personality and Political Pluralism,* ed. Leicester C. Webb. Victoria: Melbourne University Press, 1958.

Detienne, Marcel. *Dionysos Slain.* Trans. Mireille Muellner and Leonard Muellner. Baltimore: Johns Hopkins University Press, 1979.

Deutsch, Helene. *The Psychology of Women: A Psychoanalytic Interpretation.* 2 vols. London: Research Books, 1947.

———. *A Psychoanalytic Study of the Myth of Dionysus and Apollo.* New York: International Universities Press, 1969.

———. "The Significance of Masochism in the Mental Life of Women." In *The Psychoanalytic Reader,* ed. Robert Fliess. New York: International Universities Press, 1969.

Devor, Holly. *Gender Blending: Confronting the Limits of Duality.* Bloomington: Indiana University Press, 1989.

Dijkstra, Bram. *Idols of Perversity.* New York: Oxford University Press, 1986.

Dilman, Ilham. *Freud and the Mind.* Oxford: Basil Blackwell, 1984.

Diner, Helen. *Mothers and Amazons: The First Feminist History of Culture.* Ed. and trans. John Philip Lundian. New York: Julian Press, 1965.

Dinnerstein, Dorothy. *The Mermaid and the Minotaur: Sexual Arrangements and Human Malaise.* New York: Harper & Row, 1976.

Djilas, Milovan. *The New Class.* New York: Holt, Rinehart & Winston, 1957.

———. *The Unperfect Society: Beyond the New Class.* New York: Harcourt, Brace & World, 1969.

———. *Memoir of a Revolutionary.* Trans. Dremla Willen. New York: Harcourt Brace Jovanovich, 1973.

———. *Parts of a Lifetime.* Eds. Michael and Deborah Milenkovitch. New York: Harcourt Brace Jovanovich, 1975.

Dodds, E. R. *The Greeks and the Irrational.* Berkeley: University of California Press, 1951.

Doi, Takeo. *The Anatomy of Dependence.* Trans. John Bester. Tokyo: Kodansha International, 1973.

———. *The Anatomy of Self.* Trans. Mark A. Harbison. Tokyo: Kodansha International, 1986.

Dollard, John, Leonard W. Doob, Neal E. Miller, O. H. Mowrer, and Robert R. Sears. *Frustration and Aggression.* New Haven: Yale University Press in association with the Institute of Human Relations, 1939.

Donovan, Josephine. *Feminist Theory.* New York: Frederick Ungar, 1985.

Douglas, Mary. *Natural Symbols*. New York: Pantheon Books, 1970.

Dreyfus, Hubert L., and Stuart E. Dreyfus. "Making a Mind versus Modeling the Brain: Artificial Intelligence Back at a Branchpoint." *Daedalus* (Winter 1988): 15–43.

Duberman, Lucile. *Gender and Sex in Society*. New York: Praeger, 1975.

Durden-Smith, Jo, and Diane deSimone. *Sex and the Brain*. New York: Warner Books, 1983.

Dworkin, Andrea. *Woman Hating*. New York: E. P. Dutton, 1974.

———. *Right-Wing Women*. New York: Perigee Books, 1983.

———. *Intercourse*. New York: Free Press, 1987.

Eagle, Morris N. *Recent Developments in Psychoanalysis*. New York: Mc-Graw-Hill, 1984.

Eckstein, Alice R. "The Third Reich and Goethe." *Spring* (1941): 52.

Edelson, M. "Psychoanalysis as Science." *Journal of Nervous and Mental Disease* 165 (1977): 1–28.

Edinger, Edward F. *Ego and Archetype*. Baltimore: Penguin Books, 1972.

Edwards, Chilperic, trans. *The Hammurabi Code and the Sinaitic Legislation*. Port Washington, N.Y.: Kennikat Press, 1971.

Ehrenzweig, Albert. *Psychoanalytic Jurisprudence*. Dobbs Ferry, N.Y.: Oceana Publications, 1971.

Eibl-Eibesfeldt, Irenaus. *The Biology of Peace and War: Men, Animals, and Aggression*. New York: Viking Press, 1979.

Einstein, Albert. *The World as I See It*. Trans. Alan Harris. London: J. Lane, 1934.

———. *Ideas and Opinions*. New York: Bonanza Books, 1954.

Eisenstein, Hester, and Alice Jardine, eds. *The Future of Difference*. New Brunswick: Rutgers University Press, 1985.

Eisler, Riane. *The Chalice and the Blade: Our History, Our Future*. San Francisco: Harper & Row, 1987.

Eisner, Robert. *The Road to Daulis*. Syracuse: Syracuse University Press, 1987.

El Saadawi, Nawal. *The Hidden Face of Eve*. Trans. Sherif Hetata. Boston: Beacon Press, 1980.

Eliade, Mircea. *Patterns in Comparative Religion*. Trans. Rosemary Sheed. London: Sheed & Ward, 1958.

———. *The Sacred and the Profane*. Trans. Willard R. Trask. New York: Harcourt, Brace & World, 1959.

———. *Myths, Dreams, and Mysteries*. Trans. Philip Mairet. New York: Harper & Row, 1960.

———. *Images and Symbols*. Trans. Philip Mairet. New York: Sheed & Ward, 1961.

――――. *Myth and Reality*. Trans. Willard R. Trask. New York: Harper & Row, 1963.

Eliot, T. S. *Sweeney Agonistes: Fragments of an Aristophanic Melodrama*. London: Faber and Faber, 1932.

Ellenberger, Henri F. *The Discovery of the Unconscious*. New York: Basic Books, 1970.

Elliot, Gil. *Twentieth Century Book of the Dead*. New York: Scribner's, 1972.

The Encyclopedia of Philosophy. 8 vols. Ed. in chief. Paul Edwards. New York: MacMillan, 1967.

Endleman, Robert. *Psyche and Society*. New York: Columbia University Press, 1981.

Engels, Frederich. *Anti-Duhring: Herr Eugen Duhring's Revolution In Science*. Trans. Emile Burns. New York: International Publishers, 1939.

――――. *Selected Correspondence, 1846–1895*. Trans. Dona Torr. Westport, Conn.: Greenwood Press, 1942.

Erikson, Erik H. *Childhood and Society*. New York: Norton, 1963.

――――. *Identity and the Life Cycle*. New York: W. W. Norton, 1980.

Estrich, Susan. *Real Rape*. Cambridge: Harvard University Press, 1987.

Euclid. *Elements*. Trans. H. S. Hall and F. H. Stevens. London: Mac-Millan, 1904.

Euripides. *The Bacchae*. Trans. Geoffrey S. Kirk. Englewood Cliffs: N.J.: Prentice-Hall, 1970.

Evans, Arthur. *The God of Ecstasy*. New York: St. Martin's Press, 1988.

Eyer, Alvin. "Clitoridectomy for the Cure of Certain Cases of Masturbation in Young Girls." *International Medical and Surgical Journal* (November 1894): 261.

Eysenck, Hans. *Decline and Fall of the Freudian Empire*. Harmondsworth: Viking Press, 1985.

Eysenck, Hans, and Glenn D. Wilson. *The Experimental Study of Freudian Theories*. London: Methuen, 1973.

Farrell, B. A. *The Standing of Psychoanalysis*. Oxford: Oxford University Press, 1981.

Fast, Irene. "Developments in Gender Identity: Gender Differentiation in Girls." *International Journal of Psycho-Analysis* 60 (1979): 443.

――――. *Gender Identity: A Differentiation Model*. Hillsdale, N.J.: Analytic Press, 1984.

――――. *Event Theory: A Piaget-Freud Integration*. Hillsdale, N.J.: Erlbaum, 1985.

Faust, Beatrice. *Women, Sex, and Pornography*. London: Melbourne House, 1980.

Felman, Shoshana. *Jacques Lacan and the Adventure of Insight*. Cambridge: Harvard University Press, 1987.

Fenichel, Otto. "Psychoanalysis as the Nucleus of a Future Dialectical-Materialistic Psychology." *American Image* 24 (1967): 290–311.

Ferenczi, Sandor. *Sex in Psychoanalysis*. Trans. Ernest Jones. New York: Basic Books, 1950.

———. *Further Contributions to the Theory and Technique of Psycho-analysis*. Comp. and trans. by John Rickman, Jane Isabel Suttie and others. London: Hogarth Press, 1950.

———. *First Contributions to Psycho-Analysis*. Trans. Ernest Jones. London: Hogarth Press, 1952.

———. *Final Contributions to the Problems and Methods of Psycho-analysis*. Ed. Michael Balint. Trans. Eric Mosbacher and others. New York: Basic Books, 1955.

Ferguson, John. *The Religions of the Roman Empire*. Ithaca: Cornell University Press, 1970.

Ferguson, Kathy E. *The Feminist Case against Bureaucracy*. Philadelphia: Temple University Press, 1984.

Fierz-David, Linda. *Women's Dionysian Initiation*. Trans. Gladys Phelan. Dallas: Spring Publications, 1988.

Fine, Reuben. *The Psychoanalytic Vision: A Controversial Reappraisal of the Freudian Revolution*. New York: Free Press, 1981.

Fisher, Elizabeth. *Woman's Creation*. Garden City, N.Y.: Doubleday, Anchor Press, 1979.

Fisher, Helen E. *The Sex Contract*. New York: William Morrow, 1982.

Fisher, J. H. "Obtaining and Presenting Evidence in Sex Cases." *The Criminal Law Quarterly* 4 (1961–62): 150–59.

Flaubert, Gustave. *The Letters of Gustave Flaubert, 1830–1857*. Ed. and trans. Francis Steegmuller. Cambridge and London: Harvard University Press, 1980.

Formanek, Ruth. "On the Origins of Gender Identity." In *Early Female Development*, ed. Dale Mendell. New York: Spectrum Publications, 1982.

Frank, Jerome. *Law and the Modern Mind*. New York: Brentano's, 1930.

Frankfort, Henri. *Kingship and the Gods*. Chicago: University of Chicago Press, 1948.

Frankl, Viktor E. *The Unconscious God*. New York: Washington Square Press, 1975.

———. *The Unheard Cry for Meaning*. New York: Washington Square Press, 1978.

———. *Man's Search for Meaning*. New York: Washington Square Press, 1984.

Franklin, H. B. "From Empire to Empire: Billy Budd, Sailor." in *Herman Melville: Reassessments,* ed. A. R. Lee. London: Vision, 1984.

Fraser, Jessie E. "Heracles: An Introduction." *Spring* (1966): 24–38.

Fraser, Nancy, and Linda J. Nicholson. "Social Criticism without Philosophy: An Encounter between Feminism and Postmodernism." In *Feminism/Postmodernism,* ed. Linda J. Nicholson, New York: Routledge and Kegan Paul, 1990.

Frazer, Sir James George. *The Golden Bough: The Dying God,* (1911).

———. *Adonis, Attis, Osiris.* London: Macmillan, 1930.

———. *The Illustrated Golden Bough.* Gen. ed. Mary Douglas. Garden City, N.Y.: Doubleday, 1978.

Freeman, Derek. *Margaret Mead and Samoa: The Making and Unmaking of an Anthropological Myth.* Cambridge: Harvard University Press, 1983.

French, Marilyn. *Beyond Power.* New York: Summit Books, 1985.

Freud, Anna. *The Ego and the Mechanisms of Defence.* Trans. Cecil Baines. New York: International Universities Press, 1946.

———. "Some Remarks on Infant Observation." *Psycho-analytic Study of the Child* 8 (1953): 9–19.

———. "Problems of Infantile Neurosis: A Discussion." *Psycho-analytic Study of the Child* 9 (1954): 9–71.

———. "A Discussion of Dr. John Bowlby's Paper 'Grief and Mourning in Infancy and Early Childhood.' " *Psycho-analytic Study of the Child* 15 (1960): 53–62.

Freud, Sigmund. *The Origins of Psychoanalysis: Letters to Wilhelm Fliess: Drafts and Notes, 1887–1902.* Ed. Marie Bonaparte, Anna Freud, and Ernst Kris. New York: Basic Books, 1954.

———. *The Freud/Jung Letters.* Ed. William McGuire. Trans. Ralph Manheim and R. F. C. Hull. Princeton: Princeton University Press, 1974.

———. *The Standard Edition to the Complete Works of Sigmund Freud.* 24 vols. Ed. James Strachey. London: Hogarth Press, 1960–1974.

———. *The Complete Letters of Sigmund Freud to Wilhelm Fliess 1887–1904.* Ed. and trans. Jeffrey Moussaieff Masson. Cambridge: Harvard University Press, 1985.

———. *A Phylogenetic Fantasy: Overview of the Transference Neuroses.* Ed. Ilse Grubich-Simitis. Trans. Axel Hoffer and Peter T. Hoffer. Cambridge: Harvard University Press, 1987.

Frey-Rohn, Liliane. *From Freud to Jung.* Trans. Fred E. Engreen and Evelyn K. Engreen. New York: G. P. Putnam's Sons for the C. G. Jung Foundation for Analytical Psychology, 1974.

Friedman, Richard C., Ralph M. Richart, and Raymond L. Vande Wiele, eds. *Sex Differences in Behavior*. New York: John Wiley & Sons, 1974.

Fromm, Erich. *Escape from Freedom*. New York: Avon Books, 1941.

———. *The Art of Loving*. New York: Harper & Row, 1956.

———. *Beyond the Chains of Illusion*. New York: Simon & Schuster, 1962.

———. *The Anatomy of Human Destructiveness*. New York: Holt, Rinehart & Winston, 1973.

Frye, Northrop. *The Great Code: The Bible and Literature*. New York: Harcourt Brace Jovanovich, 1982.

Fustel de Coulages, Numa Denis. *The Ancient City*. Garden City, N.Y.: Doubleday, 1956.

Gabriel, Yiannis. *Freud and Society*. London: Routledge & Kegan Paul, 1983.

Gagnon, John H., and William Simon. *Sexual Conduct*. Chicago: Aldine, 1973.

Gallop, Jane. *The Daughter's Seduction: Feminism and Psychoanalysis*. Ithaca: Cornell University Press, 1982.

———. *Reading Lacan*. Ithaca: Cornell University Press, 1985.

Garner, Shirley Nelson, Claire Kahane, and Madelon Sprengnether, eds. *The (M)other Tongue*. Ithaca: Cornell University Press, 1985.

Gay, Peter. *Freud for Historians*. New York: Oxford University Press, 1985.

———. *The Godless Jew: Freud, Atheism, and the Making of Psychoanalysis*. New Haven: Yale University Press, 1987.

———. *Freud: A Life for Our Time*. New York: Norton, 1988.

Gill, Merton M., and Philip S. Holzman, eds. *Psychology versus Metapsychology: Psychoanalytic Essays in Memory of George S. Klein*. New York: International Universities Press, 1976.

Gilligan, Carol. *In a Different Voice*. Cambridge: Harvard University Press, 1982.

Gilman, Sander L. "Freud and the Prostitute: Male Stereotypes of Female Sexuality in Fin-de-siècle Vienna." *Journal of the American Academy of Psychoanalysis*, 9 (1981): 337–60.

Gilman, Sander L., ed. *Introducing Psychoanalytic Theory*. New York: Brunner/Mazel, 1982.

Gimbutas, Marija. *The Goddesses and Gods of Old Europe*. Berkeley: University of California Press, 1974.

Girard, René. *Violence and the Sacred*. Trans. Patrick Gregory. Baltimore: Johns Hopkins University Press, 1977.

Goldberg, Arnold, ed. *The Future of Psychoanalysis*. New York: International Universities Press, 1983.

Goldberg, Steven. *The Inevitability of Patriarchy*. New York: William Morrow, 1973–74.

Goldenberg, Naomi R. *Changing of the Gods: Feminism and the End of Traditional Religions*. Boston: Beacon Press, 1979.

Goldman, Robert. "Playing with a Bad Boy." *California Monthly* 94 (June–July 1984).

Goldstein, Joseph. "Psychoanalysis and Jurisprudence." *Yale Law Journal* 77 (1968): 1053.

Govinda, Lama Anagarika. *Creative Meditation and Multi-dimensional Consciousness*. Wheaton, Ill.: Theosophical Publishing House, 1976.

Graves, Robert. *The White Goddess: A Historical Grammar on Poetic Myth*. London: Faber & Faber, 1952.

———. *The Greek Myths*. Rev. ed. 12 vols. Harmondsworth, Middlesex: Penguin Books, 1960.

Gray, Elizabeth Dodson. *Green Paradise Lost*. Wellesley, Mass.: Roundtable Press, 1981.

Greene, Bob. "Bar Wars." *Esquire* (November 1986).

Greenfield, Barbara. "The Archetypal Masculine: Its Manifestation in Myth, and Its Significance for Women." *Journal of Analytical Psychology* 28 (1983): 33–50.

Greer, Germaine. *Sex and Destiny: The Politics of Human Fertility*. New York: Harper & Row, 1984.

Gregor, Thomas. *Anxious Pleasures: The Sexual Lives of an Amazonian People*. Chicago: University of Chicago Press, 1985.

Griffin, Susan. *Woman and Nature: The Roaring Inside Her*. New York: Harper & Row, 1978.

———. *Pornography and Silence: Culture's Revenge against Nature*. New York: Harper & Row, 1981.

———. *Made from This Earth*. New York: Harper & Row, 1982.

Griffiths, Morwenna, and Margaret Whitford, eds. *Feminist Perspectives in Philosophy*. Bloomington: Indiana University Press, 1988.

Groddeck, Georg Walther. *The Book of the It*. New York: Vintage Books, 1961.

———. *The Meaning of Illness: Selected Psychoanalytic Writings*. Selected by Lore Schacht. Trans. Gertrud Mander. London: Hogarth Press, 1977.

Grossman, William I. "Discussion of 'Freud and Female Sexuality.' " *The International Journal of Psycho-Analysis* 57 (1976): 301.

Groth, A. Nicholas, and H. Jean Birnbaum. "Adult Sexual Orientation and Attraction to Underage Persons." *Archives of Sexual Behavior* 7 (1978): 175–81.

Gruen, Arno. *The Betrayal of the Self: The Fear of Autonomy in Men and*

Women. Trans. Hildegard Hannum and Hunter Hannum. New York: Grove Press, 1986.

Grunbaum, Adolf. *The Foundations of Psychoanalysis*. Berkeley: University of California Press, 1984.

Grunberger, Béla. *Narcissism: Psychoanalytic Essays*. Trans. Joyce S. Diamanti. New York: International Universities Press, 1979.

Guettel, Charnie. *Marxism and Feminism*. Toronto: Women's Press, 1974.

Gurian, Jay P., and Julia M. Gurian. *The Dependency Tendency: Returning to Each Other in Modern America*. Lanham, Md.: University Press of America, 1983.

Guterbock, Carl E. *Bracton and His Relation to the Roman Law*. Trans. Brinton Cox. Littleton, Colo.: Fred B. Rothman, 1979.

Gutting, Gary, ed. *Paradigms and Revolutions*. Notre Dame: University of Notre Dame Press, 1980.

Hall, C. S. *The Meaning of Dreams*. New York: Harper, 1953.

Hall, Nor. *The Moon and the Virgin*. New York: Harper & Row, 1980.

———. *Those Women*. Dallas: Spring Publications, 1988.

Hamilton, Victoria. *Narcissus and Oedipus*. London: Routledge & Kegan Paul, 1982.

Harding, M. Esther. *The Parental Image: Its Injury and Reconstruction*. New York: G. P. Putnam's Sons, 1965.

———. *Woman's Mysteries: Ancient and Modern*. New York: Harper & Row, 1971.

Harding, Sandra. *The Science Question in Feminism*. Ithaca: Cornell University Press, 1986.

Hare, R. M. *The Language of Morals*. New York: Oxford University Press, 1964.

———. *Freedom and Reason*. New York: Oxford University Press, 1965.

Harris, Marvin. *The Rise of Anthropological Theory*. New York: Crowell, 1968.

———. *Cannibals and Kings: The Origins of Cultures*. New York: Random House, 1977.

———. *Cultural Materialism: The Struggle for a Science of Culture*. New York: Random House, 1979.

Harris, Ronald Walter. *Science, Mind, and Method*. Oxford: Blackwell, 1960.

Harrison, Jane. *Prolegomena to the Study of Greek Religion*. London: Merlin Press.

Hart, H. L. A. *The Concept of Law*. Oxford University Press, 1961.

Hartsock, Nancy C. M. *Money, Sex, and Power*. Boston: Northeastern University Press, 1983.

Hatfield, Elaine, Sue Sprecher, and Jane Traupmann. "Men's and Wom-

en's Reactions to Sexually Explicit Films: A Serendipitous Finding."
    Archives of Sexual Behavior 7 (1978): 583–92.

Hawkes, Jacquetta. *Dawn of the Gods*. Toronto: Clarke, Irwin in association with Chatto & Windus, 1968.

Hayek, F. A. *The Constitution of Liberty*. Chicago: University of Chicago Press, 1960.

Hayford, Harrison, and Merton M. Sealts, eds. *Billy Budd, Sailor (An Inside Narrative)*. Chicago: University of Chicago Press, 1962.

Hegel, G. W. F. *The Philosophy of Right*. Trans. T. M. Knox. Oxford: Clarendon Press, 1952.

————. *Lectures on the History of Philosophy*. Trans. E. S. Haldane. New York: Humanities Press, 1955.

————. *Phenomenology of Spirit*. Trans. A. V. Miller. Oxford: Clarendon Press, 1977.

Heilbroner, Robert L. *An Inquiry into the Human Prospect*. New York: W. W. Norton, 1974.

————. *The Nature and Logic of Capitalism*. New York: W. W. Norton, 1985.

Herdt, Gilbert H. *Guardians of the Flutes*. New York: McGraw-Hill, 1981.

————. *Rituals of Manhood*. Berkeley: University of California Press, 1982.

————. *Ritualized Homosexuality in Melanesia*. Berkeley: University of California Press, 1984.

Herman, Judith L. *Father-Daughter Incest*. Cambridge: Harvard University Press, 1981.

Heschel, Abraham J. *The Prophets*. New York: Harper & Row, 1962.

Hesiod. *Theogony, Works and Days, Shield*. Trans. Apostolos N. Athanassakis. Baltimore: Johns Hopkins University Press, 1983.

Hilberman, Elaine. "Overview: The 'Wife-Beater's Wife' Reconsidered." *American Journal of Psychiatry* 137 (1980); 1336–47.

Hillman, James. "Dionysus in Jung's Writings." *Spring* (1972): 191.

————. *The Myth of Analysis*. Chicago: Northwestern University Press, 1972.

————. *Re-Visioning Psychology*. New York: Harper & Row, 1975.

Hirschon, Renée, ed. *Women and Property—Women as Property*. London: Croom Helm, 1984.

Hite, Shere. *The Hite Report: A Nationwide Study on Female Sexuality*. New York: Macmillan, 1976.

————. *The Hite Report on Male Sexuality*. New York: Alfred A. Knopf, 1981.

Hobbes, Thomas. *Leviathan*. New York: E. P. Dutton, 1950.

Holcombe, Lee. *Wives and Property: Reform of the Married Women's Property Law in Nineteenth-Century England.* Toronto: University of Toronto Press, 1983.

Holdsworth, Sir William. *A History of English Law.* 4th ed. 9 vols. London: Methuen, 1936.

Holliday, Laurel. *The Violent Sex: Male Psychobiology and the Evolution of Consciousness.* Guerneville, Calif.: Bluestocking Books, 1978.

Holt, Robert R., "Freud's Mechanistic and Humanistic Images of Man. In *Psychoanalysis and Contemporary Science: An Annual of Integrative and Interdisciplinary Studies,* vol. 1, ed. Robert R. Holt and Emanuel Peterfreund. New York: Macmillan, 1972, at 3.

Honey, Margaret, and John Broughton. "Feminine Sexuality: An Interview with Janine Chasseguet-Smirgel." *Psychoanalytic Review* 74 (1985): 527.

Hopper, Stanley R. "Myth, Dream, and Imagination." In *Myths, Dreams, and Religion,* ed. Joseph Campbell. New York: E. P. Dutton, 1970.

Horney, Karen. *Neurosis and Human Growth.* New York: W. W. Norton, 1950.

———. *Feminine Psychology.* New York: W. W. Norton, 1967.

Hosken, Fran P. *The Hosken Report: Genital and Sexual Mutilation of Females.* Lexington, Mass.: Women's International Network News, 1982.

Houser, Caroline. *Dionysos and His Circle, Ancient through Modern.* Cambridge, Mass.: Fogg Art Museum, Harvard University, 1979.

Hrdy, Sarah Blaffer. *The Woman That Never Evolved.* Cambridge: Harvard University Press, 1981.

Hubbs, Joanna. *Mother Russia: The Feminine Myth in Russian Culture.* Bloomington: Indiana University Press, 1988.

Hume, David. *A Treatise of Human Nature.* 2d ed. Ed. L. A. Selby-Bigge. Oxford: Clarendon Press, 1978.

Hutton, Ernest Hirschlaff. *The Origins of Science.* London: Allen & Unwin, 1962.

Hyde, Janet Shibley, and Marcia C. Linn, eds. *The Psychology of Gender: Advances through Meta-Analysis.* Baltimore: Johns Hopkins University Press, 1986.

Iida, Sueharu, ed. *Nihon Shoki Shinko* (New Lectures on Japanese Tales). Vol. I. Tokyo: Meibunsha, 1964.

Illich, Ivan. *Gender.* New York: Pantheon Books, 1982.

Inhelder, Barbel, and Jean Piaget. *Early Growth of Logic in the Child.* New York: W. W. Norton, 1964.

International Commission of Jurists. "Report on Human Rights and Mental Patients in Japan." Geneva: I.C.J., 1985.

Irigaray, Luce. *Speculum of the Other Woman*. Trans. Gillian C. Gill. Ithaca: Cornell University Press, 1985.

―――. *This Sex Which Is Not One*. Trans. Catherine Porter. Ithaca: Cornell University Press, 1985.

Jacobi, Jolande. *Complex/Archetype/Symbol in the Psychology of C. G. Jung*. Trans. Ralph Manheim. Princeton: Princeton University Press, 1959.

―――. *The Psychology of C. G. Jung*. New Haven and London: Yale University Press, 1973.

Jacobson, Nolan Pliny. *Buddhism and the Contemporary World*. Carbondale, Ill.: Southern Illinois University Press, 1983.

―――. *Understanding Buddhism*. Carbondale, Ill.: Southern Illinois University Press, 1986.

Jacoby, Mario A. *Social Amnesia: A Critique of Contemporary Psychology from Adler to Laing*. Boston: Beacon Press, 1975.

―――. *The Longing for Paradise*. Trans. Myron B. Gubitz. Boston: Sigo Press, 1985.

Jacoby, Russell. *The Repression of Psychoanalysis*. New York: Basic Books, 1983.

Jaggar, Alison M. *Feminist Politics and Human Nature*. Totowa, N.J.: Rowman & Allanheld, 1983.

James, Edwin Oliver. *The Cult of the Mother-Goddess: An Archaeological and Documentary Study*. London: Thames & Hudson, 1959.

James, I. *Daemonlogogie*. Ed. G. B. Harrison. Reprint. New York: Barnes & Nobles, 1966; Edinburgh: R. Wald-grove, 1597.

Janssen-Jurreit, Marielouise. *Sexism*. Trans. Verne Moberg. New York: Farrar, Straus & Giroux, 1982.

Janus, Sam, Barbara Bess, and Carol Saltus. *A Sexual Profile of Men in Power*. Englewood Cliffs, N.J.: Prentice-Hall, 1977.

"Japanese Women." *Economist* 307 (1988): 19.

Jardine, Alice. *Gynesis: Configurations of Woman and Modernity*. Ithaca: Cornell University Press, 1985.

―――. "Men in Feminism: Odor di Uomo or Compagnons de Route?" In *Men in Feminism*, ed. Alice Jardine and Paul Smith. New York: Methuen, 1987.

Johnson, Buffie. *Lady of the Beasts*. San Francisco: Harper & Row, 1988.

Jones, Ernest. *The Life and Work of Sigmund Freud*. Vol. 1: *The Formative Years and the Great Discoveries*. New York: Basic Books, 1953.

―――. *The Life and Work of Sigmund Freud*. Vol. 2; *Years of Maturity*. New York: Basic Books, 1955.

―――. *The Life and Work of Sigmund Freud*. Vol. 3; *The Last Phase*. New York: Basic Books, 1957.

Jung. C. G. *The Collected Works of C. G. Jung.* Bollingen Series 20. 20 vols. Princeton: Princeton University Press, 1957–79.

———. *Memories, Dreams, Reflections.* New York: Vintage Books, 1965.

———. *The Freud/Jung Letters.* Ed. William McGuire. Trans. Ralph Manheim and R. F. C. Hull. Princeton: Princeton University Press, 1974.

Jurjevich, R. M. *The Hoax of Freudism: A Study of Brainwashing the American Professionals and Laymen.* Philadelphia: Dorrance, 1974.

Kairys, David, ed. *The Politics of Law.* New York: Pantheon Books, 1982.

Kamiya, Masako. "Women in Japan." *University of British Columbia Law Review* 20 (1986): 447.

Kantorowicz, Ernst H. *The King's Two Bodies.* Princeton: Princeton University Press, 1957.

Kantorowicz, Herman. *Bractonian Problems.* Glasgow: Jackson, 1941.

Kardiner, Abram, Ralph Linton, Cora du Bois, and James West. *The Psychological Frontiers of Society.* New York: Columbia University Press, 1945.

Kariel, Henry. "Postmodernism at the End." *Strategies* 1 (Fall 1988): 50–62.

———. *The Desperate Politics of Post-modernism.* Amherst, Mass.: University of Massachusetts Press, 1989.

Kasulis, T. P. *Zen Action/Zen Person.* Honolulu: University Press of Hawaii, 1981.

Kaufmann, Walter, ed. and trans. *Basic Writings of Nietzsche.* New York: Modern Library, 1968.

———. *Discovering the Mind.* Vols. 1–3. New York: McGraw-Hill, 1980.

———. *Discovering the Mind.* Vol. 1, *Goethe, Kant, and Hegel.* New York: McGraw-Hill, 1980.

———. *Discovering the Mind.* Vol. 2, *Nietzsche, Heidegger, and Buber.* New York: McGraw-Hill, 1980.

———. *Discovering the Mind.* Vol. 3, *Freud versus Adler and Jung.* New York: McGraw-Hill, 1980.

Kaufmann, Yehezkel. *The Religion of Israel.* Trans. Moshe Greenberg. Chicago: University of Chicago Press, 1960.

Kawashima, Takeyoshi. "The Status of the Individual in the Notion of Law, Right, and Social Order in Japan." In *The Status of the Individual in East and West,* ed. Charles A. Moore. Honolulu: University of Hawaii Press, 1968.

Keller, Evelyn Fox. *Reflections on Gender and Science.* New Haven: Yale University Press, 1985.

Kennedy, H. A. A. *St. Paul and the Mystery Religions.* London: Hodder and Stoughton, 1913.

Kenyon, J. P., ed. "James I on Monarchy: Speech to Parliament." In *The Stuart Constitution, 1603–1688*. Cambridge: Cambridge University Press, 1966.

Kerenyi, Carl. *Dionysus*. Princeton: Princeton University Press, 1976.

Kern, Fritz. *Kingship and Law in the Middle Ages*. New York: Frederick A. Praeger, 1956.

Keuls, Eva C. *The Reign of the Phallus*. New York: Harper & Row, 1985.

Kirk, G. S., J. E. Raven, and M. Schofield. *The Presocratic Philosophers*. Cambridge: Cambridge University Press, 1957.

Kleeman, J. A. "The Establishment of Core Gender Identity in Normal Girls." *Archives of Sexual Behavior* 1 (1971): 103–29.

———. "Freud's Views on Early Sexuality in the Light of Direct Child Observation." *Journal of the American Psychoanalytic Association* 24 (suppl.) (1976): 3–28.

Klein, George S. *Perception, Motives, and Personality*. New York: Alfred A. Knopf, 1970.

———. *Psychoanalytic Theory: An Exploration of Essentials*. New York: International Universities Press, 1976.

Klein, Josephine. *Our Need for Others and Its Roots in Infancy*. London: Tavistock Publications, 1987.

Klein, Melanie. "Infant Analysis." *International Journal of Psycho-analysis* 7 (1926): 31–63.

———. "On Observing the Behavior of Young Infants." In *Developments in Psychoanalysis* by Melanie Klein, Paula Hiemann, Susan Isaacs, and Joan Riviere. London: Hogarth Press, 1952.

———. "Our Adult World and Its Roots in Infancy." *Human Relations* 12 (1959): 291–303.

———. *The Psycho-analysis of Children*. Trans. Alix Strachey. London: Hogarth Press, 1959.

Klein, Melanie, Paula Heimann, and R. E. Money-Kyrle, eds. *New Directions in Psycho-analysis: The Significance of Infant Conflict in the Pattern of Adult Behavior*. New York: Basic Books, 1956.

Kleinbaum, Abby Wettan. *The War against the Amazons*. New York: McGraw-Hill, 1983.

Kline, Morris. *Mathematics in Western Culture*. New York: Oxford University Press, 1954.

Kline, Paul. *Fact and Fantasy in Freudian Theory*. Reprint. London: Methuen, 1981.

Kofman, Sarah. *The Enigma of Woman*. Trans. Catherine Porter. Ithaca, N.Y.: Cornell University Press, 1985.

Kohlberg, Lawrence. "Cognitive-Developmental Analysis of Children's Sex-Role Concepts and Attitudes." In *The Development of Sex Differ-*

ences, ed. Eleanor E. Maccoby. Stanford: Stanford University Press, 1966, at 82.

———. *The Philosophy of Moral Development.* San Francisco: Harper & Row, 1981.

Kojève, Alexandre. *Introduction to the Reading of Hegel: Lectures on the Phenomenology of Spirit.* Assembled by Raymond Queneau. Ed. Allan Bloom. Trans. James H. Nichols, Jr. New York: Basic Books, 1969.

Kolodny, Annette. *The Lay of the Land.* Chapel Hill: University of North Carolina Press, 1975.

Koonz, Claudia. *Mothers in the Fatherland.* New York: St. Martin's Press, 1987.

Kramer, Samuel N. *The Sumerians: Their History, Culture, and Character.* Chicago: University of Chicago Press, 1963.

Krull, Marianne. *Freud and His Father.* Trans. Arnold J. Pomerans. New York: W. W. Norton, 1986.

Kuhn, Thomas S. *The Structure of Scientific Revolutions.* 2d ed. Chicago: University of Chicago Press, 1970.

Lacan, Jacques. *Speech and Language in Psychoanalysis.* Trans. Anthony Wilden. Reprint. Baltimore: Johns Hopkins University Press, 1976. Originally pub. as *The Language of the Self: The Function of Language in Psychoanalysis.* Baltimore: Johns Hopkins University Press, 1968.

———. *Ecrits.* Trans. Alan Sheridan. New York: W. W. Norton, 1977.

———. *The Four Fundamental Concepts of Psycho-Analysis.* Trans. Alan Sheridan. New York: W. W. Norton, 1977.

Lakoff, George. *Women, Fire, and Dangerous Things.* Chicago: University of Chicago Press, 1987.

Langer, Susanne K. *An Introduction to Symbolic Logic.* Rev. ed. New York: Dover Publications, 1953.

Lao Tsu. *Tao Te Ching.* Trans. Gia-Fu Feng and Jane English. New York: Vintage Books, 1972.

La Planche, Jean, and J.-B. Pontalis. "Fantasy and the Origins of Sexuality." *International Journal of Psycho-analysis* 49 (1968): 1–18.

Laslett, Peter, ed. *Patriarcha and Other Political Works of Sir Robert Filmer.* Oxford: Basil Blackwell, 1949.

Lawson, F. H. *A Common Law Lawyer Looks at the Civil Law.* Ann Arbor: University of Michigan Law School, 1955.

———. "The Creative Use of Legal Concepts." *New York University Law Review* 32 (1957): 909–25.

Lebra, Takie S. *Japanese Patterns of Behavior.* Honolulu: University Press of Hawaii, 1976.

Lederer, Wolfgang. *The Fear of Women.* New York and London: Grune & Stratton, 1968.

Lee, Orlan. *Legal and Moral Systems in Asian Customary Law.* San Francisco: Chinese Materials Center, 1978.

Lefkowitz, Mary R., and Maureen B. Fant. *Women's Life in Greece and Rome.* Baltimore: Johns Hopkins University Press, 1982.

Lemaire (Rifflet-Lemaire), Anika. *Jacques Lacan.* Trans. David Macey. London: Routledge & Kegan Paul, 1977.

Lenin, V. I. "Women and Society." In *The Woman Question.* New York: International Publishers, 1951.

Lerner, Gerda. *The Creation of Patriarchy.* New York: Oxford University Press, 1986.

Levin, Ira. *The Stepford Wives.* New York: Dell, 1979.

Levin, Jack, and James Alan Fox. *Mass Murder.* New York: Plenum Press, 1985.

Lévi-Strauss, Claude. *Structural Anthropology.* Trans. Clarie Jacobson and Brooke Grundfest Schoepf. Garden City, N.Y.: Doubleday, 1967.

————. *Myth and Meaning: Five Talks for Radio.* Toronto and Buffalo: University of Toronto Press, 1978.

————. *Anthropology and Myth: Lectures, 1951–1982.* Trans. Roy Willis. Oxford and New York: Blackwell, 1987.

Levy, Gertrude Rachel. *The Gate of Horn: A Study of the Religious Conceptions of the Stone Age and Their Influence upon European Thought.* London: Faber and Faber, 1948.

Levy, Howard S. *Chinese Foot-Binding: The History of a Curious Erotic Custom.* New York: Walton Rawls, 1966.

Lewin, Karl Kay. *Sexual Self-destruct: Conscience of the West.* St. Louis, Mo.: Warren H. Green, 1980.

Lichtenberg, Joseph D. *Psychoanalysis and Infant Research.* Hillsdale, N.J.: Analytic Press, 1983.

Lieberman, E. James. *Acts of Will: The Life and Work of Otto Rank.* New York: Free Press, 1985.

Linden, Robin Ruth, Darlene R. Pagano, Diana E. H. Russell, and Susan Leigh Star, eds. *Against Sadomasochism: A Radical Feminist Analysis.* East Palo Alto, Calif.: Frog in the Well, 1982.

Lips, Hilary M., and Nina Lee Colwill. *The Psychology of Sex Differences.* Englewood Cliffs, N.J.: Prentice-Hall, 1978.

Lloyd-Jones, Hugh. *The Justice of Zeus.* 2d ed. Berkeley: University of California Press, 1983.

Lorenz, Konrad. *On Aggression.* Trans. Marjorie Kerr Wilson. New York: Harcourt, Brace & World, 1966.

Lothane, Zvi. "Love, Seduction, and Trauma." *The Psychoanalytic Review* 74 (1987): 83–105.

Lovelock, J. E. *Gaia*. Oxford and New York: Oxford University Press, 1979.

Lowen, Alexander. *The Betrayal of the Body*. New York: Macmillan, 1967.

Luckmann, Thomas. *The Invisible Religion*. New York: Macmillan, 1967.

Lyotard, Jean-Francois. *The Postmodern Condition: A Report on Knowledge*. Trans. G. Bennington and B. Massumi. Minneapolis: University of Minnesota Press, 1984.

MacCabe, Colin, ed. *The Talking Cure: Essays in Psychoanalysis and Language*. London: Macmillan, 1981.

MacCannell, Juliet Flower. *Figuring Lacan: Criticism and the Cultural Unconscious*. London: Croom Helm, 1986.

MacKinnon, Catharine A. "Feminism, Marxism, Method, and the State: An Agenda for Theory." *Signs* 7 (1982): 515.

———. "Feminism, Marxism, Method, and the State: Toward Feminist Jurisprudence." *Signs* 8 (1983): 635.

———. *Feminism Unmodified*. Cambridge: Harvard University Press, 1987.

———. *Toward a Feminist Theory of the State*. Cambridge: Harvard University Press, 1989.

MacLean, Paul D. "A Mind of Three Minds: Educating the Triune Brain." *Yearbook of the National Society for the Study of Education* 77 (1978): 308–42.

———. "A Triangular Brief on the Evolution of Brain and Law." *Journal of Social Biological Structure* 5 (1982): 369–79.

———. "Brain Roots of the Will-to-Power." *Zygon* 18 (December 1983): 359.

———. Editorial: "Evolutionary Psychiatry and the Triune Brain." *Psychological Medicine* 15 (1985): 219–221.

McCulloch, Warren S. *Embodiments of Mind*. Cambridge: M.I.T. Press, 1965.

McElroy, Wendy, ed. *Freedom, Feminism, and the State*. Washington, D.C.: Cato Institute, 1982.

McGuire, William, ed. *The Freud/Jung Letters*. Trans. Ralph Manheim and R. F. C. Hull. Princeton: Princeton University Press, 1974.

Maccoby, E., ed. *The Development of Sex Differences*. Stanford: Stanford University Press, 1966.

Mahler, Margaret S. *The Memoirs of Margaret S. Mahler*. Compil. and ed. Paul Stepansky. New York: Free Press, 1988.

Mahler, Margaret S., Fred Pine, and Anni Bergman. *The Psychological Birth of the Human Infant*. New York: Basic Books, 1975.

Maine, Sir Henry Sumner. *Ancient Law*. London: John Murray, 1861.

Maitland, F. W., ed. *Select Passages From the Works of Bracton and Azo*. Vol. 8. London: B. Quaritch, for the Selden Society, 1895.

Malcolm, Janet. *In the Freud Archives*. New York: Alfred A. Knopf, 1983.

Malinowski, Bronislaw. *Sex and Repression in Savage Society*, New York: Meridian Books, 1927.

——. *Magic, Science and Religion, and Other Essays*. New York: Free Press, 1948.

Marcuse, Herbert. *Eros and Civilization*. Boston: Beacon Press, 1955.

Markale, Jean. *Women of the Celts*. Trans. A. Mygind, C. Haunch, and P. Henry. Rochester, Vermont: Inner Traditions International, 1986.

Maroney, Heather J., and Meg Luxton, eds. *Feminism and Political Economy: Women's Work, Women's Struggles*. London: Methuen, 1987.

Masson, Jeffrey Moussaieff. "The Persecution and Expulsion of Jeffrey Masson as Performed by Members of the Freudian Establishment and Reported by Janet Malcom of the *New Yorker*." *Mother Jones* 9 (December 1984).

——. *A Dark Science: Women, Sexuality, and Psychiatry in the Nineteenth Century*. New York: Farrar, Straus & Giroux, 1986.

——. *The Assault on Truth: Freud's Suppression of the Seduction Theory*. New York: Farrar, Straus & Giroux, 1984.

Mates, Benson, *Stoic Logic*. Berkeley and Los Angeles: University of California Press, 1961.

Mattoon, Mary Ann. "Politics and Individuation." *Spring* (1978): 77–87.

Maude, H. E. "The Evolution of the Gilbertese 'Boti.' " Presented at the 10th Pacific Scientific Congress, Honolulu, 1961.

May, Rollo. *Freedom and Destiny*. New York: W. W. Norton, 1981.

Mayo, Katherine. *Mother India*. London: Jonathan Cape, 1927, reprinted 1932.

Mead, Margaret. *Coming of Age in Samoa*. New York: Morrow, 1928.

Mehta, Ved. "Profiles: Mahatma Gandhi and His Apostles." Part 3; "The Company They Keep." *New Yorker*, 24 May 1976, 41.

Mellaart, James. *Çatal Hüyük*. New York: McGraw-Hill, 1967.

Melville, Herman. *Billy Budd*, Chicago: University of Chicago Press, 1963.

Memmi, Albert. *Dependence: A Sketch for a Portrait of the Dependent*. Trans. Philip A. Facey. Boston: Beacon Press, 1984.

Mendell, Dale, ed. *Early Female Development*. New York: Spectrum Publications, 1982.

Merchant, Carolyn. *The Death of Nature*. New York: Harper & Row, 1980.

Metzger, B. M. "Considerations of Methodology in the Study of the Mystery Religions and Early Christianity." *Harvard Theological Review* 47 (1955): 1–20.

Milgram, Stanley. *Obedience to Authority*. New York: Harper & Row, 1974.

Miller, Alice. *Thou Shalt Not Be Aware: Society's Betrayal of the Child*. Trans. Hildegarde Hannum and Hunter Hannum. New York: Farrar, Straus, & Giroux, 1984.

Mills, Patricia Jagentowicz. "Hegel and 'The Woman Question': Recognition and Intersubjectivity." In *The Sexism of Social and Political Theory: Women and Reproduction from Plato to Nietzsche;* eds. Lorenne M. G. Clark and Lynda Lange. Toronto: University of Toronto Press, (1979).

Minister of Justice and Attorney General of Canada. *Sexual Offences against Children*. Report of the Committee on Sexual Offences Against Children and Youths. 2 vols. Ottawa: Canadian Publications Centre, 1984.

Minsky, Marvin. *The Society of Mind*. New York: Simon & Schuster, 1985.

Miquel, Juan. "Stoic Logic and Roman Jurisprudence." In *The Western Idea of Law*. J. C. Smith and David N. Weisstub. Trans. George H. Kendal. Scarborough, Ont.: Butterworths, 1983.

Mishima, Yukio. *Confessions of a Mask*. New York: New Directions Publishing, 1958.

———. *Death in Midsummer and Other Stories*. New York: New Directions Publishing, 1966.

———. *Decay of the Angels*. New York: Washington Square Press, 1975.

———. *Kyoko No Ie* (Kyoko's House). Vol. 11 in *Mishima Yukio Zenshu* (Complete Works of Yukio Mishima). Tokyo: Shinkosha, 1974.

———. *On Hagakure: The Samurai Ethic and Modern Japan*. New York: Basic Books, 1977.

———. *Runaway Horses*. New York: Alfred A. Knopf, 1973.

———. *The Sea of Fertility*. Tetratogy Series. New York: Washington Square Press, 1975.

———. *The Temple of the Golden Pavilion*. New York: Berkley Medallion, 1971.

Mitchell, Douglas D., *Amaeru: The Expression of Reciprocal Dependency Needs in Japanese Politics and Law*. Boulder, Colo.: Westview Press, 1977.

Mitchell, Gary D. *Human Sex Differences: A Primatologist's Perspective*. New York: Van Nostrand Reinhold, 1981.

Mitchell, Juliet. *Psycho-analysis and Feminism.* New York: Pantheon Books, 1974.

Mitchell, Juliet, and Ann Oakley, eds. *What Is Feminism?* New York: Pantheon Books, 1986.

Mitchell, Juliet, and Jacqueline Rose, eds. *Feminine Sexuality: Jacques Lacan and the Ecole Freudienne.* Trans. Jacqueline Rose. London: Macmillan, 1982.

Moberly, Elizabeth R. *Psychogenesis: The Early Development of Gender Identity.* London and Boston: Routledge & Kegan Paul, 1982.

Monaghan, Patricia. *The Book of Goddesses and Heroines.* New York: Dutton, 1981.

Money, J. "Ablatio Penis: Normal Male Infant Sex-reassigned as a Girl." *Archives of Sexual Behaviour* 4 (1975): 65.

Money, John, and Anke A. Ehrhardt. *Man and Woman, Boy and Girl: The Differentiation and Dimorphism of Gender Identity from Conception to Maturity.* Baltimore: Johns Hopkins University Press, 1972.

Montague, Ashley. *The Natural Superiority of Women.* New York: Lancer Books, 1953.

———. *Man and Aggression.* New York: Oxford University Press, 1968.

Montgrain, Noel. "On the Vicissitudes of Female Sexuality: The Difficult Path from 'Anatomical Destiny' to Psychic Representation." *International Journal of Psycho-analysis* 64 (1983): 169.

Mooij, Antoine. "The Symbolic Father." *Approaches to Discourse, Poetics, and Psychiatry.* Papers from the 1985 Utrecht Summer School of Critical Theory. Ed. Iris M. Zavala, Teun A. Van Dijk, and Myriam Diaz-Diocaretz. Amsterdam: John Benjamins, 1987.

Mooney, James. "The Ghost Dance Religion and the Sioux Outbreak of 1890." *Annual Report of the Bureau of American Ethnology.* Washington, 1896, xiv. Quoted in Mircea Eliade, *Patterns in Comparative Religion.* Trans. Rosemary Sheed. London: Sheed & Ward, 1953, 246; and in Janet Bord and Colin Bord, *Earth Rites.* London: Granada Publishing, 1982, 1.

Moore, Burness E. "Freud and Female Sexuality: A Current View." *International Journal of Psycho-analysis* 57 (1976): 287.

Moore, Michael S. *Law and Psychiatry.* Cambridge: Cambridge University Press, 1984.

Morgan, Marabel. *The Total Woman.* New York: Pocket Books, 1973.

Moser, Charles Allen. "An Exploratory-Descriptive Study of a Self-defined S/M (Sadomasochistic) Sample." Ph.D. San Francisco, 1979.

Muller, F. Max, ed. *The Sacred Books of the East.* 50 vols. Delhi: Motilal Banarsidass, 1964.

Murdock, James. *A History of Japan*. London: Kegan, Paul, Trench, Trubner, 1925.

Nagel, E. "Methodological Issues in Psychoanalytic Theory." In *Psychoanalysis, Scientific Method, and Philosophy: A Symposium,* ed. Sidney Hook. New York: New York University Press, 1959.

Napier, A. David. *Masks, Transformations, and Paradox*. Berkeley: University of California Press, 1986.

Needles, William. "Orgastic Loss of Consciousness: Its Possible Relationship to Freud's Theoretical Nihilism." *International Journal of Psycho-Analysis* 54 (1973): 315.

Nelson, Marie Coleman, and Jean Ikenberry, eds. *Psychosexual Imperatives*. New York: Human Sciences Press, 1979.

Neumann, Erich. *The Origins and History of Consciousness*. Trans. R. F. C. Hull. Princeton: Princeton University Press, 1954.

———. *The Great Mother*. Trans. Ralph Manheim. Princeton: Princeton University Press, 1955, 2d ed., 1963.

New Larousse Encylopedia of Mythology. Trans. Richard Aldington and Delano Ames. London: Hamlyn, 1983.

Nietzsche, Friedrich. "The Birth of Tragedy." In *Basic Writings of Nietzsche*. Ed. and trans. Walter Kaufman. New York: Modern Library, 1968.

Nock, Arthur D., "Hellenistic Mysteries and Christian Sacraments." In *Essays on Religion and the Ancient World*. Vol. 2, ed. Zeph Stewart. Oxford: Clarendon Press, 1972, at 791.

Northrop, F. S. C. *Science and First Principles*. New York: Macmillan, 1931.

———. "The Mathematical Background and Content of Greek Philosophy," in *Philosophical Essays for Alfred North Whitehead*. London: Longmans, Green, 1936.

———. *The Logic of the Sciences and the Humanities*. New York: Macmillan, 1947.

———. *The Complexity of Legal and Ethical Experience*. Boston: Little, Brown, 1959.

———. "The Comparative Philosophy of Comparative Law." *Cornell Law Review* 45 (1960): 617–58.

———. "The Epistemology of Legal Judgments." *Northwestern University Law Review* 58 (1964): 732.

Northrop, F. S. C., and Helen H. Livingston, eds. *Cross-Cultural Understanding: Epistemology in Anthropology*. New York: Harper & Row, 1964.

O'Brien, Mary. "Reproducing Marxist Man." In *The Sexism of Social and Political Theory,* ed. Lorenne M. G. Clark and Lynda Lange. Toronto: University of Toronto Press, 1979.

————. *The Politics of Reproduction*. Boston: Routledge & Kegan Paul, 1981.

O'Faolain, Julia, and Lauro Martines, eds. *Not in God's Image*. New York: Harper & Row, 1973.

O'Flaherty, Wendy Doniger. *Women, Androgynes, and Other Mythical Beasts*. Chicago: University of Chicago Press, 1980.

Oakley, A. *Sex, Gender, and Society*. London: Maurice Temple Smith, 1972.

Ochs, Carol. *Behind the Sex of God*. Boston: Beacon Press, 1977.

Ochshorn, Judith. *The Female Experience and the Nature of the Divine*. Bloomington: Indiana University Press, 1981.

Odajnyk, Volodymyr Walter. *Jung and Politics*. New York: Harper & Row, 1976.

Ogilvy, James A. *Many Dimensional Man: Decentralizing Self, Society, and the Sacred*. New York: Oxford University Press, 1977.

Okin, S. M. *Women in Western Political Thought*. Princeton: Princeton University Press, 1979.

Olson, Carl, ed. *The Book of the Goddess*. New York: Crossroad, 1983.

Ortner, Sherry B. "Is Female to Male as Nature Is to Culture?" In *Woman, Culture, and Society,* ed. Michelle Zimbalist Rosaldo and Louise Lamphere. Stanford: Stanford University Press, 1974.

Otsuka, Hisau, Takeo Doi, and Takeyoshi Kawashima. *'Amae' to Shakai Kaguku*. Tokyo: Kobundo, 1976.

Otto, Walter F. *Dionysus, Myth and Cult*. Bloomington: Indiana University Press, 1965; Dallas: Spring Publications, 1981.

Pagels, Elaine. *The Gnostic Gospels*. New York: Random House, 1979.

Parens, Henri, and Leon J. Saul. *Dependence in Man*. New York: International Universities Press, 1971.

Paris, Ginette. *Pagan Meditations*. Dallas: Spring Publications, 1986.

Parmenides. *A Text with Translation, Commentary, and Critical Essays,* ed. and trans. Leonardo Taran. Princeton: Princeton University Press, 1965.

Pasche, Francis. *À Partir de Freud*. Paris: Payot, 1969.

Patai, Raphael. *The Hebrew Goddess*. New York: Avon Books, 1978.

Pateman, Carole. *The Sexual Contract*. Stanford: Stanford University Press, 1988.

Paul, Diana Y. *Women in Buddhism*. 2d ed. Berkeley: University of California Press, 1985.

Peers, E. Allison. *The Mystics of Spain*. London: George Allen & Unwin, 1951.

Perera, Sylvia Brinton. *Descent to the Goddess*. Toronto: Inner City Books, 1981.

Perry, John Weir. *Lord of the Four Quarters*. New York: Collier Books, 1966.

———. "Reflections of the Nature of the Kingship Archetype." *Journal of Analytical Psychology* 11 (1966): 147–61.

Peterfreund, Emanuel. *Information, Systems, and Psychoanalysis*. New York: International Universities Press, 1971.

———. "The Need for a New General Theoretical Frame of Reference for Psychoanalysis." *Psychoanalytic Quarterly* 44 (1975): 534–49.

———. "Some Critical Comments of Psychoanalytic Conceptualizations of Infancy." *International Journal of Psycho-analysis* 59 (1978): 427–41.

Peters, Edward. *Torture*. New York: Basil Blackwell, 1985.

Phillips, John A. *Eve: The History of an Idea*. New York: Harper & Row, 1984.

Piaget, Jean. *The Moral Judgment of the Child*. Trans. Marjorie Gabain. New York: Free Press, 1965.

———. *Six Psychological Studies*. Trans. Anita Tenzer and David Elkind. New York: Random House, 1967.

———. *Structuralism*. Trans. Chaninah Maschle. New York: Harper & Row, 1970.

Picken, S. D. B. *Buddhism, Japan's Cultural Identity*. Tokyo: Kodansha International, 1982.

Pinckney, E. R., and C. Pinckney. *The Fallacy of Freud and Psychoanalysis*. Englewood Cliffs, N.J.: Prentice-Hall, 1965.

Plaskow, Judith, and Joan Arnold Romero, eds. *Women and Religion*. Rev. ed. Missoula, Mont.: Scholars' Press, 1974.

Plato. *The Republic*. New York: Oxford University Press, 1945.

Pleck, Joseph H. *The Myth of Masculinity*. Cambridge: MIT Press, 1981.

Plucknett, Theodore F. T. *Early English Legal Literature*. London: Cambridge University Press, 1958.

Pollock, G. H. "Freud as Scientist and Psychoanalysis as Science." In *The Annual of Psychoanalysis* 8. New York: International Universities Press, 1980.

Pollock, Sir Frederick, and F. W. Maitland. *The History of the English Law*. Cambridge: Cambridge University Press, 1968.

Pomeroy, Sarah B. *Goddesses, Whores, Wives, and Slaves*. New York: Schocken Books, 1975.

———. *Women in Hellenistic Egypt: From Alexander to Cleopatra*. New York: Schocken Books, 1984.

Popper, Karl R. *Conjectures and Refutations*. London: Routledge & Kegan Paul, 1963.

Power, Margaret. "The Foraging Adaptation of Chimpanzees, and the

Recent Behaviors of the Provisioned Apes in Gombe and Mahale National Parks, Tanzania." *Human Evolution* 1 (1986): 251–66.

———. *Mutual Dependence: An Anthropological View of Chimpanzee and Human Social Organization*. Cambridge: Cambridge University Press, in press.

Preston, James J., ed. *Mother Worship: Themes and Variations*. Chapel Hill: University of North Carolina Press, 1982.

Pringsheim, Fritz. "The Unique Character of Classical Roman Law." *Journal of Roman Studies* 34 (1944): 60.

Progoff, Ira. *Jung's Psychology and Its Social Meaning*. Garden City, N.Y.: Anchor Books, 1973.

Rachman, Stanley, ed. *Critical Essays on Psychoanalysis*. Oxford: Pergamon Press, 1963.

Ragland-Sullivan, Ellie. *Jacques Lacan and the Philosophy of Psychoanalysis*. Urbana: University of Illinois Press, 1986.

Rand, Ayn. "An Answer to Readers (About a Woman President)." *The Objectivist* 7 (December 1968): 1–3.

Randall, J. H. *Hellenistic Ways of Deliverance and the Making of the Christian Synthesis*. New York: Columbia University Press, 1970.

Rank, Otto. *Truth and Reality*. Trans. Jessie Taft. New York: W. W. Norton, 1936.

———. *The Myth of the Birth of the Hero and Other Writings*. ed. Philip Freund. New York: Vintage Books, 1959.

———. *Art and Artist: Creative Urge and Personality Development*. New York: Agathon Press, 1968.

———. *The Double: A Psychoanalytic Study*. Ed. and trans. Harry Tucker, Jr. New York: New American Library, 1971.

Rawson, Beryl, ed. *The Family in Ancient Rome*. London: Croom Helm, 1986.

Réage, Pauline. *Story of O*. Trans. Sabine d'Estree. New York: Ballantine, 1965.

Redfearn, Joseph W. T. "The Nature of Archetypal Activity: The Integration of Spiritual and Bodily Experience." *The Journal of Analytical Psychology* 18 (1973): 127.

Redfield, Robert. "Maine's Ancient Law in the Light of Primitive Societies." *The Western Political Quarterly* 3 (1950): 586–89. Also in J. C. Smith and David Weisstub, *The Western Idea of Law*. Scarborough, Ont.: Butterworths, 1983, 81–83.

Reed, Evelyn. *Woman's Evolution from Materiarchal Clan to Patriarchal Family*. New York: Pathfinder Press, 1975.

Reich, Wilhelm. *Dialectical Materialism and Psychoanalysis*. London: Socialist Reproduction, 1929.

————. *The Mass Psychology of Fascism*. Trans. Mary Higgins. New York: Farrar, Straus & Giroux, 1970.

Reitzenstein, Richard. *Hellenistic Mystery-Religions*. Trans. John E. Steely. Pittsburgh: Pickwick Press, 1978.

Reppen, Joseph, ed. *Analysts at Work*. Hillsdale, N.J.: Analytic Press, 1985.

Reppen, Joseph, and Maurice Charney, eds. *The Psychoanalytic Study of Literature*. Hillsdale, N.J.: Analytic Press, 1985.

Rich, Adrienne. *Of Woman Born: Motherhood as Experience and Institution*. New York: W. W. Norton, 1976.

————. *On Lies, Secrets, and Silence: Selected Prose, 1966–1978*. New York: W. W. Norton, 1979.

Richards, Janet Radcliffe. *The Sceptical Feminist*. London: Routledge & Kegan Paul, 1980.

Richardson, Henry Gerald. *Bracton: The Problem of His Text*. London: Selden Society, 1965.

Riley, Patrick. "Introduction to the Reading of Alexandre Kojeve." *Political Theory* 9 (1981): 5–48.

Ripa, C. *Baroque and Roccoco Pictorial Imagery*. Trans. E. A. Maser. Reprint. New York: Dover, 1971.

Roazen, Paul. *Freud and His Followers*. New York: New York University Press, 1984.

Robbins, Rossell Hope. *The Encyclopedia of Witchcraft and Demonology*. New York: Crown, 1959.

Robertson, Heather. "Portrait of a Sex Killer." *Chatelain* (November 1983): 69.

Robinson, John Mansley. *An Introduction to Early Greek Philosophy*. Boston: Houghton Mifflin, 1968.

Robinson, R. E., S. C. Coval, and J. C. Smith. "The Logic of Rights." *University of Toronto Law Journal* 33 (1983): 267–78.

Roheim, Geza. *Psychoanalysis and Anthropology*. New York: International Universities Press, 1968.

Rosaldo, Michelle Zimbalist, and Louise Lamphere, eds. *Woman, Culture, and Society*. Stanford: Stanford University Press, 1984.

Roszak, Betty, and Theodore Roszak, eds. *Masculine/Feminine*. New York: Harper & Row, 1969.

Rousseau, Jean Jacques. *The Social Contract*. Trans. G. D. H. Cole. London: Dent, 1947.

Roth, Michael S. *Psychoanalysis as History*. Ithaca: Cornell University Press, 1987.

Rubenstein, Richard L. *The Cunning of History*. New York: Harper & Row, 1978.

Rubinstein, B. B. "Psychoanalytic Theory and the Mind-Body Problem." In *Psychoanalysis and Current Biological Thought,* ed. Norman S. Greenfield and William C. Lewis. Madison: University of Wisconson Press, 1965.

———. "Explanation and Mere Description." In *Motives and Thought,* ed. Robert R. Holt. New York: International Universities Press, 1967.

———. "The Problem of Confirmation in Clinical Psychoanalysis." *Journal of the American Psychoanalytic Association* 28 (1980): 397–417.

Rudnytsky, Peter L. *Freud and Oedipus.* New York: Columbia University Press, 1987.

Rush, Florence. *The Best-kept Secret: Sexual Abuse of Children.* Englewood Cliffs, N.J.: Prentice-Hall, 1980.

Russell, Diana E. H. *Rape in Marriage.* New York: Macmillan, 1982.

Russell, Jeffrey Burton. *Satan: The Early Christian Tradition.* Ithaca: Cornell University Press, 1981.

———. *Mephistopheles: The Devil in the Modern World.* Ithaca: Cornell University Press, 1986.

Ryle, Gilbert. *The Concept of Mind.* New York: Barnes & Noble, 1949.

Sagan, Eli. *At the Dawn of Tyranny.* New York: Alfred A. Knopf, 1985.

Sambursky, S. *Physics of the Stoics.* New York: Macmillan, 1959.

———. *The Physical World of the Greeks.* Trans. Merton Dagut. New York: Collier Books, 1962.

———. "Structural and Dynamic Elements in the Greek Conception of Physical Reality." In *Cross-cultural Understanding: Epistemology in Anthropology.* Ed. F. S. C. Northrop and Helen H. Livingston. New York: Harper & Row, 1964.

———. *Physical Thought from the Presocratics to the Quantum Physicists.* New York: Pica Press, 1975.

SAMOIS, ed. *Coming to Power.* Boston: Alyson Publications, 1982.

Samuels, Andrew. *Jung and the Post-Jungians.* London: Routledge & Kegan Paul, 1985.

Sanday, Peggy Reeves. *Female Power and Male Dominance.* Cambridge: Cambridge University Press, 1981.

Sandler, Joseph, with Anna Freud. *The Analysis of Defense: The Ego and the Mechanisms of Defense Revisited.* New York: International Universities Press, 1985.

Sangharakshita, Bhikshu. *A Survey of Buddhism.* Boulder: Shambhala, 1980.

Sanson, G. B. *A Short Cultural History of Japan.* New York: D. Appleton Century, 1936.

Sawyer, Roger. *Children Enslaved.* London: Routledge, & Kegan Paul, 1988.

Sayers, Janet. *Biological Politics: Feminist and Anti-Feminist Perspectives*. London: Tavistock Publication, 1982.

——. *Sexual Contradictions: Psychology, Psychoanalysis, and Feminism*. London and New York: Tavistock Publications, 1986.

Scales, Ann C. "The Emergence of Feminist Jurisprudence: An Essay." *Yale Law Journal* 95 (1986): 1373–403.

——. "Towards a Feminist Jurisprudence." *Indiana Law Journal*, 56 (1980–81): 375–444.

Schafer, Roy. *A New Language for Psychoanalysis*. New Haven: Yale University Press, 1976.

Schmidt, Gunter. "Male-Female Differences in Sexual Arousal and Behavior during and after Exposure to Sexually Explicit Stimuli." *Archives of Sexual Behavior* 4 (1975): 353.

Schneider, Michael. *Neurosis and Civilization: A Marxist/Freudian Synthesis*. Trans. Michael Roloff. New York: Seabury Press, 1975.

Schneiderman, Stuart. *Returning to Freud*. New Haven and London: Yale University Press, 1980.

——. *Jacques Lacan: The Death of an Intellectual Hero*. Cambridge: Harvard University Press, 1983.

Schopenhauer, Arthur. *The World as Will and Idea*. trans. R. B. Haldane and J. Kemp. Garden City, N.Y.: Dolphin Books, 1961.

Schulz, Fritz. *Principles of Roman Law*. London: Oxford University Press, 1936.

——. *History of Roman Legal Science*. London: Oxford University Press, 1946.

Schur, Max. *Freud: Living and Dying*. New York: International Universities Press, 1972.

Schwab, Gustav. *Gods and Heroes*. Trans. Olga Marx and Ernst Morwitz. Greenwich, Conn.: Fawcett Publications, 1946.

Scott, Gini Graham. *Dominant Women, Submissive Men*. New York: Praeger, 1983.

Scott, Hilda. *Does Socialism Liberate Women?* Boston: Beacon Press, 1974.

Scott, Joan Wallach. *Gender and the Politics of History*. New York: Columbia University Press, 1988.

Scott, S. P., trans. *The Civil Law*. New York: AMS Press, 1973.

Scrutton, Sir Thomas Edward. *The Influence of the Roman Law on the Law of England*. London: Cambridge, 1885.

Searle, John. *Minds, Brains, and Science*. Cambridge: Harvard University Press, 1984.

Shakespeare, William. *The Merchant of Venice*. In *The Comedies and Tragedies of Shakespeare*, Vol. 2. New York: Random House, 1944.

Sheleff, Leon Shakolshy. "The Illusions of Law—Psychoanalysis and

Jurisprudence in Historical Perspective." *International Journal of Law and Psychiatry* 9 (1986): 143–58.

Sherfey, Mary Jane. *The Nature and Evolution of Female Sexuality.* New York: Random House, 1973.

Sherman, Charles P. *Roman Law in the Modern World.* Vol. 1. New York: Baker, Voorhis, 1937.

Shinsho, H. "Buddhism of One Great Vehicle (Mahayana)." In *The Japanese Mind,* ed. C. A. Moore. Honolulu: East-West Center Press, 1967.

Showerman, Grant. *The Great Mother of the Gods.* Chicago: Argonaut, 1969.

Singer, June. *Androgyny: Toward a New Theory of Sexuality.* Garden City, N.Y.: Doubleday, Anchor Press, 1976.

Sjöö, Monica, and Barbara Mor. *The Great Cosmic Mother.* New York: Harper & Row, 1987.

Slater, Philip E. *The Glory of Hera.* Boston: Beacon Press, 1968.

Small, Meredith F., ed. *Female Primates: Studies by Women Primatologists.* New York: Alan R. Liss, 1984.

Smith, Hedrick. *The Russians.* New York: Quadrangle/New York Times, 1976.

Smith, J. C. "The Theoretical Constructs of Western Contractual Law." In *Cross-cultural Understanding: Epistemology in Anthropology,* ed. F. S. C. Northrop and Helen H. Livingston. New York: Harper & Row, 1964.

———. "The Unique Nature of the Concepts of Western Law." *Canadian Bar Review* 46 (1968): 191–225.

———. *Legal Obligation.* London: Athlone Press, 1976.

———. "The Sword and Shield of Perseus: Some Mythological Dimensions of Law." *International Journal of Law* 6 (1983): 235.

———. "Gods and Goddesses of the Quadrant: Some Further Thoughts on the Mythical Dimensions of the Law." *International Journal of Law* (1984): 219.

Smith, J. C., and David N. Weisstub. "The Evolution of Western Legal Consciousness." *International Journal of Law and Psychiatry* 2 (1979): 215–34.

———. *The Western Idea of Law.* Scarborough, Ont.: Butterworths, 1983.

Socarides, Charles W. *Homosexuality.* New York: Jason Aronson, 1978.

Sokolowski, Robert. "Natural and Artificial Intelligence." In *Daedalus* (Winter 1988): 45–64.

Solzhenitsyn, Aleksandr I. *The Gulag Archipelago, 1918–1956: An Experiment in Literary Investigation, I–II.* Trans. Thomas P. Whitney. New York: Harper & Row, 1973.

————. *The Gulag Archipelago, 1918–1956: An Experiment in Literary Investigation, III–IV*. Trans. Thomas P. Whitney. New York: Harper & Row, 1975.

————. *The Gulag Archipelago, 1918–1956: An Experiment in Literary Investigation, V–VII*. Trans. Harry Willetts. New York: Harper & Row, 1978.

Spence, George. *The Equitable Jurisdiction of the Courts of Chancery*. 2 vols. Philadelphia: Lea & Blanchard, 1846–49.

Spielrein, Sabina. "Die Destruktion als Ursache des Werdens" (Destruction as the Cause of Becoming). *Jahrbuch für Psychoanalytische und Psychopathologische Forschungen* 4 (1912): 465.

Spiro, Melford E. *Oedipus in the Trobriands*. Chicago: University of Chicago Press, 1982.

Spretnak, Charlene. *Lost Goddesses of Early Greece*. Boston: Beacon Press, 1978.

Stacey, Judith. *Patriarchy and Socialist Revolution in China*. Berkeley: University of California Press, 1983.

Stafford, William T. *Billy Budd and the Critics*. San Francisco: Wadsworth, 1961.

Stannard, David E. *Shrinking History*. Oxford: Oxford University Press, 1980.

Stanton, Martin. *Outside the Dream: Lacan and French Styles of Psychoanalysis*. London: Routledge & Kegan Paul, 1983.

Starhawk (Miriam Simos). *The Spiral Dance: A Rebirth of the Ancient Religion of the Great Goddess*. San Francisco: Harper & Row, 1979.

————. *Truth or Dare: Encounters with Power, Authority, and Mystery*. San Francisco: Harper & Row, 1987.

Stechler, Gerald, and Samuel Kaplan. "The Development of the Self: A Psychoanalytic Perspective." *Psychoanalytic Study of the Child* 35 (1980): 85–105.

Steele, Daniel G., and C. Eugene Walker. "Male and Female Differences in Reaction to Erotic Stimuli and Related to Sexual Adjustment." *Archives of Sexual Behavior* 3 (1974): 459–70.

Steele, Robert S. *Freud and Jung: Conflicts of Interpretation*. London: Routledge & Kegan Paul, 1982.

Stein, Murray. "The Devouring Father." in *Fathers and Mothers: Five Papers on the Archetypal Background of Family Psychology,* ed. J. Hillman, E. Neuman, M. Stein, A. Vitale, and V. von der Heydt. Zurich: Spring Publications, 1973.

Steinman, Debra L., John P. Wincze, Sakheim, David H. Barlow, and Matig Mavissakalian. "A Comparison of Male and Female Patterns of Sexual Arousal." *Archives of Sexual Behavior* 10 (1981): 529–47.

Stepansky, Paul E., ed. *Freud: Appraisals and Reappraisals*. Hillsdale, N.J.: Analytic Press, 1986.

Stern, Daniel N. *The Interpersonal World of the Infant*. New York: Basic Books, 1985.

Stern, Raphael, ed. *Theories of the Unconscious and Theories of the Self*. Hillsdale, N.J.: Analytic Press, 1987.

Stevens, Anthony. *Archetype: A Natural History of the Self*. London: Routledge & Kegan, 1982.

Stevens, Richard. *Freud and Psychoanalysis*. Milton Keynes, England: Open University Press, 1983.

Stokes, Henry Scott. *The Life and Death of Yukio Mishima*. New York: Farrar, Straus, & Giroux, 1974.

Stoller, Robert J. *Sex and Gender: On the Development of Masculinity and Femininity*. New York: Science House, 1968.

———. *Perversion: The Erotic Form of Hatred*. New York: Pantheon Books, 1975.

———. *Sexual Excitement: Dynamics of Erotic Life*. New York: Pantheon Books, 1979.

———. *Observing the Erotic Imagination*. New Haven: Yale University Press, 1985.

———. *Presentations of Gender*. New Haven: Yale University Press, 1985.

———. "Perversion and the Desire to Harm." In *Theories of the Unconscious and Theories of the Self*, ed. Raphael Stern. Hillsdale, N.J.: Analytic Press, 1987.

Stone, Alan. "Psychoanalysis and Jurisprudence Revisited." *American Criminal Law Review* 10 (1972): 357.

Stone, Merlin. *When God Was a Woman*. New York: Harcourt Brace Jovanovich, 1976.

———. *Ancient Mirrors of Womanhood*. Boston: Beacon Press, 1979.

Storr, Anthony. *Human Aggression*. New York: Atheneum, 1968.

Strouse, Jean, ed. *Women and Analysis: Dialogues on Psychoanalytic Views of Femininity*. New York: Grossman Publishers, 1974.

Sullivan, Harry Stack. *Collected Works*. New York: Norton, 1940–64.

Summers, Montague, ed. and trans. *The Malleus Maleficarum of Heinrich Kramer and James Sprenger*. New York: Dover Publications, 1971. First pub. London: John Rodker, 1928.

Suzuki, D. T., E. Fromm, and R. de Martino, eds. *Zen Buddhism and Psychoanalysis*. New York: Harper & Brothers, 1960.

Symons, Donald. *The Evolution of Human Sexuality*. New York: Oxford University Press, 1979.

Takamure, Itsu. *Takamura Itsue Zenshū*. Vol. 1, *Bokei sei no Kenkyu*. Tokyo: Rironsha, 1966–67.

————. *Takamura Itsue Zenshū*. Vol. 2, *Sho Seilcon no Kenkyu*. Tokyo: Rironsha. 1966–67.

Talbot, Michael. *Mysticism and the New Physics*. New York: Bantam Books, 1981.

Tay, Alice Erh-Soon. "The Status of Women in the Soviet Union." *American Journal of Comparative Law* 20 (1972): 662–92.

Taylor, Charles. *Hegel*. Cambridge: Cambridge University Press, 1975.

————. *Hegel and Modern Society*. Cambridge: Cambridge University Press, 1979.

Teubal, Savina J. *Sarah, the Priestess*. Athens, Ohio: Swallow Press, 1984.

Theweleit, Klaus. *Male Fantasies*. Vol. 1, *Women, Floods, Bodies, History*. Trans. Stephen Conway. Minneapolis: University of Minnesota Press, 1987.

————. *Male Fantasies*. Vol. 2, *Male Bodies: Psychoanalyzing the White Terror*. Trans. Erica Carter and Chris Turner. Minneapolis: University of Minnesota Press, 1989.

Thomas, Ivor. "Greek Mathematics." In *Men and Numbers,* ed. James R. Newman. New York: Simon & Schuster, 1956.

Thompson, William Irwin. *The Time Falling Bodies Take to Light*. New York: St. Martin's Press, 1981.

Thornton, E. M. *Freud and Cocaine: The Freudian Fallacy*. London: Blond & Briggs, 1983.

Tigunait, Rajmani. *Seven Systems of Indian Philosophy*. Honesdale, Penn.: Himalyan Publications, 1983.

Tillich, Hannah. *From Time to Time*. New York: Stein & Day, 1973.

Todd, Ian A. *Çatal Hüyük in Perspective*. Menlo Park, Calif.: Cummings Publishing, 1976.

Tolstoy, Leo. "The Kreutzer Sonata." In *Illustrated Editor,* vol. 9, at 307. Boston: Dana Estes, 1904.

Tsurumi, E. Patricia. Review of "Amaeru: The Expression of Reciprocal Dependency Needs in Japanese Politics and Law." *Pacific Affairs* 51 (1978/79): 310.

Tucker, Robert C. *Philosophy and Myth in Karl Marx*. 2d ed. Cambridge: Cambridge University Press, 1972.

Turkle, Sherry. *Psychoanalytic Politics*. New York: Basic Books, 1978.

————. *The Second Self*. New York: Simon & Schuster, 1984.

————. "Artificial Intelligence and Psychoanalysis: A New Alliance." *Daedalus,* (Winter 1988): 241–68. Issued as Vol. 117, No. 1, of the "Proceedings of the American Academy of Arts and Sciences."

Turnbull, Colin. *The Mountain People*. London: Jonathan Cape, 1973.

Turnbull, Herbert Westren. "The Great Mathematicians." In *Men and*

Numbers, ed. James R. Newman. New York: Simon & Schuster, 1956.

Tustin, Frances. *Autism and Childhood Psychosis.* London: Hogarth Press, 1972.

———. *Autistic States in Children.* London: Routledge & Kegan Paul, 1981.

Tylor, E. B. *Anthropology: An Introduction to the Study of Man and Civilization.* 2d ed. London: John Murray, 1881.

Tyrrell, William Blake. *Amazons: A Study in Athenian Mythmaking.* Baltimore: Johns Hopkins University Press, 1984.

Ulanov, Ann Belford. *Receiving Woman: Studies in the Psychology and Theology of the Feminine.* Philadelphia: Westminster Press, 1981.

Ulanov, Ann Belford, and Barry Ulanov. *The Witch and the Clown: Two Archetypes of Human Sexuality.* Wilmette, Ill.: Chiron Publications, 1987.

Underwood, Richard A. "Myth, Dream, and the Vocation of Contemporary Philosophy." In *Myths, Dreams, and Religion,* ed. Joseph Campbell. New York: E. P. Dutton, 1970.

United States Commission on Civil Rights. *Under the Rule of Thumb: Battered Women and the Administration of Justice.* A Report of the U.S. Commission on Civil Rights. Washington: Commission, 1982.

Valzelli, Luigi. *Psychobiology of Aggression and Violence.* New York: Raven Press, 1981.

Van Herik, Judith. *Freud on Femininity and Faith.* Berkeley: University of California Press, 1982.

Van Melsen, Andrew G. *From Atomos to Atom.* trans. Henry J. Koren. Pittsburgh: Duquesne University Press, 1952.

Vernant, Jean-Pierre. *Myth and Society in Ancient Greece.* Sussex: Harvester Press, 1980.

Vinogradoff, Sir Paul. *Roman Law in Medieval Europe.* 3d ed. Oxford: Oxford University Press, 1961.

Vitale, Augusto. "Saturn: The Transformation of the Father." In *Fathers and Mothers, Five Papers on the Archetypal Background of Family Psychology,* ed. J. Hillman, E. Neuman, M. Stein, A. Vitale, and V. von der Heydt. Zurich: Spring Publications, 1973.

von Cles-Reden, Sibylle. *The Realm of the Great Goddess.* Trans. Eric Mosbacher. Englewood Cliffs, N.J.: Prentice Hall, 1961.

von der Heydt, Vera. "On the Father in Psychotherapy." In *Fathers and Mothers: Five Papers on the Archetypal Background of Family Psychology,* ed. J. Hillman, E. Neuman, M. Stein, A. Vitale, and V. von der Heydt. Zurich: Spring Publications, 1973.

von Franz, Marie-Louise. *Number and Time*. Evanston: Northwestern University Press, 1974.

———. *Projection and Re-Collection in Jungian Psychology*. Trans. William H. Kennedy. La Salle, Ill.: Open Court Publishing, 1980.

Wagatsuma, Hirosh. Review of "Amaeru: The Expression of Reciprocal Dependency Needs in Japanese Politics and Law." *Journal of Asian Studies* 39 (1979/80): 173.

Walker, Barbara G. *The Woman's Encyclopedia of Myths and Secrets*. New York: Harper & Row, 1983.

———. *The Crone: Woman of Age, Wisdom, and Power*. San Francisco: Harper & Row, 1985.

———. *The Skeptical Feminist*. San Francisco: Harper & Row, 1987.

Walker, Lenore E. *The Battered Woman*. New York: Harper & Row, 1979.

Wallace, Edwin R. *Freud and Anthropology*. New York: International Universities Press, 1983.

Warner, Marina. *Monuments and Maidens: The Allegory of the Female Form*. London: Weidenfeld & Nicolson, 1985.

Watkins, Mary M. *Waking Dreams*. New York: Gordon & Brean, 1976.

Wedderburn, A. J. M. "Paul and the Hellenistic Mystery Cults: On Posing the Right Questions." In *La Soteriologia dei Culti Orientali nell'Impero Romano* (Preliminary studies of Eastern religions in the Roman Empire.), ed. Ugo Bianchi and Maarten J. Vermaseren. Leiden: E. J. Brill, 1982.

Wedeck, Harry E. *Treasury of Witchcraft*. New York: Philosophical Library, 1961.

Wehr, Gerhard. *Jung: A Biography*. Boston: Shambhala Publications, 1987.

Weinberg, Martin S., Colin J. Williams, and Charles Moser. "The Social Constituents of Sadomasochism." *Social Problems* 31 (1984): 379–89.

Weininger, Otto. *Geschlecht und Charakter: Eine Prinzipielle Untersuchung* (Sex and Character). Vienna: Verlag Wilhelm Braumuller, 1905.

Weinstein, Fred, and Gerald M. Platt. *Psychoanalytic Sociology*. Baltimore: Johns Hopkins University Press, 1973.

Weisstub, David N. "The Theoretical Relationship between Law and Psychiatry." *International Journal of Law and Psychiatry* 1 (1978).

West, D. J. *Sexual Crimes and Confrontations*. Aldershot, England: Gower Publishing, 1987.

West, Robin, "In the Interest of the Governed: A Utilitarian Justification for Substantive Judicial Review." *Georgia Law Review* 18 (1984): 469–528.

————. "Authority, Autonomy, and Choice: The Role of Consent in the Moral and Political Visions of Franz Kafka and Richard Posner." *Harvard Law Review* 99 (1985): 384–428.

————. "Jurisprudence as Narrative: An Aesthetic Analysis of Modern Legal Theory." *New York University Law Review* 60 (1985): 145–211.

————. "Liberalism Rediscovered: A Pragmatic Definition of the Liberal Vision." *University of Pittsburgh Law Review* 46 (1985): 673–738.

————. "Law, Rights, and Other Totemic Illusions: Legal Liberalism and Freud's Theory of the Rule of Law." *University of Pennsylvania Law Review* 134 (1986): 817–82.

————. "Submission, Choice, and Ethics: A Rejoinder to Judge Posner." *Harvard Law Review* 99 (1986): 1449–59.

————. "Jurisprudence and Gender." *University of Chicago Law Review* 55 (1988): 1–72.

Westrup, C. W. *Introduction to Early Roman Law.* Vols. 1–5, London: Oxford, 1934–54.

Whitmont, Edward C. *The Symbolic Quest.* Princeton: Princeton University Press, 1969.

————. *Return of the Goddess.* New York: Crossroad, 1982.

Whyte, Lancelot Law. *The Unconscious before Freud.* New York: Basic Books, 1960.

Wiens, D. H. "Mystery Concepts in Primitive Christianity and in Its Environment," in *Aufstieg und Niedergang der Romischen Welt* 2:23.2. Eds. Hildegard Temporini and W. Waase. Berlin: Walter De Gruyter, 1980.

Wigmore, John Henry. *Evidence in Trials at Common Law.* (Wigmore on Evidence) 10 vols. Rev. by James H. Chadbourn. Boston: Little, Brown, 1970.

Wilson, Glenn. *The Secrets of Sexual Fantasy.* London: J. M. Dent & Sons, 1978.

Winnicott, D. W. "The Observation of Infants in a Set Situation." *International Journal of Psycho-analysis* 22 (1941): 239–49.

————. "The Baby as a Person." *Child-Family Digest* 8 (1953): 34–43.

————. "The Ordinary Devoted Mother and Her Baby." *Child-Family Digest* 8 (1953): 23–35.

————. "The Innate Morality of the Baby." *Child-Family Digest* 9 (1953): 66–71.

————. *Mother and Child: A Primer of First Relationships.* New York: Basic Books, 1957.

————. "Birth Memories, Birth Trauma, and Anxiety." In *Collected Pa-*

pers: Through Paediatrics to Psycho-analysis. London: Tavistock Publications, 1958.

———. "The Theory of the Parent-Infant Relationship." *International Journal of Psycho-analysis* 41 (1960): 585–95.

———. *The Child, the Family, and the Outside World.* Harmondsworth: Penguin Books, 1964.

———. *The Maturational Processes and the Facilitating Environment.* London: Hogarth Press, 1965.

Wolf, Margery. *Revolution Postponed: Women in Contemporary China.* Stanford: Stanford University Press, 1985.

Wolff, Hans Julius. *Roman Law: An Historical Introduction.* Norman: University of Oklahoma Press, 1951.

Wolff, Larry. *Postcards from the End of the World: Child Abuse in Freud's Vienna.* New York: Atheneum, 1988.

Wolff, Robert Paul. *In Defense of Anarchism.* New York: Harper & Row, 1970.

Wolkstein, Diane, and Samuel N. Kramer. *Inanna, Queen of Heaven and Earth: Her Stories and Hymns from Sumer.* New York: Harper & Row, 1983.

Woodbine, George E. "The Roman Element in Bracton's 'De Adquirendo Rerum Dominio'." *Yale Law Journal* 31 (1921–22): 827.

Woodman, Marion. *Addiction to Perfection.* Toronto: Inner City Books, 1982.

Workman, Herbert B. *The Evolution of the Monastic Ideal.* Boston: Beacon Press, 1962. First pub. London: Epworth Press, 1913.

Wright, George. "Stoic Midwives at the Birth of Jurisprudence." *The American Journal of Jurisprudence* 23 (1983): 169–88.

Wynne-Edwards, Vero C. *Animal Dispersion in Relation to Social Behavior.* New York: Hafner Publishing, 1962.

Yeats, W. B. "The Second Coming." In *The Collected Poems.* London: Macmillan, 1952, at 610.

Yoshifumi, U. "The Status of the Individual in Mahayana Buddhist Philosophy." In *The Japanese Mind,* ed. Charles A. Moore. Honolulu: East-West Center Press, 1967.

Yukawa, Hideyi. *Creativity and Intuition.* Tokyo: Kodansha International, 1973.

Zolla, Elemire. *The Androgyne: Reconciliation of Male and Female.* New York: Crossroad Publishing, 1981.

The Zondervan Pictorial Encyclopedia of the Bible. 5 vols. Gen. ed. Merrill Tenney. Grand Rapids, Mich.: Zondervan Corp., 1976.

Zukav, Gary. *The Dancing Wu Li Masters.* New York: William Morrow, 1979.

NAME INDEX

487

SUBJECT INDEX